FINANCIAL ACCOUNTING

FINANCIAL ACCOUNTING

AN INTRODUCTION TO CONCEPTS, METHODS, AND USES
Second Edition

Sidney Davidson, Ph.D., CPA
The University of Chicago

Clyde P. Stickney, D.B.A., CPA
Dartmouth College

Roman L. Weil, Ph.D., CPA, CMA
The University of Chicago

The Dryden Press
Hinsdale, Illinois

Copyright © 1979 by The Dryden Press
A division of Holt, Rinehart and Winston, Publishers
All rights reserved
Library of Congress Catalog Card Number: 78—56202
ISBN: 0-03-045296-1
Printed in the United States of America
9   074   987654321

Whatever be the detail with which you cram your students, the chance of their meeting in after-life exactly that detail is almost infinitesimal; and if they do meet it, they will probably have forgotten what you taught them about it. The really useful training yields a comprehension of a few general principles with a thorough grounding in the way they apply to a variety of concrete details. In subsequent practice the students will have forgotten your particular details; but they will remember by an unconscious common sense how to apply principles to immediate circumstances.

Alfred North Whitehead
The Aims of Education and Other Essays

PREFACE

The second edition of this book has the same principal objectives as the first. We view the introductory course in financial accounting as having the following purposes:

• To help the student develop a sufficient understanding of the basic concepts underlying financial statements so that the concepts can be applied to new and different situations.

• To train the student in accounting terminology and methods so that financial statements currently published in corporate annual reports can be interpreted, analyzed, and evaluated.

Most introductory financial accounting textbooks share these, or similar, objectives. The critical differences between textbooks relate to the relative emphases on concepts, methods, and uses.

1. Concepts We emphasize the rationale for, and implications of, important accounting concepts. The ability to "conceptualize" material covered is an important part of the learning process. Without such conceptualization, students will have difficulty focusing on relevant issues in new and different situations. Accordingly, we have identified the important accounting concepts early in each chapter. Following these are several numerical examples illustrating their application. Numerous short problems are included at the end of each chapter to check the students' ability to apply the concepts to still different problem situations.

2. Methods We attempt to place sufficient emphasis on accounting procedures so that students can interpret, analyze, and evaluate published financial statements, but not so much emphasis on the procedures that they get bogged down in detail. The determination of just how much accounting procedure is "enough" is a problem faced by all writers of accounting textbooks. Most feel, as we do, that the most effective way to learn accounting concepts is to work numerous problems and exercises. However, when too much emphasis is placed on accounting procedures, there is a tendency for students to be lulled into the security of thinking they understand accounting concepts when they actually do not. The mixture of concepts and procedures in this book is one with which we have experimented extensively and that we have found effective in classroom use.

Our experience is that students do not understand the accounting implications of an event until they can construct the journal entry for that event. Throughout this book, we show journal entries in describing the nature of accounting events. Moreover, most chapters contain questions that require the analysis of transactions with debits and credits. Do not conclude, however, by a glance at this text, that it is primarily procedural. We are more concerned that our students learn concepts; the procedures are required for learning the concepts. Furthermore, we believe that this is the most effective way to train both professional accountants and those who wish merely to be informed users of financial statements.

3. Uses   We attempt to bridge the gap between the preparation of financial statements and the uses to which the statements might be put. We give extensive consideration to the effects of alternative accounting principles on the measurement of earnings and financial position and to the types of interpretations that should and should not be made. A complete set of financial statements and related notes is presented in Appendix A at the back of the book. Discussion of these financial statements is integrated into each chapter as appropriate. We have also included numerous user-oriented cases at the ends of most chapters.

CHANGES IN THIS EDITION

The major changes in the second edition are as follows:

1   The discussion in Chapter 1 of the environment of financial accounting is expanded to include material on the setting of accounting standards and the role of financial statement objectives in this process.
2   The procedure for preparing the statement of changes in financial position in Chapter 5 uses a conventional, "single" T-account rather than a "double" T-account. Our experience is that students have less difficulty with the single T-account approach since it extends techniques studied in Chapters 2 through 4. The double T-account used in the first edition unnecessarily hindered the learning process. The types of transactions considered in Chapter 5 have been simplified, but the use of the "funds" statement in the remainder of the book has been increased.
3   The material on financial statement analysis in Chapter 6 places greater emphasis on analyzing trends in financial ratios for a particular firm over time rather than on comparing a firm's ratios with industry averages or those of other, comparable firms.
4   The discussion of accounting for monetary assets in Chapter 7 is expanded to include new material on cash and marketable securities.
5   Disclosures of replacement cost data are incorporated into the chapters on inventories (Chapter 8) and depreciable assets (Chapter 9).

6 Chapter 10 on accounting for liabilities includes expanded discussions of leases and pensions, the latter in an appendix.

7 Chapter 12 on accounting for intercorporate investments has been revised to provide a better sequencing of topics. We begin with minority investments in common stock and discuss the cost and equity methods. We then move to majority investments and the preparation of consolidated financial statements. The discussion of the purchase and pooling of interest methods of accounting for corporate acquisitions has been moved to the end of the chapter and expanded. This placement is made not to deemphasize its importance but to alleviate the confusion that sometimes results when students try to relate corporate acquisitions and accounting for minority investments.

8 A new chapter on current issues in financial reporting is included. The topics covered in this edition are general price-level accounting, interim and segment reporting, and the establishment of financial statement objectives.

9 We have prepared many user-oriented problems and cases that require the student to analyze or interpret financial statement data for actual firms. See the last problems at the ends of Chapters 5 through 14.

ORGANIZATION

This book is divided into four major parts as outlined below:

One	Overview of Financial Statements	Chapter 1
Two	Accounting Concepts and Methods	Chapters 2–6
Three	Measuring and Reporting Assets and Equities	Chapters 7–12
Four	Current Issues in Financial Reporting	Chapters 13–14

The four parts may be viewed as four tiers, or steps, for coverage of the material. Part One (Chapter 1) presents a general overview of the principal financial statements and the nature of accounting. Part Two (Chapters 2 through 6) discusses the basic accounting model used to generate the principal financial statements. Part Three (Chapters 7 through 12) considers the specific accounting principles or methods used in preparing the financial statements. Finally, Part Four (Chapters 13–14) serves as a synthesis for the entire book. This organization reflects our view that learning can take place most effectively when the student starts with a broad picture, then breaks up that broad picture into smaller pieces until the desired depth is achieved, and finally synthesizes so that the relationship between the parts and the whole can be kept in perspective.

Chapter 1 presents a brief description of the purpose and concepts underlying the three principal financial statements: the balance sheet, the income statement, and the statement of changes in financial position. The economic, social, and political environment within which these statements are generated is also considered. Particular attention is given to the process by which "generally accepted accounting principles" are set.

Many students feel deluged with the multitude of new terms and concepts after reading Chapter 1. Most of these same students admit later, however, that the broad overview was useful in piecing material together as they later explored individual topics in greater depth.

Chapters 2 through 5 present the basic accounting model that generates the three principal financial statements. In each case, we begin with a description of the important concepts underlying each statement. The accounting procedures employed to generate the statements are then described and illustrated. One of the unique features of the book is the integration in Chapter 4 of the accounting entries for transactions during a period with the related adjusting entries at the end of the period. We have found that when these two types of entries are discussed in separate chapters, students lose sight of the fact that both kinds of entries are required to measure net income and financial position.

Another unique aspect of the text is the early coverage, in Chapter 5, of the statement of changes in financial position. We have two purposes in placing it here. First, this placement elevates the statement to its rightful place among the three principal financial statements. Students can thereby integrate the concepts of profitability and liquidity more effectively and begin to understand that one does not necessarily accompany the other. When the funds statement is covered at the end of the course (in many cases, when time is running out), there is a tendency for the student to think it is less important. Our second purpose for placing this chapter early in the book is that it serves to cement understanding of the basic accounting model in Chapters 2 through 4: Preparing the statement of changes in financial position requires the student to work "backwards" from the balance sheet and income statement to reconstruct the transactions that took place.

Chapter 6 introduces the topic of financial statement analysis. We place it here to serve as a partial synthesis of the first five chapters. Students at this point ask how information in the statements might be used. This chapter presents an opportunity to answer some of these questions, even if at only an elementary level. Effective financial statement analysis requires an understanding of the specific accounting methods discussed in Part Three. Chapter 6 therefore serves as a springboard for what is to come.

Chapters 7 through 12 discuss the various "generally accepted accounting principles" employed in generating financial statements. In each chapter, we not only describe and illustrate the application of the various accounting methods but also consider their effect on the financial statements. This approach reflects our view that students should be able to interpret and analyze published financial statements and to understand the effect of alternative accounting methods on such assessments. We have placed some of the more complicated topics in chapter-end appendixes to provide flexibility in coverage. Some instructors may not wish to use this more advanced material.

The students who have used the first edition of this book have found that Chapter 13, which synthesizes much of the material in the first twelve chapters, is in many ways the most useful in the book. Explicit consideration is given to the combined effects of alternative accounting methods on the financial statements and the significance of alternative accounting methods on financial statement analysis. Problems **16** and **17** at the end of Chapter 13 are major review problems for the whole book. Chapter 14 explores briefly several important financial accounting issues that are under active discussion.

A comprehensive glossary of financial accounting is included at the end of the book. This glossary serves as a useful reference tool for accounting and other business terms and provides additional descriptions of a few topics considered only briefly in the text, such as *accounting changes.*

RELATED MATERIALS ACCOMPANYING THE TEXT

The following materials have been prepared for use with the text:

Instructor's Manual   The instructor's manual, in addition to including responses to all questions and solutions to all exercises and problems, presents suggested course outlines for courses of varying lengths, a list of chapter objectives, helpful teaching hints, detailed lecture and discussion outlines including the numbers of particularly germane problems, several supplementary discussion cases, and about 75 pages of sample examination questions and problems. The instructor's manual includes a list of check figures for various problems in the text. These check figures can be photocopied and distributed to students if the instructor so desires. Finally, the manual contains a set of learning objectives for each chapter, which can be distributed to students.

Study Guide   A study guide has been prepared by LeBrone C. Harris, James E. Moon, and William L. Stephens. This study guide includes a listing of highlights from each chapter and is then followed by numerous short true/false, matching, and multiple-choice questions, with answers.

Transparencies   A set of transparencies is available for many of the exhibits in the text and the problems at the ends of the chapters.

ACKNOWLEDGMENTS

We gratefully acknowledge the helpful criticisms and suggestions of our colleagues and others who reviewed the manuscript at various stages: David D. Anderson, David O. Green, Earl Ludman, James M. Patell, A. W. Richardson, Katherine Schipper, and Shyam Sunder.

Our work on this revision was further aided by reviews from Norman D. Berman, New York University; Paul Danos, University of Michigan; Donald W. Fair, Florida International University; Michael R. Gaines, Portland State University; John S. Quinn, College of William and Mary; and Robert D. Ronay, University of Minnesota.

Some of our former students helped us to improve the clarity of the Questions and Problems and to de-bug the solutions. We thank Linda S. Fiffer, Ellen K. Hochman, and Kamyar Jabbari for their help; Daniel A. Lasman was especially productive.

Thomas Horton and Daughters, Inc., has graciously given us permission to reproduce material from *Accounting: The Language of Business*, published by them. The Sortus, Sundance, and Julius problems were adapted from ones prepared by George H. Sorter. These problems involve working backwards from one financial statement to another, and we have found them useful in cementing understanding.

We thank the following people for their hard work in helping us to prepare the manuscript for this book: Barbara Haskell, Mardine McReynolds, Raymonde Rousselot, and K. Xenophon-Rybowiak. Ellen C. Rutherford and Cherie Worman prepared the index.

Finally, we thank Nedah Abbott of The Dryden Press for her assistance and patience in the preparation of this book.

S.D.
C.P.S.
R.L.W.

CONTENTS

FINANCIAL ACCOUNTING

PART ONE
OVERVIEW OF FINANCIAL STATEMENTS

CHAPTER 1
OVERVIEW OF FINANCIAL STATEMENTS AND REPORTING PROCESS

A major function of accounting is providing information useful for making decisions. For example, a corporate treasurer might use a statement of estimated cash receipts and disbursements in deciding if short-term borrowing is necessary. A production manager might use a report on the productivity of various employees in deciding how a special order is to be routed through a factory. A sales manager might use a report on the cost of producing and selling different product lines in recommending the prices that should be charged and the products that should be emphasized by the sales staff. The preparation of reports for use by persons within a firm is referred to as *managerial accounting*. Users of information within a firm are generally free to specify the types of information they need for their decisions; managerial accounting reports are prepared to conform to these needs.

In contrast, *financial accounting* is concerned with the preparation of reports for use by persons outside, or external to, a firm. For example, a bank may desire information on the cash-generating ability of a firm in deciding whether or not to grant a bank loan. A potential investor may desire information on a firm's profitability before deciding to purchase shares of its common stock.

The format and content of financial accounting reports tend to be more standardized than is the case in managerial accounting. Considering the large number of uses and users of financial accounting reports, there is a need for some degree of uniformity in reporting among firms. The most common reports for external users are the financial statements included in annual reports to stockholders and potential investors. These financial statements are prepared in accordance with "generally accepted accounting principles." Such "principles" have evolved over time or have been made "acceptable" by decree from some official body. Much of this text is devoted to a discussion of the underlying assumptions, rationale, and implications of specific generally accepted accounting principles. Since this text is an introduction to financial accounting, we do not specifically consider managerial accounting reports.

The objective of this chapter is to provide an overview of the principal financial statements and a brief description of the financial reporting process. We begin by considering the purpose and content of each of the financial statements. We then discuss the nature of generally accepted accounting principles and the process through which they are developed. Because this chapter merely introduces material to be covered in greater depth in later chapters, more questions are raised than are answered. We feel, however, that it is helpful to have an overview of financial accounting before embarking on a study of the concepts and procedures employed in preparing various accounting reports.

PRINCIPAL FINANCIAL STATEMENTS

The annual report to stockholders typically includes a letter from the company's president summarizing activities of the past year and assessing the company's prospects for the coming year. Also included are pictures of the firm's products and employees and similar promotional material. The section of the annual report containing the financial statements is composed of the following:

1 Statement of financial position
2 Statement of net income
3 Statement of changes in financial position
4 Various supporting statements or schedules
5 Notes to the financial statements
6 Opinion of the independent certified public accountant.

Statement of Financial Position

The comparative statement of financial position of the Jonathan Electronics Corporation, as of December 31, 1978 and 1979, is presented in Exhibit 1.1. As its title suggests, this statement attempts to present an overall view of Jonathan Electronics Corporation's financial position as of the ends of 1978 and 1979. Several aspects of this statement should be noted.

Statement at a Moment in Time   The statement of financial position presents a snapshot of the firm's financial position as of a given date. (In Exhibit 1.1, one column reports the financial position as of December 31, 1978, and the other, as of December 31, 1979.) The statement presents amounts or levels or *stocks* of various items. (Note here that we are not referring to shares of stock.) *Stocks* are to be contrasted with *flows*. A stock is a measure of the amount of an item at a particular time, whereas a flow is a measure of the increase or decrease in an item over a period of time. For example, to say that Jonathan Electronics Corporation had cash in the amount of $75,000 on December 31, 1978, and $125,000 on December 31, 1979, is to say something about the firm's stock of cash on these particular dates. A parallel statement about flows is to say that the firm's cash receipts and disbursements during the period were such that the cash balance increased, or changed, by $50,000.

EXHIBIT 1.1
Jonathan Electronics Corporation
Comparative Statement of
Financial Position
December 31, 1978 and 1979

ASSETS

Current Assets:[a]	December 31 1978	1979
Cash	$ 75,000	$ 125,000
Accounts Receivable from Customers	75,000	200,000
Merchandise Inventory (at acquisition cost)	150,000	225,000
Total Current Assets	$ 300,000	$ 550,000
Noncurrent Assets (at acquisition cost):[a]		
Land	$ 200,000	$ 200,000
Equipment (net of accumulated depreciation)	700,000	1,000,000
Buildings (net of accumulated depreciation)	800,000	750,000
Total Noncurrent Assets	$1,700,000	$1,950,000
Total Assets	$2,000,000	$2,500,000

LIABILITIES AND STOCKHOLDERS' EQUITY

Current Liabilities:[a]		
Accounts Payable to Suppliers	$ 125,000	$ 160,000
Salaries Payable to Employees	25,000	40,000
Income Taxes Payable to Federal Government	50,000	200,000
Total Current Liabilities	$ 200,000	$ 400,000
Noncurrent Liabilities:[a]		
Bonds Payable to Lenders (due 1998)	600,000	700,000
Total Liabilities	$ 800,000	$1,100,000
Stockholders' Equity		
Common Stock	$ 500,000	$ 500,000
Retained Earnings	700,000	900,000
Total Stockholders' Equity	$1,200,000	$1,400,000
Total Liabilities and Stockholders' Equity	$2,000,000	$2,500,000

[a] The current and noncurrent classification of assets and liabilities is discussed later in this chapter.

Concepts of Assets and Equities   The statement of financial position presents a listing of the firm's *assets, liabilities,* and *owners' equity.* When the corporate form of organization is used, ownership is evidenced by shares of stock, and the owners' equity is frequently referred to as *stockholders' equity.*

Assets are economic resources. An asset is an item that has the ability or potential to provide future services or benefits to a firm. For example, cash can be used to purchase merchandise inventory or equipment. Merchandise inventory can be sold to customers for an amount the firm hopes will be larger than was paid for it. Equipment can be used in transporting the merchandise inventory to customers.

Liabilities are creditors' claims on the resources of a firm. Jonathan Electronics Corporation acquired merchandise inventory from its suppliers but has not yet paid for a portion of the purchases. As a result, these creditors have a claim on the assets of the company. Labor services have been provided by employees for which payment has not been made as of December 31 of each year. These employees likewise have a claim on the assets of the firm. Creditors' claims, or liabilities, result from benefits previously received by a firm, and typically have a specified amount and date at which they become due.

Stockholders' equity is the owners' claim on the assets of a firm. Unlike creditors, the owners have a residual interest. That is, owners have a claim on all assets in excess of those required to meet creditors' claims. The stockholders' equity is generally comprised of two parts: contributed capital and retained earnings. Contributed capital reflects the assets invested by the original stockholders in exchange for an ownership interest. Retained earnings represent the earnings, or profits, realized by a firm since its formation in excess of dividends distributed to stockholders. In other words, retained earnings are earnings reinvested by management for the benefit of the stockholders. Management directs the use of a firm's assets so that over time more assets are received than are given up in obtaining them. This increase in assets, after any claims by creditors, belongs to the firm's owners. Most firms reinvest a large percentage of their earnings for growth and expansion rather than distributing all earnings as dividends.

Liabilities plus stockholders' equity are referred to as *total equities*, or simply *equities.*

Equality of Assets and Equities   As the statement of financial position for Jonathan Electronics Corporation indicates, there is an equality between (1) assets and (2) liabilities plus stockholders' equity. That is,

$$\text{Assets} = \text{Liabilities} + \text{Stockholders' Equity.}$$

The significance of this equality can be grasped by considering the nature of each of the three components. Assets are resources of the firm. Liabilities and stockholders' equity are the claims on these resources. Thus:

$$\text{Resources} = \text{Claims on Resources.}$$

In the statement of financial position, we view the resources from two viewpoints: a listing of the assets under the control of the firm and a listing of the parties external to the firm who have a claim on these assets. Because of the equality of total assets and total equities, the statement of financial position is often called a *balance sheet.*

Balance Sheet Classification   The assets and liabilities are classified in the balance sheet as being either *current* or *noncurrent*.

Current assets include cash and other assets that are expected to be turned into cash, or sold, or consumed within approximately 1 year from the date of the balance sheet. Cash, temporary investments in securities, accounts receivable from customers, and merchandise inventories are the most common current assets. Current liabilities include liabilities that are expected to be paid within 1 year. Accounts payable to suppliers, salaries payable to employees, and taxes payable to governmental agencies are examples of current liabilities. Noncurrent assets typically are held and used for several years; they provide a firm with longer-term productive capacity. Noncurrent liabilities plus stockholders' equity are a firm's longer-term sources of capital. The usefulness of the classification of assets and equities as current or noncurrent is discussed when we consider the third principal statement, the statement of changes in financial position.

Valuation   The dollar amount shown for each asset and liability listed in the statement of financial position of Jonathan Electronics Corporation is based on one of two valuation bases: (1) cash, or current cash-equivalent, valuation, or (2) acquisition, or historical, cost valuation.

Cash is stated at the amount of cash on hand or in the bank. Accounts receivable are shown at the amount of cash expected to be collected from customers. Liabilities are generally shown at the amount of cash required to discharge debts. These assets and liabilities are sometimes referred to as *monetary items* because they are valued on a cash, or current cash-equivalent, basis.

The remaining assets are shown at either unadjusted or adjusted acquisition cost. For example, merchandise inventory and land are shown at the amount of cash or other resources that the firm originally sacrificed to acquire those assets. Equipment and buildings are likewise shown at acquisition cost, but this amount is adjusted downward to reflect the portion of the assets' services that has been used since acquisition. A large proportion of Jonathan Electronics Corporation's assets are shown at either unadjusted or adjusted acquisition cost. It is unlikely that these amounts are equal to the amounts the company could realize if the assets were sold or the amounts the company would have to pay to replace them.

Common stock is stated at the amount originally invested by owners when the firm's stock was first sold. Retained earnings is the sum of all prior years' earnings in excess of dividends. Because of its link with earnings and the valuation of assets and liabilities, retained earnings is, in effect, measured using a combination of the current cash-equivalent and acquisition-cost valuation bases.

Assets and Equities Not Shown   After having studied carefully the balance sheet of Jonathan Electronics Corporation, several possible resources of the firm are noteworthy because of their absence. Consider, for example, the value of a well-trained labor force, dynamic managerial leadership, superior technological abilities, or the good reputation of the company. These and several other intangible, but perhaps more important, resources are excluded from most firms' balance sheets.

We have considered briefly several important asset and liability valuation and inclusion issues here to point out possible deficiencies in the balance sheet as an indicator of a firm's financial position at any moment in time. These issues are considered more fully in later chapters.

Statement of Net Income

The statement of net income of Jonathan Electronics Corporation for the year 1979 is presented in Exhibit 1.2. This statement indicates the *earnings*, or *profits*, of the company for the year. Note several aspects of this second principal financial statement.

EXHIBIT 1.2
Jonathan Electronics Corporation
Statement of Net Income
For the Year 1979

Revenues:	
Sale of Merchandise	$2,250,000
Sale of Engineering Services	140,000
Interest on Customers' Uncollected Accounts	10,000
Total Revenues	$2,400,000
Less Expenses:	
Cost of Merchandise Sold	$ 900,000
Salaries Expense	400,000
Depreciation Expense	200,000
Selling and Administrative Expenses	350,000
Interest Expense	50,000
Income Tax Expense	200,000
Total Expenses	$2,100,000
Net Income	$ 300,000

Statement Reports Activities over Time The income statement presents the results of earnings activity over time and therefore reports *flows*. In contrast, the balance sheet presents a statement of the firm's assets and equities at a specific point in time and reports *stocks*.

Concepts of Net Income, Revenue, and Expense The terms *net income, earnings,* and *profits* are synonymous and used interchangeably in corporate annual reports and throughout this text. The generation of earnings is a primary activity of most business firms, and the income statement is intended to provide a measure of how successful a firm was in achieving this goal for a given time span. Net income is defined as the difference between revenues and expenses for a period.

Revenues are a measure of the inflows of assets (or reductions in liabilities) from selling goods and providing services to customers. During 1979, Jonathan Electronics Corporation sold merchandise and provided engineering and financing services. From its customers, Jonathan Electronics Corporation received either cash or promises to pay cash in the near future. These promises to pay are called Accounts Receivable from Customers. Thus, revenues were generated, leading to an increase in assets.

Expenses are a measure of the outflows of assets (or increases in liabilities) used up in generating revenues. The cost of merchandise sold (an expense) is measured by the acquisition cost of merchandise that was sold to customers. Salaries expense is the amount of cash payments or promises to make future cash payments (Salaries Payable) to employees for services received in helping generate revenues during the period. Depreciation expense is a measure of the services of equipment and buildings used during 1979. For each expense there is either a reduction in an asset or an increase in a liability. A firm strives to generate an excess of net asset inflows from revenues over net asset outflows or expirations from expenses required in generating the revenues. When expenses for a period exceed revenues, a firm incurs a *net loss*. The net income measure may be used as an indicator of a firm's accomplishments (revenues) relative to the efforts required (expenses) in pursuing its activities.

Relationship to Balance Sheet   The income statement articulates, or links, with the balance sheets as of the beginning and end of the period. Recall that retained earnings represents the sum of all prior earnings of a firm in excess of dividends. The amount of net income for the year helps explain the change in retained earnings between the beginning and end of the year. During 1979, Jonathan Electronics Corporation had net income of $300,000. Assume that dividends declared and paid were $100,000. The change in retained earnings during 1979 can therefore be explained as follows:

Retained Earnings, December 31, 1978 (stock)	$700,000
Add Net Income for the Year 1979 (flow).........................	300,000
Subtract Dividends Declared and Paid (flow)	(100,000)
Retained Earnings, December 31, 1979 (stock)	$900,000

Net income for the period also articulates with changes in the other components of the balance sheet. If we subtract the amount for each balance sheet component at the beginning of the period from the corresponding amount at the end of the period, we get the *change* in each component during the period, as follows:

$$\begin{matrix} \text{Change in} \\ \text{Assets} \end{matrix} = \begin{matrix} \text{Change in} \\ \text{Liabilities} \end{matrix} + \begin{matrix} \text{Change in} \\ \text{Contributed} \\ \text{Capital} \end{matrix} + \begin{matrix} \text{Change in} \\ \text{Retained} \\ \text{Earnings} \end{matrix} .$$

In explaining the change in retained earnings for 1979 of Jonathan Electronics Corporation, we saw that the change in retained earnings is equal to net income minus dividends. Thus:

$$\begin{array}{c} \text{Change in} \\ \text{Assets} \end{array} = \begin{array}{c} \text{Change in} \\ \text{Liabilities} \end{array} + \begin{array}{c} \text{Change in} \\ \text{Contributed} \\ \text{Capital} \end{array} + \begin{array}{c} \text{Net} \\ \text{Income} \end{array} - \text{Dividends}$$

or:

$$\text{Net Income} = \begin{array}{c} \text{Change in} \\ \text{Assets} \end{array} - \begin{array}{c} \text{Change in} \\ \text{Liabilities} \end{array} - \begin{array}{c} \text{Change in} \\ \text{Contributed} \\ \text{Capital} \end{array} + \text{Dividends}.$$

Assets may be increased (decreased) by an increase (decrease) in liabilities, contributed capital, or net income. Net income is usually associated with an increase in assets or a decrease in liabilities. The significance of these relationships between the balance sheet and income statement is considered in more depth in later chapters. The relationships are introduced here to indicate that the amounts of assets and liabilities included in the balance sheet at the beginning and end of a period are closely related to the revenues and expenses reported in the income statement for the period.

Measurement of Revenues and Expenses   As was the case with assets and equities on the balance sheet, the measurement of revenues and expenses is based on either (1) cash, or cash-equivalent, values or (2) acquisition costs. The amount reported as revenue from the sale of merchandise or services is a measure of the expected amount of cash to be received from customers. Salary, selling and administrative, interest, and income tax expenses are stated as the amount of cash the firm was required to pay for the services received. In contrast, cost of merchandise sold is measured by the acquisition cost of inventory that was sold, and depreciation expense is measured in terms of the acquisition cost of the services of the equipment and buildings that were used during the year.

Revenues and Expenses Excluded   The balance sheet shows assets such as inventory, land, equipment, and buildings at acquisition cost. The income statement shows expenses such as cost of merchandise sold and depreciation expense at an appropriate portion of this acquisition cost. The income statement thus excludes any changes in the economic value of those assets. For example, land was acquired for $200,000 several years ago. Suppose that this land had a current appraised value of $500,000 at the end of 1979. This increase in value is not normally recognized as revenue on the income statement until the land is sold. The economist views changes in the market value of a firm's assets as part of its income. The accountant generally recognizes changes in the value of assets only at the time assets are sold. Thus, we see one important difference between the economist's and accountant's definitions of income.

Statement of Changes in Financial Position

The third principal financial statement of Jonathan Electronics Corporation, the statement of changes in financial position, is presented in Exhibit 1.3. This statement explains the change in *working capital* for the year. Working capital is equal to current

EXHIBIT 1.3
Jonathan Electronics Corporation
Statement of Changes in
Financial Position
For the Year 1979

Working Capital, January 1, 1979		$100,000
Working Capital Increased by:		
Operations:		
Revenues Increasing Working Capital	$2,400,000	
Expenses Decreasing Working Capital	(1,900,000)	
Total from Operations	$ 500,000	
Proceeds from Issue of Bonds, due 1998	100,000	
Total Increases in Working Capital		600,000
Working Capital Decreased by:		
Dividends Declared and Paid	$ 100,000	
Equipment and Buildings Acquired	450,000	
Total Decreases in Working Capital		(550,000)
Working Capital, December 31, 1979		$150,000

assets less current liabilities. Of what significance is a statement explaining or analyzing the changes in working capital for the year? This might be best understood
with an example.

Example Diversified Technologies Corporation began business in 1975. In its first
4 years of operations, it had net income of $100,000, $300,000, $800,000, and
$1,500,000, respectively. The company has retained all of its earnings for growth and
expansion. Early in 1979, the company learned that it was running out of cash despite
the retention of earnings. A careful study of the problem revealed that, although the
company was operating profitably, it was expanding inventories, buildings, and equipment so fast that funds were not being generated quickly enough to keep pace with
its recent growth.

The foregoing illustration is a common phenomenon among business firms. Cash
and near-cash resources (for example, accounts receivable from customers) are not
generated in sufficient amounts or at the proper times to finance ongoing or growing
operations. Whereas the income statement is a report on the profits of a firm, the
statement of changes in financial position is a report on the flow of funds into and
out of a firm.

The definition of "funds" could be cash only, or cash plus accounts receivable, or
some other definition. Most published statements of changes in financial position
use a broader definition of funds. Funds are defined as cash plus those assets expected
to be turned into cash within approximately 1 year (that is, current assets) less those
obligations expected to require the payment of cash within approximately 1 year
(that is, current liabilities). Working capital (= current assets − current liabilities)

then, represents a pool of excess cash or near-cash resources that can be used to finance ongoing or growing operations.

For Jonathan Electronics Corporation, working capital is increased as a result of (1) generating revenues in the form of cash or accounts receivable and (2) issuing long-term bonds for cash. Working capital is decreased as a result of reporting expenses such as (1) cost of merchandise sold (which reduces merchandise inventory), (2) salaries expense (which reduces cash or increases salaries payable), and (3) selling and administrative expenses (which reduce cash or increase accounts payable). Working capital is also decreased (4) when dividends are declared and (5) when equipment and buildings are purchased for cash. In the statement of changes in financial position, revenues that increase working capital and expenses that decrease working capital are grouped together to obtain the net increase or decrease in working capital from operations. Other sources of working capital (issuance of bonds) and uses of working capital (declaration of dividends, purchase of equipment and buildings) are then presented.

If the firm is to continue operating successfully, it must generate more working capital from revenues than it uses up for expenses. Sufficient working capital must also be generated from operations to replace equipment and buildings. In some cases the firm can borrow from long-term investors to replenish working capital, but future operations must generate sufficient working capital to repay these loans. The statement of changes in financial position, therefore, provides information about the principal financing and investing activities of a firm and may be used in assessing the financial health of a company. Several additional aspects of this statement should be noted.

Statement Reports Activities over Time   The statement of changes in financial position indicates the increases and decreases in working capital during the year and, like the income statement, reports flows.

Relationship to Balance Sheet and Income Statement   The statement of changes in financial position helps explain the change in working capital (current assets minus current liabilities) between the beginning and end of the period. In this way, the statement articulates or links with the balance sheet. To demonstrate the relationship of this statement to the balance sheet, we again determine the change in each balance sheet component between the beginning and the end of the period as follows:

$$\begin{matrix} \text{Change in} \\ \text{Current} \\ \text{Assets} \end{matrix} + \begin{matrix} \text{Change in} \\ \text{Noncurrent} \\ \text{Assets} \end{matrix} = \begin{matrix} \text{Change in} \\ \text{Current} \\ \text{Liabilities} \end{matrix} + \begin{matrix} \text{Change in} \\ \text{Noncurrent} \\ \text{Liabilities} \end{matrix} + \begin{matrix} \text{Change in} \\ \text{Stockholders'} \\ \text{Equity} \end{matrix}$$

Rearranging:

$$\begin{matrix} \text{Change in} \\ \text{Current} \\ \text{Assets} \end{matrix} - \begin{matrix} \text{Change in} \\ \text{Current} \\ \text{Liabilities} \end{matrix} = \begin{matrix} \text{Change in} \\ \text{Noncurrent} \\ \text{Liabilities} \end{matrix} + \begin{matrix} \text{Change in} \\ \text{Stockholders'} \\ \text{Equity} \end{matrix} - \begin{matrix} \text{Change in} \\ \text{Noncurrent.} \\ \text{Assets} \end{matrix}$$

As we discuss in Chapter 5, the change in working capital can be explained or analyzed by looking at changes in noncurrent liabilities (for example, long-term borrowing from creditors), changes in stockholders' equity (for example, net income and dividends), and changes in noncurrent assets (for example, purchase of equipment and buildings). Net income for the period partially explains the change in working capital, so that the income statement and the statement of changes in financial position are related.

We might summarize the relationship between the three statements as follows:

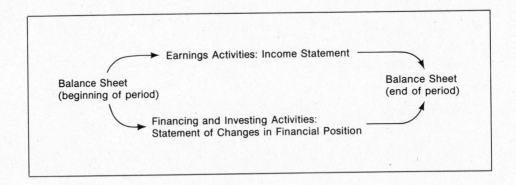

Supporting Statements or Schedules

The statements of financial position, net income, and changes in financial position shown in the annual report are usually highly condensed for easy comprehension by the average reader. Some readers are interested in details omitted from these condensed versions. The annual report, therefore, typically includes schedules that provide more detail for some of the items reported in the three main statements. For example, separate schedules must be provided to explain the change in contributed capital and retained earnings, and may be provided to explain changes in other items in the balance sheet.

Notes to the Financial Statements

Every set of published financial statements is supplemented by explanatory notes. These notes are an integral part of the statements. As later chapters make clear, a firm must select the accounting methods followed in preparing its financial statements from a set of generally accepted methods. The notes indicate the actual accounting methods used by the firm. The notes also disclose additional information that elaborates on items presented in the three principal statements. To understand fully a firm's balance sheet, income statement, and statement of changes in financial position, a careful reading of the notes is required. We do not present notes to the financial statements for the Jonathan Electronics Corporation because they would not mean much at this stage. Do not conclude, however, that the notes are unimportant merely because we have omitted them from the statements presented in this chapter.

Auditors' Opinion

An important section of the annual report to the stockholders is the opinion of the independent Certified Public Accountant on the financial statements, supporting schedules, and notes. The accountant's opinion is frequently described as the *Accountant's Report,* or sometimes merely as the *Opinion* or *Certificate.* It is often called the report of the *Auditor* or *Certified Public Accountant.*

The auditor's opinion generally follows a standard format, with some variations to meet specific circumstances. An auditor's opinion on the financial statements of Jonathan Electronics Corporation in the standard format might be as follows:

> We have examined the comparative balance sheets of Jonathan Electronics Corporation as of December 31, 1978 and 1979, and the related statements of net income and changes in financial position for the year 1979. Our examination was made in accordance with generally accepted auditing standards, and accordingly included such tests of the accounting records and such other auditing procedures as we considered necessary in the circumstances.
>
> In our opinion, the aforementioned financial statements present fairly the financial position of Jonathan Electronics Corporation at December 31, 1978 and 1979, and the results of its operations and changes in financial position for the year 1979 in conformity with generally accepted accounting principles applied on a basis consistent with that of the preceding year.

The opinion usually contains two paragraphs—a *scope* paragraph and an *opinion* paragraph. The scope paragraph indicates the financial presentations covered by the opinion and affirms that auditing standards and practices generally accepted by the accounting profession have been adhered to unless otherwise noted and described. Exceptions to the statement that the auditor's "examination was made in accordance with generally accepted auditing standards" are seldom, if ever, seen in published annual reports. There are occasional references to the auditor's having relied on financial statements examined by other auditors, particularly for subsidiaries or for data from prior periods.

The opinion expressed by the auditor in the second paragraph is the heart of the accountant's report. The opinion may be *unqualified* or *qualified.* The great majority of opinions are unqualified; that is, there are no exceptions or qualifications to the auditor's opinion that the statements "present fairly the financial position . . . and the results of operations and the changes in financial position . . . in conformity with generally accepted accounting principles applied on a consistent basis."

Qualifications to the opinion result primarily from material uncertainties regarding valuation or realization of assets, outstanding litigation or tax liabilities, or accounting inconsistencies between periods caused by changes in the application of accounting principles. An opinion qualified as to fair presentation is usually noted by the phrase *subject to;* an opinion qualified as to consistency in application of accounting principles is usually noted by *except for,* with an indication of the auditor's approval of the change.

A qualification so material that the auditor feels an opinion cannot be expressed as to the fairness of the financial statements as a whole must result in either a *disclaimer of opinion* or an *adverse opinion*. Adverse opinions and disclaimers of opinion are extremely rare in published reports.

A member of the American Institute of Certified Public Accountants (AICPA) is expected to adhere to the pronouncements of the body designated by the AICPA as the official source of generally accepted accounting principles.[1] As will be discussed later in this chapter, the official authoritative body from 1938 to 1959 was the Committee on Accounting Procedure and from 1959 to 1973 was the Accounting Principles Board. Since 1973, the Financial Accounting Standards Board has been given the authority for specifying generally accepted accounting principles. A Certified Public Accountant may not, in general, attest that statements are in conformity with generally accepted accounting principles when the statements contain material departures from rulings of those bodies. If, however, the CPA can demonstrate that, because of unusual circumstances, departures are required so that the statements are not misleading, then the CPA may attest to statements with material departures from generally accepted accounting principles. The grounds for justifying departures are so stringent, however, that such departures are seldom, if ever, seen in published financial statements.

NATURE AND DEVELOPMENT OF ACCOUNTING PRINCIPLES

Frequent references are made throughout this book to "generally accepted accounting principles." These "principles" are the accounting methods and procedures used by firms in preparing their financial statements. In this section, we consider the nature of these principles and the process through which they are developed.

Nature of Principles in Accounting

Principles in accounting differ from those in fields such as physics and mathematics. In physics and other natural sciences, the criterion for evaluating a principle is the degree to which the predictions indicated by the principle or theory correspond with physically observed phenomena. In mathematics, a principle (or theorem) is judged on its internal consistency with the structure of definitions and underlying axioms. In accounting, principles are judged on their general acceptability by preparers and users of accounting reports. Unlike those in the physical sciences, principles in accounting do not naturally exist awaiting discovery. Unlike mathematics, there is no structure of definitions and concepts in accounting that can be used unambiguously in developing accounting principles. For example, one generally accepted accounting principle is that land is to be stated at its acquisition, or historical, cost as long as it is held by a firm. Changes in the market value of the land are not reflected in the financial statements until the land is sold. This accounting principle cannot be

---

[1]   Rule 203, *Code of Professional Ethics,* AICPA, March 1973.

"proven" to be correct. It has simply been judged to be the generally acceptable method of accounting for land. (Recently, however, experience with inflation has led many accountants and financial statement users to question the relevance of historical-cost valuations.)

Development of Principles in Accounting

The discussion above concerning the nature of accounting principles suggests that their development is essentially a political process. Various persons or groups have power, or authority, in the decision process that yields generally accepted accounting principles. Some of the more important participants are described below.

Congress In the Securities Act of 1933, the Congress accepted the ultimate legal authority to prescribe the methods of accounting used in preparing financial statements for stockholders of publicly held corporations. Congress has delegated its authority to the Securities and Exchange Commission (SEC), an agency of the federal government. Whereas the SEC has legal authority to prescribe accounting principles, since 1938 it has delegated most of the responsibility for developing accounting principles to the accounting profession.[2] In most cases, the SEC serves as an advisor or consultant on proposed accounting procedures. In a few instances, the SEC has effectively exerted its legal authority by disagreeing with positions taken within the accounting profession.

The SEC does prescribe the form of financial statements submitted to it and has issued rulings in certain areas. Among its publications are the following:

Regulation S-X. A document pertaining to the form and content of financial statements required to be filed with the SEC.

Accounting Series Releases. A series of opinions on accounting principles that together with *Regulation S-X* are the primary statements on the form and content of financial statements filed with the Commission.

Staff Accounting Bulletins. A series of reports prepared by the SEC staff that discuss certain reporting issues in greater depth than provided in *Regulation S-X* or the *Accounting Series Releases.*

Accounting Profession The accounting profession is composed of practicing accountants, financial managers, controllers, academicians, and others. Each of these groups has its own professional organization or association (American Institute of Certified Public Accountants, National Association of Accountants, Financial Executives Institute, American Accounting Association). The professional organizations sometimes express positions, or opinions, on proposed accounting principles. Most of the specification of accounting principles has been carried out, however, by officially appointed committees or boards within the accounting profession. Between

---

[2] *Accounting Series Release No. 4,* Securities and Exchange Commission, 1938. The SEC reaffirmed its delegation of responsibility by recognizing the Financial Accounting Standards Board in *Accounting Series Release No. 150,* December 1973.

1938 and 1959, the Committee on Accounting Procedure of the American Institute of Certified Public Accountants issued Bulletins on various topics. Between 1959 and 1973, the Accounting Principles Board (APB) of the American Institute of Certified Public Accountants issued Opinions. These Bulletins and Opinions were considered to constitute generally accepted accounting principles. The APB was composed of individuals from within the accounting profession, with heavy representation from public accounting firms.

Since mid-1973, the Financial Accounting Standards Board (FASB) has been the principal agency outside of the federal government responsible for developing accounting principles. The FASB differs from the APB in two important respects. First, the FASB includes substantial representation from several groups of statement users in addition to members from the public accounting profession. Second, the members of the FASB are employed on a full-time basis and have severed all relations with their previous firms or universities. This severance of relations increases the independence of Board members, and reduces chances for undue influence by their previous employers. The FASB periodically issues Statements on Financial Accounting Standards which have the authority of being considered generally accepted accounting principles.

Whereas Congress and the SEC have the legal authority to prescribe accounting principles and the FASB has responsibility for doing so, several professional accounting organizations have influence on the decision process.

The *American Institute of Certified Public Accountants* (AICPA) is the national organization of certified public accountants. Its publications and committees are influential in the development of accounting principles and practices. It actively promulgates standards of ethics and reviews conduct within the profession. Among its influential publications are the following:

Journal of Accountancy. A monthly periodical containing articles, pronouncements, announcements, and practical sections of direct interest to the practicing members of the profession.

Accounting Research Bulletins Nos. 1–51 (1939–1959). A series of statements on accounting problems that contributed greatly to the narrowing of differences and inconsistencies in accounting practice and to the development and recognition of generally accepted accounting principles.

Opinions of the Accounting Principles Board Nos. 1–31 (1962–1973). A series of statements on accounting problems and generally accepted accounting principles. These pronouncements remain in effect unless superseded by statements of the Financial Accounting Standards Board.

Accounting Research Studies. A series of monographs on accounting problems that provide a basis for further development of generally accepted accounting principles in the particular area.

Statements on Auditing Standards. No. 1 (1973) of this series is a codification of all statements on auditing standards previously issued by the AICPA. Later numbers of the series deal with specific auditing procedures. These publications form the basis of compliance with the first paragraph of the auditor's report (illustrated in this chapter) with respect to the scope of the examination.

Two publications of the American Institute of Certified Public Accountants are of special interest to students and scholars:

Accountants' Index. A series published each quarter (with annual summaries) in which the literature pertaining to the field for the period covered is indexed in detail. The index service is also obtainable through an on-line computer system.

Accounting Trends and Techniques. An annual publication presenting a survey of the accounting aspects of financial reports of some 600 industrial and commercial corporations. It presents statistical tabulations on specific practices, terminology, and disclosures together with illustrations taken from individual annual reports.

In addition to the national organization, there are state societies of certified public accountants that contribute to maintaining high levels of professional performance and to developing procedures and practices.

The *American Accounting Association* is primarily an organization for accountants in academic work, but it is open to all who are interested in accounting. It participates in the development of generally accepted accounting principles and practice, and it promotes the academic phases of accounting theory, research, and instruction. Among its influential publications are the following:

The Accounting Review. A quarterly periodical containing articles and sections covering a broad span of subjects related to accounting practice, research, and instruction for purposes of both external and internal reporting.

Accounting and Reporting Standards for Corporate Financial Statements. A comprehensive presentation of accounting principles for external reporting purposes. The principles enumerated frequently indicate the direction toward which the Association feels accounting reporting should be moving rather than necessarily a reflection of currently accepted accounting principles.

A Statement of Basic Accounting Theory. An integrated statement for educators, practitioners, and others interested in accounting. The statement seeks to identify the field of accounting, to establish standards by which accounting information can be judged, to point out possible improvements in accounting practice, and to present a useful framework for scholars who wish to extend the uses of accounting.

A Statement on Accounting Theory and Theory Acceptance. A description of the process through which accounting theory is developed and validated. Whereas the two preceding publications focus on the content of accounting principles and theories, this publication is more concerned with the process of developing the principles and theories.

The *National Association of Accountants* is a national society generally open to all engaged in activities closely associated with managerial accounting. Among its publications are the following:

Management Accounting. A monthly periodical.

Research Series. A series of monographs on subjects of internal and external accounting.

Accounting Practice Reports. A series of summaries of surveys on current practice in a limited area of accounting.

The *Financial Executives Institute* is an organization of financial executives of large businesses, such as chief accountants, controllers, treasurers, and financial vice-presidents. Among its publications are *Financial Executive,* a monthly periodical, and a number of studies on problems confronting accounting and financial management.

Income tax legislation and administration have had a substantial impact on adequate accounting and reporting. Although the income tax requirements in themselves do not establish principles and practices for general external reporting, their influence on the choice of acceptable procedures is substantial. At the federal level, in addition to the *Internal Revenue Code* passed by the Congress, there are the *Regulations* and *Rulings* of the Internal Revenue Service, and the opinions of the United States Tax Court.

The *Cost Accounting Standards Board* (CASB) has been authorized by Congress to set accounting standards for cost determination by defense contractors under federal contracts. Most of the work of the CASB does not directly affect the form of published financial statements, but the standards announced by the CASB have considerable weight in practice where the FASB has not established a standard.

Financial Statement Users   The FASB seeks representation from those doing security analysis and thus some representation from user interests. Professional organizations of financial statement users, such as the Financial Analysts Federation and the Investment Bankers Association, frequently comment on proposed accounting principles to the FASB and SEC. Any individual user of financial statements can, of course, comment on existing or proposed accounting principles to the FASB, SEC, or a member of Congress.

Illustration of the Political Process   The SEC and the FASB both play important roles in the current power structure for developing accounting principles. The amount of authority that the SEC exercises and the amount that is delegated to the FASB varies with the problem area under consideration and with the pressure exerted on the SEC by Congress and others.

An example of the manner in which the political process functions in developing generally accepted accounting principles is described by Horngren,[3] a former member of the Accounting Principles Board. The accounting principle of concern in his discussion is the valuation of marketable securities using current market prices. You will not be able to follow all of the technical aspects of the example, but you should be able to observe the workings of the political process.

> The heart of the issue concerning marketable securities deals with when portfolio gains and losses should be recognized. There is a variety of views ranging from predominant present practice (whereby only realized gains and losses are included in income) to some version of spreading (whereby all gains and losses from changes in market prices are included in income but on some three- to ten-year

---

[3]   Charles T. Horngren, "The Marketing of Accounting Standards," *Journal of Accountancy,* October 1973, pp. 61–66.

moving-average, long-term yield basis) to a flow-through approach (whereby all gains and losses are included in income as the prices of marketable securities fluctuate from quarter to quarter).

Another set of issues concerns whether portfolio losses or gains belong in an income statement in the first place. Instead, some accountants believe that a two-statement approach is needed. If adopted, a separate statement of realized and unrealized gains would be used.

An intensive study of this topic was begun in September 1968. Heavy interaction persisted between the APB and all interested parties, particularly representatives of the insurance industry, whose income statements would be dramatically affected by any new accounting standards. In May 1971, there was a two-day public hearing on the issues.

After about three years of spasmodic deliberations, the APB was ready to issue an exposure draft of an Opinion. The Board had narrowed its preferences to two methods using one income statement: either flow-through or spreading. In September 1971, the Board approved a draft favoring flow-through. The draft was to be "mini-exposed" to the SEC, the insurance industry and others who had been actively involved. The intention of the Board was to have full public exposure of the Opinion after the October APB meeting.

The insurance companies were bitterly opposed to flow-through. They blitz-krieged Washington. The SEC, armed with its own preferences and buttressed by industry reactions, informed the APB that it could not support flow-through. At this point, flow-through was a dead duck because higher management (the SEC) had, in effect, overruled the APB.

At its October meeting, the APB again discussed the topic. Because flow-through was no longer an acceptable alternative, the Board changed its preferences to either spreading or a two-statement approach. The Board voted in favor of a two-statement approach, although strong voices were raised in support of spreading. In November, these alternatives were explored with the SEC and the insurance industry. At its December meeting, the Board was informed that the fire and casualty companies had also strongly objected to the spreading method. One potent spokesman for the SEC found some merit in the spreading method, but he informed the Board that the SEC would not impose it or any solution on an industry that was adamantly opposed to it. So spreading was dead.

The Board then discussed two alternatives: (1) some version of a two-statement method and (2) a modification of predominant current practice whereby all companies in all industries would show marketable securities at market value in the balance sheet, unrealized gains and losses in stockholders' equity, and only realized gains and losses in the income statement. However, the fire and casualty companies also vigorously opposed the two-statement method.

Note how the feasible alternatives changed in response to the likelihood of acceptability. The constraints became more binding as the months wore on:

1 September—flow-through or spreading
2 October—spreading or two-statement
3 December—two-statement or slight modification of status quo.

Discussions of various versions of the December alternatives were renewed in early 1972. But the Board could not resolve the issues and the SEC was non-committal on anything except "no flow-through." During the course of the discussions, the top managements of 15 or 20 large insurance companies met together about the issue more than once and also with the SEC commissioners at least once.

The marketable securities scenario was concluded by an APB report to the SEC in March 1972 that summarized the APB deliberations and the alternatives. However, the report offered no preferred solution.

Future Development of Accounting Principles

Unless Congress or the SEC unexpectedly decides to exert its legal authority, we see little reason for the future development of accounting principles to differ materially from that in the past. The process will continue to be a political one, with opposing viewpoints attempting to exert influence on the decision process. Positions taken or opinions rendered by participants in this process must be not only carefully developed but also effectively marketed if the positions are to become generally acceptable to the persons involved in preparing and using financial statements.

ACCOUNTING TERMINOLOGY

A firm's Annual Report to Stockholders reaches a large group of readers. The members of this group vary in their understanding of business and accounting. If accounting is to fulfill its potential contribution, it should address this broad group of users. Thus, there is a need for a terminology based as much as possible on that of the general citizenry.

Accounting terminology generally follows common usage. Occasionally, however, commonly used words are given restricted technical meanings. For example, the word "reserve" in common usage indicates that a pool of something is earmarked or set aside, but in accounting terminology its meaning is altogether different. The term "surplus" may mean "too much" in commonly used terminology, but this is not its meaning when used in accounting. We attempt to prevent the possible confusion that can arise out of these and other similar altered usages of common terminology. Students of accounting can therefore use their vocabulary as developed for general communication. You will find it necessary to learn a rather limited vocabulary of new technical terms and to become aware of technical meanings assigned to a few common words such as *allowance, cost, credit, expense,* and *revenue.* A glossary of accounting terms and other terms with special meanings in accounting appears at the back of this book. The first question at the end of each chapter lists the important accounting terms used in that chapter. Use the glossary to aid in reviewing the meaning of those terms.

SUMMARY

This chapter provides an overview of the three principal financial statements and describes the nature and development of generally accepted accounting principles. Perhaps more questions have been raised than answered. We feel, however, that it is helpful to have an overview of the field of financial accounting before embarking on a study of the concepts and procedures employed in preparing various accounting reports.

Chapters 2–5 discuss and illustrate the concepts and procedures underlying the balance sheet, income statement, and statement of changes in financial position. Chapter 6 considers techniques for analyzing and interpreting financial statements. Chapters 7–12 explore more fully the principles of accounting for individual assets and equities, and Chapter 13 provides a synthesis of generally accepted accounting principles. Chapter 14 explores several important current issues in financial reporting, including accounting for inflation.

Now we turn to the study of financial accounting. We recognize that most readers of this book will not choose careers in the field of accounting. Accordingly, emphasis is placed not only on the compilation of the accounting data and preparation of reports, but also on the uses of accounting data for those who will receive it in the form of various reports. Regardless of the reader's interest in accounting, we have found that the most effective means of comprehending the concepts and procedures discussed in this book is careful study of the numerical examples presented in the chapters and diligent working of several problems at the end of each chapter. Frequent reference should also be made to the detailed set of financial statements and notes presented in Appendix A at the back of the book for International Corporation. By the time you have completed your study of the material in this book, you should be able to understand all the items included in these financial statements. These suggestions should be kept in mind as you proceed with your study of accounting.

QUESTIONS AND PROBLEMS

1 Review the meaning of the following concepts or terms introduced in this chapter:
   a Financial accounting.
   b Managerial accounting.
   c Generally accepted accounting principles.
   d Balance sheet.
   e Assets.
   f Liabilities.
   g Stockholders' equity.
   h Retained earnings.
   i Income, earnings, profit.
   j Net loss.
   k Revenue.
   l Expense.

    m Working capital.
    n Stocks and flows.
    o Articulate.
    p Unqualified opinion.
    q Qualified opinion.
    r Adverse opinion.
    s SEC.
    t FASB.
    u CPA.
    v CASB.

2 Distinguish between financial accounting and managerial accounting. Suggest several ways in which the managers of a firm might use information presented in the three principal externally directed financial statements discussed in this chapter.

3 Generally accepted accounting principles are the methods of accounting used by publicly held firms in preparing their financial statements. A principle in physics, such as the law of gravity, serves as a basis for developing theories and explaining the relationships among physical objects. In what ways are generally accepted accounting principles similar to and different from principles in physics?

4 How would the principal financial statements of a not-for-profit hospital, library, or university differ from those presented in the chapter?

5 Prepare a balance sheet of your personal assets, liabilities, and owner's equity. How does the presentation of owners' equity on your balance sheet differ from that in Exhibit 1.1?

6 Suggest procedures you could follow in determining the amounts at which the following resources might be stated on a balance sheet if they were to be recognized as assets:
    a Well-known trademark or other product symbol.
    b Well-trained employee labor force.

7 Suggest reasons why the definition of "funds" in a statement of changes in financial position presented to a bank for a 6-month bank loan might differ from the definition of funds in a statement presented to stockholders and potential investors.

8 Does the unqualified or clean opinion of a certified public accountant indicate that the financial statements are free of errors and misrepresentations? Explain.

9 Assets such as buildings and equipment generally decrease in value or depreciate over time as those assets are used. Accountants measure depreciation by recognizing as an expense each period a portion of the acquisition cost of these assets based on some systematic procedure (for example, an equal amount each year of the asset's useful life). Economists measure depreciation as the decrease in the amount at which the building or equipment could be sold between the beginning and end of the period.

You are planning to acquire the assets of a steel company and must determine the price you are willing to pay. Which of these two methods of measuring depreciation and asset values do you think provides the more useful information?

10 Various items are classified on the balance sheet or income statement in one of the following ways:

CA—Current assets CC—Contributed capital
NA—Noncurrent assets RE—Retained earnings
CL—Current liabilities NI—Income statement item (revenue or expense)
NL—Noncurrent liabilities X—Item would generally not appear on a
  balance sheet or income statement

Using the letters above, indicate the classification of each of the following items:
a Factory. NA
b Interest revenue. NI
c Common stock issued by a corporation. CC
d Goodwill developed by a firm (see Glossary). X
e Automobiles used by sales staff. NA
f Cash on hand. CA
g Unsettled damage suit against a firm. NL
h Commissions earned by sales staff. NI
i Supplies inventory. CA
j Note payable, due in 3 months. CL
k Increase in market value of land held. X
l Dividends. RE
m Employee payroll taxes payable. CL

11 Determine the missing balance sheet amounts in each of the four independent cases below. Only items marked "?" need be calculated.

	a	b	c	d
Noncurrent Assets	$700,000	$2,000,000	$360,000	?
Stockholders' Equity	?	1,550,000	380,000	$370,000
Total Assets	?	?	500,000	?
Current Liabilities	250,000	400,000	*	**
Current Assets	320,000	?	*	**
Noncurrent Liabilities	300,000	?	?	400,000
Total Liabilities and Stockholders' Equity	?	2,800,000	?	950,000

* Working capital = current assets − current liabilities = $40,000.
** Working capital = current assets − current liabilities = $60,000.

12 The comparative balance sheets of the Sedwick Corporation as of December 31, 1978, and December 31, 1979, are presented below:

**Sedwick Corporation
Comparative Balance Sheets
December 31, 1978 and 1979**

	December 31, 1978	December 31, 1979
Total Assets	$200,000	$400,000
Liabilities	$ 40,000	$ 60,000
Capital Stock	100,000	200,000
Retained Earnings	60,000	140,000
Total Liabilities and Stockholders' Equity	$200,000	$400,000

Dividends declared and paid during 1979 were $30,000.
a Determine net income for the year ending December 31, 1979, by analyzing the change in retained earnings.
b Determine net income for the year ending December 31, 1979, by analyzing the changes in assets, liabilities, and contributed capital during the year. (Hint: Refer to the last equation on p. 9.)

13 Determine the missing amount affecting retained earnings for the year 1979 in each of the independent cases below.

	a	b	c	d	e
Retained Earnings, December 31, 1978	$200,000	? *455,000*	$320,000	$75,000	$70,000
Net Income	50,000	$120,000	180,000	*55,000*	(50,000)*
Dividends Declared and Paid	20,000	75,000	*50,000*	40,000	? *10,000*
Retained Earnings December 31, 1979	? *230,000*	500,000	450,000	90,000	10,000

* Net loss.

14 Determine the change in working capital for 1979 in each of the independent cases below.

Noncurrent Assets	a	b	c	d
January 1, 1979	$ 70,000	$400,000	$250,000	$400,000
December 31, 1979	100,000	500,000	300,000	350,000
Noncurrent Liabilities				
January 1, 1979	70,000	200,000	100,000	200,000
December 31, 1979	80,000	250,000	250,000	180,000
Stockholders' Equity				
January 1, 1979	40,000	160,000	100,000	200,000
December 31, 1979	40,000	200,000	100,000	240,000

If you cannot determine the required relation from the discussion in this chapter, you can get help by referring to the *working capital equation* in the Glossary at the back of the book.

15 B. Stephens, L. Harris, and G. Winkle, recent business school graduates, set up a management consulting practice on December 31, 1978, by issuing common stock for $750,000. The accounting records of the S, H, & W Corporation as of December 31, 1979, reveal the following:

Balance Sheet Items:

Cash	$ 80,000
Accounts Receivable from Clients	195,000
Supplies Inventory	5,000
Office Equipment (net of depreciation)	85,000
Office Building (net of depreciation)	480,000
Accounts Payable to Suppliers	20,000
Payroll Taxes Payable	5,000
Income Taxes Payable	20,000
Common Stock	750,000

Income Statement Items:

Revenue from Consulting Services	$400,000
Rental Revenue (from renting part of building)	30,000
Property Taxes and Insurance Expense	40,000
Salaries Expense	220,000
Depreciation Expense	60,000
Income Tax Expense	50,000

Dividend Information:

Dividends Declared and Paid	$ 10,000

a Prepare an income statement for S, H, & W Corporation for the year ending December 31, 1979. Refer to Exhibit 1.2 for help in designing the format of the statement.

b Prepare a comparative balance sheet for S, H, & W Corporation on December 31, 1978, and December 31, 1979. Refer to Exhibit 1.1 for help in designing the format of the statement.

c Prepare an analysis of the change in retained earnings during 1979.

16 Indicate the effect of each of the independent transactions below on working capital (current assets minus current liabilities) using + (increase), − (decrease), 0 (no net effect). (Hint: You may want to use the equation for the change in net working capital presented in the section on the statement of changes in financial position in preparing your responses.)

a Issue of capital stock for cash.

b Acquisition of land for cash.

c Issue of 20-year bonds for cash.

d Issue of common stock for land.

e Purchase of merchandise inventory from suppliers by agreeing to pay within 2 months.

f Payment of liability to supplier in part **e**.

    g Rendering of legal services to a client and receipt from the client of a promise to pay within 3 months.

    h Collection of the client's account in part **g**.

    i Declaration and immediate payment of a cash dividend to stockholders.

17 Refer to the financial statements and notes of International Corporation presented in Appendix A at the back of the book. After studying carefully these financial statements, respond to the following questions.

    a With respect to the consolidated balance sheet:

       (1) Justify the inclusion of "marketable securities," "inventories," and "plant equipment—net" as assets.

       (2) Identify the valuation methods used in determining the amounts for the various assets shown on International Corporation's balance sheet. (Note: You must refer to some of International Corporation's notes to respond to this question.)

       (3) What justification can you see for excluding International Corporation's investment in a well-trained labor force or its good reputation with customers from its balance sheet?

       (4) Liabilities and stockholders' equities represent sources of or claims on the assets of a firm. In what sense are "accounts payable—trade," "accrued payrolls and payroll deductions," and "retained earnings" sources of or claims on the assets of International Corporation?

       (5) Speculate as to the meaning of the following items on International Corporation's balance sheet: "cost of uncompleted contracts in excess of related billings," "estimated realizable value-discontinued businesses," "cumulative preferred stock," and "treasury stock." (Note: You may want to use the Glossary at the back of the book in responding to this question.)

       (6) The "net worth" of a firm has been described as the excess of a firm's assets over its liabilities. Assume that you have agreed to purchase all of the preferred and common stock of International Corporation for its net worth as of December 31, 19X1. Is $2,001,692,000, the total stockholders' equity, a reasonable price to pay? Why or why not?

    b With respect to the consolidated income statement:

       (7) Net income is defined as the excess of revenues over expenses. Using only numerical amounts, rearrange the items in International Corporation's income statement for 19X1 into the following equation:

$$\text{Net Income} = \text{Revenues} - \text{Expenses.}$$

       (8) Revenues are a measure of the inflows of assets (or reductions in liabilities) from selling goods and services to customers. Justify the inclusion of "sales" and "equity in income (loss) from nonconsolidated subsidiaries and affiliated companies" as revenues.

       (9) Expenses are a measure of the outflows of assets (or increases in liabilities) used up in generating revenues. Justify the inclusion of "cost of goods sold," "depreciation," and "income taxes" as expenses.

      (10) Assuming that "minority interest," "cumulative preferred stock," "common stock," "capital in excess of par value," and "treasury stock" are considered "contributed capital," demonstrate that the following equation is valid for 19X1:

$$\frac{\text{Net}}{\text{Income}} = \frac{\text{Change in}}{\text{Assets}} - \frac{\text{Change in}}{\text{Liabilities}} - \frac{\text{Change in}}{\text{Contributed}} + \text{Dividends.}$$

(11) Net income has been described as a measure of the increase in wealth of a firm for a particular period of time. Do you agree?

c With respect to the consolidated statement of changes in financial position:

(12) Using the current asset and current liability accounts on the consolidated balance sheet of International Corporation, demonstrate that the net change in working capital for 19X1 is a decrease of $194,290,000.

(13) The factors causing a change in working capital can be classified as follows:

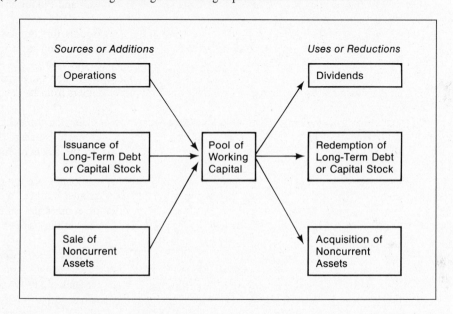

Classify each of the sources and applications of working capital for International Corporation for 19X1 into one of these six categories.

(14) Demonstrate that the following equation is valid for International Corporation for 19X1. Use the definitions in part (10) of this problem.

$$\frac{\text{Change in}}{\text{Current}} - \frac{\text{Change in}}{\text{Current}} = \frac{\text{Change in}}{\text{Noncurrent}} + \frac{\text{Change in}}{\text{Stockholders'}} - \frac{\text{Change in}}{\text{Noncurrent}}$$
$$\text{Assets} \qquad \text{Liabilities} \qquad \text{Liabilities} \qquad \text{Equity} \qquad \text{Assets}$$

d Assume that you are a credit officer for a bank contemplating a loan of $500,000,000 to International Corporation as of February 1, 19X2. The loan is to be repaid with interest on July 31, 19X2. What information from International Corporation's financial statements would you find useful in making this decision?

e Assume that you are an independently wealthy investor contemplating the purchase of $500,000,000 of International Corporation's common stock. What information from International Corporation's financial statements would you find useful in making this decision?

PART TWO
ACCOUNTING CONCEPTS AND METHODS

CHAPTER 2
MEASURING FINANCIAL POSITION—VALUATION PRINCIPLES AND ACCOUNTING PROCEDURES

Chapter 1 introduced the balance sheet, sometimes called the statement of financial position, as one of the three principal financial statements. You will recall that the balance sheet presents a snapshot of the resources of a firm (assets) and claims on those resources (liabilities and owners' equity) as of a specific moment in time. The balance sheet derives its name from the fact that it shows the following balance, or equality:

$$Assets = Liabilities + Owners' \ Equity.$$

That is, a firm's resources are in balance with, or equal to, the claims on those resources by creditors and owners. In the balance sheet, we view resources from two angles: a listing of the specific forms in which they are held (for example, cash, inventory, equipment); and a listing of the persons or interests that have a claim on them (for example, suppliers, employees, governments, stockholders). Our introduction to the balance sheet in Chapter 1 left several important questions unanswered:

1 What limits are set in defining the business entity for which the statement is prepared?
2 Which resources of a firm are recognized as assets?
3 What valuations are placed on these assets?
4 How are assets classified, or grouped, within the balance sheet?
5 Which claims against a firm's assets are recognized as liabilities?
6 What valuations are placed on these liabilities?
7 How are liabilities classified within the balance sheet?
8 What valuation is placed on the owners' equity in a firm, and how is the owners' equity disclosed?

In seeking answers to these questions, we must explore briefly several accounting concepts and conventions that underlie the balance sheet. This discussion not only provides a background for understanding the statement as it is currently prepared, but also permits an assessment of alternative methods of measuring financial position. After this brief introduction to accounting theory, we describe and then illustrate the accounting procedures used in recording transactions and events for presentation in a balance sheet.

UNDERLYING CONCEPTS AND CONVENTIONS

Accounting Entity

Business activities are carried on through various units, or entities. The identification of the business entity is the starting point in designing an accounting system that will provide data for financial statements. Most problems of identifying the business entity are caused by differences between the definition of the entity used in accounting, or the *accounting entity,* and the definition of the entity prescribed by law, or the *legal entity.* In accounting we attempt to emphasize substance over form; that is, we focus on the unit, or entity, engaged in business activity even though it may not be recognized as a separate legal entity.

Example 1   Joan Webster operates a hardware store in her neighborhood as a sole proprietorship. According to the laws of most states, Webster's business assets and personal assets are mingled. That is, suppliers of merchandise to the hardware store can obtain payment for their claims from some or all of her personal assets if business assets are insufficient. Even so, the accounting entity is the hardware store alone, since this is the organizational unit carrying on the business activity.

Example 2   Bill White and Roger Green own and manage an apartment complex, called the Leisure Living Apartments, as a partnership. Under the laws of most states, their personal assets as well as the business assets are subject to the claims of creditors. Even so, the accounting entity is the apartment complex alone, since this is the organizational unit carrying on the business activity.

Example 3   The Domestic Corporation operates through its subsidiaries in 23 states. Each subsidiary is organized as a separate legal corporation under the laws of the state in which it is located. The accounting entity is a combination (or consolidation) of Domestic Corporation and all of its 23 subsidiary corporations, since these legally separate units operate as a single business entity. For purposes of internal performance evaluation by management, however, Domestic Corporation might treat each subsidiary as a separate reporting entity. Thus, we see that the scope of the accounting entity can be related to the purpose to be served by the financial statements.

The accounting entity for which a set of financial statements has been prepared can be determined from the heading of each statement. For the three examples above, the headings might read: Webster's Hardware Store, Leisure Living Apartments, and Domestic Corporation and Consolidated Subsidiaries.

Asset Recognition

Assets are resources that have the potential for providing a firm with future economic services or benefits. In short, *an asset is a future benefit.* The resources that are recognized as assets are those (1) for which the firm has acquired rights to their future use as a result of a past transaction or exchange and (2) for which the value of the future benefits can be measured, or quantified, with a reasonable degree of precision.

Example 1   Miller Corporation sold merchandise and received a note from the customer who agreed to pay $1,000 within 3 months. This note receivable is an asset of Miller Corporation, since a right has been established to receive a definite amount of cash in the future as a result of the previous sale of merchandise.

Example 2   Miller Corporation acquired manufacturing equipment costing $20,000 and agreed to pay the seller over 2 years. After the final payment, legal title to the equipment will be transferred to Miller Corporation. The equipment is Miller's asset, even though Miller Corporation does not possess legal title, since it has obtained the rights and responsibilities of ownership and can sustain those rights as long as the payments are made on schedule.

Example 3   Miller Corporation plans to acquire a fleet of new trucks next year to replace those wearing out. These new trucks are not now assets, since no exchange has taken place between Miller Corporation and a supplier and, therefore, no right to the future use of the trucks has been established.

Example 4   Miller Corporation has developed a good reputation with its employees, customers, and citizens of the community. This good reputation is expected to provide benefits to the firm in its future business activities. A good reputation, however, is generally *not* recognized as an asset. Although Miller Corporation has made various expenditures in the past to develop the reputation, the future benefits are considered to be too difficult to quantify with any degree of precision to warrant recognition as an asset.

Most of the difficulties in deciding which items to recognize as assets are related to unexecuted or partially executed contracts. In Example 3, suppose that Miller Corporation entered into a contract with a local truck dealer to acquire the trucks next year at a cash price of $50,000. Miller Corporation has acquired rights to future benefits, but the contract has not been executed. Unexecuted contracts of this nature are generally not recognized as assets in accounting. Miller Corporation will recognize an asset for the trucks when they are received next year.

To take the illustration one step further, assume that Miller Corporation advances the truck dealer $10,000 of the purchase price upon signing the contract. Miller Corporation has acquired rights to future benefits and has exchanged cash. Current accounting practice would treat the $10,000 advance as a deposit on the purchase of equipment and report it as an asset under a title such as Advances to Suppliers. The trucks would not be shown as assets at this time, however, because Miller Corporation is not yet deemed to have received sufficient future rights to justify their inclusion in the balance sheet. Similar asset-recognition questions arise when a firm leases buildings and equipment under long-term leases or manufactures custom-design products for particular customers. These issues are discussed more fully in later chapters.

Asset Valuation Methods

An amount must be assigned to each asset in the balance sheet. Several methods of determining this amount might be used.

Acquisition or Historical Cost   The acquisition, or historical cost, of an asset is the amount of cash payment (or cash-equivalent value of other forms of payment) made in acquiring the asset. This amount is generally determinable by referring to contracts, invoices, and canceled checks. Since a firm is not compelled to acquire a given asset, it must expect the future benefits from that asset to be at least as large as its acquisition cost. Historical cost, then, is a lower limit on the amount that a firm considered the future benefits of the asset to be worth at the time of acquisition.

Current Value—Replacement Cost   Each asset might be shown on the balance sheet at its current value. One measure of current value is the current cost of replacing it. Current replacement cost is often referred to as an *entry value,* because it represents the amount required currently to acquire, or "enter" into, the rights to receive future benefits from the asset.

   For assets purchased frequently, such as merchandise inventory, current replacement cost can frequently be determined by consulting suppliers' catalogs or price lists. The replacement cost of assets purchased less frequently, such as land, buildings, and equipment, is more difficult to determine. A major problem in using current replacement cost is caused by the absence of well-organized secondhand markets for many used assets. Determining current replacement cost in these cases requires determining the cost of a similar new asset and then adjusting that amount downward somehow for the services of the asset already used. There may be difficulties, however, in finding a similar asset. With technological improvements and other quality changes, equipment purchased currently will likely be quite different from that acquired 10 years previously but that is still being used. Thus, there may be no similar equipment on the market for which replacement cost can be determined. Alternatively, the current replacement cost of an asset capable of rendering equivalent services might be substituted when the replacement cost of the specific asset is not readily available. The approach, however, is also subject to a high degree of subjectivity in the identification of assets with equivalent service potential.

Current Value—Net Realizable Value   Another measure of current value is the net amount of cash (selling price less selling costs) that the firm would receive if it sold each asset separately. This amount is often referred to as an *exit value,* because it reflects the amount obtainable if the firm currently disposed of the asset, or "exited" ownership. In determining net realizable value, it is generally assumed that the asset would be sold in an orderly fashion, rather than through a forced sale at some "distress" price.

Measuring net realizable value entails difficulties similar to those in measuring current replacement cost. There may be no well-organized secondhand market for used equipment, particularly when the equipment is specially designed for a single firm's needs. In this case, the current selling price of the asset (value in exchange) may be substantially less than the value of the future benefits to the firm from using the asset (value in use).

Current Value – Present Value of Future Net Cash Flows   A third measure of current value can be obtained from estimates of future cash flows. An asset is a resource that provides future benefits. This future benefit is the ability of an asset either to generate future net cash receipts or to reduce future cash expenditures. For example, accounts receivable from customers will lead directly to future cash receipts. Merchandise inventory can be sold for cash or promises to pay cash. Equipment can be used to manufacture products that can then be sold for cash. A building that is owned reduces future cash outflows for rental payments. Since these cash flows represent the future services, or benefits, of assets, they might be used in the valuation of assets. Because cash can be invested to yield interest revenue over time, today's value of a stream of future cash flows, called the *present value,* is worth less than the sum of the cash amounts to be received or saved over time. The balance sheet is to be prepared as of a current date. If future cash flows are to be used to measure an asset's value, then the future net cash flows must be "discounted" to find their present value as of the date of the balance sheet. The discounting methodology is described in Chapter 10, but the following example should help in understanding the general approach.

Example   Miller Corporation sold merchandise to a reliable customer, General Models Company, who promised to pay $10,000 one year from the date of sale. General Models Company signed a "promissory note" to that effect and gave the note to Miller Corporation. Miller Corporation judges that if it invests $9,100 today, it could earn about 10 percent on the investment in a year. At the end of 1 year, it would therefore receive about $10,000. Hence, the *present value* of $10,000 to be received 1 year from today is not $10,000, but is about $9,100. (Miller Corporation is indifferent between receiving approximately $9,100 today and $10,000 one year from today.) The asset represented by General Model Company's promissory note has a present value of $9,100. If the note was stated on the balance sheet as of the date of sale at the present value of the future cash flows, it would be shown at approximately $9,100.

Using discounted cash flows to determine balance sheet amounts for individual assets entails several problems. One is the uncertainty of the amounts of future cash flows. The amounts to be received can depend on whether or not competitors introduce new products, the rate of inflation, and many other factors. A second problem is allocating the cash receipts from selling a single item of merchandise inventory to all of the assets involved in its production and distribution (for example, equipment, buildings, sales staff's automobiles). A third problem is selecting the appropriate rate to be used in discounting the future cash flows back to the present. Is the interest rate at which the firm could borrow the appropriate one? Or is the rate at which the firm could invest excess cash the one that should be used? Or is the appropriate rate the firm's cost of capital (a concept introduced in managerial accounting and finance courses)?

Determining the Appropriate Valuation Method

In selecting a valuation method, we should choose the one that is most appropriate for the financial report being prepared.

Example 1   Miller Corporation is preparing its income tax return for the current year. The Internal Revenue Code and Regulations specify that acquisition or adjusted acquisition cost is the valuation method that must be used in most instances.

Example 2   A fire recently destroyed the manufacturing plant, equipment, and inventory of Miller Corporation. The firm's fire insurance policy provides coverage in an amount equal to the cost of replacing the assets that were destroyed. Current replacement cost at the time of the fire is the appropriate valuation method to be used in support of the insurance claim.

Example 3   Miller Corporation plans to dispose of one of its manufacturing divisions because it has been operating unprofitably. In deciding on the lowest price to accept for the division, the net realizable value of each asset is the valuation method that should be used.

Example 4   Brown Corporation is considering the purchase of Miller Corporation. In deciding on the highest price to be paid, Brown Corporation would be interested in the present value of the future cash flows to be realized from owning Miller Corporation. In this case, Miller Corporation's assets (and liabilities) should be stated at the net present value of the future cash flows.

Generally Accepted Accounting Asset Valuation Methods

The asset valuation method appropriate for financial statements issued to stockholders and other investors is perhaps less obvious. The financial statements currently prepared by publicly held firms are based on one of two valuation methods—one for monetary assets and one for nonmonetary assets.

Monetary assets, such as cash and accounts receivable, are generally shown on the balance sheet at their current cash, or cash-equivalent, values. Cash is stated at the amount of cash on hand or in the bank. Accounts receivable from customers are stated at the amount of cash expected to be collected in the future. If the period of time until a receivable is to be collected spans more than 1 year, then the expected future cash receipt is discounted to a present value. Most accounts receivable, however, are collected within 1 to 3 months. The amount of future cash flows is approximately equal to the present value of these flows, and the discounting process is ignored.

Nonmonetary assets, such as merchandise inventory, land, buildings, and equipment, are stated at acquisition cost, in some cases adjusted downward for depreciation reflecting the services of the assets that have been consumed.

The acquisition cost of an asset may include more than its invoice price. Cost includes all expenditures made or obligations incurred in order to put the asset into usable condition. Transportation cost, costs of installation, handling charges, and any other necessary and reasonable costs incurred in connection with the asset up to the time it is put into service should be considered as part of the total cost assigned to the asset. For example, the cost of an item of equipment might be calculated as follows:

Invoice Price of Equipment	$8,000
Less: 2 Percent Discount for Prompt Cash Payment	160
Net Invoice Price	$7,840
Transportation Cost	232
Installation Costs	694
Total Cost of Equipment	$8,766

The acquisition cost of this equipment to be recorded in the accounting records is $8,766.

Instead of disbursing cash or incurring a liability, other forms of consideration (for example, common stock, merchandise inventory, land) may be given in acquiring an asset. In these cases, acquisition cost is measured by the market value of the consideration given or the market value of the asset received, depending on which market value is more readily determinable.

Foundations for Acquisition Cost   Accounting's use of acquisition-cost valuations for nonmonetary assets rests on three important concepts or conventions. First, a firm is assumed to be a *going concern.* That is, it is assumed that the firm will remain in operation long enough for all of its current plans to be carried out. Any increases in the market prices of assets held will be realized in the normal course of business by way of higher prices for the firm's products. Current selling prices of the individual assets are therefore assumed to be largely unimportant. Second, acquisition-cost valuations are considered to be more objective than those obtained from using the other valuation methods. *Objectivity* in accounting refers to the ability of several independent measurers to come to the same conclusion about the valuation of an asset. It is relatively easy to obtain consensus on what constitutes the acquisition cost of an asset. Differences among measurers can arise in determining an asset's current replacement cost, net realizable value, or present value of future cash flows. A reasonable degree of consensus is necessary if financial statements are to be subject to audits by independent accountants. Third, acquisition cost generally provides more conservative valuations of assets (and measures of earnings) relative to the other valuation methods. Many accountants feel that the possibility of misleading financial statement users will be minimized when assets are stated at lower rather than higher amounts. Thus, *conservatism* has evolved as a convention to justify acquisition-cost valuations.

The preceding description of generally accepted accounting valuation methods is not intended to justify them. Whether the acquisition costs, current replacement costs, net realizable values, or present values of future cash flows of a firm's assets are more relevant to investors' decisions is an empirical question and one for which a definitive answer has not yet been provided.

Asset Classification

The classification of assets within the balance sheet varies widely in published annual reports. The principal asset categories are described below.

Current Assets   The term *current assets* "is used to designate cash and other assets or resources commonly identified as those which are reasonably expected to be realized in cash or sold or consumed during the normal operating cycle of the business."[1] Included in this category are cash, marketable securities held as short-term investments, accounts and notes receivable net of allowance for uncollectible accounts, inventories of merchandise, raw materials, supplies, work in process, and finished goods and prepaid operating costs. Prepaid costs, or prepayments, are current assets to the extent that if they were not paid in advance, then current assets would be required to be used to acquire them within the next operating cycle.

Investments   The section of the balance sheet labeled "Investments" includes primarily the investments in securities of other firms where the purpose of the investment is long term in nature. For example, shares of common stock of a supplier might be purchased to help assure continued availability of raw materials. Or shares of common stock of a firm in another area of business activity might be acquired to permit the acquiring firm to diversify its operations. When one corporation (the parent) owns more than 50 percent of the voting stock in another corporation (the subsidiary), consolidated financial statements are usually prepared. That is, the specific assets, liabilities, revenues, and expenses of the subsidiary are merged, or consolidated, with those of the parent corporation. When consolidated financial statements are prepared, the account, Investment in Subsidiary, is eliminated as part of the consolidation process. Intercorporate investments in securities shown in the Investments section of the balance sheet are therefore investments in firms whose financial statements have not been consolidated with the parent or investor firm. Consolidated financial statements are discussed in Chapter 12.

The holders of a firm's long-term bonds may require that cash be set aside periodically so that sufficient funds will be available to retire, or redeem, the bonds at maturity. The funds are typically given to a trustee, such as a bank or insurance company, which invests the funds received. Funds set aside for this purpose are shown in a Sinking Fund account and classified under Investments on the balance sheet.

---

[1]   *Accounting Research Bulletin No. 43*, Chapter 3.A, AICPA, 1953.

Property, Plant, and Equipment   Property, plant, and equipment (sometimes called *plant assets* or *fixed assets*) includes the tangible, long-lived assets used in a firm's operations over a period of years and generally not acquired for resale. This category includes land, buildings, machinery, automobiles, furniture, fixtures, computers, and other equipment. The amount shown on the balance sheet for each of these items (except land) is acquisition cost less accumulated depreciation. Frequently, only the net balance, or book value, is disclosed on the balance sheet. Land is presented at acquisition cost.

Intangible Assets   Intangible assets include such items as patents, trademarks, franchises, and goodwill. The expenditures made by the firm in developing intangible assets are usually not recognized as assets, because of the difficulty of determining the existence and amount of future benefits.

Liability Recognition

A liability represents an obligation of a firm to make payment of a reasonably definite amount at a reasonably definite future time for benefits or services received currently or in the past.

Example 1   Miller Corporation purchased merchandise inventory and agreed to pay the supplier $5,000 within 30 days. This obligation is a liability, since Miller Corporation has received the goods and must pay a definite amount at a reasonably definite future time.

Example 2   Miller Corporation borrowed $2 million by issuing long-term bonds. Annual interest payments of 8 percent must be made on December 31 of each year, and the $2 million principal must be repaid in 20 years. This obligation is also a liability, because Miller Corporation has received the cash and must repay the debt in a definite amount at a definite future time.

Example 3   Miller Corporation provides a 3-year warranty on its products. The obligation to maintain the products under warranty plans creates a liability. The selling price for its products implicitly includes a charge for future warranty services. As customers pay the selling price, Miller Corporation receives a benefit (that is, the cash received). Past experience provides a basis for estimating the proportion of customers who will seek services under the warranty agreement and the expected cost of providing warranty services. Thus, the amount of the obligation can be estimated with a reasonable degree of accuracy, and it is shown as a liability.

Example 4   Miller Corporation has signed an agreement with its employees' labor union, promising to increase wages 6 percent and to provide for medical and life insurance. This agreement does not immediately give rise to a liability, since services have not yet been received from employees that would require any payments for wages and insurance. As labor services are received, a liability will arise.

The most troublesome questions of liability recognition relate to unexecuted contracts. The labor union agreement in Example 4 above is an unexecuted contract. Other examples include leases, pension agreements, and purchase-order commitments. Whether or not unexecuted contracts should be recognized as liabilities has been and continues to be controversial.

Liability Valuation

Most liabilities are monetary in nature. Those due within 1 year or less are stated at the amount of cash expected to be paid to discharge the obligation. If the payment dates extend more than 1 year into the future (for example, as in the case of the bonds in Example 2 above), the liability is stated at the present value of the future cash outflows.

A liability that is discharged by delivering goods or rendering services, rather than by paying cash, is nonmonetary. For example, magazine publishers typically collect cash for subscriptions, promising delivery of magazines over many months. Cash is received currently, whereas the obligation under the subscription is discharged by delivering magazines in the future. Theaters and football teams receive cash for season tickets and in return incur an obligation to admit the ticket holder to future performances. Landlords receive cash in advance and are obligated to let the tenant use the property. Such nonmonetary obligations are included among liabilities. They are stated, however, at the amount of cash received rather than at the expected cost of publishing the magazines or of providing the theatrical or sporting entertainment. The title frequently used for liabilities of this type is Advances from Customers.

Liability Classification

Liabilities in the balance sheet are typically classified in one of the following categories.

Current Liabilities The term *current liabilities* "is used principally to designate obligations whose liquidation is reasonably expected to require the use of existing resources properly classified as current assets, or the creation of other current liabilities."[2] Included in this category are liabilities to merchandise suppliers, employees, and governmental units. Notes and bonds payable are also included to the extent that they will require the use of current assets within a relatively short period of time, typically during the next 12 months.

Long-Term Debt Obligations having due dates, or maturities, more than 1 year after the balance sheet date are generally classified as long-term debt. Included are bonds, mortgages, and similar debts, as well as some obligations under long-term leases.

---

[2]   *Ibid.*

Other Long-Term Liabilities   Obligations not properly considered as current liabilities or long-term debt are classified as *other long-term liabilities,* or *indeterminate-
term liabilities.* Included are such items as deferred income taxes and some deferred
pension obligations.

Owners' Equity Valuation and Disclosure

The owners' equity, or interest, in a firm is a residual interest.[3] That is, the owners
have a claim on all assets not required to meet the claims of creditors. The valuation
of the assets and liabilities included in the balance sheet therefore determines the
valuation of total owners' equity.

The remaining question concerns the manner of disclosing this total owners' equity.
From Chapter 1, you will recall that a distinction is drawn between contributed capital and earnings retained by a firm. In preparing the balance sheet for a corporation,
the amounts contributed directly by stockholders for an interest in the firm (that is,
capital stock) are generally separated from the subsequent earnings realized by the
firm in excess of dividends declared (that is, retained earnings).

In addition, the amount received from stockholders is usually further disaggregated
into the *par* or *stated value* of the shares and *amounts contributed in excess of par value
or stated value.* The par or stated value of a share of stock is a somewhat arbitrary
amount assigned to comply with corporation laws of each state. As a result, the distinction between par or stated value and amounts contributed in excess of par or
stated value is of questionable informational value, but is typically shown nonetheless.
(These fine points of accounting for owners' equity are discussed in Chapter 11.)

Example 1   Stephens Corporation was formed on January 1, 1979. It issued 15,000
shares of $10 par value common stock for $10 cash per share. During 1979, Stephens
Corporation had net income of $30,000 and paid dividends of $10,000 to stockholders.
The stockholders' equity section of the balance sheet of Stephens Corporation on
December 31, 1979, is as follows:

Common Stock (par value of $10 per share,	
15,000 shares issued and outstanding)	$150,000
Retained Earnings	20,000
Total Stockholders' Equity	$170,000

Example 2   Instead of issuing $10 par value common stock as in Example 1, assume
that Stephens Corporation issued 15,000 shares of $1 par value common stock for $10
cash per share. (The market price of a share of common stock depends on the economic value of the firm and not on the par value of the shares.) The stockholders'

---

[3]   Although owners' equity is equal to assets minus liabilities, accounting provides an independent method
for determining the amount. This method is presented in this and the next two chapters.

equity section of the balance sheet of Stephens Corporation on December 31, 1979, is as follows:

Common Stock (par value of $1 per share,
  15,000 shares issued and outstanding) . . . . $ 15,000
Capital Contributed in Excess of Par Value 135,000
Retained Earnings   20,000
Total Stockholders' Equity $170,000

The balance sheets of firms that are organized as sole proprietorships or partnerships, rather than as corporations, do not distinguish between contributed capital and earnings retained in the business. The designation of par or stated value is also not used, since these forms of organization do not issue capital stock.

Example 3   Joan Webster operates her hardware store as a sole proprietorship. She contributed $20,000 on January 1, 1979, and used the cash to rent a building, acquire display equipment, and purchase merchandise inventory. During 1979, she had net income of $15,000 and withdrew $10,000 cash for personal use. The owner's equity section of the balance sheet of Webster's Hardware Store on December 31, 1979, is as follows:

Joan Webster, Capital . . . . $25,000[a]
Total Owner's Equity $25,000

[a] $20,000 + $15,000 − $10,000 = $25,000.

Example 4   Bill White and Roger Green own and manage an apartment complex as a partnership. Each partner contributed $50,000 cash to form the partnership on January 1, 1979. During 1979, net income from the apartment complex was $40,000, which the partners shared equally. Bill White withdrew $10,000 and Roger Green withdrew $5,000 from the partnership. The owners' equity section of the balance sheet on December 31, 1979, for the apartment complex is as follows:

Bill White, Capital . . . . $ 60,000[a]
Roger Green, Capital . . . .   65,000[b]
Total Owners' Equity $125,000

[a] $50,000 + (.50 × $40,000) − $10,000 = $60,000.
[b] $50,000 + (.50 × $40,000) − $ 5,000 = $65,000.

ACCOUNTING PROCEDURES FOR PREPARING THE BALANCE SHEET

Now that we have explored the concepts and conventions underlying the balance sheet, we are ready to consider the manner in which these concepts and conventions are applied in preparing the statement. Our objective is to develop a sufficient understanding of the accounting process that generates the balance sheet so that the resulting statement can be interpreted and analyzed.

Dual Effects of Transactions on the Balance Sheet Equation

The equality between total assets and total equities (liabilities plus owners' equity) in the balance sheet equation is maintained by reporting the effects of *each* transaction in a way that maintains the equation. Any single transaction will have one of the following four effects or some combination of these effects:

1   It increases both an asset and an equity.
2   It decreases both an asset and an equity.
3   It increases one asset and decreases another asset.
4   It increases one equity and decreases another equity.

To illustrate the dual effects of various transactions on the balance sheet equation, consider the following selected transactions for Miller Corporation during January 1979:

Transaction	Assets	=	Liabilities	+	Stock-holders' Equity
(1) On January 1, 1979, 20,000 shares of $10 par value common stock are issued for $200,000 cash. (Increase in both an asset and an equity.)	+$200,000		0	+	$200,000
Subtotal	$200,000	=	0	+	$200,000
(2) Equipment costing $75,000 is purchased for cash on January 5, 1979. (Increase in one asset and decrease in another asset.)	− 75,000 + 75,000				
Subtotal	$200,000	=	0	+	$200,000
(3) Merchandise inventory costing $20,000 is purchased from a supplier on account on January 15, 1979. (Increase in both an asset and an equity.)	+ 20,000		+$20,000		
Subtotal	$220,000	=	$20,000	+	$200,000
(4) The supplier in (3) is paid $10,000 of the amount due on January 31, 1979. (Decrease in both an asset and an equity.)	− 10,000		− 10,000		
Subtotal	$210,000	=	$10,000	+	$200,000
(5) The supplier in (3) accepts 500 shares of common stock at par value in settlement of $5,000 of the amount owed. (Increase in one equity and decrease in another equity.)			− 5,000	+	5,000
Total—January 31, 1979	$210,000	=	$ 5,000	+	$205,000

Purpose and Use of Accounts

It would be possible to prepare a balance sheet for Miller Corporation as of January 31, 1979, using information from the preceding analysis. Total assets are $210,000. We would need to retrace the effects of each transaction on total assets to determine what portion of the $210,000 represents cash, merchandise inventory, and equipment. Likewise, the effects of each transaction on total liabilities and stockholders' equity would have to be retraced to determine which liability and stockholders' equity amounts comprise the $210,000 total. Even with just a few transactions during the accounting period, this approach to preparing a balance sheet would be cumbersome. Considering the thousands of transactions during the accounting period for most firms, some more practical approach to accumulating amounts for the balance sheet is necessary. To accumulate the changes that take place in each balance sheet item, we use a device known as an *account*.

Requirement for an Account   The requirement for a satisfactory account is simple. Since a balance sheet item that changes can only increase or decrease, all an account need do is to provide for accumulating the increases and decreases that have taken place during the period for a single balance sheet item. The balance carried forward from the previous statement is added to the total increases; the total decreases are deducted, and the result is the amount of the new balance for the current balance sheet.

Form of an Account   The account may take many possible forms, and several are commonly used in accounting practice.

Perhaps the most useful form of the account for textbooks, problems, and examinations is the skeleton account, usually called the *T-account*. This form of the account is not used in actual practice, except perhaps for memorandums or preliminary analyses. However, it satisfies the requirement of an account and it is easy to use. As the name indicates, the T-account is shaped like the letter T and consists of a horizontal line bisected by a vertical line. The name or title of the account is written on the horizontal line. One side of the space formed by the vertical line is used to record increases in the item and the other side to record the decreases. Spaces for dates and other information can, of course, be provided.

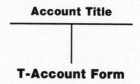

The form that the account takes in actual records depends on the type of accounting system being used. In manual systems the account may be more elaborate than a T-account; in punched-card systems the account may take the form of a group of cards; in computer systems it may be a group of similarly coded items on a tape. Whatever its form, an account contains the opening balance as well as the increases and decreases in the balance that result from the transactions of the period.

Placement of Increases and Decreases in the Account   Given the two-sided account, we must choose which side will be used to record increases and which, decreases. By long-standing custom, the following rules are used:

1 Increases in assets are entered on the left side and decreases in assets on the right side.
2 Increases in liabilities are entered on the right side and decreases in liabilities on the left side.
3 Increases in owners' equity are entered on the right side and decreases in owners' equity on the left side.

This custom has an element of logic. A common form of balance sheet shows assets on the left and liabilities and owners' equity on the right. Following this example, asset balances should appear on the left side of accounts; equity balances should appear on the right. But asset balances will appear on the left only if asset increases are recorded on the left side of the account. Similarly, right-hand equity balances can be produced only by recording equity increases on the right. When each transaction is properly analyzed into its dual effects on the accounting equation, and when the above three rules for recording the transaction are followed, then every transaction results in equal amounts in entries on the left- and right-hand sides of various accounts.

Debit and Credit   Two terms may now be added to our vocabulary, *debit* (Dr.) and *credit* (Cr.). These terms have an interesting history, but today they should be thought of merely as convenient abbreviations. *Debit* is an abbreviation for "record an entry on the left side of an account" when used as a verb and is an abbreviation for "an entry on the left side of an account" when used as a noun or adjective. *Credit* is an abbreviation for "record an entry on the right side of an account" when used as a verb and is an abbreviation for "an entry on the right side of an account" when used as a noun or adjective. These terms have no other meaning in accounting. More convenient abbreviations than *debit* and *credit* certainly seem possible, but these have become part of the accounting language through centuries of use and are not likely to be displaced. Often, however, the word *charge* is used instead of *debit*, both as a noun and as a verb. In terms of balance sheet categories, a debit or charge indicates (1) an increase in an asset, (2) a decrease in a liability, or (3) a decrease in an owners' equity item. A credit indicates (1) a decrease in an asset, (2) an increase in a liability, or (3) an increase in an owners' equity item.

Any previous associations or meanings of the terms debit and credit should be disregarded in accounting. In popular parlance, to credit people with something means to give them favorable recognition for some achievement, and to debit them means to charge something unfavorable against them. These terms have, however, no such implications in accounting. The best approach is simply to accept the terms *debit* and *credit* as technical terms meaning *left* and *right*.

In order to maintain the equality of the balance sheet equation, the amounts debited to various accounts for each transaction must equal the amounts credited to various accounts. Likewise, the sum of balances in accounts with debit balances at the end of each period must equal the sum of balances in accounts with credit balances.

Summary of Account Terminology and Procedure The conventional use of the account form and the terms debit and credit can be summarized graphically with the use of the skeleton account form, as follows:

Any Asset Account	
Beginning Balance Increases + Dr.	Decreases – Cr.
Ending Balance	

Any Liability Account	
Decreases – Dr.	Beginning Balance Increases + Cr.
	Ending Balance

Any Owners' Equity Account	
Decreases – Dr.	Beginning Balance Increases + Cr.
	Ending Balance

Reflecting the Dual Effects of Transactions in the Accounts

We are now ready to illustrate the manner in which the dual effects of transactions are reflected in the accounts. We begin by creating three separate T-accounts, one for assets, one for liabilities, and one for stockholders' equity. The dual effects of the transactions of Miller Corporation for January 1979, described earlier in the chapter, are entered in the T-accounts as shown in Exhibit 2.1.

EXHIBIT 2.1
Summary T-Accounts Showing the Transactions of Miller Corporation

	Assets =		Liabilities +		Stockholders' Equity	
	Increases (Dr.)	Decreases (Cr.)	Decreases (Dr.)	Increases (Cr.)	Decreases (Dr.)	Increases (Cr.)
(1) Issue of Common Stock for Cash	200,000					200,000
(2) Purchase of Equipment for Cash	75,000	75,000				
(3) Purchase of Merchandise on Account	20,000			20,000		
(4) Payment of Cash to Supplier in (3)		10,000	10,000			
(5) Issuance of Common Stock to Supplier in (3)			5,000			5,000
Balance	210,000	=		5,000 +		205,000

You will note that the amount entered on the left side of, or debited to, the accounts for each transaction is equal to the amount entered on the right side of, or credited to, the accounts. Recording equal amounts of debits and credits for each transaction ensures that the balance sheet equation will always be in balance. At the end of January 1979, the assets account has a debit balance of $210,000. The sum of the balances in the liabilities and stockholders' equity accounts is a credit balance of $210,000.

A balance sheet could be prepared for Miller Corporation from the information in the T-accounts. As was the case in the earlier illustration, however, it would be necessary to retrace the entries in the accounts during the period to determine which individual assets, liabilities, and stockholders' equity items make up the total assets of $210,000 and the total equities of $210,000.

So that the amount of each asset, liability, and stockholders' equity item can be determined directly, a separate account is used for each balance sheet item, rather than for the three broad categories alone. The recording procedure is the same, except that we must now consider which specific asset or equity account is debited and credited.

The transactions of Miller Corporation for January 1979 are recorded in Exhibit 2.2, using separate T-accounts for each balance sheet item. The number in parentheses refers to the five transactions we have been considering for Miller Corporation.

EXHIBIT 2.2
**Individual T-Accounts Showing
the Transactions of
Miller Corporation**

Cash (Asset)				Accounts Payable (Liability)	
Increases (Dr.)	Decreases (Cr.)			Decreases (Dr.)	Increases (Cr.)
(1) 200,000	75,000 (2)			(4) 10,000	20,000 (3)
	10,000 (4)			(5) 5,000	
Balance 115,000					5,000 Balance

Merchandise Inventory (Asset)				Common Stock (Stockholders' Equity)	
Increases (Dr.)	Decreases (Cr.)			Decreases (Dr.)	Increases (Cr.)
(3) 20,000					200,000 (1)
					5,000 (5)
Balance 20,000					205,000 Balance

Equipment (Asset)	
Increases (Dr.)	Decreases (Cr.)
(2) 75,000	
Balance 75,000	

We can see that the total assets of Miller Corporation of $210,000, as of January 31, 1979, comprise $115,000 in cash, $20,000 in merchandise inventory, and $75,000 in equipment. Total equities of $210,000 comprise $5,000 of accounts payable and $205,000 of common stock.

The balance sheet can be prepared using the amounts shown as balances in the T-accounts. The balance sheet of Miller Corporation after the five transactions of January 1979 is shown in Exhibit 2.3.

EXHIBIT 2.3
Miller Corporation
Balance Sheet
January 31, 1979

Assets		Liabilities and Stockholders' Equity	
Cash	$115,000	Accounts Payable	$ 5,000
Merchandise Inventory	20,000	Common Stock	205,000
Equipment	75,000	Total Liabilities and	
Total Assets	$210,000	Stockholders' Equity	$210,000

AN OVERVIEW OF THE ACCOUNTING PROCESS

The double-entry recording framework is employed in processing the results of various transactions and events through the accounts so that financial statements can be prepared periodically. The accounting system designed around this recording framework generally involves the following operations:

1 Entering the results of each transaction in the *general journal* in the form of a *journal entry,* a process called *journalizing*
2 Posting the journal entries from the general journal to the accounts in the *general ledger*
3 Preparing a *trial balance* of the accounts in the general ledger
4 Making *adjusting* and *correcting* journal entries to accounts listed in the trial balance and posting them to the appropriate general ledger accounts
5 Preparing financial statements from a trial balance after adjusting and correcting entries.

Each of these operations is described further and illustrated using the transactions of Miller Corporation during January 1979.

Journalizing

Each transaction is initially recorded in the general journal in the form of a *journal entry.* The standard journal entry format is as follows:

Date Account Debited .... Amount Debited
       Account Credited .... Amount Credited
       Explanation of transaction or event being journalized.

The *general journal* is merely a book or other device containing a listing of journal entries. The general journal is often referred to as the "book of original entry," since transactions initially enter the accounting system through it.

The journal entries for the five transactions of Miller Corporation during January 1979 are presented below.

(1) Jan. 1, 1979	Cash...	200,000	
	Common Stock		200,000
	20,000 shares of $10 par value common stock are issued for cash.		
(2) Jan. 5, 1979	Equipment....................................	75,000	
	Cash		75,000
	Equipment costing $75,000 is purchased for cash.		
(3) Jan. 15, 1979	Merchandise Inventory........................	20,000	
	Accounts Payable		20,000
	Merchandise inventory costing $20,000 is purchased on account.		
(4) Jan. 31, 1979	Accounts Payable.............................	10,000	
	Cash		10,000
	Liabilities of $10,000 are paid with cash.		
(5) Jan. 31, 1979	Accounts Payable.............................	5,000	
	Common Stock		5,000
	500 shares of $10 par value common stock are issued in settlement of a liability of $5,000.		

In addition to their role in the processing of accounting data, journal entries are also useful tools for indicating the effects of various transactions on a firm's financial statements and in preparing solutions to the problems at the end of each chapter. You will not completely understand an accounting event until you can analyze the event into its required debits and credits and can prepare the journal entry. Consequently, journal entries are employed as tools of analysis throughout this text.

Posting

At periodic intervals (for example, weekly or monthly), the transactions journalized in the general journal are entered, or posted, to the individual accounts in the general ledger. The *general ledger* is usually a book with a separate page for each account. The general ledger may also take the form of an access number in a computer's memory bank. The skeleton, or T-account, described earlier serves as a useful surrogate for a general ledger account. The journal entries from the general journal of Miller Corporation would be posted to the general ledger accounts in the manner shown previously in Exhibit 2.2.

As with journal entries, T-accounts are useful tools in preparing solutions to accounting problems and are used extensively in this text.

Trial Balance Preparation

A trial balance is a listing of each of the accounts in the general ledger with its balance as of a particular date. The trial balance of Miller Corporation on January 31, 1979, is presented in Exhibit 2.4.

EXHIBIT 2.4
Miller Corporation
Unadjusted Trial Balance
January 31, 1979

Account	Amounts in Accounts With Debit Balances	Amounts in Accounts With Credit Balances
Cash	$115,000	
Merchandise Inventory	20,000	
Equipment	75,000	
Accounts Payable		$ 5,000
Common Stock		205,000
Totals	$210,000	$210,000

An equality between the sum of debit and the sum of credit account balances serves as a check on the arithmetic accuracy of the manner in which the double-entry recording procedure has been carried out during the period. If the trial balance is out of balance, it is necessary to retrace the steps followed in processing the accounting data to locate the source of the error.

Trial Balance Adjustment and Correction

Any errors detected in the processing of accounting data must be corrected. Such corrections are generally few in number. A more important type of adjustment is often necessary to account for unrecorded events that help to determine financial position at the end of the period and net income for the period. This type of adjustment is considered more fully in Chapters 3 and 4. Most corrections and adjustments are made by preparing a journal entry, entering it in the general journal, and then posting it to the general ledger accounts.

Financial Statement Preparation

The balance sheet and income statement can be prepared from the trial balance after adjustments and corrections. Since correcting or adjusting entries are not required for Miller Corporation, the balance sheet presented in Exhibit 2.3 is correct as presented. In subsequent chapters, we consider the accounting procedures for preparing the income statement and the statement of changes in financial position.

The accounting process might be summarized as shown in Figure 2.1. The results of various transactions and events are processed through the accounting system following a flow beginning with the journalizing operation and ending with the financial statements.

The audit of the financial statements by the independent accountant typically flows in the opposite direction. The auditor begins with the financial statements prepared by management and then traces various items back through the accounts to

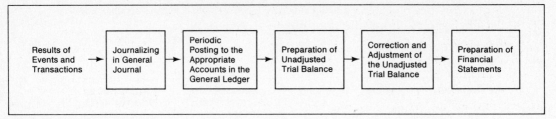

FIGURE 2.1
Summary of the
Accounting Process

the source documents (for example, sales invoices, canceled checks) that support the entries made in the general journal. Thus, it is possible to move back and forth among source documents, journal entries, general ledger postings, and the financial statements.

BALANCE SHEET ACCOUNT TITLES

The following list shows balance sheet account titles that are commonly used. The descriptions should help in understanding the nature of various assets, liabilities, and owners' equities as well as in selecting appropriate terms for solving problems. Alternative account titles can be easily devised. The list is not intended to exhaust all the account titles used in this book or appearing in the financial statements of publicly held firms.

Assets

Cash on Hand. Coins and currency, and such items as bank checks and money orders. The latter items are merely claims against individuals or institutions, but by custom are called "cash."

Cash in Bank. Strictly speaking, merely a claim against the bank for the amount deposited. Cash in bank consists of demand deposits, against which checks can be drawn, and time deposits, usually savings accounts and certificates of deposit. In published statements, the two items of Cash on Hand and Cash in Bank usually are combined under the title *Cash.*

Marketable Securities. Government bonds, or stocks and bonds of corporations. The word *marketable* implies that they can be bought and sold readily through a security exchange such as the New York Stock Exchange.

Accounts Receivable. Amounts due from customers of a business from the sale of goods or services. The collection of cash occurs some time after the sale. These accounts are also known as "charge accounts" or "open accounts." An alternative title is *Customers' Accounts.* The general term Accounts Receivable is used in financial statements to describe the figure representing the total amount receivable but, of course, the firm keeps a separate record for each customer.

Notes Receivable. Amounts due from customers or from others to whom loans have been made or credit extended, when the claim has been put into writing in the form of a promissory note.

Interest Receivable. Interest on assets such as promissory notes or bonds that has accrued, or come into existence, through the passing of time but that has not been collected as of the date of the balance sheet.

Merchandise Inventory. Goods on hand that have been purchased for resale, such as canned goods on the shelves of a grocery store or suits on the racks of a clothing store. This item is frequently shown simply as *Merchandise.*

Finished Goods Inventory. Completed but unsold manufactured products.

Work-in-Process Inventory. Partially completed manufactured products.

Raw Materials Inventory. Unused materials from which manufactured products are to be made. Sometimes combined with supplies under the title *Stores.*

Supplies Inventory. Lubricants, cleaning rags, abrasives, and other incidental materials used in manufacturing operations. Stationery, computer cards, pens, and other office supplies. Bags, twine, boxes, and other store supplies. Gasoline, oil, spare parts, and other delivery supplies. Alternative titles, such as *Factory Supplies, Office Supplies, Store Supplies,* and *Delivery Supplies,* could be used.

Prepaid Insurance. Insurance premiums paid for future coverage. An alternative title is *Unexpired Insurance.*

Prepaid Rent. Rent paid in advance of future use of land, buildings, or equipment.

Advances to Suppliers. The general name used to indicate payments made in advance for goods to be received at a later date. If no cash is paid by a firm when it places an order, then no asset is recognized.

Investments. The cost of shares of stock in other companies, where the firm's purpose is to hold the shares for relatively long periods of time.

Land. Land occupied by buildings or used in operations.

Buildings. Factory buildings, store buildings, garages, warehouses, and so forth.

Machinery and Equipment. Lathes, ovens, tools, boilers, computers, motors, bins, cranes, conveyors, and so forth.

Furniture and Fixtures. Desks, tables, chairs, counters, showcases, scales, and other such store and office equipment. Other titles, such as *Office Furniture and Fixtures* and *Store Furniture and Fixtures,* could be used.

Office Machines. Typewriters, adding machines, bookkeeping equipment, calculators, and so forth. Sometimes combined with Furniture and Fixtures.

Automobiles. Delivery trucks, sales staff's cars, and so forth.

Accumulated Depreciation. This account shows the cumulative amount of the cost of long-term assets (such as buildings and machinery) that has been allocated to prior periods in measuring net income or to the costs of production. The amount in this account is subtracted from the acquisition cost of the long-term asset to which it relates in determining the *net book value* of asset to be shown in the balance sheet.

Leasehold. The right to use property owned by someone else.

Organization Costs. Amounts paid for legal and incorporation fees, for printing the certificates for shares of stock, and for accounting and any other costs incurred in organizing the business so it can begin to function. This asset is seen most commonly on the balance sheets of corporations.

Patents. A right granted for up to 17 years by the federal government to exclude others from manufacturing, using, or selling a certain process or device. Under current generally accepted accounting principles, research and development costs must be treated as an expense in the year incurred rather than being recognized as an asset with future benefits.[4] (This treatment seems to us to be at odds with good accounting theory.) As a result, a firm that develops technology will not normally show it as an asset. On the other hand, a firm that purchases a patent from another firm or from an individual will recognize the patent as an asset. This inconsistent treatment of internally developed and externally purchased patents is discussed more fully in Chapter 9.

Goodwill. An amount paid by one firm in acquiring another business enterprise that is greater than the sum of the values assignable to other assets. A good reputation and other desirable attributes are generally not recognized as assets by the firm that creates or develops them. However, when one firm acquires another firm, these desirable attributes are indirectly recognized as assets, since they are a factor in determining the valuation of goodwill.

Liabilities

Accounts Payable. Amounts owed for goods or services acquired under an informal credit agreement. These accounts are usually payable within 1 or 2 months. The same items appear as Accounts Receivable on the creditor's books.

Notes Payable. The face amount of promissory notes given in connection with loans from the bank or the purchase of goods or services. The same items appear as Notes Receivable on the creditors' books.

Payroll Taxes Payable. Amounts withheld from wages and salaries of employees for federal and state payroll taxes and the employer's share of such taxes.

Withheld Income Taxes. Amounts withheld from wages and salaries of employees for income taxes that have not yet been remitted to the taxing authority. This is a tentative income tax on the earnings of employees, and the employer acts merely as a tax-collecting agent for the federal and state governments. A few cities also levy income taxes, which the employer must withhold from wages.

Interest Payable. Interest on obligations that has accrued or accumulated with the passage of time but that has not been paid as of the date of the balance sheet. The liability for interest is customarily shown separately from the face amount of the obligation.

Income Taxes Payable. The estimated liability for income taxes, accumulated and unpaid, based on the taxable income of the business from the beginning of the taxable year to the date of the balance sheet. Since sole proprietorships and partnerships do not pay federal income taxes directly, this term will appear only on the books of a corporation or other taxable entity.

Advances from Customers. The general name used to indicate payments received

---

[4]   Financial Accounting Standards Board, "Accounting for Research and Development Costs," *Statement of Financial Accounting Standards No. 2,* 1974.

in advance for goods to be delivered or services to be furnished to customers in the future. If no cash is received when a customer places an order, then no liability is shown.

Rent Received in Advance. An example of a nonmonetary liability. The business owns a building that it rents to a tenant. The tenant has prepaid the rental charge for several months in advance. The amount applicable to future months cannot be considered a component of income until the rent is earned as service is rendered with the passage of time. Meanwhile the advance payment results in a liability payable in services (that is, in the use of the building). On the records of the tenant the same amount would appear as an asset, Prepaid Rent.

Mortgage Payable. Long-term promissory notes that have been given greater protection by the pledge of specific pieces of property as security for their payment. If the loan or interest is not paid according to the agreement, the property can be sold for the benefit of the creditor.

Bonds Payable. Amounts borrowed by the business for a relatively long period of time under a formal written contract or indenture. The loan is usually obtained from a number of lenders, each of whom receives one or more bond certificates as written evidence of his or her share of the loan.

Debenture Bonds. The most common type of bond, except in the railroad and public utility industries. This type of bond carries no specific security or collateral; instead it is issued on the basis of the general credit of the business. If other bonds have a prior claim on the assets of the business, then the debenture is called *subordinated.*

Convertible Bonds. A bond that the holder can *convert* into or "trade in" for shares of common stock. The number of shares to be received when the bond is converted into stock, the dates when conversion can occur, and other details are specified in the bond indenture.

Capitalized Lease Obligations. The present value of future commitments for cash payments to be made in return for the right to use property owned by someone else.

Deferred Income Taxes. Certain income tax payments are delayed beyond the current accounting period. This item, which appears on the balance sheet of most U.S. corporations, is discussed in Chapter 10.

Owners' Equity

Common Stock. Amounts received for the par or stated value of a firm's principal class of voting stock.

Preferred Stock. Amounts received for the par value of a class of a firm's stock that has some preference relative to the common stock. This preference is usually with respect to dividends and to assets in the event the corporation is liquidated. Sometimes preferred stock is convertible into common stock.

Capital Contributed in Excess of Par or Stated Value. Amounts received from the issuance of common or preferred stock in excess of such shares' par value or stated value. This account is also referred to as *Additional Paid-in Capital* or sometimes as *Premium on Preferred* (or *Common*) *Stock.*

Stock Warrants. The amount in this account represents the amount the firm received for issuing certificates that permit the holders to purchase shares of stock at a specified price. The rights contained in stock warrants are usually exercisable for only a limited period.

Retained Earnings. An account reflecting the increase in net assets since the business was organized as a result of generating earnings in excess of dividend declarations. When dividends are declared, net assets are distributed, and retained earnings are reduced by an equal amount.

Treasury Shares. This account shows the cost of shares of stock originally issued but subsequently reacquired by the corporation. Treasury shares are not entitled to dividends and are not considered to be "outstanding" shares. The cost of treasury shares is almost always shown on the balance sheet as a deduction from the total of the other shareholders' equity accounts. Accounting for treasury shares is discussed in Chapter 11.

A balance sheet that includes many of the accounts described in this section is presented in Appendix A, Exhibit A.2, for International Corporation.

SUMMARY

The balance sheet, or statement of financial position, is composed of three major classes of items—assets, liabilities, and owners' equity.

Resources are recognized as assets when a firm has acquired rights to their future use as a result of a past transaction or exchange and when the value of the future benefits can be measured with a reasonable degree of precision. Monetary assets are, in general, stated at their current cash, or cash-equivalent, values. Nonmonetary assets are stated at acquisition cost, in some cases adjusted downward for the cost of services that have been consumed.

Liabilities represent obligations of a firm to make payments of a reasonably definite amount at a reasonably definite future time for benefits already received. Owners' equity is the difference between total assets and total liabilities and, for corporations, is typically segregated into contributed capital and retained earnings.

The equality of total assets and total equities (liabilities plus owners' equity) is maintained by recording the effects of each transaction in a dual manner in the accounts. The double-entry recording framework is summarized as follows:

Asset Accounts		=	**Liability Accounts**		+	**Owners' Equity Accounts**	
Increases (Debits)	Decreases (Credits)		Decreases (Debits)	Increases (Credits)		Decreases (Debits)	Increases (Credits)

The dual effects of each transaction are initially recorded in journal-entry form in the general journal. These journal entries are then posted to the appropriate asset, liability, and owners' equity accounts in the general ledger. A trial balance of the ending balances in the general ledger accounts is prepared periodically as a check on the mathematical accuracy of the double-entry recording procedure. Any necessary adjustments or corrections of the account balances in the trial balance are then made in the general journal and posted to the accounts in the general ledger. The financial statements are prepared from the adjusted and corrected trial balance. The procedures for preparing the income statement are discussed in Chapters 3 and 4. The statement of changes in financial position is considered in Chapter 5.

QUESTIONS AND PROBLEMS

1 Review the meaning of the following concepts or terms discussed in this chapter.
  a Accounting entity.
  b Legal entity.
  c Sole proprietorship.
  d Partnership.
  e Corporation.
  f Acquisition cost.
  g Current replacement cost.
  h Net realizable value.
  i Present (discounted) value.
  j Monetary assets.
  k Nonmonetary assets.
  l Going concern.
  m Objectivity.
  n Conservatism.
  o Fixed assets.
  p Par value.
  q Stated value.
  r Debit.
  s Charge.
  t Credit.
  u Journal entry.
  v General journal.
  w General ledger.
  x T-account.
  y Trial balance.

2 How can you determine from a balance sheet whether the enterprise is a corporation, partnership, or sole proprietorship?

3 Conservatism is generally regarded as a convention in accounting. Indicate who might be hurt by conservatively stated accounting reports.

4 When a customer opens an account at a department store, the account is referred to as a *charge account.* When merchandise purchased on account is returned to the store, the customer is given *credit* for the returned merchandise. How is the use of the terms *charge* and *credit* in the department store context consistent with the definitions of *charge* and *credit* in accounting?

5 Identify the accounting entity in each of the following situations:
  a John MacDonald owns and directs the operations of three hamburger outlets in the Chicago area.
  b U.S. International Corporation operates through outlets located throughout the United

States. Twelve foreign-held firms have been granted rights to distribute U.S. International Corporation's products in foreign countries.

   c   John Walker and Ken Wardlow have agreed to share equally the cost of constructing a fence between their properties.
   d   Residents of a nearby community have organized to lobby against a bill before the state legislature. Funds to support their endeavor have been raised from various citizens.

6 Indicate whether or not each of the following items would be recognized as assets by a firm according to current generally accepted accounting principles.
   a   The cash received from a customer for goods to be delivered in a future accounting period. ASSETS
   b   A contract signed by a customer to purchase $1,000 of goods next year. NOT ASSETs not execute contract
   c   A favorable reputation. NOT Assets
   d   A patent on a new invention developed by a firm. NA.
   e   A good credit standing. NA .
   f   A delivery truck. A
   g   A degree in engineering from a reputable university, awarded to the firm's chief engineer. NA.

7 Indicate whether or not each of the following events immediately gives rise to an asset. If an asset is recognized, state an account title and amount.
   a   An investment of $8,000 is made in a government bond. The bond will have a maturity value of $10,000 in 3 years. Long term investment $8000
   b   An order for $600 of merchandise is received from a customer. NA
   c   Merchandise inventory with a list price of $300 is purchased, with payment being made in time to secure a 2-percent discount for prompt payment. A Merchandise inventory $294
   d   Notice has been received from a manufacturer that materials billed at $4,000, with payment due within 30 days, have been shipped by freight. The seller retains title to the materials until they are received by the buyer. NA
   e   A contract is signed for the construction of a specially designed piece of machinery. The terms are $5,000 down upon signing the contract and the balance of $8,000 upon delivery of the equipment. Consider this question from the standpoint of the purchaser. A Deposit supply $5,000
   f   A check for $900 is sent to a landlord for 2 months' rent in advance (consider from the standpoint of the tenant, often called the *lessee*). A rent pay in advance $900
   g   A check for $1,000 is written to obtain an option to purchase a tract of land. The price of the land is $32,500. Consider from the standpoint of the person writing the check. A
   h   Bonds with a face value of $100,000 are purchased for $96,000. The bonds mature in 25 years. Interest is payable by the issuer of the bonds at the rate of 8 percent annually. A investment 96,000

8 Indicate whether or not each of the following events immediately gives rise to the recognition of an asset. If an asset is recognized, state an account title and amount.
   a   Raw materials with an invoice price of $6,200 are purchased on account from Williams Wholesalers.
   b   Defective raw material purchased in part **a** for $200 is returned to Williams Wholesalers.
   c   The bill of Williams Wholesalers (see parts **a** and **b**) is paid promptly. A discount of 2 percent offered by the seller for prompt payment is taken.
   d   A machine is purchased for $15,000 cash.
   e   The cost of transporting the new machine in part **d** to the plant site is paid in cash, $350.
   f   Material and labor costs incurred in installing the machine in part **d** total $200 and are paid in cash.

9 In each of the following transactions, give the title(s) and amount(s) of the asset(s) that would appear on the balance sheet.

a A firm purchases a delivery truck with a list price of $10,000. The dealer allows a discount of $650 from list price for payment in cash. Dealer preparation charges on the truck amount to an extra $150. The dealer collects a 5-percent sales tax on the price paid for the truck and preparation charges. In addition, the dealer collects a $65 fee to be remitted to the state for this year's license plates and $400 for a 1-year insurance policy provided by the dealer's insurance agency. The firm pays a body shop $50 for painting the firm's name on the truck.

b A firm acquires a building that has been appraised at $1 million by a certified real estate appraiser. The firm pays for the building by giving up shares in the General Electric Company at a time when equivalent shares traded on the New York Stock Exchange for $1,050,000.

c A firm acquires a building that has been appraised at $1 million by a certified real estate appraiser. The firm pays for the building by giving up shares in Small Timers, Inc., whose shares are traded only on the Cincinnati Stock Exchange. The last transaction in shares of Small Timers, Inc., occurred 4 days prior to this asset swap. Using the prices of the most recent trades, the shares of stock of Small Timers, Inc., given in exchange for the building have a market value of $1,050,000.

10 Give an illustration, other than those in the text, of each of the following:

a A situation in which property is not shown as an asset on the balance sheet of the firm that has possession of the property.

b A situation in which property is shown as an asset on the balance sheet of a firm even though the firm does not have legal title to the property.

11 A group of investors owns an office building, which is rented unfurnished to tenants. The building was purchased 5 years previously from a construction company and, at that time, was expected to have a useful life of 40 years. Indicate the procedures you might follow in determining the amount at which the building would be stated under each of the following valuation methods.

a Acquisition cost.

b Adjusted acquisition cost.

c Current replacement cost.

d Net realizable value.

e Present value of future cash flows.

12 Indicate whether or not each of the following items is recognized as a liability by a firm according to current generally accepted accounting principles.

a Unpaid wages of employees.

b A tenant's obligation to maintain a rented office building in good repair.

c The amount payable by a firm for a newspaper advertisement that has appeared but for which payment is not due for 30 days.

d An incompetent brother-in-law of the firm's president, who is employed in the business.

e The reputation for not paying bills promptly.

f The outstanding common stock of a corporation.

g An obligation to deliver merchandise to a customer next year for which cash has been received.

h An obligation to provide rental services to a tenant who has paid 3 months' rent in advance.

13 Indicate whether or not each of the following events immediately gives rise to the recognition of a liability. If a liability is recognized, state an account title and amount.

   a A landscaper agrees to improve land owned by the company. The agreed price for the work is $425. Consider from the standpoint of the company. *N L*

   b Additional common stock with a par value of $50,000 is issued for $62,500. *L . under owner equity 62500*

   c A check for $24 is received for a 2-year future subscription to a magazine. *advance payment $24*

   d A construction company agrees to build a bridge for $2 million. A down payment of $200,000 is received upon signing the contract, and the remainder is due when the bridge is completed. *L . construction down payment $ 200,500*

   e During the last pay period, employees earned wages amounting to $24,500 that they have not been paid. The employer is also liable for payroll taxes of 8 percent of the wages earned. *L . wage payable $24500 Tax Payable $ 1960*

   f A landlord receives $900 for 3 months' rent in advance. *L . Rent in advance $900*

   g A 60-day, 8-percent loan for $10,000 is obtained at a bank. *L Note payable $10,000*

   h A firm signs a contract to purchase at least $5,000 worth of merchandise during the next 3 months. *N L*

14 Some of the assets of one firm correspond to the liabilities of another firm. For example, an account receivable on the seller's balance sheet would be an account payable on the buyer's balance sheet. For each of the following items, indicate whether it is an asset or a liability and give the corresponding account title on the balance sheet of the other party to the transaction

   a Advances by Customers.

   b Bonds Payable.

   c Cash in Bank.

   d Interest Receivable.

   e Prepaid Insurance.

   f Rental Fees Received in Advance.

15 The assets of a business total $950,000, and liabilities total $700,000. Present the owners' equity section of the balance sheet under the following assumptions:

   a The business is a sole proprietorship owned by William Gleason.

   b The business is a partnership. William Gleason has a 35-percent interest, John Morgan has a 40-percent interest, and David Johnson has a 25-percent interest.

   c The business is a corporation. Outstanding common stock was originally issued for $180,000, of which $100,000 represented par value. The remainder of the owners' equity represents accumulated, undistributed earnings.

16 Information may be classified with respect to a balance sheet in one of the following ways:

   (1) Asset.

   (2) Liability.

   (3) Owners' equity.

   (4) Item would not appear on the balance sheet as conventionally prepared.

Using the numbers above, indicate the appropriate classification of each of the following items:

   a Salaries payable.

   b Retained earnings.

c Notes receivable.
d Unfilled customers' orders.
e Land.
f Interest payable.
g Work-in-process inventory.
h Mortgage payable.
i Organization costs.
j Advances by customers.
k Advances to employees.
l Patents.
m Good credit standing.
n Common stock.

17 Information may be classified with respect to a balance sheet in one of the following ways:

(1) Asset.
(2) Liability.
(3) Owners' equity.
(4) Item would not appear on the balance sheet as conventionally prepared.

Using the numbers above, indicate the appropriate classification of each of the following items:
a Preferred stock.
b Furniture and fixtures.
c Potential liability under lawsuit (case has not yet gone to trial).
d Prepaid rent.
e Capital contributed in excess of par value.
f Cash on hand.
g Goodwill.
h Estimated liability under warranty contract.
i Raw materials inventory.
j Rental fees received in advance.
k Bonds payable.
l Unexpired insurance.

18 Indicate the effects of the transactions below on the balance sheet equation using the following format:

Transaction Number	Assets	=	Liabilities + Owners' Equity
(1)	+$50,000		+$50,000
Subtotal	$50,000	=	$50,000

(1) Five thousand shares of $10-par value common stock are issued at par value for cash.
(2) Merchandise is purchased on account for $24,300.
(3) Store equipment is purchased for $4,800. A check is drawn for $1,000 and the balance is payable over 3 years under an installment contract.
(4) Store supplies costing $650 are purchased for cash.

(5) A 60-day promissory note is issued to the supplier in (2) for the amount due.

(6) A check is issued for $600 covering 2 months' rent in advance on office space.

19 Indicate the effects of the transactions below on the balance sheet equation using the following format:

Transaction Number	Assets	=	Liabilities	+	Owner's Equity
(1)	+$50,000		0		+$50,000
Subtotal	$50,000	=	0	+	$50,000

(1) Shares of common stock are issued to stockholders for cash, $50,000.

(2) Equipment is purchased on an installment contract for $18,000; terms are $3,000 payable immediately and the balance in three quarterly installments.

(3) A check for $900 is issued to Roger White to reimburse him for costs incurred in organizing and promoting the corporation.

(4) A check for $600 is issued for 3 months' rent in advance for office space.

(5) Office equipment is purchased for $950. A down payment of $250 is made, with the balance payable in 30 days.

(6) A patent on a machine process is purchased for $30,000 cash.

(7) $275 is paid to Express Transfer Company for delivering the equipment purchased in (2).

(8) The first payment on the equipment installment contract is made.

(9) Supplies are purchased on account, $800.

20 Indicate the effects of the transactions below on the T-accounts for Assets, Liabilities, and Owners' Equity using the following format:

Assets		=	**Liabilities**		+	**Owners' Equity**	
Increases (Dr.)	Decreases (Cr.)		Decreases (Dr.)	Increases (Cr.)		Decreases (Dr.)	Increases (Cr.)
(1) 100,000							100,000 (1)

(1) 10,000 shares of $10-par value common stock are issued at par value for cash.

(2) Land and building costing $75,000 are acquired with the payment of $15,000 cash and the assumption of a 20-year, 8-percent mortgage for the balance. The land is to be stated at $10,000 and the building at $65,000.

(3) A used lathe is purchased for $3,250 cash.

(4) Raw materials costing $5,400 are acquired on account.

(5) Defective raw materials purchased in (4) and costing $750 are returned to the supplier. The account has not yet been paid.

(6) The supplier in (4) is paid the amount due, less a 2-percent discount for prompt payment.

(7) A fire insurance policy providing $100,000 coverage beginning next month is obtained. The 1-year premium of $425 is paid in cash.

21 Set up T-accounts for the following accounts, indicate whether each account is an asset, liability, or owners' equity item, and enter the transactions described below:

Cash   Accounts Payable
Merchandise Inventory   Note Payable
Prepaid Insurance   Mortgage Payable
Building   Common Stock—Par Value
Equipment   Capital Contributed in Excess of Par Value

(1) Twenty thousand shares of $10-par value stock are issued for $18 cash per share.
(2) A building costing $400,000 is acquired. A cash payment of $50,000 is made, and a long-term mortgage is assumed for the balance of the purchase price.
(3) Equipment costing $4,000 and merchandise inventory costing $6,000 are acquired on account.
(4) A 3-year fire insurance policy is taken out and the $600 premium is paid in advance.
(5) A 90-day, 6-percent note is issued to the bank for an $8,000 loan.
(6) Payments of $7,000 are made to the suppliers in **(3)**.

22 Express the following transactions of the Harris Grocery Store, a sole proprietorship, in journal-entry form. You may omit explanations for the journal entries.

(1) John Harris contributes $25,000 cash to help set up the grocery store.
(2) A 60-day, 8-percent note is signed in return for an $8,000 loan from the bank.
(3) A building is rented, with the annual rental of $5,000 paid in advance.
(4) Display equipment costing $8,000 is acquired. A check is issued.
(5) Merchandise inventory costing $25,000 is acquired. A check for $4,000 is issued, with the remainder payable in 30 days.
(6) A contract is signed with a nearby restaurant under which the restaurant agrees to purchase $4,000 of groceries each week. A check is received for the first 2 weeks' orders in advance.

23 Express the following independent transactions in journal-entry form. If an entry is not required, indicate the reason. You may omit explanations for the journal entries.

(1) Bonds of the Sommers Company with a face value of $50,000 and annual interest at the rate of 8 percent are purchased for $51,500 cash.
(2) A check for $4,000 is received by a fire insurance company for premiums on policy coverage over the next 2 years.
(3) A corporation issues 30,000 shares of $12-par value common stock in exchange for land, building, and equipment. The land is to be stated at $40,000, the building at $260,000, and the equipment at $100,000.
(4) A contract is signed by a manufacturing firm agreeing to purchase 100 dozen machine tool parts over the next 2 years at a price of $40 per dozen.
(5) Five thousand shares of $1-par value preferred stock are issued to an attorney for legal services rendered in organization of the corporation. The bill for the services is $8,500.
(6) A coupon book, redeemable in movie viewings, is issued for $50 cash by a movie theater.

(7) A firm has been notified that it is being sued for $20,000 damages by a customer who incurred losses as a result of purchasing defective merchandise.

(8) Merchandise inventory costing $3,000, purchased on account, is found to be defective and returned to the supplier for full credit.

24 The transactions of the Electronics Appliance Corporation during September 1979 are as follows:

(1) The firm issues 4,000 shares of $10-par value common stock at par value for cash.

(2) A factory building is leased for the 3 years beginning October 1, 1979. Monthly rental payments are $5,000. Two months' rent is paid in advance.

(3) Factory equipment costing $27,500 is purchased. A check for $5,000 is issued, and a long-term mortgage liability is assumed for the balance.

(4) The labor costs of installing the new equipment in **(3)** are $450 and are paid in cash.

(5) Raw materials are purchased on account for $6,100.

(6) A check for $900 is received from a customer as a deposit on a special order for equipment that Electronics plans to manufacture. The contract price is $4,800.

(7) Office equipment with a list price of $950 is acquired. After deducting a discount of $25, a check is issued in full payment.

(8) The company hires three employees to begin work October 1. A cash advance of $200 is given to one of the employees.

(9) The firm's attorney is given 600 shares of common stock in payment for legal services rendered in the organization of the corporation. The bill for the services is $6,000.

a Enter the transactions in T-accounts. Indicate whether each account is an asset, liability, or owners' equity item. Cross-reference each entry to the appropriate transaction number.

b Prepare a balance sheet for Electronics Appliance Corporation as of September 30, 1979.

25 The Standard Manufacturing Corporation is organized on January 1, 1979. During January 1979, the following transactions occur:

(1) The corporation issues 10,000 shares of $10-par value common stock for $180,000 in cash.

(2) The corporation issues 30,000 shares of common stock in exchange for land, building, and equipment. The land is to be stated at $100,000, the building at $260,000, and the equipment at $180,000.

(3) The corporation issues 1,000 shares of common stock to an attorney in payment of legal services rendered in obtaining the corporate charter.

(4) Raw materials costing $85,000 are acquired on account from various suppliers.

(5) Manufacturing equipment with a list price of $5,000 is acquired. After deducting a $500 discount, the net amount is paid in cash.

(6) Freight charges of $250 for delivery of the equipment in **(5)** are paid in cash.

(7) Raw materials costing $600 are found to be defective and returned to the supplier for full credit. The raw materials had been purchased on account [see **(4)**], and no payment had been made as of the time that the goods were returned.

(8) A contract is signed for the rental of a fleet of automobiles beginning February 1, 1979. The rental for February of $1,200 is paid in advance.

(9) Invoices for $50,000 of raw materials purchased in (4) are paid, after deducting a discount of 2 percent for prompt payment.

(10) Fire and liability insurance coverage is obtained from Midwest Insurance Company. The 1-year policy, beginning February 1, 1979, carries a $360 premium, which has not yet been paid.

(11) A contract is signed with a customer for $10,000 of merchandise that Standard plans to manufacture. The customer advanced $3,500 toward the contract price.

(12) A warehouse costing $50,000 is acquired. A down payment of $5,000 is made, and a long-term mortgage is assumed for the balance.

(13) Raw materials inventory with a list price of $1,000 is found to be defective and returned to the supplier. This inventory has already been paid for in (9). The returned raw materials are the only item purchased from this particular supplier during January 1979.

(14) The firm purchased 5,000 shares of $10-par value common stock of the General Electronics Corporation for $85,000. This investment is made as a short-term investment of excess cash. The shares of General Electronics Corporation are traded on the New York Stock Exchange.

The following assumptions will help you resolve certain accounting uncertainties: (i) Transactions (2) and (3) occurred on the same day as transaction (1). (ii) The invoices paid in (9) are the only purchases for which discounts were made available to the purchaser.

a Enter these transactions in T-accounts. Indicate whether each account is an asset, liability, or owners' equity item. Cross-reference each entry to the appropriate transaction number.

b Prepare a balance sheet as of January 31, 1979.

26 The following transactions occur during June 1979 for the Snyder Book Store, a sole proprietorship, in preparation for its opening for business on July 1, 1979.

(1) J. R. Snyder contributes $5,000 in cash, 200 shares of Western Corporation common stock, and an inventory of books to be sold. The stock of Western Corporation is quoted on the New York Stock Exchange at $13 per share on the day it is contributed, and will be sold when additional cash is needed. The books are to be stated at $1,750.

(2) Three months' rent on a store building is paid in advance in cash. The bookstore will occupy the building on July 1. The monthly rental is $200.

(3) Store fixtures are purchased for $3,000, of which $500 is paid in cash. A note, to be paid in 10 equal monthly installments beginning August 1, is signed for the balance.

(4) Books with an invoice price of $2,100 are purchased on account.

(5) A one-year insurance policy on the store's contents beginning July 1, 1979, is purchased. The premium of $120 is paid by check.

(6) A check for $250 is issued to the Darwin Equipment Co. for a cash register and other operating equipment.

(7) Merchandise costing $1,500 is ordered from a publisher. Delivery is scheduled for July 15.

(8) The merchandise purchased in (4) is paid for by check. Payment is made in time to obtain a 2-percent cash discount for prompt payment. These are the only purchases for which discounts are available.

(9) An operating license for the year beginning July 1, 1979, is obtained from the city. The fee of $150 is paid by check.

    a Enter these transactions in T-accounts. Indicate whether each account is an asset, liability, or owners' equity item. Cross-reference each entry to the appropriate transaction number.

    b Prepare a balance sheet for this sole proprietorship as of June 30, 1979.

27 Priscilla Mullins and Miles Standish form a partnership to operate a laundry and cleaning business to be known as Pilgrim's One Day Laundry and Cleaners. The following transactions occur in late June 1979, prior to the grand opening on July 1, 1979.

    (1) Standish contributes $500 cash and cleaning equipment that is to be stated at $4,500.

    (2) Mullins contributes $4,000 cash and a delivery truck to be stated at $1,500.

    (3) The July rent for the business premises of $300 is paid in advance.

    (4) Cleaning supplies are purchased on account from the Wonder Chemical Company for $1,500.

    (5) Insurance coverage on the equipment and truck for a 1-year period beginning July 1, 1979, is purchased for $275 cash.

    (6) The firm borrows $1,000 from the First National Bank. A 90-day, 8-percent note is signed, with principal and interest payable at maturity.

    (7) The Wonder Chemical Company account is paid in full after deducting a 2-percent discount for prompt payment.

    (8) A cash register is purchased for $900. A down payment of $50 is made, and a note is signed for the remainder, payable in 10 equal installments beginning August 1.

    a Enter these transactions in T-accounts. Indicate whether each account is an asset, liability, or owners' equity item. Cross-reference each entry to the appropriate transaction number.

    b Prepare a balance sheet for the partnership as of June 30, 1979.

28 Most of the financial records of the Rowland Novelty Company were removed by an employee who, apparently, took all the cash on hand from the store on October 31. From supplementary records, the following information is obtained:

    (1) According to the bank, cash in bank was $5,730.

    (2) Amounts payable to creditors were $4,720.

    (3) Rowland's initial contribution to the business was $15,000 and the total interest in the business at the time of the theft was $17,500.

    (4) Cost of merchandise on hand was $11,380.

    (5) A 1-year fire insurance policy was purchased on September 1 for $900.

    (6) Furniture and fixtures are rented from the Anderson Office Supply Company for $200 per month. The rental for October has not been paid.

    (7) A note for $1,200 was given by a customer. Interest due at October 31 was $45.

    (8) Payments due from other customers amounted to $1,915.

    (9) Rowland purchased a license from the city for $300 on July 1. The license allows retail operations for 1 year.

    a Determine the probable cash shortage.

    b Prepare a well-organized balance sheet presenting the financial position immediately preceding the theft.

29 Comment on any unusual features of the following balance sheet of the Western Sales Corporation.

Western Sales Corporation
Balance Sheet
For the Year Ended
December 31, 1979

ASSETS

Current Assets:

Cash and Certificates of Deposit	$ 86,500	
Accounts Receivable—Net	193,600	
Merchandise Inventory	322,900	$ 603,000

Investments (substantially at cost):

Investment in U.S. Treasury Notes	$ 60,000	
Investment in Eastern Sales Corp.	196,500	256,500

Fixed Assets (at cost):

Land	$225,000	
Buildings and Equipment—Net	842,600	1,067,600

Intangibles and Deferred Charges:

Prepaid Insurance	$ 1,200	
Prepaid Rent	1,500	
Goodwill	2	2,702
Total Assets		$1,929,802

LIABILITIES AND STOCKHOLDERS' EQUITY

Current Liabilities:

Accounts Payable	$225,300	
Accrued Expenses	10,900	
Income Taxes Payable	89,200	$ 325,400

Long-Term Liabilities:

Bonds Payable	$500,000	
Pensions Payable	40,600	
Contingent Liability	100,000	640,600

Stockholders' Equity:

Common Stock—$10-par value, 50,000 shares issued and outstanding	$625,000	
Earned Surplus	338,802	963,802
Total Liabilities and Stockholders' Equity		$1,929,802

30 A set of condensed balance sheets for International Harvester Company and Subsidiaries for each of the years 1967 through 1976 is presented in Exhibit 2.5. Using only the information provided in these comparative balance sheets, describe the major changes that have occurred in the structure of this firm's assets and equities during this 10-year period. (Hint: You might want to begin by expressing various balance sheet components as a percentage of other components. For example, current assets are 62.3 percent of total assets at the end of the 1976 accounting period.)

EXHIBIT 2.5
International Harvester Company and Subsidiaries
Comparative Condensed Balance Sheets
December 31, 1967 to 1976
(Amounts in Millions)

Assets	1967	1968	1969	1970	1971	1972	1973	1974	1975	1976
Current Assets	$1,157.8	$1,211.1	$1,304.9	$1,411.1	$1,461.3	$1,726.6	$1,895.5	$2,257.1	$2,308.7	$2,228.0
Property, Plant, and Equipment—Net	496.9	511.8	547.6	575.8	564.9	541.5	569.5	654.4	657.7	710.3
Investments	134.6	148.1	157.5	191.2	221.5	268.7	310.0	357.3	430.4	495.8
Other Assets	15.8	21.4	19.2	39.2	27.3	37.5	37.7	58.2	113.6	140.8
Total Assets	$1,805.1	$1,892.4	$2,029.2	$2,217.3	$2,275.0	$2,574.3	$2,812.7	$3,327.0	$3,510.4	$3,574.9
Liabilities and Stockholders' Equity										
Current Liabilities	$ 410.7	$ 442.4	$ 553.9	$ 644.7	$ 669.5	$ 881.3	$1,006.8	$1,309.8	$1,093.8	$1,004.2
Long-Term Debt	264.4	298.1	312.7	402.2	431.3	465.1	497.0	625.3	938.2	922.9
Deferred Income Taxes	—	—	7.4	23.6	24.7	29.9	24.3	27.7	34.5	67.0
Total Liabilities	$ 675.1	$ 740.5	$ 874.0	$1,070.5	$1,125.5	$1,376.3	$1,528.1	$1,962.8	$2,066.5	$1,994.1
Stockholders' Equity	1,130.0	1,151.9	1,155.2	1,146.8	1,149.5	1,198.0	1,284.6	1,364.2	1,443.9	1,580.8
Total Liabilities and Stockholders' Equity	$1,805.1	$1,892.4	$2,029.2	$2,217.3	$2,275.0	$2,574.3	$2,812.7	$3,327.0	$3,510.4	$3,574.9

31 Financial analysts typically use information from all three of the principal financial statements discussed in Chapter 1 (that is, balance sheet, income statement, and statement of changes in financial position) in making their analyses and interpretations. It is possible, however, to make some general observations about changes in the structure of a firm's assets and equities by studying comparative balance sheets only. These general observations are then examined further by studying the income statement and statement of changes in financial position.

Refer to the comparative balance sheet and related notes of International Corporation in Appendix A at the back of the book. Using this financial statement only, describe the most significant changes that occurred in the structure of International Corporation's assets and equities between 19X0 and 19X1. (Hint: You may want to begin your analysis by expressing various balance sheet components as a percentage of other components. For example, current assets represent 58.4 percent of total assets on December 31, 19X1.)

CHAPTER 3
INCOME STATEMENT—
MEASUREMENT PRINCIPLES

The second principal financial statement considered is the income statement. This statement provides a measure of the earnings performance of a firm for some particular period of time. As we discussed in Chapter 1 and illustrated for the Jonathan Electronics Corporation in Exhibit 1.2, *net income,* or *earnings,* is equal to revenues minus expenses.

Revenues measure the inflow of net assets (assets less liabilities) from selling goods and providing services. Expenses measure the outflow of net assets that are used up, or consumed, in the process of generating revenues. As a measure of earnings performance, revenues reflect the services rendered by the firm and expenses indicate the efforts required or expended.

This chapter considers the accounting principles and conventions that underlie the income statement. We begin by discussing the concept of the accounting period, the span of time over which earnings performance is measured. Next we describe and illustrate two common methods of measuring performance, the cash basis and the accrual basis. We then discuss the criteria for recognizing and measuring revenues and expenses. Finally, the classification of items within the income statement is considered. Chapter 4 describes the accounting procedures used in applying these principles and conventions in preparing the income statement.

THE ACCOUNTING PERIOD CONVENTION

The income statement is a report on earnings performance over a specified period of time. Years ago, the length of this period varied substantially among firms. Income statements were prepared at the completion of some activity, such as after the round-trip voyage of a ship between England and the colonies or at the completion of a construction project.

The earnings activities of most modern firms are not so easily separated into distinguishable projects. Instead, the income-generating activity is carried on continually. For example, a plant is acquired and used in manufacturing products for a period of 40 years or more. Delivery equipment is purchased and used in transporting merchandise to customers for 4, 5, or more years. If the preparation of the income statement were postponed until all earnings activities were completed, the report might never be prepared and, in any case, would be too late to help a reader appraise performance and make decisions. An accounting period of uniform length is used to facilitate timely comparisons and analyses among firms.

An accounting period of *1 year* underlies the principal financial statements distributed to stockholders and potential investors. Most firms prepare their annual reports using the calendar year as the accounting period. A growing number of firms, however, use a *natural business year*. The use of a natural business year is an attempt to measure performance at a time when most earnings activities have been substantially concluded. The ending date of a natural business year varies from one firm to another. For example, Sears uses a natural business year ending on January 31, which comes after completion of the Christmas shopping season and before the start of the Easter season. American Motors uses a year ending September 30, the end of its model year. A. C. Nielsen (producers of television ratings and other surveys) uses a year ending August 31, just prior to the beginning of the new television season.

ACCOUNTING METHODS FOR MEASURING PERFORMANCE

When measuring earnings performance for the accounting period, some activities will have been started and completed within the period. For example, during a particular accounting period, merchandise might be purchased from a supplier, sold to a customer on account, and the account collected in cash. Few difficulties are encountered in measuring performance in these cases. The difference between the cash received from customers and the cash disbursed to acquire, sell, and deliver the merchandise represents earnings from this series of transactions.

Many earnings activities, however, are started in one accounting period and completed in another. Buildings and equipment are acquired in one period but used over a period of several years. Merchandise is sometimes purchased in one accounting period and sold during the next period, whereas cash is collected from customers during a third period. A significant problem in measuring performance for specific accounting periods concerns the determination of the amount of revenues and expenses to be recognized from earnings activities that are in process as of the beginning of the period or are incomplete as of the end of the period. Two approaches to measuring earnings performance are (1) the cash basis of accounting, and (2) the accrual basis of accounting.

Cash Basis of Accounting

Under the *cash basis of accounting,* revenues from selling goods and providing services are recognized in the period when cash is received from customers. Expenses are typically reported in the period in which expenditures are made for merchandise, salaries, insurance, taxes, and similar items. To illustrate the measurement of performance under the cash basis of accounting, consider the following example.

Donald and Joanne Allens open a hardware store on January 1, 1979. They contribute $10,000 in cash and borrow $6,000 from a local bank. The loan is repayable on June 30, 1979, with interest charged at the rate of 10 percent per year. A store building is rented on January 1, and 2 months' rent of $2,000 is paid in advance. The premium of $1,200 for property and liability insurance coverage for the year ending December 31, 1979, is paid on January 1. During January, merchandise costing $20,000 is acquired, of which $13,000 is purchased for cash and $7,000 is purchased on account. Sales to customers during January total $25,000, of which $17,000 is sold for cash and $8,000 is sold on account. The acquisition cost of the merchandise sold during January is $16,000, and various employees are paid $2,500 in salaries.

Exhibit 3.1 presents a performance report for Allens' Hardware Store for the month of January 1979 using the cash basis. Cash receipts from sales of merchandise of $17,000 represent the portion of the total sales of $25,000 made during January which was collected in cash. Whereas merchandise costing $20,000 was acquired during January, only $13,000 cash was disbursed to suppliers, and only this amount is subtracted in measuring performance under the cash basis. Cash expenditures during January for salaries, rent, and insurance are also subtracted in measuring performance, without regard to whether or not the services acquired were fully consumed by the end of the month. Cash expenditures made for merchandise and services exceeded cash receipts from customers during January by $1,700.[1]

EXHIBIT 3.1
Allens' Hardware Store
Performance Measurement on a
Cash Basis
For the Month of January 1979

Cash Receipts from Sales of Merchandise		$17,000
Less Cash Expenditures for Merchandise and Services:		
Merchandise	$13,000	
Salaries	2,500	
Rental	2,000	
Insurance	1,200	
Total Cash Expenditures		18,700
Excess of Cash Expenditures over Cash Receipts		($1,700)

As a basis for measuring performance for a particular accounting period (for example, January 1979 for Allens' Hardware Store), the cash basis of accounting is subject to

[1] Note that, under the cash method, cash received from owners and through borrowing is not included in the performance report. Only those cash receipts and disbursements from the firm's operating and investing activities are included.

two important and somewhat related criticisms. First, the cost of the efforts required in generating revenues is not adequately matched with those revenues. Performance of one period therefore gets mingled with the performance of preceding and succeeding periods. The store rental payment of $2,000 provides rental services for both January and February, but under the cash basis, the full amount is subtracted in measuring performance during January. Likewise, the annual insurance premium provides coverage for the full year, whereas under the cash basis of accounting, none of this insurance cost will be subtracted in measuring performance during the months of February through December.

The longer the period over which future benefits are received, the more serious is this criticism of the cash basis of accounting. Consider, for example, the investments of a capital-intensive firm in buildings and equipment that might be used for 10, 20, or more years. The length of time between the purchase of these assets and the collection of cash for goods produced and sold can span many years.

A second, and probably less serious, criticism of the cash basis of accounting is that it postpones unnecessarily the time when revenue is recognized. In most cases, the sale (delivery) of goods or rendering of services is the critical event in generating revenue. The collection of cash is relatively routine, or at least highly predictable. In these cases, recognizing revenue at the time of cash collection may result in reporting the effects of earnings activities one or more periods after the critical revenue-generating activity has occurred. For example, sales to customers during January by Allens' Hardware Store totaled $25,000. Under the cash basis of accounting, $8,000 of this

---

EXHIBIT 3.2
Allens' Hardware Store
Income Statement
For the Month of January 1979
(Accrual Basis of Accounting)

Sales Revenue		$25,000
Less Expenses:		
Cost of Goods Sold	$16,000	
Salaries Expense	2,500	
Rent Expense	1,000	
Insurance Expense	100	
Interest Expense	50	
Total Expenses		19,650
Net Income		$ 5,350

---

amount will not be recognized until February or later, when the cash is collected. If the credit standings of customers have been checked prior to making sales on account, it is highly probable that cash will be collected, and there is little reason to postpone recognition of the revenue.

The cash basis of accounting is used principally by lawyers, accountants, and other professional people who have relatively small investments in multiperiod assets, such as buildings and equipment, and who tend to collect cash from their clients soon after services are rendered. Most such firms actually use a *modified cash basis of accounting,* under which the costs of buildings, equipment, and similar items are treated as assets when purchased. A portion of the acquisition cost is then recognized as an expense when services of these assets are consumed. Except for the treatment of these long-lived assets, revenues are recognized at the time cash is received and expenses are reported when cash disbursements are made. Some physicians and dentists with relatively heavy investments in equipment use the modified cash basis of accounting.

Most individuals use the cash basis of accounting for the purpose of computing personal income and personal income taxes. Where inventories are an important factor in generating revenues, such as for a manufacturing or merchandising firm, the Internal Revenue Code prohibits a firm from using the cash basis of accounting in its income tax returns.

Accrual Basis of Accounting

Under the *accrual basis of accounting,* revenue is recognized when some critical event or transaction occurs that is related to the earnings process. In most cases, this critical event is the sale (delivery) of goods or the rendering of services. The nature and significance of this critical event are discussed later in the chapter. Under the accrual basis of accounting, costs incurred are reported as expenses in the period when the revenues to which they relate are recognized. Thus, an attempt is made to *match* expenses with associated revenues. When particular types of costs incurred cannot be closely identified with specific revenue streams, they are treated as expenses of the period in which services of an asset are consumed or future benefits of an asset disappear.

Exhibit 3.2 presents an income statement for Allens' Hardware Store for January 1979 using the accrual basis of accounting. The entire $25,000 of sales during January is recognized as revenue even though cash in that amount has not yet been received. Because of the high probability that outstanding accounts receivable will be collected, the critical revenue-generating event is the sale of the goods rather than the collection of cash from customers. The acquisition cost of the merchandise sold during January is $16,000. Recognizing this amount as cost-of-goods-sold expense leads to an appropriate matching of sales revenue and merchandise expense in the income statement. Of the advance rental payment of $2,000, only $1,000 applies to the cost of services consumed during January. The remaining rental of $1,000 applies to the month of February. Likewise, only $100 of the $1,200 insurance premium represents coverage used up during January. The remaining $1,100 of the insurance premium provides coverage for February through December and will be recognized as an expense during those months. The interest expense of $50 represents 1 month's interest on the $6,000 bank loan at an annual rate of 10 percent ($= \$6,000 \times .10 \times \frac{1}{12}$). Although the interest will not be paid until the loan becomes due on June 30, 1979, the firm benefited from having the funds available for its use during January and an appropriate portion of the total interest cost on the loan should be recognized as a January expense. The salaries, rental, insurance, and interest expenses, unlike the cost of merchandise sold, cannot be associated directly with revenues recognized during the period. These costs are therefore reported as expenses of January to the extent services were consumed during the month.

The accrual basis of accounting provides a better measure of earnings performance for Allens' Hardware Store for the month of January than does the cash basis, both because revenues are measured more accurately and because expenses are associated more closely with reported revenues. Likewise, the accrual basis will provide a superior measure of performance for future periods, since activities of those periods will be charged with their share of the costs of rental, insurance, and other services to be consumed.

Several important questions regarding the recognition of revenues and expenses have not yet been considered:

1 When, or at what point(s), within the earnings process is revenue recognized (that is, what is the nature of the critical revenue-generating event)?
2 How do we measure or determine the amount of revenue to be recognized?
3 When, or at what point(s), within the earnings process are expenses reported (that is, what is the nature of the matching convention)?
4 How do we measure or determine the amount of expenses to be reported?

We consider the principles employed in measuring revenues and expenses in the next two sections.

REVENUE RECOGNITION AND MEASUREMENT PRINCIPLES

In reporting revenue, we are concerned with *when* it arises (a timing question) and *how much* is recognized (a measurement question).

Timing of Revenue Recognition

The earnings process for the acquisition and sale of merchandise might be depicted as shown in Figure 3.1. Revenue could conceivably be recognized at the time of purchase, sale, or cash collection, at some point(s) between these events, or even continuously. To answer the timing question, we must have a set of criteria for revenue recognition.

FIGURE 3.1
Earnings Process for the Acquisition and Sale of Merchandise

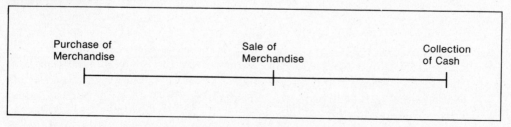

Criteria for Revenue Recognition   The criteria currently required to be met before revenue is recognized are as follows:

1 All, or a substantial portion, of the services to be provided have been performed.
2 Cash, receivables, or some other asset susceptible to reasonably precise measurement has been received.

For the vast majority of firms involved in selling goods and services, revenue is recognized at the time of sale (delivery). This method of recognizing revenues is called the *completed-sale,* or in some contexts the *completed-contract,* method of revenue recognition. The goods have been transferred to the buyer or the services have been performed. Future services, such as for warranties, are likely to be insignificant, or if significant, can be estimated with reasonable precision. An exchange between an independent buyer and seller has occurred which provides an objective measure of the amount of revenue. If the sale is made on account, past experience and an assessment of customers' credit standings provide a basis for predicting the amount of cash that will be collected. The sale of the goods or services is therefore the critical revenue-generating event. Under the accrual basis of accounting, revenue is typically recognized at the time of sale.

In a few instances, revenue may be recognized either earlier or later than the point of sale. These possibilities are discussed later in the chapter.

Measurement of Revenue

The amount of revenue recognized is generally measured by the cash or cash-equivalent value of other assets received from customers. As a starting point, this amount is the agreed-upon price between buyer and seller at the time of sale. Some adjustments to this amount may be necessary, however, if revenue is recognized in a period prior to the collection of cash.

Uncollectible Accounts   If some portion of the sales for a period is not expected to be collected, the amount of revenue recognized for that period must be adjusted for estimated uncollectible accounts arising from those sales. Logic suggests that this adjustment of revenue should occur in the period when revenue is recognized and not in a later period when specific customers' accounts are determined to be uncollectible. If the adjustment is postponed, reported income of subsequent periods will be affected by earlier decisions to extend credit to customers. Thus, the performance of the firm for both the period of sale and the period when the account is judged uncollectible would be measured inaccurately. These problems are considered further in Chapter 7.

Example   Champion's Department Store had sales to customers during 1979 as follows: cash sales, $400,000; sales on account, $600,000. Based on past experience, Champion's estimates that 2 percent of all sales on account will never be collected. The amount of revenue recognized by Champion's for 1979 under the accrual method is determined as follows:

Cash Sales	$ 400,000
Credit Sales	600,000
Total Sales—Gross	$1,000,000
Estimated Uncollectibles (2% $\times$ $600,000)	(12,000)
Total Sales—Net	$ 988,000

Sales Discounts and Allowances Customers may take advantage of discounts for prompt payment, or allowances may be granted for unsatisfactory merchandise. In these cases, the amount of cash eventually to be received can be expected to be less than the stated selling price. Appropriate reductions should therefore be made at the time of sale in determining the amount of revenue to be recognized.

Delayed Payments If the period between the sale of the goods or services and the time of cash collection extends over several years and there is no provision for explicit interest payments, it is likely that the selling price includes an interest charge for the loan conveying the right to delay payment. Under the accrual basis of accounting, this interest element should be recognized as interest revenue during the periods between sale and collection when the loan is outstanding. To recognize all potential revenue entirely in the period of sale would be to recognize too soon the return for services rendered over time in lending money. Thus, when cash collection is to be delayed, the measure of current revenue should be the selling price reduced to account for the interest element applicable to future periods. Only the *present value* of the amount to be received should be recognized as revenue during the period of sale. For most accounts receivable, the period between sale and collection spans only 2 to 3 months. The interest element is likely to be relatively insignificant in these cases. As a result, in accounting practice no reduction for interest on delayed payments is made for receivables to be collected within 1 year or less. This procedure is a practical expedient rather than a strict following of the underlying accounting theory.

EXPENSE RECOGNITION AND MEASUREMENT PRINCIPLES

Analogous to the questions raised regarding revenue recognition, we are confronted with the questions of *when* expenses are recognized and at *what amount* they are stated.

Timing of Expense Recognition

Recall that assets represent resources providing future benefits to the firm. *Expenses* are a measurement of the assets consumed in generating revenue. Assets may be referred to as *unexpired costs* and expenses as *expired costs* or "gone assets." Our attention focuses on the question of when the asset expiration takes place. The critical question is "When have asset benefits expired—leaving the balance sheet—and become expenses—entering the income statement as reductions in owners' equity?" Thus:

Balance Sheet	**Income Statement**
Assets or Unexpired Costs	$\longrightarrow$ Expenses or Expired Costs

Expense Recognition Criteria   The criteria presently employed by accountants in making the timing decision may be summarized as follows:

1 Asset expirations, or expenses, directly associated with particular types of revenue are recognized as expenses in the period in which the revenues are recognized. This treatment is called the *matching convention,* because cost expirations are matched with revenues.
2 Asset expirations, or expenses, not directly or easily associated with revenues are treated as expenses of the period in which services are consumed in operations.

Product or Production Costs   The cost of goods or merchandise sold is perhaps the easiest expense to associate with revenue. At the time of sale, the asset physically changes hands. Revenue is recognized, and the cost of the merchandise transferred is treated as an expense.

A *merchandising firm* purchases inventory and later sells it without changing its physical form. The inventory is shown as an asset stated at acquisition cost on the balance sheet. Later, when the inventory is sold, the same amount of acquisition cost is shown as an expense (cost of goods sold) on the income statement.

A *manufacturing firm,* on the other hand, incurs various costs in changing the physical form of the goods it produces. These costs are typically of three types: (1) direct material, (2) direct labor, and (3) manufacturing overhead (sometimes called indirect manufacturing costs). Direct material and direct labor costs can be associated directly with particular products manufactured. Manufacturing overhead includes a mixture of costs that provide a firm with a capacity to produce. Examples of manufacturing overhead costs are expenditures for utilities, property taxes, and insurance on the factory, as well as depreciation on manufacturing plant and equipment. The services of each of these items are used up, or consumed, during the period while the firm is creating new assets, the inventory of goods being worked upon or held for sale. Benefits from direct material, direct labor, and manufacturing overhead are, in a sense, transferred to, or become embodied in, the asset represented by units of inventory. Since the inventory items are assets until sales are made to customers, the various direct material, direct labor, and manufacturing overhead costs incurred in producing the goods are treated as unexpired, but converted, costs and included in the valuation of the manufacturing inventory under the titles Work-in-Process Inventory and Finished Goods Inventory. Such costs, which are assets transformed from one form to another, are called *product costs.* Product costs are assets; they become expenses only when the goods in which they are embodied are sold.

Selling Costs   In most cases, the costs incurred in selling, or marketing, a firm's products relate to the units sold during the period. For example, salaries and commissions of the sales staff, sales literature used, and most advertising costs are incurred in generating revenue currently. Since these selling costs are associated with the revenues of the period, they are reported as expenses in the period when the services provided by these costs are consumed. It can be argued that some selling costs, such as advertising and other sales promotion, provide future-period benefits for a firm and should continue to be treated as assets. However, distinguishing what portion of the cost relates to the current period to be recognized as an expense and what portion relates to future periods to be treated as an asset can be extremely difficult. Therefore, accountants typically treat selling and other marketing activity costs as expenses of the period when the services are used. These selling costs are treated as *period expenses* rather than as assets, even though they may enhance the future marketability of a firm's products.

Administrative Costs   The costs incurred in administering, or directing, the activities of the firm cannot be closely associated with units produced and sold and are, therefore, like selling costs, treated as period expenses. Examples include the president's salary, accounting and data-processing costs, and the costs of conducting various supportive activities such as legal services and corporate planning.

Summary of Cost Flows   Exhibit 3.3 summarizes the treatment of various costs incurred by a manufacturing firm.

EXHIBIT 3.3
Treatment of Various Costs
Incurred by a Manufacturing Firm

Cost Item	Product Cost (Asset)	Period Expense — Selling	Period Expense — Administrative
I. Salaries			
A. President of Company[a]			X
B. Vice-President for Sales		X	
C. Vice-President for Manufacturing	X		
D. Production Supervisor	X		
E. Sales Staff		X	
F. Accountant (general office)[a]			X
II. Materials and Supplies			
A. Raw Materials Purchased for Future Productive Use	X		
B. Raw Materials Used in the Factory	X		
C. Sales Pamphlets Distributed		X	
D. Data-Processing Supplies Used			X
E. Cleaning Supplies Used in Factory	X		
III. Other			
A. Insurance on Factory Building	X		
B. Insurance on Sales Staff's Automobiles		X	
C. Insurance on Office Building			X
D. Depreciation on Factory Equipment	X		
E. Depreciation on General Office Data-Processing Equipment			X
F. Maintenance of Sales Staff's Automobiles		X	

[a] Might in principle be allocated between Product Cost and Period Expense in proportion to time spent on these functions. In practice, this allocation is seldom done because it is not worth the trouble.

The flow of costs for materials and services through the stages of acquisition, production, and sale can be diagrammed as shown in Figure 3.2.

Measurement of Expenses

Expenses are costs expired, or assets consumed, during the period. The amount of an expense is therefore the amount of the expired asset. Thus, the basis for expense measurement is the same as for asset valuation. Since assets are primarily stated at acquisition cost on the balance sheet, expenses are measured by the acquisition cost of the assets that were either sold or used during the period.

INCOME RECOGNITION OTHER THAN AT POINT OF SALE

Income is revenues less expenses. The criteria discussed earlier for recognizing revenue were:

1 All, or a substantial portion of the services to be provided have been performed.
2 Cash, receivables, or some other asset susceptible to reasonably precise measurement has been received.

These criteria may sometimes be met prior to the time of sale or may sometimes not be

FIGURE 3.2
Diagram of Cost Flows

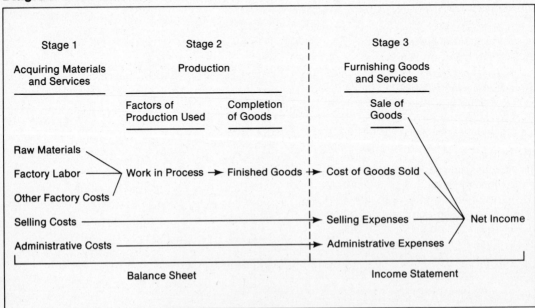

met until after the time of sale. In these cases, revenue may be recognized either earlier or later. There is an effort, however, to match expenses with associated revenues.

Recognition at the Time of Production

On some long-term construction projects, the buyer and the seller agree in advance on the contract price and the timing of cash payments. Revenue from these long-term contracts is often recognized during the period of construction. The earnings process for a particular long-term construction project may span several years. If the firm waited until the project was completed to recognize revenue, the efforts and accomplishments of several accounting periods would be recognized in the one period when the contract was completed. This approach would give an unsatisfactory measure of performance for each period during the contract. In these cases, some firms use the *percentage-of-completion method* of recognizing revenue. A portion of the total contract price, based on the degree of completion of the work, is recognized as revenue each period. This proportion is determined using either engineers' estimates of the degree of completion or the ratio of costs incurred to date to the total expected costs for the contract.

Although future services required on these long-term construction contracts can be substantial at any given time, the costs to be incurred in providing these services can often be estimated with reasonable precision. The existence of a contract indicates that a buyer has been obtained and a price for the construction services has been set. Cash is usually collected from the buyer as construction progresses or the assessment of the customer's credit standing leads to a reasonable expectation that the contract price will be received in cash after construction is completed. Construction activities are therefore the critical revenue-generating events. The actual schedule of cash collections is *not* significant for the revenue recognition process when the percentage-of-completion method is used.

Some firms involved with construction contracts postpone the recognition of revenue until the construction project and the sale are completed. This method is the same as the completed-sale basis, but is often referred to as the *completed-contract method* of recognizing revenue. In some cases, the completed-contract method is used because the contracts are of such short duration (such as 3 or 6 months) that earnings reported with the percentage-of-completion method and the completed-contract method are not significantly different. In these cases, the completed-contract method is used because it is generally easier to implement. Some firms use the completed-contract method in situations when a specific buyer has not been obtained during the periods while construction is progressing, as is sometimes the case in constructing residential housing. In these cases, future selling efforts are required and substantial uncertainty may exist regarding the contract price ultimately to be established and the amount of cash to be received.

The primary reason for a contractor's not using the percentage-of-completion method when a contract exists is the uncertainty of total costs to be incurred in carrying out the project. If total costs cannot be reasonably estimated, the percentage of total costs incurred by a given date also cannot be estimated, and the percentage of services already rendered (revenue) cannot be determined.

Recognition at the Point of Cash Collection

Occasionally, estimating the amount of cash or other assets that will be received from customers is extremely difficult. Therefore, an objective measure of the services rendered and the benefits to be received cannot be made at the time of the sale. Under these circumstances, revenue is recognized at the time of cash collection. But, unlike the cash method of accounting, there is an attempt to match expenses with revenues.

Installment Method   The recognition of revenue at the time of cash collection is sometimes followed by land development companies. These companies typically sell undeveloped land and promise to develop it over several future years. The buyer makes a nominal down payment and agrees to pay the remainder of the purchase price in installments over 10, 20, or more years. In these cases, future development of the land is a significant aspect of the earnings process. Also, substantial uncertainty often exists as to the ultimate collectibility of the installment notes, particularly those not due until several years in the future. The customer can always elect to stop making payments, merely losing the right to own the land.

    The critical revenue-generating event in this case is the collection of cash. When revenue is recognized as the periodic cash collections are received and costs incurred in generating the revenue are matched as closely as possible with the revenue (for example, if 40 percent of the purchase price is collected, then 40 percent of the cost of the land is recognized as an expense), the firm is using the *installment method* of accounting. The installment method is similar to the cash basis of accounting, since revenue is recognized only as cash is received. In the installment method, however, an effort is made to match expenses with associated revenues.

    For most sales of goods and services, past experience and an assessment of customers' credit standings provide a sufficient basis for predicting the amount of cash to be received. The installment method is not allowed in these situations, and revenue is recognized at the time of sale.[2]

Cost-Recovery-First Method   Under circumstances where there is such great uncertainty about cash collection that the installment method is allowed, the *cost-recovery-first method* of income recognition can also be used. (It is, in our opinion, preferable under these circumstances.) Under this method, costs of generating revenues are matched dollar for dollar with cash receipts until all such costs are recovered. Only when cumulative cash receipts exceed total costs will profit (that is, revenue without any matching expenses) be shown in the financial statements.

    Although the installment method and the cost-recovery-first method are permitted under generally accepted accounting principles when great uncertainty exists about cash collection, they are used only rarely in financial reporting. The installment method is allowable for income tax reporting under certain circumstances, even when cash collections are assured. Retailers and other firms selling on extended payment plans often use the installment method for income tax reporting (while recognizing

---

[2]   APB *Opinion No. 10,* paragraph 12, footnote 8, 1966.

revenue at the time of sale for financial reporting). The cost-recovery-first method is not permitted for income tax reporting.

Recognition Between Purchase and Sale

The period between the acquisition, or production, and the sale of merchandise and other salable goods is referred to as a *holding period.* The current market prices of these assets could change during this holding period. Such changes are described as *unrealized holding gains and losses,* because a transaction or exchange has not taken place.

Unrealized holding gains could be recognized as they occur. Accountants typically wait, however, until the asset is sold or exchanged in an arm's-length transaction before recognizing the gain. At that time, an inflow of net assets subject to objective measurement is presumed to have taken place. Since the accountant assumes that the firm is a going concern, the unrealized gain will eventually be recognized as revenue in the ordinary course of business in a future period. The recognition of revenue and the valuation of assets are therefore closely associated. Nonmonetary assets are typically stated at acquisition cost until sold. At the time of sale, an inflow of net assets occurs (for example, cash, accounts receivable), and revenue reflecting the previously unreported unrealized gain is recognized. This treatment of unrealized holding gains has the effect of shifting income from periods when the asset is held and the market price increases to the later period of sale. The longer the holding period (as, for example, land held for several decades), the more is reported income likely to be shifted to later periods.

Current accounting practices do not treat unrealized holding *losses* in the same way as unrealized holding *gains,* particularly on inventory items and marketable securities. If the current market prices of inventory items and marketable securities decrease below acquisition cost during the holding period, the asset is usually written down. As a result, the unrealized loss is recognized in the period of price decline. This treatment of losses rests on the convention that earnings should be reported conservatively. Considering the estimates and predictions required in measuring revenues and expenses, some accountants feel it is desirable to provide a conservative measure of earnings so statement users will not be misled into thinking the firm is doing better than it really is.

The inconsistent treatment of unrealized gains and unrealized losses does not seem warranted. The arguments used against recognizing unrealized gains apply equally well to unrealized losses. If gains cannot be determined objectively prior to sale, then how can losses be measured prior to sale? If losses can be measured objectively prior to sale, then why cannot gains? We consider the accounting treatment of unrealized holding gains and losses further in Chapters 7, 8, and 12.

Summary Illustration of Income Recognition Methods

As a summary of much of the material covered thus far in this chapter, Exhibit 3.4 presents a comprehensive illustration of income recognition. The illustration relates

EXHIBIT 3.4
Comprehensive Illustration of Revenue and Expense Recognition
(All Dollar Amounts in Thousands)

Period	Cash Basis of Accounting[a]			Percentage-of-Completion Method			Completed-Contract Method		
	Revenue	Expense	Income	Revenue	Expense	Income	Revenue	Expense	Income
1	$ 500	$ 800	$ (300)	$1,000[d]	$ 800	$ 200	$ —	$ —	$ —
2	500	2,000	(1,500)	2,500[e]	2,000	500	—	—	—
3	1,000	2,000	(1,000)	2,500[e]	2,000	500	6,000	4,800	1,200
4	2,000	—	2,000	—	—	—	—	—	—
5	2,000	—	2,000	—	—	—	—	—	—
Total	$6,000	$4,800	$1,200	$6,000	$4,800	$1,200	$6,000	$4,800	$1,200

Period	Installment Method[b]			Cost-Recovery-First Method[c]		
	Revenue	Expense	Income	Revenue	Expense	Income
1	$ 500	$ 400[f]	$ 100	$ 500	$ 500	$ 0
2	500	400[f]	100	500	500	0
3	1,000	800[g]	200	1,000	1,000	0
4	2,000	1,600[h]	400	2,000	2,000	0
5	2,000	1,600[h]	400	2,000	800	1,200
Total	$6,000	$4,800	$1,200	$6,000	$4,800	$1,200

a The cash basis is not allowed for tax or financial reporting if inventories are a material factor in generating income.
b The installment method is allowed for financial reporting only if extreme uncertainty exists as to the amount of cash to be collected from customers. Its use for tax purposes is not affected by the collectibility of cash.
c The cost-recovery-first method is allowed for financial reporting only if extreme uncertainty exists as to the amount of cash to be collected from customers. It is not permitted for tax purposes.
d $800/$4,800 × $6,000.
e $2,000/$6,000 × $6,000.
f $500/$6,000 × $4,800.
g $1,000/$6,000 × $4,800.
h $2,000/$6,000 × $4,800.

to a contract for the construction of a bridge for $6 million. The expected and actual pattern of cash receipts and disbursements under the contract is as follows:

Period	Expected and Actual Cash Receipts	Expected and Actual Cash Expenditures
1	$ 500,000	$ 800,000
2	500,000	2,000,000
3	1,000,000	2,000,000
4	2,000,000	—
5	2,000,000	—
Total	$6,000,000	$4,800,000

The bridge was completed in period 3. Exhibit 3.4 indicates the revenues, expenses, and income recognized each period under the contract using the cash method, the percentage-of-completion method, the completed-contract (completed-sale) method, the installment method, and the cost-recovery-first method. Not all five methods of income recognition could be justified for financial reporting, nor could they all be used on the tax return in this case. They are presented merely for illustrative purposes. Note that the total revenues, expenses, and income recognized for the 5 years are the same for all methods. In historical cost accounting over long enough time periods, income is equal to cash inflows less cash outflows. There is, however, a significant difference in the patterns of annual income, depending on the accounting method.

FORMAT AND CLASSIFICATION WITHIN THE INCOME STATEMENT

The income statement might contain some or all of the following sections or categories, depending on the nature of the firm's income for the period:

1 Income from continuing operations
2 Income, gains, and losses from discontinued operations
3 Adjustments for changes in accounting principles
4 Extraordinary gains and losses
5 Earnings per share

The great majority of income statements include only the first section. The other sections are added if necessary. The income statement for International Corporation on page 579 of Appendix A contains several of these classifications of income.

Income from Continuing Operations   Revenues, gains, expenses, and losses from the continuing areas of business activity of a firm are presented in the first section of the income statement. A heading such as "Income from Continuing Operations" is used if there are other sections in the income statement.

Income, Gains, and Losses from Discontinued Operations   If a firm sells a major division or segment of its business during the year or contemplates its sale within a short time after the end of the accounting period, Accounting Principles Board

Opinion No. 30 requires that any income, gains, and losses related to that segment be disclosed separately from ordinary, continuing operations in a section of the income statement entitled "Income, Gains, and Losses from Discontinued Operations."[3] This section follows the section presenting Income from Continuing Operations.

Adjustments for Changes in Accounting Principles   A firm that changes its principles, or methods, of accounting during the period is required in some cases to disclose the effects of the change on current and prior years' net income.[4] This information is presented in a separate section, after Income, Gains, and Losses from Discontinued Operations.

Extraordinary Gains and Losses   Extraordinary gains and losses are presented in a separate section of the income statement. For an item to be classified as *extraordinary*, it must generally meet both of the following criteria (one exception is the gain or loss on bond retirement, which is considered to be extraordinary):

1   Unusual in nature
2   Infrequent in occurrence.[5]

An example of an item likely to be extraordinary for most firms is a loss from expropriation or confiscation of assets by a foreign government. Since 1973, when Accounting Principles Board Opinion No. 30 was issued, extraordinary items are seldom seen in published annual reports (except for gains or losses on bond retirements, which are discussed in depth in Chapter 10).

Earnings per Share   Earnings-per-share data must be shown in the body of the income statement in order to receive an unqualified accountant's opinion.[6] Earnings per common share is conventionally calculated by dividing net income minus preferred stock dividends by the average number of outstanding common shares during the accounting period. For example, assume that a firm had net income of $500,000 during the year 1979. Dividends declared and paid on outstanding preferred stock were $100,000. The average number of shares of outstanding common stock during 1979 was 1 million shares. Earnings per common share would be $.40 [= ($500,000 − $100,000)/1,000,000].

If a firm has securities outstanding that can be converted into or exchanged for common stock, it may be required to present two sets of earnings-per-share amounts: *primary earnings per share* and *fully diluted earnings per share.* For example, some firms issue convertible bonds or convertible preferred stock, which can be exchanged directly for shares of common stock. Also, many firms have employee stock option

---

[3]   APB *Opinion No. 30,* 1973.
[4]   APB *Opinion No. 20,* 1971.
[5]   APB *Opinion No. 30,* 1973; Financial Accounting Standards Board, *Statement of Financial Accounting Standards No. 4,* 1975.
[6]   APB *Opinion No. 15,* 1969.

EARNING/share = Net income / # of Common stock share outstanding

plans under which shares of the company's common stock may be acquired by employees under special arrangements. If these convertible securities were converted or stock options were exercised and additional shares of common stock were issued, the amount conventionally shown as earnings per share would probably decrease, or become *diluted*. When a firm has outstanding securities that, if exchanged for shares of common stock, would decrease earnings per share by 3 percent or more, a dual presentation of primary and fully diluted earnings per share is required.[7]

SUMMARY

Net income is determined for discrete accounting periods in order to facilitate appraisals of earnings performance among firms and over time for a given firm. Most business firms use the accrual basis of accounting for measuring earnings and financial position. A few firms use the cash basis.

Under the cash basis, revenue is recognized when cash is received, and expenses are reported when cash disbursements for merchandise, salaries, taxes, and similar items are made. The cash basis suffers from two weaknesses: (1) It unnecessarily defers the recognition of revenue, and (2) it recognizes expenses in periods that may differ from those when economic benefits are received as revenues.

The accrual basis of accounting is not subject to these important weaknesses of the cash basis. Revenue is generally recognized when merchandise is sold or services are rendered to customers. Costs incurred in generating revenues are recognized as expenses of the period in which the associated revenues are recognized. Costs incurred that cannot be closely associated with particular revenue items are treated as expenses of the period in which the services of assets are consumed. Factory costs for labor, material, and overhead, called product costs, do not become expenses until the goods in which these costs are embodied are sold.

Firms involved in selling goods and services under long-term contracts sometimes recognize revenue on a percentage-of-completion, or production, basis. A portion of the contract price is recognized as revenue for each accounting period during the contract, and an appropriate amount of the costs incurred in generating the revenue is recognized as expense.

When substantial uncertainty exists regarding the amount of cash to be collected from customers for goods sold or services rendered, some firms recognize revenue using the installment method. Revenue is recognized when cash is received, and proportional amounts of the costs incurred are recognized as expenses. Under such circumstances of substantial uncertainty, the cost-recovery-first method could be used.

Unless information is provided to the contrary, all illustrations and problems in this book assume that the accrual basis of accounting is used and that revenue is recognized at the time goods are sold or services are rendered.

---

[7]   *Ibid.*

Primary Earning /share = $\dfrac{\text{Net income} - \text{Preferred stock dividends}}{\text{\# of C.S. share outstanding}}$

QUESTIONS AND PROBLEMS

1 Review the meaning of the following concepts or terms discussed in this chapter.
  a Revenue.
  b Expense.
  c Net income.
  d Loss.
  e Accounting period.
  f Natural business year or fiscal period.
  g Accrual basis of accounting.
  h Cash basis of accounting.
  i Percentage-of-completion method.
  j Completed-sales or completed-contract method.
  k Installment method.
  l Cost-recovery-first method.
  m Conservatism.
  n Unexpired cost.
  o Expired cost.
  p Product cost.
  q Period expense.
  r Matching convention.
  s Manufacturing overhead.
  t Flow of costs.
  u Income from continuing operations.
  v Income from discontinued operations.
  w Adjustments for accounting principles changes.
  x Extraordinary gains and losses.
  y Primary earnings per share.
  z Fully diluted earnings per share.

2 What factors give rise to the need for generating accounting information on a time, or accounting period, basis rather than on a project basis?

3 What factors would a firm be likely to consider in its decision to use the calendar year versus a fiscal year as its accounting period?

4 If one of the purposes of the accounting period concept is to elicit more timely information for making comparisons across firms, why is the accounting period not the same for all firms (for example, a year ending on November 30 of each year)?

5 Which of the following types of businesses are likely to have a natural business year?
  a A ski resort in Colorado.
  b A major league baseball team.
  c A radio and television repair firm.
  d An automobile manufacturer.

6 Conservatism is generally regarded as a convention in accounting. Indicate who might be hurt by conservatively stated accounting reports.

7 What is the significance of complete and incomplete earnings activities in measuring performance?

8 Distinguish between a revenue and a cash receipt. Under what conditions will they be the same?

9 Distinguish between an expense and a cash disbursement. Under what conditions will they be the same?

10 What is the basic difference between a product cost and a period expense?

11 "It is easy enough to see why material and labor costs become part of the cost of manufactured goods, but it is hard to see why indirect factory costs should be considered a part of production costs, since they do not enter into the products." Comment.

12 Indicate the amount of revenue, if any, in each of the following transactions, assuming the accrual basis of accounting is used.
  a Goods that cost $700 are sold for $800 cash.
  b Goods that cost $700 are sold on account for $800.
  c Goods that cost $800 are sold on account for $800.
  d Goods that cost $850 are sold for $800 cash.
  e Cash of $800 is received from customers to apply to their accounts.
  f A deposit of $800 is received on a $20,000 order for goods.
  g Bonds are issued for $20,000 cash.
  h Shares of common stock are issued for $20,000 cash.

13 Under the accrual basis of accounting, cash receipts and disbursements may precede, coincide with, or follow the period in which revenues and expenses are recognized. Give an example of each of the following:
  a A cash receipt that precedes the period in which revenue is recognized.
  b A cash receipt that coincides with the period in which revenue is recognized.
  c A cash receipt that follows the period in which revenue is recognized.
  d A cash disbursement that precedes the period in which expense is recognized.
  e A cash disbursement that coincides with the period in which expense is recognized.
  f A cash disbursement that follows the period in which expense is recognized.

14 Assume that the accrual basis of accounting is used and that revenue is recognized at the time the goods are sold or services are rendered. How much revenue is recognized during the month of May in each of the following transactions?
  a Collection of cash from customers during May for merchandise sold and delivered in April, $5,200. 0
  b Sales of merchandise during May for cash, $3,600. $3600
  c Sales of merchandise during May to customers to be collected in June, $5,400. $5,400
  d A store building is rented to a toy shop for $600 a month, effective May 1. A check for $1,200 for 2 months' rent is received on May 1. $600
  e Data in part **d**, except that collection is received from the tenant in June. $600

15 Assume that the accrual basis of accounting is used and that revenue is recognized at the time goods are sold or services are rendered. Indicate the amount of expense recognized during March, if any, in each of the following situations:
   a Rent is paid on March 1, $1,800, for the 2 months starting at that time. $900
   b An advance on the April salary is paid to an employee on March 28, $100. $0
   c Property taxes on a store building for the year of $2,400 were paid in January. $200
   d An employee earned $900 of commissions during March, but has not yet been paid. $900
   e The cost of equipment purchased on March 26, to be put into operation on April 1, is $5,000.
   f $800 of supplies were purchased during March. On March 1, supplies were on hand that cost $400. At March 31, supplies that cost $300 were still on hand. $900
   g Data of part **f,** except that $200 of supplies were on hand at March 1. $700
   h At March 1, the balance in the Prepaid Insurance account was $4,800. The insurance policy had 12 months to run at that time. $400

16 How would you allocate the cost of the following assets over their useful lives?
   a A building with an estimated useful life of 30 years.
   b A road leading to a timber tract. The road would normally last for 14 years before extensive reconstruction would be necessary, but it is expected that the timber will all be cut in 5 years.
   c Rent prepaid for 2 years on a warehouse in Minneapolis.
   d A truck with an estimated service life of 90,000 miles.
   e Rent prepaid for a year on a shop used for boat repairs at a summer resort. The shop is open only from June 1 to September 1.
   f An ore deposit owned by a mining company.

17 Indicate which of the following transactions involve the immediate recognition of revenue under the accrual basis of accounting:
   a The delivery of an issue of a magazine to subscribers.
   b The sale of an automobile by an automobile agency.
   c A collection of cash from accounts receivable debtors.
   d The borrowing of money at a bank.
   e The sale of merchandise on account.
   f The collection of cash by a barber for a haircut.
   g The rendering of dry-cleaning services on account.
   h The issue of shares of preferred stock.
   i The sale of tickets by a symphony box office for a concert to be given in 2 weeks.
   j Same as part **i,** except that sale was made by Ticketron, a ticket broker.

18 In which of the following situations should there be an immediate recognition of revenue under the accrual basis of accounting?
   a The shipment of goods that have been paid for in advance.
   b The receipt of an order for a carload of merchandise.
   c The interest earned on a savings account between interest payment dates.
   d The issue of additional shares of common stock for cash.
   e The completion of production of a batch of shoes by a shoe factory.
   f The deduction of union dues from an employee's paycheck (from the standpoint of the employer).
   g Transaction **f** from the standpoint of the union when the dues are received from the employer.
   h The sale of a season ticket to a series of concerts.

19 Assume that the accrual basis of accounting is used and that revenue is recognized at the time goods are sold or services are rendered. Indicate the amount of revenue or expense recognized during November in each of the following situations.

    a A bank loaned a customer $10,000 on June 1. The loan was repaid on November 30 with interest at the rate of 8 percent per year.

    b Same as part **a** except the loan is repayable on February 28 of next year.

    c Marketable securities costing $4,500 plus broker's commission of $90 are purchased on November 10.

    d A cashier leaves town with $3,000 of the firm's money during November. The loss is covered by insurance (consider from the standpoint of the firm).

    e An insurance company received insurance premiums of $7,200 during November for 24 months' coverage beginning November 1.

20 Indicate the amount of revenue recognized, if any, from each of the following related events assuming that the accrual basis of accounting is used.

    a Purchase orders are received from regular customers for $5,000 of merchandise. A 2-percent discount is allowed, and generally taken, for prompt payment.

    b The customers' orders are filled and shipped by way of the company's trucking division.

    c The merchandise is received by customers in the correct quantities and according to specifications (except as to price; see part **d**).

    d Invoices totaling $5,400 are sent to the customers. The increase in amount is due to price increases that occurred since the latest price catalog was sent to customers.

    e Checks in the amount of $5,292 ($= .98 \times \$5,400$) are received from customers in payment of the merchandise.

    f On reinspection, several days later, merchandise with a gross invoice price of $500 is found to be defective by customers and returned for appropriate credit.

21 Give the amount of expense recognized, if any, from each of the following related events, assuming that the accrual basis of accounting is used.

    a The purchasing department notifies the stockroom that the supply of $\frac{1}{2}$-inch plywood has reached the minimum point and should be reordered.

    b A purchase order is sent to Central Lumber Company for $8,000 of the material.

    c An acknowledgment of the order is received. It indicates that delivery will be made in 15 days but that the price has been raised to $8,400.

    d The shipment of plywood arrives and is checked by the receiving department. The correct quantity has been delivered.

    e The purchase invoice arrives. The amount of $8,400 is subject to a 2-percent discount if paid within 10 days.

    f On reinspection, plywood with a gross invoice price of $100 is found to be defective and returned to the supplier.

    g The balance of the amount due the Central Lumber Company is paid in time to obtain the discount.

    h The plywood is sold to customers for $10,000.

22 Indicate whether each of the following types of wages and salaries are **(1)** product costs or **(2)** period expenses:

    a Cutting-machine operators.

    b Delivery labor.

    c Factory janitors.

    d Factory payroll clerks.

    e Factory superintendent.

    f General office secretaries.
    g Guards at factory gate.
    h Inspectors in factory.
    i Maintenance workers who service factory machinery.
    j Night watch force at the factory.
    k General office clerks.
    l Operator of a lift truck in the shipping room.
    m President of the firm.
    n Sales manager.
    o Shipping room workers.
    p Sweepers who clean retail store.
    q Traveling salespersons.

23 Indicate whether each of the following types of materials and supplies are **(1)** product costs, or **(2)** period expenses:
    a Cleaning lubricants for factory machines.
    b Paper for central office computer.
    c Glue used in assembling products.
    d Supplies used by factory janitor.
    e Gasoline used by salespersons.
    f Sales promotion pamphlets distributed.
    g Materials used in training production workers.

24 Indicate whether each of the following costs are **(1)** period expenses, **(2)** product costs, or **(3)** some balance sheet account other than those for product costs.
    a Office supplies used. (1)
    b Salary of factory supervisor. (2)
    c Purchase of a fire insurance policy on the store building for the 3-year period beginning next month. (3) *prepaid insurance account (asset)*
    d Expiration of 1 month's protection of the insurance in **c.** (1)
    e Property taxes for the current year on the factory building. (2)
    f Wages of truck drivers who deliver finished goods to customers. (1)
    g Wages of factory workers who install a new machine. (3)
    h Wages of mechanics who repair and service factory machines. (2)
    i Salary of the president of the company. (1)
    j Depreciation of office equipment. (1)
    k Factory supplies used. (2)

25 The results of various transactions and events are classified within the income statement in one of the following three sections: **(1)** income from continuing operations, **(2)** income, gains, and losses from discontinued operations, and **(3)** extraordinary items. Using the appropriate number, identify the classification of each of the transactions or events below. State any assumptions you feel are necessary.
    a Depreciation expense for the year on a company's automobile used by its president.
    b Uninsured loss of a factory complex in Louisiana as a result of a hurricane.
    c Gain from the sale of marketable securities.
    d Loss from the sale of a delivery truck.
    e Loss from the sale of a division that conducted all of the firm's research activities.
    f Earnings during the year up to the time of sale of the division in part **e.**
    g Loss in excess of insurance proceeds on an automobile destroyed during an accident.

h Loss of plant, equipment, and inventory held in a South American country when confiscated by the government of that country.

26 Discuss when revenue is likely to be recognized by firms in each of the following types of businesses:

a A shoe store. *Time paid the cost*

b A ship-building firm constructing an aircraft carrier under a government contract. *% complete of contract or contract complt*

c A real estate developer selling lots on long-term contracts with small down payments.

d A clothing manufacturer. *← cloth is sell*   *Installment base*

e A citrus-growing firm. *← when it sell*

f A producer of television movies, where the rights to the movies for the first 3 years are sold to a television network and all rights thereafter revert to the producer.

g A residential real estate developer who constructs only "speculative" houses and then later sells the houses to buyers. *sell of each house*

h A producer of fine whiskey that ages from 6 to 12 years before sale. *time when sale*

i A savings and loan association lending money for home mortgages. *time pass*

j A travel agency. *confirm agreement*

k A printer who prints only custom-order stationery. *when orders is place*

l A seller of trading stamps to food stores redeemable by food store customers for various household products.

m A wholesale food distributor.

n A livestock rancher.

o A shipping company that loads cargo in one accounting period, carries cargo across the ocean in a second accounting period, and unloads the cargo in a third period. The shipping is all done under contract, and cash collection of shipping charges is relatively certain.

27 Carlson's Department Store had sales to customers during 1979 as follows: cash sales, $400,000; sales on account, $500,000. Based on past experience, Carlson's estimates that .5 percent of goods sold will be returned because of defects. The customers are given full credit for the returned merchandise, and the defective merchandise is scrapped. Carlson's also estimates that 2 percent of all sales on account will never be collected. Under the accrual basis of accounting, how much revenue should Carlson's report for sales during 1979?

28 Wobilt's Department Store had sales to customers during 1979 as follows: cash sales, $1,500,000; sales on account, $1,200,000. Past experience indicates that 1 percent of goods will be returned because of defects. Customers are given full credit for returned merchandise, and the defective merchandise is scrapped. Wobilt's Department Store also estimates that 3 percent of sales on account will be uncollectible. Of the merchandise purchased on account and subsequently paid for, 40 percent is paid in time to obtain a 2-percent cash discount for prompt payment. Under the accrual basis of accounting, how much revenue should Wobilt's Department Store report for sales during 1979? Assume that merchandise purchased for cash is just as likely to be returned as merchandise purchased on account.

29 J. Thompson opened a hardware store on January 1, 1979. Thompson invested $6,000 and borrowed $6,000 from the local bank. The loan is repayable on June 30, 1979, with interest at the rate of 8 percent per year.

Thompson rented a building on January 1, and paid 2 months' rent in advance in the amount of $1,000. Property and liability insurance coverage for the year ending December 31, 1979, was paid on January 1 in the amount of $600.

Thompson purchased $18,000 of merchandise inventory on account on January 2 and paid $6,000 of this amount on January 25. The cost of merchandise on hand on January 31 was $10,000.

During January, cash sales to customers totaled $8,000 and sales on account totaled $4,000. Of the sales on account, $1,000 were collected as of January 31.

Other costs incurred and paid in cash during January were as follows: utilities, $300; salaries, $550; taxes, $150.

a Prepare an income statement for January, assuming that Thompson uses the accrual basis of accounting with revenue recognized at the time goods are sold (delivered).

b Prepare an income statement for January, assuming that Thompson uses the cash basis of accounting.

c Which basis of accounting do you feel provides a better indication of the operating performance of the hardware store during January? Why?

30 Management Consultants, Inc., opened a consulting business on July 1, 1979. Roy Bean and Sarah Bower each contributed $5,000 cash for shares of the firm's common stock. The corporation borrowed $6,000 from a local bank on August 1, 1979. The loan is repayable on July 31, 1980, with interest at the rate of 10 percent per year.

Office space was rented on August 1, with 2 months' rent paid in advance. The remaining monthly rental fees of $600 per month were made on the first of each month beginning October 1. Office equipment with a 3-year life was purchased for cash on August 1 for $3,600.

Consulting services rendered for clients between August 1 and December 31, 1979, were billed at $12,000. Of this amount, $8,000 was collected by year-end.

Other costs incurred and paid in cash by the end of the year were as follows: utilities, $350; salary of secretary, $5,500; supplies used, $250. Unpaid bills at year-end are as follows: utilities, $50; salary of secretary, $800; supplies used, $40.

a Prepare an income statement for the 5 months ended December 31, 1979, assuming that the corporation uses the accrual basis of accounting, with revenue recognized at the time services are rendered.

b Prepare an income statement for the 5 months ended December 31, 1979, assuming that the corporation uses the cash basis of accounting.

c Which basis of accounting do you feel provides a better indication of operating performance of the consulting firm for the period? Why?

31 Feltham Company acquired used machine tools costing $75,000 from various sources. These machine tools were then sold to Mock Corporation. Delivery costs paid by Feltham Company totaled $4,500. Mock Corporation had agreed to pay $100,000 cash for these tools. Finding itself short of cash, however, Mock Corporation offered $110,000 of its par-value bonds to Feltham Company. These bonds promised 8 percent interest per year. At the time the offer was made, the bonds could have been sold in public bond markets for $98,000.

Feltham Company accepted the offer and held the bonds for 3 years. During the 3 years, it received interest payments of $8,800 per year, or $26,400 total. At the end of the third year, Feltham Company sold the bonds for $95,000.

a What profit or loss did Feltham Company recognize on the sale of machine tools to Mock Corporation?

b What profit or loss would Feltham Company have recognized on the sale of machine tools if it had sold the bonds for $98,000 immediately upon receiving them?

c What profit or loss would Feltham Company have recognized on the sale of machine tools if it had held the bonds to maturity, receiving $8,800 each year for another 5 years and $110,000 at the time the bonds matured?

32 The Humbolt Electric Company received a contract late in 1978 to build a small electricity-generating unit. The contract price was $700,000 and it was estimated that total costs would be $600,000. Estimated and actual construction time was 15 months and it was agreed that payments would be made by the purchaser as follows:

March 31, 1979	$ 70,000
June 30, 1979	105,000
September 30, 1979	203,000
December 31, 1979	161,000
March 31, 1980	161,000
	$700,000

Estimated and actual costs of construction incurred by the Humbolt Electric Company were as follows:

January 1–March 31, 1979	$120,000
April 1–June 30, 1979	120,000
July 1–September 30, 1979	180,000
October 1–December 31, 1979	120,000
January 1–March 31, 1980	60,000
	$600,000

The Humbolt Electric Company prepares financial statements quarterly at March 31, June 30, and so forth.

Determine the amount of revenue, expense, and net income for each quarter under each of the following methods of revenue recognition:
a Production (percentage-of-completion) method.
b Sales (completed-contract) method.
c Cash collection (installment) method.
d Cash collection (cost-recovery-first) method.
e Which method do you feel provides the best measure of Humbolt's performance under this contract? Why?
f Under what circumstances would the methods not selected in part e provide a better measure of performance?

33 The Webster Corporation produces a single product at a cost of $5 each, all of which is paid in cash when the unit is produced. The selling cost consists of a sales commission of $3 a unit and is paid in cash at the time of shipment. The selling price is $10 a unit; all sales are made on account. No uncollectible accounts are expected, and no costs are incurred at the time of collection.

During 1979, the firm produced 200,000 units, shipped 150,000 units, and collected $1 million from customers. During 1980, the firm produced 125,000 units, shipped 160,000 units, and collected $2 million from customers.

Determine the amount of net income for 1979 and 1980:
a If revenue and expense are recognized at the time of production.
b If revenue and expense are recognized at the time of shipment.

   c If revenue and expense are recognized at the time of cash collection.

   d A firm experiencing growth in its sales volume will often produce more units during a particular period than it sells. In this way, inventories can be built up in anticipation of an even larger sales volume during the next period. Under these circumstances, will recognition of revenue and expense at the time of production, shipment, or cash collection generally result in the largest reported net income for the period? Explain.

   e A firm experiencing decreases in its sales volume will often produce fewer units during a period than it sells in an effort to reduce the amount of inventory on hand for next period. Under these circumstances, will recognition of revenue and expense at the time of production, shipment, or cash collection generally result in the largest reported net income for a period? Explain.

34 The Acme Construction Company contracted on May 15, 1979, to build a bridge for the city for $4,500,000. Acme estimated the cost of constructing the bridge would be $3,600,000. Acme incurred $1,200,000 in construction costs during 1979, $2,000,000 during 1980, and $400,000 during 1981 in completing the bridge. The city paid $1,000,000 during 1979, $1,500,000 during 1980, and the remaining $2,000,000 of the contract price at the time the bridge was completed and approved in 1981.

   a Determine the net income (revenues less expenses) of Acme on the contract during 1979, 1980, and 1981, assuming that the percentage-of-completion method is used.

   b Repeat part **a**, assuming that the completed-contract method is used.

   c Repeat part **a**, assuming that the cash collection (installment) method is used.

   d Repeat part **a**, assuming that the cash collection (cost-recovery-first) method is used.

   e Which method do you feel provides a better measure of Acme's performance under this contract? Why?

   f Under what circumstances would the method not selected in part **e** provide a better measure of performance?

35 R and D Corporation conducts research and development services for several business clients. In most cases, R and D Corporation contracts with clients for specific development work on existing products. In other cases, R and D Corporation conducts basic research in an area and then attempts to market any new technologies or designs that are developed.

   In January 1979, scientists at R and D Corporation began work developing a synthetic energy source. During 1979, $780,000 of costs were incurred in this effort. Late in July 1980, potentially promising results emerged in the form of a substance the scientists called Energitol. Costs incurred through the end of July 1980 were $420,000. At this point, R and D Corporation attempted to sell the formulas and rights of Energitol to Diversified Industries, Incorporated, for $5,000,000. Diversified Industries, Incorporated, however, was reluctant to sign before further testing was done. It did wish, though, to have the first option to acquire the formulas and rights to Energitol if future testing showed that the product would be profitable. It therefore paid R and D Corporation $20,000 for an option to be able to acquire the formulas and rights to Energitol anytime before December 31, 1980. Costs incurred during the remainder of 1980 in testing the product were $540,000.

   On December 28, 1980, Diversified Industries, Incorporated, exercised its option and agreed to purchase the formulas and rights to Energitol for $5,000,000. Diversified Industries, Incorporated, paid $500,000 immediately, with the remainder payable in five equal annual installments on December 31, 1981, to December 31, 1985.

   On March 15, 1981, R and D Corporation delivered the formulas and samples of Energitol to Diversified Industries, Incorporated. Additional costs incurred during 1981 by R and D Corporation totaled $240,000.

a When do you feel that revenue should be recognized by R and D Corporation from its work on Energitol? Why?

b You may assume that the total costs of $1,980,000 actually incurred over the years 1979–81 were accurately estimated during 1979. Determine the amount of revenue and expense for each year from 1979 to 1985, assuming that the accrual basis of accounting is used and revenue is recognized:

(1) At the time the option is sold.

(2) At the time the option is exercised.

(3) At the time the formulas are delivered.

(4) As cash is collected using the installment method.

36 Pickin Chicken, Incorporated, and Country Delight, Incorporated, both sell franchises for their chicken restaurants. The franchisee receives the right to use the franchisor's products and to benefit from national training and advertising programs. The franchisee agrees to pay $50,000 for exclusive franchise rights in a particular city. Of this amount, $20,000 is paid upon signing the franchise agreement and the remainder is payable in five equal annual installments of $6,000 each.

Pickin Chicken, Incorporated, recognizes franchise revenue as franchise agreements are signed, whereas Country Delight, Incorporated, recognizes franchise revenue on an installment basis. In 1979, both companies sold eight franchises. In 1980, they both sold five franchises. In 1981, neither company sold a franchise.

a Determine the amount of revenue recognized by each company during 1979, 1980, 1981, 1982, 1983, 1984, and 1985.

b When do you feel that franchise revenue should be recognized? Why?

37 Comment on any unusual features of the following income statement of Nordic Enterprises, Inc.

Nordic Enterprises, Inc.
Income Statement
December 31, 1979

Revenues and Gains:

Sales Revenue	$1,964,800	
Rental Revenue	366,900	
Interest Revenue	4,600	
Gain on Sale of Equipment	2,500	
Gain on Sale of Subsidiary	643,200	$2,982,000

Expenses and Losses:

Cost of Goods Sold	$1,432,900	
Depreciation Expense	226,800	
Salaries Expense	296,900	
Interest Expense	6,600	
Loss of Plant Due to Fire	368,800	
Income Tax Expense	200,000	
Dividends Expense	100,000	2,632,000
Net Income		$ 350,000

---

38 Exhibit 3.5 presents comparative income statements for International Harvester Company and Subsidiaries for the years 1972 through 1976. Using the information in these income statements (as well as any relevant balance sheet data provided in Problem **30** at the end of Chapter 2), describe the major changes that have occurred in the profitability of this company during the 5-year period. (Hint: You might want to begin by expressing various income statement items as a percentage of sales.)

EXHIBIT 3.5
International Harvester Company
and Subsidiaries
Income Statements
For the Years 1972 through 1976
(Amounts in Millions
Except per-Share Data)
(Problem 38)

	1972	1973	1974	1975	1976
Sales	$3,412.9	$4,091.8	$4,863.5	$5,246.0	$5,488.1
Cost of Goods Sold	(2,867.8)	(3,425.9)	(4,086.2)	(4,384.5)	(4,536.7)
Gross Profit	$ 545.1	$ 665.9	$ 777.3	$ 861.5	$ 951.4
Selling and Administrative Expenses	(347.2)	(411.5)	(428.1)	(491.9)	(509.9)
Interest Expense	(95.5)	(136.4)	(196.9)	(234.4)	(220.1)
Income Taxes	(46.0)	(40.7)	(68.5)	(59.7)	(95.6)
Income from Nonconsolidated Subsidiaries	28.9	31.5	32.0	40.4	48.3
Income from Continuing Operations	$ 85.3	$ 108.8	$ 115.8	$ 115.9	$ 174.1
Income (Loss) from Discontinued Operations	1.3	(1.9)	2.2	(44.6)	—
Extraordinary Gains	—	7.4	6.1	—	—
Adjustment for Change in Accounting Principle	—	—	—	8.1	—
Net Income	$ 86.6	$ 114.3	$ 124.1	$ 79.4	$ 174.1
Earnings (Loss) Per Share:					
Continuing Operations	$ 3.12	$ 3.93	$ 4.16	$ 4.09	$ 6.02
Discontinued Operations	.05	(.07)	.08	(1.61)	—
Extraordinary Gains	—	.27	.22	—	—
Change in Accounting Principle	—	—	—	.29	—
Net Income	$ 3.17	$ 4.13	$ 4.46	$ 2.77	$ 6.02

CHAPTER 4
INCOME STATEMENT— ACCOUNTING PROCEDURES

Chapter 3 introduced the important accounting concepts underlying income measurement and reporting. Net income is measured and reported for relatively brief, discrete time periods, such as a quarter or a year, to permit timely disclosure of earnings performance and to facilitate comparisons among firms and for a given firm over time. Net income for virtually all publicly held firms is measured on the accrual, rather than the cash, basis of accounting. Under the accrual basis, revenue is generally recognized in the period when the sale is made or services are rendered. Expenses are recognized in the period when the services of assets have been used up or consumed in generating revenue. An attempt is made to match expenses with the revenues to which they relate. In this chapter, we describe and illustrate the accounting procedures for recording the results of various events and transactions leading to the preparation of the income statement. As was the case in describing the accounting procedures underlying the balance sheet in Chapter 2, our objective is to develop a sufficient understanding of the recording process so that the income statement can then be interpreted and analyzed. We begin by providing an overview of the accounting procedures and then illustrating their application for a merchandising firm. The accounting procedures for a manufacturing firm are described in the appendix to this chapter.

OVERVIEW OF ACCOUNTING PROCEDURES

Relationship Between Balance Sheet and Income Statement

Net income, or earnings, for a period is measured by the excess of revenues over expenses. Dividends to stockholders may be declared out of earnings of the current year or of prior years. Earnings in excess of dividends declared become a component of the Retained Earnings account on the balance sheet. The following disaggregation of the balance sheet equation helps to show the relation of revenues, expenses, and dividends to the components of the balance sheet.

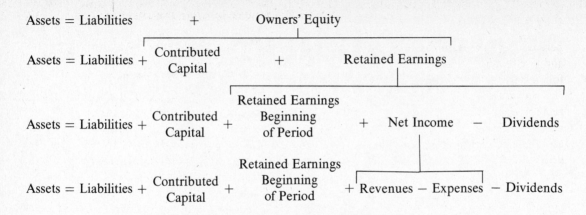

Purpose and Use of Individual Revenue and Expense Accounts

Revenue and expense amounts could be recorded directly in the Retained Earnings account. For example, the sale of merchandise on account results in an increase in assets (accounts receivable) and retained earnings (sales revenue) and a decrease in assets (merchandise inventory) and retained earnings (cost of merchandise sold). Measurement of the *amount* of net income would be relatively simple if revenues and expenses were recorded directly in the Retained Earnings account. Net income would be determined from the following equation:

$$\text{Net Income} = \frac{\text{Retained Earnings}}{\text{End of Period}} - \frac{\text{Retained Earnings}}{\text{Beginning of Period}} + \text{Dividends}.$$

In preparing an income statement, however, we are interested in the components of net income: the sources of revenue and the types of expenses. To facilitate the preparation of the income statement, individual revenue and expense accounts are maintained during the accounting period. These accounts begin the accounting period with a zero balance. During the period, revenues and expenses are recorded in the accounts as they arise. At the end of the period, the balance in each revenue and expense account represents the cumulative revenues and expenses *for the period*. These amounts are reported in the income statement, which shows the net income of the period.

Since revenues and expenses are basically components of retained earnings, the balance in each revenue and expense account is transferred at the end of the period to the Retained Earnings account. Each revenue and expense account will then have a zero balance after the transfer. Retained earnings will be increased (or decreased) by the amount of net income (or net loss) for the period.

The end result of maintaining separate revenue and expense accounts during the period and transferring their balances to the Retained Earnings account at the end of the period is the same as if revenues and expenses were initially recorded directly in the Retained Earnings account. The purpose of using separate revenue and expense accounts is to facilitate the preparation of the income statement in which specific types of revenues and expenses are disclosed. Once this purpose has been served, the usefulness of separate revenue and expense accounts *for a given accounting period* has ended. Having been reduced to a zero balance at the end of the accounting period, these accounts begin the following accounting period with a zero balance and are therefore ready for entry of the revenue and expense amounts of the following period.

The process of transferring the balances in revenue and expense accounts to retained earnings is referred to as the *closing process,* since each revenue and expense account is closed, or reduced to a zero balance. Because revenue and expense accounts accumulate amounts for only a single accounting period, they are called *temporary accounts.* On the other hand, the accounts on the balance sheet reflect the cumulative changes in each account from the time the firm was first organized, and are not closed each period. The balances in these accounts at the end of one period are carried over as the beginning balances of the following period. Balance sheet accounts are called *permanent accounts.*

Debit and Credit Procedures for Revenues, Expenses, and Dividends

Since revenues, expenses, and dividends are components of retained earnings, the recording procedures for these items are the same as for any other transaction affecting equity accounts.

Owners' Equity	
Decreases (Debit)	Increases (Credit)
	Issue of Capital Stock
Expenses	Revenues
Dividends	

Revenue is a measure of the amount of services rendered. It is reflected in the accounts as an increase in net assets (increase in assets or decrease in liabilities) and an increase in owners' equity. The usual journal entry to record a revenue transaction is therefore

Asset (A) Increase or Liability (L) Decrease . . . . Amount
   Revenue (OE) . . . . Amount
Typical entry to recognize revenue.

Expense is a measure of the net assets used up or consumed in generating revenue. It is reflected in the accounts as a decrease in net assets (decrease in assets or increase in liabilities) and a decrease in owners' equity. The usual journal entry to record an expense is therefore

Expense (OE) . . . . Amount
   Asset (A) Decrease or Liability (L) Increase . . . . Amount
Typical entry to record expense.

Dividends are distributions to owners of assets generated by earnings of the current and prior years. As we shall discuss in Chapter 11, dividends may be paid either in cash or in other assets. Although the accounting procedures for dividends are similar regardless of the form of the distribution, we shall assume that cash is used unless information is provided to the contrary. The usual entry to record the declaration of a dividend by the board of directors of a corporation is

Retained Earnings (OE) . . . .   Amount
   Dividends Payable (L) . . . .   Amount
Typical entry to record dividend declaration.

An alternative method of recording the dividend is to debit an account, Dividends Declared. This temporary account is called an *income distribution* account. At the end of the accounting period, the balance in the Dividends Declared account is closed to the Retained Earnings account, thereby reducing the balance of Retained Earnings. The end result under both procedures is a debit to Retained Earnings and a credit to Dividends Payable for the amount of dividends declared during the period.

When the dividend is paid, the journal entry is

Dividends Payable (L) . . . .   Amount
   Cash (A) . . . .   Amount
Typical entry to record dividend payment.

A conceptual error sometimes made is that of treating dividends as an expense on the income statement. *Dividends are not expenses*; rather, they represent *distributions of earnings* of the current and prior years to the owners of the firm. They are not costs incurred in *generating* revenues. Because the account, Dividends Declared, is closed in a manner similar to an expense account at the end of the accounting period, the second method of recording the dividend leads some students to regard dividends as expenses. We therefore prefer that dividends declared be debited directly to the Retained Earnings account.

Before illustrating the recording procedures for revenues and expenses, it may be helpful to review briefly the steps in the accounting process.

Review of the Accounting Process

The steps in the accounting process and the purpose of each were discussed in Chapter 2 and are summarized as follows:

Journalizing   Each transaction or series of transactions during the period is recorded in journal entry form in the general journal (or in a special journal that supplements the general journal).

Posting   At periodic intervals, the entries in the general journal are posted to the accounts in the general ledger.

Trial Balance   At the end of the accounting period, the balance in each general ledger account is determined and a trial balance is prepared. A trial balance is a listing of all accounts in the general ledger. Accounts with debit balances are totaled separately from accounts with credit balances. If the recording process has been carried out properly, the total amount in accounts having debit balances must equal the total amount in accounts having credit balances.

Adjusting Entries   During the period, some accounting events may be only partially recorded, not recorded at all, or recorded incorrectly. Before the financial statements can be prepared at the end of the period, the omissions must be accounted for and the errors corrected. The entries to do this are known as *adjusting* entries. These entries are made so that revenues and expenses are reported in the correct accounts and amounts and so that balance sheet accounts show appropriate amounts of assets and equities at the end of the period.

Closing Entries   The revenue and expense accounts, as well as the Dividend Declared account if used, are closed at the end of the accounting period by transferring the balance in each account to Retained Earnings.

Statement Preparation   The balance sheet, income statement, statement of changes in financial position, and any desired supporting schedules (for example, an analysis of changes in the Cash, Buildings and Equipment, or Retained Earnings accounts) are then prepared.

ILLUSTRATION OF THE ACCOUNTING PROCESS FOR A MERCHANDISING FIRM

Stephen's Shoe Store, Inc., has been in business since 1976. A trial balance taken from its general ledger accounts on January 1, 1979, the first day of an accounting period, is shown in Exhibit 4.1. To facilitate understanding, in this illustration the asset accounts are designated (A), the liability accounts (L), and the owners' equity accounts (OE). Trial balances do not usually contain such designations.

EXHIBIT 4.1
Stephen's Shoe Store, Inc.
Trial Balance
January 1, 1979

	Accounts with Debit Balances	Accounts with Credit Balances
Cash (A)	$ 60,000	
Accounts Receivable (A)	140,000	
Allowance for Uncollectible Accounts (XA)		$ 14,000
Merchandise Inventory (A)	350,000	
Land (A)	200,000	
Building and Equipment (A)	1,050,000	
Accumulated Depreciation (XA)		170,000
Accounts Payable (L)		270,000
Bonds Payable (L)		200,000
Common Stock (OE)		500,000
Additional Paid-in Capital (OE)		400,000
Retained Earnings (OE)		246,000
Total	$1,800,000	$1,800,000

Note that the revenue and expense accounts are not included in this trial balance; they have zero balances at the beginning of an accounting period. Two of the accounts in the trial balance, Allowance for Uncollectible Accounts and Accumulated Depreciation, have not previously been considered. These accounts are presented on the balance sheet as deductions from Accounts Receivable and from Building and Equipment, respectively. (See Exhibit 4.7 for balance sheet presentation of these accounts.) Because of this manner of disclosure, they are referred to as *contra accounts.* A contra account accumulates amounts that are subtracted from the amount in another account. The nature and use of these contra accounts are discussed later in this illustration. An asset contra account is designated XA in the trial balance.

Journalizing

The transactions of Stephen's Shoe Store during 1979 and the appropriate journal entries at the time of the transactions follow.

(1) Merchandise costing $710,000 is purchased on account.

Merchandise Inventory (A)	710,000	
Accounts Payable (L)		710,000

(2) Sales during the year are $1,250,000, of which $450,000 are for cash and the remainder are on account.

Cash (A)	450,000	
Accounts Receivable (A)	800,000	
Sales Revenue (OE)		1,250,000

(3) The cost of merchandise sold during 1979 is $780,000.

Cost of Goods Sold (OE)	780,000	
Merchandise Inventory (A)		780,000

(4) Salaries of $220,000 are paid in cash during the year.

Salaries Expense (OE)	220,000	
Cash (A)		220,000

(5) Customers' accounts of $650,000 are collected.

Cash (A)	650,000	
Accounts Receivable (A)		650,000

(6) Payments of $540,000 are made to merchandise suppliers for purchases on account.

Accounts Payable (L)	540,000	
Cash (A)		540,000

(7) A premium of $3,000 is paid on January 1, 1979, for a 3-year property and liability insurance policy.

Prepaid Insurance (A)	3,000	
Cash (A)		3,000

The debit in this entry, made on January 1, 1979, is to an asset account, since the insurance provides 3 years of coverage beginning on that date. The entry to reduce the Prepaid Insurance account and to record the insurance expense for 1979 is one of the adjusting entries made at the end of the accounting period.

(8) Warehouse space not needed in the company's operations is rented out for 1 year beginning December 1, 1979. The annual rental of $1,200 is received at that time.

Cash (A)	1,200	
Rental Fees Received in Advance (L)		1,200

(9) Annual interest on the long-term bonds outstanding at the rate of 8 percent is paid on December 31, 1979.

Interest Expense (OE)	16,000	
Cash (A)		16,000

(10) A 90-day note was received from a customer on December 1, 1979. The note replaced the customer's open account receivable balance of $10,000 arising from an earlier sale. The note bears interest at the rate of 9 percent per year.

Notes Receivable (A)	10,000	
Accounts Receivable (A)		10,000

(11) The board of directors declared a cash dividend of $30,000 on December 28, 1979. The dividend is to be paid on January 20, 1980.

Retained Earnings (OE)	30,000	
Dividends Payable (L)		30,000

Posting

The entries in the general journal are posted to the appropriate general ledger accounts. In this illustration, the posting operation takes place on December 31, 1979. The T-accounts in Exhibit 4.2 show the opening balances from the trial balance in Exhibit 4.1 and the effects of transactions (1) through (11).

EXHIBIT 4.2
Stephen's Shoe Store, Inc.
T-Accounts Showing Beginning and Ending Balances and Transactions During 1979

Cash (A)

Debit		Credit	
Bal. 1/1	60,000	220,000	(4)
(2)	450,000	540,000	(6)
(5)	650,000	3,000	(7)
(8)	1,200	16,000	(9)
Bal. 12/31	382,200		

Accounts Receivable (A)

Debit		Credit	
Bal. 1/1	140,000	650,000	(5)
(2)	800,000	10,000	(10)
Bal. 12/31	280,000		

Allowance for Uncollectible Accounts (XA)

Debit	Credit	
	14,000	Bal. 1/1
	14,000	Bal. 12/31

Notes Receivable (A)

Debit		Credit
Bal. 1/1	0	
(10)	10,000	
Bal. 12/31	10,000	

Merchandise Inventory (A)

Debit		Credit	
Bal. 1/1	350,000	780,000	(3)
(1)	710,000		
Bal. 12/31	280,000		

Prepaid Insurance (A)

Debit		Credit
Bal. 1/1	0	
(7)	3,000	
Bal. 12/31	3,000	

Land (A)

Debit		Credit
Bal. 1/1	200,000	
Bal. 12/31	200,000	

Building and Equipment (A)

Debit		Credit
Bal. 1/1	1,050,000	
Bal. 12/31	1,050,000	

Accumulated Depreciation (XA)

Debit	Credit	
	170,000	Bal. 1/1
	170,000	Bal. 12/31

Accounts Payable (L)

Debit		Credit	
		270,000	Bal. 1/1
(6)	540,000	710,000	(1)
		440,000	Bal. 12/31

Dividends Payable (L)

Debit	Credit	
	0	Bal. 1/1
	30,000	(11)
	30,000	Bal. 12/31

Rental Fees Received in Advance (L)

Debit	Credit	
	0	Bal. 1/1
	1,200	(8)
	1,200	Bal. 12/31

Bonds Payable (L)

	200,000 Bal. 1/1
	200,000 Bal. 12/31

Additional Paid-in Capital (OE)

	400,000 Bal. 1/1
	400,000 Bal. 12/31

Common Stock (OE)

	500,000 Bal. 1/1
	500,000 Bal. 12/31

Retained Earnings (OE)

(11) 30,000	246,000 Bal. 1/1
	216,000 Bal. 12/31

Sales Revenue (OE)

	0 Bal. 1/1
	1,250,000 (2)
	1,250,000 Bal. 12/31

Salaries Expense (OE)

Bal. 1/1 0	
(4) 220,000	
Bal. 12/31 220,000	

Interest Expense (OE)

Bal. 1/1 0	
(9) 16,000	
Bal. 12/31 16,000	

Cost of Goods Sold (OE)

Bal. 1/1 0	
(3) 780,000	
Bal. 12/31 780,000	

Trial Balance Preparation

The trial balance prepared at the end of the accounting period before adjusting and closing entries is called an *unadjusted trial balance.* The unadjusted trial balance of Stephen's Shoe Store as of December 31, 1979, is shown in Exhibit 4.3. The amounts in the unadjusted trial balance are taken directly from the ending balances in the T-accounts shown in Exhibit 4.2.

EXHIBIT 4.3
Stephen's Shoe Store, Inc.
Unadjusted Trial Balance
December 31, 1979

	Accounts with Debit Balances	Accounts with Credit Balances
Cash (A)	$ 382,200	
Accounts Receivable (A)	280,000	
Allowance for Uncollectible Accounts (XA) ..		$ 14,000
Notes Receivable (A)	10,000	
Merchandise Inventory (A)	280,000	
Prepaid Insurance (A)	3,000	
Land (A)	200,000	
Building and Equipment (A)	1,050,000	
Accumulated Depreciation (XA)		170,000
Accounts Payable (L)		440,000
Dividends Payable (L)		30,000
Rental Fees Received in Advance (L)		1,200
Bonds Payable (L)		200,000
Common Stock (OE)		500,000
Additional Paid-in Capital (OE)		400,000
Retained Earnings (OE)		216,000
Sales Revenue (OE)		1,250,000
Cost of Goods Sold (OE)	780,000	
Salaries Expense (OE)	220,000	
Interest Expense (OE)	16,000	
Totals	$3,221,200	$3,221,200

Adjusting and Correcting Entries

The entries in the general journal made during the year result primarily from transactions between the firm and outsiders (for example, suppliers, employees, customers, and governmental units). Other events continually occur, however, for which no specific transaction signals the requirement for a journal entry, but which must be considered in measuring net income for the period and financial position at the end of the period. For example, building and equipment are continually used in the process of generating revenue. Because the services of these assets are consumed during the period, a portion of their acquisition cost must be recorded as an expense. Similarly, insurance coverage expires continually throughout the year. Because the services of the asset are gradually consumed, a portion of the asset, Prepaid Insurance, must be recorded as an expense.

Other kinds of events occur that affect the revenues and expenses of the period but for which a transaction with an outsider will not occur until a subsequent period. For example, salaries and wages are earned by administrative employees during the last several days of the current accounting period, but they will not be paid until the following accounting period. Such salaries and wages, although payable in the next period, are expenses of the current period when the labor services are consumed. Similarly, interest accrues on a firm's notes receivable or payable. Interest will be collected or paid in a subsequent period, but a portion of the interest should be recognized as revenue or expense in the current period.

Adjusting entries are prepared at the end of the accounting period. These entries alter the balances in the general ledger accounts in order to recognize all revenues and expenses for the proper reporting of net income and financial position. Several examples of adjusting entries are illustrated for Stephen's Shoe Store in the following sections.

Recognition of Accrued Revenues and Receivables Revenue is earned as services are rendered. For example, rent is earned as a tenant uses the property. Interest, a "rent" for the use of money, is earned as time passes on a loan. It is usually not convenient, however, to record these amounts as they accrue day by day. At the end of the accounting period, there may be some situations in which revenue has been earned but for which no entry has been made, either because cash has not been received or the time has not arrived for a formal invoice to be sent to the customer. A claim has come into existence that, although it may not be due immediately, should appear on the balance sheet as an asset and be reflected in the revenues of the period. The purpose of the adjusting entry for interest eventually receivable by the lender is to recognize on the balance sheet the right to receive cash in an amount equal to the interest already earned and to recognize the same amount as revenue on the income statement for the period.

Stephen's Shoe Store received a 90-day note from a customer on December 1, 1979. At year end, the note is included as an asset on the trial balance. Interest earned during December, however, is not reflected in the unadjusted trial balance. The note earns interest at the rate of 9 percent per year. By convention in business practice, interest rates stated on loans are almost always stated as annual interest rates. Also, by convention, a year equal to 360 days is usually assumed to simplify the calculation of interest earned. Interest of $75 is earned by Stephen's Shoe Store, Inc., during December. This amount is equal to the $10,000 principal times the 9 percent annual interest rate times the elapsed 30 days divided by 360 days ($75 = $100,000 × .09 × 30/360). The adjusting entry to recognize the asset, Interest Receivable, and the interest earned, is

(12) Interest Receivable (A) 75
    Interest Revenue (OE)   75

Recognition of Accrued Expenses and Payables   As various services are received, their cost should be reflected in the financial statements, whether or not payment has been made or an invoice received. Here, also, it is frequently not convenient to record these amounts day by day. It is likely that some adjustment of expenses and liabilities will be necessary at the end of the accounting period.

Salaries and wages earned during the last several days of the accounting period that will not be paid until the following accounting period illustrate this type of adjustment. According to payroll records, employees of Stephen's Shoe Store earned salaries of $12,000 during the last several days of 1979 that were not recorded at year-end. The adjusting entry is

(13) Salaries Expense (OE) 12,000
        Salaries Payable (L)   12,000

Other examples of this type of adjusting entry include costs incurred for utilities, taxes, and interest.

Allocation of Prepaid Operating Costs   Another type of adjustment arises because assets are acquired for use in the operations of the firm but are not completely used during the accounting period in which they are acquired. For example, Stephen's Shoe Store paid $3,000 on January 1, 1979, for a 3-year insurance policy. During 1979, one-third of the coverage expired, so $1,000 of the premium should be reflected as insurance expense. The balance sheet on December 31, 1979, should show $2,000 of prepaid insurance among the assets, since only this portion of the premium is a future benefit—the asset of insurance coverage to be received over the next 2 years.

The nature of the adjusting entry to record an asset expiration as an expense depends on the recording of the original payment. If the payment resulted in a debit to an asset account, the adjusting entry must reduce the asset and increase the expense for the services used up during the accounting period. Stephen's Shoe Store recorded the payment of the insurance premium on January 1, 1979, as follows:

(7) Prepaid Insurance (A) 3,000
        Cash (A)   3,000

The adjusting entry is, therefore,

(14) Insurance Expense (OE) 1,000
        Prepaid Insurance (A)   1,000

Insurance expense for 1979 is $1,000, and prepaid insurance in the amount of $2,000 is shown as an asset on the balance sheet on December 31, 1979.

Instead of debiting an asset account at the time the premium is paid, some firms debit an expense account. For example, Stephen's Shoe Store might have recorded the original premium payment as follows:

(7a) Insurance Expense (OE) 3,000
        Cash (A)   3,000

Since many operating costs become expenses in the period in which the expenditure is made (for example, monthly rent, office supplies), this second procedure for recording expenditures during the year sometimes reduces the number of adjusting entries that must be made at year-end. In the situation with the insurance policy, however, not all of the $3,000 premium paid is an expense of 1979. If the original journal entry had been (7a), the adjusting entry would then be

(14a) Prepaid Insurance (A)	2,000	
Insurance Expense (OE)		2,000

After the original entry in (7a) and the adjusting entry in (14a), insurance expense for 1979 is reflected in the accounts at $1,000, and prepaid insurance at $2,000. The *end result* of these two approaches to recording the original payment of the premium is the same. The *adjusting entries,* however, are quite different.

Recognition of Depreciation   When assets such as buildings, machinery, furniture, and trucks are purchased, their acquisition cost is debited to appropriate asset accounts. Although these assets may provide services for a number of years, eventually their future benefits will expire. Therefore, the portion of an asset's cost that will expire is spread systematically over its estimated useful life. The charge made to the current operations for the portion of the cost of such assets consumed during the current period is called *depreciation* expense. Depreciation involves nothing new in principle; it is identical with the procedure for prepaid operating costs presented previously. For example, the cost of a building is a prepayment for a series of future services, and depreciation allocates the cost of the services to the periods in which services are received and used.

Various accounting methods are used in allocating the acquisition cost of long-lived assets to the periods of benefit. One widely used method is the *straight-line method.* Under this procedure, an equal portion of the acquisition cost less estimated salvage value is allocated to each period of the asset's estimated useful life. The depreciation charge for each period is determined as follows:

$$\frac{\text{Acquisition Cost}-\text{Estimated Salvage Value}}{\text{Estimated Useful Life in Periods}} = \frac{\text{Depreciation Charge for}}{\text{Each Period}}$$

Internal records indicate that the Building and Equipment account of Stephen's Shoe Store is composed of a store building with an acquisition cost of $800,000 and a group of items of equipment with an acquisition cost of $250,000. At the time the building was acquired, it had an estimated 40-year useful life and a zero salvage value. Depreciation expense for each year of the building's life is calculated to be

$$\frac{\$800,000 - \$0}{40 \text{ years}} = \$20,000 \text{ per year.}$$

At the time the equipment was acquired, it had an estimated useful life of 6 years and an estimated salvage value of $10,000. Annual depreciation is, therefore,

$$\frac{\$250,000 - \$10,000}{6 \text{ years}} = \$40,000 \text{ per year.}$$

The adjusting entry to record depreciation of $60,000 (= $20,000 + $40,000) for 1979 is

(15) Depreciation Expense (OE)   60,000
        Accumulated Depreciation (XA)   60,000

The credit in entry (15) could have been made directly to the Building and Equipment account, because the credit records the portion of the asset's cost which has expired, or become an expense, during 1979. The same end result is achieved by crediting the Accumulated Depreciation account, a contra-asset account, and then deducting the balance in this account from the acquisition cost of the assets in the Building and Equipment account on the balance sheet. Using the contra account enables the financial statements to show both the acquisition cost of the assets in use and the portion of that amount that has previously been recognized as an expense. Showing both acquisition cost and accumulated depreciation amounts separately provides a rough indication of the relative age of the firm's long-lived assets.

Note that the Depreciation Expense account includes only depreciation for the current accounting period, while the Accumulated Depreciation account reflects the cumulative depreciation charges on the present assets since acquisition. The Accumulated Depreciation account is sometimes referred to as Allowance for Depreciation.

Valuation of Accounts Receivable   When sales are made to customers on account, it is usually expected that some of the accounts will not be collected. In Chapter 3, we indicated that the primary objective in accounting for uncollectible accounts is to ensure that sales revenue of the period reflects only the amount of cash expected to be collected. That is, adjustments for anticipated uncollectible accounts should be charged against sales revenue *in the period of the sale.* The principal accounting problem here arises from the fact that individual accounts may not be judged uncollectible until some time after the period of sale. An estimate of the probable amount of uncollectible accounts must therefore be made in the period of sale.

Based on past experience, Stephen's Shoe Store estimates that 2 percent of sales on account during the year will ultimately become uncollectible. Since sales on account during 1979 were $800,000, the adjusting entry to provide for estimated uncollectible accounts of $16,000 (= .02 × $800,000) is

(16) Sales, Uncollectible Accounts Adjustment (OE)   16,000
        Allowance for Uncollectible Accounts (XA)   16,000

The debit entry is to an income statement account. Since revenue should be stated at the amount expected to be collected in cash, the amount in this account is preferably deducted from sales revenue on the income statement as a contra account. Many firms, however, debit an expense account, such as Bad Debt Expense or Uncollectible Accounts Expense, which is included in the expense section rather than the revenue section of the income statement. The effect on net income is the same in either case.

The credit entry to recognize estimated uncollectible accounts is to a balance sheet account that is shown as a contra to Accounts Receivable. The net amount, accounts receivable less estimated uncollectibles, indicates the amount of cash expected to be collected from customers. Using the contra account permits the disclosure of the total receivables outstanding as well as the estimated amount that will be collected.

At periodic intervals, individual customers' accounts are reviewed to assess their collectibility. Accounts deemed to be uncollectible are eliminated or "written off." Stephen's Shoe Store determined on December 31, 1979, that specific customers' accounts totaling $15,000 would never be collected. The adjusting entry to write off these individual accounts is

(17) Allowance for Uncollectible Accounts (XA)   15,000
         Accounts Receivable (A)   15,000

Note that net income is not affected by the write-off of the specific customers' accounts. Net income is affected in the period of sale when a provision is made for uncollectible accounts [for example, entry (16) and similar entries made in prior years]. When the $15,000 of specific customers' accounts is written off at the end of 1979, there is no additional effect on net income. Also note that the amount, accounts receivable less estimated uncollectibles, on the balance sheet is not affected by the write-off, since both the asset and contra asset are reduced by an equal amount. We consider further the accounting treatment of uncollectible accounts in Chapter 7.

Valuation of Liabilities   When cash is received from customers before merchandise is sold or services are rendered, the cash receipt creates a liability. For example, Stephen's Shoe Store received $1,200 on December 1, 1979, as 1 year's rent on warehouse space. When the cash was received, the liability account, Rental Fees Received in Advance, was credited. One month's rent has been earned as of December 31, 1979. The adjusting entry is

(18) Rental Fees Received in Advance (L).   100
         Rent Revenue (OE)   100

The remaining $1,100 of the advance rental is yet to be earned and is carried on the December 31, 1979, balance sheet as a liability.

Correction of Errors   Various errors and omissions may be discovered at the end of the accounting period as the process of checking, reviewing, and auditing is carried out. For example, the sales for 1 month during the year might have been recorded as $38,700 instead of $37,800. Or the sale to a specific customer might not have been

EXHIBIT 4.4
Stephen's Shoe Store, Inc.
Trial Balance Before and After Adjusting Entries[a]
December 31, 1979

Accounts	Unadjusted Trial Balance Debit	Unadjusted Trial Balance Credit	Adjusting Entries Debit	Adjusting Entries Credit	Adjusted Trial Balance Debit	Adjusted Trial Balance Credit
Cash (A)	$ 382,200				$ 382,200	
Accounts Receivable (A)	280,000			15,000 (17)	265,000	
Allowance for Uncollectible Accounts (XA)		$ 14,000	15,000 (17)	16,000 (16)		$ 15,000
Notes Receivable (A)	10,000				10,000	
Interest Receivable (A)			75 (12)		75	
Merchandise Inventory (A)	280,000				280,000	
Prepaid Insurance (A)	3,000			1,000 (14)	2,000	
Land (A)	200,000				200,000	
Building and Equipment (A)	1,050,000				1,050,000	
Accumulated Depreciation (XA)		170,000		60,000 (15)		230,000
Accounts Payable (L)		440,000				440,000
Salaries Payable (L)				12,000 (13)		12,000
Dividends Payable (L)		30,000				30,000
Rental Fees Received in Advance (L)		1,200	100 (18)			1,100
Bonds Payable (L)		200,000				200,000
Common Stock (OE)		500,000				500,000
Additional Paid-In Capital (OE)		400,000				400,000
Retained Earnings (OE)		216,000				216,000
Sales Revenue (OE)		1,250,000				1,250,000
Interest Revenue (OE)				75 (12)		75
Rent Revenue (OE)				100 (18)		100
Cost of Goods Sold (OE)	780,000				780,000	
Salaries Expense (OE)	220,000		12,000 (13)		232,000	
Interest Expense (OE)	16,000				16,000	
Insurance Expense (OE)			1,000 (14)		1,000	
Depreciation Expense (OE)			60,000 (15)		60,000	
Sales, Uncollectible Accounts Adjustment (OE)			16,000 (16)		16,000	
Totals	$3,221,200	$3,221,200	$104,175	$104,175	$3,294,275	$3,294,275

[a] This convenient tabular form is often called a *work sheet*. Most work sheets are more elaborate than this one, but their purpose is the same—to display data in a form for easy computations and financial statement preparation. The typical work sheet would not show just two final columns called Adjusted Trial Balance, but would show four columns: Income Statement Debit and Credit, and Balance Sheet Debit and Credit. The horizontal sum of the amounts in an income account is shown in the appropriate debit or credit income statement column of the work sheet. The horizontal sum of the amounts in a balance sheet account is shown in the appropriate debit or credit balance sheet column of the work sheet. See the Glossary at *work sheet* for an example.

recorded. Entries must be made at the end of the accounting period to correct for these errors. There were no such errors in the accounts of Stephen's Shoe Store.

Trial Balance After Adjusting Entries   The adjusting entries are posted or entered in the general ledger in the same manner as entries made during the year. A trial balance of the general ledger accounts after adjusting entries are made could be prepared. Such a trial balance is called an *adjusted trial balance* and is useful in preparing the financial statements. Exhibit 4.4 presents the trial balance data before and after adjusting entries for Stephen's Shoe Store. The exhibit indicates the effect of the adjustment process on the various accounts. The number in parentheses identifies the debit and credit components of each adjusting entry.

Closing of Temporary Accounts

The purpose of the closing process is to transfer the balances in the temporary revenue and expense accounts (and income distribution accounts, if any) to retained earnings. Temporary accounts with debit balances are closed by crediting each such account in an amount equal to its balance at the end of the period and debiting Retained Earnings. The usual closing entry for temporary accounts with debit balances is

Retained Earnings (OE)	X	
Accounts with Debit Balances (OE) (specific account titles)		X

Temporary accounts with credit balances are closed by debiting the temporary account and crediting Retained Earnings. The usual closing entry for temporary accounts with credit balances is

Accounts with Credit Balances (OE) (specific account titles)	X	
Retained Earnings (OE)		X

After closing entries, the balances in all temporary accounts are zero. The former debit (credit) balances in temporary accounts become debits (credits) in the Retained Earnings account.

Each temporary revenue and expense account could be closed by a separate entry. Some recording time is saved, however, by closing all revenue and expense accounts in a single entry as follows:

(19) Sales Revenue (OE)	1,250,000	
Interest Revenue (OE)	75	
Rent Revenue (OE)	100	
Cost of Goods Sold (OE)		780,000
Salaries Expense (OE)		232,000
Interest Expense (OE)		16,000
Insurance Expense (OE)		1,000
Depreciation Expense (OE)		60,000
Sales, Uncollectible Accounts Adjustment (OE)		16,000
Retained Earnings (OE)		145,175

The amount credited to Retained Earnings is the difference between the amounts debited to revenue accounts and the amounts credited to expense and sales adjustments accounts. This amount is the net income for the period.[1]

An alternative closing procedure uses a temporary "Income Summary" account. Individual revenue and expense accounts are first closed to the Income Summary account. The income statement is prepared using information on the individual revenues and expenses in the Income Summary account. The balance in the Income Summary account, representing net income for the period, is then closed to Retained Earnings.

For example, the entry to close the Sales Revenue account under this alternative procedure is

```
(19a)  Sales Revenue (OE) ....................................  1,250,000
           Income Summary (OE) ...................................           1,250,000
```

The entry to close the Cost of Goods Sold account is

```
(19b)  Income Summary (OE) ...................................  780,000
           Cost of Goods Sold (OE) ...............................           780,000
```

Similar closing entries are made for the other revenue and expense accounts. The Income Summary account will have a credit balance of $145,175 after all revenue and expense accounts have been closed. The balance in the Income Summary account is then transferred to Retained Earnings:

```
(19c)  Income Summary (OE) ...................................  145,175
           Retained Earnings (OE) ................................           145,175
```

The end result of both closing procedures is the same. Revenue and expense accounts, as well as the Income Summary account if one is used, have zero balances after closing entries, and the Retained Earnings account is increased by the net income for the period of $145,175. Exhibit 4.5 shows the Income Summary account for Stephen's Shoe Store after all revenue and expense accounts have been closed at the end of the period.

---

[1] The amount credited to Retained Earnings in the closing entry is called a *plug*. When making some journal entries in accounting, often all debits are known, as are all but one of the credits (or vice versa). Since the double-entry recording procedure requires equal debits and credits, the unknown quantity can be found by subtracting the sum of the known credits from the sum of all debits (or vice versa). This process is known as *plugging*.

EXHIBIT 4.5
Illustration of Income Summary Account for Stephen's Shoe Store, Inc.

Income Summary Account (OE)				Retained Earnings (OE)	
Cost of Goods Sold	780,000	1,250,000 Sales Revenue			246,000 Beginning Balance
Salaries Expense	232,000	75 Interest Revenue			
Interest Expense	16,000	100 Rent Revenue	Dividends 30,000		145,175 Net Income ←
Insurance Expense	1,000	1,250,175			
Depreciation Expense	60,000				361,175 Ending Balance
Sales, Uncollectible Accounts Adjustment	16,000				
To Close Income Summary Account	145,175				
	1,250,175				

Financial Statement Preparation

The income statement, balance sheet, and any desired supporting schedules can be prepared from information in the adjusted trial balance. The income statement of Stephen's Shoe Store for 1979 is presented in Exhibit 4.6. The comparative balance sheets for December 31, 1978 and 1979, are presented in Exhibit 4.7. An analysis of changes in retained earnings is presented in Exhibit 4.8.

EXHIBIT 4.6
Stephen's Shoe Store, Inc.
Income Statement
For the Year Ending
December 31, 1979

Revenues:

Sales Revenue	$1,250,000		
Less Sales, Uncollectible Accounts Adjustment	16,000		
Net Sales Revenue		$1,234,000	
Interest Revenue		75	
Rent Revenue		100	
Total Revenues			$1,234,175

Less Expenses:

Cost of Goods Sold	$ 780,000		
Salaries Expense	232,000		
Interest Expense	16,000		
Insurance Expense	1,000		
Depreciation Expense	60,000		
Total Expenses		1,089,000	
Net Income		$ 145,175	

EXHIBIT 4.7
Stephen's Shoe Store, Inc.
Comparative Balance Sheet
December 31, 1978 and 1979

ASSETS

Current Assets:	December 31, 1978		December 31, 1979	
Cash		$ 60,000		$ 382,200
Accounts Receivable	$ 140,000		$ 265,000	
Less Allowance for Uncollectible Accounts	14,000		15,000	
Accounts Receivable—net		126,000		250,000
Notes Receivable		—		10,000
Interest Receivable		—		75
Merchandise Inventory		350,000		280,000
Prepaid Insurance		—		2,000
Total Current Assets		$ 536,000		$ 924,275

Property, Plant, and Equipment				
Land		$ 200,000		$ 200,000
Building and Equipment—at acquisition cost	$1,050,000		$1,050,000	
Less: Accumulated Depreciation	170,000		230,000	
Building and Equipment—net		880,000		820,000
Total Property, Plant, and Equipment		$1,080,000		$1,020,000
Total Assets		$1,616,000		$1,944,275

LIABILITIES AND STOCKHOLDERS' EQUITY

Current Liabilities:				
Accounts Payable		$ 270,000		$ 440,000
Salaries Payable		—		12,000
Dividends Payable		—		30,000
Rental Fees Received in Advance		—		1,100
Total Current Liabilities		$ 270,000		$ 483,100

Long-Term Debt:				
Bonds Payable		200,000		200,000
Total Liabilities		$ 470,000		$ 683,100

Stockholders' Equity:				
Common Stock—at par value		$ 500,000		$ 500,000
Additional Paid-in Capital		400,000		400,000
Retained Earnings		246,000		361,175
Total Stockholders' Equity		$1,146,000		$1,261,175
Total Liabilities and Stockholders' Equity		$1,616,000		$1,944,275

EXHIBIT 4.8
Stephen's Shoe Store, Inc.
Analysis of Changes in
Retained Earnings
For the Year Ending
December 31, 1979

Retained Earnings, December 31, 1978		$246,000
Net Income	$145,175	
Less Dividends	30,000	
Increase in Retained Earnings.................................		115,175
Retained Earnings, December 31, 1979		$361,175

SUMMARY

Measurements of net income *for the period* and of financial position *at the end of the period* are closely related. Revenues result from selling goods or rendering services to customers and lead to increases in assets or decreases in liabilities. Expenses indicate that services have been consumed in generating revenue and result in decreases in assets or increases in liabilities. Since revenues represent provisional increases in owners' equity, revenue transactions are recorded by crediting (increasing) an owners' equity account for the specific type of revenue and by debiting either an asset or liability account. Expenses represent provisional decreases in owners' equity and are recorded by debiting (decreasing) an owners' equity account for the specific type of expense and crediting either an asset or a liability account. After the revenue and expense accounts have accumulated the revenues earned and expenses recognized during the period, the balances in these temporary accounts are transferred, or closed, to the Retained Earnings account at the end of the period.

Some events will not be recorded as part of the regular day-to-day recording process during the period because no explicit transaction between the firm and some external party (such as a customer, creditor, or governmental unit) has taken place to signal the requirement for a journal entry. Such events require an adjusting entry at the end of the period so that periodic income and financial position can be properly reported on an accrual basis.

APPENDIX 4.1
The Accounting Process for a Manufacturing Firm

The principal difference between accounting for merchandising and for manufacturing firms is the treatment of inventories. As discussed in Chapter 3, a merchandising firm acquires inventory items in finished form ready for sale. The acquisition cost of these items is reflected in the asset account, Merchandise Inventory, until the units

EXHIBIT 4.9
Flow of Manufacturing Costs Through the Accounts

Raw Materials Inventory (A)

Cost of Raw Materials Purchased	Raw Materials Costs Incurred in Manufacturing

→

Work-in-Process Inventory (A)

Raw Materials Costs Incurred in Manufacturing	Manufacturing Cost of Units Completed and Transferred to Storeroom
Direct Labor Costs Incurred in Manufacturing	
Overhead Costs Incurred in Manufacturing	

→

Finished Goods Inventory (A)

Manufacturing Cost of Units Transferred from Factory	Manufacturing Cost of Units Sold

→

Cost of Goods Sold (OE)

Manufacturing Cost of Units Sold	

Cash (A) or Wages Payable (L)

	Direct Labor Costs Incurred in Manufacturing

→

Cash (A), Accumulated Depreciation (XA), Other Accounts

	Overhead Costs Incurred in Manufacturing

→

are sold. At the time of sale, the cost of the items sold is transferred from the asset account, Merchandise Inventory, to the expense account, Cost of Goods Sold.

A manufacturing firm, on the other hand, incurs various costs in transforming raw materials into finished products. These manufacturing costs are generally classified as direct material (or raw material), direct labor, and manufacturing overhead. Until the units being produced are sold, manufacturing costs are treated as product costs—assets—and accumulated in various inventory accounts.

Separate inventory accounts are used for items at various stages of completion. The Raw Materials Inventory account includes the cost of raw materials purchased but not yet transferred to production. The balance in the Raw Materials Inventory account indicates the cost of raw materials on hand in the raw materials storeroom or warehouse. When raw materials are issued to producing departments, the cost of the materials is transferred from the Raw Materials Inventory account to the Work-in-Process Inventory account. The Work-in-Process Inventory account accumulates the costs incurred in producing units during the period. The Work-in-Process Inventory account is debited for the cost of raw materials transferred from the raw materials storeroom, the cost of direct labor services used, and the manufacturing overhead costs incurred (for example, factory utilities, taxes, insurance, and depreciation). The Work-in-Process Inventory account is credited for the total manufacturing cost of units completed in the factory and transferred to the finished goods storeroom. The Finished Goods Inventory account includes the total manufacturing cost of units completed but not yet sold. At the time of sale, the cost of units sold is transferred from the Finished Goods Inventory account to the Cost-of-Goods-Sold account. This flow of manufacturing costs through the various inventory accounts is summarized in Exhibit 4.9.

Illustration of the Accounting Process for a Manufacturing Firm

The accounting process for a manufacturing firm is illustrated with information about the operations of the Moon Manufacturing Company. The Company was formed on December 31, 1978, with the issuance of 10,000 shares of $10 par value common stock for $30 per share. The firm began business on January 1, 1979. Transactions during January 1979 are described below, and the appropriate journal entries are provided:

(1) A building costing $200,000 and equipment costing $50,000 are acquired for cash.

Building (A)	200,000	
Equipment (A)	50,000	
Cash (A)		250,000

(2) Raw materials costing $25,000 are purchased on account.

Raw Materials Inventory (A)	25,000	
Accounts Payable (L)		25,000

(3) Raw materials costing $20,000 are issued to producing departments.

Work-in-Process Inventory (A)	20,000	
Raw Materials Inventory (A)		20,000

(4) The total payroll for January is $60,000. Of this amount, $40,000 is paid to factory workers, and $20,000 is paid to selling and administrative personnel.

Work-in-Process Inventory (A)	40,000	
Salaries Expense (OE)	20,000	
Cash (A)		60,000

Recall from Chapter 3 that nonmanufacturing costs are recorded as expenses of the period in which the services are consumed, since these costs rarely create assets with future benefits. Journal entry (4) illustrates the difference between the recording of a product cost and a period expense.

(5) The expenditures for utilities during January are $1,200. Of this amount, $1,000 is attributable to manufacturing, and $200 to selling and administrative activities.

Work-in-Process Inventory (A)	1,000	
Utilities Expense (OE)	200	
Cash (A)		1,200

(6) Depreciation on building and equipment during January is as follows: factory, $8,000; selling and administrative, $2,000.

Work-in-Process Inventory (A)	8,000	
Depreciation Expense (OE)	2,000	
Accumulated Depreciation (XA)		10,000

(7) The manufacturing cost of units completed during January and transferred to the finished goods storeroom is $48,500.

Finished Goods Inventory (A)	48,500	
Work-in-Process Inventory (A)		48,500

(8) Sales during January total $75,000, of which $25,000 is on account.

Cash (A)	50,000	
Accounts Receivable (A)	25,000	
Sales Revenue (OE)		75,000

(9) The manufacturing cost of the goods sold during January is $42,600.

Cost of Goods Sold (OE)	42,600	
Finished Goods Inventory (A)		42,600

The manner in which the various costs incurred flow through the accounts may be further illustrated by entering these journal entries in T-accounts as shown in Exhibit 4.10.

EXHIBIT 4.10
Moon Manufacturing Company
T-Accounts Showing Transactions
During 1979

Raw Materials Inventory (A)				Work-in-Process Inventory (A)			
(2)	25,000	20,000	(3)	(3)	20,000	48,500	(7)
				(4)	40,000		
				(5)	1,000		
				(6)	8,000		
Bal. 12/31	5,000			Bal. 12/31	20,500		

Finished Goods Inventory (A)				Cost of Goods Sold (OE)		
(7)	48,500	42,600	(9)	(9)	42,600	
Bal. 12/31	5,900			Bal. 12/31	42,600	

Cash (A)				Accounts Receivable (A)		
Bal. 1/1	300,000	250,000	(1)	(8)	25,000	
(8)	50,000	60,000	(4)			
		1,200	(5)			
Bal. 12/31	38,800			Bal. 12/31	25,000	

Building (A)			Equipment (A)		
(1)	200,000		(1)	50,000	
Bal. 12/31	200,000		Bal. 12/31	50,000	

Accumulated Depreciation (XA)				Salaries Expense (OE)		
		10,000	(6)	(4)	20,000	
		10,000	Bal. 12/31	Bal. 12/31	20,000	

Sales Revenue (OE)			
		75,000	(8)
		75,000	Bal. 12/31

Accounts Payable (L)			
		25,000	(2)
		25,000	Bal. 12/31

Utilities Expense (OE)			Depreciation Expense (OE)		
(5)	200		(6)	2,000	
Bal. 12/31	200		Bal. 12/31	2,000	

Exhibit 4.11 presents an income statement for Moon Manufacturing Company for January 1979.

EXHIBIT 4.11
Moon Manufacturing Company
Income Statement
For the Month of January 1979

Sales Revenue		$75,000
Less Expenses:		
Cost of Goods Sold	$42,600	
Salaries Expense	20,000	
Utilities Expense	200	
Depreciation Expense	2,000	
Total Expenses		64,800
Net Income		$10,200

Summary of the Accounting for Manufacturing Operations

The accounting procedures for the selling and administrative costs of manufacturing and merchandising firms are quite similar. These costs are treated as expenses of the period in which services are consumed. The accounting procedures for a manufacturing firm differ from those of a merchandising firm primarily in the treatment of inventories. A manufacturing firm incurs various costs in transforming raw materials into finished products. Until the units produced are sold, manufacturing costs are accumulated in inventory accounts—the Work-in-Process Inventory account or the Finished Goods Inventory account—depending on the stage of completion of each unit being produced. Product costs are therefore debited to inventory (asset) accounts until the time of sale.

QUESTIONS AND PROBLEMS

1 Review the meaning of the following concepts or terms discussed in this chapter:
  a Revenue.
  b Expense.
  c Expense versus dividend.
  d Temporary and permanent accounts.
  e General journal entries.
  f Adjusting entries.
  g Closing entries.
  h Unadjusted trial balance.
  i Adjusted trial balance.
  j Contra account.
  k Accrual basis of accounting.

    l Merchandise inventory.
    m Raw materials inventory.
    n Work-in-process inventory.
    o Finished goods inventory.
    p "Flow of costs."
    q Work sheet.

2 "Revenue and expense accounts are useful accounting devices, but they could be dispensed with." What is an alternative to using them?

3 After the books have been closed, what classes of accounts will have zero balances? What classes of accounts will have nonzero balances?

4 Why are revenue and expense accounts closed at the end of each period?

5 "Despite the earning of substantial amounts of revenue during the period, retained earnings decreased instead of increased." Explain.

6 What is the purpose of using contra accounts? What is the alternative to using them?

7 In the business world many transactions are routine and repetitive. Since accounting records business transactions, many accounting entries are also routine and repetitive. Because of the double-entry system and its often desirable redundancy, knowing one-half of an entry permits a reasoned guess about the other half. The items below give the account name for one-half of an entry. Indicate your best guess as to the name of the account of the *routine* other half of the entry. Also indicate whether the other account is increased or decreased by the transaction.
    a Debit: Cost of Goods Sold.
    b Debit: Accounts Receivable.
    c Credit: Accounts Receivable.
    d Debit: Accounts Payable.
    e Credit: Accounts Payable.
    f Credit: Accumulated Depreciation.
    g Debit: Retained Earnings.
    h Credit: Prepaid Insurance.
    i Debit: Property Taxes Payable.
    j Debit: Merchandise Inventory.

8 The particular time when various events and transactions are recorded in the accounts is often a matter of clerical efficiency. For each of the items below, describe the likely entry during each month and the adjusting entry at the end of each month, assuming that financial statements are prepared monthly.
    a The rental on buildings and equipment of $600 is paid in advance at the beginning of each month.
    b Property taxes for the calendar year of $3,600 are paid on July 1.
    c Selling and office supplies, $375, are purchased once each month but used each day in small amounts.
    d A firm rents out excess office space at the rate of $500 a month, payable in advance for each calendar quarter of the year.

9 Give the journal entry that should be made upon the receipt of each of the following invoices by the South Appliance Company, assuming that no previous entry has been made.

(1) From Western Electric Supply Company, $864, for repair parts purchased.

(2) From Touch & Rose, certified public accountants, $200, for services in filing income tax returns.

(3) From the General Electric Company, $9,560, for refrigerators purchased.

(4) From the White Stationery Company, $150, for office supplies purchased.

(5) From the Showy Sign Company, $470, for a neon sign acquired.

(6) From Schutheis and Schutheis, attorneys, $750, for legal services in changing from the corporate to the partnership form of organization.

(7) From the Bell Telephone Company, $46, for telephone service for next month.

(8) From the Madison Avenue Garage, $52, for gasoline and oil used by the delivery truck.

(9) From the Municipal Electric Department, $126, for electricity used for lighting last month.

10 Give the journal entry to record each of the transactions below as well as any necessary adjusting entries on December 31, 1979, assuming that the accounting period is the calendar year and the books are closed on December 31.

   a Morrissey's Department Store had sales of $400,000 during 1979. Of this total, $250,000 were for cash and $150,000 were on account. Accounts totaling $120,000 were collected. Past experience indicates that 2 percent of sales on account will probably become uncollectible. Specific accounts totaling $2,500 were determined to be uncollectible during the year.

   b Harrison's Supply Company received a 90-day note from a customer on December 1, 1979. The note in the face amount of $2,000 replaced an open account receivable of the same amount. The note is due with interest at 8 percent per year on March 1, 1980.

   c Thompson's Wholesale Company purchased a 3-year insurance policy on September 1, 1979, paying the 3-year premium of $10,800 in advance.

   d William's Products Company acquired a machine on July 1, 1979, for $10,000 cash. The machine is expected to have a $2,000 salvage value and a 4-year life.

   e Greer Electronics Company acquired an automobile on September 1, 1978, for $6,000 cash. The automobile is expected to have $1,200 salvage value and a 4-year life.

   f Devine Company rented out excess office space for the 3-month period beginning December 15, 1979. The first month's rent of $7,200 was received on this date.

   g Prentice Products Corporation began business on November 1, 1979. It acquired office supplies costing $6,000 on account. Of this amount, $5,000 was paid by year-end. A physical inventory indicates that office supplies costing $2,500 were on hand on December 31, 1979.

11 The Merchandise Supply Company received a $6,000, 3-month, 12-percent promissory note, dated December 1, 1979, from Virdon Stores to apply on its open accounts receivable.

   a Present journal entries for the Merchandise Supply Company from December 1, 1979, through collection at maturity. The books are closed quarterly. Include the closing entry.

   b Present journal entries for Virdon Stores from December 1, 1979, through payment at maturity. The books are closed quarterly. Include the closing entry.

12 Selected transactions of the Kessinger Co. are described below. Present dated journal entries for these transactions and adjusting entries at the end of each month from January 15, 1979, through July 1, 1979. Assume that only the notes indicated were outstanding during this period. The accounting period is 1 month.

(1) The company issued a $2,000, 2-month, 12-percent promissory note on January 15, 1979, in lieu of payment on an account due that date to the White Wholesale Company.

(2) The note in **(1)** and interest were paid at maturity.

(3) The company issued a $4,000, 3-month, 12-percent promissory note to the White Wholesale Company on the date of purchase of merchandise, April 1, 1979.

(4) The note in **(3)** and interest were paid at maturity.

13 On January 1, 1979, the Office Supplies Inventory account of the Harris Company had a balance of $2,200. During the ensuing quarter, supplies were acquired on account in the amount of $6,000. On March 31, 1979, the inventory was taken and calculated to amount to $1,500.

Present journal entries to record the above acquisition and adjustments at the end of March in accordance with each of the following sets of instructions, which might be established in an accounting systems manual:

a An expense account is to be debited at the time supplies are acquired.

b An asset account is to be debited at the time supplies are acquired.

14 The sales, all on account, of the Devine Company in 1979, its first year of operation, were $600,000. Collections totaled $450,000. At December 31, 1979, it was estimated that $1\frac{1}{2}$ percent of sales on account during the year would likely be uncollectible. On that date, specific accounts in the amount of $3,500 were written off.

Present journal entries for the transactions and adjustments of 1979 related to sales and customers' accounts.

15 In recording the adjusting entries of the Hammond Sales Company, Inc., at the end of 1979, the following adjustments were omitted:

(1) Depreciation on the delivery truck of $1,500.

(2) Insurance expired on the delivery truck of $300.

(3) Interest accrued on notes payable of $75.

(4) Interest accrued on notes receivable of $165.

Indicate the effect (exclusive of income tax implications) of these omissions on the following items in the financial statements prepared on December 31, 1979.

a Current assets.

b Noncurrent assets.

c Current liabilities.

d Selling expenses.

e Net income.

f Retained earnings.

16 Present journal entries for each of the following separate sets of data:

a On January 15, 1979, a $4,000, 2-month, 12-percent note was received by the company. Present adjusting entries at the end of each month and the entry for collection at maturity.

b The company uses one Merchandise Inventory account to record the beginning inventory and purchases during the period. The balance in this account on December 31, 1979, was $480,000. The inventory of merchandise on hand at that time was $90,000. Present the adjusting entry.

c The company rents out part of its building for office space at the rate of $600 a month, payable in advance for each calendar quarter of the year. The quarterly rental was received on February 1, 1979. Present collection and adjusting entries for the quarter. Assume that the books are closed monthly.

d The company leases branch office space at $2,000 a month. Payment is made by the company on the first of each 6-month period. Payment of $12,000 was made on July 1,

1979. Present payment and adjusting entries through August 31, 1979. Assume that the books are closed monthly.

e The balance of the Prepaid Insurance account on October 1, 1979, was $200. On December 1, 1979, the company renewed its only insurance policy for another 3 years beginning on that date by payment of $3,960. Present journal entries for renewal and adjusting entries through December 31, 1979. Assume that the books are closed quarterly.

f The Office Supplies on Hand account had a balance of $300 on December 1, 1979. Purchases of supplies in the amount of $480 were recorded in the Office Supplies Expense account during the month. The inventory of office supplies on December 31, 1979, was $290. Present any necessary adjusting entry at December 31, 1979.

g An office building was constructed at a cost of $260,000. It was estimated that it would have a useful life of 50 years from the date of occupancy, October 31, 1979, and a residual value of $20,000. Present the adjusting entry for the depreciation of the building in 1979. Assume that the books are closed annually at December 31.

h Experience indicates that 1 percent of the accounts arising from sales on account will not be collected. Sales on account during 1979 were $200,000. A list of uncollectible accounts totaling $500 as of December 31, 1979, was compiled. Present journal entries for the annual provision for uncollectible accounts and the write-off of specific customers' accounts as of December 31, 1979. The books are closed annually.

17 a Machine A costs $10,000, has accumulated depreciation of $4,000 as of year-end, and is being depreciated on a straight-line basis over 10 years with an estimated salvage value of zero. How old is machine A as of year-end?

b Machine B has accumulated depreciation (straight-line basis) of $6,000 at year-end. The depreciation charge for the year is $2,000. The estimated salvage value of the machine at the end of its useful life is zero. How old is machine B as of year-end?

18 Determine the missing items in each of the independent cases below:

	a	b	c	d
Retained Earnings, January 1, 1979	$ 45,000	?	$875,000	$965,000
Retained Earnings, December 31, 1979	?	$520,000	805,000	985,000
Revenues—1979	220,000	?	660,000	680,000
Expenses—1979	165,000	680,000	?	640,000
Net Income—1979	?	355,000	?	?
Dividends—1979	30,000	75,000	10,000	?

19 Determine the missing items in each of the independent cases below:

	a	b	c	d
Stockholders' Equity January 1, 1979	?	$46,400	$21,400	$34,700
Stockholders' Equity December 31, 1979	$159,600	?	30,150	47,500
Stock Issued in 1979	28,600	15,000	0	2,500
Dividends in 1979	4,000	21,000	?	2,100
Net Income (Loss) in 1979	(7,200)	36,100	19,300	?

20 The adjusted trial balance of the Life Photographers, Incorporated, at June 30, 1979, is as follows:

Life Photographers, Inc.
Adjusted Trial Balance
June 30, 1979
(Problem 20)

Accounts Payable		$ 3,636
Accounts Receivable	$ 3,900	
Accumulated Depreciation		2,000
Advertising Expense	1,500	
Cameras and Equipment	15,500	
Cash	2,994	
Common Stock		10,000
Depreciation Expense—Cameras and Equipment	180	
Depreciation Expense—Furniture and Fixtures	105	
Electricity Expense	300	
Equipment Repairs Expense	180	
Furniture and Fixtures	9,600	
Insurance Expense	330	
Photographic Supplies Expense	1,950	
Photographic Supplies on Hand	3,390	
Prepaid Insurance	270	
Rent Expense	1,425	
Retained Earnings		14,138
Revenue—Commercial Photography		18,090
Revenue—Printing Service		4,680
Salaries Expense	10,800	
Telephone Expense	120	
	$52,544	$52,544

a Present the journal entries to close the revenue and expense accounts directly to Retained Earnings as of June 30, 1979.

b Set up in T-account form the revenue, expense, and retained earnings accounts. Insert the trial balance amounts and record the closing entries from part **a**.

21 The trial balance of the Riteway Barber Shop on July 1, 1979, the first day of an accounting period, is as follows:

Cash	$1,200	
Supplies Inventory	300	
Prepaid Magazine Subscriptions	60	
Furniture and Equipment	7,000	
Accumulated Depreciation		$1,000
Accounts Payable, Republic Supply Company		400
Rent Payable		200
Equipment Contract Payable		2,000
Pat Simson, Capital		2,480
Jill Evans, Capital		2,480
	$8,560	$8,560

A summary of the business for the month of July is as follows:

(1) Cash received from customers for services rendered during July, $2,000.

(2) Payment of an installment on the equipment contract, $400 plus interest for 1 month on the old balance at 9 percent.

(3) Payment of rent for June and July, $400.

(4) Supplies purchased on account from the Republic Supply Company, $200.

(5) Payment for newspapers for the month, $8.

(6) Payments to the Republic Supply Company, $440.

(7) A bill is received from the Bright Laundry Service for laundry service for the month, $50.

(8) Supplies used, $340.

(9) Magazine subscription expirations applicable to the month of July, $10.

(10) Depreciation applicable to furniture and equipment for the month of July, $100.

(11) Each partner drew $400 for her personal use.

a Open T-accounts for the accounts listed in the trial balance and insert the beginning balances. Record the transactions for the month of July in the T-accounts, opening additional T-accounts for individual revenue and expense accounts as needed.

b Prepare an adjusted, preclosing trial balance as of July 30, 1979, to check the accuracy of your entries.

22 A corporation known as the Stevens Collection Agency is organized by Betty Stevens and Charles Kirby on January 1, 1979. The business of the firm is to collect overdue accounts receivable of various clients on a commission basis. The following transactions occurred during January:

(1) Stevens contributes office supplies worth $2,000 and cash of $13,000. She is issued stock certificates for 500 shares with a par value of $30 a share.

(2) Kirby contributes $2,000 in cash and office equipment valued at $10,000. He is issued stock certificates for 400 shares.

(3) The Stevens agency collects $600 on an account that was turned over to it by the Giggly Market. The commission earned is 50 percent of the amount collected.

(4) The stenographer's salary during the month is paid, $800.

(5) A bill is received from Lyband and Linn, certified public accountants, for $300 to cover the cost of installing a computer system.

(6) The amount due the Giggly Market [see **(3)**] is paid.

(7) An office is leased for the year beginning February 1, 1979, and the rent for 3 months is paid in advance. A check is drawn for $1,200.

(8) An automobile is purchased for $3,500; $2,500 is paid by check, and an installment contract, payable to the Scotch Automobile Sales Company, is signed for the balance.

a Open T-accounts and record the transactions during January.

b Prepare an adjusted, preclosing trial balance as of January 31, 1979. Indicate, by **"R"** or **"E"**, accounts that are revenue or expense accounts.

23 The balance sheet accounts of Blake's Radio Shop at July 1, 1979, are as follows:

Cash	$1,720	
Repair Parts Inventory	600	
Office Supplies Inventory	80	
Equipment	2,000	
Accumulated Depreciation		$ 200
Accounts Payable		2,200
Brenda Blake, Capital		2,000
	$4,400	$4,400

A summary of the transactions for July is as follows:

(1) Performed repair services, for which $800 in cash was received immediately.
(2) Performed additional repair work, $300, and sent bills to customers for this amount.
(3) Paid creditors, $500.
(4) Took out insurance on equipment on July 1, and issued a check to cover 1 year's premium of $84.
(5) Paid $50 for a series of advertisements that appeared in the local newspaper during July.
(6) Issued check for $120 for rent of shop space for July.
(7) Paid telephone bill for the month, $30.
(8) Collected $150 of the amount charged to customers in item (2).
(9) The insurance expired during July is calculated at $7.
(10) Cost of repair parts used during the month, $130.
(11) Cost of office supplies used during July, $30.
(12) Depreciation of equipment for the month is $24.

a Open T-accounts and insert the July 1 balances. Record the transactions for the month in the T-accounts, opening additional T-accounts for individual revenue and expense accounts as needed.
b Prepare an adjusted, preclosing trial balance at July 31, 1979.
c Enter closing entries in the T-accounts using an Income Summary account.
d Prepare an income statement for the month of July and a balance sheet as of July 31, 1979.

24 The trial balance of Safety Cleaners and Dyers at February 28, 1979, is shown below. The books have not been closed since December 31, 1978.

Cash	$ 3,560	
Accounts Receivable	15,200	
Supplies Inventory	4,800	
Prepaid Insurance	1,040	
Equipment	65,000	
Accumulated Depreciation		$ 10,600
Accounts Payable		6,980
P. O. Grey, Capital		60,000
Sales		46,060
Salaries and Wages Expense	26,600	
Cost of Outside Work	2,040	
Advertising Expense	900	
Rent Expense	1,200	
Power, Gas, and Water Expense	880	
Supplies Used	—	
Depreciation Expense	—	
Miscellaneous Expense	2,420	
	$123,640	$123,640

A summary of the transactions for the month of March 1979 is as follows:

(1) Sales: For cash, $24,000; on account, $15,800.
(2) Collections on account, $20,000.

(3) Purchases of outside work (cleaning done by wholesale cleaners), $1,800, on account.

(4) Purchases of supplies, on account, $3,800.

(5) Payments on account, $5,000.

(6) March rent paid, $1,000.

(7) Supplies used (for the quarter), $6,340.

(8) Depreciation (for the quarter), $3,420.

(9) March salaries and wages of $21,120 are paid.

(10) Bills received but not recorded or paid by the end of the month: advertising, $400; power, gas, and water, $580.

(11) Insurance expired (for the quarter), $600.

a Open T-accounts and enter the trial balance amounts.

b Record the transactions for the month of March in the T-accounts, opening additional T-accounts as needed. Cross-number the entries.

c Enter closing entries in the T-accounts using an Income Summary account.

d Prepare an adjusted, preclosing trial balance at March 31, 1979, an income statement for the 3 months ending March 31, 1979, and a balance sheet as of March 31, 1979.

25 The following data relate to the manufacturing activities of the Haskell Company during March 1979.

	March 1	March 31
Raw Materials Inventory	$42,400	$46,900
Work-in-Process Inventory	75,800	63,200
Finished Goods Inventory	44,200	46,300

Factory costs incurred during the month:

Raw Materials Purchased	$ 60,700
Labor Services Received	137,900
Heat, Light, and Power	1,260
Factory Rent	4,100

Expirations of previous factory acquisitions and prepayments:

Depreciation on Factory Equipment	$1,800
Prepaid Insurance Expired	1,440

a Determine the cost of raw materials used during March.

b Determine the cost of the units completed during March and transferred to the finished goods storeroom.

c Determine the cost of goods sold during March.

26 The following data relate to the manufacturing activities of the Cornell Company during June 1979.

	June 1	June 30
Raw Materials Inventory	$22,600	$18,900
Factory Supplies Inventory	3,600	2,700
Work-in-Process Inventory	88,600	96,500
Finished Goods Inventory	64,300	61,900

Factory costs incurred during the month:

Raw Materials Purchased	$366,000
Factory Supplies Purchased	6,800
Labor Service Received	292,100
Heat, Light, and Power	3,300
Factory Insurance	2,000

Expirations of previous factory acquisitions and prepayments:

Depreciation on Factory Equipment	$20,800
Prepaid Rent Expired	2,400

a Determine the cost of raw materials and factory supplies used during June.
b Determine the cost of units completed during June and transferred to the finished goods storeroom.
c Determine the cost of goods sold during June.

27 Melton Plastics Company was incorporated on September 16, 1979. By September 30, 1979, the firm was ready to begin operations. The trial balance at that date was as follows:

Cash	$387,200	
Raw Materials Inventory	19,200	
Factory Equipment	136,000	
Accounts Payable		$ 22,400
Capital Stock		520,000
	$542,400	$542,400

The following data relate only to the manufacturing operations of the firm during October:

(1) Materials purchased on account, $161,600.
(2) Wages and salaries earned during the month, $148,000.
(3) Raw materials requisitioned and put into process during the month, $168,800.
(4) Equipment was acquired during the month at a cost of $112,000. A check for $40,000 was issued, and an equipment contract payable in eight equal monthly installments was signed for the remainder.
(5) Additional payments by check:

Raw Materials Suppliers	$140,000
Payrolls	112,420
Factory Building Rent	6,000
Utilities	2,920
Insurance Premiums (for 1 year from October 1, 1979)	9,600
Miscellaneous Factory Costs	26,400
	$297,340

(6) Invoices received but unpaid at October 31, 1979:

City Water Department	$ 120
Hoster Machine Supply Company, for additional equipment	2,400

(7) Depreciation on equipment for the month, $1,200.

(8) One month's insurance expiration is recorded.

(9) The cost of parts finished during October was $281,750.

a   Open T-accounts and enter the amounts from the opening trial balance.

b   Record the transactions during the month in the T-accounts, opening additional accounts as needed.

c   Prepare an adjusted trial balance at October 31, 1979.

28 This problem is a continuation of Problem 27, Melton Plastics Company. In addition to the manufacturing activities described in that problem, the following transactions relating to selling and administrative activities occurred during October 1979.

(10) Sales, on account, $340,600.

(11) Collections from customers, $330,000.

(12) Salaries earned during the month: Sales, $30,800; office, $31,200.

(13) Payments by check:

Sales Salaries	$27,630
Office Salaries	27,550
Advertising During October	7,200
Rent of Office and Office Equipment for October	2,200
Office Supplies	1,600
Miscellaneous Office Costs	1,400
Miscellaneous Selling Costs	2,800
Total	$70,380

(15) The inventory of finished goods on October 31, 1979, is $59,000.

a   Employing the T-accounts of Problem 27 and additional accounts as needed, record the selling and administrative activities for the month in the T-accounts.

b   Prepare a combined statement of income and retained earnings for the month.

c   Enter closing entries in the T-accounts using an Income Summary account.

d   Prepare a balance sheet as of October 31, 1979.

29 On July 1, 1978, the accounts of the Tampa Manufacturing Company contained the following balances:

Debit Balances		**Credit Balances**	
Cash	$ 110,000	Accumulated Depreciation	$ 30,000
Accounts Receivable	220,000	Accounts Payable	56,000
Raw Materials Inventory	80,000	Wages Payable	24,000
Work-in-Process Inventory	230,000	Capital Stock	1,000,000
Finished Goods Inventory	170,000	Retained Earnings	200,000
Factory Supplies Inventory	20,000		
Manufacturing Equipment	480,000		
Total	$1,310,000	Total	$1,310,000

Transactions for the month of July are listed below in summary form:

(1) Sales, all on account, were $310,000.

(2) Labor services furnished by employees during the period (but as yet unpaid) amounted to $80,000. All labor is employed in the factory.

(3) Factory supplies were purchased for $8,500; payment was made by check.

(4) Raw materials purchased on account, $100,000.

(5) Collections from customers, $335,000.

(6) Payment of $108,000 was made to raw materials suppliers.

(7) Payments to employees total $78,500.

(8) Rent of the factory building for the month, $8,000, was paid.

(9) Depreciation of manufacturing equipment for the month, $12,000.

(10) Other manufacturing costs incurred and paid, $40,000.

(11) All selling and administrative services are furnished by Clark and Company for $10,000 per month. Their bill was paid by check.

(12) Raw materials used during month, $115,000.

(13) Factory supplies used during month, $8,000.

(14) Cost of goods completed during month, $258,000.

(15) Goods costing $261,500 were shipped to customers during the month.

a   Open T-accounts and record the July 1, 1979, amounts. Record transactions (1) through (15) in the T-accounts, opening additional accounts as needed.

b   Prepare an adjusted, preclosing trial balance as of July 31, 1979.

c   Prepare a combined statement of income and retained earnings for July 1979.

d   Enter closing entries in the T-accounts using an Income Summary account.

e   Prepare a balance sheet as of July 31, 1979.

30 The trial balance of the Handy Harriet's Hardware Store on September 30, 1979, is as follows:

Cash	$ 86,500	
Accounts Receivable	54,500	
Merchandise Inventory	136,300	
Prepaid Insurance	800	
Equipment	420,000	
Allowance for Uncollectible Accounts		$ 6,500
Accumulated Depreciation		166,000
Accounts Payable		66,300
Note Payable		10,000
Salaries Payable		2,500
Capital Stock		300,000
Retained Earnings		146,800
Total	$698,100	$698,100

Transactions during October and additional information are as follows:

(1) Sales, all on account, total $150,000.

(2) Merchandise inventory purchased on account from various suppliers is $88,400.

(3) Rent for the month of October of $22,000 is paid.

(4) Salaries paid to employees during October are $38,700.

(5) Accounts receivable of $63,800 are collected.

(6) Accounts payable of $73,200 are paid.

(7) Miscellaneous expenses of $8,200 are paid in cash.

(8) The premium on a 1-year insurance policy was paid on June 1, 1979.

(9) Equipment is depreciated over a 10-year life. Estimated salvage value of the equipment is considered to be negligible.

(10) Employee salaries earned during the last two days of October but not paid are $4,300.

(11) Based on past experience, the firm estimates that 1 percent of all sales on account will become uncollectible.

(12) Specific customers' accounts of $3,800 are determined to be uncollectible.

(13) The note payable is a 90-day, 12-percent note issued on September 30, 1979.

(14) Merchandise inventory on hand on October 31, 1979, totals $151,500.

a Prepare general journal entries to reflect the transactions and other events during October. Indicate whether each entry records a transaction during the month **(T)** or is an adjusting entry at the end of the month **(A)**.

b Set up T-accounts and enter the opening balances in the accounts on September 30, 1979. Record the entries from part **a** in the T-accounts, creating additional accounts as required.

c Prepare an adjusted, preclosing trial balance as of October 31, 1979.

d Prepare an income statement for the month of October.

e Enter the appropriate closing entries at the end of October in the T-accounts, assuming that the books are closed each month. Use an Income Summary account.

f Prepare a balance sheet as of October 31, 1979.

31 The following unadjusted trial balance is taken from the books of the Kathleen Clothing Company at July 31, 1979. The company closes its books monthly.

Accounts Payable		$ 12,695
Accounts Receivable	$ 18,000	
Accumulated Depreciation		8,240
Advances by Customers		540
Allowance for Uncollectible Accounts		1,200
Capital Stock		40,000
Cash	9,000	
Equipment	2,640	
Depreciation Expense	—	—
Dividends Payable	—	—
Furniture and Fixtures	12,000	
Income Tax Expense	—	—
Income Tax Payable		3,500
Insurance Expense	—	—
Leasehold	10,800	
Merchandise Cost of Goods Sold	—	—
Merchandise Inventory	49,500	
Miscellaneous Expenses	188	
Prepaid Insurance	450	
Rent Expense	—	—
Retained Earnings		13,068
Salaries and Commissions Expense	2,020	
Salaries and Commissions Payable		500
Sales		25,000
Sales, Uncollectible Accounts Adjustment	—	—
Supplies Inventory	145	
	$104,743	$104,743

Additional data:

(1) Depreciation on equipment is to be calculated at 20 percent of cost per year (assume zero salvage value).

(2) Depreciation on furniture and fixtures is to be calculated at 15 percent of cost per year (assume zero salvage value).

(3) The leasehold represents long-term rent paid in advance by Kathleen. The monthly rental charge is $400.

(4) One invoice of $340 for the purchase of merchandise from the Peoria Company on account was recorded during the month as $430. The account has not yet been paid.

(5) Commissions unpaid at July 31, 1979, are $380. All salaries have been paid. The balance in the Salaries and Commissions Payable account represents the amount of commissions unpaid at July 1.

(6) Merchandise with a sales price of $250 was recently delivered to a customer, and charged to Accounts Receivable, although the customer had paid $250 in advance.

(7) The estimated uncollectible account rate is 1 percent of the charge sales of the month. Charge sales were 80 percent of the sales of the month.

(8) An analysis of outstanding customers' accounts indicates that two accounts totaling $240 should be written off as uncollectible.

(9) The balance in the Prepaid Insurance account relates to a 3-year policy that went into effect on January 1, 1979.

(10) A dividend of $2,000 was declared on July 31, 1979.

(11) The inventory of merchandise on July 31, 1979, was $30,500.

Present adjusting journal entries at July 31, 1979. Use only the accounts listed in the trial balance.

32 (Problems **32** through **34** are adapted from problems by George H. Sorter.) Sortus Company presents the following incomplete trial balances as well as a statement of cash receipts and disbursements:

Debits	1/1/79	12/31/79
Cash	$?	$?
Accounts and Notes Receivable	41,000	50,000
Merchandise Inventory	49,500	52,000
Interest Receivable	700	500
Prepaid Miscellaneous Services	5,200	5,500
Building, Machinery, & Equipment	47,000	47,000
Total Debits	$?	$?
Credits		
Accounts Payable (Miscellaneous Services)	$ 2,500	$ 3,000
Accounts Payable (Merchandise)	41,000	53,000
Property Taxes Payable	1,500	1,000
Accumulated Depreciation	12,000	14,000
Mortgage Payable	30,000	25,000
Capital Stock	25,000	25,000
Retained Earnings	?	?
Total Credits	$211,200	$?

Cash Receipts	**Year 1979**
1. Collection from Credit Customers	$150,000
2. Cash Sales	66,000
3. Collection of Interest	1,000
	$217,000

Less: Cash Disbursements	
4. Payment to Suppliers of Merchandise	$120,000
5. Repayment on Mortgage	5,000
6. Payment of Interest	500
7. Payment to Suppliers of Miscellaneous Services	60,000
8. Payment of Property Taxes	1,200
9. Payment of Dividends	2,000
	$188,700
Increase in Cash Balance for Year	$ 28,300

Prepare a combined statement of income and retained earnings for the year of 1979. (Hint: Set up T-accounts for each of the balance sheet accounts listed in the trial balance and enter the amounts shown on January 1, 1979, and December 31, 1979. Starting with the cash receipts and disbursements for the year, reconstruct the transactions that took place during the year and enter them in the appropriate T-accounts. The effect of earning activities for the year is already reflected in the Retained Earnings account because the trial balance shown is post-closing.)

33 The Sundance Company presents the following trial balance at the beginning of 1979 and the adjusted, preclosing trial balance at the end of 1979.

Debits	**1/1/79**	**12/31/79**
Cash	$ 30,000	$ 25,000
Accounts Receivable	54,000	62,000
Merchandise Inventory	68,000	76,000
Prepayments	4,000	3,000
Land, Buildings, and Equipment	40,000	46,000
Cost of Goods Sold	—	87,000
Interest Expense	—	1,000
Other Operating Expenses	—	32,000
Total Debits	$196,000	$332,000

Credits		
Accumulated Depreciation	$ 24,000	$ 27,000
Interest Payable	1,000	—
Accounts Payable	45,000	51,000
Mortgage Payable	25,000	20,000
Capital Stock	80,000	80,000
Retained Earnings	21,000	19,000
Sales	—	135,000
Total Credits	$196,000	$332,000

All goods and services acquired during the year were purchased on account. All sales were made on account. The Other Operating Expenses account includes depreciation charges and expirations of prepayments.

Prepare a schedule showing all cash transactions for the year 1979. Dividends declared during the year were debited to Retained Earnings. (Hint: Set up T-accounts for each of the accounts listed in the trial balance and enter the amounts shown as of January 1, 1979, and December 31, 1979. Starting with the entries in revenue and expense accounts, reconstruct the transactions which took place during the year and enter the amounts in the appropriate T-accounts. The effect of earning activities for the year is not yet reflected in the Retained Earnings account because the trial balance is preclosing.)

34 The following data relate to the Julius Company:

(1) Postclosing trial balance at December 31, 1979:

Debits

Cash	$ 40,000
Marketable Securities	100,000
Accounts Receivable	100,000
Merchandise Inventory	158,000
Prepayments for Miscellaneous Services	16,600
Land, Buildings, and Equipment	180,000
Total Debits	$594,600

Credits

Accounts Payable (for merchandise)	$110,000
Interest Payable	1,600
Taxes Payable	21,000
Notes Payable (6%, long-term)	80,000
Accumulated Depreciation	62,000
Capital Stock	270,000
Retained Earnings	50,000
Total Credits	$594,600

(2) Income statement for 1979:

Sales		$800,000
Less Expenses:		
Cost of Goods Sold	$520,000	
Depreciation Expense	10,000	
Taxes Expense	20,000	
Other Operating Expenses	201,500	
Interest Expense	4,800	
Total Expenses		756,300
Net Income		$ 43,700
Less: Dividends		20,000
Increase in Retained Earnings		$ 23,700

(3) Summary of cash receipts and disbursements in 1979:

Cash Receipts

Cash Sales	$178,000	
Collections from Credit Customers	580,000	
Total Receipts		$758,000

Cash Disbursements

Payment to Suppliers of Merchandise	$501,000	
Payment to Suppliers of Miscellaneous Services	185,000	
Payment of Taxes	30,000	
Payment of Interest	4,800	
Payment of Dividends	20,000	
Purchase of Marketable Securities	40,000	
Total Disbursements		780,800

Excess of Disbursements over Receipts . . . . $ 22,800

(4) Purchases of merchandise during the period, all on account, were $510,000. All "Other Operating Expenses" were credited to Prepayments.

a Prepare a balance sheet at January 1, 1979.

b What is the interest payment date on the long-term notes?

35 Refer to the Consolidated Statements of Income and Retained Earnings and the Consolidated Balance Sheet for International Corporation in Appendix A at the back of the book. Respond to each of the following questions. Be sure to show supporting computations for your response.

a Assume that marketable securities with a cost of $15,600,000 were sold during 19X1. Determine the acquisition cost of marketable securities purchased during the year.

b Assuming that all sales during 19X1 were made on account and that $14,000,000 of accounts receivable were written off as uncollectible during 19X1, determine the amount of cash collections from customers during the year.

c Refer to the assumptions made in part **b**. Determine the provision for uncollectible accounts during 19X1.

d Assume that "Other Current Liabilities" include dividends payable of $15,300,000 on December 31, 19X0 and $16,700,000 on December 31, 19X1. Determine the amount of dividends paid during 19X1.

e Assume that the cost of plant and equipment acquired during 19X1 totaled $187,517,000. Determine the acquisition cost of plant and equipment sold or otherwise disposed of during the year.

CHAPTER 5
FLOWS OF FUNDS AND THE STATEMENT OF CHANGES IN FINANCIAL POSITION

Chapter 1 pointed out that three major financial statements are generally deemed useful to those interested in understanding the financial activities of a business. Chapter 2 discussed the balance sheet, a snapshot of financial position at a given time. Chapters 3 and 4 considered the income statement, a report on revenues and expenses for a period. This chapter discusses a third major statement, the statement of changes in financial position, which reports flows of funds for a period. The discussion includes the rationale for the statement, the alternative meanings of the term *funds,* and the accounting procedures for preparing the statement. Example statements of changes in financial position appear in Exhibits 1.3, 5.7, 11.2, and A.3 (Appendix A at the back of the book).

RATIONALE FOR THE STATEMENT OF CHANGES IN FINANCIAL POSITION

Solinger Electric Corporation was formed during January 1976 to operate a retail electrical supply business. The net income from operating the business has increased each year since opening, from $3,000 in 1976 to $20,000 in 1979. The firm has had increasing difficulty, however, paying its monthly bills as they become due. Management is puzzled as to how net income could be increasing while at the same time the firm continually finds itself strapped for cash.

The experience of Solinger Electric Corporation is not unusual. Many firms, particularly those experiencing rapid growth, discover that their cash position is deteriorating despite an excellent earnings record. The statement of changes in financial position provides information that is useful in assessing changes in a firm's *liquidity* (its holdings of cash and other assets that could be readily turned into cash), by reporting on the flows of funds into and out of the business during a period.

139

EXHIBIT 5.1
Solinger Electric Corporation
Income Statement and Statement of
Cash Receipts and Disbursements
For the Year 1979

	Income Statement		Statement of Cash Receipts and Disbursements
Sales Revenue	$125,000	Collections from Customers	$ 90,000
Less Expenses:		Less Disbursements:	
Cost of Goods Sold	$ 60,000	To Merchandise Suppliers	$ 50,000
Salaries	20,000	To Employees	19,000
Depreciation	10,000	—	0
Other	15,000	To Other Suppliers	13,000
Total Expenses	$105,000	Total Disbursements to Suppliers and Employees	$ 82,000
Net Income	$ 20,000	Net Cash Inflow from Operations	$ 8,000
		Receipts from Issuing Long-Term Bonds	100,000
		Total Receipts from Operations and Bond Issue	$108,000
		Disbursements for Dividends	$ 10,000
		Disbursements for Equipment	125,000
		Total Disbursements for Dividends and Equipment	$135,000
		Net Decrease in Cash	$ 27,000

Income Flows and Cash Flows

Revenues and expenses reported in the income statement for a period differ in amount from cash receipts and disbursements for the period. (We pointed out this fact in Chapter 3 when we illustrated the cash basis and sales basis of accounting for Allens' Hardware Store in Exhibits 3.1 and 3.2.) Revenues and expenses differ from cash receipts and disbursements for two principal reasons.

1 The accrual basis of accounting is used in determining net income. Thus, the recognition of revenues does not necessarily coincide with the receipts of cash from customers, and the recognition of expenses does not necessarily coincide with disbursements of cash to suppliers, employees, and other creditors.
2 The firm receives cash from sources that are not related directly to the earnings process, such as from issuing capital stock or bonds. Similarly, the firm makes cash disbursements, for such things as dividends or the acquisition of equipment, that are not related directly to generating this period's earnings.

Exhibit 5.1 shows the relationship between the revenues and expenses and the cash receipts and disbursements of Solinger Electric Corporation during 1979. Although sales revenue was $125,000, only $90,000 was collected from customers. The remaining amount of sales was not collected by the end of the year and is reflected in the increase in the Accounts Receivable account on the balance sheet. Likewise, the cost of goods sold was $60,000, but only $50,000 cash was disbursed to suppliers during the year.[1] Similar differences between income flows and cash flows can be seen for salaries and for other expenses. Next, note that there is no specific cash flow associated with depreciation expense during 1979. Cash was used in some earlier periods for the acquisition of buildings and equipment, but the amount of cash spent earlier was not reported then as an expense in accrual accounting. Rather, it was reflected in the balance sheet as an increase in the asset account for buildings and equipment. Now that the buildings and equipment are being used, the cost of the assets' services used is reported as expense of the period.

Thus, although the operating activities generated $20,000 in net income, these activities led to an increase in cash of only $8,000 during 1979. But the firm engaged in other activities affecting cash during 1979, as is reported near the bottom of Exhibit 5.1. Cash in the amount of $100,000 was received from the issue of bonds, $10,000 was disbursed for dividends, and $125,000 was disbursed for the acquisition of new equipment. The result of all of the firm's activities is a decrease in cash of $27,000. Whereas earnings led to an increase in net assets of $20,000, the firm finds itself with $27,000 less cash. The firm is probably in a better overall position at the end of the year than at the beginning although its cash position has deteriorated.

---

[1] We have simplified the illustration. In a realistic situation, some of the receipts would have been from collection of receivables existing at the start of the year. Similarly, some of the payments would have been for liabilities existing at the start of the year.

EXHIBIT 5.2
Solinger Electric Corporation
Statements of Cash Receipts and Disbursements and Increases and Decreases in Working Capital
For the Year 1979

Statement of Cash Receipts and Disbursements

Collections from Customers	$ 90,000
Less Disbursements:	
To Merchandise Suppliers	$ 50,000
To Employees	19,000
To Other Suppliers	13,000
Total Disbursements to Suppliers and Employees	$ 82,000
Net Cash Inflow from Operations	$ 8,000
Receipts from Issuing Long-Term Bonds	100,000
Total Receipts from Operations and Bond Issue	$108,000
Disbursements for Dividends	$ 10,000
Disbursements for Equipment	125,000
Total Disbursements for Dividends and Equipment	$135,000
Net Decrease in Cash	$ 27,000

Statement of Increases and Decreases in Working Capital

Increase in Working Capital from Operations:	
Sales Revenue	$125,000
Less Decreases in Working Capital from Operations:	
Inventory Sold	$ 60,000
Salaries Paid or Earned and Accrued	20,000
Other Expenses Paid or Accrued	15,000
Total Decreases in Working Capital from Operations	$ 95,000
Net Increase in Working Capital from Operations	$ 30,000
Increase in Working Capital from Issuing Long-Term Bonds	100,000
Total Increases in Working Capital from Operations and Bond Issue	$130,000
Decrease in Working Capital for Dividends Declared	$ 10,000
Decrease in Working Capital for Equipment Acquired	125,000
Total Decreases in Working Capital for Dividends Declared and Equipment Acquired	$135,000
Net Decrease in Working Capital	$ 5,000

Cash Flows and Working Capital Flows

The statement of changes in financial position reports on the flows of funds into and out of a business during a period. Funds were viewed as "cash" in Exhibit 5.1. The term "funds" is, however, a general one which can have different meanings, depending on the circumstances. Consider the following two questions which the management of Solinger Electric Corporation might raise:

1 Does the firm have sufficient funds to acquire new equipment tomorrow?
2 Will the firm have sufficient funds to acquire new equipment within the next 6 months?

In answering the first question, management is likely to consider the amount of cash on hand and in its bank account. It would also consider if the equipment could be acquired on account from one of its regular suppliers. In answering the second question, management would, in addition, consider if the firm had marketable securities or other assets that could be sold for cash during the next 6 months. It should be clear, however, that *time is the important factor* in answering the questions about available funds. When the time horizon is short, the meaning of funds must be more restrictive than when the time horizon is longer.

The statements of changes in financial position of most publicly held firms use a definition of funds broader than cash. In most published annual reports, the statement explains the change in the net current asset position, or *working capital,* of the firm. That is, funds are defined as the difference between current assets (cash, readily marketable securities, accounts receivable, inventories and current prepayments) and current liabilities (accounts payable, salaries payable, and other short-term obligations). Current assets are those assets that are either cash or are expected to be turned into cash, or sold, or consumed within the operating cycle, usually 1 year. Current liabilities are obligations expected to be discharged or paid within approximately 1 year. Thus, the amount of working capital at a particular time represents the excess of cash and near-cash assets over near-term claims on these liquid assets. This broader definition of funds is considered by many to provide more useful information to investors and other users of a firm's financial statements than does the more restrictive definition of funds as cash alone. Still, some analysts find cash to be a useful definition of funds. The appendix to this chapter discusses the statement of change in financial position when funds are defined as cash only.

Exhibit 5.2 shows the relationship between the cash receipts or disbursements and the increases or decreases of working capital of Solinger Electric Corporation during 1979. Some revenues, $90,000, are collected in cash, but others, $35,000, are not. The $35,000 of revenues not collected in cash result in an increase in the amount of accounts receivable. Because accounts receivable is a current asset, the effect of revenues is to increase the amount of working capital by $125,000 (= $90,000 + $35,000). Most firms collect their accounts receivable shortly after sale, so the working capital definition of funds may give a more meaningful indication of the effect of revenues on the firm's liquidity.

On the other hand, liquidity is decreased not only when salaries are actually paid, but when obligations to workers are incurred that must be discharged within a short time. Using a working capital definition of funds, rather than a cash definition, may give the reader of financial statements more insight about decreases in a firm's current and near-term liquidity than does a cash definition. For example, the Solinger Electric Corporation's Salaries Expense and Other Operating Expenses resulted in a $32,000 (= $19,000 + $13,000) decrease in cash but a $35,000 reduction in working capital. The current liabilities for these items (for example, Salaries Payable and Accounts Payable to Other Suppliers) must therefore have increased by $3,000 (= $35,000 − $32,000). The firm's liquidity is affected by the need to pay current obligations in the near future, and the obligations should be considered in assessing liquidity.

Note that depreciation expense does not affect either cash flows or working capital flows. Whereas operations generated a net cash inflow of $8,000, working capital from operations increased by $30,000. An increase in accounts receivable caused most of the $22,000 difference.

Objective of the Statement of Changes in Financial Position

The statement of changes in financial position presents information on the sources (increases) and uses (decreases) of working capital during a period. The major sources and uses are depicted graphically in Figure 5.1 and are described below.

1 *Sources—operations.* The excess of revenues increasing working capital over expenses using working capital is the most important source of funds. When

FIGURE 5.1
Sources and Uses of Working Capital

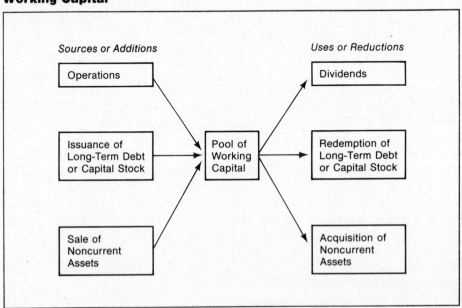

assessed over several years, working capital from operations indicates the extent to which the operating or earnings activities have generated more working capital than is used up. The excess from operations can then be used for dividends, acquisition of buildings and equipment, or repayment of long-term debt if necessary.

2 *Sources—issuance of long-term or capital stock.* In the long run, a firm must generate most of its funds from operating activities. Potential shareholders are not willing to invest in unprofitable firms. Neither are banks willing to lend large amounts of funds to firms that do not generate profits. A potentially profitable firm finds that it can raise funds by issuing shares to owners or by borrowing. The amount of funds that can be generated by issuing stock or by borrowing is limited, however, by the degree of the firm's past success and the marketplace's assessment of the firm's prospects.

3 *Sources—sale of noncurrent assets.* The sale of buildings, equipment, and other noncurrent assets results in an increase in working capital. These sales generally cannot be viewed as a major source of financing for an ongoing firm, since the amounts received from the sales are not likely to be sufficient to replace the assets sold.

4 *Uses—dividends.* Dividends are generally a recurring use of working capital, since most publicly held firms are reluctant to omit the payment of dividends, even during a year of poor earnings performance.

5 *Uses—redemption of long-term debt or capital stock.* In most instances, publicly held firms redeem or pay long-term debt at maturity with the proceeds of another bond issue. Thus, these redemptions often have little effect on the *net* change in working capital. Some firms also occasionally reacquire or redeem their own capital stock for various reasons (discussed in Chapter 11).

6 *Uses—acquisition of noncurrent assets.* The acquisition of noncurrent assets such as buildings and equipment usually represents an important use of working capital. These assets must be replaced as they wear out, and additional noncurrent assets must be acquired if a firm is to grow.

Firms sometimes issue long-term debt or capital stock directly to the vendor, or seller, in acquiring buildings, equipment, or other noncurrent assets. These transactions technically do not affect a working capital account. However, the transaction is reported in the statement of changes in financial position as though two transactions took place: the issuance of long-term debt or capital stock for cash and the immediate use of the cash in the acquisition of noncurrent assets. This is called the *dual transactions assumption.* Such a transaction would normally be disclosed in the statement of changes in financial position as both a source and use of working capital of equal amounts.

Uses of Information in the Statement of Changes in Financial Position

The statement of changes in financial position provides information that may be used in:

1 Assessing changes in a firm's liquidity, and

2   Assessing changes in the structure of a firm's assets and equities.

Liquidity   Perhaps the most important factor not reported on the balance sheet and income statement alone is how the operations of a period affected the liquidity of a firm. It is easy to assume that increased earnings mean increased cash or other liquid assets. Such an assumption may be incorrect. The successful firm may acquire a new plant, so that it has less funds after a good year than before. On the other hand, increased liquidity can accompany reduced earnings. Consider, for example, a firm that is gradually reducing the scope of its operations. Such a firm is likely to report reduced net income or even losses over time. But because it is not replacing plant and equipment, it is likely to be accumulating cash or other liquid assets.

When one uses information from the statement of changes in financial position in assessing changes in liquidity, the working capital definition of funds must be kept in mind. If near-term liquidity is of interest, then funds should be redefined as cash. The procedures for converting working capital provided by operations to cash flow provided by operations are discussed in the appendix to this chapter.

Structure of Assets and Equities   In addition to providing information about changes in a firm's liquidity during a period, the statement of changes in financial position also indicates the major transactions causing changes in the structure of a firm's assets and equities. For example, acquisitions and sales of specific types of noncurrent assets (buildings, equipment, patents) are reported. Likewise, issues and redemptions of long-term debt and capital stock are disclosed. These transactions are difficult to observe by looking at either the income statement or balance sheet alone. For example, the change in the account, "Buildings and Equipment—Net of Accumulated Depreciation," could be attributable to depreciation charges, to acquisition of new buildings and equipment, to disposition of old buildings and equipment, or to a combination of these. The income statement and comparative balance sheets do not provide sufficient information about these three items individually for the reader to disaggregate the net change in the account during the period. A statement of changes in financial position is required to report this information.

In describing the relationship of the statement of changes in financial position to the other basic financial statements, the Accounting Principles Board stated that it

> . . . is related to both the income statement and the balance sheet and provides
> information that can be obtained only partially, or at most in piecemeal form,
> by interpreting them. . . . The [statement of changes in financial position]
> cannot supplant either the income statement or balance sheet but is intended to
> provide information that the other statements either do not provide or provide
> only indirectly about the flow of funds and changes in financial position during
> a period.[2]

---

[2]   APB *Opinion No. 19,* 1971.

ANALYSIS OF THE EFFECTS OF TRANSACTIONS ON WORKING CAPITAL

Algebraic Formulation

The effects of various transactions on working capital might be seen by reexamining the accounting equation. In doing so, we use the following notation:

CA   represents current assets
CL   represents current liabilities
NCA   represents noncurrent assets
NCL   represents noncurrent liabilities
OE   represents owners' equity
Δ represents the change in an item, whether positive (an increase) or negative (a decrease) from the beginning of a period to the end of the period.

The accounting equation states that:

$$\text{Assets} = \text{Liabilities} + \text{Owners' Equity}$$
$$\text{CA} + \text{NCA} = \text{CL} + \text{NCL} + \text{OE}.$$

Furthermore, this equation must be true for balance sheets constructed at both the start of the period and the end of the period. If the start-of-the-period and end-of-the period balance sheets maintain the accounting equation, then the following equation must also be valid:

$$\Delta\text{CA} + \Delta\text{NCA} = \Delta\text{CL} + \Delta\text{NCL} + \Delta\text{OE}.$$

Rearranging terms in this equation, we get the working capital equation:

$$\Delta\text{CA} - \Delta\text{CL} = \Delta\text{NCL} + \Delta\text{OE} - \Delta\text{NCA}.$$

Working capital is equal to current assets minus current liabilities, so the left-hand side of the above equation represents the net change in working capital. The right-hand side of the equation, reflecting changes in all *nonworking* capital accounts, must also be equal in amount to the net change in working capital. The equation states that increases in working capital (left-hand side) are equal to, or caused by, the increases in noncurrent liabilities plus the increase in owners' equity less the increase in noncurrent assets (right-hand side). Next, we illustrate how the changes in the noncurrent accounts on the right-hand side bring about the change in working capital on the left-hand side.

Illustration of Transactions Analysis

We can analyze some typical transactions to demonstrate how the equation is maintained and how working capital is affected.

Assume that the following events occur during 1979 for the Solinger Electric Corporation, considered earlier in Exhibits 5.1 and 5.2.[3]

1   Merchandise costing $70,000 is acquired on account.
2   Merchandise costing $60,000 is sold to customers on account for $125,000.
3   Salaries of $19,000 are paid in cash.
4   Other expenses of $13,000 are paid in cash.
5   Cash collections of customers' accounts total $90,000.
6   Cash payments to suppliers of merchandise total $50,000.
7   Salaries earned but not paid as of December 31, 1979, are accrued, $1,000.
8   Other expenses not paid as of December 31, 1979, are accrued, $2,000.
9   Depreciation for 1979 is recorded, $10,000.
10 Long-term debt is issued for cash, $100,000.
11 Dividends of $10,000 are declared and paid.
12 Equipment costing $125,000 is acquired for cash.

The effects of these transactions on the working capital equation

$$\Delta CA - \Delta CL = \Delta NCL + \Delta OE - \Delta NCA$$

are analyzed in Exhibit 5.3. Working capital decreased by $5,000 during 1979. Both sides of the equation show this net change. The net change in working capital during a period (left-hand side of the equation) can therefore be explained, or analyzed, by focusing on the changes in nonworking capital accounts (right-hand side of the equation). For Solinger Electric Corporation, the net decrease in working capital of $5,000 is explained as follows:

Increases in Working Capital:
  From Operations . . . . $ 30,000
  From Issuing Long-Term Debt   100,000
    Total Increases $130,000
Decreases in Working Capital:
  For Dividends . . . . $ 10,000
  For Acquisition of Equipment   125,000
    Total Decreases $135,000
Net Decrease in Working Capital . . . . $ 5,000

Note several aspects of the transactions analysis in Exhibit 5.3. First, the recording of depreciation for the period does not affect working capital. A noncurrent asset is decreased and owners' equity is decreased. No working capital accounts are affected. (Working capital was reduced in the period when the noncurrent asset was acquired.) Second, some transactions during the year have no net effect on working capital, since they merely result in transfers among working capital accounts. Several examples

---

[3]   To simplify this illustration, we have not provided information on the amounts in balance sheet accounts on January 1, 1979. As will become evident later in the chapter, however, some cash receipts and disbursements represent settlements of beginning-of-the-period receivables and payables.

EXHIBIT 5.3
Analysis of the Effects of Solinger Electric Corporation's Transactions During 1979 on Working Capital and Nonworking Capital Accounts

TRANSACTIONS	Working Capital Changes				Nonworking Capital Changes			
	ΔCA	− ΔCL	=		ΔNCL +	ΔOE −	ΔNCA	
(1) Merchandise costing $70,000 is acquired on account, increasing a current asset and a current liability	$ 70,000	$70,000	=		0 +	0 −	0	
(2) Merchandise costing $60,000 is sold to customers on account for $125,000, increasing a current asset, accounts receivable, by $60,000, decreasing the current asset, inventory, by $60,000, and increasing owners' equity by $65,000	$125,000 (−$60,000)	0	=		0 +	$65,000 −	0	
(3) Salaries of $19,000 are paid in cash, decreasing a current asset and owners' equity	(−$19,000)	0	=		0 +	(−$19,000) −	0	
(4) Other expenses of $13,000 are paid in cash, decreasing a current asset and owners' equity	(−$13,000)	0	=		0 +	(−$13,000) −	0	
(5) Cash collections of customers' accounts total $90,000, increasing the current asset, cash, and decreasing the current asset, accounts receivable	$90,000 (−$90,000)	0	=		0 +	0 −	0	
(6) Cash payments to suppliers of merchandise total $50,000, decreasing a current asset and a current liability	(−$50,000)	(−$50,000)	=		0 +	0 −	0	
(7) Salaries of $1,000 earned but not paid as of December 31, 1979, are accrued, increasing a current liability and decreasing owners' equity	0	$ 1,000	=		0 +	(−$1,000) −	0	
(8) Other expenses of $2,000 not paid as of December 31, 1979, are accrued, increasing a current liability and decreasing owners' equity	0	$ 2,000	=		0 +	(−$2,000) −	0	
(9) Depreciation for 1979 of $10,000 is recorded, decreasing owners' equity and noncurrent assets	0	0	=		0 +	(−$10,000) −	(−$10,000)	
Total from Operations	$ 53,000	$23,000	=		0 +	$20,000 −	(−$10,000)	
(10) Long-term debt is issued for cash, $100,000, increasing a current asset and a noncurrent liability	$100,000	0	=		$100,000 +	0 −	0	
(11) Dividends of $10,000 are declared and paid, decreasing a current asset and owners' equity	(−$10,000)	0	=		0 +	(−$10,000) −	0	
(12) Equipment costing $125,000 is acquired for cash, decreasing a current asset and increasing noncurrent assets	(−$125,000)	0	=		0 +	0 −	$125,000	
Totals	$ 18,000	$23,000	=		$100,000 +	$10,000 −	$115,000	
Net Change in Working Capital and Nonworking Capital		−$5,000	=			−$5,000		

are the purchase of merchandise on account, the collection of accounts receivable, and the payment of accounts payable. These transactions, therefore, do not explain the *change* in working capital during the period.

The information necessary to prepare the statement of changes in financial position could be generated, or developed, using the transactions analysis approach illustrated in Exhibit 5.3. This approach quickly becomes cumbersome, however, as the number of transactions increases. In addition, there are numerous transactions during the year that have no net effect on working capital (for example, collection of accounts receivable, payment of accounts payable). These transactions can effectively be ignored in explaining the change in working capital. In the next section, we describe an alternative procedure for preparing the statement of changes in financial position which uses the T-account discussed in previous chapters.

PREPARATION OF THE STATEMENT OF CHANGES IN FINANCIAL POSITION

As with the balance sheet and income statement, it is not essential that you know how to prepare a statement of changes in financial position in order to use it effectively. Nevertheless, learning how to construct this statement facilitates understanding its rationale and content. In this section, we present a step-by-step procedure for preparing the statement of changes in financial position. We then illustrate this procedure using the transactions of Solinger Electric Corporation for 1979.

The Procedure and an Illustration

Step 1   Obtain balance sheets for the beginning and end of the period covered by the statement of changes in financial position. The comparative balance sheets of Solinger Electric Corporation for December 31, 1978 and 1979, are presented in Exhibit 5.4. Properly prepared balance sheets classify both assets and equities as either current or noncurrent. The distinction between current and noncurrent items is essential to the preparation of the statement of changes in financial position when funds are defined as working capital.

Step 2   Prepare a "T-account" *work sheet*. In preparing a T-account work sheet, first prepare a master T-account titled "Working Capital." This account is merely an aggregation of the individual current asset and current liability accounts into a single summary account. An example of this master T-account is shown in the top portion of Exhibit 5.5. Note that this T-account has sections labeled "From Operations" and "Other (Nonoperating)" sources and uses. Transactions affecting working capital during the period are classified under one of these headings to aid in the preparation of the statement of changes in financial position. This procedure is explained later in this section. The beginning and ending amounts of working capital are then entered in the master T-account. The beginning and ending amounts of working capital for Solinger Electric Corporation are $45,000 (= $90,000 − $45,000) and $40,000

EXHIBIT 5.4
Solinger Electric Corporation
Comparative Balance Sheets for
December 31, 1978 and 1979

ASSETS

	December 31, 1978	December 31, 1979
Current Assets		
Cash	$ 30,000	$ 3,000
Accounts Receivable	20,000	55,000
Merchandise Inventory	40,000	50,000
Total Current Assets	$ 90,000	$108,000
Noncurrent Assets		
Buildings and Equipment (Cost)	$100,000	$225,000
Accumulated Depreciation	(30,000)	(40,000)
Total Noncurrent Assets	$ 70,000	$185,000
Total Assets	$160,000	$293,000

EQUITIES

	December 31, 1978	December 31, 1979
Current Liabilities		
Accounts Payable—Merchandise Suppliers ...	$ 30,000	$ 50,000
Accounts Payable—Other Suppliers	10,000	12,000
Salaries Payable	5,000	6,000
Total Current Liabilities	$ 45,000	$ 68,000
Noncurrent Liabilities		
Bonds Payable	$ 0	$100,000
Owners' Equity		
Capital Stock	$100,000	$100,000
Retained Earnings	15,000	25,000
Total Owners' Equity	$115,000	$125,000
Total Equities	$160,000	$293,000

(= $108,000 − $68,000) respectively. The check marks indicate that the figures are balances. The number at the top of the T-account is the opening balance; the one at the bottom is the closing balance. Note that the master T-account, Working Capital, is another means of expressing the left-hand side of the working capital equation in Exhibit 5.3.

After the master T-account for Working Capital has been prepared (as at the top of Exhibit 5.5), the work sheet is completed by preparing T-accounts for *each* noncurrent asset and noncurrent equity account. Enter the beginning and ending balances in each account for the period as given in Exhibit 5.4. The lower portion of Exhibit 5.5 shows the T-accounts for each noncurrent asset and noncurrent equity. Note that these individual T-accounts are another means of expressing the right-hand side of the working capital equation in Exhibit 5.3.

EXHIBIT 5.5
T-Account Work Sheet for
Solinger Electric Corporation

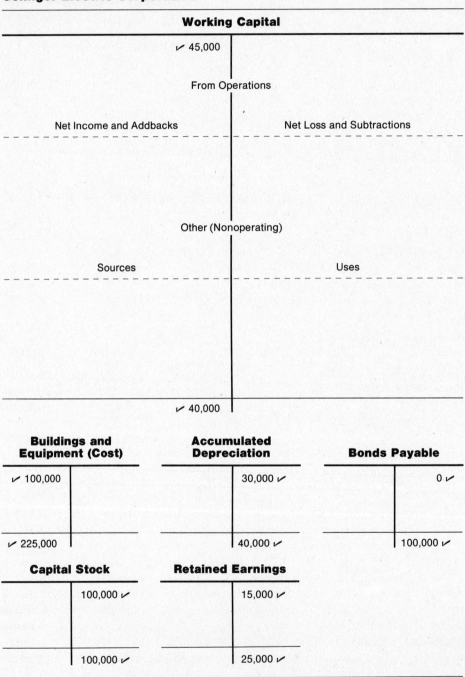

Working Capital

✔ 45,000	

From Operations

Net Income and Addbacks	Net Loss and Subtractions

Other (Nonoperating)

Sources	Uses

✔ 40,000	

Buildings and Equipment (Cost)	**Accumulated Depreciation**	**Bonds Payable**
✔ 100,000	30,000 ✔	0 ✔
✔ 225,000	40,000 ✔	100,000 ✔

Capital Stock	**Retained Earnings**
100,000 ✔	15,000 ✔
100,000 ✔	25,000 ✔

The T-account work sheet for Solinger Electric Corporation after completion of Step 2 is shown in Exhibit 5.5.

Step 3   Explain the change in the master working capital account between the beginning and end of the period by explaining or accounting for the change in the balance of each nonworking capital account during the period. This step is accomplished by *reconstructing the entries originally recorded in the accounts during the period.* The reconstructed entries are written in the appropriate T-accounts. You will see that once the net change in each of the nonworking capital accounts has been accounted for, sufficient information will have been generated to account for the net change in working capital. That is, if you have explained the changes in the right-hand side of the working capital equation, you will also have explained the causes of the changes in working capital itself on the left-hand side.

The process of reconstructing the transactions during the year is usually easiest if supplementary information is accounted for first. Assume that the following information is obtained concerning the Solinger Electric Corporation for 1979:

1   Net income is $20,000.
2   Depreciation expense is $10,000.
3   Dividends declared and paid total $10,000.

The analytical entry to record the information concerning net income is

```
(1) Working Capital (Operations—Net Income) .........................   20,000
       Retained Earnings ...........................................              20,000
    Entry recorded in T-account work sheet.
```

To understand this entry, review the process of recording revenues and expenses and the closing entries for those temporary accounts from Chapter 4. All of the journal entries that together record the process of earning $20,000 net income are equivalent to the following single journal entry:

```
Net Assets (= All Assets − All Liabilities) ............................   20,000
    Retained Earnings ...............................................              20,000
Summary entry equivalent to recording earnings of $20,000.
```

In the analytic entry (1) above, the debit results in showing a provisional increase in working capital from operations in an amount equal to net income for the period. In the summary journal entry, we debit Net Assets. The initial assumption at this stage of preparing the statement of changes in financial position is that all of the net assets generated by the earnings process were *current* net assets (or working capital).

Some portion of the items recognized as expenses and deducted in determining net income does not, however, decrease working capital (refer to Exhibit 5.2). The portion of the expenses that does not affect working capital is added to the provisional increase in working capital to calculate the net amount of working capital from operations. Such an adjustment for an expense not using working capital is illustrated for depreciation expense in entry (2).

(2) Working Capital (Operations—Depreciation Expense Addback)   10,000
      Accumulated Depreciation   10,000
      Entry recorded in T-account work sheet.

Since depreciation expense was deducted in calculating net income but did not reduce working capital, the amount of depreciation expense must be added back to net income in determining the amount of working capital provided by operations. The results of entries (1) and (2) might be summarized as follows:

Working Capital (Operations—Net Income and Addbacks)   30,000
      Retained Earnings   20,000
      Accumulated Depreciation   10,000

This combined entry shows that the operating activities of Solinger Electric Corporation resulted in a $30,000 increase in working capital during 1979. That is, revenues increasing working capital exceeded expenses using working capital (total expenses less depreciation expense) by $30,000.

    The supplementary information concerning dividends declared and paid of $10,000 is recorded as follows:

(3) Retained Earnings   10,000
      Working Capital (Other Uses—Dividends)   10,000
      Entry recorded in T-account work sheet.

Once the supplementary information has been reflected in the T-accounts, it is necessary to make inferences about the reasons for the remaining changes in the nonworking capital accounts. (If the statement of changes in financial position were being prepared for an actual firm, such inferences might not be necessary, since sufficient information regarding the change in each account is likely to be available from the firm's accounting records.) The Buildings and Equipment (Cost) account shows a net increase of $125,000 (= $225,000 − $100,000). Because we have no other information, we must assume or deduce that buildings and equipment costing $125,000 were acquired during the year. The analytical entry is

(4) Buildings and Equipment (Cost)   125,000
      Working Capital (Other Uses—Acquisitions of Buildings
          and Equipment)   125,000
      Entry recorded in T-account work sheet.

The Bonds Payable account increased $100,000 during 1979. Because we have no other information, we must assume or deduce that long-term bonds were issued during the year. The analytical entry is

(5) Working Capital (Other Sources—Long-Term Bond Issue)   100,000
      Bonds Payable   100,000
      Entry recorded in T-account work sheet.

Exhibit 5.6 presents the T-account work sheet for Solinger Electric Corporation for 1979 after analytic entry (5). All changes in the nonworking capital T-accounts have been explained. If the work has been done correctly, the change in the Working Capital account has also been explained by the entries in the master Working Capital account.

EXHIBIT 5.6
T-Account Work Sheet for Solinger Electric Corporation

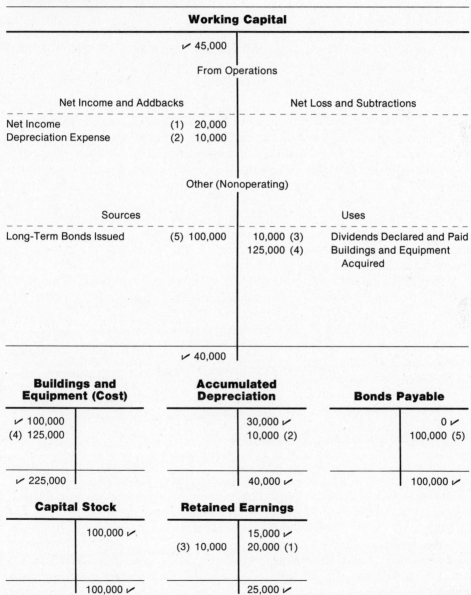

Working Capital

✔ 45,000

From Operations

Net Income and Addbacks			Net Loss and Subtractions
Net Income	(1)	20,000	
Depreciation Expense	(2)	10,000	

Other (Nonoperating)

Sources					Uses
Long-Term Bonds Issued	(5)	100,000	10,000	(3)	Dividends Declared and Paid
			125,000	(4)	Buildings and Equipment Acquired

✔ 40,000

Buildings and Equipment (Cost)		**Accumulated Depreciation**		**Bonds Payable**	
✔ 100,000			30,000 ✔		0 ✔
(4) 125,000			10,000 (2)		100,000 (5)
✔ 225,000			40,000 ✔		100,000 ✔

Capital Stock		**Retained Earnings**	
	100,000 ✔		15,000 ✔
		(3) 10,000	20,000 (1)
	100,000 ✔		25,000 ✔

Exhibit 5.6 shows the sum of the debit entries in the Working Capital account to be $130,000, whereas the sum of the credit entries is $135,000. There is an excess of credits over debits in the account of $5,000, which accounts for the decrease in working capital from $45,000 to $40,000 during the year.

We can see in Exhibit 5.6 that operations provided working capital of $30,000 (= $20,000 + $10,000), whereas new bond issues provided $100,000 of working capital. Working capital of $135,000 was used: $10,000 for dividends and $125,000 for new buildings and equipment.

Step 4   The final step is the preparation of the formal statement of changes in financial position. The statement for Solinger Electric Corporation is shown in Exhibit 5.7. Section I presents the sources and uses of working capital. This section of the statement is prepared directly from information in the master Working Capital account.

Section II of the Statement of Changes in Financial Position analyzes the changes in the individual current asset and current liability accounts. That is, the manner in which the net change in working capital (explained in Section I of the statement) affects the various working capital accounts is analyzed in Section II. The information needed for preparing Section II is obtained from the comparative balance sheets in Exhibit 5.4.

The information in Section II of the statement is necessary for a complete assessment of a firm's liquidity and changes in the structure of its assets and equities. The net change explained in Section I can result from the offsetting of much larger increases and decreases in individual current asset and current liability accounts.

For example, cash decreased by $27,000, whereas accounts receivable increased by $35,000 during the year. Together, this represents an increase of $8,000 in the firm's most liquid assets. However, most of the increased liquidity does not reflect cash immediately available to pay liabilities or to make purchases. Instead, cash must first be collected from customers. Financial statement readers interested in assessing changes in the structure of the firm's working capital would find the information in Section II of the statement of changes in financial position to be useful.

Interpretation of the Statement

In published annual reports, the amount of working capital provided by operations is typically derived by starting with net income and then adding back expenses that do not use working capital and subtracting revenues, if any, that do not provide working capital. This format is illustrated in the statement for Solinger Electric Corporation in Exhibit 5.7. Because depreciation expense is added to net income to determine working capital provided by operations, some readers of financial statements incorrectly conclude that depreciation expense is a source of working capital. As Exhibit 5.3 illustrated, the recording of depreciation expense does not affect a working capital account. A noncurrent asset is decreased and an owners' equity account is decreased. Working capital is not affected.

EXHIBIT 5.7
Solinger Electric Corporation
Statement of Changes in
Financial Position
For the Year 1979

SECTION I. SOURCES AND USES OF WORKING CAPITAL

Sources of Working Capital:

Operations

Net Income	$20,000	
Add Back Expenses Not Using Working Capital:		
Depreciation	10,000	
Total Sources from Operations		$ 30,000
Proceeds from Long-Term Bonds Issued		100,000
Total Sources of Working Capital		$130,000

Other Uses of Working Capital:

Dividends	$ 10,000
Acquisition of Buildings and Equipment	125,000
Total Uses of Working Capital	$135,000
Net Decrease in Working Capital During the Year (Sources Minus Uses)	$ 5,000

SECTION II. ANALYSIS OF CHANGES IN WORKING CAPITAL ACCOUNTS

Current Asset Item Increases (Decreases):

Cash	$(27,000)	
Accounts Receivable	35,000	
Merchandise Inventory	10,000	
Net Increase (Decrease) in Current Asset Items		$ 18,000

Current Liability Increases (Decreases):

Accounts Payable—Merchandise Suppliers	$20,000	
Accounts Payable—Other Suppliers	2,000	
Salaries Payable	1,000	
Net Increase (Decrease) in Current Liability Items		23,000
Net Decrease in Working Capital During the Year (Net Increase in Current Liability Items Minus Net Increase in Current Asset Items)		$ 5,000

Working capital from operations results from selling goods and services to customers. If no sales are made, then there will be no working capital provided by operations regardless of how large the depreciation charge may be. Remember, depreciation is *not* a source of working capital. Rather, it is an expense that reduces net income, but does not use working capital.

Depreciation Is Not a Source of Funds   Refer to the income statement of Solinger Electric Corporation (Exhibit 5.1) and the working capital from operations section of the statement of changes in financial position (Exhibit 5.7). These are reproduced in condensed form in Exhibit 5.8. Ignore income taxes for a moment. Suppose that depreciation for 1979 had been $25,000 rather than $10,000. Then the condensed income statement and working capital from operations would appear as in Exhibit 5.9. Note that the total working capital from operations remains $30,000, which is the difference between revenues and all expenses that did use working capital. The only effects on working capital of transactions involving long-term assets are that: (1) working capital is used when a long-term asset is acquired, and (2) working capital is provided when the asset is sold. Do not commit the common error in interpreting the statement of changes in financial position of thinking that depreciation is a source of funds.

EXHIBIT 5.8
Solinger Electric Corporation
Year 1979
Depreciation $10,000

Income Statement		Working Capital from Operations	
Revenues	$125,000	Net Income	$20,000
Expenses Except Depreciation . . .	(95,000)	Add Back Expenses Not Using	
	$ 30,000	Working Capital:	
Depreciation Expense	(10,000)	Depreciation	10,000
		Total Working Capital from	
Net Income.	$ 20,000	Operations	$30,000

EXHIBIT 5.9
Solinger Electric Corporation
Year 1979
Depreciation $25,000

Income Statement		Working Capital from Operations	
Revenues	$125,000	Net Income	$ 5,000
Expenses Except Depreciation . . .	(95,000)	Add Back Expenses Not Using	
	$ 30,000	Working Capital:	
		Depreciation	25,000
Depreciation Expense	(25,000)	Total Working Capital from	
Net Income.	$ 5,000	Operations	$30,000

At a more sophisticated level, however, when income taxes are a factor, depreciation does affect funds flow. Depreciation is a factor in the determination of net income reported in the financial statement. Depreciation is also a deduction from otherwise taxable income on tax returns. The larger is depreciation on tax returns, the smaller is taxable income, and the smaller is the current payment for income taxes. We discuss the effect of depreciation on income taxes in Chapters 9 and 10.

Alternative Presentation of Working Capital from Operations   An alternative procedure for deriving working capital from operations is to list all revenue items that provide working capital and then subtract all expense items that use working capital. This approach is illustrated in the right-hand column of Exhibit 5.2 (and in Exhibit 1.3). This alternative presentation is appealing to us because depreciation expense does not appear as an element in the determination of working capital provided by operations. The latter presentation, although acceptable, is rarely used in published financial statements.

Extension of the Illustration

The illustration for Solinger Electric Corporation considered so far in this chapter is simpler than the typical published statement of changes in financial position in at least four respects:

1 There are only a few balance sheet accounts whose changes are to be explained.
2 Several types of more complex transactions that affect the sources of working capital from operations are not involved.
3 Each transaction recorded in step 3 involves only one debit and one credit.
4 Each explanation of a nonworking capital account change involves only one transaction, except for the Retained Earnings account.

Most of the complications that arise in interpreting published statements of changes in financial position arise from accounting events that are not discussed until later chapters. As we discuss these transactions, we shall illustrate their effects on the statement of changes in financial position. We can illustrate now one complication caused by a supplementary disclosure. Suppose that the firm sold some of its buildings and equipment during the year. For now, and until we address the issue again in Chapter 9, we assume that the firm disposes of existing buildings and equipment at their book value; the cash proceeds from disposition are equal to acquisition cost less accumulated depreciation of the assets. With this assumption, there will be no gain or loss on disposition.

Let us reconsider Solinger Electric Corporation with the following new information. Solinger Electric Corporation sold some equipment during 1979. This equipment cost $10,000 and was sold for $3,000 at a time when accumulated depreciation on the equipment sold was $7,000. The actual entry made during the year to record the sale of the equipment was as follows:

Cash	3,000	
Accumulated Depreciation	7,000	
Buildings and Equipment (Cost)		10,000

Journal entry for sale of equipment.

Assume that the comparative balance sheets as shown in Exhibit 5.4 are correct and thus that the net decrease in working capital for 1979 is still $5,000. The entries in the T-accounts must be altered to reflect this new information. The following entry in the T-accounts is required to recognize the effect of the sale of equipment:

(1a) Working Capital (Other Sources—Proceeds from Sale of Equipment)   3,000
     Accumulated Depreciation   7,000
       Buildings and Equipment (Cost)   10,000
     Entry recorded in T-account work sheet.

The debit to Working Capital (Other Sources—Proceeds from Sale of Equipment) shows the proceeds of the sale.

As a result of entry (1a), the T-accounts for Buildings and Equipment (Cost) and Accumulated Depreciation would appear as follows:

Buildings and Equipment (Cost)		Accumulated Depreciation	
✔ 100,000			30,000 ✔
	10,000 (1a)	(1a) 7,000	
✔ 225,000			40,000 ✔

When it comes time to explain the change in the account, Buildings and Equipment (Cost), the T-account indicates that there is an increase of $125,000 and a credit entry (1a) of $10,000 to recognize the sale of equipment. The net increase in the Buildings and Equipment (Cost) account can only be accounted for, given the decrease already entered, by assuming that new buildings and equipment have been acquired during the period for $135,000.

The reconstructed entry to complete the explanation of the change in this account would be as follows:

(4a) Buildings and Equipment (Cost)   135,000
     Working Capital (Other Uses—Acquisition of Buildings
       and Equipment)   135,000
     Entry recorded in T-account work sheet.

Likewise, when the change in the T-account for Accumulated Depreciation is explained, there is a net credit change of $10,000 and a debit entry (1a) of $7,000 to recognize the sale. Thus, the depreciation charge for 1979 must have been $17,000. The reconstructed entry to complete the explanation of the change in the Accumulated Depreciation account would be as follows:

(2a) Working Capital (Operations—Depreciation Expense Addback)   17,000
     Accumulated Depreciation   17,000
     Entry recorded in T-account work sheet.

A revised T-account work sheet for Solinger Electric Corporation incorporating the new information on the sale of equipment is presented in Exhibit 5.10.

EXHIBIT 5.10
Revised T-Account Work Sheet
For Solinger Electric Corporation

Working Capital

✓ 45,000		

From Operations

Net Income and Addbacks			Net Loss and Subtractions
Net Income	(1)	20,000	
Depreciation Expense	(2a)	17,000	

Other (Nonoperating)

Sources				Uses
Sale of Equipment	(1a)	3,000		
Long-Term Bonds Issued	(5)	100,000	10,000 (3)	Dividends Declared and Paid
			135,000 (4a)	Buildings and Equipment Acquired

✓ 40,000

Buildings and Equipment (Cost)		Accumulated Depreciation		Bonds Payable	
✓ 100,000			30,000 ✓		0 ✓
(4a) 135,000	10,000 (1a)	(1a) 7,000	17,000 (2a)		100,000 (5)
✓ 225,000			40,000 ✓		100,000 ✓

Capital Stock		Retained Earnings	
	100,000		15,000 ✓
		(3) 10,000	20,000 (1)
	100,000 ✓		25,000 ✓

STATEMENT OF CHANGES IN FINANCIAL POSITION

Format of the Statement of Changes in Financial Position in Published Financial Statements

The statement of changes in financial position usually explains and discloses the changes in working capital (current assets minus current liabilities) during the period. The statement also discloses other significant changes in financial position, even though the transactions or events do not affect working capital directly. For example, the issue of capital stock in the acquisition of land would be an event disclosed in the statement.

Classification Within the Statement of Changes in Financial Position

The sources and uses of working capital or financial resources presented in the first section of the statement of changes in financial position might be classified as being related to

1 Earnings activities
2 Financing activities
3 Income distributions of the firm
4 Investing activities.

The first item generally reported on the statement is the amount of working capital provided (or used) by operations. This item indicates whether the earnings activities of the firm (that is, acquiring and selling goods or services) have resulted in an increase or decrease in working capital. If a firm is to continue operating effectively over a period of years, the operating activities must generate sufficient working capital so that inventory can be replaced and creditors' claims can be paid. Operations must also generate, or provide, working capital so that plant and equipment can be replaced as they wear out. Working capital provided (or used) by operations is therefore an important indicator of the firm's financial health, particularly when working capital flows are assessed over several years.

Working capital from operations is separated into continuing and discontinued operations much as the income statement itself is separated. For example, as explained in Note 2 of Appendix A on page 583, International Corporation planned to dispose of its trade book publishing and book club activities. The income statement effects of these activities are separately reported in the income statement on page 579 in Exhibit A.1. The statement of changes in financial position also reflects the decision to discontinue the book publishing and book club activities. See Exhibit A.3 on page 581.

If a firm reports an extraordinary gain or loss in the income statement, then the effects of the extraordinary item (net of income tax effects) on working capital must be disclosed separately in the statement of changes in financial position. For example, the uninsured loss of merchandise inventory as a result of a tornado would likely represent an extraordinary loss on the income statement and an extraordinary use of working capital on the statement of changes in financial position.

The sources and uses of working capital from financing activities include the issuance and redemption of common or preferred stock or long-term bonds. The sources and uses of working capital from investing activities include the purchase and sale of land, buildings, equipment, and other noncurrent assets. The declaration of dividends (income distribution) is a use of working capital.

Whereas the first section of the statement of changes in financial position presents the sources and uses of working capital or financial resources, the second section summarizes the change in each of the working capital accounts.

A comprehensive example of a statement of changes in financial position for International Corporation is presented in Exhibit A.3 on page 581.

SUMMARY

Generally accepted accounting principles require that a statement of changes in financial position be presented whenever a firm presents an income statement and a balance sheet. The statement of changes in financial position reports on flows of funds into and out of a business during a period. The critical element in defining funds is the time horizon relevant for measuring liquidity. The shorter the time horizon, the more restrictive the definition. Funds are usually defined as working capital (current assets minus current liabilities), but occasionally funds may be defined simply as cash. The appendix to this chapter deals with the more restrictive definition of funds as cash only.

The statement of changes in financial position discloses the sources of funds from operations separately from the nonoperating sources and uses. The primary source of funds is usually operations. Understanding the notion of funds provided by operations is particularly important to understanding the statement of changes in financial position. Net income is derived from revenues and expenses computed on an accrual basis. The statement of changes in financial position converts net income from the accrual basis to a report of funds flows. Funds provided by operations are rarely equal to net income.

The statement of changes in financial position is basically derived from an analysis of changes in balance sheet accounts during the accounting period. If the double-entry recording process has been applied properly, the net change in funds (working capital or cash or whatever) accounts during the period will equal the net change in all nonfunds accounts. By reconstructing the entries made in nonfunds accounts and explaining their net change during the period, the net change in the funds accounts is also explained.

The format of the statement of changes in financial position is organized in two sections. The sources and uses of funds are presented first, followed by an analysis of the changes in the individual funds accounts. Most published statements of changes in financial position show the derivation of funds provided by operations by beginning with net income and then adding expenses that do not use funds and subtracting revenues that do not provide funds.

APPENDIX 5.1
Cash as Funds

The illustrations for Solinger Electric Corporation in the chapter used working capital as the definition of funds. As we discussed in the chapter, there are several possible definitions of funds. Time is the critical dimension in deciding upon the appropriate definition. The shorter the time horizon, the more liquid an item must be before it can be considered to be funds. At the extreme short end, when the horizon must be as short as possible, cash is the only item of funds.

A few corporations use cash (or cash and marketable securities) as their definition, although most major corporations define funds as working capital. There appears to be a trend among major corporations toward a more restrictive definition of funds, one that excludes some items from working capital. For example, within the last decade the General Electric Company decided to remove inventories from its definition of funds. GE is aware that for every dollar's worth of inventory held for a year, the company incurs costs of around $0.25 for storage, insurance, and the like. GE's management knows that it is good policy, other things being equal, to reduce the amount of inventory carried. GE's management consciously undertook a policy of holding down inventories. The corporation felt it was more, rather than less, liquid as a result, since less cash was tied up in inventory. In order to reflect this increase in liquidity in the financial statements, GE removed inventory from its definition of funds on the statement of changes in financial position. When GE increases inventory, it now shows that increase as a *use of funds*.

Not many firms use a definition of funds as restrictive as cash only, but many financial analysts are interested in a cash-only definition of funds. In this section, we illustrate the procedures for constructing a statement of changes in financial position when cash is the only component of funds. The procedures closely parallel those illustrated in the chapter for funds defined as working capital. Using any definition of funds intermediate on the liquidity spectrum between cash and working capital is easy once one understands how to treat the two extreme points.

Using the same symbols introduced earlier on page 147, the funds equation with a cash-only definition of funds becomes

$$\Delta\text{Cash} = \Delta\text{CL} + \Delta\text{NCL} + \Delta\text{OE} - \Delta\text{CA (Other than Cash)} - \Delta\text{NCA}.$$

One important purpose of the statement of changes in financial position is to enable the reader to separate those sources of funds caused by ongoing operations of the firm from those resulting from the sale of assets and financing transactions such as security issues. Most analysts rightly think that, over the long run, a firm that cannot generate funds from operating activities will not survive. The importance of funds from operations is highlighted in the statement of changes in financial position by the separation of operating sources from nonoperating sources of funds. Just as before, increases in asset accounts other than cash are a *use* of funds, whereas increases in liabilities are a *source* of funds.

Most of the changes in current asset and current liability accounts should be considered as operating sources or uses of cash, but there are occasional exceptions. For example, an increase in the balance in the liability account, Dividends Payable, reduces the use of cash for dividends declared rather than reducing the use of cash for operating purposes.

Similarly, a change in the marketable securities balance might be excluded from the operating section of the statement. Other special items may also be exceptions, but for each such item, the facts of the case should be scrutinized to see if an exception to the general rule should be made. The general rule is that changes in working capital items other than cash are included in the operating section of the statement of changes in financial position if "funds" is defined as cash.

The Procedure and an Illustration

We illustrate the construction of a statement of changes in financial position with a cash-only definition of funds for the Solinger Electric Corporation for 1979. The steps outlined below parallel those described earlier on pages 151–156 for a working capital definition of funds.

Step 1   Obtain balance sheets for the beginning and end of the period. The comparative balance sheets of Solinger Electric Corporation for December 31, 1978 and 1979, are presented on page 151 in Exhibit 5.4.

Step 2   Prepare a T-account work sheet. First prepare a master account titled *Cash*. This account will show the change in cash for the period and after the work sheet is complete, it will show the causes of that change in cash. The master account will show sections "From Operations" and "Other (Nonoperating)" to separate the two kinds of transactions affecting cash.

After the master T-account for Cash has been prepared (as at the top of Exhibit 5.11), the work sheet is completed by preparing T-accounts for *each noncash account*. These accounts are shown at the bottom of Exhibit 5.11 for the Solinger Electric Company. The beginning and ending balances in the accounts for the period are entered in each of the separate T-accounts. The T-account work sheet for Solinger Electric Company after completion of step 2 is shown in Exhibit 5.11.

Step 3   Explain the change in the master Cash account by explaining the changes in the noncash accounts. This step is accomplished by reconstructing on the work sheet the entries originally recorded in the accounts during the periods. The reconstructed entries are written in the appropriate T-accounts. Once the net change in each of the noncash accounts has been explained, then sufficient information will have been generated to explain the net change in cash. We start with the supplementary information, which, for the Solinger Electric Corporation for 1979, is

1 Net income is $20,000.
2 Depreciation expense is $10,000.
3 Dividends declared and paid total $10,000.

EXHIBIT 5.11
T-Account Work Sheet for
Solinger Electric Corporation
(Using Cash as Funds)

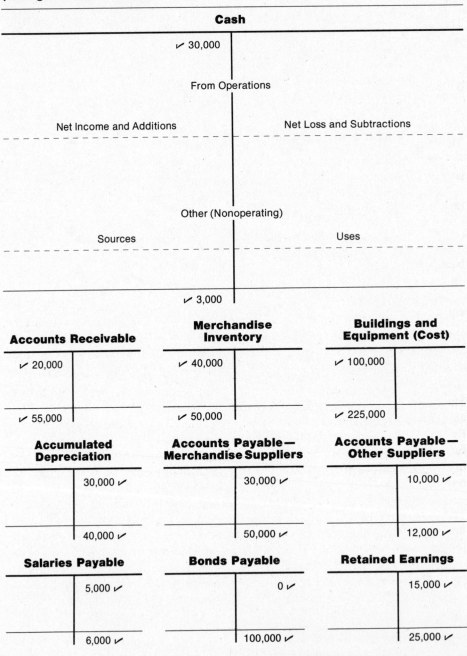

The analytical entry to record the information concerning net income is

(1) Cash (Operations—Net Income) 20,000
      Retained Earnings 20,000
    Entry recorded in T-account work sheet.

The reason for this entry is the same as that given under entry (1) on page 153. You may refer to that explanation for review if it seems necessary.

The supplementary information about depreciation is recorded with entry (2):

(2) Cash (Operations—Depreciation Expense Addback) 10,000
      Accumulated Depreciation 10,000
    Entry recorded in T-account work sheet.

This entry is explained in an earlier example, on page 154.

The supplementary information concerning dividends declared and paid of $10,000 is recorded as follows:

(3) Retained Earnings 10,000
      Cash (Other Uses—Dividends) 10,000
    Entry recorded in T-account work sheet.

Next, we explain the changes in the noncash accounts in order of their appearance on the work sheet.

The Accounts Receivable account shows an increase of $35,000. The analytical entry to record this assumed information in the work sheet is

(4) Accounts Receivable 35,000
      Cash (Operations—Subtractions) 35,000
    Entry recorded in T-account work sheet.

The operations of the period led to increased sales. Not all of these sales resulted in an increase in cash. Some of the increase in sales resulted in an increase in Accounts Receivable. Here, we are defining funds as Cash only; thus not all sales increased funds. Because we start the statement of changes in financial position with Net Income, in deriving the amount of Cash from Operations we must *subtract that portion of revenues not producing cash,* such as the increase in Accounts Receivable.

The next noncash account showing a change is that for Merchandise Inventory. That account shows an increase during the year of $10,000. As the operations of the firm have expanded, so has the amount carried in inventory. The analytical entry in the work sheet to explain the change in Merchandise Inventory is

(5) Merchandise Inventory 10,000
      Cash (Operations—Subtractions) 10,000
    Entry recorded in T-account work sheet.

Solinger Electric Corporation found it necessary to increase the amount of inventory carried to make possible increased future sales. An increase in inventory is ordinarily an operating use of cash. Because we start the statement of changes in financial position with net income, in deriving cash from operations we must subtract from net income the incremental investment in inventories during the year.

The next noncash account showing a change is that for Buildings and Equipment (Cost). The entry here and the reason for it are essentially the same as in the earlier example [see entry (4) on page 154]:

```
(6) Buildings and Equipment (Cost) ................................   125,000
        Cash (Other Uses—Acquisitions of Buildings and Equipment) .......          125,000
        Entry recorded in T-account work sheet.
```

Acquisition of buildings and equipment is a nonoperating use of cash.

The next noncash account showing a change is that for Accounts Payable—Merchandise Suppliers. As the amounts carried in inventory have increased, so has the amount owed to suppliers of inventory. The analytical entry to explain the increase in the amount of Accounts Payable—Merchandise Suppliers is

```
(7) Cash (Operations—Net Income and Additions) ......................   20,000
        Accounts Payable—Merchandise Suppliers ........................          20,000
        Entry recorded in T-account work sheet.
```

Ordinarily, one thinks of using cash to acquire inventory. Suppliers who allow us to pay later for goods and services received now are effectively supplying us with cash. Thus an increase in the amount of accounts payable for inventory results from a transaction where inventory increased but cash did not decrease, which is equivalent to saying that an increase in payables is a source of cash, even if only a temporary one.[4] The increase in cash resulting from increased payables for inventory is an operating source of funds.

The next noncash account showing a change is Accounts Payable—Other Suppliers. As the scope of operations has increased, so has the amount owed to others. The analytical entry to explain the increase in the amount of Accounts Payable—Other Suppliers is

```
(8) Cash (Operations—Net Income and Additions) ........................   2,000
        Accounts Payable—Other Suppliers ................................          2,000
        Entry recorded in T-account work sheet.
```

The reasoning behind this entry is the same as for entry (7), just above. Creditors

---

[4]   The actual degree to which such a source is temporary is controversial. We are inclined to argue that when a growing business increases the amount of accounts payable, that increase is likely to result in a relatively permanent increase in funds provided by creditors. A growing firm is likely to increase the amount of payables even more in subsequent periods as operations continue to increase. Arguments of this sort are beyond the scope of the current discussion; we return to them in Chapter 10.

who permit a firm to owe them more are effectively a source of cash. The same reasoning applies to our own employees who are owed an increased amount of Salaries Payable, the next noncash account showing a change. The analytic entry to record the increase in Salaries Payable is

(9) Cash (Operations—Net Income and Additions) 1,000
    Salaries Payable 1,000
    Entry recorded in T-account work sheet.

Employees who do not demand immediate payment for salaries earned have provided their employer with cash, at least temporarily.

The final noncash account showing a change not yet explained is Bonds Payable. It shows a net increase of $100,000 for the year. The analytic entry in the T-account work sheet to explain the change in bonds payable is

(10) Cash (Other Sources—Long-Term Bond Issue) 100,000
    Bonds Payable 100,000

The explanation of this entry is the same as for entry (5) on page 154 in the earlier example.

Exhibit 5.12 presents the T-account work sheet for a cash-only definition of funds for Solinger Electric Company for 1979. All changes in the noncash T-accounts have been explained with the 10 entries. If the work is correct, the causes of the change in the Cash account have been presented in the entries in the master Cash account.

Step 4   The final step is the preparation of a formal statement of changes in financial position. The statement for Solinger Electric Corporation is presented in Exhibit 5.13. It is prepared directly from the information provided in the master T-account for Cash in the completed work sheet.

Converting Working Capital Provided by Operations to Cash Provided by Operations

The preceding sections have illustrated the construction of the statement of changes in financial position, first using a working capital definition of funds and then using a cash definition of funds. Most published financial statements use working capital as the definition of funds. If the analyst wishes to convert such a statement to one using a cash definition, then the analyst can use the procedures illustrated earlier or the following shortcuts.

1 Begin with the amount of working capital provided by operations as previously determined.
2 Add the amount of the change in current operating accounts (other than cash) that experienced a net credit change during the period. These are decreases in receivables, inventories, and prepayments and increases in current operating liability accounts.

EXHIBIT 5.12
T-Account Work Sheet for Solinger Electric Corporation (Using Cash as Funds)

Cash

✓ 30,000

From Operations

Net Income and Additions				Net Loss and Subtractions
Net Income	(1)	20,000	35,000 (4)	Increased Accounts Receivable
Depreciation Expense	(2)	10,000	10,000 (5)	Increased Merchandise Inventory
Increased Accounts Payable to Merchandise Suppliers	(7)	20,000		
Increased Accounts Payable to Other Suppliers	(8)	2,000		
Increased Salaries Payable	(9)	1,000		

Other (Nonoperating)

Sources				Uses
Long-Term Bonds Issued	(10)	100,000	10,000 (3)	Dividends Declared and Paid
			125,000 (6)	Buildings and Equipment Acquired

✓ 3,000

Accounts Receivable	
✓ 20,000	
(4) 35,000	
✓ 55,000	

Merchandise Inventory	
✓ 40,000	
(5) 10,000	
✓ 50,000	

Buildings and Equipment (Cost)	
✓ 100,000	
(6) 125,000	
✓ 225,000	

Accumulated Depreciation	
	30,000 ✓
	10,000 (2)
	40,000 ✓

Merchandise Suppliers	
	30,000 ✓
	20,000 (7)
	50,000 ✓

Accounts Payable Other Suppliers	
	10,000 ✓
	2,000 (8)
	12,000 ✓

Salaries Payable	
	5,000 ✓
	1,000 (9)
	6,000 ✓

Bonds Payable	
	0 ✓
	100,000 (10)
	100,000 ✓

Retained Earnings	
	15,000 ✓
(3) 10,000	20,000 (1)
	25,000 ✓

EXHIBIT 5.13
Solinger Electric Corporation
Statement of Changes in
Financial Position
Cash Definition of Funds
For the Year 1979

Sources of Cash
Operations

Net Income	$20,000	
Additions:		
Depreciation Expense Not Using Cash	10,000	
Increased Accounts Payable		
To Suppliers of Merchandise	20,000	
To Other Suppliers	2,000	
Increased Salaries Payable	1,000	
Subtractions:		
Increased Accounts Receivable	(35,000)	
Increased Merchandise Inventory	(10,000)	
Total Sources from Operations		$ 8,000
Proceeds of Long-Term Bonds Increase		100,000
Total Sources of Cash		$108,000
Nonoperating Uses of Cash		
Dividends		$ 10,000
Acquisition of Buildings and Equipment		125,000
Total Nonoperating Uses of Cash		$135,000
Net (Decrease) in Cash for Year: Sources − Uses		($ 27,000)
Net (Decrease) in Cash Account for Year: From Balance Sheet		($ 27,000)

3 Subtract the amount of the change in current operating accounts (other than cash) that experienced a net debit change during the period. These are increases in receivables, inventories, and prepayments and decreases in current operating liability accounts.
4 The result is the cash flow provided by operations.

We saw in Exhibit 5.2 that the working capital provided by operations during 1979 by Solinger Electric Corporation was $30,000, whereas the cash flow provided by operations was $8,000. Exhibit 5.14 illustrates the procedure for converting working capital to cash flow provided by operations.

The rationale for the additions and the subtractions in this procedure may be better understood by considering Salaries Payable and Accounts Receivable.

EXHIBIT 5.14
Solinger Electric Corporation
Conversion of Working Capital
Provided by Operations to Cash
Flow Provided by Operations

Working Capital Provided by Operations		$30,000
Add the Net Change in Current Operating Asset Accounts (Except Cash) That Decreased and Current Operating Liability Accounts That Increased During the Period (Credit Changes):		
Accounts Payable—Merchandise Suppliers	$20,000	
Accounts Payable—Other Suppliers	2,000	
Salaries Payable	1,000	
Total Additions		23,000
Subtract the Net Change in Current Operating Asset Accounts (Except Cash) That Increased and Current Operating Liability Accounts That Decreased During the Period (Debit Changes):		
Accounts Receivable	$35,000	
Merchandise Inventory	10,000	
Total Subtractions		(45,000)
Cash Flow Provided by Operations		$ 8,000

The change in the Salaries Payable account is explained as follows:

Salaries Payable, December 31, 1978	$ 5,000
Plus Salaries Expense—1979	20,000
Less Salaries Paid in Cash—1979	(19,000)
Salaries Payable, December 31, 1979	$ 6,000

The amount of working capital provided by operations reflects a $20,000 use of working capital relating to salary expense during the period. Since only $19,000 was disbursed to employees, $1,000 (= $20,000 − $19,000) must be added back to working capital from operations to determine cash flow from operations.

The change in the Accounts Receivable account is explained as follows:

Accounts Receivable, December 31, 1978	$ 20,000
Plus Sales on Account—1979	125,000
Less Cash Collections from Customers—1979	(90,000)
Accounts Receivable, December 31, 1979	$ 55,000

The amount of working capital provided by operations reflects a $125,000 source of working capital relating to sales on account during the period. Since only $90,000 was collected in cash, $35,000 (= $125,000 − $90,000) must be subtracted from working capital provided by operations to determine cash flow provided by operations.

QUESTIONS AND PROBLEMS

1 Review the meaning of the following concepts or terms discussed in this chapter.
  a Funds flow.
  b Liquidity.
  c Cash as funds.
  d Working capital as funds.
  e Working capital equation.
  f Source of funds.
  g Use of funds.
  h Statement of changes in financial position.
  i Working capital provided by operations.
  j Cash provided by operations.
  k Dual transactions assumption.
  l Analysis of changes in working capital accounts.
  m Depreciation is not a source of funds.
  n Liquidity may be unrelated to earnings.

2 What is the objective of a statement of changes in financial position?

3 Can the statement of changes in financial position substitute for the balance sheet? The income statement?

4 The statement of changes in financial position indicates that the board of directors of the Calex Company declared dividends of $500,000 during the year. The comparative balance sheets show Dividends Payable of $80,000 at the start of the year and $100,000 at the end of the year. How much cash was distributed in dividends during the year?

5 Given the following balance sheet accounts for the Turney Company at the end of a year, determine the amount of Turney Company's working capital at the end of the year:

Taxes Payable	$ 1,000
Work-in-Process Inventory	2,000
Advances from Customers	3,000
Accumulated Depreciation	4,000
Common Stock (Par)	5,000
Merchandise Inventory	6,000
Accounts Payable	7,000
Mortgage Payable	8,000
Accounts Receivable	9,000
Buildings and Equipment	10,000
Additional Paid-in Capital	11,000
Investments	12,000

6 The following items were found in the financial statements of Maher Company for 1980:

Sales	$180,000
Depreciation Expense	90,000
Income Taxes	20,000
Other Expenses	40,000
Common Stock Issued During Year	35,000

Prepare a portion of the statement of changes in financial position (working capital definition of funds) to present working capital from operations for the year 1980.

7 Exhibit 5.15 shows a simplified statement of changes in financial position for a period. Ten of the lines in the statement are numbered. Other lines are various subtotals and grand totals; these are to be ignored in the remainder of the problem. Assume that the accounting cycle is complete for the period and that all of the financial statements have been prepared. Then it is discovered that a transaction has been overlooked. That transaction is recorded in the accounts and all of the financial statements are corrected. For each of the following transactions, indicate which of the numbered lines of the funds statement is affected.

EXHIBIT 5.15
Simplified Funds Statement
for a Period
(Problems 7, 8, and 9)

Sources of Funds:
From Operations:

Net Income	(1)
Additions for Expenses Not Using Funds	+ (2)
Subtractions for Revenues Not Producing Funds	− (3)
Total Funds Provided by Operations	S1

Other Sources:

Issues of Long-Term Debt and Owners' Equity	(4)
Proceeds of Dispositions of Noncurrent Assets	(5)
	S2
Total Sources of Funds	S1 + S2

Uses of Funds

Income Distributions (Dividends)	(6)
Acquisition of Noncurrent Assets	(7)
Retirement of Noncurrent Debt and Equity Securities	(8)
Total Uses of Funds	S3
Sources of Funds Minus Uses of Funds =	
Change in Funds for Year, (S1 + S2 − S3) = (9) − (10)	T

Analysis of Changes in Funds Accounts

Increase in Funds	(9)
Decrease in Funds	(10)
Increases in Funds Minus Decreases in Funds =	
Change in Funds for Year, (9) − (10) = (S1 + S2 − S3)	T

Define funds as working capital. If net income, line (1), is affected, be sure to indicate whether it decreases or increases. Ignore income tax effects.

a Depreciation expense on cash register.

b Purchase of machinery for cash.

c Declaration of a cash dividend on common stock; the dividend has not been paid at the close of the fiscal year.

d Issue of preferred stock for cash.

e Issue of common stock for cash.

f Proceeds of sale of common stock investment, a noncurrent asset, for cash. The investment was sold for book value.

g Merchandise Inventory is sold for a price in excess of cost, but payment is received in the form of a long-term note receivable.

8 Refer to the instructions in the preceding question: Repeat those instructions for the following transactions.

a Amortization of patent, treated as an expense.

b Amortization of patent, charged to production activities.

c Acquisition of a factory site by issue of capital stock.

d Purchase of inventory on account.

e Uninsured fire loss of merchandise inventory.

f Collection of an account receivable.

g Issue of bonds for cash.

9 Refer to Exhibit 5.15 and to the instructions in Problem **7.** Now define funds as cash only. Expand the meanings of lines (2) and (3) of Exhibit 5.15 as follows:

Line (2): Additions for Expenses Not Using Cash, for Decreases in Current Asset Accounts Other than Cash, and for Increases in Current Liabilities.

Line (3): Subtractions for Revenues Not Producing Cash, for Increases in Current Asset Accounts Other than Cash, and for Decreases in Current Liabilities.

Analyze the effects of the transactions on the funds statement for the period.

a Use transactions **a–g** of Problem **7.**

b Use transactions **a–g** of Problem **8.**

10 One writer stated that:

Depreciation expense was the chief source of funds for growth in industries.

A reader criticized this statement by replying:

The fact remains that if the companies listed had elected, in any year, to charge off $10 million more depreciation than they did charge off, they would not thereby have added one dime to the total of their funds available for plant expansion or for increasing inventories or receivables. Therefore, to speak of depreciation expense as a source of funds has no significance in a discussion of fundamentals.

Comment on these statements, including income tax effects.

11 Refer to the Appendix to Chapter 4 and the accounting for a manufacturing firm. A manufacturing firm records depreciation on factory machinery (or equipment or buildings) with an entry such as the following:

Work-in-Process Inventory 10,000

    Accumulated Depreciation (Factory Machinery) 10,000

Assume that none of the work in process was completed during the current accounting period. All sales were made from Finished Goods Inventory and there were no transfers from Work-in-Process Inventory to Finished Goods Inventory.

a Under these unrealistic assumptions, trace the effects of the above entry on the balance sheet accounts. Think about the totals of current assets, all assets, liabilities, and all equities.

b What is the effect of the above entry on working capital?

c Aside from income tax effects, can depreciation be a source of funds? Explain.

d What can you generalize from the above answers to a more realistic situation where part of the goods produced during the current period were sold?

12 The comparative balance sheet of the Kanodia Company showed a balance in the Buildings and Equipment account at December 31, 1979, of $24,600,000; at December 31, 1978, the balance was $24,000,000. The Accumulated Depreciation account showed a balance of $8,600,000 at December 31, 1979, and $7,600,000 at December 31, 1978. The Statement of Changes in Financial Position reports that expenditures for buildings and equipment for the year totaled $1,300,000. The income statement indicates a depreciation charge of $1,200,000 for the year and a gain of $53,000 from the disposition of buildings and equipment in the determination of the net income.

Determine the acquisition cost and accumulated depreciation of the buildings and equipment retired during the year and the proceeds from their disposition.

13 Condensed financial statement data for the Harris Company are shown below.

Harris Company
Comparative Balance Sheets
(Problems 13, 14, and 15)

ASSETS	January 1, 1979	December 31, 1979
Cash	$ 12,000	$ 14,000
Accounts Receivable	36,000	40,000
Inventory	63,000	64,000
Land	11,000	11,000
Buildings and Equipment (Cost)	300,000	313,000
Less Accumulated Depreciation	(160,000)	(167,000)
Total Assets	$262,000	$275,000

LIABILITIES AND STOCKHOLDERS' EQUITY		
Accounts Payable	$ 45,000	$ 48,000
Notes Payable (Current)	14,000	13,000
Mortgage Payable	40,000	40,000
Common Stock	100,000	104,000.
Retained Earnings	63,000	70,000
Total Liabilities and Stockholders' Equity	$262,000	$275,000

Harris Company
Statement of Income
and Retained Earnings
For the Year 1979

Revenues		$100,000
Expenses:		
Cost of Goods Sold	$50,000	
Wages and Salaries	15,000	
Depreciation	11,000	
Income Taxes	7,000	
Total		83,000
Net Income		$ 17,000
Dividends on Common Stock		10,000
Addition to Retained Earnings for Year		$ 7,000
Retained Earnings, January 1, 1979		63,000
Retained Earnings, December 31, 1979		$ 70,000

Supplementary Information: Equipment costing $5,000 and with $4,000 of accumulated depreciation was sold for $1,000.

a Prepare a T-account work sheet for the statement of changes in financial position for the year 1979. Use a working capital definition of funds.

b Prepare a statement of changes in financial position for the year 1979. Use a working capital definition of funds.

14 (This problem should not be attempted until Problem **13** has been worked.) Refer to Problem **13** concerning Harris Company. Convert working capital provided by operations to cash flow provided by operations.

15 Refer to Problem **13** concerning Harris Company. Work parts **a** and **b** defining funds as cash.

16 Condensed financial statement data for the Victoria Company for the year are shown on page 178.

Expenditures on new Plant and Equipment for the year amounted to $221,000. Old Plant and Equipment that had cost $64,000 were sold during the year. It was sold for cash at book value.

a Prepare an income statement (including a reconciliation of retained earnings) for the year.

b Prepare a Statement of Changes in Financial Position for the Victoria Company for the year defining funds as working capital. Support the Statement of Changes in Financial Position with a T-account work sheet.

Victoria Company
Postclosing Trial Balance
Comparative Data
(Problems 16, 17, and 18)

Debits:	January 1	December 31
Cash	$ 54,000	$ 47,000
Accounts Receivable	156,000	184,000
Plant and Equipment (Cost)	1,703,000	1,860,000
	$1,913,000	$2,091,000

Credits:		
Accounts Payable	$ 61,000	$ 69,000
Accumulated Depreciation	491,000	560,000
Long-Term Debt	225,000	360,000
Capital Stock	611,000	611,000
Retained Earnings	525,000	491,000
	$1,913,000	$2,091,000

INCOME STATEMENT DATA	
Sales	$1,040,000
Cost of Goods Sold (excluding depreciation)	740,000
Selling and Administrative Expenses	203,000
Depreciation Expense	110,000
Interest Charges	10,000
Other Expenses	11,000

17 (This problem should not be attempted until Problem **16** has been worked.) Refer to the data of Problem **16** for the Victoria Company. Convert working capital provided by operations to cash provided by operations.

18 Refer to the data of Problem **16** for the Victoria Company. Work part **b** defining funds as cash.

19 Condensed financial statement data of the Alberta Company for the years ending December 31, 1978, 1979, and 1980 are presented on page 179.

The original cost of the noncurrent assets sold during 1979 was $108,000. These assets were sold for cash at their net book value. Prepare a statement of changes in financial position for the year 1979 with *funds* defined as working capital. Support the statement with a T-account work sheet.

20 Refer to the data of Problem **19**. Prepare a T-account work sheet and a statement of changes in financial position for 1980 with *funds* defined as working capital. Noncurrent assets were sold during the year at book value. Expenditures on new noncurrent assets amounted to $318,000 during 1980.

Alberta Company
Postclosing Trial Balance
Comparative Data
(Problems 19 and 20)

Debits:	12/31/78	12/31/79	12/31/80
Current Assets	$ 290,000	$ 322,000	$ 342,000
Noncurrent Assets	1,616,000	1,679,000	1,875,000
Total Debits	$1,906,000	$2,001,000	$2,217,000
Credits:			
Current Liabilities	$ 81,000	$ 80,000	$ 83,000
Accumulated Depreciation	697,000	720,000	745,000
Long-Term Debt	106,000	90,000	135,000
Capital Stock	377,000	423,000	514,000
Retained Earnings	645,000	688,000	740,000
Total Credits	$1,906,000	$2,001,000	$2,217,000

Alberta Company
Income and Retained Earnings
Statement Data

	1979	1980
Sales	$910,000	$970,000
Interest and Other Revenue	5,000	7,000
Cost of Goods Sold (Excluding Depreciation)	370,000	413,000
Selling and Administrative Expenses	320,000	301,000
Depreciation	87,000	98,000
Federal Income Taxes	55,000	66,000
Dividends Declared	40,000	47,000

21 Financial statement data for the Perkerson Supply Company for the years ending December, 31, 1979, and December 31, 1980, are presented on page 180.

Additional Information:

(1) Net income for the year was $159,000; dividends declared and paid were $82,000.
(2) Depreciation expense for the year was $210,000 on buildings and machinery.
(3) Machinery originally costing $53,000 and with accumulated depreciation of $26,000 was sold for $27,000.

Prepare a statement of changes in financial position for the Perkerson Supply Company for 1980 with funds defined as working capital. Support the statement with a T-account work sheet.

Perkerson Supply Company
Comparative Balance Sheets
(Problems 21, 22, and 23)

ASSETS

Current Assets	12/31/79	12/31/80
Cash	$ 267,000	$ 240,000
Accounts Receivable	223,000	325,000
Inventory	521,000	671,000
Total Current Assets	$1,011,000	$1,236,000

Noncurrent Assets		
Land	$ 142,000	$ 153,000
Buildings and Machinery	3,364,000	3,556,000
Less Accumulated Depreciation	(857,000)	(1,041,000)
Total Noncurrent Assets	$2,649,000	$2,668,000

Total Assets	$3,660,000	$3,904,000

LIABILITIES AND STOCKHOLDERS' EQUITY

Current Liabilities		
Accounts Payable	$ 138,000	$ 231,000
Taxes Payable	117,000	104,000
Other Short-Term Payables	301,000	392,000
Total Current Liabilities	$ 556,000	$ 727,000

Noncurrent Liabilities		
Bonds Payable	995,000	971,000
Total Current Liabilities	$1,551,000	$1,698,000

Shareholders' Equity		
Common Stock	$ 807,000	$ 827,000
Retained Earnings	1,302,000	1,379,000
Total Shareholders' Equity	$2,109,000	$2,206,000

Total Liabilities and Shareholders' Equity	$3,660,000	$3,904,000

22 (This problem should not be attempted until Problem **21** has been worked.) Refer to Problem **21** concerning the Perkerson Supply Company. Convert working capital provided by operations to cash provided by operations.

23 Refer to Problem **21** concerning the Perkerson Supply Company. Work the problem using a definition of funds as only cash.

24 The Quinta Company presents the following postclosing trial balance and statement of changes in financial position for the year 1979.

Investment, and equipment, and land were sold for cash at their net book value. The accumulated depreciation of the equipment sold was $20,000. Current liabilities were $75,000 at the start of the year and $125,000 at the end of the year.

Prepare a balance sheet for the beginning of the year, January 1, 1979.

Quinta Company
Postclosing Trial Balance,
December 31, 1979
(Problem 24)

Debit Balances:

Working Capital (= Current Assets − Current Liabilities)	$200,000
Land	40,000
Buildings and Equipment	500,000
Investments (Noncurrent)	100,000
Total Debits	$840,000

Credit Balances:

Accumulated Depreciation	$200,000
Bonds Payable	100,000
Common Stock	200,000
Retained Earnings	340,000
Total Credits	$840,000

Quinta Company
Statement of Changes in
Financial Position
For the Year 1979

SOURCES OF WORKING CAPITAL

A. From Operations:

Net Income		$200,000
Addbacks for Depreciation Expense Not		
Using Working Capital		60,000
Total Sources from Operations		$260,000

B. Proceeds from Issues of Securities and Debt:

Capital Stock Issue	$60,000	
Bond Issue	40,000	
Total Proceeds		100,000

C. Proceeds of Disposition of Noncurrent Assets:

Sale of Investments	$40,000	
Sale of Buildings and Equipment	15,000	
Sale of Land	10,000	
Total Proceeds		65,000

Total Sources of Working Capital . . . . | | $425,000 |

USES OF WORKING CAPITAL

A. Dividends $200,000
B. Acquisition of Buildings and Equipment   130,000

Total Uses of Working Capital $330,000
Increase in Working Capital During the Year
(Sources Minus Uses) . . . . $ 95,000

Net Increase in Working Capital Items
(Net Current Asset Item Increases Minus
Net Current Liability Item Increases) . . . . $ 95,000

25 The purpose of this problem is to convince you that depreciation expense uses no funds and that depreciation is not a source of funds. To carry out this exercise, get one writing pen, a dollar's worth of change, and a piece of paper. Put 40 cents, the writing pen, and the piece of paper on the other side of the desk and put 60 cents on your side of the desk.

(1) Your balance sheet now looks like the one shown below.

My Balance Sheet as of Now
(Problem 25)

Assets		**Equities**	
Cash	$0.60	Contributed Capital	$0.60

(2) You are about to acquire a *noncurrent* asset, one long-lived writing pen. The pen costs 40 cents.
(3) Acquire the pen by exchanging 40 cents for the pen which is now across the desk. Record the following journal entry:

Noncurrent Assets 0.40
    Cash 0.40

(4) Acquire the piece of paper, a current asset item, by trading 5 cents for the paper which is now across the desk. Record the following journal entry:

Current Asset—Paper Inventory 0.05
    Cash 0.05

(5) Sign your name on the piece of paper you now have with the pen you acquired. (No journal entry required.)
(6) Because of a sudden surge in your popularity, your autograph has become valuable. Sell your autograph to the other side of the table for 80 cents. Record the following journal entry:

Cash 0.80
    Sales 0.80

(7) The accounting period is over. Record an adjusting entry to recognize 10 cents depreciation for the period on the writing pen:

Depreciation on Noncurrent Assets 0.10
    Accumulated Depreciation on Noncurrent Assets 0.10

(8) Depreciation on Noncurrent Assets is, in this case, a cost of work-in-process inventory that is to be counted as part of Cost of Goods Sold. Record the following journal entry to measure Cost of Goods Sold.

Cost of Goods Sold 0.15
    Depreciation on Noncurrent Assets 0.10
    Current Asset—Paper Inventory 0.05

(9) Close all temporary accounts with the following entry:

Sales 0.80
    Cost of Goods Sold 0.15
    Retained Earnings 0.65

a Ignore income taxes. Prepare an income statement for the period just ended and a balance sheet as of the end of the period.
b Prepare a statement of changes in financial position for the period just ended. Start with net income and adjustments thereto.

Note: Observe that depreciation used no funds not otherwise counted in the nonoperating sources and uses. Funds were provided by selling one autograph. Notice that your funds on hand at the end of the period do not depend on the amount of depreciation on the pen for the period. If this is not clear, repeat **a** and **b** assuming depreciation of $0.30 or $0.00 in step **(7)**.

26 The Johns and White Company, incorporated in 1969, manufactures a line of small electrical appliances for sale to local discount houses. At the time of incorporation, Johns and White each contributed $150,000, and a venture capital firm supplied $250,000. Business was good and profits grew steadily with only a slight decrease in the rate of growth of profits during the years 1973 and 1974. By 1976, Johns and White had bought out the venture capital firm's interest and were in sole command of the company.

In 1977, feeling that the only constraint on their profitability was their limited manufacturing capacity, Johns and White began buying and rehabilitating old factories and equipping them to manufacture the Johns and White line of products. Johns and White intended to quadruple their 1977 manufacturing capacity by 1981. They financed the expansion through retained earnings and a series of 90-day revolving notes with a local bank. During the years 1977, 1978, and 1979 Johns and White's profits continued to grow.

In late January 1980, Johns and White were informed simultaneously by their largest supplier and the bank that they had insufficient funds to cover their outstanding bills with the supplier. Johns and White were mystified. Over the years they had kept a careful watch on their profitability to ensure that they maintained their steady rate of growth of earnings. Their earnings for 1979 had been their highest ever. Over the years, however, they had paid little attention to their liquidity or working capital.

In consultation with the bank, it was brought out that Johns and White would need a large sum of money in the near future to finance inventories and continue formal operations. However, the bank stated that Johns and White had already borrowed beyond prudent levels and that the bank could not extend further loans to Johns and White under the existing terms. The terms imposed by the bank for a new loan would be such that not only would profitability be decreased due to the high interest rate on the additional loan and further expansion plans curtailed for the foreseeable future, but that Johns and White felt they would no longer be in full control of the Company.

Explain what happened to Johns and White Company through the use of comparative statements of changes in financial position. Comparative balance sheets and income statements are presented here for the relevant periods.

Johns and White Company
Comparative Balance Sheets
(Problem 26)

ASSETS

Current Assets	12/31/79	12/31/78	12/31/77	12/31/76
Cash	$ 17,000	$ 23,000	$ 38,000	$ 35,000
Accounts Receivable	101,000	89,000	79,000	71,000
Inventory	118,000	119,000	116,000	112,000
Total Current Assets	$236,000	$231,000	$233,000	$218,000
Noncurrent Assets				
Land	$ 39,000	$ 32,000	$ 22,000	$ 10,000
Plant and Equipment	400,000	279,000	193,000	143,000
Accumulated Depreciation	(85,000)	(67,000)	(51,000)	(42,000)
Total Long-Term Assets	$354,000	$244,000	$164,000	$111,000
Total Assets	$590,000	$475,000	$397,000	$329,000

LIABILITIES AND STOCKHOLDERS' EQUITY

Current Liabilities				
Accounts Payable	$ 96,000	$ 81,000	$ 73,000	$ 61,000
Income Taxes Payable	9,000	7,000	6,000	6,000
Total Current Liabilities	$105,000	$ 88,000	$ 79,000	$ 67,000
Noncurrent Liabilities				
Notes Payable	$199,000	$142,000	$104,000	$ 70,000
Mortgage Payable	27,000	17,000	8,000	—
Total Long-Term Liabilities	$226,000	$159,000	$112,000	$ 70,000
Total Liabilities	$331,000	$247,000	$191,000	$137,000
Stockholders' Equity				
Common Stock	$ 55,000	$ 55,000	$ 55,000	$ 55,000
Retained Earnings	204,000	173,000	151,000	137,000
Total Stockholders' Equity	$259,000	$228,000	$206,000	$192,000
Total Liabilities and Stockholders' Equity	$590,000	$475,000	$397,000	$329,000

Johns and White Company
Comparative Income Statements
For the Years Ended December 31

	1979	1978	1977
Sales	$387,000	$339,000	$298,000
Cost of Goods Sold	$260,000	$250,000	$242,000
Depreciation Expense	18,000	16,000	9,000
Interest Expense	30,000	18,000	8,000
Other Expenses (Except Taxes)	27,000	19,000	16,000
Income Taxes	21,000	14,000	9,000
Total Expenses	$356,000	$317,000	$284,000
Net Income	$ 31,000	$ 22,000	$ 14,000

27 Refer to Exhibit A.3 on page 581, the Statement of Changes of Financial Position for
International Corporation for the years 19X0 and 19X1. Answer each of the following
questions.
   a What definition of *funds* does International Corporation use? How can you tell?
   b What was the total amount of funds provided by operations for the year 19X1?
   c Management of International Corporation is concerned that its "Inventories and Costs
   of Uncompleted Contracts in Excess of Related Billings" are not particularly liquid
   assets. Management has been attempting to reduce these amounts over the last several
   years. Moreover, management has been attempting to increase the amount of "Billings
   on Uncompleted Contracts in Excess of Related Costs," which is a form of nonmonetary
   liability similar to "Advances from Customers." What would be the funds position at
   the ends of each of 19X0 and 19X1 if "Inventories," "Costs of Uncompleted Contracts
   in Excess of Related Billings," and "Billings on Uncompleted Contracts in Excess of
   Related Costs" were excluded from funds? By how much more or less would funds have
   increased for the year 19X1 after this exclusion as compared to the reported change in
   funds for the year 19X1?
   d How would you assess the change in liquidity of International Corporation during 19X1?

28 The discussion in the appendix to this chapter points out that suppliers and employees
who do not demand immediate cash payments for their goods and services are effectively
supplying a firm with cash, at least temporarily. In parallel, when a firm does not demand
immediate payment for sales, but instead accepts an increased amount of accounts receivable, it is in effect using its own liquidity to supply cash to customers. Other things being
equal, a firm would like to restrict severely the amount of cash loaned interest free to customers (through accounts receivable) and increase without limit the amount of cash borrowed interest free from suppliers and employees (through accounts and wages payable).
   Shown here are excerpts from the financial statements of Safeway Stores and of Sears,
Roebuck & Co. for three recent years. Both of these companies are retailers—Safeway
carries out most of its operations in grocery stores where most sales are for cash, whereas
Sears' makes many credit sales in its department stores. Some of Sears' credit sales, those
for which payment is to be made more than 1 month or so after the sale, carry explicit
interest charges to the customer. There are no interest charges on the remainder of Sears'
credit sales.

Analyze the data given in Exhibit 5.16. Determine which company seems to be more successful in financing its operations with interest-free capital. Which company seems to be doing better over the three years reported on here? On what analysis do you base your answer?

EXHIBIT 5.16
Safeway Stores and Sears
(Problem 28)

	Dollar Amounts in Millions		
	Year 1	Year 2	Year 3
	Safeway Stores		
Non-Interest-Bearing Accounts Receivable	$ 29	$ 33	$ 40
Non-Interest-Bearing Accounts Payable	530	525	636
Total Equities	1,490	1,575	1,709
Sales	8,185	9,717	10,443
Net Income	79	149	106
	Sears, Roebuck & Co.		
Non-Interest-Bearing Accounts Receivable	$ 230	$ 222	$ 227
Total Accounts Receivable	4,979	5,201	5,672
Accounts Payable	843	1,120	991
Total Equities	11,339	11,577	12,771
Sales	13,101	13,640	14,950
Net Income	511	523	695

---

29 Some accountants, financial analysts, and others feel that dividend payments to owners are important to potential investors in a firm's common shares. They disagree as to the best accounting measures with which to predict dividend declarations. Some argue that net income is best, others argue that working capital from operations is best, and still others argue that cash from operations is best. It is not possible for us to explore in depth the theoretical and empirical ramifications of this question. Exhibit 5.17 provides, however, data from six recent years for three well-known companies—American Telephone & Telegraph Co., General Electric Company, and Sears, Roebuck & Co. What inferences, if any, can you draw from these data about the relations between dividends and the various accounting measures shown? (Hint: You might find it useful to compute the percentage changes in the data series from year to year.)

EXHIBIT 5.17
Information from Financial Statements of Three Companies
(Problem 29)

	Dollar Amounts in Millions					
American Telephone & Telegraph Co.	**Year 1**	**Year 2**	**Year 3**	**Year 4**	**Year 5**	**Year 6**
Net Income	$2,199	$2,189	$2,240	$2,532	$ 2,947	$ 3,170
Working Capital from Operations	6,933	7,064	7,659	9,448	10,871	12,385
Cash from Operations	8,088	7,639	6,899	9,757	10,675	13,397
Dividends	1,346	1,428	1,428	1,483	1,591	1,808
Sears, Roebuck & Co.						
Net Income	$ 441	$ 464	$ 551	$ 614	$ 680	$ 511
Working Capital from Operations	1,057	1,008	1,087	1,159	1,348	1,233
Cash from Operations	1,053	814	1,058	923	1,264	1,253
Dividends	208	208	232	252	275	291
General Electric Company						
Net Income	$ 278	$ 328	$ 472	$ 530	$ 585	$ 608
Working Capital from Operations	777	883	1,046	1,129	1,320	1,431
Cash from Operations	1,018	996	1,012	826	1,464	1,131
Dividends	235	235	250	255	273	291

Source: Compustat.

CHAPTER 6
INTRODUCTION TO FINANCIAL STATEMENT ANALYSIS

A major function of accounting and financial reporting is helping investors make investment decisions. For example, assume that you recently inherited $25,000 and must decide what to do with the bequest. You have narrowed the investment decision either to depositing the money in a savings account at a local bank or to purchasing shares of common stock of Horrigan Corporation, currently selling for $40 per share. Your decision will be based on the *return* anticipated from each investment and the *risk* associated with that return.

The bank is currently paying interest at the rate of 6 percent annually on savings deposits. Since it is unlikely that the bank will go out of business (and if it does, the federal government provides insurance), you are virtually certain of earning 6 percent each year.

The return from investing in the shares of common stock of Horrigan Corporation has two components. First, the firm paid a cash dividend in 1979, their most recent year, of $.625 per share, and it is anticipated that this dividend will continue in the future. Second, the market price of the stock is likely to change between the date the shares are purchased and the date in the future when they are sold. The difference between the eventual selling price per share and the $40 purchase price, often called a *capital gain*, is a second component of the return from buying the stock.

Compared to the savings account interest, the return from the common stock investment is more risky. Future dividends and market price changes are likely to be associated, at least partially, with the profitability of the firm. Future income might be less than is currently anticipated if competitors introduce new products that erode Horrigan Corporation's share of its sales market. Future income might be greater than currently anticipated if Horrigan Corporation makes important discoveries or introduces successful new products.

The market price of Horrigan Corporation's shares will probably also be affected by economy-wide factors such as inflation and unemployment. Also, specific industry factors such as raw materials shortages or government antitrust actions may influence the market price of the shares. Since most individuals prefer less risk to more risk, you will probably demand a higher expected return from the purchase of Horrigan Corporation's shares than if you invest the inheritance in a savings account.

There are numerous sources of information that might be consulted in assessing the return and risk of investment alternatives. One such source is the financial statements prepared by firms and distributed periodically to stockholders and potential investors as part of the firm's annual report. These financial statements, based on the results of past activities, can be analyzed in order to obtain useful information for predicting future rates of return and for assessing risk.

In this chapter we introduce some of the basic concepts and methods of financial statement analysis. Comprehensive analysis and interpretation require an understanding of specific generally accepted accounting principles discussed in Chapters 7 through 12. Thus, this chapter provides a bridge between the preceding introductory chapters and the more advanced ones that follow.

OBJECTIVES OF FINANCIAL STATEMENT ANALYSIS

The first question likely to be raised in analyzing a set of financial statements is "What do I look for?" Most financial statement analysis is directed at some aspect of either a firm's *profitability* or a firm's *liquidity.*

For example, assume that you are interested in acquiring a firm's common stock and wish to predict future dividends and market price changes for the stock. Dividends and market price changes are likely to be affected, at least partially, by the future profitability of the firm. The firm's past earnings performance can be analyzed as a basis for predicting its future profitability.

Suppose instead that you wished to acquire a firm's long-term bonds. Your return will be primarily in the form of periodic contractual interest receipts. Of particular concern here is the likelihood that the firm will have sufficient cash available to make the required periodic interest payments when due and to repay the principal at maturity. The focus of financial statement analysis in this case is the long-term solvency, or long-run cash-generating ability, of the firm.

Finally, assume that you plan to extend a loan to a firm, expecting repayment of the loan with interest in 6 months. The focus of financial statement analysis in this case is the short-term liquidity of the firm.

Before analyzing a set of financial statements, it is important that the objective of the analysis be clearly specified. The analytical techniques used will differ, as we show in this chapter, depending on the purpose of the analysis.

USEFULNESS OF RATIOS

The various items in financial statements may be difficult to interpret in the form in which they are presented. For example, the profitability of a firm may be difficult to assess by looking at the amount of net income alone. It is helpful to compare earnings with the assets or capital required to generate those earnings. This relationship, and other important ones between various items in the financial statements, can be expressed in the form of ratios. Some ratios compare items within the income statement; some use only balance sheet data; others relate items from more than one statement. Ratios are useful tools of financial statement analysis because they conveniently summarize data in a form that is more easily understood, interpreted, and compared.

Ratios are, by themselves, difficult to interpret. For example, does a rate of return on common stock of 8.6 percent reflect a good performance? Once calculated, the ratios must be compared with some standard. Several possible standards might be used:

1 The planned ratio for the period being analyzed
2 The corresponding ratio during the preceding period for the same firm

---

EXHIBIT 6.1
Horrigan Corporation
Comparative Balance Sheets
(Dollar Amounts in Millions)

	December 31			
ASSETS	**1976**	**1977**	**1978**	**1979**
Cash	$ 10	$ 10	$ 8	$ 10
Marketable Securities	—	4	—	2
Accounts Receivable (net)	26	36	46	76
Inventories	14	30	46	83
Total Current Assets	$ 50	$ 80	$100	$171
Land	$ 20	$ 30	$ 60	$ 60
Building	150	150	150	190
Equipment	70	192	276	313
Less Accumulated Depreciation	(40)	(52)	(66)	(84)
Total Noncurrent Assets	$200	$320	$420	$479
Total Assets	$250	$400	$520	$650
LIABILITIES AND SHAREHOLDERS' EQUITY				
Accounts Payable	$ 25	$ 30	$ 35	$ 50
Salaries Payable	10	13	15	20
Income Taxes Payable	5	7	10	20
Total Current Liabilities	$ 40	$ 50	$ 60	$ 90
Bonds Payable	50	50	100	150
Total Liabilities	$ 90	$100	$160	$240
Common Stock ($10 par value)	$100	$150	$160	$160
Additional Paid-in Capital	20	100	120	120
Retained Earnings	40	50	80	130
Total Shareholders' Equity	$160	$300	$360	$410
Total Liabilities and Shareholders' Equity	$250	$400	$520	$650

3 The corresponding ratio for a similar firm in the same industry

4 The average ratio for other firms in the same industry.

Difficulties encountered in using each of these bases for comparison are discussed later.

In the sections that follow we describe several ratios that are useful for assessing profitability, short-term liquidity, and long-term solvency. To demonstrate the calculation of various ratios, we use data for Horrigan Corporation for the years 1977 and 1979 as shown in Exhibit 6.1 (comparative balance sheets), Exhibit 6.2 (comparative income statements), and Exhibit 6.3 (comparative statements of changes in financial position). Our analysis for Horrigan Corporation is based on a study of the changes in its various ratios over the 3-year period. Such an analysis is referred to as *time-series analysis*. Comparison of a given firm's ratios with those of other firms for a particular period is referred to as *cross-section analysis*. Cross-section analysis requires an understanding of the accounting principles used by different firms and is considered in Chapter 13.

MEASURES OF PROFITABILITY

Usually the most important question asked about a business is "How profitable is it?" Most financial statement analysis is directed at various aspects of this question. Some measures of profitability relate earnings to resources or capital employed, other computations relate earnings and various expenses to sales, whereas a third group seeks to explain profitability by measuring the efficiency with which inventories, receivables, or other assets have been managed.

EXHIBIT 6.2
Horrigan Corporation
Comparative Income Statements
(Dollar Amounts in Millions)

	For the Year Ended December 31		
	1977	1978	1979
Sales	$210	$310	$475
Less Expenses:			
Cost of Goods Sold	$119	$179	$280
Selling	36	38	46
Administrative	12	13	15
Depreciation	12	14	18
Interest	5	10	16
Total	$184	$254	$375
Net Income Before Taxes	$ 26	$ 56	$100
Income Tax Expense	10	22	40
Net Income	$ 16	$ 34	$ 60

EXHIBIT 6.3
Horrigan Corporation
Comparative Statements of
Changes in Financial Position
(Dollar Amounts in Millions)

	For the Year Ended December 31		
Sources of Working Capital	**1977**	**1978**	**1979**
Operations:			
Net Income	$ 16	$ 34	$ 60
Add Back Expenses Not Using Working Capital:			
Depreciation	12	14	18
Working Capital Provided by Operations	$ 28	$ 48	$ 78
Other Sources:			
Issuance of Bonds	—	50	50
Issuance of Common Stock	130	30	—
Total Sources	$158	$128	$128
Uses of Working Capital			
Dividends	$ 6	$ 4	$ 10
Purchase of Land	10	30	—
Purchase of Building	—	—	40
Purchase of Equipment	122	84	37
Total Uses	$138	$118	$ 87
Net Change in Working Capital	$ 20	$ 10	$ 41

Analysis of Effects of Increases
(Decreases) in Working Capital

Cash	$—	$ (2)	$ 2
Marketable Securities	4	(4)	2
Accounts Receivable	10	10	30
Inventories	16	16	37
Accounts Payable	(5)	(5)	(15)
Salaries Payable	(3)	(2)	(5)
Income Taxes Payable	(2)	(3)	(10)
Net Changes in Working Capital	$ 20	$ 10	$ 41

Rate of Return on Assets

The most important profitability ratio for assessing management's performance in using assets to generate earnings is the *rate of return on assets*. This ratio is often called the *return on investment,* or *ROI,* or the *all-capital earnings rate.*

Management's performance in using assets is independent of how the acquisition of those assets has been financed. Thus, the earnings figure used in calculating the rate of return on assets is income before deducting any payments or distributions to the providers of capital. Because interest is a payment to a furnisher of capital, interest expense should not be deducted in measuring the return on total assets. To derive income before interest charges, it is usually easier to start with net income and add to that figure. The amount added to net income is not, however, the interest expense shown on the income statement. Because interest expense is deductible in determining taxable income, interest expense does not reduce *aftertax* net income by the full amount of interest expense. The amount added back to net income is interest expense reduced by income tax effects.

For example, interest expense for Horrigan Corporation for 1979 as shown in Exhibit 6.2 is $16 million. The income tax rate is assumed to be 40 percent of pretax income. The income tax saved, because interest is deductible in determining taxable income, is $6.4 million (= .40 × $16 million). The amount of interest expense net of income tax savings that is added back to net income is therefore $9.6 million (= $16 million − $6.4 million). There is no need to add back dividends paid to stockholders, because they are not deducted as an expense in calculating net income.

Because the earnings rate *during the year* is being determined, the measure of investment should reflect the average amount of assets during the year. A crude, but usually satisfactory, figure for average total assets is one-half the sum of total assets at the beginning and at the end of the year.

The calculation of rate of return on assets for Horrigan Corporation for 1979 is as follows:[1]

$$\frac{\text{Net Income Plus Aftertax Interest Expense}}{\text{Average Total Assets}} = \frac{\$60 + (\$16 - \$6.4)}{\frac{1}{2}(\$520 + \$650)} = 11.9 \text{ percent.}$$

Thus, for each dollar of assets used, the management of Horrigan Corporation was able to earn $.119 during 1979 before payments to the suppliers of capital. The rate of return on assets was 5.8 percent in 1977 and 8.7 percent in 1978. Thus, the rate of return has increased steadily during this 3-year period.

Disaggregating the Rate of Return on Assets

One means of studying changes in the rate of return on assets is to disaggregate the ratio into two other ratios as follows:

$$\begin{matrix}\text{Rate of} \\ \text{Return} \\ \text{on Assets}\end{matrix} = \begin{matrix}\text{Profit Margin Ratio} \\ \text{(before interest expense} \\ \text{and related income tax effects)}\end{matrix} \times \begin{matrix}\text{Total Assets} \\ \text{Turnover} \\ \text{Ratio}\end{matrix}$$

---

[1] Throughout the remainder of this chapter, we omit reference to the fact that the amounts for Horrigan Corporation are in millions of dollars.

or

$$\frac{\text{Net Income Plus}\atop\text{Aftertax Interest}\atop\text{Expense}}{\text{Average Total}\atop\text{Assets}} = \frac{\text{Net Income Plus}\atop\text{Aftertax Interest}\atop\text{Expense}}{\text{Sales}} \times \frac{\text{Sales}}{\text{Average Total}\atop\text{Assets}}.$$

The profit margin ratio is a measure of a firm's ability to control the level of costs, or expenses, relative to revenues generated. By holding down costs, a firm will be able to increase the profits from a given amount of revenue and thereby improve its profit margin ratio. The total assets turnover ratio is a measure of a firm's ability to generate revenues from a particular level of investment in assets.

Exhibit 6.4 shows the disaggregation of the rate of return on assets for Horrigan Corporation for 1977, 1978, and 1979 into profit margin and total assets turnover ratios. Much of the improvement in the rate of return on assets between 1977 and 1978 can be attributed to an increase in the profit margin ratio from 9.05 percent to 12.90 percent. The total assets turnover ratio remained relatively stable between

---

EXHIBIT 6.4
**Disaggregation of Rate of Return
on Assets for Horrigan Corporation
for the Years 1977, 1978, and 1979**

$$\frac{\text{Net Income Plus}\atop\text{Aftertax Interest}\atop\text{Expense}}{\text{Average Total}\atop\text{Assets}} = \frac{\text{Net Income Plus}\atop\text{Aftertax Interest}\atop\text{Expense}}{\text{Sales}} \times \frac{\text{Sales}}{\text{Average Total}\atop\text{Assets}}$$

1977: $\dfrac{\$16 + (\$5 - \$2)}{\frac{1}{2}(\$250 + \$400)} = \dfrac{\$16 + (\$5 - \$2)}{\$210} \times \dfrac{\$210}{\frac{1}{2}(\$250 + \$400)}$

5.8 percent $=$ 9.05 percent $\times$ .646

1978: $\dfrac{\$34 + (\$10 - \$4)}{\frac{1}{2}(\$400 + \$520)} = \dfrac{\$34 + (\$10 - \$4)}{\$310} \times \dfrac{\$310}{\frac{1}{2}(\$400 + \$520)}$

8.7 percent $=$ 12.90 percent $\times$ .674

1979: $\dfrac{\$60 + (\$16 - \$6.4)}{\frac{1}{2}(\$520 + \$650)} = \dfrac{\$60 + (\$16 - \$6.4)}{\$475} \times \dfrac{\$475}{\frac{1}{2}(\$520 + \$650)}$

11.9 percent $=$ 14.65 percent $\times$ .812

these two years. On the other hand, most of the improvement in the rate of return on assets between 1978 and 1979 can be attributed to the increased total assets turnover. The firm was able to generate $.812 of sales from each dollar invested in assets during 1979 as compared to $.674 of sales per dollar of assets in 1978. The increased total assets turnover coupled with an improvement in the profit margin ratio permitted Horrigan Corporation to increase its rate of return on assets during 1979. We must analyze the changes in the profit margin ratio and total assets turnover ratio in greater depth to pinpoint the causes of the changes in Horrigan Corporation's profitability over this 3-year period. We return to this analysis shortly.

Improving the rate of return on assets can be accomplished by increasing the profit margin ratio, the rate of asset turnover, or both. Some firms, however, may have little flexibility in altering some of these components. For example, a firm committed under a 3-year labor union contract may have little control over wage rates paid. Or a firm operating under market- or government-imposed price controls may not be able to increase the prices of its products. In these cases, the opportunities for improving the profit margin ratio may be limited. In order to increase the rate of return on assets, the level of investment in assets such as inventory, plant, and equipment must be reduced or, to put it another way, revenues per dollar of assets must be increased.

Analyzing Changes in the Profit Margin Ratio

Profit, or net income, results from subtracting various expenses from revenues. To identify the reasons for a change in the profit margin ratio, changes in a firm's expenses must be examined. One approach is to express individual expenses and net income as a percentage of sales. Such an analysis is presented in Exhibit 6.5 for Horrigan Corporation. Note that we have altered somewhat the conventional income statement format in this analysis by subtracting interest expense (net of its related income tax effects) as the last expense item. The percentages on the line, Income Before Interest and Related Income Tax Effect, correspond (except for rounding) to the profit margin ratios (before interest and related tax effects) shown in Exhibit 6.4.

The analysis in Exhibit 6.5 indicates that the improvement in the profit margin ratio over the 3 years for Horrigan Corporation can be attributed primarily to decreases in selling, administrative, and depreciation expenses as a percentage of sales. The reasons for these decreasing percentages should be explored further with management. Does the decrease in selling expenses as a percentage of sales reflect a reduction in the rate of advertising expenditures that could hurt future sales? Does the decrease in depreciation expense as a percentage of sales reflect a failure to expand plant and equipment as sales have increased? On the other hand, do these decreasing percentages merely reflect the realization of economies of scale as fixed selling, administrative, and depreciation expenses are being spread over a larger number of units?[2] The amount or trend in a particular ratio cannot, by itself, be the basis for investing or not

---

[2] This phenomenon is called *operating leverage* and is discussed more fully in financial management textbooks.

EXHIBIT 6.5
Net Income and Expenses as a
Percentage of Sales for
Horrigan Corporation for
1977, 1978, and 1979

	For the Year Ended December 31		
	1977	**1978**	**1979**
Sales	100.0%	100.0%	100.0%
Less Operating Expenses:			
Cost of Goods Sold	56.7%	57.7%	58.9%
Selling	17.1	12.3	9.7
Administrative	5.7	4.2	3.2
Depreciation	5.7	4.5	3.8
Total	85.2%	78.7%	75.6%
Income Before Income Taxes and Interest	14.8%	21.3%	24.4%
Income Taxes at 40 percent	5.7	8.4	9.7
Income Before Interest and Related			
Income Tax Effect	9.1%	12.9%	14.7%
Interest Expense Net of Income Tax Effect	1.5	1.9	2.1
Net Income	7.6%	11.0%	12.6%

investing in a firm. Ratios merely indicate areas where additional analysis is required. For example, the increasing percentage of cost of goods sold to sales should be explored further. It may reflect a successful, planned pricing policy of reducing gross margin (selling price less cost of goods sold) in order to increase the volume of sales. On the other hand, the replacement cost of inventory items may be increasing without corresponding increases being made in selling prices. Or, the firm may be accumulating excess inventories that are physically deteriorating or becoming obsolete.

Analyzing Changes in the Total Assets Turnover Ratio

The total assets turnover ratio depends on the turnover ratios for its individual asset components. Three turnover ratios are commonly calculated: accounts receivable turnover, inventory turnover, and fixed asset turnover.

Accounts Receivable Turnover The rate at which accounts receivable turn over gives an indication of their nearness to being converted into cash. The accounts receivable turnover is calculated by dividing net sales on account by average accounts receivable. For Horrigan Corporation, the accounts receivable turnover for 1979, assuming all sales are on account (that is, none are for immediate cash), is calculated as follows:

$$\frac{\text{Net Sales on Account}}{\text{Average Accounts Receivable}} = \frac{\$475}{\frac{1}{2}(\$46 + \$76)} = 7.79 \text{ times per year.}$$

The concept of accounts receivable turnover is often expressed in terms of the average number of days receivables are outstanding before cash is collected. The calculation is to divide the accounts receivable turnover ratio into 365 days. The average number of days that accounts receivable are outstanding for Horrigan Corporation for 1979 is 46.9 days (= 365 days/7.79 times per year). Thus, on average, accounts receivable are collected approximately $1\frac{1}{2}$ months after the date of sale. The interpretation of this average collection period depends on the terms of sale. If the terms of sale are "net 30 days," the accounts receivable turnover indicates that collections are not being made in accordance with the stated terms. Such a ratio would warrant a review of the credit and collection activity for an explanation and for possible corrective action. If the firm offers terms of "net 45 days," then the results indicate that accounts receivable are being handled well.

Inventory Turnover   The inventory turnover ratio is considered to be a significant indicator of the efficiency of operations for many businesses. It is calculated by dividing cost of goods sold by the average inventory during the period. The inventory turnover for Horrigan Corporation for 1979 is calculated as follows:

$$\frac{\text{Cost of Goods Sold}}{\text{Average Inventory}} = \frac{\$280}{\frac{1}{2}(\$46 + \$83)} = 4.34 \text{ times per year.}$$

Thus, inventory is typically on hand an average of 84.1 days (= 365/4.34) before it is sold.

The interpretation of the inventory turnover figure involves two opposing considerations. Management would like to sell as many goods as possible with a minimum of capital tied up in inventories. An increase in the rate of inventory turnover between periods would seem to indicate more profitable use of the investment in inventory. On the other hand, management does not want to have so little inventory on hand that shortages result and customers are turned away. An increase in the rate of inventory turnover in this case may mean a loss of customers and thereby offset any advantage gained by decreased investment in inventory. Some trade-offs are therefore required in deciding the optimum level of inventory for each firm and thus the desirable rate of inventory turnover.

The inventory turnover ratio is sometimes calculated by dividing sales, rather than cost of goods sold, by the average inventory. As long as there is a relatively constant relationship between selling prices and cost of goods sold, changes in the *trend* of the inventory turnover can usually be identified with either measure. It is inappropriate to use sales in the numerator if the inventory turnover ratio is to be used to calculate the average number of days inventory is on hand until sale.

Plant Asset Turnover The plant asset turnover ratio is a measure of the relationship between sales and the investment in plant assets such as property, plant, and equipment. It is calculated by dividing sales by average plant assets during the year. The plant assets turnover ratio for Horrigan Corporation for 1979 is

$$\frac{\text{Sales}}{\text{Average Fixed Assets}} = \frac{\$475}{\frac{1}{2}(\$420 + \$479)} = 1.06 \text{ times per year.}$$

Thus, for each dollar invested in fixed assets during 1979, $1.06 was generated in sales.

Changes in the plant asset turnover ratio must be interpreted carefully. Investments in plant assets (for example, production facilities) are often made several periods before the time when sales are generated from products manufactured in the plant. Thus, a low or decreasing rate of plant asset turnover may be indicative of an expanding firm preparing for future growth. On the other hand, a firm may cut back its capital expenditures if the near-term outlook for its products is poor. Such action could lead to an increase in the plant asset turnover ratio.

We noted earlier that the total assets turnover for Horrigan Corporation was relatively steady between 1977 and 1978 but increased dramatically in 1979. Exhibit 6.6 presents the four turnover ratios we have discussed for Horrigan Corporation over this 3-year period. The accounts receivable turnover ratio increased steadily over the 3 years, indicating either more careful screening of credit applications or more effective collection efforts. The inventory turnover ratio decreased during the 3 years. Coupling this result with the increasing percentage of cost of goods sold to sales shown in Exhibit 6.5 indicates that there may be excessive investments in inventories that are physically deteriorating or becoming obsolete.

Most of the increase in the total assets turnover between 1978 and 1979 can be attributed to an increase in the plant assets turnover. We note in the statement of changes in financial position for Horrigan Corporation in Exhibit 6.3 that total capital expenditures on land, building, and equipment have decreased over the 3-year period. The reasons for this decrease should be investigated.

Summary of the Analysis of the Rate of Return on Assets This section began by stating that the rate of return on assets is a useful measure for assessing management's performance. The rate of return on assets was then disaggregated into profit margin

EXHIBIT 6.6
Asset Turnover Ratios for
Horrigan Corporation for the Three
Years 1977, 1978, and 1979

	1977	1978	1979
Total Assets Turnover	.646	.674	.812
Accounts Receivable Turnover	6.77	7.56	7.79
Inventory Turnover	5.41	4.71	4.34
Plant Asset Turnover	.81	.84	1.06

and total assets turnover components. The profit margin ratio was in turn disaggregated by relating various expenses and net income to sales. The total assets turnover was further analyzed by calculating turnover ratios for accounts receivable, inventory, and fixed assets.

Rate of Return on Common Stock Equity

The investor in a firm's common stock is probably more interested in the *rate of return on common stock equity* than the rate of return on assets. To determine the amount of earnings assignable to common stock equity, the earnings allocable to any preferred stock equity, usually the dividends on preferred stock declared during the period, must be deducted from net income. The capital provided during the period by common shareholders can be determined by averaging the aggregate par value of common stock, capital contributed in excess of par value on common stock, and retained earnings (or by deducting the equity of preferred shareholders from total shareholders' equity) at the beginning and end of the period.

The rate of return on common stock equity of Horrigan Corporation for 1979 is calculated as

$$\frac{\text{Net Income} - \text{Dividends on Preferred Stock}}{\text{Average Common Shareholders' Equity}} = \frac{\$60-\$0}{\frac{1}{2}(\$360 + \$410)} = 15.6 \text{ percent.}$$

The rate of return on common stock equity of Horrigan Corporation, 15.6 percent, is larger in this case than the rate of return on assets (11.9 percent). The return to the common stock equity is larger than the rate of return on assets because the payments to the other suppliers of capital (for example, creditors and bondholders) are less than the overall 11.9-percent rate of return generated from capital that they provided. Observe that current liabilities carry no explicit interest payment and bonds carry an average interest rate of less than 11 percent (= $16/$150).

The common stock equity earned a higher rate of return only because the shareholders undertook more risk in their investment. They were placed in a riskier position because the firm incurred debt obligations with fixed payment dates. In each of the years 1977 through 1979 the rate of return on assets exceeded the average cost of debt so that the rate of return on common stock equity exceeded the rate of return on assets. The phenomenon of common shareholders trading extra risk for a potentially higher return is called *financial leverage* and is described next.

Financial Leverage: Trading on the Equity

Financing with debt and preferred stock to increase the potential return to the residual common shareholders' equity is referred to as *financial leverage* or *trading on the equity*. So long as a higher rate of return can be earned on assets than is paid for the capital used to acquire those assets, then the rate of return to owners can be increased. Exhibit 6.7 explores this phenomenon. Leveraged Company and No-Debt Company both have $100,000 of assets. Leveraged Company borrows $40,000 at a 10-percent annual rate. No-Debt Company raises all its capital from owners. Both companies pay income taxes at the rate of 40 percent.

EXHIBIT 6.7
Effects of Leverage on Rate of Return of Shareholders' Equity (Income Tax Rate Is 40 Percent of Pretax Income)

	Long-Term Equities		Income After Taxes but Before Interest Charges[a]	Aftertax Interest Charges[b]	Net Income	Rate of Return on Total Assets[c] (Percent)	Rate of Return on Common Shareholders' Equity (Percent)
	Long-Term Borrowing at 10 Percent per Year	Shareholders' Equity					
Good Earnings Year							
Leveraged Company	$40,000	$ 60,000	$10,000	$2,400	$ 7,600	10.0%	12.7%
No-Debt Company	—	100,000	10,000	—	10,000	10.0	10.0
Neutral Earnings Year							
Leveraged Company	40,000	60,000	6,000	2,400	3,600	6.0	6.0
No-Debt Company	—	100,000	6,000	—	6,000	6.0	6.0
Bad Earnings Year							
Leveraged Company	40,000	60,000	4,000	2,400	1,600	4.0	2.7
No-Debt Company	—	100,000	4,000	—	4,000	4.0	4.0

[a] But not including any income tax savings caused by interest charges. Income before taxes and interest for *good* year is $16,667; for *neutral* year is $10,000; for *bad* year is $6,667.
[b] $40,000 (borrowed) × .10(interest rate) × [1 − .40(income tax rate)]. The numbers shown in the preceding column for aftertax income do not include the effects of interest charges on taxes.
[c] In each year, the rate of return on assets is the same for both companies as the rate of return on common shareholders' equity for No-Debt-Company, 10 percent, 6 percent, and 4 percent, respectively.

Consider first a "good" earnings year. Both companies earn $10,000 before interest charges (but after taxes except for tax effects of interest charges).[3] This represents a rate of return on assets for both companies of 10 percent (= $10,000/$100,000). Leveraged Company's net income is $7,600 [= $10,000 − (1 − .40 tax rate) × (.10 interest rate × $40,000 borrowed)], representing a rate of return on common shareholders' equity of 12.7 percent (= $7,600/$60,000). Net income of No-Debt Company is $10,000, representing a rate of return on shareholders' equity of 10 percent. Leverage increased the rate of return to shareholders of Leveraged Company, since the capital contributed by the long-term debtors earned 10 percent but required an aftertax interest payment of only 6 percent [= (1 − .40 tax rate) × (.10 interest rate)]. This additional 4-percent return on each dollar of assets increases the return to the common shareholders.

Although leverage increased the return to the common stock equity during the "good" earnings year, the increase would be larger if a larger proportion of the assets were financed with long-term borrowing and the firm were made more risky. For example, assume that the assets of $100,000 were financed with $50,000 of long-term borrowing and $50,000 of shareholders' equity. Net income of Leveraged Company in this case would be $7,000 [= $10,000 − (1 − .40 tax rate) × (.10 × $50,000 borrowed)]. The rate of return on common stock equity would be 14 percent (= $7,000/$50,000). This rate compares with a rate of return on common stock equity of 12.7 percent when long-term debt was only 40 percent of the total capital provided.

Financial leverage increases the rate of return on common stock equity when the rate of return on assets is larger than the aftertax cost of debt. The greater the proportion of debt in the capital structure, however, the greater the risk borne by the common shareholders. Debt cannot, of course, be increased without limit. As more debt is added to the capital structure, the risk of default or insolvency becomes greater. Lenders, including investors in a firm's bonds, will require a higher and higher return (interest rate) to compensate for this additional risk. A point will be reached when the aftertax cost of debt will exceed the rate of return that can be earned on assets. At this point, leverage can no longer increase the potential rate of return to common stock equity. For most large manufacturing firms, liabilities represent between 30 percent and 60 percent of total capital.

Exhibit 6.7 also demonstrates the effect of leverage in a "neutral" earnings year and in a "bad" earnings year. In the "neutral" earnings year, the rate of return to common shareholders is neither increased nor decreased by leverage, since the return on assets is 6 percent and the aftertax cost of long-term debt is 6 percent. In the "bad" earnings year, the return on assets of 4 percent is less than the aftertax cost of debt of 6 percent. The return on common stock equity therefore drops—to only 2.7 percent— below the rate of return on assets. Clearly, financial leverage can work in two ways. It can enhance owners' rate of return in good years, but owners run the risk that bad earnings years will be even worse than they would be without the borrowing.

---

[3] That is, income before taxes and before interest charges is $16,667; $10,000 = (1 − .40) × $16,667.

Earnings per Share of Common Stock

Earnings per common share of common stock is determined by dividing net income applicable to common shareholders by the average number of common shares outstanding during the period.

Earnings per share for Horrigan Corporation for 1979 is calculated as follows:

$$\frac{\text{Net Income} - \text{Preferred Stock Dividend}}{\text{Weighted Average Number of Shares Outstanding During the Period}} = \frac{\$60 - \$0}{16 \text{ shares}^4} = \$3.75 \text{ per share.}$$

Earnings per share were $1.28 (= $16/12.5) for 1977 and $2.19 (= $34/15.5) for 1978.

If a firm has securities outstanding that can be converted into or exchanged for common stock, it may be required to present two earnings-per-share amounts: *primary earnings per share* and *fully diluted earnings per share.* For example, some firms issue convertible bonds or convertible preferred stock that can be exchanged directly for shares of common stock. Also, many firms have employee stock option plans under which shares of the company's common stock may be acquired by employees under special arrangements. If these convertible securities were converted or stock options were exercised and additional shares of common stock were issued, the amount conventionally shown as earnings per share would probably decrease, or become *diluted.* When a firm has outstanding securities that, if exchanged for shares of common stock, would decrease earnings per share by 3 percent or more, a dual presentation of primary and fully diluted earnings per share is required.[5]

Primary Earnings per Share   In determining earnings per share, adjustments may be made to the conventionally determined amount for securities that are nearly the same as common stock. These securities are called *common stock equivalents.* Common stock equivalents are securities whose principal value arises from their capability of being exchanged for, or converted into, common stock rather than only for their own periodic cash yields over time. Stock options and warrants are always common stock equivalents. Convertible bonds and convertible preferred stock may or may not be common stock equivalents. A test is employed to determine if the return from these convertible securities at the date of their issue is substantially below the return available from other debt or preferred stock investments. If so, the presumption is that the securities derived their value primarily from their conversion privileges and are therefore common stock equivalents. Adjustments are made in calculating primary earnings per share for the dilutive effects of securities classified as common stock equivalents.

---

4   Exhibit 6.1 indicates that the par value of a common share is $10 and that the common stock account has a balance of $160 million throughout 1979. The shares outstanding were therefore 16 million.

5   APB *Opinion No. 15,* 1969.

Fully Diluted Earnings per Share   As the title implies, fully diluted earnings per share indicates the maximum possible dilution that would occur if all options, warrants, and convertible securities outstanding at the end of the accounting period were exchanged for common stock. This amount, therefore, represents the maximum limit of possible dilution that could take place on the date of the balance sheet. All securities convertible into or exchangeable for common stock, whether or not classified as common stock equivalents, enter into the determination of fully diluted earnings per share.

Firms that do not have convertible or other potentially dilutive securities outstanding compute earnings per share in the conventional manner. Firms with outstanding securities that have the potential for materially diluting earnings per share as conventionally determined must present dual earnings-per-share amounts.

Comparisons of Earnings per Share Among Companies   Comparisons of rates of growth over time in earnings per share among companies can often be misleading. Assume, for example, that two companies earn identical rates of return on shareholders' equity, but one company declares and pays dividends equal to net income each year whereas the other retains all its earnings, paying no dividends. Assume that the number of common shares outstanding does not change for either company. Then, the earnings per share of the first company, the one paying dividends, will remain level, whereas the earnings per share amounts of the second company, the one retaining earnings, will grow over time (at a rate equal to the rate of return on shareholders' equity). The second company may appear to be doing better, but the earnings-per-share data indicate merely that the management of the second company has more assets per share with which to work. Problem **15** at the end of the chapter explores this phenomenon.

Price-Earnings Ratio

Earnings-per-share amounts are often compared with the market price of the stock. This is usually expressed as a *price-earnings ratio* (= market price per share/earnings per share). For example, the common stock of Horrigan Corporation is selling for $40 per share at the end of 1979. The price-earnings ratio, often called the P/E ratio, is 11.27 to 1 (= $40/$3.55). This ratio is often presented in tables of stock market prices and in financial periodicals. The relationship is sometimes expressed by saying that "the stock is selling at 11.5 times earnings."

The relation between earnings and market price per share might be expressed as a rate (= earnings per share/market price per share). This calculation, 8.9 percent (= $3.55/$40) for Horrigan Corporation, is seen less often than the price-earnings ratio.

MEASURES OF SHORT-TERM LIQUIDITY

Investors or creditors whose claims will become payable in the near future are interested in the short-term liquidity or "nearness to cash" of a firm's assets. One tool for predicting whether or not cash will be available when the claims become due is a budget of cash receipts and disbursements for several months or quarters in the future. Such budgets are often prepared for management and used internally for planning cash requirements. Budgets of cash receipts and disbursements are not generally available for use by persons outside a firm. Investors must therefore use other tools in assessing short-term liquidity.

The statement of changes in financial position is one published source of information for assessing liquidity. The amount of working capital provided by operations indicates the extent to which the operating activities have generated sufficient working capital for the payment of dividends and the acquisition of fixed assets. The statement also discloses the extent to which additional financing has been used for those purposes. Exhibit 6.8 indicates that working capital provided by operations for Horrigan Corporation increased each year between 1977 and 1979.

Additional insights into the impact of operations on liquidity can be obtained by converting working capital provided by operations to cash flow provided by operations. Exhibit 6.8 presents the analysis for Horrigan Corporation. Cash flow provided by operations increased each year but by a smaller amount than working capital provided by operations. A substantial portion of the cash flow generated each year was reinvested in inventory. Nevertheless, operations appear to be having a positive effect on cash flows.

EXHIBIT 6.8
Horrigan Corporation
Conversion of Working Capital
Provided by Operations to Cash
Flow Provided by Operations
for the Years 1977, 1978, and
1979 (Dollar Amounts in Millions)

	1977	1978	1979
Working Capital Provided by Operations	$28	$48	$78
Add Increases in Current Liabilities:			
Accounts Payable	5	5	15
Salaries Payable	3	2	5
Income Taxes Payable	2	3	10
Subtract Increases in Current Asset Accounts Other Than Cash and Marketable Securities:			
Accounts Receivable	(10)	(10)	(30)
Inventories	(16)	(16)	(37)
Cash Flow Provided by Operations	$12	$32	$41

Several ratios are also useful in assessing the short-term liquidity of a firm. The most popular ones are the current ratio, quick ratio, and accounts receivable turnover ratio.

Current Ratio

The *current ratio* is calculated by dividing current assets by current liabilities. It is commonly expressed as a ratio such as "2 to 1" or "2:1," meaning that current assets are twice as large as current liabilities. The current ratio of Horrigan Corporation on December 31, 1976, 1977, 1978, and 1979 is:

$$\frac{\text{Current}}{\text{Ratio}} = \frac{\text{Current Assets}}{\text{Current Liabilities}}$$

December 31, 1976: $\dfrac{\$\,50}{\$\,40}$ = 1.25 to 1.0

December 31, 1977: $\dfrac{\$\,80}{\$\,50}$ = 1.60 to 1.0

December 31, 1978: $\dfrac{\$100}{\$\,60}$ = 1.67 to 1.0

December 31, 1979: $\dfrac{\$171}{\$\,90}$ = 1.90 to 1.0.

This ratio is presumed to indicate the ability of the concern to meet its current obligations, and is therefore of particular significance to short-term creditors. Although an excess of current assets over current liabilities is generally considered desirable from the creditor's viewpoint, changes in the trend of the ratio may be difficult to interpret. For example, when the current ratio is larger than 1 to 1, an increase of equal amount in both current assets and current liabilities results in a decline in the ratio, whereas equal decreases result in an increased current ratio.

If a corporation has a particularly profitable year, the large current liability for income taxes may cause a decline in the current ratio. In a recession period, business is contracting, current liabilities are paid, and even though the current assets may be at a low point, the ratio will often go to high levels. In a boom period, just the reverse effect might occur. In other words, a very high current ratio may accompany unsatisfactory business conditions, whereas a falling ratio may accompany profitable operations.

Furthermore, the current ratio is susceptible to "window dressing"; that is, management can take deliberate steps to produce a financial statement that presents a better current ratio at the balance sheet date than the average or normal current ratio. For example, toward the close of a fiscal year normal purchases on account may be delayed. Or loans to officers, classified as noncurrent assets, may be collected and the proceeds used to reduce current liabilities. These actions may be taken so that the current ratio will appear as favorable as possible in the annual financial statements at the balance sheet date.

Although the current ratio is probably the most common ratio presented in statement analysis, there are limitations in its use as discussed above. Its trends are difficult to interpret and, if overemphasized, it can easily lead to undesirable business practices as well as misinterpretation of financial condition.

Quick Ratio

A variation of the current ratio, usually known as the *quick ratio* or *acid-test ratio,* is computed by including in the numerator of the fraction only those current assets that could be converted quickly into cash. The items customarily included are cash, marketable securities, and receivables, but it would be better to make a study of the facts in each case before deciding whether or not to include receivables and to exclude inventories. In some businesses the inventory of merchandise might be converted into cash more quickly than the receivables of other businesses.

Assuming that the accounts receivable of Horrigan Corporation are included but that inventory is excluded, the quick ratio on December 31, 1976, 1977, 1978, and 1979 is:

$$\frac{\text{Quick}}{\text{Ratio}} = \frac{\text{Cash, Marketable Securities,}\ \text{Accounts Receivable}}{\text{Current Liabilities}}$$

December 31, 1976: $\dfrac{\$36}{\$40}$ = .90 to 1.0

December 31, 1977: $\dfrac{\$50}{\$50}$ = 1.0 to 1.0

December 31, 1978: $\dfrac{\$54}{\$60}$ = .90 to 1.0

December 31, 1979: $\dfrac{\$88}{\$90}$ = .98 to 1.0.

Whereas the current ratio increased steadily over the 3-year period, the quick ratio remained relatively constant. The increase in the current ratio is caused primarily by a buildup of inventories.

Accounts Receivable Turnover Ratio

The accounts receivable turnover ratio, discussed earlier in the section on profitability ratios, also provides useful information about a firm's liquidity. The ratio is calculated by dividing net sales on account by the average amount of accounts receivable during the period. In assessing short-term liquidity, it is generally desirable to re-express the ratio in terms of the average number of days accounts receivable are outstanding. Using the accounts receivable turnover amounts from Exhibit 6.5, the average number of days Horrigan Corporation's receivables were outstanding during 1977, 1978, and 1979 were:

$$\begin{array}{c} \text{Average Number of Days} \\ \text{Accounts Receivable Are} \\ \text{Outstanding} \end{array} = \frac{365}{\begin{array}{c} \text{Accounts Receivable} \\ \text{Turnover Ratio} \end{array}}$$

$$1977: \quad \frac{365}{6.77} = \quad 53.9 \text{ days}$$

$$1978: \quad \frac{365}{7.56} = \quad 48.3 \text{ days}$$

$$1979: \quad \frac{365}{7.79} = \quad 46.9 \text{ days.}$$

Over the 3-year period, the accounts receivable of Horrigan Corporation have become more liquid.

Other Short-Term Liquidity Ratios

Several other ratios are sometimes used to assess short-term liquidity. One ratio relates cash *inflow* from operations to the average amount of current liabilities during a period. This ratio is intended to provide information similar to the current ratio but is not as susceptible to year-end window dressing. Another ratio sometimes encountered is the *defensive interval*.[6] It is calculated by dividing the average daily cash expenditures for operating expenses into a firm's most liquid assets, generally cash, marketable securities, and accounts receivable. The defensive interval is the number of days the firm could theoretically remain in business without additional sales or new financing. In studies of bond default and bankruptcy, this ratio has been found to be a good predictor.

Summarizing the analysis of Horrigan Corporation's short-term liquidity, we have noted the following:

1 Working capital and cash flow provided by operations have been positive and growing at a reasonably stable rate with sales and net income. Operations are now the primary source of liquid assets for the firm.
2 The current ratio has been improving over the last 3 years, but most of the improvement is caused by a buildup of inventories.
3 The average collection period for accounts receivable has been decreasing during the past 3 years, indicating that they are becoming more liquid or that collection policy has been more stringent, or both.

---

[6] George H. Sorter and George Benston, "Appraising the Defensive Position of a Firm: The Interval Measure," *The Accounting Review*, Vol. 35 (October 1960): 633–640.

MEASURES OF LONG-TERM SOLVENCY

Measures of long-term solvency are used in assessing the firm's ability to meet interest and principal payments on long-term debt and similar obligations as they become due. If the payments cannot be made on time, the firm becomes *insolvent* and may have to be reorganized or liquidated.

Perhaps the best indicator of long-term solvency is a firm's ability to generate profits over a period of years. If a firm is profitable, it will either generate sufficient capital from operations or be able to obtain needed capital from creditors and owners. The measures of profitability discussed previously are therefore applicable for this purpose as well. Two other commonly used measures of long-term solvency are debt ratios and the number of times that interest charges are earned.

Debt Ratios

There are several variations of the debt ratio, but the one most commonly encountered in financial analysis is the *long-term debt ratio*. It reports the portion of the firm's long-term capital that is furnished by debt holders. To calculate this ratio, divide total noncurrent liabilities by the sum of total noncurrent liabilities and total shareholders' equity.

Another form of the debt ratio is the *debt-equity ratio*. To calculate the debt-equity ratio, divide total liabilities (current and noncurrent) by total equities (liabilities plus stockholders' equity = total assets).

The two forms of the debt ratio for Horrigan Corporation on December 31, 1976, 1977, 1978, and 1979, are shown in Exhibit 6.9. In general, the higher these ratios, the higher the likelihood that the firm may be unable to meet fixed interest and

---

EXHIBIT 6.9
Horrigan Corporation
Debt Ratios

$$\text{Long-Term Debt Ratio} = \frac{\text{Total Noncurrent Liabilities}}{\text{Total Noncurrent Liabilities Plus Stockholders' Equity}}$$

$$\text{Debt-Equity Ratio} = \frac{\text{Total Liabilities}}{\text{Total Liabilities Plus Stockholders' Equity}}$$

Dec. 31, 1976: $\dfrac{\$ 50}{\$210} = 24$ percent

Dec. 31, 1976: $\dfrac{\$ 90}{\$250} = 36$ percent

Dec. 31, 1977: $\dfrac{\$ 50}{\$350} = 14$ percent

Dec. 31, 1977: $\dfrac{\$100}{\$400} = 25$ percent

Dec. 31, 1978: $\dfrac{\$100}{\$460} = 22$ percent

Dec. 31, 1978: $\dfrac{\$160}{\$520} = 31$ percent

Dec. 31, 1979: $\dfrac{\$150}{\$560} = 27$ percent

Dec. 31, 1979: $\dfrac{\$240}{\$650} = 37$ percent

principal payments in the future. The decision for most firms is how much financial leverage with its attendant risk they can afford to assume. Funds obtained from issuing bonds or borrowing from a bank have a relatively low interest cost but require fixed, periodic payments that increase the likelihood of bankruptcy.

In assessing the debt ratios, analysts customarily vary the standard in direct relation to the stability of the firm's earnings. The more stable the earnings, the higher the debt ratio that is considered acceptable or safe. The debt ratios of public utilities are customarily high, on the order of 60 to 70 percent. The stability of public utility earnings makes these ratios acceptable to many investors who would be dissatisfied with such large leverage for firms with less stable earnings.

Because several variations of the debt ratio appear in corporate annual reports, care in making comparisons of debt ratios among firms is necessary.

Interest Coverage: Times Interest Charges Earned

Another measure of long-term solvency is the *number of times that interest charges are earned*, or covered. This ratio is calculated by dividing net income before interest and income tax expenses by interest expense. For Horrigan Corporation, the times interest earned ratios for 1977, 1978, and 1979 are:

$$\frac{\text{Times Interest}}{\text{Charges Earned}} = \frac{\text{Net Income Before Interest and Income Taxes}}{\text{Interest Expense}}$$

$$1977: \quad \frac{\$16 + \$5 + \$10}{\$5} = 6.2 \text{ times}$$

$$1978: \quad \frac{\$34 + \$10 + \$22}{\$10} = 6.6 \text{ times}$$

$$1979: \quad \frac{\$60 + \$16 + \$40}{\$16} = 7.3 \text{ times.}$$

Thus, whereas the bonded indebtedness increased sharply during the 3-year period, the growth in net income before interest and income taxes was sufficient to provide increasing coverage of the fixed interest charges.

The purpose of this ratio is to indicate the relative protection of bondholders and to assess the probability that the firm will be forced into bankruptcy by a failure to meet required interest payments. If periodic repayments of principal on long-term liabilities are also required, the repayments might also be included in the denominator of the ratio. The ratio would then be described as the *number of times that fixed charges were earned*, or covered.

The times interest or fixed charges earned ratios can be criticized as measures for assessing long-term solvency because the ratios use earnings rather than cash flows in the numerator. Interest and other fixed payment obligations are paid with cash, and not with earnings. When the value of the ratio is relatively low (for example, two to three times), some measure of cash flows, such as cash flows from operations, may be preferable in the numerator.

LIMITATIONS OF RATIO ANALYSIS

For convenient reference, Exhibit 6.10 summarizes the calculation of the ratios discussed in this chapter.

The analytical computations discussed in this chapter have a number of limitations that should be kept in mind by anyone preparing or using them. Several of the more important limitations are the following:

EXHIBIT 6.10
Summary of Financial Statement Ratios

Ratio	Numerator	Denominator
Rate of Return on Assets	Net Income + Interest Expense[a] (net of tax effects)	Average Total Assets During the Period
Profit Margin Ratio (before interest effects)	Net Income + Interest Expense (net of tax effects)	Sales
Various Expense Ratios	Various Expenses	Sales
Total Assets Turnover Ratio	Sales	Average Total Assets During the Period
Accounts Receivable Turnover Ratio	Net Sales on Accounts	Average Accounts Receivable During the Period
Inventory Turnover Ratio	Cost of Goods Sold	Average Inventory During the Period
Plant Asset Turnover Ratio	Sales	Average Plant Assets During the Period
Rate of Return on Common Stock Equity	Net Income − Preferred Stock Dividends	Average Common Shareholders' Equity During the Period
Earnings per Share of Stock[b]	Net Income − Preferred Stock Dividends	Weighted Average Number of Common Shares Outstanding During the Period
Current Ratio	Current Assets	Current Liabilities
Quick or Acid-Test Ratio	Highly Liquid Assets (ordinarily, cash, marketable securities, and receivables)[c]	Current Liabilities
Long-Term Debt Ratio	Total Noncurrent Liabilities	Total Noncurrent Liabilities Plus Shareholders' Equity
Debt-Equity Ratio	Total Liabilities	Total Equities (liabilities plus shareholders' equity)
Times Interest Charges Earned	Net Income Before Interest and Income Taxes	Interest Expense

---

[a] If a consolidated subsidiary is not owned entirely by the parent corporation, the minority interest share of earnings must also be added back to net income. See the description in Chapter 12.
[b] This calculation can be more complicated when there are convertible securities, options, or warrants outstanding.
[c] Receivables could conceivably be excluded for some firms and inventories included for others. Such refinements are seldom employed in practice.

1 The ratios are based on financial statement data and are therefore subject to the same criticisms as the financial statements (for example, use of acquisition cost rather than current replacement cost or net realizable value; the latitude permitted firms in selecting from among various generally accepted accounting principles).
2 Changes in many ratios are highly associated, or correlated, with each other. For example, the changes in the current ratio and quick ratio between two different times are often in the same direction and approximately proportional. It is therefore not necessary to compute all the ratios to assess a particular factor.
3 When comparing the size of a ratio between periods for the same firm, one must recognize conditions that have changed between the periods being compared (for example, different product lines or geographical markets served, changes in economic conditions, changes in prices).
4 When comparing ratios of a particular firm with those of similar firms, one must recognize differences between the firms (for example, use of different methods of accounting, differences in the method of operations, type of financing, and so on).

Results of financial statement analyses cannot be used by themselves as direct indications of good or poor management. Such analyses merely indicate areas that might be investigated further. For example, a decrease in the turnover of raw materials inventory, ordinarily considered to be an undesirable trend, may reflect the accumulation of scarce materials that will keep the plant operating at full capacity during shortages when competitors have been forced to restrict operations or to close down. Ratios derived from financial statements must be combined with an investigation of other facts before valid conclusions can be drawn.

SUMMARY

We began this chapter by raising the question: Should you invest your inheritance in a savings account or in the shares of common stock of Horrigan Corporation. Our analysis of Horrigan Corporation's financial statements indicates that it has been a growing, profitable company with few indications of either short-term liquidity or long-term solvency problems. At least three additional inputs are necessary before making the investment decisions. First you must consider other sources of information besides the financial statements to determine if relevant information for projecting rates of return or for assessing risk needs to be considered. Second, you must decide your attitude toward or willingness to assume, risk. Third, you must decide if you think the stock market price of the shares makes them an attractive purchase.[7] It is at this stage in the investment decision that the analysis becomes particularly subjective.

-----

[7] Other important factors cannot be discussed here, but are in finance texts. Perhaps the most important question of all is how a particular investment fits in with the investor's entire portfolio. Modern research suggests that the suitability of a potential investment depends more on the attributes of the other components of an investment portfolio and the risk attitude of the investor than it does on the attributes of the potential investment itself.

QUESTIONS AND PROBLEMS

1 Review the meaning of the following concepts or terms discussed in this chapter.
  a Risk and return.
  b Profitability.
  c Short-term liquidity.
  d Long-term solvency.
  e Time-series analysis.
  f Cross-section analysis.
  g Rate of return on assets.
  h Profit margin and expense ratios.
  i Total assets turnover ratio.
  j Accounts receivable turnover ratio.
  k Inventory turnover ratio.
  l Plant asset turnover ratio.
  m Rate of return on common stock equity.
  n Operating leverage.
  o Financial leverage.
  p Earnings per share.
  q Primary earnings per share.
  r Fully diluted earnings per share.
  s Price-earnings ratio.
  t Current ratio.
  u Quick ratio.
  v Long-term debt ratio.
  w Debt-equity ratio.
  x Times interest charges earned.

2 Describe several factors that might limit the comparability of a firm's current ratio over several periods.

3 Describe several factors that might limit the comparability of one firm's current ratio with that of another firm in the same industry.

4 Under what circumstances will the rate of return on the common stock equity be more than the rate of return on assets? Under what circumstances will it be less?

5 In calculating the inventory turnover, when might the use of the average of the beginning and ending inventories lead to an inaccurate result?

6 Illustrate with amounts how a decrease in working capital can accompany an increase in the current ratio.

7 It has been suggested that for any given firm at a particular time there is an optimal inventory turnover ratio. Explain.

8 A company president recently stated: "The operations of our company are such that we can use effectively only a small amount of financial leverage." Explain.

9 The following data are taken from the 1979 annual reports of Alabama Company and Carolina Company.

	Alabama Co.	Carolina Co.
Sales	$2,000,000	$2,400,000
Expenses Other Than Interest and Income Taxes	1,700,000	2,150,000
Interest Expense	100,000	50,000
Income Tax Expense at 40 Percent	80,000	80,000
Net Income	120,000	120,000
Average Total Assets During the Year	1,500,000	1,000,000

a Determine the rate of return on assets for each company.
b Disaggregate the rate of return in part **a** into profit margin and total assets turnover components.
c Comment on the relative performance of the two companies.

10 Net income attributable to common stockholders' equity of Florida Corporation during 1979 was $250,000. Earnings per share were $.50 during the period. The average common stockholders' equity during 1979 was $2,500,000. The market price at year-end was $6.00 per share.
a Determine the rate of return on common stockholders' equity for 1979.
b Determine the rate of return currently being earned on the market price of the stock (the ratio of earnings per common share to market price per common share).
c Why is there a difference between the rates of return determined in parts **a** and **b**?

11 The revenues of Lev Company were $1,000 for the year. A financial analyst computed the following ratios for Lev Company using the year-end balances for balance sheet amounts.

Debt/Equity Ratio (all liabilities/all equities)	$73\frac{1}{3}$%
Income Tax Expense as a Percentage of Pretax Income	40%
Income as a Percentage of Revenue	12%
Rate of Return on Shareholders' Equity	10%
Rate of Return on Assets	6%

From this information, compute each of the following items.
a Interest expense.
b Income tax expense.
c Total expenses.
d Net income.
e Total assets.
f Total liabilities.

12 Refer to the data below for the Adelsman Company.

	Year 1	Year 2	Year 3
Rate of Return on Common Shareholders' Equity	8%	10%	11%
Earnings per Share	$3.00	$4.00	$4.40
Times Interest Charges Earned	10	5	4
Debt-Equity Ratio (liabilities/all equities)	20%	50%	60%

The income tax rate was 40 percent in each year and 100,000 common shares were outstanding throughout the period.

a Did the company's profitability increase over the 3-year period? How can you tell? (Hint: Compute the rate of return on assets.)

b Did risk increase? How can you tell?

c Are shareholders better off in year 3 than in year 1?

13 The following information is taken from the annual reports of two companies, one of which is a retailer of quality men's clothes and the other of which is a discount household goods store. Neither company had any interest-bearing debt during the year. Identify which of these companies is likely to be the clothing retailer and which is likely to be the discount store. Explain.

	Company A	Company B
Sales	$3,000,000	$3,000,000
Net Income	60,000	300,000
Average Total Assets	600,000	3,000,000

14 The Borrowing Company has total assets of $100,000 during the year. It has borrowed $20,000 at a 10 percent annual rate and pays income taxes at a rate of 40 percent of pretax income. Shareholders' equity is $80,000.

a What must net income be for the rate of return on shareholders' equity to equal the rate of return on assets (the all capital earnings rate)?

b What is the rate of return on shareholders' equity for the net income determined above in part a?

c What must income before interest and income taxes be to achieve this net income?

d Repeat parts a, b, and c assuming borrowing of $80,000 and shareholders' equity of $20,000.

e Compare the results from the two different debt-equity relations. What generalizations can be made?

15 Company A and Company B both start the year 1978 with $1 million of shareholders' equity and 100,000 shares of common stock outstanding. During 1978 both companies earn net income of $100,000, a rate of return of 10 percent on shareholders' equity. Company A declares and pays $100,000 of dividends to common shareholders at the end of 1978, whereas Company B retains all its earnings, declaring no dividends. During 1979, both companies earn net income equal to 10 percent of shareholders' equity at the beginning of 1979.

a Compute earnings per share for Company A and for Company B for 1978 and for 1979.

b Compute the rate of growth in earnings per share for Company A and Company B, comparing earnings per share in 1979 with earnings per share in 1978.

c Using the rate of growth in earnings per share as the criterion, which company's management appears to be doing a better job for its shareholders? Comment on this result.

16 (CMA adapted.) The Virgil Company is planning to invest $10 million in an expansion program that is expected to increase income before interest and taxes by $2.5 million. Currently, Virgil Company has total equities of $40 million, 25 percent of which is debt and 75 percent of which is shareholders' equity, represented by 1 million shares. The expansion can be financed with the issuance of 200,000 new shares at $50 each or by issuing long-term debt at an annual interest rate of 10 percent. The following is an excerpt from the most recent income statement.

Earnings Before Interest and Taxes	$10,500,000
Less: Interest Charges	500,000
Earnings Before Income Taxes	$10,000,000
Income Taxes (at 40 percent)	4,000,000
Net Income	$ 6,000,000

Assume that Virgil Company maintains its current earnings on its present assets, achieves the planned earnings from the new program, and that the tax rate remains at 40 percent.
a What will be earnings per share if the expansion is financed with debt?
b What will be earnings per share if the expansion is financed by issuing new shares?
c At what level of earnings before interest and taxes will earnings per share be the same, whichever of the two financing programs is used?
d At what level of earnings before interest and taxes will the rate of return on shareholders' equity be the same, whichever of the two financing plans is used?

17 Merchandise inventory costing $30,000 is purchased on account. Indicate the effect (increase, decrease, no effect) of this transaction on (1) working capital and (2) the current ratio, assuming that current assets and current liabilities immediately prior to the transaction were as follows:
a Current assets, $120,000; current liabilities, $120,000.
b Current assets, $120,000; current liabilities, $150,000.
c Current assets, $120,000; current liabilities, $80,000.

18 Assuming an excess of current assets over current liabilities, indicate the effect of the following upon the current ratio:
a Collection of an account receivable.
b Payment of an account payable.
c Acquisition of merchandise on account.
d Acquisition of merchandise for cash.
e Acquisition of machinery on account.
f Acquisition of machinery for cash.
g Sale of marketable securities at less than book value.
h Sale of an investment at less than book value.

19 Assuming an excess of current assets over current liabilities, indicate the effect of the following upon the current ratio:
a The acquisition of government bonds for cash.
b The borrowing of funds from a bank on a non-interest-bearing note.
c The issuance of bonds for cash.
d The payment of a short-term note at the bank.
e The recording of accrued interest on a note receivable.
f The receipt of a non-interest-bearing, 2-month note from a customer to apply to an account receivable.
g The sale of machinery and equipment at less than book value.

20 Following is a schedule of the current assets and current liabilities of the Lewis Company:

Current Assets	Dec. 31, 1979	Dec. 31, 1978
Cash	$ 355,890	$ 212,790
Accounts Receivable	389,210	646,010
Inventories	799,100	1,118,200
Prepayments	21,600	30,000
Total Current Assets	$1,565,800	$2,007,000
Current Liabilities		
Accounts Payable	$ 152,760	$ 217,240
Accrued Payroll, Taxes, etc.	126,340	318,760
Notes Payable	69,500	330,000
Total Current Liabilities	$ 348,600	$ 866,000

The Lewis Company operated at a loss during 1979.

a   Calculate the current ratio for each date.

b   Explain how the improved current ratio is possible under the 1979 operating conditions.

21 The following information relates to the activities of Tennessee Corporation and Kentucky Corporation for 1979.

	Tennessee Corp.	Kentucky Corp.
Sales on Account, 1979	$4,050,000	$2,560,000
Accounts Receivable, December 31, 1978	960,000	500,000
Accounts Receivable, December 31, 1979	840,000	780,000

a   Compute the accounts receivable turnover of each company.

b   Determine the average number of days that accounts receivable are outstanding for each company.

c   Which company is managing its accounts receivable more efficiently?

22 Indicate the effects (increase, decrease, no effect) of each of the independent transactions below on (1) rate of return on common stock equity, (2) current ratio, and (3) debt-equity ratio. State any necessary assumptions.

a   Merchandise inventory costing $120,000 is sold on account for $150,000.

b   Collections from customers on accounts receivable total $100,000.

c   A provision is made for estimated uncollectible accounts, $15,000.

d   Specific customers' accounts totaling $10,000 are written off as uncollectible.

e   Merchandise inventory costing $205,000 is purchased on account.

f   A machine costing $40,000 and on which $30,000 depreciation had been taken is sold for $8,000.

g   Dividends of $80,000 are declared. The dividends will be paid during the next accounting period.

23 Indicate the effects (increase, decrease, no effect) of the independent transactions below on (1) earnings per share, (2) working capital, and (3) quick ratio, where accounts receivable are *included* but merchandise inventory is *excluded* from "quick assets." State any necessary assumptions.

a Merchandise inventory costing $240,000 is sold on account for $300,000.

b Dividends of $160,000 are declared. The dividends will be paid during the next accounting period.

c Merchandise inventory costing $410,000 is purchased on account.

d A machine costing $80,000 and on which $60,000 depreciation had been taken is sold for $16,000.

e Merchandise inventory purchased for cash in the amount of $7,000 is returned to the supplier because it is defective. A cash reimbursement is received.

f 10,000 shares of $10 par value common stock were issued on the last day of the accounting period for $15 per share. The proceeds were used to acquire the assets of another firm composed of the following: accounts receivable, $30,000; merchandise inventory, $60,000; plant and equipment, $100,000. The acquiring firm also agreed to assume current liabilities of $40,000 of the acquired company.

g Marketable securities costing $16,000 are sold for $20,000.

24 The following data are taken from the financial statements of the Press Company:

	Dec. 31, 1979	Dec. 31, 1978
Current Assets	$210,000	$180,000
Noncurrent Assets	275,000	255,000
Current Liabilities	78,000	85,000
Long-Term Liabilities	75,000	30,000
Common Stock (10,000 shares)	300,000	300,000
Retained Earnings	32,000	20,000

	1979 Operations
Net Income	$72,000
Interest Expense	3,000
Income Taxes (40% rate)	48,000
Dividends Declared	60,000

Calculate the following ratios:

a Rate of return on total capital.

b Rate of return on stockholders' equity.

c Earnings per share of common stock.

d Current ratio (both dates).

e Times interest earned.

f Debt-equity ratio (both dates).

25 Refer to the financial statements of Jonathan Electronics Corporation in Chapter 2 and calculate the following:

a Rate of return on total capital. The income tax rate is 40 percent.

b Rate of return on stockholders' equity.

    c Earnings per share. (500,000 shares were outstanding throughout the year.)
    d Profit margin ratio.
    e Inventory turnover.
    f Current ratio (both dates).
    g Debt-equity ratio (both dates).
    h Times interest earned.

26 The income statements and balance sheets of Illinois Corporation and Ohio Corporation are presented below:

Income Statements
for the Year 1979

	Illinois Corp.	Ohio Corp.
Sales	$4,300,000	$3,000,000
Less Expenses:		
Cost of Goods Sold	$2,800,000	$1,400,000
Selling and Administrative Expenses	330,000	580,000
Interest Expense	100,000	200,000
Income Tax Expense	428,000	328,000
Total Expenses	$3,658,000	$2,508,000
Net Income	$ 642,000	$ 492,000

Balance Sheets
December 31, 1979

Assets	Illinois Corp.	Ohio Corp.
Cash	$ 100,000	$ 50,000
Accounts Receivable (Net)	700,000	400,000
Merchandise Inventory	1,200,000	750,000
Plant and Equipment (Net)	4,000,000	4,800,000
Total Assets	$6,000,000	$6,000,000
Equities		
Accounts Payable	$ 572,000	$ 172,000
Income Taxes Payable	428,000	328,000
Long-Term Bonds Payable (10 percent)	1,000,000	2,000,000
Capital Stock	2,000,000	2,000,000
Retained Earnings	2,000,000	1,500,000
Total Equities	$6,000,000	$6,000,000

Assume that the balances in asset and equity accounts at year-end approximate the average balances during the period. The income tax rate is 40 percent. On the basis of this information, which company is

a More profitable?

b More liquid?

c More secure in terms of long-term solvency?

Use financial ratios, as appropriate, in doing your analysis.

27 The following information is taken from the financial statements of the Eastern Oil Company for the year ending December 31, 1978 and 1979.

**Eastern Oil Company
Consolidated Statement of
Financial Position**

	(in millions of dollars)	
ASSETS	December 31, 1979	December 31, 1978
Cash	$ 921.0	$ 866.1
Receivables (Net)	1,198.3	1,173.2
Inventories	1,676.0	1,566.0
Plant and Equipment (Net)	11,930.4	11,305.3
Other Noncurrent Assets	4,589.5	4,331.2
Total Assets	$20,315.2	$19,241.8
EQUITIES		
Current Liabilities	$ 3,329.7	$ 3,240.1
Long-Term Liabilities	5,392.6	5,051.0
Capital Stock (average shares outstanding in 1979: 224,100,000; in 1978: 221,000,000)	2,640.5	2,608.4
Retained Earnings	8,952.4	8,342.3
Total Equities	$20,315.2	$19,241.8

**Eastern Oil Company
Statement of Income for the
Years 1979 and 1978**

	(in millions of dollars)	
Revenues	**1979**	**1978**
Sales	$20,361.7	$18,143.3
Other Revenue	801.4	553.4
Total Revenues	$21,163.1	$18,696.7
Expenses		
Crude Oil and Product Costs	$ 6,283.8	$ 5,520.7
Selling and Administrative Expenses	11,806.8	10,415.2
Interest Expenses	261.7	241.6
Income Taxes Expense	1,349.2	1,209.2
Total Expenses	$19,701.5	$17,386.7
Net Income to Stockholders	$ 1,461.6	$ 1,310.0

On the basis of this information, assess the relative **(a)** profitability, **(b)** liquidity, **(c)** solvency of the firm as between 1978 and 1979. Assume that the balances in the asset and equity accounts at year-end approximate the average balances during the period. Also assume an income tax rate of 48 percent.

28 Following are comparative balance sheets, income statement, and statement of changes in financial position of Solinger Electric Corporation for 1979. Income taxes are 40 percent of pretax income.

  a Calculate the following ratios for Solinger Electric Corporation for 1979.

    (1) Rate of return on assets.
    (2) Rate of return on common stock equity.
    (3) Earnings per share.
    (4) Accounts receivable turnover (assuming that all sales are made on account).
    (5) Inventory turnover.
    (6) Plant asset turnover.
    (7) Current ratio on December 31, 1978, and December 31, 1979.
    (8) Quick ratio on December 31, 1978, and December 31, 1979 (assuming that merchandise inventories are excluded from quick assets).
    (9) Debt-equity ratio on December 31, 1978, and December 31, 1979.
    (10) Times interest charges earned ratio.

  b Was Solinger Electric Corporation successfully leveraged during 1979?
  c Assume that the bonds were issued on November 1, 1979. At what annual interest rate were the bonds apparently issued?
  d If Solinger Electric Corporation earns the same rate of return on assets in 1980 as it realized in 1979, and issues no more debt, will the firm be successfully leveraged in 1980?
  e Determine the amount of cash flow provided by operations during 1979.

Solinger Electric Corporation
Comparative Balance Sheets
for December 31, 1978 and 1979

ASSETS

Current Assets	December 31, 1978	December 31, 1979
Cash	$ 30,000	$ 3,000
Accounts Receivable	20,000	55,000
Merchandise Inventory	40,000	50,000
Total Current Assets	$ 90,000	$108,000

Noncurrent Assets		
Buildings and Equipment (Cost)	$100,000	$225,000
Accumulated Depreciation	(30,000)	(40,000)
Total Noncurrent Assets	$ 70,000	$185,000
Total Assets	$160,000	$293,000

EQUITIES

Current Liabilities		
Accounts Payable—Merchandise Suppliers	$ 30,000	$ 50,000
Accounts Payable—Other Suppliers	10,000	12,000
Salaries Payable	5,000	6,000
Total Current Liabilities	$ 45,000	$ 68,000

Noncurrent Liabilities		
Bonds Payable	0	100,000
Total Liabilities	$ 45,000	$168,000

Owners' Equity		
Capital Stock ($10 par value)	$100,000	$100,000
Retained Earnings	15,000	25,000
Total Owners' Equity	$115,000	$125,000
Total Equities	$160,000	$293,000

Solinger Electric Corporation
Income Statement
for the Year 1979

Sales Revenue	$125,000
Less Expenses:	
Cost of Goods Sold	$ 60,000
Salaries	19,667
Depreciation	10,000
Interest	2,000
Income Taxes	13,333
Total Expenses	$105,000
Net Income	$ 20,000

Solinger Electric Corporation
Statement of Changes in
Financial Position
for the Year 1979

SECTION I. SOURCES AND USES OF WORKING CAPITAL

Sources of Working Capital
Operations
Net Income $20,000
   Add Back Expenses Not Using Working Capital:
Depreciation   10,000
   Total Sources from Operations . . . . $ 30,000
Proceeds from Long-Term Bonds Issued   100,000
   Total Sources of Working Capital $130,000

Uses of Working Capital
Dividends . . . . $ 10,000
Acquisition of Buildings and Equipment   125,000
   Total Uses of Working Capital $135,000
Net Decrease in Working Capital During the Year
   (Sources Minus Uses) . . . . $ 5,000

SECTION II. ANALYSIS OF CHANGES IN WORKING CAPITAL ACCOUNTS

Current Asset Item Increases (Decreases)
Cash . . . . $(27,000)
Accounts Receivable   35,000
Merchandise Inventory   10,000
Net Increase (Decrease) in Current Asset Items . . . . $ 18,000

Current Liability Increases (Decreases)
Accounts Payable—Merchandise Suppliers $20,000
Accounts Payable—Other Suppliers   2,000
Salaries Payable   1,000
Net Increase (Decrease) in Current Liability Items   23,000
Net Decrease in Working Capital During the Year (Net
   Increase in Current Liability Items Minus Net Increase in
   Current Asset Items) . . . . $ 5,000

29 Presented below are comparative balance sheets, income statement, and statement of changes in financial position of Nykerk Electronics Corporation for 1979.

Nykerk Electronics Corporation
Comparative Balance Sheets

ASSETS	($ in Thousands)	
	December 31	
Current Assets	**1979**	**1978**
Cash	$ 1,300	$ 1,100
Marketable Securities	300	300
Accounts Receivable (Net)	2,600	2,500
Inventories	7,300	6,900
Total Current Assets	$11,500	$10,800
Noncurrent Assets		
Plant and Equipment	$ 5,200	$ 4,500
Less Accumulated Depreciation	1,300	1,000
Net Plant and Equipment	$ 3,900	$ 3,500
Land	1,200	1,200
Total Noncurrent Assets	$ 5,100	$ 4,700
Total Assets	$16,600	$15,500

LIABILITIES AND SHAREHOLDERS' EQUITY		
Current Liabilities		
Accounts Payable	$ 1,600	$ 1,700
Accrued Payables	800	900
Income Taxes Payable	300	200
Notes Payable	1,900	1,200
Total Current Liabilities	$ 4,600	$ 4,000
Long-Term Liabilities		
Bonds Payable (8 percent)	$ 2,000	$ 2,100
Mortgage Payable	200	200
Total Long-Term Liabilities	$ 2,200	$ 2,300
Total Liabilities	$ 6,800	$ 6,300
Shareholders' Equity		
Preferred Stock (6 percent, $100 par)	$ 2,000	$ 2,000
Common Stock ($1 par)	500	500
Additional Paid-in Capital	2,500	2,500
Total Contributed Capital	$ 5,000	$ 5,000
Retained Earnings	4,800	4,200
Total Shareholders' Equity	$ 9,800	$ 9,200
Total Liabilities and Shareholders' Equity	$16,600	$15,500

Nykerk Electronics Corporation
Statement of Income
and Retained Earnings
Year of 1979

Revenues		($ in Thousands)
Sales		$26,500
Less Sales Allowances, Returns, and Discounts		600
Net Sales		$25,900
Interest and Other Revenues		200
Total Revenues		$26,100

Expenses		
Cost of Goods Sold		$20,500
Selling and Administrative Expenses:		
Selling Expenses	$2,120	
Administrative Expenses	1,000	
Depreciation	300	
Total Selling and Administrative Expenses		3,420
Interest Expense		180
Income Tax Expense		800
Total Expenses		$24,900
Net Income to Shareholders		$ 1,200

Dividends		
Dividends on Preferred Shares	$ 120	
Dividends on Common Shares	480	
Total Dividends		600
Addition to Retained Earnings for Year		$ 600
Retained Earnings, January 1, 1979		4,200
Retained Earnings, December 31, 1979		$ 4,800

Nykerk Electronics Corporation
Statement of Changes
in Financial Position
Year of 1979
($ in thousands)

Sources of Working Capital:		
Net Income	$1,200	
Add Back Expenses Not Using Working Capital:		
Depreciation Expense	300	
Working Capital Provided by Operations		$1,500
Uses of Working Capital:		
Preferred Stock Dividend	$ 120	
Common Stock Dividend	480	
Purchase of Plant and Equipment	700	
Redemption of Bonds Payable	100	1,400

Increase in Working Capital for the Year .... $ 100
Analysis of Increases (Decreases) in Working Capital Amounts
Cash .... $ 200
Marketable Securities 0
Accounts Receivable (Net) 100
Inventories 400
Accounts Payable 100
Accrued Payables 100
Income Taxes Payable .... (100)
Notes Payable .... (700)

Increase in Working Capital for the Year .... $ 100

---

a Calculate the following ratios for Nykerk Electronics Corporation for 1979.

  (1) Rate of return on assets.
  (2) Rate of return on common stock equity.
  (3) Earnings per share.
  (4) Accounts receivable turnover (assuming that all sales are made on account).
  (5) Inventory turnover.
  (6) Plant asset turnover.
  (7) Current ratio on December 31, 1978, and December 31, 1979.
  (8) Quick ratio on December 31, 1978, and December 31, 1979.
  (9) Debt-equity ratio on December 31, 1978, and December 31, 1979.
  (10) Times interest charges earned ratio.

b Determine the amount of cash flow provided by operations for 1979. For this purpose, do not include the change in Notes Payable in the analysis.
c Was Nykerk Electronics Corporation successfully leveraged during 1979?

30 Refer to the financial statements of International Corporation in Appendix A at the back of the book.
  Calculate the amount of the following ratios for 19X1.

(1) Rate of return on assets. Assume an income tax rate of 40 percent in computing after-tax interest charges. In computing income before charges to suppliers of capital, do not subtract the $2,452,000 shown as the minority interest in net income of consolidated subsidiaries. That is, add the $2,452,000 back to net income. Minority interest is explained in Chapter 12.
(2) Rate of return on common stock equity.
(3) Accounts receivable turnover (assuming that all sales are made on account).
(4) Inventory turnover (cost of uncompleted contracts in excess of related billings is to be ignored in this calculation).
(5) Plant asset turnover.
(6) Current ratio on December 31, 19X0, and December 31, 19X1.

(7) Quick ratio on December 31, 19X0, and December 31, 19X1 (assuming that quick assets includes cash, marketable securities, and customer receivables).

(8) Debt-equity ratio on December 31, 19X0, and December 31, 19X1 (assuming that minority interest is considered to be part of shareholders' equity).

(9) Times interest charges earned ratio (also add back the minority interest in net income of consolidated subsidiaries and subtract the $10,000,000 income tax savings from losses of discontinued operations).

31 One approach to financial statement analysis is to prepare common-size statements. These statements express each financial statement item as a percentage of some base, such as total assets, total equities, or total revenues. Presented below are common-size balance sheets for Horrigan Corporation as discussed in the chapter.

Horrigan Corporation
Common-Size Balance Sheets

	December 31			
ASSETS	**1976**	**1977**	**1978**	**1979**
Cash	4.0%	2.5%	1.5%	1.5%
Marketable Securities	—	1.0	—	.3
Accounts Receivable (net)	10.4	9.0	8.8	11.7
Inventories	5.6	7.5	8.9	12.8
Total Current Assets	20.0%	20.0%	19.2%	26.3%
Land	8.0%	7.5%	11.5%	9.2%
Building	60.0	37.5	28.9	29.2
Equipment	28.0	48.0	53.1	48.2
Less Accumulated Depreciation	(16.0)	(13.0)	(12.7)	(12.9)
Total Noncurrent Assets	80.0%	80.0%	80.8%	73.7%
Total Assets	100.0%	100.0%	100.0%	100.0%

LIABILITIES AND STOCKHOLDERS' EQUITY				
Accounts Payable	10.0%	7.5%	6.8%	7.7%
Salaries Payable	4.0	3.3	2.9	3.1
Income Taxes Payable	2.0	1.7	1.9	3.0
Total Current Liabilities	16.0%	12.5%	11.6%	13.8%
Bonds Payable	20.0	12.5	19.2	23.1
Total Liabilities	36.0%	25.0%	30.8%	36.9%
Common Stock	40.0%	37.5%	30.8%	24.6%
Additional Paid-in Capital	8.0	25.0	23.0	18.5
Retained Earnings	16.0	12.5	15.4	20.0
Total Stockholders' Equity	64.0%	75.0%	69.2%	63.1%
Total Liabilities and Stockholders' Equity	100.0%	100.0%	100.0%	100.0%

a Assuming that the ratio analysis presented in the chapter had not yet been performed, what significant changes in the structure of Horrigan Corporation's assets and equities can you observe from the common-size statement above?

b In what respects are the changes observed in part a consistent with the ratio analysis presented in the chapter?

c In what respects are the changes observed in part a inconsistent with the ratio analysis presented in the chapter?

32 Exhibit 6.11 shows five items from the financial statements for three companies for a recent year.

EXHIBIT 6.11
Comparison of Operations and Investment
(Problem 32)

For Year	Company A	Company B	Company C
Operating Revenues	$28,947,200	$13,639,900	$9,716,900
Income Before Interest and Dividends[a]	4,295,800	824,600	156,400
Net Income to Common Shareholders[b]	2,915,800	522,600	148,600
Average During Year			
Total Assets	77,107,200	10,885,000	1,532,400
Common Shareholders' Equity . .	29,769,200	5,118,800	743,830

[a] Net Income + Interest Charges × (1 − Tax Rate).
[b] Net Income − Preferred Stock Dividends.

---

a Compute the income to sales (or income to operating revenues) ratio for each company. Which company seems to be the most successful according to this ratio?

b How many dollars of sales on average does each of the companies make for each dollar's worth of average assets held during the year?

c Compute the rate of return on assets for each company. Which company seems to be the most successful according to this ratio?

d Compute the rate of return on common shareholders' equity for each company. Which company seems to be the most successful according to this ratio?

e The three companies are American Telephone & Telegraph, Safeway Stores, and Sears, Roebuck and Company. (Dollar amounts shown are actually in thousands.) Which of the companies corresponds to A, B, and C? What clues did you use in reaching your conclusion?

33 In this problem, you become a financial analyst/detective. The condensed financial statements in Exhibit 6.12 are constructed on a percentage basis. In all cases, total sales revenues are shown as 100.00%. All other numbers were divided by sales revenue for the year.

EXHIBIT 6.12
Data for Ratio Detective Exercise
(Problem 33)

Balance Sheet at End of Year	Company Numbers						
	(1)	**(2)**	**(3)**	**(4)**	**(5)**	**(6)**	**(7)**
Current Receivables.....	0.31%	29.11%	6.81%	25.25%	3.45%	38.78%	17.64%
Inventories	7.80	0.00	3.14	0.00	6.45	14.94	20.57
Net Plant and Equipment*	8.50	9.63	11.13	19.88	49.87	15.59	37.60
All Other Assets	2.16	7.02	25.59	32.93	24.05	15.54	30.07
Total Assets..........	18.78%	45.76%	46.67%	78.06%	83.83%	84.85%	105.88%
*Cost of Plant and Equipment (Gross)	14.64%	14.80%	19.57%	29.03%	79.03%	24.80%	59.73%
Current Liabilities	6.08%	9.82%	6.41%	17.49%	14.83%	35.28%	27.68%
Long-Term Liabilities	2.12	7.96	0.00	0.00	0.00	8.33	1.33
Owners' Equity.........	10.58	27.98	40.25	60.57	69.00	41.24	76.86
Total Equities	18.78%	45.76%	46.67%	78.06%	83.83%	84.85%	105.88%
Income Statement for Year							
Revenues	100.00%	100.00%	100.00%	100.00%	100.00%	100.00%	100.00%
Cost of Goods Sold (Excluding Depreciation) or Operating Expenses[a]...	78.97	53.77	48.21	59.07	68.62	60.88	33.29
Depreciation...........	1.04	1.39	1.72	2.07	4.07	1.09	3.02
Interest Expense	0.16	.52	0.00	0.08	0.02	1.35	0.73
Advertising Expense	0.00	0.00	11.43	0.06	4.39	2.93	2.28
Research and Development Expense	0.00	1.00	0.00	0.00	0.15	0.00	9.06
Income Taxes..........	1.28	.53	9.59	6.52	7.87	3.78	8.55
All Other Items (Net)	17.06	18.88	18.58	24.52	6.40	24.39	27.66
Total Expenses.........	98.50%	76.08%	89.53%	92.32%	91.51%	94.41%	84.59%
Net Income	1.50%	23.92%	10.47%	7.68%	8.49%	5.59%	15.41%

The 13 companies (all corporations except for the accounting firm) shown here represent the following industries:

(1) Advertising and public opinion survey firm.
(2) Beer brewery
(3) Department store chain (that carries its own receivables)
(4) Distiller of hard liquor
(5) Drug manufacturer
(6) Finance company (lends money to consumers)
(7) Grocery store chain
(8) Insurance company
(9) Manufacturer of tobacco products, mainly cigarettes

Balance Sheet at End of Year	Company Numbers					
	(8)	**(9)**	**(10)**	**(11)**	**(12)**	**(13)**
Current Receivables	12.94%	9.16%	25.18%	27.07%	13.10%	653.94%
Inventories	15.47	56.89	79.53	0.00	1.62	0.00
Net Plant and Equipment*	70.29	28.36	19.22	2.64	251.62	2.88
All Other Assets	18.37	26.42	24.72	223.91	23.68	200.37
Total Assets	117.08%	120.82%	148.65%	253.63%	290.01%	857.18%
*Cost of Plant and Equipment (Gross)	167.16%	42.40%	35.08%	4.45%	320.90%	3.81%
Current Liabilities	19.37%	33.01%	20.42%	161.37%	28.01%	377.56%
Long-Term Liabilities	20.62	34.07	36.09	10.62	115.50	280.79
Owners' Equity	77.09	53.74	92.13	81.63	146.51	198.83
Total Equities	117.08%	120.82%	148.65%	253.63%	290.01%	857.18%
Income Statement for Year						
Revenues	100.00%	100.00%	100.00%	100.00%	100.00%	100.00%
Cost of Goods Sold (Excluding Depreciation) or Operating Expenses[a] . . .	81.92	57.35	42.92	82.61	45.23	47.69
Depreciation	5.81	1.90	1.97	0.05	14.55	0.00
Interest Expense	1.23	2.69	3.11	1.07	7.15	24.33
Advertising Expense	0.00	6.93	13.04	0.00	0.00	0.00
Research and Development Expense	0.76	0.00	0.00	0.00	0.71	0.00
Income Taxes	2.15	7.47	10.63	3.92	8.73	12.89
All Other Items (Net)	3.81	14.82	17.99	2.97	11.51	−5.57
Total Expenses	95.68%	91.16%	89.66%	90.62%	87.89%	79.35%
Net Income	4.32%	8.84%	10.34%	9.38%	12.11%	20.65%

[a] Represents operating expenses for the following companies: Advertising/public opinion survey firm, insurance company, finance company, and the public accounting partnership.

(10) Public accounting (CPA) partnership
(11) Soft drink bottler
(12) Steel manufacturer
(13) Utility company.

Use whatever clues you can to identify who is who. As an aid to identifying which company is which, you may find the data in the accompanying Exhibit 6.13 to be helpful. This exhibit is adapted from data published by Dun & Bradstreet, Inc., and is reproduced here with their permission. The ratios shown are median ratios for several individual firms of the business type listed. There is not a perfect relation between the ratios shown for a given type of business and that same ratio for the particular company shown in Exhibit 6.12.

EXHIBIT 6.13
Key Business Ratios
Median Ratios for Business
of the Types Indicated
(Problem 33)

Type of Business	Current Ratio (times) (1)	Net Income as a Percentage of Sales (2)	Rate of Return in Shareholders' Equity (3)	Shareholders' Equity[a] as a Percentage of Sales (4)	Inventory as a Percentage of Sales (5)
Department Store . .	2.81	1.61%	5.47%	27.5%	17.5%
Grocery Store	1.63	0.94	12.78	7.8	6.2
Beer, Wine, and Alcoholic Beverages	1.96	1.58	11.91	12.2	12.5
Tobacco and Tobacco Products	2.25	0.93	11.85	8.3	6.3
Blast Furnace, Steel Works, and Rolling Mills	2.46	4.45	10.31	38.6	21.3
Drugs	2.46	6.15	14.37	45.7	22.7
Soft Drinks, Bottled and Canned	2.10	6.46	19.05	27.7	5.1

Source: Dun & Bradstreet, Inc., © 1977, *Key Business Ratios.* The document from which these data are developed lists 14 ratios for about 90 kinds of businesses. The entire document can be ordered at no cost from Public Relations Department, Dun & Bradstreet, Inc., 99 Church Street, New York, New York 10007.
[a] Dun & Bradstreet uses tangible shareholders' equity for this ratio. They subtract from owners' equity shown in the balance sheet in the net book value of intangible assets.

34 On October 2, 1975, W. T. Grant Company filed for bankruptcy protection under Chapter XI of the Bankruptcy Act. At that time, it reported assets of $1.02 billion and liabilities of $1.03 billion. The company had operated at a profit for most years prior to 1974, but reported an operating loss of $177 million for its fiscal year January 31, 1974 to January 31, 1975.

The accompanying Exhibits 6.14–6.17 contain:

(1) Balance sheet and income statements issued in 1975, and the statements of changes in financial position for W. T. Grant Company for the 1971 through 1975 fiscal periods
(2) Additional financial information about W. T. Grant Company, the retail industry, and the economy for the same period as above.

Prepare an analysis which explains the major causes of Grant's collapse. You may find it useful to refer to financial and nonfinancial data presented in other sources such as the *Wall Street Journal* in addition to that presented here.

EXHIBIT 6.14
W. T. Grant Company
Balance Sheet
(Dollar Amounts in Thousands)
(Problem 34)

Assets	January 31, 1975
Cash and Marketable Securities	$ 79,642
Accounts Receivable (Net)	399,968
Inventories	407,357
Other Current Assets	37,814
Total Current Assets	$ 924,781
Investments	52,264
Property, Plant, and Equipment (Net)	101,932
Other Assets	3,789
Total Assets	$1,082,766

Liabilities and Shareholders' Equity	
Short-Term Loans	$ 600,985
Accounts Payable	146,921
Current Deferred Taxes	2,000
Total Current Liabilities	$ 749,906
Long-Term Debt	216,341
Deferred Taxes	—
Other Long-Term Liabilities	2,183
Total Liabilities	$ 968,430
Preferred Stock	$ 7,465
Common Stock	18,599
Additional Paid-in Capital	83,914
Retained Earnings	37,674
Total	$ 147,652
Less Cost of Treasury Stock	(33,316)
Total Shareholders' Equity	$ 114,336
Total Liabilities and Shareholders' Equity	$1,082,766

EXHIBIT 6.15
W. T. Grant Company
Income Statement
(Dollar Amounts in Thousands)
(Problem 34)

	Fiscal Year Ending January 31, 1975
Sales	$1,761,952
Income from Concessions	4,238
Total	$1,766,190
Less Expenses:	
Cost of Goods Sold	1,303,267
Selling, General and Administrative Expenses	540,953
Store Closing Expenses	24,000
Net Credit Expense (Income)	161,467
Other Interest Expense	37,771
Net Operating Income	$ (301,268)
Other Income:	
Interest	1,390
Gain on Retirement of Long-Term Debt	1,986
Earnings Before Income Taxes and Equity in Earnings of Unconsolidated Subsidiaries	$ (297,892)
Less Income Tax Expense (Credits)	
Current	(19,439)
Deferred	(98,027)
Income Before Equity in Earnings of Unconsolidated Subsidiaries	$ (180,426)
Equity in Earnings of Unconsolidated Subsidiary	3,086
Net Income (Loss)	$ (177,340)

EXHIBIT 6.16
W. T. Grant Company
Statement of Changes in
Financial Position
(Dollar Amounts in Thousands)
(Problem 34)

	Fiscal Year Ending January 31				
Sources of Working Capital	**1971**	**1972**	**1973**	**1974**	**1975**
Operations:					
Net Income	$39,577	$ 35,212	$37,787	$ 8,429	$(177,340)
Less Equity in Earnings of					
Unconsolidated Subsidiaries	(2,777)	(2,383)	(3,403)	(3,570)	(331)
Plus: Depreciation	9,619	10,577	12,004	13,579	14,587
Deferred Taxes	233	1,145	2,262	2,724	(14,649)
Other	74	(520)	(558)	(498)	(2,013)
Total from Operations	$46,726	$ 44,031	$48,092	$ 20,664	$(179,746)
Sale of Common Stock to Employees	5,218	7,715	3,491	2,584	886
Issuance of Long-Term Debt	—	100,000	—	100,000	—
Other	—	2,229	2,403	259	—
Total Sources	$51,944	$153,975	$53,986	$123,507	$(178,860)
Applications of Working Capital					
Dividends	$20,821	$ 21,139	$21,141	$ 21,122	$ 4,457
Acquisition of Property, Plant, and					
Equipment	16,141	25,918	26,251	23,143	15,535
Acquisition of Treasury Stock	13,224	—	11,466	133	—
Reacquisition of Preferred Stock	948	308	252	618	—
Retirement of Long-Term Debt	1,538	1,615	1,584	6,074	3,995
Investments in Securities	436	5,951	2,216	5,700	5,282
Other	47	3,575	(80)	904	627
Total Applications	$53,155	$ 58,506	$62,830	$ 57,694	$ 29,896
Net Increase (Decrease) in Working					
Capital	$ (1,211)	$ 95,469	$(8,844)	$ 65,813	$(208,756)

ANALYSIS OF CHANGES IN WORKING CAPITAL ACCOUNTS

	Fiscal Year Ending January 31				
	1971	**1972**	**1973**	**1974**	**1975**
Current Asset Increases (Decreases):					
Cash	$ 1,032	$ 15,842	$(18,908)	$ 15,008	$ 33,691
Accounts Receivable	51,464	57,593	65,427	56,047	(121,351)
Merchandise Inventories	38,365	38,184	100,857	51,104	(43,280)
Prepayments	208	427	1,270	651	11,032
Current Liabilities Decreases (Increases):					
Bank Loans	(64,288)	8,680	(152,293)	(63,063)	(147,898)
Accounts Payable	(9,828)	(13,995)	15,888	2,781	8,125
Salaries Payable	(470)	(161)	(3,325)	4,322	3,870
Taxes Payable	(17,394)	(12,496)	(17,760)	2,895	81,978
Other Accruals	(300)	1,395	—	(3,932)	(34,923)
Net Increase (Decrease) in Working					
Capital	$(1,211)	$ 95,469	$ 8,844	$ 65,813	$(208,756)

EXHIBIT 6.17
Additional Information
(Problem 34)

	Fiscal Year Ending January 31				
W. T. Grant Company	**1971**	**1972**	**1973**	**1974**	**1975**
Range of Stock Price, Dollar per Share[a] ...	$41\frac{7}{8}$–$70\frac{5}{8}$	$34\frac{3}{4}$–$48\frac{3}{4}$	$9\frac{7}{8}$–$44\frac{3}{8}$	$9\frac{5}{8}$–41	$1\frac{1}{2}$–$11\frac{3}{8}$
Earnings per Share in Dollars	$2.64	$2.25	$2.49	$ .76	$(12.74)
Dividends per Share in Dollars	$1.50	$1.50	$1.50	$1.50	$ .30
Number of Stores	1,116	1,168	1,208	1,189	1,152
Total Store Area, Thousands of Square Feet	38,157	44,718	50,619	53,719	54,770
Retail Industry[b]	**1970**	**1971**	**1972**	**1973**	**1974**
Total Retail Sales in Millions of Dollars	$364,571	$408,850	$448,379	$503,317	$537,782
Number of Variety Stores (such as W. T. Grant)	7,056	6,972	7,498	8,212	8,714
Aggregate Economy[c]	**1970**	**1971**	**1972**	**1973**	**1974**
Gross National Product in Millions of Dollars	$1,075.3	$1,107.5	$1,171.1	$1,233.4	$1,210
Bank Short-Term Lending Rate	8.48%	6.32%	5.82%	8.30%	11.28%

[a] Source: Standard and Poor's Stock Reports.
[b] Source: Standard Industry Surveys.
[c] Source: Survey of Current Business.

PART THREE
MEASURING AND REPORTING ASSETS AND EQUITIES

CHAPTER 7
CASH, MARKETABLE SECURITIES, AND RECEIVABLES

By now, you have been exposed to all of the basic concepts and procedures of financial accounting. We have discussed the purpose of accounting, its theoretical framework, some of its procedures, and introduced financial statement analysis. From this point onward, we shall be concerned with the application of generally accepted accounting principles to individual assets and equities. The chapters are arranged in approximate balance sheet order. Current assets are the subject of Chapters 7 and 8. This chapter emphasizes liquid, cash-like, or "quick" assets, and Chapter 8 emphasizes inventories. Chapter 9 discusses noncurrent assets. Chapters 10 and 11 consider the right-hand side of the balance sheet—liabilities and owners' equity. Chapter 12, somewhat out of "balance sheet order," focuses on accounting for long-term investments in securities of other companies.

LIQUIDITY AND MONEY-LIKE ASSETS

As Chapters 5 and 6 pointed out, liquidity is essential for business operations. An insolvent company, one that cannot pay its bills and meet its commitments as they mature, will not survive no matter how large its owners' equity. Most bankrupt companies show positive owners' equity on their balance sheets at the time of bankruptcy. Bankruptcy is usually caused by an inability to meet debts as they become due. One of the largest bankruptcies of recent times occurred in 1970 when the Penn Central Transportation Company was placed into bankruptcy by its parent holding company, the Penn Central Company. At that time, Penn Central Transportation Company had almost $2 billion of stockholders' equity, including some $500 million of retained earnings. Nevertheless, the company became insolvent because it could not meet "only" a few hundred million dollars in current obligations at that time.

Money-like assets are an important determinant of a firm's liquidity. Cash, marketable securities, accounts receivable, and notes receivable are the principal liquid assets of a business. In previous chapters, we have seen that these assets are *generally* stated at their current cash, or cash-equivalent, values on the balance sheet. In this chapter, we explore in greater depth various inclusion and valuation questions related to each of these liquid assets. Some consideration is also given to liquidity management. The objective of the chapter is to develop a sufficient understanding of the methods of accounting and reporting for money-like assets so that an assessment can be made of a firm's liquidity at a moment in time and changes in that liquidity over time.

CASH

Cash is the most liquid asset. It is also the most vulnerable because of its susceptibility to theft or embezzlement. In this section, we consider cash inclusions and valuation as well as cash management and control.

Cash Inclusions and Valuation

To be included in "Cash" on the balance sheet, items should be freely available for use as a medium of exchange. Included in this category are coins, currency, travelers' checks, undeposited checks, and other cash on hand. Also included is cash in the bank in the form of demand deposits, savings accounts, and certificates of deposit. Although there are generally certain restrictions on the immediate withdrawal of funds from savings accounts and certificates of deposit, they are considered to be sufficiently available for use as a medium of exchange to be included in "cash." Foreign currency is also included unless there are restrictions on a firm's ability to use the currency. For example, foreign currency held by a division located in a country that significantly restricts the outflow of capital would probably not be included. Also, funds set aside or restricted for a particular purpose would not be included. For example, firms are often required to establish "sinking funds" to retire outstanding debt. The cash in a sinking fund would be reported under "Investments," rather than included in "Cash," on the balance sheet.

Compensating balances are frequently excluded from "Cash." A compensating balance generally takes the form of a minimum checking account balance that must be maintained in connection with a borrowing arrangement with a bank. For example, a firm might borrow $5 million from a bank and agree to maintain a 10 percent (= $500,000) compensating balance in an interest-free checking account. This arrangement results in a reduction of the amount effectively borrowed and an increase in the interest rate effectively paid by the borrower. Unless compensating balances are adequately disclosed, incorrect assessments of a firm's liquidity can occur.

With respect to reports submitted to the Securities and Exchange Commission, the SEC requires that legally restricted deposits held as compensating balances against short-term borrowing arrangements be stated separately from "Cash" but included among Current Assets. Similar compensating balances held against long-term borrowing arrangements should be included under noncurrent assets, preferably Investments. In cases where compensating balance arrangements exist but the firm is not legally precluded from using the cash, the nature of the arrangements and the amounts involved should be disclosed in a footnote to the financial statements.[1]

Once a determination is made as to which items are to be included in "Cash," there are few valuation problems. Cash is normally stated at its face amount. Foreign currency must be translated to its U.S. dollar-equivalent amount using the exchange rate in effect on the date of the balance sheet.

Cash Management

The management of cash involves two primary considerations. First, management must establish a system of internal controls to ensure that cash is properly safeguarded from theft or embezzlement. Typical internal control procedures include the separation of duties of individuals handling various cash receipt and disbursement tasks, the immediate depositing of cash receipts, the disbursement of cash only by authorized checks, and the regular preparation of bank account reconciliations. The appendix to this chapter describes some of the internal control procedures for cash.

A second management concern is that cash balances be regulated in such a way that neither too much nor too little cash is available at any time. Cash on hand or in checking accounts generally does not earn interest. In fact, during inflationary periods, idle cash loses purchasing power and therefore decreases in real value. A firm, therefore, does not want to maintain excessive cash balances. On the other hand, a firm does not want to find itself so short of cash that it is unable to meet its obligations as they become due or unable to take advantage of cash discounts.

One effective tool in cash management is the preparation of a weekly or monthly budget of cash receipts and disbursements. Such a budget will indicate both the time and amount when excess cash will be available for investment or when additional borrowing will become necessary. There have also been several quantitative models suggested for determining the optimal cash balance.[2]

MARKETABLE SECURITIES

A business may find itself with more cash than it needs for current and near-term business purposes. Rather than allow cash to remain unproductive, the business may invest some of its currently excess cash in income-yielding securities, such as U.S. government bonds or stocks or bonds of other companies. Such uses of liquid assets are known as investments in *marketable securities* or *temporary investments* and are alternatives to putting cash in savings accounts or certificates of deposit. In this section, we consider the classification and valuation of marketable securities. Chapter 12 discusses the accounting for long-term investments.

---

[1]   *Accounting Series Release No. 148,* "Amendments to Regulations S-X and Related Interpretations and Guidelines Regarding the Disclosure of Compensating Balances and Short-Term Borrowing Arrangements," Securities and Exchange Commission, 1973.
[2]   See Hans E. Daellenback, "Are Cash Management Models Worthwhile?" *Journal of Financial and Quantitative Analysis,* September 1974, pp. 607–626.

Classification of Marketable Securities

Securities are classified as "marketable securities" and shown among Current Assets as long as they can be readily converted into cash *and* management intends to do so when it needs to raise cash. Securities that do not meet both of these criteria are included under Investments on the balance sheet.

Example 1   Morrissey Manufacturing Corporation invested $150,000 of temporarily excess funds in U.S. Treasury notes. The notes mature in 3 months. This investment is properly classified among "marketable securities" since the notes can be sold at any time and even if not sold, the cash will be collected within 3 months.

Example 2   Suppose that Morrissey Manufacturing Corporation in Example 1 above had acquired 20-year bonds of Greer Electronics Company instead of the U.S. Treasury notes. Its intent in acquiring the bonds was the same as before, the invest-ment of temporarily excess cash. These bonds would likewise be classified as "market-able securities" since they can be traded in an established marketplace.

Example 3   West Corporation acquired 10 percent of the outstanding shares of Has-kell Corporation on the open market for $10 million. West Corporation plans to hold these shares as a long-term investment. Even though the shares of Haskell Corpora-tion are readily marketable, they would not be classified as "marketable securities," since West Corporation does not intend to turn the securities into cash within a reasonably short period. These securities would be classified under Investments on the balance sheet.

In published financial statements, all securities properly classified as "marketable securities" are grouped together and shown on a single line on the balance sheet. As we shall see below, however, a distinction is made for accounting purposes between *marketable debt securities* and *marketable equity securities*.

Valuation of Marketable Securities

Marketable securities, as with other assets, are initially recorded at acquisition cost. Acquisition cost includes the purchase price plus any commissions, taxes, and other costs incurred. For example, if marketable securities are acquired for $10,000 and $800 is paid in commissions and taxes, the entry is

Marketable Securities	10,800	
Cash		10,800

Dividends on marketable securities are recognized when declared. Interest is recog-nized when earned. Assuming that $125 of dividends were declared and $150 of interest were earned on the marketable securities above and these amounts were immediately received in cash, the entry is

Cash	275	
Dividend Revenue		125
Interest Revenue		150

Thus far, there is nothing about the valuation of marketable securities that has not already been covered in previous chapters. In the next section, however, we see for marketable equity securities a situation where a departure from historical-cost accounting is required.

Marketable Equity Securities   Financial Accounting Standards Board Statement No. 12[3] requires that the portfolio of marketable equity securities (that is, common stock, preferred stock, stock options, and warrants) be stated at the lower of acquisition cost or market at the end of each period. Under the *lower-of-cost-or-market method,* decreases in the market value of a portfolio of marketable equity securities are recognized as losses each period as they arise. Any subsequent increases in the market value of the portfolio up to the original acquisition cost must likewise be recognized as gains. In no case can the portfolio be stated at an amount greater than the original acquisition cost. The procedures for applying the lower-of-cost-or-market method are illustrated below.

Example 4   Nurnberg Company acquired marketable equity securities during 1979 and 1980 as shown below:

| | | | Market Value on | |
| | | Acquisition | | |
Security	Date Acquired	Cost	Dec. 31, 1979	Dec. 31, 1980
A Company	11/1/79	$10,000	$11,000	$13,000
B Company	12/1/79	20,000	18,000	17,000
C Company	2/1/80	30,000	—	26,000
D Company	4/1/80	40,000	—	41,000

The entry to record the acquisitions of shares in A Company and B Company during 1979 is

Marketable Securities	30,000	
Cash		30,000

At the end of 1979, the portfolio of marketable equity securities (that is, the securities of A Company and B Company) had an aggregate acquisition cost of $30,000 (= $10,000 + $20,000) and an aggregate market value of $29,000 (= $11,000 + $18,000). A write-down of $1,000 is required to recognize the unrealized loss.

Unrealized Loss on Valuation of Marketable Equity Securities	1,000	
Allowance for Excess of Cost of Marketable Equity Securities over Market Value		1,000

The loss account should appear in the income statement for 1979 among the expenses. The allowance account should be shown as a contra account to marketable securities on the balance sheet at the end of 1979.

---

[3]   Financial Accounting Standards Board, *Statement of Financial Accounting Standards No. 12,* 1975.

The entry to record the acquisitions during 1980 is

Marketable Securities	70,000	
Cash		70,000

At the end of 1980, the portfolio of marketable equity securities has an aggregate acquisition cost of $100,000 (= $10,000 + $20,000 + $30,000 + $40,000) and an aggregate market value of $97,000 (= $13,000 + $17,000 + $26,000 + $41,000). The balance in the allowance account before adjustment is still $1,000. An additional write-down of $2,000 is required.

Unrealized Loss on Valuation of Marketable Equity Securities	2,000	
Allowance for Excess of Cost of Marketable Equity Securities		
over Market Value		2,000

The marketable securities would be shown on the December 31, 1980, balance sheet at $97,000 (= $100,000 acquisition cost less $3,000 allowance).

To take the example one step further, assume that there were no acquisitions or dispositions of marketable equity securities during 1981 and that the market value of the portfolio at the end of 1981 was $102,000. The portfolio of securities would be written back up, but not to an amount greater than original acquisition cost. The entry would be

Allowance for Excess of Cost of Marketable Equity Securities		
over Market Value	3,000	
Recovery of Unrealized Loss on Valuation of Marketable Equity Securities		3,000

The debit entry above brings the balance in the allowance account to zero. The Recovery of Unrealized Loss on Valuation of Marketable Equity Securities account is included in the income statement for 1981 as a form of revenue or gain.

When individual marketable equity securities are sold, the realized gain or loss is the difference between the selling price and the acquisition cost of the individual securities, regardless of the balance in the allowance account. For example, assume that the securities of B Company were sold during 1980 for $17,500. The entry to record the sale would be

Cash	17,500	
Realized Loss on Sale of Marketable Securities	2,500	
Marketable Securities		20,000

Realized Loss = $17,500 proceeds of sale less $20,000 *original* cost.

The realized loss would be included in the determination of net income for 1980. The aggregate acquisition cost of the portfolio at the end of 1980 would now be $80,000 (= $10,000 + $30,000 + $40,000). The aggregate market value would likewise be $80,000 (= $13,000 + $26,000 + $41,000). Since the allowance account has a balance of $1,000 carried over from 1979, the following entry is necessary at the end of 1980 to reduce the allowance account:

Allowance for Excess of Cost of Marketable Equity Securities
over Market Value   1,000
   Recovery of Unrealized Loss on Valuation of Marketable Equity Securities   1,000

The securities will now be shown at $80,000 on the December 31, 1980, balance sheet.

Since these items are viewed as temporary investments, it is likely that there would be more buying and selling during the periods than indicated in the previous illustration. The acquisition costs and market values of the equity securities in the portfolio at the end of the period must be reported; to make the required adjusting entry, these two amounts must be compared with the acquisition cost and market value of the equity securities in the portfolio at the start of the period, even though the individual equity securities in the portfolio may have changed drastically during the period. The financial statements must include the following disclosures relating to marketable equity securities:

1 Aggregate cost and aggregate market value of the portfolio at each balance sheet date
2 The gross unrealized gain or the gross unrealized loss at the most recent balance sheet date
3 The unrealized gain or loss (that is, the change in the allowance account) included in net income each period
4 The realized gain or loss included in income each period
5 Any significant changes in the net unrealized gain or loss or the net realized gain or loss after the most recent balance sheet date but prior to the issuance of the financial statements.

Marketable Debt Securities   FASB Statement No. 12 addressed itself only to marketable equity securities. The accounting for marketable debt securities follows *Accounting Research Bulletin No. 43,* which prescribed acquisition cost as the valuation method except that "where market value is less than cost by a substantial amount and it is evident that the decline in market value is not due to a mere temporary condition, the amount to be included as a current asset should not exceed the market value."[4]

As a practical matter, many firms have adopted the lower-of-cost-or-market method for marketable debt securities during the past decade. The issuance of FASB Statement No. 12 has made this practice even more acceptable. The lower-of-cost-or-market method is usually applied to the portfolio of marketable equity securities separately from the portfolio of marketable debt securities.

Evaluation of Lower of Cost or Market   The lower-of-cost-or-market valuation method provides only a partial solution to accounting for marketable securities. Since at least 1939, accounting theorists have argued that marketable securities should be

---

[4] *Accounting Research Bulletin No. 43,* Chapter 3A, par. 9, AICPA, 1953.

shown at market value, whether greater or less than cost. Their very marketability makes valuing them on a current basis reasonably objective. The market value of the securities is the most relevant value for assessing a firm's liquidity. The FASB has taken the position, however, that permitting the write-up of marketable securities to an amount greater than acquisition cost would be a departure from historical-cost accounting, a move the FASB does not feel is appropriate yet. The case for market values for marketable securities is so strong that it is likely to be the first area where upward revaluations from acquisition cost will become acceptable.

ACCOUNTS RECEIVABLE

The third liquid asset to be considered in this chapter is accounts receivable. Accounts receivable typically arise when sales of goods or services are made on account. The entry is

Accounts Receivable	250	
Sales Revenue		250

Receivables sometimes also arise from transactions other than sales. For example, advances might be made to officers or employees, deposits might be made to guarantee performance or cover potential damages, or claims may be made against insurance companies, governmental bodies, common carriers, or others. These receivables are classified as either current assets or investments, depending on the expected collection date. In this section, we focus on trade accounts receivable. We consider their valuation and their management.

Accounts Receivable Valuation

Accounts receivable are initially recorded at the amount owed by customers. This amount is reduced for estimated uncollectible accounts, sales discounts, and sales returns and allowances. The reporting objective is to state accounts receivable at the amount expected to be collected in cash. It is also desirable that the charge against income for uncollectible accounts, sales discounts, and sales returns and allowances be made in the period when the related revenue is recognized. In this way, a proper periodic measurement of revenue will be achieved.

Uncollectible Accounts

Whenever credit is extended to customers, there will almost certainly be some accounts that will never be collected. The uncollectible amount will vary among different types of enterprises both as to its relative significance and as to its regularity. In recording uncollectible accounts, the practice is sometimes followed of waiting until a customer's account has clearly been demonstrated to be uncollectible and then recognizing a loss when the account is written off. If it is decided that the account receivable of Robert S. Thomley for $135 has become uncollectible, the entry would be

Bad Debt Expense 135
   Accounts Receivable—Robert S. Thomley 135
To record loss from account receivable which has become uncollectible.

This "direct write-off" method is not appropriate when such losses are significant in amount, occur frequently, and are reasonably predictable, as in retail stores. The direct write-off method usually fails to recognize an uncollectible amount in the accounting period when the sale occurs and revenue from it is recognized. Too much income is reported in the period of sale and too little in the period of write-off. The period of the sale on account to customers is the appropriate time for the adjustment, not the later period when the firm discovers that a specific account is uncollectible.

A better procedure is known as the *allowance method.* This method involves:

1 Estimating the amount of uncollectible accounts that will occur at some time in connection with the sales of each period.
2 Making an adjusting entry reducing the reported revenue of the period for the estimated uncollectible amount, and
3 Making a corresponding adjustment to the amount of accounts receivable so that the balance sheet figure reports the amount expected to be collected.

The entry involves a debit to Sales, Uncollectible Accounts Adjustment, which is an account contra to Sales, and a credit to Allowance for Uncollectible Accounts, which is an account contra to the total of Accounts Receivable. The credit must be made to a contra account rather than to Accounts Receivable because no specific, individual account is being written off at the time of entry.[5] Since the Allowance for Uncollectible Accounts is a contra to Accounts Receivable, its balance at the end of the period appears on the balance sheet as a deduction from Accounts Receivable. The Sales, Uncollectible Accounts Adjustment account, as a revenue contra, is deducted from sales revenue on the income statement.

To illustrate the allowance method, assume that 2 percent of the credit sales made during the present period will never be collected. If sales on account are $35,000, then the entry to reduce revenue and reduce the amount of Accounts Receivable to the amount expected to be collected would be

Sales, Uncollectible Accounts Adjustment 700
   Allowance for Uncollectible Accounts 700
To record estimate of uncollectible accounts arising from current period's sales (.02 × $35,000).

When a particular customer's account is judged uncollectible, it is written off against the Allowance for Uncollectible Accounts. If, for example, it is decided that a balance of $135 due from Robert S. Thomley will not be collected, the entry to charge off the account is

---

[5] Recall that Accounts Receivable is a master, or "control" account showing the total of all amounts receivable from specific customers. There is a separate account for each customer in a subsidiary ledger; the Accounts Receivable account merely records their total.

Allowance for Uncollectible Accounts 135
   Accounts Receivable 135
To write off Robert S. Thomley's account.

Under the allowance method, the revenue for the period of sale is reduced by the amount of uncollectibles that is estimated to arise from that period's sales. Some time later, when the attempts at collection are finally abandoned, the specific account is written off. Net assets are not affected by writing off the specific account. The reduction in net assets took place earlier, when the Allowance for Uncollectibles was credited in the entry recognizing the estimated amount of eventual uncollectibles.

Rationale for the Revenue Contra Presentation

In practice, many firms do not treat the adjustment for estimated uncollectibles as a reduction in revenue. Instead the adjustment is treated as an administrative or selling expense, reported in the income statement as Bad Debt Expense. Net income for the period is the same whether the uncollectibles charge is treated as a revenue contra or as an expense provided that the same method for estimating the *amount* of uncollectibles is used.

We prefer to treat the adjustment for estimated uncollectibles as a reduction in revenue, not as an expense. To justify this preference, we ask, "What is the optimal amount of uncollectible accounts for a firm?" For most firms, the optimal amount of uncollectibles is not zero. If a firm is to have no uncollectible accounts, it must screen credit customers carefully, which is costly. Furthermore, the firm would deny credit to many customers who would pay their bills even though they could not pass a most stringent credit check. Some of the customers who are denied credit will take their business elsewhere and sales will be lost. So long as the revenue collected from credit sales to a given class of customers exceeds the cost of goods sold and the selling expenses to that class of customers, the firm will be better off selling to that class rather than losing the sales. The rational firm should prefer granting credit to a class of customers who have a high probability of paying their bills, rather than losing their business, even though there may be some uncollectible accounts.

For example, if gross margin—selling price less cost of goods sold—on new credit sales is 20 percent of credit sales, then a firm could afford uncollectible accounts of up to 20 percent of the new credit sales and still show increased net income, so long as selling and administrative expenses remain constant.

An expense is a "gone asset." Accounts that prove uncollectible are not assets, because the rational firm made credit sales expecting that a small percentage of those sales would never be collected. Hence, the amount of uncollectibles was never an asset or revenue in the first place. Thus we reach the conclusion that the amount of the uncollectible accounts should be treated as an adjustment in determining revenue, not as a "gone asset" or expense.

We do not suggest, of course, that a firm grant credit indiscriminately or ignore collection efforts for uncollected accounts receivable. We do suggest that a cost/benefit analysis of credit policy will probably dictate a strategy that results in some amount of uncollectible accounts, an amount that is reasonably predictable before any sales are made.

Estimating Uncollectibles

There are two basic methods used for calculating the amount of the adjustment for uncollectible accounts. These are the *percentage-of-sales method* and the *aging-of-accounts-receivable method.*

Percentage-of-Sales Method   The easiest method in most cases is to multiply the total sales on account during the period by an appropriate percentage, because it seems reasonable to assume that uncollectible account amounts will vary directly with the volume of credit business. (The example on page 244 used the percentage-of-sales method.) The percentage to be used can be determined by a study of the experience of the business or by an inquiry into the experience of similar enterprises. The rates found in use will generally be within the range of $\frac{1}{4}$ percent to 2 percent of credit sales.

To illustrate, assume that sales on account total $150,000, and experience indicates that the appropriate percentage of uncollectible accounts is 2 percent. The entry is

Sales, Uncollectible Accounts Adjustment   3,000
   Allowance for Uncollectible Accounts   3,000
To provide for estimate of uncollectibles as determined by a percentage of sales.

If cash sales occur in a relatively constant proportion to credit sales, the percentage, proportionately reduced, can be applied to the total sales for the period. The total sales amount may be more readily available than that for sales on account.

Aging-of-Accounts-Receivable Method   Another method of calculating the amount of the adjustment, often called *aging the accounts,* involves classifying each customer's account as to the length of time during which the accounts have been uncollected. Common intervals used for classifying individual accounts receivable are

1 Not yet due
2 Past due 30 days or less
3 Past due 31 to 60 days
4 Past due 61 to 180 days
5 Past due more than 180 days.

The presumption is that the balance in the Allowance for Uncollectible Accounts should be large enough to cover substantially all accounts receivable past due for more than 6 months and smaller portions of the more recent accounts. The actual portions are estimated from past experience.

As an example of the adjustment to be made, assume that the present balance in the Accounts Receivable account is $85,000 and the balance in the Allowance for Uncollectible Accounts before the adjusting entry for the period is $3,600. An aging of the accounts receivable balance ($85,000), shown in Exhibit 7.1, results in an estimate that $6,800 of the accounts will probably become uncollectible. The adjustment requires that the Allowance for Uncollectible Accounts balance be $6,800, an increase of $3,200. The adjusting entry at the end of the period is

Sales, Uncollectible Accounts Adjustment   3,200
  Allowance for Uncollectible Accounts   3,200
To increase Allowance account to $6,800 as determined by an aging analysis.

Even when the percentage method is used, aging the accounts should be done periodically as an occasional check on the accuracy of the percentage being used. If the aging analysis shows that the balance in the Allowance for Uncollectible Accounts is apparently too large or too small, the percentage of sales to be charged to the contra-revenue account can be raised or lowered so that the apparent error will work itself out through future adjustments.

EXHIBIT 7.1
Illustration of Aging Accounts Receivable

Classification of Accounts	Amount	Estimated Uncollectible Percentage	Estimated Uncollectible Amounts
Not yet due	$68,000	0.5%	$ 340
1–30 days past due	6,000	6.0	360
31–60 days past due	3,000	25.0	750
61–180 days past due	5,000	50.0	2,500
Over 180 days past due	3,000	95.0	2,850
	$85,000		$6,800

When the percentage-of-sales method is used, the periodic provision for uncollectible accounts (for example, $3,000), is merely added to the amounts provided in previous periods in the account, Allowance for Uncollectible Accounts. When the aging method is used, the balance in the account, Allowance for Uncollectible Accounts, is adjusted (for example, by $3,200) to reflect the desired ending balance. If the percentage used under the percentage-of-sales method is reasonably accurate, the *balance* in the allowance account should be approximately the same at the end of each period under these two methods of estimating uncollectible accounts.

Exhibit 7.2 illustrates the operation of the allowance method for uncollectibles over two periods. In the first period the percentage method is used. In the second period the aging method is used. Normally, a firm would use the same method in all periods.

EXHIBIT 7.2
Review of the Allowance Method of Accounting for Uncollectible Accounts

Transactions in the First Period:
(1) Sales are $800,000.
(2) Cash of $737,000 is collected from customers in payment of their accounts.
(3) At the end of the first period, it is estimated that uncollectibles will be 2 percent of sales; $.02 \times \$800,000 = \$16,000$.
(4) Specific accounts totaling $6,000 are written off as uncollectible.
(5) The revenue, revenue contra, and other temporary accounts are closed.

Transactions in the Second Period:
(6) Sales are $1,000,000.
(7) Specific accounts totaling $17,000 are written off during the period as information on their uncollectibility becomes known. The debit balance of $7,000 will remain in the Allowance account until the adjusting entry is made at the end of the period; see (9).
(8) Cash of $973,000 is collected from customers in payment of their accounts.
(9) An aging of the accounts receivable, as in Exhibit 7.1, shows that the amount in the Allowance account should be $12,000. The amount of the adjustment is $19,000. It is determined as the difference between the desired $12,000 credit balance and the current $7,000 debit balance in the Allowance account.
(10) The revenue, revenue contra, and other temporary accounts are closed.

Cash		Accounts Receivable		Allowance for Uncollectible Accounts	
		(1) 800,000			16,000 (3)
(2) 737,000			737,000 (2)		
			6,000 (4)	(4) 6,000	
Bal. ?		Bal. 57,000			10,000 Bal.
		(6) 1,000,000			
			17,000 (7)	(7) 17,000	
(8) 973,000			973,000 (8)		
					19,000 (9)
Bal. ?		Bal. 67,000			12,000 Bal.

Sales, Uncollectible Accounts Adjustment		Sales Revenue	
(3) 16,000			800,000 (1)
	Closed (5)	(5) Closed	
(9) 19,000			1,000,000 (6)
	Closed (10)	(10) Closed	

Sales Discounts

Often the seller of merchandise offers a reduction from its invoice price for prompt payment. Such reductions are called *sales discounts* or *cash discounts*.[6] Discounts should be considered as a reduction in sales revenue in the period of the sale. There is nothing incongruous in the proposition that goods may have two prices: a cash price or a higher price if goods are sold on credit. The cash discount is offered, not only as an interest allowance on funds paid before the bill is due—the implied interest rate is unreasonably large—but also as an incentive for prompt payment so that additional bookkeeping and collection costs can be avoided. To state it more realistically, the goods are sold for a certain price if prompt payment is made, and a penalty is added in the form of a higher price if the payment is delayed. The bills rendered by many public utilities illustrate this more realistic approach. The amount of sales discount made available to customers, then, should be considered as one of the adjustments in the determination of net sales revenue.

The need to prepare operating statements for relatively short periods leads to alternative possibilities for recording sales discounts and determining the amount of sales discounts reported for a period. The theoretical issue is whether the amount of cash discount should be deducted from sales revenue in the period when the sales revenue is recognized or in the period of cash collection. In determining the amount of sales discounts recognized for a period, the major alternatives are the following:

1 To recognize discounts when taken by the customer, without regard to the period of sale (called the *gross price method*)
2 To estimate the total amount of discounts that will be taken on the sales made during the period (called the *allowance method*)
3 To record sales amounts reduced by all discounts made available to customers and to recognize additional revenue when a discount lapses (called the *net price method*).

These methods are discussed in advanced accounting texts.

Sales Returns

When a customer returns merchandise, the sale has, in effect, been canceled, and an entry that reverses the recording of the sale would be appropriate. In analyzing sales activities, however, management may be interested in the amount of goods returned. If so, a Sales Returns account, a contra to Sales, is used to accumulate the amount of returns for a particular period.

A cash refund, such as might be made in a retail store when a customer returns merchandise that had been purchased for cash, would be entered as

Sales Returns	23	
Cash on Hand		23

---

[6] See the Glossary at the back of the book for the definition of a *discount* and a summary of the various contexts where this word is used in accounting.

Return of goods by a customer who buys "on account" would usually involve the preparation of a credit memorandum, which is, in effect, the reverse of a sales invoice. The credit memorandum lists the goods that have been returned and indicates the amount that is to be allowed the customer. The entry to record the issuance of the credit would normally be a debit to the Sales Returns account and a credit to the Accounts Receivable account. The Sales Returns account is a revenue contra account. The net amount of sales for the period will reflect the amount of such returns.

Somewhat misleading sales and income amounts can result if goods are returned in a period after the one of sale. If there is no adjustment, the sales and income amounts for the period of sale are overstated, since they reflect transactions that are later canceled. Further, sales and revenue amounts are correspondingly understated in the period when the goods are returned. It would be possible to use the same type of estimated allowance procedure for returns that was illustrated for uncollectible accounts, but since the amounts involved are usually relatively small, it is not customary to do so.

Another type of distortion may occur: The costs that have been incurred in making the sale, other than the cost of the goods, constitute a loss to the business and should not, strictly speaking, be charged against other completed sales. Occasionally, a charge is made to the customer for delivery costs both ways on returned goods or a deduction is made for loss in value of the goods from handling and shipment, but usually the privilege of return without penalty is granted as a part of the service of the merchant. It would be difficult, if not impossible, to isolate the costs relating to a particular returned sale. Further, some accountants argue that these costs are normal—necessary for ongoing business operations—and can therefore logically be absorbed as costs of making the sales that are not returned. There are techniques for meeting some of the foregoing considerations, but they are beyond the scope of this discussion.

Sales Allowances

A *sales allowance* is a reduction in price granted to a customer, usually after the goods have been delivered and found to be unsatisfactory or damaged. Again, as in the case of sales returns, the effect is a reduction in the sales revenue, but it may be desirable to accumulate the amount of such adjustments as a separate item. A revenue contra account, Sales Allowances, may be used for this purpose, or a combined account title, Sales Returns and Allowances, may be employed. The record-keeping problems are similar to those caused by sales returns.

Presentation of Sales Adjustments in the Income Statement

In discussing the complications that accompany accounts receivable, we have introduced several adjustments to sales that are accumulated in revenue contra accounts. All these adjustments—for uncollectible accounts, for discounts, for returns, and for allowances—are illustrated in the Caral Company's income statement, Exhibit 7.3, for the month of June 1979. Caral Company uses the gross price method for recording sales-related transactions. See also Exhibit 7.4 on page 255.

EXHIBIT 7.3
Income Statement Illustration of
Sales and Sales Adjustments
Caral Company
Partial Income Statement
for the Month Ended June 30, 1979

Revenues

Sales—Gross		$51,523
Less Sales Adjustments:		
Discounts Taken[a]	$2,367	
Allowances	1,126	
Uncollectible Accounts Adjustment	1,030	
Returns	857	
Total Sales Adjustments		5,380
Net Sales		$46,143

[a] The gross price method is used. If the net price method were used, discounts taken would not be shown and there would be an *addition* to revenue for the amount of sales discounts that lapsed.

Turning Receivables into Cash

In some cases, a firm may find itself temporarily short of cash and unable to obtain financing from its usual sources. In such instances, accounts receivable can be used to obtain financing. A firm may *assign* its accounts receivable to a bank or finance company to obtain a loan. The borrowing company physically maintains control of the accounts receivable, collects amounts remitted by customers, and then forwards the proceeds to the lending institution. Alternatively, the firm may *pledge* its accounts receivable to the lending agency. If the borrowing firm is unable to make loan repayments when due, the lending agency has the power to sell the accounts receivable in order to obtain payment. Finally, the accounts receivable may be *factored* to a bank or finance company to obtain cash. In this case, the accounts receivable are in effect sold to the lending institution and it physically controls the receivables and collects payments from customers. If accounts receivable have been assigned or pledged, a footnote to the financial statements should indicate this fact. The collection of such accounts receivable will not increase the liquid resources available to the firm to pay general trade creditors. Accounts receivable that have been factored will not appear on the balance sheet, since they have been sold.

NOTES RECEIVABLE

Many business transactions involve written promises to pay sums of money at a future date. These written promises are called promissory notes. The holder of a promissory note has a liquid asset, notes receivable. A promissory note is a written contract in which one person, known as the *maker,* promises to pay to another person, known as the *payee,* a definite sum of money. The money may be payable either on demand or at a definite future date. The maker may be a group of individuals and there may also be more than one payee. The amount is usually payable to the order of the payee, so that the note can readily be transferred from one holder to another. A note may or may not provide for the payment of interest in addition to the principal amount.

Promissory notes are used most commonly in connection with obtaining loans at banks or other institutions, the purchase of various kinds of property, and as a temporary settlement of an open or charge-account balance when payment cannot be made within the usual credit period. A note may be *secured* by a mortgage on real estate (land and buildings) or personal property (machinery and merchandise), or by the deposit of specific collateral (stock certificates, bonds, and so forth). If the secured note is not collected at maturity, the lender can take possession of the real estate, personal property, or other collateral, sell it, and apply the proceeds to the repayment of the note. Any proceeds in excess of the amount due under the note are then paid to the borrower. Alternatively, the note may be *unsecured,* in which case it has about the same legal position as an account receivable.

Calculation of Interest Revenue

Interest is the price paid for the use of borrowed funds. From the lender's point of view, it is a type of revenue. The interest price is usually expressed as a percentage rate of the principal, with the rate being stated on an annual basis. Thus, a 2-month, 12-percent note would have interest equal to 2 percent of the principal; a 3-month, 6-percent note would have interest equal to $1\frac{1}{2}$ percent of principal, and so on. Since interest is a payment for the use of borrowed funds for a period of time, it accrues with the passage of time. Although interest accrues every day (indeed, every time the clock ticks), firms usually record interest only at the time payments are made or received or at the end of an accounting period.

Most short-term notes receivable from customers are based on *simple interest* calculations.[7] The general formula for the calculation of simple interest is

$$\text{Interest} = \text{Base (Principal or Face)} \times \text{Interest Rate} \times \text{Elapsed Time.}$$

The calculation of simple interest for a year or for any multiple or fraction of a year is an elementary arithmetic computation. For example, the interest at the rate of 8 percent a year on $2,000 is $160 for 1 year, $320 for 2 years, $80 for 6 months, and so on. The calculation for shorter periods, although still not an involved mathematical problem, is complicated by the odd number of days in a year and the variations in the number of days in a month. Simple interest at the rate of 8 percent a year on $2,000 for 90 days would be $2,000 $\times$ .08 $\times$ 90/365, or $39.45, if an exact computation were made. For many purposes, especially the calculation of accrued interest, a satisfactory approximation of the correct interest can be obtained by assuming that the year has 360 days and that each month is one-twelfth of a year. Thus, 30 days is the

---

[7] Most long-term notes involve *compound interest,* which is discussed in Appendix B at the end of the book.

equivalent of 1 month, and 60 days is the equivalent of 2 months or one-sixth of a year. Under this method, the interest at 8 percent on $2,000 for 90 days would be the same as the interest for 3 months or one-quarter of a year, or $40. Keep in mind that nearly all quotations of simple interest rates state the rate per year, unless some other period is specifically mentioned. In the formula for simple interest, Principal × Rate × Elapsed Time, "time" should be expressed in terms of years, since the rate is the rate per year.

For the sake of uniformity and simplicity, we shall use the following rules in connection with the calculation of interest throughout the text and problems:

1 When the maturity terms are given in months, consider 1 month to be one-twelfth of a year; 3 months to be one-fourth of a year; 6 months to be one-half of a year, and so on, regardless of the actual number of days in the period. This is equivalent to regarding any 1-month period as being 30 days in a 360-day year.
2 When the maturity terms are given in days, use the 360-day year. Consider 30 days to be one-twelfth of a year, 60 days to be one-sixth of a year, 17 days to be 17/360 of a year, and so on. Determine maturity dates and elapsed time by using the actual number of days.
3 When the maturity terms are given in actual dates, such as 60 days from April 1, the first day is not counted and the last day is. That is, all transactions are assumed to occur at the close of a business day. Thus, 60 days from April 1 is May 31.

Accounting for Interest-Bearing Notes Receivable

The notes to be discussed in this section, so-called interest-bearing notes, are those that indicate a face, or principal, amount together with explicit interest at a stated rate for the time period stated in the note.[8] For example, the basic elements of such a note might read: "Sixty days after date (June 30, 1979), the Suren Company promises to pay to the order of the Mullen Company $3,000 with interest from date at the rate of 12 percent per annum." At the maturity date, August 30, 1979, the maturity value would be the face amount of $3,000 plus interest of $60 calculated in accordance with the preceding discussion ($60 = $3,000 × .12 × 60/360), or a total of $3,060.

Among the types of transactions related to a note receivable discussed in this section are the following: receipt of note, interest recognition at an interim date, transfer prior to maturity, and collection at maturity dates.

Receipt of Note and Collection at Maturity Promissory notes usually are received from customers in connection with sales or with the settlement of an open account receivable. The customer is usually the maker, but the customer may transfer a note that has been received from another. It is common practice to allow the customer full credit for the face value and accrued interest, if any, although a different value might be agreed upon in some instances.

---

[8] Non-interest-bearing notes, those for which the face amount is the same as the maturity value and implicit interest is included in the principal, involve compound interest calculations and are discussed in Chapter 10.

If, on June 30, 1979, the Mullen Company were to receive a 60-day, 12-percent note for $3,000, dated July 1, 1979, from the Suren Company, to apply on its account, the entry would be

June 30	Notes Receivable	3,000	
	Accounts Receivable—Suren Company		3,000

Assuming the accounting period of the Mullen Company to be the calendar year, the entry upon collection at maturity would be

Aug. 30	Cash on Hand	3,060	
	Notes Receivable		3,000
	Interest Revenue		60

Assuming the accounting period of the Mullen Company to be 1 month, the interest adjustment at the interim date, July 31, would be

July 31	Interest Receivable	30	
	Interest Revenue		30
	($3,000 × .12 × 30/360 = $30.)		

The entry upon collection at maturity would then be

Aug. 30	Cash on Hand	3,060	
	Notes Receivable		3,000
	Interest Receivable		30
	Interest Revenue		30

At the maturity date, the note may be collected, as illustrated above, renewed, partially collected with renewal of the balance, or dishonored by the maker. These other possibilities involve more advanced accounting procedures and are not discussed in this book.

Transfer of Notes Receivable To obtain cash, a note may be transferred to another party *without recourse.* This procedure is equivalent to a sale of the note, because the transferor has no further liability even if the maker fails to pay at maturity.

If Mullen Company transferred without recourse the 60-day, 12-percent, $3,000 note to Lane Trust Company for $3,030 one month after the date of the note, the entry would be

July 31	Cash	3,030	
	Notes Receivable		3,000
	Interest Revenue		30
	To record transfer of note without recourse.		

Most businesses that "purchase" notes are, however, unwilling to acquire them without recourse. Such firms do not want to be responsible for investigating the creditworthiness of the maker or for any collection efforts required for dishonored notes. Consequently, most notes that are transferred are done so *with recourse.*

A transfer with recourse places a potential or "contingent" liability on the transferor if the maker fails to pay at maturity. This contingent liability is assumed when the transferor signs or "endorses" the note with only a signature or with a signature together with wording such as "pay to the order of . . . " Such a transfer is not a closed, or completed, transaction because of the possibility that the endorser will have to pay the note in case the maker defaults at maturity.

Contingent liabilities, such as those for notes transferred with recourse or for the potential loss arising from an unsettled damage suit, are discussed in Chapter 11. Contingent liabilities are not shown directly in the accounts, but are merely disclosed in notes to the balance sheet.

If Mullen Company transferred with recourse the 60-day, 12-percent $3,000 note to Lane Trust Company 1 month after the date of the note, the entry would be the same as if the note was transferred without recourse. If Mullen Company prepared financial statements before Lane Trust Company collected from the maker, however, the notes to Mullen's balance sheet would contain a statement such as the following:

Contingent Liabilities. The firm is contingently liable for a note transferred and accrued interest thereon to the Lane Trust Company. The face value of the transferred note is $3,000.

ILLUSTRATION OF BALANCE SHEET PRESENTATION

The balance sheet accounts discussed in this chapter include Cash, Certificates of Deposit, Marketable Securities, Notes Receivable, and Accounts Receivable. The presentation of these items in the balance sheet is illustrated in Exhibit 7.4, which includes all of the current assets, not just the liquid assets, for the Caral Company as of June 30, 1979.

EXHIBIT 7.4
Detailed Illustration of Current
Assets on the Balance Sheet
Caral Company
Partial Balance Sheet
June 30, 1979

Current Assets

Cash on Hand (Change and Petty Cash Funds)		$ 1,000
Cash in Bank		13,000
Certificates of Deposit		8,000
Marketable Securities (At Cost, Less than Market Value of $20,000)		16,000
Notes Receivable (Note A)...		8,000
Interest Receivable on Notes		200
Accounts Receivable	$50,000	
Less: Allowance for Uncollectible Accounts	3,000	47,000
Merchandise Inventory		72,000
Prepaid Rent		3,000
Prepaid Insurance		1,800
Total Current Assets		$170,000

Note A. The amount of Notes Receivable does not include notes with a face amount of $2,000, which have been discounted with recourse at the Harris Bank. The company is contingently liable for these notes should the makers not honor the notes at maturity. The estimated amount of our liability is zero.

SUMMARY

This chapter has examined the accounting for cash and other liquid, or cash-like, assets. Among the questions addressed were the following:

1 What items are included in each of the liquid asset accounts?
2 At what amount are they stated?
3 Are there any restrictions on the use of particular liquid assets?

The appendix to this chapter discusses internal control procedures for protecting cash.

APPENDIX 7.1
Controlling Cash

Of all assets, cash is the most difficult to control—to safeguard from theft. This appendix discusses the usual procedures of accounting for and controlling cash. For internal control purposes, most firms maintain two cash accounts, Cash on Hand and Cash in Bank.

CONTROLLING CASH RECEIPTS AND DISBURSEMENTS

The system for controlling cash receipts should be designed to ensure that all money collected for the firm ends up in the firm's treasury. In most businesses, collections are received primarily through the mail in the form of bank checks or in currency and coins for cash sales. The need to control the collections of currency and coins is obvious. All collections for cash sales should be recorded promptly, either in a cash register or some other device that both records the receipts and locks in the amount of the collection. Other kinds of collections are more susceptible to mishandling because they occur less often. These include receipts from the sale of assets not normally intended to be sold, receipts from dividends and interest on investments, collections on notes receivable, proceeds of bank loans, and proceeds of stock or bond issues.

One way to provide effective control of cash receipts would be to maintain duplicate sets of records, each under separate supervision. But doing so would be expensive. The business need not undertake this expensive control device, however, if it (1) designs its cash-handling techniques so that the monthly statement received from its bank effectively serves as a duplicate record and (2) separates the functions of cash handling and record keeping. To use the bank statement as an effective cash-controlling device requires prompt depositing of all receipts and making all disbursements by check.

Undeposited Cash

If a firm follows the desirable plan of depositing all receipts intact, disbursements will usually be made only from checking accounts. Any balance in the Cash on Hand account will represent cash received since the last deposit, which usually will have been made the previous business day. A daily record of cash on hand is usually necessary. Cash registers facilitate the accumulation of cash data. There are many types, but the usual cash register is a combination of a cash drawer and a multiple-register adding machine. The transactions are entered by hand. Then they are recorded and accumulated by the register so that at the end of the day the totals are available for each of several divisions of the day's activities—the total cash sales (sometimes classified according to products or departments), total collections on account, and total sales of each salesperson.

Cash in Bank—Deposits

A deposit ticket provides the information for preparing the journal entry to record the deposit of cash funds in the checking account. The deposit ticket should be prepared in duplicate; the bank keeps the original and the firm keeps the duplicate. The duplicate is often initialed by the bank teller and used as a receipt for the deposit of the funds. The total on the deposit ticket is entered in a journal as a debit to Cash in Bank and a credit to Cash on Hand.

Cash in Bank—Issuance of Checks

The information for the entry to record checks drawn in payment of bills comes from the document authorizing the disbursement. The customary entry will be a debit to Accounts Payable and a credit to Cash in Bank.

Control of Disbursements by Check

All cash payments except for those of very small amounts should be made by check. The firm can thereby restrict the authority for payments to a few employees. Firms often provide further control by requiring that all checks be signed by two employees. Another control device is the use of a Cash Disbursements Journal or Check Register in which all checks issued are recorded. Using such a journal provides control because a single person, who is not allowed to authorize payments or to sign checks, is responsible for recording all payments.

In any case, control over disbursements should ensure that:

1 Disbursements are made only by authorized persons.
2 Adequate records support each disbursement. Such records attest that disbursement was for goods and services procured by proper authority and actually received by the business. The records attest that payment is made in accordance with the purchase contract.
3 The transaction is entered properly in the formal accounting records.
4 Authority for authorization of payment is separate from authority to pay, and record keeping is separate from both.

THE BANK STATEMENT

At the end of each month (or other regular interval), the bank sends a statement together with the canceled checks that have been paid and deducted from the depositor's account, and memorandums of any other additions or deductions that have been made by the bank. When the bank statement is received, it should be compared promptly with the record of deposits, checks drawn, and other bank items on the records of the firm.

The balance shown on the bank statement will rarely correspond to the balance of the Cash in Bank account. The two basic causes of the difference are time lag and errors. In the normal course of business activities, some items will have been recorded by either the bank or the firm without having reached the recording point on the other set of records, hence a *time lag* difference. Causes of such differences include: checks outstanding (that is, checks recorded by the drawing firm but not yet received by the bank on which they were drawn), deposits made just before the bank statement date that do not appear on the bank statement, and transactions (such as service charges and collections of notes or drafts) that have not been recorded on the firm's books. The other basic difference is caused by errors in record keeping by either the firm or the bank. The process of comparing the bank statement with the books is known as *reconciling* the bank account, and the schedule that is prepared to demonstrate the results of the comparing is called a *bank reconciliation.* A typical reconciliation schedule is shown in Exhibit 7.5. The preparation of the bank reconciliation schedule is explained below.

Preparing the Bank Reconciliation Schedule

The purpose of the bank reconciliation is to explain the difference between the book balance of Cash in Bank and the bank's statement of the firm's cash on deposit and to indicate the required adjustments of the firm's accounts. If the bank statement is used as a control device, as we suggest it should, the bank reconciliation is the final step in the monthly procedure for controlling cash receipts and disbursements. The bank reconciliation provides a convenient summary of the adjusting entries that must be made by the firm to account for previous errors in recording cash-related transactions or for cash transactions that have not yet been recorded.

Preparing the bank reconciliation schedule typically involves the following steps.

1 Enter at the top of the reconciliation schedule the balance as shown on the bank statement.
2 Enter next any deposits that have not been recorded on the bank statement. Such items usually occur because the bank has prepared the statement before the deposits for the last day or two have been recorded. If there are any time or date breaks in the list of deposits for the period, the bank should be notified promptly.
3 Enter any other adjustments of the bank's balance such as errors in recording canceled checks or deposits, or the return of checks belonging to some other customer of the bank. Errors on bank statements are infrequent.

EXHIBIT 7.5
Young Spring Company
Bank Reconciliation Schedule—
Citizens National Bank
April 1, 1979

Balance shown on bank statement, April 1, 1979		$2,323.36
Deposits of March 30 and 31, not yet recorded by bank		643.16
Check of Young Wire Co. deducted by bank in error		10.00
		$2,976.52
Outstanding checks:		
#367	$ 69.67	
#470	142.53	
#471	131.26	
#472	131.44	
#474	243.55	
#475	305.52	
Less: Total outstanding checks		1,023.97
Adjusted bank balance[a]		$1,952.55
Balance shown on books, April 1, 1979		$1,453.55
Items unrecorded on books:		
Collection of note of J. T. Munn—		
Face amount of note	$500.00	
Less collection charge	(5.00)	495.00
Less bank service charge for March		(14.00)
Adjusted book balance before correction of errors		$1,934.55
Check #467 for $168.81 was entered in the check register as $186.81. It was issued in March 1979, to pay a bill for office equipment		18.00
Adjusted book balance[a]		$1,952.55

[a] This is the amount that would be shown in the Cash in Bank account if a balance sheet were prepared as of April 1, 1979.

4 Obtain a total.
5 List the outstanding checks. A list should be prepared, beginning with the checks still outstanding from the previous period and continuing with the checks outstanding which were drawn during the current period.
6 Deduct the sum of the outstanding checks from the total obtained in step 4. The balance is the adjusted bank balance—the balance that would be shown on the bank statement if all deposits had been entered, all checks written had been returned, and no errors had been made; it is the final figure for this first section of the statement.

These steps will frequently conclude the reconciliation because this balance should correspond to the balance of the Cash in Bank account as of the bank statement date when there are no unrecorded transactions or errors. If these two amounts are not equal at this point, the following steps must be taken and shown in a second section of the reconciliation schedule.

7 Enter the Cash in Bank account balance as shown on the books as of the bank statement date.
8 Add or deduct any errors or omissions that have been disclosed in the process of reviewing the items returned by the bank. These will include such items as errors in recording deposits or checks, unnumbered checks that have not been entered in the check register, and service charges and collection fees deducted by the bank.
9 The net result is the adjusted book balance, and it must correspond to the adjusted bank balance derived in the first section. If it does not, the search must be continued for other items that have been overlooked.

Adjusting Entries from Bank Reconciliation Schedule

The bank reconciliation schedule shows two distinct kinds of differences:

1 Differences between the balance shown on the bank statement and the adjusted bank balance
2 Differences between the account balance in the firm's books and the adjusted book balance.

Only the second type of difference requires entries on the firm's books. Any deposits not credited by the bank will presumably have been recorded by the time the reconciliation is prepared and, in any event, represent funds that the depositor may assume are in the bank and available for disbursement by check.

Entries must be made for all of the differences between the firm's account balance on the books and the adjusted book balance, since they represent errors or omissions that must be corrected. The reconciliation illustrated in Exhibit 7.3 requires adjustments for bank service charges, for the collection of a note, and for the check whose amount was incorrectly recorded.[9] The entries would be

Bank Service Charge Expense	14	
Cash in Bank		14
Service charges for month of March.		
Cash in Bank	495	
Collection Expense	5	
Note Receivable, J. T. Munn		500
Note collected by bank.		
Cash in Bank	18	
Accounts Payable		18
To correct entry of check #467.		

---

[9] The bank must, of course, correct any error on its books when the mistake is called to its attention. The entry on the bank's books to correct the error shown on the reconciliation in Exhibit 7.5 is

Deposits—Young Wire Company	10	
Deposits—Young Spring Company		10
To correct posting of check charged to Young Spring Company account in error.		

SUMMARY OF ACCOUNTING FOR CASH

Management is always concerned about getting the best and safest use of its resources, and an enterprise's most valuable resource, cash, is also its most vulnerable. An internal control system is essential to the proper management of cash. One way to provide control is to maintain duplicate and independent records of cash flows, but this is not necessary if an enterprise uses the monthly bank statement as a duplicate record. Using the bank statement as an effective control device requires depositing receipts daily and making all disbursements by check or through petty cash funds. By this means the bank reconciliation serves as a control device because the bank record will reflect the cash inflows and outflows of the enterprise.

QUESTIONS AND PROBLEMS

1 Review the meaning of the following concepts or terms discussed in this chapter.
  a Liquidity.
  b Quick assets.
  c Insolvent.
  d Cash.
  e Demand deposits.
  f Certificate of deposit.
  g Foreign currency.
  h Compensating balance.
  i Marketable securities.
  j Investments (noncurrent).
  k Marketable debt securities.
  l Marketable equity securities.
  m Lower of cost or market.
  n Unrealized loss on marketable securities.
  o Recovery of unrealized loss on marketable securities.
  p Realized gain or loss on marketable securities.
  q Sales, Uncollectible Accounts Adjustment account.
  r Aging of accounts receivable.
  s Sales discounts.
  t Sales returns and allowances.
  u Simple interest.
  v Recourse.
  w Factoring.
  x Contingent liability.

2 What evidence of cash control have you observed in a cafeteria? A department store? A theater? A gasoline station?

3 The Tastee Delight ice cream stores prominently advertise on signs in the stores that the customer's purchase is free if the clerk does not present a receipt. Oakland's Original hot dog stand says that the customer's purchase is free if the cash register receipt contains a red star. What control purposes do such policies serve?

4 Current assets are defined as those assets that are expected to be turned into cash, or sold, or consumed within the next operating cycle. Cash is not always classified as a current asset, however. Explain.

5 Does application of the lower-of-cost-or-market valuation method to the portfolio of marketable equity securities or to each marketable equity security individually result in the most conservative asset values and net income amounts?

6 Which of the two methods for treating uncollectible accounts implies recognizing revenue reductions earlier rather than later? Why?

7 a An old wisdom in tennis holds that if your first serves are always good, then you are not hitting them hard enough. An analogous statement in business might be that if you have no uncollectible accounts, then you probably are not selling enough on credit. Comment on the validity of this statement.
b When are more uncollectible accounts better than fewer uncollectible accounts?
c When is a higher percentage of uncollectible accounts better than a lower one?

8 The customary method of accounting for sales returns results in adequate reporting for the returned sales when the goods are returned in the same period in which they are sold. If the goods are returned in a period subsequent to that of the sale, distortion of the reported revenue figures results. Explain how sales returns may produce each of the described effects.

9 Under what circumstances will the Allowance for Uncollectible Accounts have a debit balance during the accounting period? The balance sheet figure for the Allowance for Uncollectible Accounts at the end of the period should never show a debit balance. Why?

10 What is the effect on the financial statements of discounting, or transferring, a note with recourse versus without recourse?

11 Indicate if each of the following items should be included in "cash" on the balance sheet. If not, indicate how the item should be reported.
a Cash that has been collected from customers and is awaiting deposit in the firm's checking account.
b Cash left in cash registers each day which serves as a change fund.
c Cash set aside in a special savings account to accumulate funds to replace equipment as it wears out. The firm is not legally obligated to use the funds for this purpose.
d Cash set aside in a special savings account to accumulate funds to retire debt as it becomes due. The firm is legally obligated to use the funds for this purpose.
e A postdated check received from a customer. The check is dated 60 days after the date of the balance sheet.
f A money order received from a customer.
g Postage stamps.
h Cash in a petty cash fund which is used for small miscellaneous expenditures, such as freight charges and executive lunches.
i Cash in a checking account which must be maintained at a certain minimum level in accordance with a written loan agreement for a 6-month loan.

12 You are asked to determine the amount that should be shown as "Cash" on the balance sheet as of December 31, 1979, for Stevens Transportation Company. The following information is obtained.

a Coins, currency, and checks received from customers on December 31, 1979, but not yet deposited, $5,300.

b Amount in a petty cash fund which is maintained for making small miscellaneous cash expenditures. The fund normally has a balance of $100, but expenditures of $14 were made on December 31, 1979.

c The firm's postage meter was "filled" on December 31, 1979, and contains $500 of postage.

d The books indicate that the balance in the firm's checking account on December 31, 1979, is $45,800. When the bank statement is received on January 10, 1980, it is learned that one customer's check for $800, which was deposited on December 28, 1979, was returned for insufficient funds. In addition, the bank collected, during December 1979, a note receivable from one of Stevens' customers and added the amount to Stevens' bank account. The note had a face value of $200 and interest of $20.

e Certificate of deposit for a face value of $10,000. The certificate was acquired on July 1, 1979, and matures on June 30, 1980. Simple interest of 6 percent per year accumulates on the note and is payable at maturity with the principal.

f British sterling currency, £10,000. The exchange rate on December 31, 1979, is $2.00 per pound sterling.

13 Refer to the Simplified Funds Statement for a Period in Exhibit 5.15 on page 174. Ten of the lines in the statement are numbered. Line (2) should be expanded to say "Additions for Expense and Other Charges Against Income Not Using Funds" and line (3) should be expanded to say "Subtractions for Revenue and Other Credits to Income Not Producing Funds from Operations." Ignore the other lines in responding to the questions below.

Assume that the accounting cycle is complete for the period and that all of the financial statements have been prepared. Then, it is discovered that a transaction has been overlooked. That transaction is recorded in the accounts, and all of the financial statements are corrected. Define *funds* as *working capital*. For each of the following transactions or events, indicate which of the numbered lines of the funds statement is affected and by how much. Ignore income tax effects.

a Estimated uncollectibles equal to 2 percent of the year's sales of $1 million are recognized. An entry is made increasing the Allowance for Uncollectible Accounts.

b The specific account receivable of Eli Worman in the amount of $200 is written off by a firm using the allowance method.

c The specific account receivable of Eli Worman in the amount of $300 is written off by a firm using the direct write-off method.

d A firm owns marketable securities. Dividends of $10,000 are declared on the shares owned.

e The portfolio of marketable securities has a market value of $50,000 less than their net amount shown on the balance sheet at the end of the current accounting period. An entry is made changing the allowance account contra to marketable securities.

f The market value of the same portfolio of marketable securities referred to in part **e** has increased $20,000 by the end of the next period. An entry is made changing the allowance account for marketable securities.

14 Rogerson Corporation borrowed $1 million from State National Bank on July 1, 1979. The bank charged Rogerson Corporation interest at its prime lending rate of 8 percent. The principal and interest on the loan is repayable on June 30, 1980. Rogerson Corporation must maintain a $100,000 compensating balance in an interest-free checking account at State National Bank during the term of the loan.

   a What is the effective annual interest rate that Rogerson Corporation is paying on this loan?

   b What message to Rogerson Corporation is implicit in State National Bank's requirement that a compensating balance be maintained?

15 a Arrange the following data related to the Ayer Company in bank reconciliation form.

Adjusted bank balance	$6,853
Adjusted book balance	6,853
Balance per bank statement, October 31, 1979	7,941
Balance per books, October 31, 1979	6,075
Error in deposit of October 28; $457 deposit entered	
on books as $475	18
Outstanding checks	1,233
Payroll account check deducted from this account in error	145
Proceeds on note of W. Y. Jones, taken by the bank for collection,	
less collection fee of $4	796

   b Present journal entries on the books of the Ayer Company to record the adjustments indicated in the bank reconciliation schedule.

16 a Prepare a bank reconciliation schedule at July 31, 1979, for the Home Appliance Company from the following information:

Balance per bank statement, July 29	$1,240
Balance per ledger, July 31	714
Deposit of July 30 not recorded by bank	280
Debit memo—service charges	8
Credit memo—collection of note by bank	300

An analysis of the canceled checks returned with the bank statement reveals the following:

   Check #901 for purchase of supplies was drawn for $58 but was recorded as $85.

The manager wrote a check for traveling expenses of $95 while out of town. The check was not recorded. The following checks are outstanding:

#650	$120
#721	162
#728	300
	$582

   b Journalize the adjusting entries required by the information revealed in the bank reconciliation schedule.

17 On May 31, 1979, the books of the Locus Land Company show a debit balance in the Cash in Bank account of $4,799. The bank statement at that date shows a balance of $6,066. The deposit of May 31 of $205 is not included in the bank statement. Notice of collections made by the bank on mortgages of the company in the amount of $243, including interest of $8, and of bank service charges of $6 have not previously been received. Outstanding checks at May 31 total $1,235.

a Prepare a bank reconciliation for the Locus Land Company at May 31, 1979.

b Journalize the entries required upon preparation of the bank reconciliation schedule.

18 The following items are taken from the April 30, 1979, bank reconciliation schedule of the Porter Company. Present a journal entry required on the books of the company for each item; indicate if no adjustment is required.

(1) Outstanding checks total $1,650.

(2) A check drawn as $196 for office supplies was recorded in the appropriate journal as $169.

(3) Included among the checks returned by the bank was one for $150 drawn by the Peter Company and charged to this company in error.

(4) The deposit of April 30 of $420 was not included on the bank statement.

(5) A debit memorandum was included for service charges for April in the amount of $10.

(6) The bank collected a note of $1,750, including $50 of interest, for the company.

(7) Checks for traveling expenses of $250 had not been entered in the journal.

(8) A check was written and recorded on April 29 for the regular monthly salary of an office employee who had resigned on March 31. The check has been voided, but an entry to record the voiding has not been made. The monthly salary was $600; deductions of 8 percent for FICA taxes and $120 for withheld income taxes were made.

19 The bank reconciliation of the Clark Company at March 31, 1979, was as follows:

Balance per bank statement, March 31, 1979	$ 3,850
Unrecorded deposit	475
	$ 4,325
Outstanding checks	820
Adjusted bank and book balance, March 31, 1979	$ 3,505

The bank statement, returned checks, and other documents received from the bank at the end of April provide the following information:

Balance, April 29, 1979	$ 3,685
Deposit of March 31, 1979	475
Deposits of April 1–29 including a credit memo for a collection of a note, $808	16,160
Canceled checks issued prior to April 1, 1979	600
Canceled checks issued during April, 1979	16,200

The Cash in Bank account of the Clark Company for the month of April shows deposits of $16,190 and checks drawn of $17,015. The credit memo has not as yet been recorded on the books of the company; it represents the collection of a note with $800 face value on which $5 interest had been accrued as of March 31, 1979.

a Prepare a bank reconciliation for the Clark Company at April 30, 1979.

b Present in journal entry form any adjustment of the company's books resulting from the information determined in the bank reconciliation.

20 Indicate the classification of each of the securities below in the balance sheet of Bower Corporation on December 31, 1979.

   a U.S. Treasury Bills, acquired on October 15, 1979. The bills mature on April 15, 1980.

   b Shares of stock of Home Savings and Loan Association in which Bower Corporation maintains savings accounts and certificates of deposit.

   c Shares of Brazil Coffee Corporation, a major supplier of raw materials for Bower Corporation's products.

   d Shares of Overland Transportation Company. The shares were originally acquired as a temporary investment of excess cash. Overland Transportation Company has been so profitable that Bower Corporation plans to increase its ownership percentage, eventually obtaining 51 percent of the outstanding shares.

   e American Telephone and Telegraph Company bonds that mature in 1985. The bonds were acquired with a cash advance from a customer on a contract for the manufacture of machinery.

21 The aggregate cost and aggregate market value of the portfolio of marketable equity securities of Elliott Corporation at various dates are shown below:

Date	Aggregate Cost	Aggregate Market Value
December 31, 1979	$150,000	$140,000
December 31, 1980	160,000	154,000
December 31, 1981	170,000	175,000
December 31, 1982	180,000	178,000

Give the journal entry required at the end of each year, assuming that the accounting period is the calendar year.

22 Information relating to the marketable equity securities of Alcron Corporation is summarized below:

Security	Date Acquired	Acquisition Cost	Date Sold	Selling Price	Market Value Dec. 31, 1979	Market Value Dec. 31, 1980
A	1/5/79	$40,000	11/5/80	$43,000	$41,000	—
B	6/12/79	85,000	—	—	80,000	$82,000
C	2/22/80	48,000	—	—	—	46,000
D	3/25/80	25,000	11/5/80	23,000	—	—
E	4/25/80	36,000	—	—	—	36,000

   a Give all journal entries relating to these marketable equity securities during 1979 and 1980, assuming that the calendar year is the accounting period.

   b Indicate the manner in which marketable securities would be presented in the balance sheet and related notes on December 31, 1979.

   c Indicate the manner in which marketable securities would be presented in the balance sheet and related notes on December 31, 1980.

23 Information relating to the marketable equity securities of Webster Corporation is summarized below:

					Market Value	
Security	Date Acquired	Acquisition Cost	Date Sold	Selling Price	Dec. 31, 1979	Dec. 31, 1980
W	10/15/79	$142,000	2/15/80	$136,000	$140,000	—
X	12/28/79	56,000	11/28/80	59,000	56,500	—
Y	2/15/80	136,000	—	—	—	$139,000
Z	11/28/80	59,000	—	—	—	58,000

   a Give all journal entries relating to these marketable equity securities during 1979 and 1980, assuming that the calendar year is the accounting period.

   b Indicate the manner in which marketable securities would be presented in the balance sheet and related notes on December 31, 1979.

   c Indicate the manner in which marketable securities would be presented in the balance sheet and related notes on December 31, 1980.

24 Information relating to the marketable equity securities of TSS Company is shown below:

					Market Value	
Security	Date Acquired	Acquisition Cost	Date Sold	Selling Price	Dec. 31, 1979	Dec. 31, 1980
H	4/26/79	$18,000	2/9/80	$15,000	$16,000	—
I	5/25/79	25,000	8/10/80	26,000	24,000	—
J	11/24/79	12,000	—	—	14,000	$15,000
K	2/26/80	34,000	—	—	—	33,500
L	12/17/80	8,000	—	—	—	7,800

   a Determine the realized and the unrealized gain or loss for 1979 in accordance with FASB Statement No. 8.

   b Determine the realized and the unrealized gain or loss for 1980 in accordance with FASB Statement No. 8.

   c Repeat steps **a** and **b** but assume that lower of cost or market is applied for each security rather than the portfolio of securities. Gains and losses on sale of marketable securities will be based, in this case, on the lower-of-cost-or-market book value.

   d Does application of lower of cost or market at the level of the portfolio or at the level of individual securities result in the more conservative asset values and measures of earnings?

25 The sales, all on account, of the Nelson Company in 1978, its first year of operations, were $600,000. Collections totaled $550,000. On December 31, 1978, it was estimated that 1.5 percent of sales on account would probably be uncollectible. On that date, specific accounts in the amount of $3,000 were written off.

   The company's *unadjusted* trial balance (but after all *non*-adjusting entries were made) on December 31, 1979, included the following accounts and balances:

Accounts Receivable (Dr.)	$60,000	
Allowance for Uncollectible Accounts (Dr.)	3,000	
Sales, Uncollectible Accounts Adjustment	—	
Sales (Cr.)		$700,000

It was concluded that the estimated uncollectible account rate of 1.5 percent of sales should be applied to 1979 operations.

Present journal entries to portray the following:

a   Transactions and adjustments of 1978 related to sales and customers' accounts.

b   Transactions of 1979 resulting in the above trial balance amounts.

c   Adjustment for estimated uncollectibles for 1979.

26 The trial balance of the Wagner Company at the end of 1978, its first year of operations, included $18,000 of outstanding customers' accounts. An analysis reveals that 80 percent of the total credit sales of the year had been collected and that no accounts had been charged off as uncollectible.

The auditor estimated that 2 percent of the total credit sales would be uncollectible.

On January 31, 1979, it was concluded that the account of H. J. Williams, who had owed a balance of $300 for 6 months, was uncollectible and should be written off at that time.

On July 1, 1979, the amount owed by H. J. Williams, previously written off, was collected in full.

Present dated journal entries to record the following:

a   Adjustment for estimated uncollectible accounts on December 31, 1978.

b   Write-off of the H. J. Williams account on January 31, 1979.

c   Collection of the H. J. Williams account on July 1, 1979, assuming that it is felt that there is evidence that the account should not have been written off as uncollectible.

27 The amounts in certain accounts on January 1, 1979, and before closing entries on December 31, 1979, are shown below:

	January 1, 1979	December 31, 1979
Accounts Receivable	$400,000 Dr.	$ 480,000 Dr.
Allowance for Uncollectible Accounts	30,000 Cr.	20,000 Dr.
Sales, Uncollectible Accounts Adjustment	0	0
Sales	0	2,000,000 Cr.

During 1979, 90 percent of sales were on account. It was estimated that 3 percent of credit sales would become uncollectible. During 1979, one account for $1,500 was collected, although it had been written off as uncollectible during 1978.

a   Give the journal entries made during 1979 that explain the changes in the four accounts as listed above.

b   Give any adjusting entries required on December 31, 1979.

28 The balance sheets of Wilcox Corporation on December 31, 1978, and December 31, 1979, showed accounts receivable of $8,342,000 and $9,648,000, respectively. A footnote indicates that the balances in the Allowance for Uncollectible Accounts account at the beginning and end of 1979, after closing entries, were credits of $749,000 and $931,000, respectively. The income statement for 1979 shows that the provision for estimated uncollectible accounts was $300,000, which was 1 percent of sales. All sales are made on credit. There were no recoveries during 1979 of accounts written off in previous years. Give all the journal entries that were made during 1979 that have an effect on Accounts Receivable and Allowance for Uncollectible Accounts.

29 The data in the following schedule pertain to the first 8 years of the Gordon Company's credit sales and experiences with uncollectible accounts.

Year	Credit Sales	Related Uncollectible Accounts	Year	Credit Sales	Related Uncollectible Accounts
1	$100,000	$2,550	5	$250,000	$3,000
2	150,000	3,225	6	275,000	2,700
3	200,000	3,725	7	280,000	2,875
4	225,000	4,000	8	290,000	2,925

Gordon Company has not previously used an Allowance for Uncollectible Accounts but has merely charged accounts written off directly to Uncollectible Accounts Expense.

What percentage of credit sales for a year would you recommend that Gordon Company charge to the sales adjustment account if one were to be set up at the end of year 8?

30 Lave Company's accounts receivable show the following balances by ages:

Age of Accounts	Balance Receivable
0–30 days	$200,000
31–60 days	75,000
61–120 days	30,000
More than 120 days	15,000

The credit balance in the Allowance for Uncollectible Accounts is now $5,075.

Lave Company's independent auditors suggest that the following percentages be used to compute the estimates of amounts that will eventually prove uncollectible: 0–30 days, .5 of 1 percent; 31–60 days, 1 percent; 61–120 days, 10 percent; more than 120 days, 60 percent. Prepare a journal entry that will carry out the auditor's suggestion.

31 a The Feldman Company has a gross margin on credit sales of 30 percent. That is, cost of goods sold on account is 70 percent of sales on account. Uncollectible accounts amount to 2 percent of credit sales. If credit is extended to a new class of customers, credit sales will increase by $10,000, 8 percent of the new credit sales will be uncollectible, and selling expenses will increase by $1,000. Would Feldman Company be better or worse off if it extends credit to the new class of customers and by how much?

  b How would your answer to part **a** differ if $2,000 of the $10,000 increase in credit sales would have been made anyway as sales for cash? (Assume that the uncollectible amount on new credit sales is $800.)

  c The Norman Company has credit sales of $100,000, a gross margin on those sales of 25 percent, and 3 percent of the credit sales are uncollectible. If credit is extended to a new class of customers, sales will increase by $40,000, selling expenses will increase by $1,500, and uncollectibles will be 5 percent of *all* credit sales. Verify that Norman Company will be $4,500 better off if it extends credit to the new customers. What percentage of the new credit sales are uncollectible?

32 Calculate simple interest on a base of $6,000 for the following intervals and rates, using a 360-day year.
  a 60 days at 12 percent.
  b 60 days at 8 percent.
  c 90 days at 9 percent.
  d 60 days at 16 percent.
  e 15 days at 16 percent.

    f 6 months at 9 percent.
    g 5 months, 15 days at 12 percent.
    h 4 months, 12 days at 9 percent.

33 On May 10, 1979, the Pacific Supply Company receives a note from one of its customers, Silk Builders, Inc., to apply on its account. The 6-month, 12-percent note for $6,600, issued on May 10, 1979, is valued at its face amount.

    On July 25, 1979, the Pacific Supply Company endorses the note and transfers it with recourse to the Cobb Steel Products Company to settle an account payable. The note is valued at its face amount plus accrued interest.

    On November 12, 1979, the Pacific Supply Company was notified that the note was paid at maturity.

    a Present dated entries on the books of the Pacific Supply Company, assuming that it closes its books quarterly on March 31, June 30, and so on.

    b Present dated entries on the books of the Cobb Steel Products Company, assuming that it closes its books quarterly on March 31, June 30, and so on.

34 On November 1, 1979, the Atlantic Supply Company received a note from one of its customers to apply on its open account receivable. The 9-month, 9-percent note for $8,000, issued November 1, 1979, is valued at its face amount.

    On January 31, 1980, the Atlantic Supply Company endorses the note and transfers it with recourse to Second National Bank. The Company's checking account at this bank is increased for the proceeds, $8,100.

    On August 1, 1980, the Atlantic Supply Company is notified by the bank that the note was collected from the customer at maturity.

    Atlantic Supply Company closes its books annually on December 31.

    Present dated journal entries on the books of Atlantic Supply Company relating to this note.

35 Give the likely transaction or event that would result in making each of the independent journal entries below:

a Notes Receivable	300	
Accounts Receivable		300
b Marketable Securities	10,000	
Cash		10,000
c Sales, Uncollectible Accounts Adjustment	2,300	
Allowance for Uncollectible Accounts		2,300
d Unrealized Loss on Valuation of Marketable Equity Securities	4,000	
Allowance for Excess of Cost of Marketable Equity Securities over Market Value		4,000
e Cash	295	
Notes Receivable		285
Interest Revenue		10
f Cash	1,200	
Loss on Sale of Marketable Securities	200	
Marketable Securities		1,400
g Allowance for Uncollectible Accounts	450	
Accounts Receivable		450
h Allowance for Excess of Cost of Marketable Equity Securities over Market Value	1,000	
Recovery of Unrealized Loss on Valuation of Marketable Equity Securities		1,000

i	Bad Debt Expense	495	
	Accounts Receivable		495
j	Accounts Receivable	285	
	Allowance for Uncollectible Accounts		285

36 Refer to Problem **28** at the end of Chapter 5 on p. 186. Consider now the questions asked there.

37 A recent annual report of a major petroleum company revealed the following information (in millions of dollars).

	December 31,	
BALANCE SHEET	**Year 2**	**Year 1**
Cash	$ 1,299	$ 1,179
Marketable Securities	3,212	3,984
Accounts Receivable	5,217	4,704
Inventories:		
Crude Oil, Products, and Merchandise	3,758	3,438
Materials and Supplies	455	414
Prepayments	585	365
Total Current Assets	$14,526	$14,084
Property, Plant, and Equipment—Net	19,562	17,220
Investments and Other Assets	2,984	2,575
Total Assets	$37,072	$33,879
Notes and Loans Payable	$ 1,305	$ 1,388
Accounts Payable and Accrued Liabilities	8,073	6,705
Income Taxes Payable	782	747
Total Current Liabilities	$10,160	$ 8,840
Long-Term Debt	3,901	3,841
Deferred Income Taxes	4,000	3,429
Total Liabilities	$18,061	$16,110
Capital	$ 2,601	$ 2,596
Earnings Reinvested	16,410	15,173
Total Shareholders' Equity	$19,011	$17,769
Total Liabilities and Shareholders' Equity	$37,072	$33,879

SOURCES AND USES OF WORKING CAPITAL

Sources:	Year 2	Year 1
Net Income	$ 1,537	$ 1,342
Depreciation and Depletion	600	550
Deferred Income Taxes	571	480
Working Capital Provided from Operations	$ 2,708	$ 2,372
Additions to Long-Term Debt	60	40
Additions to Capital Stock	5	2
Uses:		
Additions to Property, Plant, and Equipment	(2,942)	(1,245)
Cash Dividends to Petroleum Company Shareholders	(300)	(250)
Additional Investments in Securities	(409)	(300)
Net Decrease/Increase in Working Capital	$ (878)	$ 619

Prepare an analysis that explains the change in cash during year 2 from $1,179 million to $1,299 million. You may want to review the procedures in the appendix to Chapter 5.

38 Refer to the financial statements for International Corporation in Appendix A at the back of the book.
   a The consolidated balance sheet shows that cash increased from $98,906,000 to $117,984,000 between the beginning and end of 19X1, an increase of $19,078,000. Prepare an analysis that explains this change, indicating the amount of cash obtained from operations, issuing bonds and stock, and other sources and the amount of cash used for dividends, acquisition of property, plant and equipment, and other uses. (Hint: You may want to review the relevant procedures in Chapter 5.)
   b Prepare an analysis that explains the change in the Marketable Securities account of International Corporation between the beginning and end of 19X1.
   c Prepare an analysis that explains the change in the account, Customers Receivables— Net, of International Corporation between the beginning and end of 19X1.

CHAPTER 8
INVENTORIES AND COST OF GOODS SOLD

In the 1970s many major U.S. corporations changed their method of accounting for inventories and cost of goods sold. As a result of the change in methods, these corporations reported net income that was smaller by hundreds of millions of dollars than would have been reported without the change. Paradoxically, these firms were actually better off as a result of the change. This chapter attempts to resolve the apparent paradox of how a firm could be better off despite the reporting of smaller net income than had been anticipated. We introduce the choices that any firm must make in accounting for inventories and show how the decisions made can affect reported expenses and net income for the period. The choices made in accounting for inventories can make two companies that are basically alike appear to be quite different.

INVENTORY TERMINOLOGY

The term *inventory,* as used in accounting and in this chapter, means a stock of goods or other items owned by the firm. Goods held for sale by a retail or wholesale business are referred to as *merchandise* or *merchandise inventory;* goods held for sale by a manufacturing concern are referred to as *finished goods.* The inventories of manufacturing firms also include *work in process* (partially completed products in the factory) and *raw materials* (materials being stored which will become part of goods to be produced). Various types of supplies that will be consumed in administrative, selling, and manufacturing operations are also frequently included in inventories on the balance sheet.

The term *inventory* is sometimes used as a verb. To inventory a stock of goods means to prepare a list of the items on hand at some specified date, to assign a unit price to each item, and to calculate the total cost of the goods.

SIGNIFICANCE OF ACCOUNTING FOR INVENTORIES

One major objective of financial accounting is to measure periodic income. The role of accounting for inventories in measuring income is the assignment of cost to various accounting periods as expenses. The total cost of goods available for sale or use during a period must be allocated between the current period's usage (cost of goods sold, an expense) and the amounts carried forward to future periods (the end-of-period inventory, an asset).

One equation applies to all inventory situations and will facilitate our discussion of accounting for inventory. In the following equation, all quantities are measured in physical units.

$$\text{Beginning Inventory} + \text{Additions} - \text{Withdrawals} = \text{Ending Inventory}$$

If we begin a period with 1,000 pounds of salt (beginning inventory), if we purchase (add) 1,500 pounds during the period, and if we use (withdraw) 1,300 pounds during the period, then there should be 1,200 pounds of salt left at the end of the period (ending inventory). More important for accounting purposes, the inventory equation can be rewritten as

$$\text{Beginning Inventory} + \text{Additions} - \text{Ending Inventory} = \text{Withdrawals}.$$

If we begin the period with 1,000 pounds of salt, if we purchase 1,500 pounds of salt, and if we observe 1,200 pounds of salt on hand at the end of the period, then we know that 1,300 pounds of salt were used, or otherwise withdrawn from inventory, during the period. The sum of Beginning Inventory plus Additions is often called "Goods Available for Sale (or Use)." In this example there are 2,500 pounds of salt available for sale (or use).

If accounting were concerned merely with keeping a record of physical quantities, there would be few problems in accounting for inventories. But, of course, accounting reports are stated in dollar amounts, not physical quantities. If all prices remained constant, inventory accounting problems would be minor, because any variation in values of inventories would be attributable solely to changes in quantities. The major problems in inventory accounting arise from fluctuations over time in the unit acquisition costs of inventory items.

Consider the inventory of goods for sale in a merchandising firm. The inventory equation can be written as follows, with all quantities measured in dollars of cost:

$$\text{Beginning Inventory} + \text{Net Purchases} - \text{Cost of Goods Sold} = \text{Ending Inventory}.$$

Rearranging terms, the equation becomes

$$\text{Beginning Inventory} + \text{Net Purchases} - \text{Ending Inventory} = \text{Cost of Goods Sold}.$$

The valuation for the ending inventory will appear on the balance sheet as the asset, Merchandise Inventory; the amount of Cost of Goods Sold will appear on the income statement as an expense of generating the sales revenue.

To illustrate, suppose that a merchandising firm (appliance store) had a beginning inventory of one toaster, which we call "toaster 1" and which cost $25. Suppose further that two toasters are purchased during the period, toaster 2 for $29 and toaster 3 for $30, and that one toaster is sold for $55. The three toasters are alike in every physical respect, and there is no way of determining which toaster was the one that was sold.

If financial statements are prepared with amounts measured in dollar terms, then some assumption must be made about which toaster was sold. The total cost of the three toasters available for sale is $84, and the average cost of the toasters is $28 [= ($25 + $29 + $30)/3]. There are at least four assumptions that can be made in applying the inventory equation to determine the Cost of Goods Sold expense for the income statement and the ending inventory for the balance sheet:

Assumed Item Sold	Cost of Goods Available for Sale (Beginning Inventory Plus Purchases)[a]	= Cost of Goods Sold (for Income Statement)	+ Ending Inventory (for Balance Sheet)
Toaster 1	$84	$25	$59
Toaster 2	84	29	55
Toaster 3	84	30	54
"Average" toaster	84	28	56

[a] Cost of Goods Available for Sale = Cost of (Toaster 1 + Toaster 2 + Toaster 3) = ($25 + $29 + $30) = $84.

As the inventory equation and the toaster example both show, the higher the Cost of Goods Sold, the lower must be the Ending Inventory. The choice of which particular pair of numbers to use—one for the income statement and one for the balance sheet—is determined by the *cost-flow assumption*. Making a cost-flow assumption is just one problem, but it is the major one, in accounting for inventories.

Problems of Inventory Accounting

Discussion of inventory accounting can be conveniently split into consideration of individual problems, considered more or less separately. The remainder of this chapter discusses four such problems:

1 Periodic and perpetual methods of keeping track of items in inventory
2 Valuation basis for items in inventory
3 Costs included in acquisition cost
4 Cost-flow assumptions for the movement of goods and prices into and out of inventory.

The income tax laws affect some of the firm's choices in accounting for inventories. We discuss the impact of income taxes at the appropriate places.

There are other inventory management problems that require attention by a successful business, but these problems are considered in managerial accounting courses. For example, the physical size of inventories can significantly influence the profitability of the firm. A firm whose inventory is too small may lose customers because of "stock-outs," whereas one whose inventory is too large will incur extra costs of holding and storing unnecessary quantities.

INVENTORY METHODS

There are two principal methods of determining the physical quantity and dollar amount of an inventory. One is known as the *periodic* inventory method and the other as the *perpetual* inventory method. The periodic method is less expensive to use than the perpetual method, but the perpetual method provides useful information not provided by the periodic method.

Periodic Inventory Method

The periodic inventory method determines the ending inventory figure by taking a physical count of units on hand at the end of an accounting period and multiplying the quantity on hand by the cost per unit. Then the inventory equation is used to determine the withdrawals that represent the cost-of-goods-sold expense (or the cost of manufacturing materials used, a product cost, or of supplies used, either a product cost or a general and administrative expense). The following form of the inventory equation is used to determine the cost of goods sold under the periodic method:

Beginning Inventory + Purchases − Ending Inventory = Cost of Goods Sold.
    (known)   (known)   (counted)   (solved for)

When the periodic method is used, no entry is made for withdrawals (cost of goods sold or used) until the end of the accounting period when the time comes to compute ending inventory and the cost of goods sold or used. To illustrate the application of the periodic method, assume that sales during the year amounted to $123,500. The entries made to record sales during the year would have the combined effect of the following entry:

Cash and Accounts Receivable 123,500
  Sales   123,500
Sales recorded for the entire year have this effect.

At the end of the year, a physical count is taken, an inventory valuation is made, and the cost of the withdrawals is determined from the inventory equation. For example,

Cost of Merchandise Inventory, January 1 . . . . $ 10,000
Plus Merchandise Purchased (Net) During the Year   100,000
Cost of Goods Available for Sale During the Year $110,000
Less Cost of Merchandise Inventory, December 31   15,000
Cost of Goods Sold During the Year . . . . $ 95,000

The cost-of-goods-sold expense is recognized in a single entry:

Cost of Goods Sold 95,000
  Merchandise Inventory   95,000
Cost of Goods Sold recognized under the periodic inventory method.

The principal disadvantage of the periodic inventory method is the assumption that all goods not accounted for by the physical inventory count have been sold or used. Any "shrinkages" (the general name for losses from such causes as breakage, theft, evaporation, and waste) are buried in the cost of goods sold or the cost of materials or supplies used. Thus, no information is generated to aid in controlling the amount of shrinkage. Furthermore, physically counting the inventory at the end of the accounting period is apt to interfere seriously with normal business operations for several days. Some firms using the periodic inventory method even close down and engage practically the entire staff on the physical count and measurement of the items on hand. Preparing operating statements more frequently than once a year is expensive when the inventory figures are obtained only by physically counting inventories.

Estimating Inventory Values When the Periodic Method Is Used   To count every item in inventory is generally expensive. Firms try to do it as seldom as possible, consistent with requirements of generally accepted accounting principles and proper inventory control. When the periodic inventory method is used and financial statements are to be prepared, say at the end of a month or quarter, reasonably good estimates of Ending Inventory and Cost-of-Goods-Sold amounts can often be obtained with the various *gross margin methods* and *retail methods*. The details of these methods are covered in intermediate accounting books, but we can introduce the general idea involved.

The foundation of these estimating methods is the fact that most businesses mark up the cost of similar kinds of merchandise by a relatively constant percentage in obtaining selling prices. For example, nearly every college bookstore sets the selling price of a textbook 25 percent more than its cost to the bookstore. Put another way, the manager of the bookstore would say that the gross margin (= retail selling price less cost) is 20 percent of selling price.[1] To take another example, men's clothing in a department store is likely to carry a selling price twice the cost to the store. The selling price of most types of retail items stands in a relatively constant percentage to their costs. This fact is used in estimating Ending Inventory and Cost of Goods Sold.

We find it easier to illustrate the procedure than to define it. The method is illustrated in Exhibit 8.1 and is often called the *gross margin method*. The gross margin percentage is defined by

$$\text{Gross Margin Percentage} = \frac{\text{Selling Price} - \text{Acquisition Cost}}{\text{Selling Price}}.$$

Assume that the data shown at the top of Exhibit 8.1 are available from the records for a month. (The kinds of information assumed available would typically be available in nearly all businesses.) In this business firm, all goods carry a gross margin percentage

---

[1]   This is one of the most confusing areas in business terminology. If you buy a share of stock for $8 and sell it for $10, both you and your stockbroker would call that a 25 percent (= $2/$8) *gain.* You would compute the gain percentage with the denominator being original cost. A retailer, however, speaks of the *markup* on an item selling for $10 that cost $8 as being 20 percent (= $2/$10). The retailer uses selling price, not cost, as the denominator. It seems illogical to do so, but it is common practice and the effective participant in the business world will have to understand these differences in terms.

of 25 percent. That is, if the selling price of an item is $100, it cost $75; $25/$100 = 25 gross margin percentage.

EXHIBIT 8.1
Illustration of Gross Margin Method
(Gross Margin Percentage is 25
Percent of Selling Price)

ASSUMED DATA

Cost of Inventory, January 1	$150,000
Invoice Cost of Purchases During January	220,000
Transportation-in on Purchases During January	2,000
Invoice Cost of Purchases Made During January but Returned to Seller During January (Purchase Returns)	7,000
Sales Made During January	300,000
Selling Price of Goods Sold During January but Returned by Customers (Sales Returns)	10,000

APPLICATION OF GROSS MARGIN METHOD TO ASSUMED DATA

Cost of Inventory, January 1		$150,000
Net Purchases:		
Purchases	$220,000	
Plus Transportation-in	2,000	
Less Purchase Returns	(7,000)	215,000
Total Cost of Goods Available for Sale		$365,000
Estimated Cost of Goods Sold:		
Sales	$310,000	
Less Sales Returns by Customers	(10,000)	
Net Sales	$300,000	
Less Estimated Gross Margin (= .25 × 300,000)	(75,000)	
Estimated Cost of Goods Sold		225,000
Estimated Cost of Ending Inventory, January 31		$140,000

The cost of goods sold and inventory at the end of January are computed as shown at the bottom of Exhibit 8.1. This method results in the precisely correct figures for cost of goods sold and ending inventory if each item has a gross margin percentage of exactly 25 percent. The method results in approximations as the individual items have different gross margin percentages whose average is 25 percent.

There are many variants of this method. In the retail methods, the gross margin percentage is itself estimated from data on costs and selling prices of goods. The variants of the retail method result from various assumptions about the fate (whether sold or not by the end of the period) of goods that have been marked down from their original retail price or that have been marked up still further from their original retail price.

Perpetual Inventory Method

Under the *perpetual* (or *continuous)* inventory method, the system of records is designed so that the cost of withdrawals is recorded at the time these assets are withdrawn from inventory. The perpetual inventory method determines the cost of withdrawals by a constant tracing of costs removed from inventory. Such entries as the following may be made from day to day.

Cost of Goods Sold	546	
Merchandise Inventory		546
To record the cost of goods withdrawn from inventory and sold.		
Work-in-Process Inventory	1,075	
Raw Material Inventory		1,075
To record the cost of raw material withdrawn from the storeroom and used in production.		

The balance in the Merchandise Inventory account or in the Raw Materials Inventory account, when postings for a period have been completed, is the cost of the goods still on hand. Operating statements can be prepared without a physical count of inventory. The perpetual inventory method uses the following form of the inventory equation to determine what should be in the ending inventory after each acquisition or withdrawal:

Beginning Inventory + Purchases − Withdrawals = Ending Inventory.
    (known)   (known)   (recorded)   (solved for)

Using a perpetual inventory system does not entirely eliminate the need to count and value the items of inventory on hand. A physical count and valuation of the goods on hand must be taken from time to time to check the accuracy of the book figures and to gauge the loss from shrinkages. The loss is the difference between the amounts in the Inventory account and the cost of the goods physically on hand. The loss would be recorded with a debit to the Cost of Goods Sold account (or perhaps to a Loss account) and a credit to the Inventory account.

Some businesses make a complete physical check at the end of the accounting period, in the same way as when the periodic inventory method is used. Usually, however, a more effective procedure can be employed. Rather than taking the inventory of all items at one time, the count may be staggered throughout the period. For example, a bookstore may check actual physical amounts of textbooks and inventory account amounts at the end of the school year, whereas the comparison for sunglasses might be done in November. All items should be counted at least once during every year. Certain items may be checked more frequently, either because of their high value or because of a high probability of errors in recording their withdrawals.

Choosing Between Periodic and Perpetual Inventory Methods

The perpetual method helps maintain up-to-date information on quantities actually on hand. Thus, its use is justified when being "out of stock" may lead to costly consequences, such as the need to shut down production lines or customer dissatisfaction.

In such cases, the perpetual inventory system might keep track of the physical quantities of inventory but not the dollar amounts.

Further, controlling losses or shrinkages is difficult if they cannot be measured. The periodic inventory method usually costs less to administer than the perpetual inventory method, but it provides no data on losses, shrinkages, and deterioration. To gather data on losses from inventory requires both a continuous record of withdrawals and periodic counts so that the amounts that the books indicate should be on hand can be compared with the actual amounts. As with other choices that have to be made in accounting, the costs of any system have to be compared with its benefits. The periodic inventory method is likely to be cost-effective when being out of stock will not be extremely costly, when there is a large volume of items with a small value per unit, or when items are hard to steal or pilfer. Perpetual methods are cost-effective when there is a small volume of high-value items or when running out of stock is costly.

BASES OF INVENTORY VALUATION

The basis of valuation for inventories significantly affects both net income and the amount at which inventories are shown on the balance sheet. At least five bases of valuation are used for one purpose or another. The most common ones, discussed below, are acquisition cost, replacement cost, net realizable value, lower of (acquisition) cost or market, and standard cost. Chapter 2 discussed the choice of valuation bases generally; much of the following is a review.

Acquisition-Cost Basis

When the acquisition-cost basis is used, units in inventory are carried at their historical cost until sold. In accounting the terms *acquisition cost* and *historical cost* are used to mean the same thing.

Use of historical or acquisition costs in accounting implies the use of the *realization convention*: Increases (or decreases) in the market value of individual assets, including items of inventory, are not recognized as gains (or losses) until the particular assets are sold. Thus, when acquisition cost is used for items in inventory, income is not affected until a sale takes place. Any changes in the value of inventory items occurring between the time of acquisition and the time of sale are not recognized. The figure shown on the balance sheet for inventory will be more or less out of date depending on how much prices have changed since the items were acquired. The longer the elapsed time since acquisition, the more likely is the current value of the inventory to differ from its acquisition cost.

Current-Value Bases

When a current-value basis is used, units in inventory are stated at a current market price. Two current-value bases are discussed below: current entry value, often called *replacement cost;* and current exit value, often called *net realizable value.*

When inventories are stated at their current value, gains and losses from changes in prices of inventory items are recognized during the holding period that elapses between acquisition (or production) and the time of sale. This phenomenon will be illustrated later in Exhibit 8.4.

Whereas an acquisition-cost basis for inventory shows objective, verifiable information that may be out of date, a current-value basis shows current information that can be more useful but the amount shown may be more difficult to obtain and to audit.

Replacement Cost   The replacement cost of an inventory item at a given time is the amount the firm would have to pay to acquire the item at that time. In computing replacement cost, it is assumed that a fair market (or arm's-length) transaction between a willing buyer and a willing seller would take place. It is also assumed that the inventory would be bought in the customary fashion in the customary quantities. Replacement cost does not imply the forced purchase of inventory by a frantic buyer from a hoarding seller (which probably implies a premium price) or purchases of abnormally large quantities (which often can be bought at a lower-than-normal price) or purchases of abnormally small quantities (which usually cost more per unit to acquire).

Net Realizable Value   The amount that a firm could realize as a willing seller in an arm's-length transaction with a willing buyer in the ordinary course of business is *net realizable value,* an exit value. Because not all items of inventory are in a form ready for sale (there may be partially complete inventory in a manufacturing firm, for example) and because a sales commission and other selling costs must often be incurred in ordinary sales transactions, net realizable value is defined as the estimated selling price of the inventory less any estimated costs to make the item ready for sale and to sell it. To take another example, agricultural products on hand at the close of an accounting period are often stated at net realizable value. It may be easier to estimate a market price less selling costs than it is to determine the historical cost of a bushel of apples that has been harvested from an orchard.

Lower-of-Cost-or-Market Basis

The lower-of-cost-or-market valuation basis is the smaller of the two amounts: acquisition cost or "market value." Market value is generally replacement cost.[2]

The American Institute of Certified Public Accountants justified the need for the lower-of-cost-or-market valuation basis as follows:

A departure from the cost basis of pricing the inventory is required when the utility of the goods is no longer as great as its cost. Where there is evidence that the utility of goods, in their disposal in the ordinary course of business, will be less

---

[2]   Actually, the definition of "market value" in the computation of lower of cost or market is more complex than mere replacement cost. Market value is replacement cost but no more than net realizable value nor less than the quantity net realizable value reduced by a "normal profit margin" on sales of items of this type. (Refer to the citation in footnote 3.) The actual definition of "market" need not concern us here, but its complexity bolsters our skepticism, expressed below, about the extent to which it is used by business firms.

than cost, whether due to physical deterioration, obsolescence, changes in price levels, or other causes, the difference should be recognized as a loss of the current period. This is generally accomplished by stating such goods at a lower level commonly designated as market.

The lower-of-cost-or-market basis for inventory valuation is thought to be a "conservative" policy because (1) losses from decreases in market value are recognized before goods are sold, but gains from increases in market value are never recorded before a sale takes place; and (2) inventory figures on the balance sheet are never greater, but may be less, than acquisition cost. An examination of the effects of using the lower-of-cost-or-market basis over a series of accounting periods shows why the "conservatism" argument is questionable. For any one unit, there is only one total gain or loss figure—the difference between its selling price and its acquisition cost; the valuation rule merely determines how this amount of gain or loss is to be spread over the accounting periods between acquisition and final disposition. When the lower-of-cost-or-market basis is used, the net income of the present period may be lower than if the acquisition cost basis were used, but if so, the net income of a later period, when the unit is sold, will be higher.

The lower-of-cost-or-market valuation basis has received wide acceptance in principle, but there is reason to believe that its practical use has not been as extensive as the attention it has received. Use of the lower-of-cost-or-market basis involves the determination of both acquisition cost and "market" information for each item in the inventory and, as the name implies, using the lesser of these two amounts as the inventory value. The difficulty of gathering the necessary information for each of the hundreds or thousands of items in an inventory, to say nothing of the difficulty of calculating the market value of work in process and finished goods on the basis of present material prices, present labor rates, and present prices for each of the other costs of production operations, certainly lends support to our opinion that the method is limited in application. It is used frequently for valuable items and for other items where the decrease in price has been significant.

Standard Costs

Standard cost is a predetermined estimate of what items of manufactured inventory *should* cost. Studies of past and estimated future cost data provide the basis for standard costs. Standard cost systems are frequently used by manufacturing firms for internal performance measurement and control. These are discussed in managerial and cost accounting texts. Standard cost is also occasionally used as the valuation basis for preparing financial statements. Units in inventory may be valued at standard cost, especially in the preparation of monthly or quarterly statements. If so, any excess of actual cost over standard cost (called an *unfavorable variance*) is usually debited to

---

[3]   *Accounting Research Bulletin No. 43,* Chapter 4, Statement 5, AICPA, 1953.
[4]   To use the terms introduced in Chapter 3, *holding losses* are reported currently, whereas *holding gains* are not reported until the goods are sold.

cost of goods sold or to other expenses of the period. If actual cost is less than standard cost, the variance is usually credited to cost of goods sold.

Generally Accepted Accounting Basis for Inventory Valuation

For the most part, accounting uses historical costs. The general rule for valuing inventories is to use the acquisition-cost basis. There are important exceptions, however. If the "market value" of inventory items is significantly less than acquisition cost, either because of price changes for this kind of inventory generally or because of physical deterioration of the particular items in an inventory, then generally accepted accounting principles require the use of lower of cost or market. This is the same thing as saying that "market values" must be used in some cases. Since the determination of market value (see footnote 2 above) requires knowledge of both replacement cost and net realizable value, it is fair to say that generally accepted accounting principles for inventory valuation require a combination of three valuation bases: acquisition cost, replacement cost, and net realizable value.

As we discuss in more detail later, the Securities and Exchange Commission requires disclosure by large firms of the replacement cost of beginning inventory, ending inventory, and cost of goods sold.

ACQUISITION OF INVENTORY

Components of Inventory Cost

All costs incurred in connection with acquiring goods and preparing them for sale should enter into the valuation of the goods as assets. For a merchandising firm, such costs logically include purchasing, transportation, receiving, unpacking, inspecting, and shelving costs as well as that portion of the bookkeeping and office cost which relates to the recording of purchases. The example on page 36 (in Chapter 2), showing the computation of the cost of some equipment, applies as well to inventory.

For a manufacturing firm, inventory costs include direct materials, direct labor, and manufacturing overhead. In the illustrations for manufacturing firms considered so far in this book, *all* production costs were debited to Work-in-Process Inventory. This procedure, called *absorption* (or *full*) *costing,* is the one most commonly used in accounting practice. An alternative procedure, known as *direct costing* (or more properly *variable costing*), has received substantial attention in recent years.

---

[5]   *Accounting Research Bulletin No. 43,* Chapter 4, referenced above.
[6]   Since the amounts involved are often relatively small, and since it is difficult to assign a definite dollar amount for many of these costs to specific purchases, the tendency in practice is to restrict the actual additions to a few significant items that can easily be identified with particular goods, such as transportation costs. The costs of operating a purchasing department, the salaries and expenses of buyers, the costs of the receiving and warehousing departments, and the costs of handling and shelving are usually treated as expenses of the period in which they are incurred, although they are logically part of the total cost of merchandise made ready for sale.

In the direct costing procedure, production costs are classified into variable manufacturing costs (those that tend to vary with output) and fixed manufacturing costs (those that tend to be relatively unaffected in the short run by the number of units produced). Non-variable (fixed) manufacturing costs are treated in the same way as selling and administrative costs; that is, they are treated as expenses assigned to the period of incurrence rather than as costs assignable to the product produced. Non-variable manufacturing costs are charged in their entirety against revenues in determining net income for the period. In the direct costing procedure, only variable manufacturing costs are classified as product costs, to be assigned to Work-in-Process Inventory and, later, to Finished Goods Inventory. Direct labor and direct materials are variable costs. Most manufacturing overhead items, such as property taxes and depreciation of equipment, are non-variable costs.

When the absorption costing method is used, reported net income from one year to the next can display strange patterns if the number of units produced differs from the number of units sold. These unusual changes in net income could lead some statement users to make incorrect interpretations about the operating performance of a firm. The direct costing procedure does not result in these unusual patterns of income. It has been suggested, therefore, that the direct costing method should be used so that more useful information will be provided for assessing operating performance.

Generally accepted accounting principles, however, do not permit a firm to use direct costing procedures in preparing financial statements. We suspect that direct costing is not generally acceptable for financial reporting primarily because it is not allowed for tax reporting. Because direct costing is not a generally accepted accounting principle, we defer to managerial accounting courses the discussion of the criticism of the absorption costing method and the suggested benefits of the direct costing method for internal management uses.

The Purchase Transaction

The procedures for recording purchases of merchandise, raw materials, and supplies vary a great deal from one business to another. Purchase transactions culminate, of course, when the goods are received and inspected and the purchase is entered into the records. From the legal point of view, purchases should be recorded in the formal accounting records when title to the goods passes. The question of when title passes is often a technical, legal matter, and the precise answer depends on a consideration of all of the circumstances of the transaction. As a convenience, therefore, the accountant usually recognizes purchases only after both the invoice and the goods are received and inspected. Adjustments may be made at the end of the accounting period in order to reflect the legal formalities at that time.

Merchandise Purchases Account

During the accounting period, acquisitions of merchandise can be debited either to the appropriate inventory account, such as Merchandise Inventory, or to a Merchandise Purchases account. (The shorter title Purchases is used in practice, but the full title is occasionally used here to avoid ambiguity.) The Merchandise Purchases account is a temporary, asset adjunct account. That is, the balance in Merchandise Purchases is closed at the end of each accounting period to the appropriate inventory account and does not appear in the balance sheet. The typical entry to record a specific purchase of merchandise is

Merchandise Purchases	350	
Accounts Payable (or Cash)		350
To record purchase of merchandise.		

At the end of the period, the closing entry, assuming that merchandise costing $1,675 was purchased during the period, would be

Merchandise Inventory	1,675	
Merchandise Purchases		1,675
To close purchases account to the inventory account.		

The special account to record purchases is used to give more complete information about purchase transactions during the period than is provided when all purchases are debited directly to the Merchandise (or Raw Materials) Inventory accounts.

Merchandise Purchases Adjustments

The invoice price of goods purchased will seldom correctly measure the total acquisition cost. Additional costs may be incurred in transporting and handling the goods, and deductions may be required for cash discounts, goods returned, and other allowances or adjustments of the invoice price. All of these adjustments could be handled through the one Merchandise Purchases account. Frequently, however, a number of contra and adjunct accounts are used for these adjustments so that a more complete analysis of the cost of purchases is available. Freight-in, Purchase Returns, Purchase Allowances, and Purchase Discounts (or Purchase Discounts Lost) are used to provide the needed detail. The treatment of purchase discounts and purchase allowances by the purchaser is analogous to the treatment of sales discounts and sales allowances by the seller discussed in Chapter 7.

Merchandise Purchases Discounts

The largest adjustment to the invoice price of merchandise purchases is likely to be that for purchase discounts. Sellers often offer a discount from the invoice price for prompt payment. For example, the terms of sale "2/10, net/30" mean that a 2-percent discount from invoice price is offered if payment is made within 10 days and the full invoice price is due in any case within 30 days.[7] The amount of discounts taken during

---

[7] Problem **4** at the end of Appendix B attempts to help you understand that the interest rate implied in these terms of sales is about *45 percent per year.* That is, a purchaser who does not take such a discount is borrowing money at an interest rate of about 45 percent per year. Most purchasers find it advantageous to take such discounts and to borrow elsewhere at lower rates.

a period is sometimes shown as a special or "other" revenue item on the income statement. Some supporters of this treatment argue that the discounts represent interest earned on cash and so should be viewed as a revenue item.

A more appropriate interpretation, however, is to treat purchase discounts as a reduction in the purchase price. As was explained in Chapter 7, there is a cash price for purchases, and if payment is delayed, there is an additional charge for the right to delay payment and for the other additional services the seller is compelled to render. To view purchase discounts as revenue would indicate that revenue may be earned simply by buying goods and paying for them with cash within a specified time even though the goods have not been sold to others. It seems more reasonable to treat discounts as a reduction in the cost of merchandise purchased and thereby to defer their effect on net income until the goods have been sold.

Some accountants who recognize the logic of treating purchase discounts as a reduction in price nevertheless suggest that purchase discounts should be treated as "other" revenue for reasons of expediency. These accountants would treat discounts on major purchases, such as equipment, as reductions in the purchase price. They would not, however, deduct purchase discounts from the gross price of merchandise when the amounts involved are too small to justify the additional record-keeping effort. There is merit in the view that precision in accounting may cost more than the benefits received from greater accuracy. Whenever the amounts involved are not material or significant, the most convenient, rather than the logically correct, procedure may be satisfactory because the effects on net income are approximately the same.

Purchase discounts are often a material item; for some firms, the total of purchase discounts has been greater than net income. In this day of electronic computers, there should be little inconvenience or extra cost incurred in treating purchase discounts as a reduction in purchase price rather than as "other" revenue.

Two alternatives for treating discounts on merchandise purchases are often used in practice: (1) Recognize the amount of discounts taken on payments made during the period, without regard to the period of purchase (gross price method); or (2) deduct all discounts made available from the gross purchase invoice prices at the time of purchase (net price method). The effects of these two methods are explained in Problem **11** at the end of this chapter.

COST-FLOW ASSUMPTIONS

Specific Identification and the Need for a Cost-Flow Assumption

If the individual units of an item can be physically identified as coming from a specific purchase, then there is no special problem in ascertaining the acquisition cost of the units withdrawn from inventory and the cost of the units still on hand. The cost can be marked on the unit or on its container, or the unit can be traced back to its purchase invoice or cost record. The inventory and cost of goods sold of an automobile dealer or of a dealer in fine diamonds or fur coats would probably be determined using specific identification of costs.

In most cases, however, new items are mixed with old units on shelves, in bins, or in other ways, and physical identification is impossible or impracticable. Moreover, it may be desirable (for reasons to be discussed in this section) to assume that cost flows differ from physical flows of goods.

The inventory *valuation* problem arises because there are *two* unknowns in the inventory equation:

Beginning Inventory + Net Purchases − Cost of Goods Sold = Ending Inventory.
    (known)   (known)   (unknown)   (unknown)

The values of the beginning inventory and net purchases are known; the values of the cost of goods sold and of ending inventory are not known. The question is whether to value the units in ending inventory using the most recent costs, the oldest costs, the average cost, or some other alternative. Of course, the question could have been put in terms of valuing the cost of goods sold, for once we determine the value of one unknown quantity, the inventory equation automatically determines the value of the other. The relation between the two unknowns, Cost of Goods Sold and Ending Inventory, in the inventory equation for historical costs is such that the higher the value assigned to one of them, the lower must be the value assigned to the other.

When prices are changing, no historical cost-based accounting method for valuing both ending inventory and cost of goods sold allows the accountant to show current values on both the income statement and the balance sheet. For example, in a period of rising prices, if current, higher acquisition prices are used in measuring cost of goods sold shown on the income statement, then older, lower acquisition prices must be used in valuing the ending inventory shown on the balance sheet. As long as cost of goods sold and ending inventory are based on acquisition costs, financial statements can present current values in the income statement or the balance sheet, but not in both. Of course, combinations of current and out-of-date information can be shown in both statements.

If more than one purchase is made of the same item at different prices, and specific identification is not feasible or possible, then some assumption must be made as to the flow of costs in order to estimate the acquisition cost applicable to the units remaining in the inventory. One of three cost-flow assumptions is typically used for this purpose. These cost-flow assumptions are:

1 First in, first out (FIFO)
2 Last in, first out (LIFO)
3 Weighted average.

The demonstrations of each of these methods that follow are based on the toaster data introduced earlier in the chapter and repeated at the top of Exhibit 8.2. The toaster example illustrates most of the important points about the cost-flow assumption required in accounting for inventories and cost of goods sold. The appendix to this chapter illustrates a more realistic, but more computationally complex, case.

EXHIBIT 8.2
Comparison of Cost-Flow Assumptions
Historical-Cost Basis

ASSUMED DATA

Beginning Inventory: Toaster 1 Cost $25
            Purchases: Toaster 2 Cost 29
                    Toaster 3 Cost 30
Cost of Goods Available for Sale $84

Sales: One Toaster for $55

FINANCIAL STATEMENTS

	Cost-Flow Assumption		
	FIFO (1)	Weighted Average (2)	LIFO (3)
Sales	$55	$55	$55
Cost of Goods Sold	25[a]	28[b]	30[c]
Gross Margin on Sales..........................	$30	$27	$25
Ending Inventory	$59[d]	$56[e]	$54[f]
Increase in Inventory for Period (= Ending Inventory − Beginning Inventory of $25)	$34	$31	$29

[a] Toaster 1 cost $25.
[b] Average toaster costs $28 (= $84/3).
[c] Toaster 3 cost $30.
[d] Toasters 2 and 3 cost $29 + $30 = $59.
[e] 2 Average toasters cost 2 × $28 = $56.
[f] Toasters 1 and 2 cost $25 + $29 = $54.

First In, First Out

The first-in, first-out cost-flow assumption, abbreviated FIFO, assigns the cost of the earliest units acquired to the withdrawals and the cost of the most recent acquisitions to the ending inventory. The cost flow assumes that the oldest materials and goods are used first. This cost-flow assumption conforms to good business practice in managing physical flows, especially in the case of items that deteriorate or become obsolete.

Column (1) of Exhibit 8.2 illustrates FIFO. Toaster 1 is assumed to be sold, whereas toasters 2 and 3 are assumed to remain in inventory. The designation FIFO refers to the cost flow of units sold. A parallel description for ending inventory is last-in, still-here, or LISH.

Last In, First Out

The last-in first-out cost-flow assumption, abbreviated LIFO, assigns the cost of the latest units acquired to the withdrawals and the cost of the oldest units to the ending inventory. Some theorists argue that LIFO matches current costs to current revenues and therefore that LIFO better measures income. Column (3) of Exhibit 8.2 illustrates LIFO. The $30 cost of toaster 3 is assumed to leave, whereas the costs of toasters 1 and 2 are assumed to remain in inventory. The designation of LIFO refers to the cost flow for units sold. A parallel description for ending inventory is first-in, still-here, or FISH.

LIFO has attracted much attention since 1939 when it first became acceptable for income tax determinations. In a period of consistently rising prices, LIFO results in a higher cost of goods sold, a lower reported periodic income, and lower current income taxes than either FIFO or weighted-average cost-flow assumptions.

LIFO corresponds to a physical assumption that the business carries a certain number of units on hand and that current operations and sales are carried on with the use of units purchased most recently.[8] There are some situations where the physical conditions justify such an assumption, such as where material is kept in a bin and new purchases are dumped in before the supply is exhausted completely. The quantity at the bottom of the bin may have been purchased many months or years ago. Most often, however, LIFO cannot be justified in terms of physical flows but is used because it produces a cost-of-goods-sold figure that is based on more up-to-date prices. In a period of rising prices, LIFO's higher (than FIFO's) cost-of-goods-sold figure reduces reported income and income taxes.

Weighted Average

To use a weighted-average method, a weighted average of the costs of all goods available for sale (or use) during the month, including the cost applicable to the beginning inventory, must be calculated.[9] The weighted-average cost is applied to the units on hand at the end of the month. Column (2) of Exhibit 8.2 illustrates the weighted-average cost-flow assumption. The weighted-average cost of toasters available for sale during the period is $28 $[= \frac{1}{3} \times (\$25 + \$29 + \$30)]$. Cost of Goods Sold is thus $28 and ending inventory is $56 $(= 2 \times \$28)$.

Comparison of Cost-Flow Assumptions

FIFO results in balance sheet figures that are closest to current cost, since the latest purchases dominate the ending inventory valuation. The cost-of-goods-sold expense tends to be out of date, however, since it assumes that the earlier prices of the beginning inventory and the earliest purchases are charged to expense. When prices change, FIFO usually leads to the highest reported net income of the three methods when prices are rising and the smallest when prices are falling.

---

[8] The LIFO assumption in the strict sense can be applied only to physically identical items such as tons of ore or pounds of cotton. LIFO can be used for style goods (for example, dresses and suits) or annual models of appliances by using a variant known as *dollar-value LIFO* or *retail-method LIFO*. These methods are beyond the scope of this discussion.

[9] This description is technically correct only when a periodic inventory method is used. The appendix to this chapter describes the procedures for applying the weighted-average method in a perpetual inventory system.

LIFO leads to opposite results. LIFO produces balance sheet figures that may be far removed from current costs and a cost-of-goods-sold figure close to current costs. Of the three cost-flow assumptions, LIFO usually implies the smallest net income when prices are rising (highest cost of goods sold), and the largest when prices are falling (lowest cost of goods sold). Also, LIFO results in the least fluctuation in reported income over the business cycle in businesses where selling prices tend to change as current prices of inventory items change.

The weighted-average cost-flow assumption falls between the other two in its effect both on the balance sheet and the income statement. It is, however, much more like FIFO than like LIFO in its effects on the balance sheet. When inventory turns over rapidly, the weighted-average inventory values are almost as close to present prices as FIFO. Weighted averages reflect all of the prices during the period in proportion to the quantities purchased at those prices as well as beginning inventory costs carried over from the previous period.

A Closer Look at LIFO

As we discussed above, LIFO usually presents a cost-of-goods-sold figure closely related to current costs. It also generally has the practical advantage of deferring income taxes. LIFO usually leads, however, to a balance sheet figure for inventory so far removed from current values as possibly to delude and confuse readers of financial statements.

For example, consider the current ratio (= current assets/current liabilities) introduced in Chapter 6. The current ratio is often used by readers of financial statements to assess the liquidity of a company. If LIFO is used in periods of rising prices while inventory quantities are increasing, the amount of inventory included in the numerator will be much smaller than if the inventory were valued at current prices. Hence, the unwary reader may underestimate the liquidity of a company that uses a LIFO cost-flow assumption. When a company uses LIFO, the SEC requires that it disclose in notes the current value of beginning and ending inventory. These disclosures are illustrated in Appendix A at the back of the book for the International Corporation in Note 9 on page 587 and later in this chapter on page 293 for the General Electric Corporation.

A second criticism of LIFO relates to dipping into old LIFO layers. A major objective of using LIFO is to reduce current taxes in periods of rising prices and rising inventory quantities. Usually LIFO produces this result. If inventory quantities decline, however, the opposite effect can occur in the year of the decline, since older, lower costs per unit leave the balance sheet and are charged to expense.

For example, if under LIFO, a firm must for some reason reduce end-of-period physical inventory quantities below what they were at the beginning of the period, then cost of goods sold will be based on the current period's purchases plus a portion of the older and lower costs in the beginning inventory. Such a firm will have larger reported income and income taxes in that period than if the firm had been able to maintain its ending inventory at beginning-of-period levels.

Assume that LIFO inventory at the beginning of 1979 consists of 46 units with a total cost of $342, as follows:

Number of Units	Year Purchased	Cost per Unit	Total Cost
10	1975	$ 5	$ 50
11	1976	6	66
12	1977	8	96
13	1978	10	130
46			$342

Assume that the cost at the end of 1979 is $12 per unit. If 1979 ending inventory is more than 46 units, then the cost of goods sold will be roughly $12 per unit. If, however, the 1979 ending inventory drops to 10 units, then all the 36 units purchased in 1976 through 1978 will also enter cost of goods sold. These 36 units cost $292 (= $66 + $96 + $130), but the current cost of comparable units is $432 (= 36 units × $12 per unit). Cost of goods sold will be $140 (= $432 − $292) smaller because of the "dip into old LIFO layers" of inventory. Income before taxes will be $140 larger than if inventory quantities had not declined from 46 to 10 units. In reality, many LIFO firms have inventory layers built up since the 1940s, and the costs of the early units are often as little as 10 percent of the current cost. For these firms, a dip into old layers will substantially increase income. A footnote from a recent annual report of the U.S. Steel Corporation illustrates this phenomenon:

> Because of the continuing high demand throughout the year, inventories of many steel-making materials and steel products were unavoidably reduced and could not be replaced during the year. Under the LIFO system of accounting, used for many years by U.S. Steel, the net effect of all the inventory changes [reductions] was to increase income for the year by about $16 million.

Finally, if matching physical flows with cost flows is considered important, then LIFO is unsatisfactory because it assumes an order of consumption that is not likely to conform to reality or to good business practice. Oldest materials are rarely sold or used last.

Recently many firms, including du Pont, General Motors, and Eastman Kodak, have switched from FIFO to LIFO. Given the rapid rate of price increases over the past decade, the switch from FIFO to LIFO has resulted in substantially lower cash payments for income taxes. For example, when du Pont and General Motors switched from FIFO to LIFO, they each lowered current income taxes by about $150 million.[10]

In spite of criticisms of LIFO on grounds that it often leads to absurd balance sheet amounts, most company managements will probably best serve their shareholders by using a LIFO cost-flow assumption in order to save income taxes because prices are likely to increase in the future rather than to decrease.

---

[10] Thus, the apparent "paradox" in the introduction to this chapter is resolved.

Income Tax Considerations

The differences between LIFO and FIFO cost-flow assumptions can lead to substantial differences in reported income. Similarly, the choices made on tax returns can lead to substantial differences in taxable income and, hence, in income tax payments. Other things being equal, the rational manager prefers lower taxes to higher taxes and would probably choose those accounting methods for tax purposes that minimize current taxes. Accounting choices for financial reporting and for tax returns can usually be made independently of one another, but generally not with respect to inventory-flow assumptions.

Conformity of Cost-Flow Assumptions In only one major area in accounting does the Internal Revenue Service require firms to use the same method for financial reporting as for tax returns. When the LIFO flow assumption is elected for tax returns, it must also be used in financial reports to owners. Once a firm has chosen to adopt LIFO, it must request permission to change back to FIFO or weighted average, and may incur a tax liability if it does so. (See Problem **18** of Chapter 13 on page 550, where Chrysler's switch from LIFO to FIFO is discussed.)

Valuation Basis and Cost-Flow Assumption The Internal Revenue Service does not permit the lower-of-cost-or-market valuation basis to be used with a LIFO cost-flow assumption. Consider the effect of allowing LIFO with lower of cost or market. When prices are rising, the LIFO cost-flow assumption results in a lower ending inventory amount and lower reported income than does FIFO. When prices are falling, the lower-of-LIFO-cost-or-market basis leads to an ending inventory amount approximately equal to that of the lower-of-FIFO-cost-or-market basis. The Internal Revenue Service is unwilling to allow a cost-flow assumption that, when compared to FIFO, results in lower taxable income when prices are rising and no higher taxable income when prices are falling. If LIFO coupled with the lower-of-cost-or-market basis were allowed, it would result in a guarantee of no worse tax position (falling prices) and the hope of a better tax position (rising prices) when compared to FIFO used with lower of cost or market.[11] If a firm selects the LIFO cost-flow assumption for income tax purposes, therefore, it must use the acquisition-cost basis of inventory valuation.

If a firm chooses the FIFO or average cost-flow assumption for income tax purposes, it can use either the acquisition cost or lower-of-acquisition-cost-or-market valuation basis. These firms should select the lower-of-cost-or-market basis, since it results in the immediate recognition of a loss whenever market price at the end of the year is less than acquisition cost.

LIFO Versus FIFO Impact on Financial Statements: An Illustration

A recent report of the General Electric Company (GE) states, in part:

Substantially all these [inventories] are valued on a last-in, first-out (LIFO) basis.

---

[11] It would be a case where "Heads, you win, tails, you break even."

. . . If the FIFO method of inventory accounting had been used by the Company, inventories would have been $783.7 million higher [at year-end] and $429.7 million higher [at the beginning of the year]. . . .

GE's beginning inventories amounted to $1,986.2 million. GE's ending inventories amounted to $2,257.0 million. Cost of goods sold was $10,137.6 million and sales were $13,413.1 million.

Let us see what we can deduce from this information about GE's reported income as it is affected by the choice of a flow assumption. The data from the annual report quoted above are shown in Exhibit 8.3 along with other amounts that can be computed from the given information.

EXHIBIT 8.3
General Electric Company
Inventory Data from Financial
Statements and Footnotes

(Amounts shown in **boldface** are given in GE's financial statements. Other amounts are computed as indicated.)

Dollar Amounts in Millions

	LIFO Cost-Flow Assumption (Actually Used)	+	Excess of FIFO over LIFO Amount	=	FIFO Cost-Flow Assumption (Hypothetical)
Beginning Inventory	**$ 1,986.2**		**$429.7**		$ 2,415.9
Purchases	10,408.4[a]		0		10,408.4
Cost of Goods Available for Sale	$12,394.6		**$429.7**		$12,824.3
Less Ending Inventory	**2,257.0**		**783.7**		3,040.7
Cost of Goods Sold	**$10,137.6**		($354.0)[b]		$ 9,783.6
Sales	**$13,413.1**		0		**$13,413.1**
Less Cost of Goods Sold . .	**10,137.6**		($354.0)		9,783.6
Gross Margin on Sales . . .	$ 3,275.5		$354.0		$ 3,629.5

Order of computation of amounts not presented in GE's financial statements:
[a] Purchases = Cost of Goods Sold + Ending Inventory − Beginning Inventory
    $10,408.4 = **$10,137.6** + **$2,257.0** − **$1,986.2**
[b] ($354.0) = **$429.7** − **$783.7**

Recall the inventory equation:

Beginning Inventory + Purchases − Ending Inventory = Cost of Goods Sold.

FIFO's higher beginning inventory increases reported cost of goods available for sale and the cost of goods sold by $429.7 million, relative to LIFO. FIFO's higher ending inventory decreases cost of goods sold by $783.7 million, relative to LIFO. Hence the cost of goods sold is $783.7 million minus $429.7 million, or $354.0 million less under FIFO than it was under LIFO. GE's pretax income would be $354.0 million more under FIFO than it was under the LIFO flow assumption actually used. GE's reported pretax income for the year was about $1 billion, so GE's reported income would have been about 35 percent larger if it had used a FIFO, rather than a LIFO, flow assumption.

Many investors and financial analysts look not merely at net income amounts, but at the rate of growth of these amounts. GE's reported pretax income in the previous year was also about $1 billion. The rate of growth of income using the LIFO flow assumption was zero, but would have been about 20 percent had GE used a FIFO flow assumption in both years.

The moral is clear: The choice of inventory-flow assumption can have an important effect on financial statements and their interpretation. During periods of substantial price change, there is no other choice between generally accepted financial accounting principles that affects financial statements for most companies as much as the inventory-flow assumption.

IDENTIFYING OPERATING MARGIN AND HOLDING GAINS

The reported net income under FIFO is generally larger than under LIFO during periods of rising prices. This higher reported net income is caused by the *recognition* of a larger *holding gain* under FIFO than under LIFO. The significance of holding gains in the determination of net income under FIFO and LIFO is illustrated in this section. The conventionally reported gross margin (sales minus cost of goods sold) is split into (1) an operating margin and (2) a realized holding gain. In addition, there is usually an unrealized holding gain that is not currently included in income.

The difference between the selling price of an item and its replacement cost at the time of sale is called an *operating margin.* This operating margin gives some indication of the relative advantage that a particular firm has in the market for its goods, such as a reputation for quality or service. The difference between the current replacement cost of an item and its acquisition cost is called a *holding gain* (or *loss*). The holding gain (or loss) reflects the change in cost of an item during the period while the inventory item is held.

To illustrate the calculation of the operating margin and holding gain, consider the example of the toasters discussed in this chapter. The acquisition cost of the three items available for sale during the period is $84. Assume that one toaster is sold for $55. The replacement cost of the toaster at the time it was sold is assumed to be $32. The current replacement cost at the end of the month for each item in ending inventory is $35. The top portion of Exhibit 8.4 illustrates the separation of the conventionally reported gross margin into the operating margin and the realized holding gain.

The operating margin is the difference between the $55 selling price and the $32 replacement cost at the time of sale. The total operating margin of $23 is the same under both the FIFO and LIFO cost-flow assumptions. The *realized holding gain* is the difference between cost of goods sold based on replacement cost and cost of goods sold based on acquisition cost. The realized holding gain under FIFO is larger than under LIFO, since the earlier purchases at lower costs are charged to cost of goods

EXHIBIT 8.4
Reporting of Operating Margins
and Holding Gains for Toasters
Periodic Inventory Method

	Cost-Flow Assumption			
	FIFO		LIFO	
Sales Revenue	$55		$55	
Less Replacement Cost of Goods Sold	32		32	
Operating Margin on Sales		$23		$23
Realized Holding Gain on Toasters:				
Replacement Cost (at Time of Sale) of Goods Sold	$32		$32	
Less Acquisition Cost of Goods Sold				
(FIFO—Toaster 1; LIFO—Toaster 3)	25		30	
Realized Holding Gain on Toasters[a]		7		2
Conventionally Reported Gross Margin[b]		$30		$25
Unrealized Holding Gain:				
Replacement Cost of Ending Inventory (2 × $35)	$70		$70	
Less Acquisition Cost of Ending Inventory (FIFO—				
Toasters 2 & 3; LIFO—Toasters 1 & 2)	59		54	
Unrealized Holding Gain on Toasters		11		16
Economic Profit on Sales and Holding Inventory				
of Toasters (Not Reported in Financial Statements)		$41		$41

[a] The SEC refers to the "Realized Holding Gains" as Inventory Profit. See *inventory profit* in the Glossary at the back of the book.
[b] Note that Exhibit 8.2 stops here.

sold under FIFO. This larger realized holding gain under FIFO is the principal reason why net income under FIFO is typically larger than under LIFO during periods of rising prices.

The calculation of an unrealized holding gain on units in ending inventory is also shown in Exhibit 8.4. The *unrealized holding gain* is the difference between the current replacement cost of the ending inventory and its acquisition cost. This unrealized holding gain on ending inventory is not reported in the income statement as presently prepared. The unrealized holding gain under LIFO is larger than under FIFO, since earlier purchases with lower costs are assumed to remain in ending inventory under LIFO. The sum of the operating margin plus all holding gains (both realized and unrealized) is the same under FIFO and LIFO. Most of the holding gain under FIFO is recognized in determining net income each period, whereas most of the holding gain under LIFO is not currently recognized in the income statement. Instead, under LIFO the unrealized holding gain remains unreported, so long as the older acquisition costs are shown on the balance sheet as ending inventory.

The total increase in wealth for a period includes both realized and unrealized holding gains. That total increase, $41, in the example, is independent of the cost-flow assumption, but is not reported in financial statements under currently accepted accounting principles.

CURRENT VALUATION BASIS REMOVES
THE NEED FOR A COST-FLOW ASSUMPTION

The preceding sections illustrate the difficulty in constructing useful financial statements in historical-cost accounting for inventory in times of changing prices. If a FIFO cost-flow assumption is used, then the income statement reports out-of-date cost of goods sold. If a LIFO cost-flow assumption is used, then the balance sheet reports out-of-date ending inventory.

If a current-value basis for inventory is used, then up-to-date information can be shown on both statements. Using a current-value basis requires a relaxation of the realization convention in accounting and requires the accountant to make estimates of current values. Whereas both of these requirements are objectionable to some accountants, others feel that the benefits outweigh the costs.

Exhibit 8.5 illustrates how the toaster example would look when both cost of goods sold and ending inventory are valued at replacement costs.

The first income figure, $23, is labeled *Distributable Income* (*Operating Margin*). This figure shows selling price less replacement cost of goods sold at the time of sale. This number has significance for companies operating in unregulated environments. The significance can perhaps be understood by considering the following assertion. If the toaster retailer pays out more than $23 in taxes and dividends, then there will be insufficient funds retained in the firm for it to replace inventory and to allow it to continue in business carrying out the same operations next period as it did this period. On the date of sale, a new toaster costs $32; the historical cost of the toaster sold, whether $25 or $30 or whatever number in between, is irrelevant to understanding the current economic conditions facing the retailer. The second income item shown in Exhibit 8.5 is called *Holding Gains*. Holding Gains of $18 occurred during the period on the toasters held in inventory. At the time of sale, the replacement cost of toasters had increased to $32. Thus, the holding gain on three toasters, on the date of sale of one of them, was $12 [= 3 × $32 − ($25 + $29 + $30)]. By the end of the accounting period there was another $6 [= 2($35 − $32)] holding gain on the two toasters still held in inventory as the replacement cost increased to $35.

The income figure shown after the inclusion of holding gains, $41, is thought to be significant by some accountants. It represents the increase in wealth of the firm without regard to the realization convention. To the economist, income is the change in wealth during the period. The economist does not care that a gain has not been realized in an arm's length transaction. So long as a firm's wealth has increased (through holding gains), then that firm is better off at the end of the period than at the start, and the firm has had income. To the economist and some accountants, income should be measured whether or not it has been realized in arm's-length transactions. Economic income, including all holding gains, is $41 in the example.

In recent years, the Securities and Exchange Commission has required major corporations to disclose the replacement cost of goods sold computed at the time of sale and the current replacement cost of ending inventory. With such information, it is possible to measure distributable income and holding gains and to assess the economic performance of business firms.

EXHIBIT 8.5
Using Replacement Cost Data to
Analyze Components of Income

ASSUMED DATA

Beginning Inventory:	Toaster 1 Cost	$25
Purchases:	Toaster 2 Cost	29
	Toaster 3 Cost	30
Historical Cost of Goods Available for Sale		$84

Sales: One Toaster for	$55
Replacement Cost of Toasters On:	
Date of Sale	$32
At End of Period	$35

INCOME STATEMENT

Sales	$55
Replacement Cost of Goods Sold	32
Distributable Income (Operating Margin)	$23
Holding Gains for Year[a]	18
Economic Income	$41

Calculation of Holding Gains for Year

Replacement Cost at Time of Sale[a]	$ 32
Replacement Cost of Ending Inventory (2 × $35)	70
Total Replacement Cost	$102
Historical Cost of Goods Available for Sale	84
Total Holding Gains for Year.................................	$ 18

[a] To give some recognition to the realization convention, the total holding gain might be divided into realized and unrealized portions. To do so requires knowing the acquisition cost of the toaster sold and that requires a cost-flow assumption. As Exhibit 8.4 indicates, if a LIFO assumption is made, then the realized holding gain is $2 and the realized income of $25 could be shown intermediate between the distributable income of $23 and the economic income of $41.

SUMMARY

Inventory measurements affect both the cost-of-goods-sold expense on the income statement for the period and the amount shown for the asset, inventory, on the balance sheet at the end of the period. The sum of the two must be equal to the beginning inventory plus the cost of purchases, at least in accounting based on acquisition costs and market transactions. The allocation between expense and asset depends on four factors:

1 The inventory method used
2 The valuation basis used
3 The types of manufacturing and other costs included in inventory
4 The cost-flow assumption used.

The first factor involves a choice between periodic and perpetual inventory methods. The second factor involves a choice among the acquisition-cost basis, the lower-of-cost-or-market basis, or some current-value basis. The third factor involves consideration of absorption and direct costing. The fourth factor concerns a choice among the FIFO, LIFO, and weighted-average cost-flow assumptions. When a current-value basis is used, then there is no need to use a cost-flow assumption, except to separate realized from unrealized holding gains.

APPENDIX 8.1
Illustration of Calculations of Inventories and Cost of Goods Sold

The chapter describes and illustrates inventory accounting problems in the context of the simplistic toaster example where three items are available for sale and one is sold. In spite of its simplicity, that example captures nearly all of the important concepts in accounting for inventories and cost of goods sold. This appendix illustrates a more realistic situation where additional complexities of calculation are considered.

The illustration in this appendix combines various combinations of periodic and perpetual methods with FIFO, weighted-average, and LIFO cost-flow assumptions. Exhibit 8.6 contains the data for additions to, and withdrawals from, the inventory of item X during June that are used in the illustrations.

EXHIBIT 8.6
Data for Illustration of Inventory Calculations

ITEM X	Units	Unit Cost	Total Cost
Beginning Inventory, June 1[a]	100	$1.00	$100
Purchases, June 7	300	1.10	330
Purchases, June 12	100	1.25	125
Total Available for Sale	500		$555
Withdrawals, June 5	25		?
Withdrawals, June 10	10		?
Withdrawals, June 15	200		?
Withdrawals, June 25	150		?
Total Withdrawals During June	385		?
Ending Inventory, June 30	115		?
Replacement Cost Per Unit, June 30		$1.35	

[a] The example contains one simplifying assumption. Beginning inventory is shown as having the same opening valuation, $100, under all cost-flow assumptions. If costs had varied in the past, then the opening unit costs would have differed for each of the cost-flow assumptions.

First In, First Out

When a FIFO cost-flow assumption is used, the unit prices to be applied to quantities on hand are usually determined by working backward through the purchases until a sufficient quantity is accumulated to cover the inventory at the end of the month. If a physical count reveals that there are 115 units on hand at June 30, the prices paid for the most recently acquired 115 units comprise the ending FIFO inventory. The most recent purchase is the one of June 12, which accounts for 100 units at a cost of $125.00. The next most recent purchase is that of June 7. The remaining 15 units of inventory are priced at the $1.10 unit price of that purchase transaction, or $16.50. The total valuation of the inventory is, then, $141.50 as shown in Exhibit 8.7.

EXHIBIT 8.7
Ending Inventory and Cost-of-Goods-Sold Determination Adopting the Periodic Inventory Method and a FIFO Cost-Flow Assumption

ITEM X

100 units @ $1.25 (from June 12 purchase)	$125.00
15 units @ $1.10 (from June 7 purchase)	16.50
Ending Inventory, June 30	$141.50
Cost of Goods Available for Sale	$555.00
Less Ending Inventory	141.50
Cost of Goods Sold	$413.50

Under FIFO, perpetual and periodic inventory systems lead to identical cost-of-goods-sold and ending inventory amounts.

Last In, First Out

LIFO, Periodic   When the periodic inventory method is used with LIFO, the value of ending inventory is determined by starting with the beginning inventory and then working forward through the purchases until sufficient units have been priced to cover the ending inventory. In the illustration, a physical count reveals that there are 115 units on hand at June 30. Thus, the prices paid for the oldest 115 units comprise the ending LIFO inventory. The oldest units on hand are those in the beginning inventory of June 1, which accounts for 100 units at a total cost of $100.00. The next oldest purchase is that of June 7. The remaining 15 units in ending inventory are priced at the $1.10 unit price of that transaction. The total value of ending inventory, assuming LIFO, is $116.50 as shown in Exhibit 8.8.

EXHIBIT 8.8
Ending Inventory and
Cost-of-Goods-Sold Determination
Adopting the Periodic Inventory
Method and a LIFO Cost-Flow
Assumption

ITEM X

100 units @ $1.00 (from beginning inventory)	$100.00
15 units @ $1.10 (from first purchase, June 7)	16.50
Ending Inventory at Cost	$116.50
Cost of Goods Available for Sale	$555.00
Less Ending Inventory	116.50
Cost of Goods Sold	$438.50

The type of calculation shown in Exhibit 8.8 is realistic only when the quantity on hand never dropped below the number of units in the beginning inventory, 100 units in the illustration. This would not be known unless perpetual inventory records were kept. This doubtful assumption weakens the logic of LIFO when a periodic inventory system is used. On the other hand, when a periodic inventory system is used, LIFO usually requires less pricing of inventory items at the end of the period. Because the quantity in the ending inventory is apt to be somewhat larger than the quantity in the beginning inventory, only the increase in units need be priced. (This increase in physical quantities with its own set of prices is often called a *LIFO inventory layer.*)

LIFO, Perpetual When LIFO is used with a perpetual inventory method, the balance carried forward after each addition to or withdrawal from inventory must be analyzed to reflect the costs applicable to the unused items. LIFO requires that the most recent costs be applied to withdrawals until the corresponding quantities have been absorbed and the balance on hand reflects the earliest purchase prices. Exhibit 8.9 illustrates the operation of LIFO with a perpetual inventory method. If prices are steadily increasing, then the cost of goods sold under LIFO with a perpetual method will never exceed, and will usually be less than, the cost of goods sold under LIFO with a periodic method. The two figures will be equal only when all additions during the period occur before any withdrawals. Most firms who use LIFO do so to save taxes. Since most of these firms do not acquire all of their additions during a period before making any withdrawals, few firms use a LIFO, perpetual combination.

Weighted Average

Weighted Average, Periodic Exhibit 8.10 illustrates the weighted-average cost-flow assumption used with a periodic method. The weighted-average cost-flow assumption is physically appropriate for liquids and not unreasonable for other types of products

EXHIBIT 8.9
**Ending Inventory and
Cost-of-Goods-Sold Determination
Adopting the Perpetual Inventory
Method and a LIFO Cost-Flow
Assumption**

ITEM X

	Received			Issued			Balance		
Date	**Units**	**Cost**	**Amount**	**Units**	**Cost**	**Amount**	**Units**	**Cost**	**Amount**
6/1							100	1.00	100.00
6/5				25	1.00	25.00	75	1.00	75.00
6/7	300	1.10	330.00				75	1.00	75.00
							300	1.10	330.00
6/10				10	1.10	11.00	75	1.00	75.00
							290	1.10	319.00
6/12	100	1.25	125.00				75	1.00	75.00
							290	1.10	319.00
							100	1.25	125.00
6/15				100	1.25	125.00	75	1.00	75.00
				100	1.10	110.00	190	1.10	209.00
6/25				150	1.10	165.00	75	1.00	75.00
Cost of Goods Sold						$436.00	40	1.10	44.00

ENDING INVENTORY COMPUTATION
75 units @ $1.00	$ 75.00
40 units @ $1.10	44.00
Ending Inventory	$119.00

ALTERNATIVE COST-OF-GOODS-SOLD COMPUTATION
Cost of Goods Available for Sale	$555.00
Less Ending Inventory	119.00
Cost of Goods Sold	$436.00

---

where distinguishing different lots is difficult. The result shown in Exhibit 8.10 is correct, strictly speaking, only if no units were used or sold until after the firm makes the last purchase that enters the computations of the weighted average. Seldom do all additions to inventory precede any withdrawals and, therefore, the logic of the method is somewhat weakened.

Weighted Average, Perpetual   The weighted-average cost-flow assumption is often the easiest to apply with a perpetual inventory system, especially where the number of purchases is less than the number of withdrawals. The technique requires the calcula-

EXHIBIT 8.10
**Ending Inventory and
Cost-of-Goods-Sold Determination
Adopting the Periodic Inventory
Method and a Weighted-Average
Cost-Flow Assumption**

ITEM X

6/1 100 units @ $1.00	$100.00
6/7 300 units @ $1.10	330.00
6/12 100 units @ $1.25	125.00
500 units @ $1.11 (= $555/500)	$555.00
Ending Inventory (115 units @ $1.11)	$127.65
Cost of Goods Available for Sale	$555.00
Less Ending Inventory	127.65
Cost of Goods Sold	$427.35

EXHIBIT 8.11
**Ending Inventory and
Cost-of-Goods-Sold Determination
Adopting the Perpetual Inventory
Method and a Moving-Average
Cost-Flow Assumption**

ITEM X

Date	Received			Issued			Balance		
	Units	Cost	Amount	Units	Cost	Amount	Units	Cost	Amount
6/1							100	$1.00	$100.00
6/5				25	$1.00	$ 25.00	75	1.00	75.00
6/7	300	$1.10	$330.00				375	1.08	405.00
6/10				10	1.08	10.80	365	1.08	394.20
6/12	100	1.25	125.00				465	1.1166	519.20
6/15				200	1.1166	223.32	265	1.1166	295.88
6/25				150	1.1166	167.49	115	1.1166	128.39
Cost of Goods Sold						$426.61			

ALTERNATIVE COST-OF-GOODS-SOLD COMPUTATION

Cost of Goods Available for Sale	$555.00
Less Ending Inventory	128.39
Cost of Goods Sold	$426.61

tion of a new average unit cost after each purchase, and this unit-cost figure is used to price all withdrawals until the next purchase is made. Hence, this method is often called the *moving-average method* when it is used in a perpetual inventory system. The illustration in Exhibit 8.11 indicates how the moving-average method operates with the use of perpetual inventory records. The inventory at the end of the month is valued at the last amount shown on the perpetual inventory form, $128.39. The unit price of $1.1166 is used only for determining the amount of subsequent withdrawals. The ending inventory of $128.39 is calculated as $295.88 less $167.49 (= 150 × $1.1166), not as 115 × $1.1166.

Operating Margin and Holding Gains

Exhibit 8.12 illustrates the identification of operating margin and holding gains for the inventory of item X. We have assumed that the 385 items withdrawn were all sold for a price of $1.50 each. In computing the replacement cost of goods sold, we use as a unit price for all goods sold on a given date the acquisition cost per unit at the most recent purchase date.

EXHIBIT 8.12
**Reporting of Operating Margins
and Holding Gains for Item X**

	Cost-Flow Assumption			
PERIODIC INVENTORY METHOD	**FIFO**		**LIFO**	
Sales Revenue from Item X (385 × $1.50)	$577.50		$577.50	
Less Replacement Cost of Goods Sold [(25 × $1.00)				
+ (10 × $1.10) + (350 × $1.25)]	473.50		473.50	
Operating Margin on Sales of Item X		$104.00		$104.00
Realized Holding Gain on Item X:				
Replacement Cost of Goods Sold	$473.50		$473.50	
Less Acquisition Cost of Goods Sold (FIFO—				
Exhibit 8.7; LIFO—Exhibit 8.8)	413.50		438.50	
Realized Holding Gain on Item X[a]		60.00		35.00
Conventionally Reported Gross Margin[b]		$164.00		$139.00
Unrealized Holding Gain on Item X:				
Replacement Cost of Ending Inventory (115 × $1.35) . . .	$155.25		$155.25	
Less Acquisition Cost of Ending Inventory (FIFO—				
Exhibit 8.7; LIFO—Exhibit 8.8)	141.50		116.50	
Unrealized Holding Gain on Item X		13.75		38.75
Economic Profit on Sales and Holding Inventory				
of Item X		$177.75		$177.75

[a] The SEC refers to this quantity as "inventory profit." See *inventory profit* in the Glossary at the back of the book.
[b] Historical-cost income statements usually omit information shown below this point.

The calculation of the operating margin and holding gain in this more realistic example follows the same procedure used in the simpler toaster example. The acquisition cost of the 500 items available for sale during the period is $555. If 385 units were sold for, say, $1.50 each, the total revenue would be $577.50. The replacement cost of the items at the time they were sold can be determined from information in Exhibit 8.6 to be $473.50 [= 25 × $1.00) + (10 × $1.10) + (350 × $1.25)]. The operating margin is $104.00 (= $577.50 − $473.50). The current replacement cost at the end of the month of the 115 units in ending inventory is $1.35 each, or a total of $155.25 (= 115 × $1.35). Thus the replacement cost of the goods sold plus the replacement cost of ending inventory is $628.75 (= $473.50 + $155.25). Total holding gain is $73.75 (= $628.75 − $555.00) and economic income is $177.75 (= $104.00 + $73.75).

The top portion of Exhibit 8.12 illustrates the separation of the conventionally reported gross margin into the operating margin and the realized holding gain. Unrealized holding gains are shown in the lower portion of the exhibit.

QUESTIONS AND PROBLEMS

1 Review the meaning of the following concepts or terms discussed in this chapter.
   a Inventory (both as a noun and as a verb).
   b Inventory equation.
   c Purchases.
   d Purchase returns.
   e Purchase discounts.
   f Shrinkages.
   g Periodic inventory method.
   h Gross margin method.
   i Perpetual inventory method.
   j Acquisition-cost basis.
   k Replacement cost.
   l Net realizable value.
   m Lower-of-cost-or-market basis.
   n Standard cost.
   o Cost-flow assumption.
   p FIFO.
   q LIFO.
   r Weighted average.
   s LIFO inventory layer.
   t Realized holding gain.
   u Unrealized holding gain.
   v Absorption (full) costing.
   w Direct (variable) costing.
   x Inventory profit.

2 Goods that cost $800 are sold for $1,000 cash. Present the normal journal entries at the time of the sale:
   a When a periodic inventory method is used.
   b When a perpetual inventory method is used.

3 Which of the two inventory methods, periodic or perpetual, would you expect to find used in each of the following situations?
   a The greeting card department of a retail store.
   b The fur coat department of a retail store.
   c Supplies storeroom for an automated production line.
   d Automobile dealership.
   e Wholesale dealer in bulk salad oil.
   f Grocery store.
   g College bookstore.
   h Diamond ring department of a jewelry store.
   i Ballpoint pen department of a jewelry store.

4 Under what circumstances would the perpetual and periodic inventory methods both yield the same inventory amount if the weighted-average flow assumption were used?

5 A noted accountant once claimed that firms which use a LIFO cost-flow assumption will find that historical cost of goods sold is *greater than* replacement cost of goods sold computed as of the time of sale. Under what circumstances is this assertion likely to be true? (Hint: Compare the effects of periodic and perpetual methods on LIFO cost of goods sold.) Do you agree that the assertion is likely to be true?

6 During a period of rising prices, will the FIFO or LIFO cost-flow assumption result in the higher ending inventory amount? The lower inventory amount? Assume no changes in physical quantities during the period.

7 Refer to the preceding question. Which cost-flow assumption will result in the higher ending inventory amount during a period of declining prices? The lower inventory amount?

8 a During a period of rising prices, will the FIFO or LIFO cost-flow assumption result in the higher cost of goods sold? The lower cost of goods sold? Assume no changes in physical quantities during the period.
   b Which cost-flow assumption, LIFO or FIFO, will result in the higher cost of goods sold during a period of declining prices? The lower cost of goods sold?

9 On December 30, 1979, merchandise amounting to $750 was received by the Perrin Company and was counted in its December 31 listing of all inventory items on hand. The invoice was not received until January 4, 1980, at which time the acquisition was recorded as of that date. The acquisition should have been recorded for 1979. Assume that the error was not discovered by the firm when the invoice was received, and that Perrin Company uses the periodic inventory method. Indicate the effect (overstatement, understatement, none) on each of the following amounts.
   a Inventory, 12/31/79.
   b Inventory, 12/31/80.
   c Cost of goods sold, 1979.
   d Cost of goods sold, 1980.
   e Net income, 1979.
   f Net income, 1980.
   g Accounts payable, 12/31/79.
   h Accounts payable, 12/31/80.
   i Retained earnings, 12/31/80.

10 Indicate the effect on Working Capital Provided by Operations of the following independent transactions. Include the effects of income taxes assuming a rate of 40 percent of pretax
income and that the same accounting methods used on the tax return are the same as on
the financial statements.

a A firm using the lower-of-cost-or-market basis for inventories writes ending inventory
down by $50,000.

b A firm has been using FIFO. It switches to LIFO during the current year and finds that
the cost of goods sold is $100,000 larger than it would have been under FIFO.

11 The chapter points out that two alternatives for treating discounts on merchandise purchases are often used in practice: (1) the gross price method, which recognizes the amount
of discounts taken on payments made during the period, without regard to the period of
purchase, and (2) the net price method, which deducts all discounts made available from
the gross purchase invoice prices at the time of purchases. This problem explains the two
methods.

Alternative 1: Gross Price Method The gross price method of accounting for purchases
records invoices at the gross price and accumulates the amount of discounts taken on payments made. Suppose that goods with a gross invoice price of $1,000 are purchased, 2/10,
net/30. (That is, a 2-percent discount from invoice price is offered if payment is made
within 10 days and the full invoice price is due, in any case, within 30 days.) The entries
to record the purchase and the payment (1) under the assumption that the payment is made
in time to take the discount, and (2) under the assumption that the payment is too late
to take advantage of the discount, are as follows:

Gross Price Method	(1) Discount Taken		(2) Discount Not Taken	
Purchases	1,000		1,000	
Accounts Payable		1,000		1,000
To record purchase.				
Accounts Payable	1,000		1,000	
Cash		980		1,000
Purchase Discounts		20		—
To record payment.				

The balance in the Purchase Discounts account is deducted from the balance in the
Purchases account in calculating net purchases for a period. Such a deduction merely
approximates the results achieved by treating purchase discounts as a reduction in purchase
price at the time of purchase. It is only an approximation because the total adjustment
includes discounts taken on payments made this period, without regard to the period
of purchase.

An accurate adjustment would require eliminating the discounts taken related to purchases of previous periods while including the amount of discounts available at the end
of the accounting period that are expected to be taken during the following period. This
refinement in the treatment of purchase discounts is seldom employed in practice.

Alternative 2: Net Price Method In recording purchases, the purchase discount is deducted from the gross purchase price immediately upon receipt of the invoice, and the net
invoice price is used in the entries. The example used previously of a $1,000 invoice price
for goods subject to a 2-percent cash discount would be recorded as follows under the
net price method:

Net Price Method	**(1) Discount Taken**		**(2) Discount Not Taken**	
Purchases	980		980	
Accounts Payable		980		980
To record purchase.				
Accounts Payable	980		980	
Purchase Discounts Lost	—		20	
Cash		980		1,000
To record payment.				

The balance in the Purchase Discounts Lost account could be added to the cost of the merchandise purchased and, therefore, viewed as an additional component of goods available for sale. We believe, however, that discounts lost should be shown as a financial or general operating expense rather than as an addition to the cost of purchases, since lost discounts may indicate an inefficient office force or inadequate financing. In this text, we treat purchase discounts lost as an expense unless an explicit contrary statement is made.

a Attempt to decide which of these two alternatives is preferable and why. You might find working part **b,** below, helpful in making your decision.

b Prepare a journal form with two pairs of columns, one headed Net Price Method and the other headed Gross Price Method. Using this journal form, show summary entries for the following events in the history of Evans and Foster, furniture manufacturers.

(1) During the first year of operations, materials with a gross invoice price of $60,000 are purchased. All invoices are subject to a 2-percent cash discount if paid within 10 days.

(2) Payments to creditors during the year amount to $53,000, settling $54,000 of accounts payable at gross prices.

(3) Of the $6,000, gross, in unpaid accounts at the end of the year, the discount time has expired on one invoice amounting to $400. It is expected that all other discounts will be taken. This expectation is reflected in the year-end adjustment.

(4) During the first few days of the next period, all invoices are paid in accordance with expectations.

12 The accounts listed below might appear in the records of a retail store. Their use is never required, but accounts such as these are often a convenience. From the name of the account and your understanding of the accounting for purchases and sales, indicate:

(1) Whether the account is a permanent account (to appear as such on the balance sheet) or a temporary account (to be closed at the end of the accounting period).

(2) The normal balance, debit or credit, in the account. If the account is a temporary one, then give the normal balance prior to closing.

(3) If the account is a temporary one, the kind of account it is closed to—balance sheet asset, balance sheet liability, balance sheet owners' equity through a revenue account, or balance sheet owners' equity through an expense (or revenue contra) account.

a Merchandise Purchases.
b Merchandise Purchase Allowances.
c Merchandise Purchase Returns.
d Purchase Returns.
e Sales Tax on Purchases.
f Freight-in on Purchases.

    g   Sales Allowances.

    h   Allowance for Sales Discounts.

    i   Federal Excise Taxes Payable on Sales.

The next two items should not be attempted until Problem **11** has been read.

    j   Purchase Discounts.

    k   Purchase Discounts Taken.

    l   Purchase Discounts Lost.

13 (This problem should not be attempted until Problem **11** has been read.) The following are selected transactions of the Wearever Shoe Store:

(1) A shipment of shoes is received from the Standard Shoe Company, $2,100. Terms 2/30, n/60.

(2) Part of the shipment of **(1)** is returned. The gross price of the returned goods is $200, and a credit memorandum for this amount is received from the Standard Shoe Company.

(3) The invoice of the Standard Shoe Company is paid in time to take the discount.

    a   Give entries on the books of the Wearever Shoe Store, assuming that the net price method is used.

    b   Give entries on the books of the Wearever Shoe Store, assuming that the gross price method is used.

14 The Salem Company began business on January 1, 1978. The information concerning merchandise inventories, purchases, and sales for the first 3 years of operations is as follows:

	1978	**1979**	**1980**
Sales	$300,000	$330,000	$450,000
Purchases	280,000	260,000	350,000
Inventories, Dec. 31:			
At cost	80,000	95,000	95,000
At market	75,000	80,000	100,000

    a   Compute the gross margin on sales (sales minus cost of goods sold) for each year, using the lower-of-cost-or-market basis in valuing inventories.

    b   Compute the gross margin on sales (sales minus cost of goods sold) for each year, using the acquisition-cost basis in valuing inventories.

    c   Indicate your conclusion whether the lower-of-cost-or-market basis of valuing inventories is "conservative" in all situations where it is applied.

15 The merchandise inventory of Parks Store was destroyed by fire on July 4. The accounting records were saved. They provided the following information:

Cost of Merchandise Inventory on Hand, January 1	$ 46,000
Purchases of Merchandise, January 1 to July 4	98,000
Sales, January 1 to July 4	120,000

The average retail markup over cost of the goods sold during the year before the fire was 50 percent of the acquisition cost.

    a   Use the gross margin method to estimate the cost of the goods on hand at the time of the fire.

    b   Give the journal entry to record the loss assuming that it was uninsured.

c Give the journal entry to record the loss assuming that all goods were fully insured for their acquisition cost.

16 Refer to the data in the preceding problem. Assume that the store owner does not know the average retail markup over cost for the destroyed goods. The accounting records show that the total sales revenue during the 4 years preceding the fire amounted to $1,000,000 and the total cost of goods sold over the same period was $650,000.

a Assuming that the ratio of sales prices to cost of goods sold for the last 4 years holds for this year, estimate the cost of the goods destroyed in the fire.

b Assume the same facts as above, except that the $1,000,000 represents the original selling price of the goods sold during the last 4 years. Certain goods were marked down before sale so that the actual sales revenue was only $975,000. Assuming that the same percentage of goods were marked down by the same price during the first 6 months of this year as in the previous 4 years, estimate the cost of the goods destroyed by the fire.

17 The inventory footnote to the 1979 annual report of the Cheral Company reads in part as follows:

> Because of continuing high demand throughout the year, inventories were unavoidably reduced and could not be replaced. Under the LIFO system of accounting, used for many years by Cheral Company, the net effect of all the inventory changes was to increase pretax income by $60,000 over what it would have been had inventories been maintained at their physical levels at the start of the year.

The price of Cheral Company's merchandise purchases was $22 per unit during 1979 after having risen steadily for many years. Cheral Company uses a periodic inventory method. Cheral Company's inventory positions at the beginning and end of the year are summarized below.

Date	Physical Count of Inventory	LIFO Cost of Inventory
January 1, 1979	30,000 units	$?
December 31, 1979	20,000 units	$260,000

a What was the average cost per unit of the 10,000 units removed from the January 1, 1979, LIFO inventory?

b What was the January 1, 1979, LIFO cost of inventory?

18 The inventory at September 1 and the purchases during September of a certain item of raw material were as follows:

9/1 Inventory	1,000 lb	$ 4,000
9/5 Purchased	3,000 lb	13,500
9/14 Purchased	3,500 lb	17,500
9/27 Purchased	3,000 lb	16,500
9/29 Purchased	1,000 lb	6,000

The inventory at September 30 is 1,800 pounds.

Assume a periodic inventory system. Compute the cost of the inventory on September 30 under each of the following cost-flow assumptions:

a FIFO.

b Weighted average.

c LIFO.

19 The following information concerning an item of raw materials is available:

Nov. 2 Inventory	....	4,000 lb @ $5
9 Issued	....	3,000 lb
16 Purchased	....	7,000 lb @ $6
23 Issued	....	3,000 lb
30 Issued	....	3,000 lb

Compute the cost of goods sold and the cost of ending inventory on November 30 for each of the following combinations of inventory systems and cost-flow assumptions.
a Periodic FIFO.
b Periodic weighted average.
c Periodic LIFO.
d Perpetual FIFO.
e Perpetual weighted average.
f Perpetual LIFO.

20 The Central Supply Company has in its inventory on May 1 three units of item K, all purchased on the same date at a price of $60 per unit. Information relative to item K is as follows:

Date	Explanation	Units	Unit Cost	Tag Number
May 1	Inventory	3	$60	K–515,516,517
3	Purchase	2	65	K–518,519
12	Sale	3		K–515,518,519
19	Purchase	2	70	K–520,521
25	Sale	1		K–516

Compute the cost of units sold in accordance with the following:
a Specific identification of units sold.
b FIFO cost-flow assumption and periodic inventory method.
c FIFO cost-flow assumption and perpetual inventory method.
d LIFO cost-flow assumption and periodic inventory method.
e LIFO cost-flow assumption and perpetual inventory method.
f Weighted-average cost-flow assumption and perpetual inventory method.
g Weighted-average cost-flow assumption and periodic inventory method.

21 The Harrison Corporation was organized and began retailing operations on January 1, 1979. Purchases of merchandise inventory during 1979 and 1980 were as follows:

	Quantity Purchased	Unit Price	Acquisition Cost
1/10/79	100,000	$ .10	$10,000
6/30/79	40,000	.15	6,000
10/20/79	20,000	.16	3,200
Total 1979	160,000		$19,200
2/18/80	30,000	$ .18	$ 5,400
7/15/80	10,000	.20	2,000
12/15/80	50,000	.22	11,000
Total 1980	90,000		$18,400

The number of units sold during 1979 and 1980 was 90,000 units and 110,000 units, respectively. Harrison Corporation uses a periodic inventory method.

a Determine the cost of goods sold during 1979 under the FIFO cost-flow assumption.

b Determine the cost of goods sold during 1979 under the LIFO cost-flow assumption.

c Determine the cost of goods sold during 1979 under the weighted-average cost-flow assumption.

d Determine the cost of goods sold during 1980 under the FIFO cost-flow assumption.

e Determine the cost of goods sold during 1980 under the LIFO cost-flow assumption.

f Determine the cost of goods sold during 1980 under the weighted-average cost-flow assumption.

g For the 2 years, 1979 and 1980, taken as a whole, will FIFO or LIFO result in reporting the larger net income? What is the difference in net income for the 2-year period under FIFO as compared to LIFO? Assume an income tax rate of 40 percent for both years.

h Which method, LIFO or FIFO, should Harrison Corporation probably prefer and why?

22 (This problem should not be attempted until Problem **21** has been done.) Assume the same data for the Harrison Corporation as given in the previous problem. In addition, assume the following:

Selling Price per Unit:

1979	$.25
1980	.30

Average Current Replacement Cost:

1979	$.15
1980	.20

Current Replacement Cost:

December 31, 1979	$.17
December 31, 1980	.22

a Prepare an analysis similar to that in Exhibit 8.4 for 1979, identifying operating margins, realized holding gains and losses, and unrealized holding gains and losses for the FIFO, LIFO, and weighted-average cost-flow assumptions.

b Repeat part **a** for 1980.

c Demonstrate that over the 2-year period, the economic profits of Harrison Corporation are independent of the cost-flow assumption.

23 On January 1, the merchandise inventory of Revsine Retail Store consisted of 1,000 units acquired for $450 each. During the year, 2,500 additional units were acquired at an average price of $600 each while 2,300 units were sold for $800 each. The replacement cost of these units at the time they were sold averaged $600 during the year. The replacement cost of units on December 31 was $700 per unit.

a Calculate cost of goods sold under both FIFO and LIFO cost-flow assumptions.

b Prepare partial statements of income showing gross margin on sales as revenues less cost of goods sold with both FIFO and LIFO cost-flow assumptions.

c Prepare partial income statements separating the gross margin on sales into operating margins and realized holding gains under both FIFO and LIFO.

d Append to the bottom of the statements prepared in part **c** a statement showing the amount of unrealized holding gains and the total of realized income plus unrealized holding gains.

e If you did the above steps correctly, the totals in part **d** are the same for both FIFO and LIFO. Is this equality a coincidence? Why or why not?

24 The Sanlex Company started the year with no inventories on hand. It manufactured two batches of inventory, which were identical except that the variable costs of producing the first batch were $120 and the variable costs of producing the second batch were $200 because of rising prices. By the end of the year, Sanlex Company had sold three-fourths of the first batch for $300 and none of the second batch. The ending inventory had a market value of $305. Total fixed manufacturing costs for the year were $160. Under the absorption costing procedure, $100 of fixed manufacturing costs allocated to units produced remained in inventory at the close of the year. Selling and administrative expenses for the year were $30.

Prepare a statement of pretax income for the Sanlex Company for the year under each of the following sets of assumptions.

a FIFO, acquisition-cost basis.

b LIFO, acquisition-cost basis.

c FIFO, lower-of-cost-or-market basis.

25 This problem tries to make clear the difference between the impact on financial statements of the choice between a FIFO and a LIFO flow assumption. Take 12 pieces of paper and mark each one with a number between 1 and 12 inclusive. Sort the pieces of paper into a pile with the numbers in consecutive order facing up, so that number 1 is on top and number 12 is on bottom. These 12 pieces of paper are to represent 12 identical units of merchandise purchased at prices increasing from $1 to $12. Assume that four of the units are purchased each period for three periods, that three units are sold each period, and that the periodic inventory method is used.

a Compute the cost of goods sold and ending inventory amounts for each of the three periods under a FIFO flow assumption.

b Compute the cost of goods sold and ending inventory amounts for each of the three periods under a LIFO flow assumption.

c Re-sort the 12 pieces of paper into decreasing order to represent declining prices for successive purchases. Compute the cost-of-goods-sold and ending inventory amounts for each of the three periods under a FIFO flow assumption.

d Repeat part **c** using a LIFO flow assumption.

e If you are not convinced that the following are all true statements, then repeat parts **a**–**d** until you are.

(1) In periods of rising prices and increasing physical inventories, FIFO implies higher reported income than does LIFO.

(2) In periods of declining prices and increasing physical inventories, LIFO implies higher reported income than does FIFO.

(3) Under FIFO, current prices are reported on the balance sheet and old prices are reported on the income statement.

(4) Under LIFO, current prices are reported on the income statement and very old prices are reported on the balance sheet.

(5) The difference between FIFO and LIFO balance sheet amounts for inventory at the end of each period after the first one is larger than the differences between FIFO and LIFO reported net income for each period after the first one.

f Assume that in period 4, only one unit (number 13) is purchased for $13, but three are sold. What additional "truth" can you deduce from comparing LIFO and FIFO cost of goods sold when physical quantities are declining?

g The LIFO portion of Figure 8.1 represents a periodic inventory method. In this part of the question, assume that in each period the first item is acquired before any sales occur. Then one item is sold; then the two items are purchased; then one more item is sold; then the last two purchases are made and the last sale occurs. (If P represents

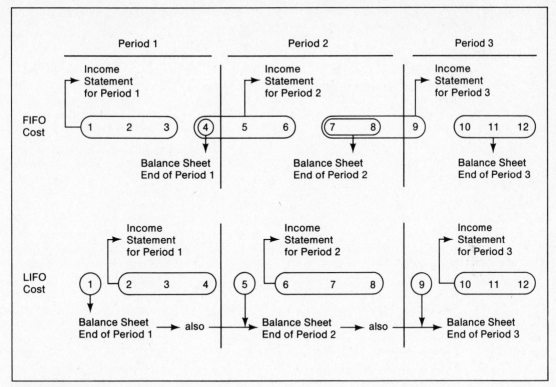

FIGURE 8.1
To Aid in Understanding Problem 25

purchase and S represents sale, the events are PSPPSPS.) Draw a figure similar to those in Figure 8.1 to represent a LIFO cost-flow assumption coupled with a perpetual inventory system. Convince yourself that in times of rising prices the LIFO cost-of-goods-sold figure with a periodic method exceeds LIFO cost of goods sold computed under a perpetual method.

26 The purpose of this problem is to help you explore the relationship between replacement cost of goods sold and historical LIFO cost of goods sold. The text makes several points in this regard:

(1) LIFO cost of goods sold is generally larger in a periodic system than in a perpetual system.

(2) LIFO cost of goods sold for most companies is insignificantly different from replacement cost of goods sold using replacement costs as of the time of sale.

(3) Historical LIFO cost of goods sold in a perpetual inventory system is likely to be larger (although not significantly) than the replacement cost of goods sold using replacement cost at the time of sale.

The accompanying data are hypothetical. They are constructed from ratios of an actual retailing firm selling grocery products. Sales revenue for the year is $2,820,000. All expenses (including income taxes) other than cost of goods sold are $144,000 for the year. Exhibit 8.13 shows cost of goods available for sale.

EXHIBIT 8.13
Data for Problem 26

	Replacement Cost of Goods Measured at	
	Sales Dates (Mid-Month)	Purchases Dates (End of Month)
December 1978	—	$ 300,000
January 1979	$ 201,000	202,000
February 1979	203,000	204,000
March 1979	205,000	206,000
April 1979	207,000	208,000
May 1979	209,000	210,000
June 1979	211,000	212,000
July 1979	213,000	214,000
August 1979	215,000	216,000
September 1979	217,000	218,000
October 1979	219,000	220,000
November 1979	221,000	222,000
December 1979	223,000	224,000
Replacement Cost of Goods Sold at Times of Sale	$2,544,000	
Cost of Goods Available for Sale		$2,856,000

The costs of the grocery items for this company increase during the year at a steady rate of about 1 percent per month. The company starts the year with an inventory equal to $1\frac{1}{2}$ months' sales. These items were acquired at the end of December 1978 for $300,000. At the end of each month during 1979, the firm is assumed to acquire inventory in physical quantities equal to the next month's sales requirements. We assume that all sales occur at mid-month during each month and that all purchases occur at the end of a month to be sold during the next month. (These artificial assumptions capture the reality of a firm acquiring inventory on average $\frac{1}{2}$ month before it is sold and inventory turnover rate of about eight times per year.) Identical physical quantities are purchased and sold each month.

Exhibit 8.13 shows the actual cost of the items purchased at the end of each month and the replacement cost of those items if they had been acquired at mid-month.

At the end of the year, ending physical inventory is equal in amount to $1\frac{1}{2}$ months' sales, which is the same as the physical quantity on hand at the start of the year.

a Compute LIFO historical cost of goods sold and net income for 1979 using a periodic inventory method.

b Compute LIFO historical cost of goods sold and net income for 1979 using a perpetual inventory method.

c Compute net income for 1979 using replacement cost of goods sold at the time of sale.

d What is the percentage difference between the largest and smallest cost-of-goods-sold figures computed in the preceding three parts?

e What is the percentage error in using LIFO cost of goods sold to approximate replacement cost of goods sold? (Compute percentage errors for both LIFO periodic and LIFO perpetual calculations.)

f Would you expect that most companies who use LIFO for tax purposes do so with a periodic inventory method or with a perpetual inventory method? Why?

27 The LIFO Company and the FIFO Company both manufacture paper and cardboard products. Prices of timber, paper pulp, and finished paper products have generally increased by about 5 percent per year through the *start of this year*. Inventory data for the beginning and end of the year are shown below.

	January 1	December 31
LIFO Company Inventory (last in, first out)	$19,695,000	$15,870,000
FIFO Company Inventory (first in, first out, lower of cost or market)	46,284,000	38,250,000

Income statements for the two companies for the year ending December 31 are as follows:

	LIFO Company	FIFO Company
Sales	$57,000,000	$129,000,000
Expenses:		
Cost of Goods Sold	$44,580,000	$108,000,000
Depreciation	5,400,000	12,000,000
General Expenses	2,220,000	5,400,000
Income Taxes		
(40 percent of pretax income)	1,920,000	1,440,000
Total Expenses	$54,120,000	$126,840,000
Net Income	$ 2,880,000	$ 2,160,000

a Assuming that the prices for timber, paper pulp, and finished paper had remained unchanged during the year, how would the two companies' respective inventory valuation methods affect the interpretation of their financial statements for the year?

b How would the answer to part **a** differ if prices at the end of the year had been lower than at the beginning of the year?

c How would the answer to part **a** differ if prices at the end of the year had been higher than at the beginning of the year?

28 The Wilson Company sells chemical compounds made from expensium. The company has used a LIFO inventory-flow assumption for many years. The inventory of expensium on January 1, 1973, consisted of 2,000 pounds from the inventory bought in 1969 for $30 a pound. The following schedule shows purchases and physical ending inventories of expensium for the years 1973 through 1978.

Year	Purchase Price per Pound During Year	Cost of Units Purchased	End-of-Year Inventory in Pounds
1973	$48	$240,000	2,000
1974	46	296,000	2,200
1975	48	368,000	3,000
1976	50	384,000	3,600
1977	50	352,000	2,600
1978	52	448,000	4,000

Because of temporary scarcities, expensium is expected to cost $62 per pound during 1979 but to fall back to $52 per pound in 1980. Sales for 1979 are expected to require 7,000 pounds of expensium. The purchasing agent suggests that the inventory of expensium be allowed to decrease from 4,000 to 600 pounds by the end of 1979 and to be replenished to the desired level of 4,000 pounds early in 1980.

The controller argues that such a policy would be foolish. If inventories are allowed to decrease to 600 pounds, then the cost of goods sold will be extraordinarily low (because the older LIFO purchases will be consumed) and income taxes will be extraordinarily high. Furthermore, he points out that the diseconomies of smaller orders during 1979, as required by the purchasing agent's plan, would lead to about $1,000 of extra costs for recordkeeping. These costs would be treated as an expense for 1979. He suggests that 1979 purchases should be planned to maintain an end-of-year inventory.

Assume that sales for 1979 do require 7,000 pounds of expensium, that the prices for 1979 and 1980 are as forecast, and that the income tax rate for Wilson Company is 40 percent.

Calculate the cost of goods sold and end-of-year LIFO inventory:

a For each of the years 1973 through 1978.
b For 1979, assuming that the controller's advice is followed so that inventory at the end of 1979 is 4,000 pounds.
c For 1979, assuming that the purchasing agent's advice is followed and inventory at the end of 1979 is 600 pounds.

Assuming that the controller's, rather than the purchasing agent's, advice is followed, calculate:

d The tax savings for 1979.
e The extra cash costs for inventory.
f Using the results derived so far, what should Wilson Company do?
g Would your advice be different if Wilson Company used a FIFO cost-flow assumption?

29 The purpose of this problem is to help you understand how to compare income as it appears in financial statements under a given cost-flow assumption (or other inventory system) with what income would have been under a different cost-flow assumption (or other inventory system). The following two relations can help. In comparing income under one set of conditions, called system F, with income under another set of conditions, called system L,

$$(I) \quad \frac{\text{Income (System F)}}{- \text{ Income (System L)}} = \frac{\text{Increase in Ending Inventory (System F)}}{- \text{ Increase in Ending Inventory (System L)}}.$$

Also,

$$(II) \quad \frac{\text{Income (System F)}}{- \text{ Income (System L)}} = \frac{\begin{array}{l}\text{[Ending Inventory (Systems F)} \\ - \text{ Ending Inventory (System L)]}\end{array}}{\begin{array}{l}- \text{ [Beginning Inventory (System F)} \\ - \text{ Beginning Inventory (System L)]}\end{array}}.$$

We use the symbols F and L to evoke the thoughts FIFO and LIFO as you read these equations, but keep in mind that the equations hold whatever comparisons are being made. For example condition F might represent a specific identification method of measuring cost of goods sold, whereas L might represent a weighted-average cost-flow assumption with a perpetual inventory method.

Some readers will prefer to see a derivation of these results. We use the following two equations:

$$\text{Margin} = \text{Revenue} - \text{Cost of Goods Sold}$$

$$\text{Cost of Goods Sold} = \text{Beginning Inventory} + \text{Purchases} - \text{Ending Inventory}.$$

We abbreviate the components of these equations as follows:

$$M = R - COGS$$

$$COGS = BI + P - EI.$$

A subscript on a symbol denotes the quantity under a particular set of inventory conditions, either F or L. Thus,

(1) $M_F = R_F - COGS_F$ and $COGS_F = BI_F + P_F - EI_F.$

(2) $M_L = R_L - COGS_L$ and $COGS_L = BI_L + P_L - EI_L.$

But note that both revenues and purchases are unaffected by the inventory conditions, so that

$$R_F = R_L \qquad \text{and} \qquad P_F = P_L.$$

Thus if we subtract equations (2) from (1), we get

$$M_F - M_L = - COGS_F + COGS_L \quad \text{and}$$

$$COGS_F - COGS_L = (BI_F - BI_L) - (EI_F - EI_L).$$

Now, if we multiply the right-hand equation by -1, we get

(3) $- COGS_F + COGS_L = (EI_F - EI_L) - (BI_F - BI_L).$

Substituting the right-hand equation's results into the left yields

(4) $M_F - M_L = (EI_F - EI_L) - (BI_F - BI_L).$

Equation (4) is the second relation mentioned above (II) as being useful in comparing inventory conditions. The first term in parentheses on the right-hand side is the difference between ending inventories, and the second is the difference between beginning inventories. If we rearrange the terms on the right-hand side of equation (4), we get

(5) $M_F - M_L = (EI_F - BI_F) - (EI_L - BI_L).$

The right-hand side of (5) is the increase in inventory during the year under conditions F minus the increase in inventory during the period under conditions L. Thus, equation (5) is the first relation (I) mentioned above as being useful in comparing incomes under two sets of inventory conditions.

Exhibit 8.2 illustrates this relation. For example, the difference between FIFO and LIFO income (or gross margins) is $5 (= $30 − $25). The difference between the FIFO and LIFO increases in inventory during the period is also $5 (= $34 − $29). This relation can also be seen in Exhibit 8.2 by comparing FIFO and weighted-average income differences ($3) or weighted-average and LIFO differences ($2).

The Burch Corporation began a merchandising business on January 1, 1978. It acquired merchandise costing $100,000 in 1978, $125,000 in 1979, and $135,000 in 1980. Information about Burch Corporation's inventory, as it would appear on the balance sheet under different inventory methods, is shown below:

Burch Corporation
Inventory Valuations for Balance
Sheet Under Various
Assumptions (Problem 29)

Date	LIFO Cost	FIFO Cost	Lower of FIFO Cost or Market
12/31/78	$40,800	$40,000	$37,000
12/31/79	36,400	36,000	34,000
12/31/80	41,200	44,000	44,000

In answering each of the following questions, indicate how the answer is deduced. You may assume that in any one year, prices moved only up or down, but not both in the same year.

a Did prices go up or down in 1978?

b Did prices go up or down in 1980?

c Which inventory method would show the highest income for 1978?

d Which inventory method would show the highest income for 1980?

e Which inventory method would show the highest income for 1979?

f Which inventory method would show the lowest income for all three years combined?

g For 1980, how much higher or lower would income be on the FIFO cost basis than it would be on the lower-of-cost-or-market basis?

h The notes to the financial statements in a recent annual report of the Westinghouse Electric Corporation contain the following statement. "The excess of current cost [of inventories] . . . over the cost of inventories valued on the LIFO basis was $230 million at [year-end] and $163 million at [the beginning of the year]." How much higher or lower would Westinghouse's pretax reported income have been if its inventories had been valued at current costs, rather than with a LIFO cost-flow assumption? Westinghouse reported $28 million net income for the year and tax expense equal to 48 percent of pretax income. By what percentage would Westinghouse's net income increase if a FIFO flow assumption had been used?

30 Exhibit 8.3 illustrated the calculation of pretax income for the General Electric Company using a LIFO and a FIFO cost-flow assumption. Shown below are General Electric Company's inventories for a period of years under the LIFO assumption actually used and under FIFO as they would have been if it had been used. Also shown is the firm's pretax income as a result of using LIFO.

 a Determine the pretax income for years 2 through 6, assuming that a FIFO cost-flow assumption had been used.

 b Calculate the percentage change in pretax income for each of the years 3 through 6 under both LIFO and FIFO (that is, the increase in pretax income in year 3 relative to year 2, the increase in pretax income in year 4 relative to year 3, and so on).

 c Calculate the percentage change in pretax income between year 2 and year 6 (that is, the 5-year period taken as a whole) under both LIFO and FIFO.

 d Did the quantity of items in inventory increase or decrease during each of the years 3 through 6? How can you tell?

**General Electric Company
(Amounts in Millions)**
(Problem 30)

End of Year	LIFO Ending Inventory	FIFO Ending Inventory
1	$1,611.7	$1,884.5
2	1,759.0	2,063.1
3	1,986.2	2,415.9
4	2,257.0	3,040.7
5	2,202.9	3,166.6
6	2,354.4	3,515.2

For the Year	Pretax Income Using LIFO
2	$ 897.2
3	1,011.6
4	1,000.7
5	1,174.0
6	1,627.5

 e Did the acquisition cost of items in inventory increase or decrease during each of the years 3 through 6? How can you tell?

 f Assume for this part that the inventory value under LIFO at the end of year 1 of $1,611.7 is the initial LIFO layer. This layer may be viewed as the bottom layer on a cake. Construct a figure showing the addition or subtraction of LIFO layers for each of the years 2 through 6.

 g The current assets and current liabilities of the General Electric Company at the end of years 2 through 6 using a LIFO cost-flow assumption are shown below.

	Amounts in Millions	
End of Year	**Current Assets**	**Current Liabilities**
2	$3,979.3	$2,869.7
3	4,485.4	3,492.4
4	5,222.6	3,879.5
5	5,750.4	4,163.0
6	6,685.0	4,604.9

Compute General Electric's current ratio for each year using the above data.

h Recompute General Electric's current ratio for each year using a FIFO cost-flow assumption for inventories. Although it is unrealistic to do so, assume for this part that there are no changes in income taxes payable or current liabilities. (To make the figures realistic after taxes, ending LIFO inventory should be increased by about *one-half* the difference between FIFO and LIFO ending inventory amounts. Why?)

31 The financial statements of the International Corporation (IC) are included in Appendix A at the back of this book.

a Refer to IC's Note 9 on page 586. Explain why the decline in inventory quantities during 19X1 caused income to increase. Is there any inconsistency in that reported decrease and the reported increase in the difference between replacement and historical cost of ending inventory? Why not?

b IC uses a LIFO cost-flow assumption. There is sufficient information given in IC's Note 9 for you to construct hypothetical financial statements both assuming that IC used a FIFO cost-flow assumption and assuming that IC used a current-value (replacement-cost) basis for inventories, without any cost-flow assumption. For each of these treatments—LIFO, FIFO, replacement cost—compute each of the following ratios (ignoring income tax effects):

(1) Current ratio.

(2) Inventory turnover ratio.

(3) Rate of return on shareholders' equity.

(When assuming a FIFO cost-flow assumption or a current-value basis for inventory, be sure to increase owners' equity by the same amount that you increase ending inventory. When you hypothetically debit ending inventory to increase it, you must also credit owners' equity.)

c What inferences can you draw from the computations done in part **b** about comparing the financial statements of a company using LIFO with ones of a company using FIFO? What inferences can you draw about the comparison of financial statements using historical-cost accounting for inventories with those based on current values measured by replacement cost?

32 Data for companies A, B, and C shown in Exhibit 8.14 are taken from the annual reports of three actual companies in the same industry for a recent year. One of these companies uses a LIFO cost-flow assumption for 100 percent of its inventories, another uses LIFO for about 60 percent of its inventories, and the other uses LIFO for about 45 percent of its inventories. From these data and the lessons of this chapter, answer the following questions, making explicit the reasoning used in each case.

EXHIBIT 8.14
Financial Statement Data
(Problems 32 and 33)

	Dollar Amounts in Millions				
	Company				
	A	**B**	**C**	**D**	**E**
Sales Revenue	$14,950	$10,445	$5,152	$15,697	$5,042
Cost of Goods Sold:[a]					
Historical-Cost Basis	13,497	8,318	3,638	10,852	3,720
Replacement-Cost Basis . . .	13,432	8,322	3,675	11,110	3,720
Net Income	695	106	108	931	383
Ending Inventory:					
Historical-Cost Basis	2,215	756	1,026	2,265	1,245
Replacement-Cost Basis . . .	2,303	875	1,056	3,540	2,169
Ratio of Net Income					
to Revenue	4.6%	1.0%	2.1%	5.9%	7.6%

[a] Excludes depreciation charges.

a From the cost-of-goods-sold data alone, which of the companies appears to be the 100-percent LIFO company? The 60-percent LIFO company? The 45-percent LIFO company?

b From the ending-inventory data alone, which of the companies appears to be the 100-percent LIFO company? The 60-percent LIFO company? The 40-percent LIFO company?

c From your answers to parts **a** and **b,** draw a conclusion as to which of the companies appears to be which.

d Note that Company A earned net income equal to 4.6 percent of sales, whereas Company B earned net income equal to 1.0 percent of sales. Can you conclude that Company A is more profitable than Company B? Why or why not? (Hint: Refer to the data and discussion in Problem **32** of Chapter 6.)

e Although all three of these companies are from the same industry, the nature of the goods sold and the operations of two of the companies are somewhat different from the nature of the goods sold and the operations of the third. Which of the three appears to be the one that is different from the other two?

33 (This problem should not be attempted until Problem **32** has been read.) Data for Company D and Company E shown in Exhibit 8.14 are taken from the annual reports of two actual companies for a recent year. One of these companies uses a LIFO cost-flow assumption for all of its inventories, whereas the other uses LIFO for only a portion. From these data and the lessons of this chapter, answer the following questions, making explicit the reasoning you used.

a Which of the two companies is more likely to be the 100-percent LIFO company?

b Data for companies A, B, and C are also shown in Exhibit 8.14. These three companies are in an industry much different from the industries that include Company D and Company E. Which of the two industries is more likely to be related to retailing and which is more likely to be related to manufacturing?

CHAPTER 9
LONG-LIVED ASSETS AND AMORTIZATION EXPENSE

In everyday language, the term *asset* means something good, something that is beneficial and that will provide benefits in the future. This definition of asset applies in accounting as well. Assets are either short-lived or long-lived. A business acquires a short-lived asset, such as cash, in one period and can use up its benefits in the same period. A long-lived asset is different: To enjoy all its benefits, the owner must use it for many years. In these cases, the accountant must apportion, or allocate, the cost of the asset over the several accounting periods of benefit. This general process is called *amortization*. Amortization of *plant assets,* which include the fixtures, machinery, equipment, and physical structures of a business, is called *depreciation*.

In addition to its plant assets, a company such as Gulf Oil has other long-lived assets. Oil companies own natural gas and oil wells. These natural resources are called *wasting assets.* Oil wells, coal mines, uranium deposits, and other natural resources are eventually used up, and amortization of the cost of these wasting assets is called *depletion.*

Businesses may also acquire *intangible assets* and, although there are many examples of them, some of the best-known ones are everyday words such as *Coca-Cola, Kleenex,* and *Kodak,* all famous trademarks. A local operator may pay several thousand dollars to acquire a McDonald's or Kentucky Fried Chicken franchise. Such franchises frequently do not have a perpetual life; the accountant must amortize their costs.

Most of this chapter is devoted to depreciation because plant assets are the most common long-lived assets, and depreciation problems are typical of almost all other amortization problems.

The problems of plant asset valuation and depreciation expense measurement can be conveniently separated into the consideration of four separate kinds of events:

1 Recording the acquisition of the asset

2 Recording its use over time

3 Recording adjustments for changes in capacity or efficiency and for repairs or improvements

4 Recording its retirement or other disposal.

ACQUISITION OF PLANT ASSETS

The cost of a plant asset includes all charges necessary to prepare it for rendering services, and it is often recorded in a series of transactions. Thus, the cost of a piece of equipment will be the sum of the entries to recognize the invoice price (less any discounts), transportation costs, installation charges, and any other costs necessary before the equipment is ready for use. When a firm constructs or fabricates its own buildings or equipment, many entries to record the labor, material, and overhead costs will normally be required before the total cost is recorded on the books. When a firm acquires a new asset in exchange for an old one, such as in a trade-in transaction or a bartered transaction, the fair market value of the assets given up plus any cash disbursed in the transaction should be used as the cost of the new asset. Trade-in transactions are discussed later in this chapter.

Repair and maintenance *costs* will almost certainly occur during the life of the asset. These costs are required to *maintain* the service level anticipated from the asset and are treated as expenses of the period. Once an asset is in service, certain costs may be incurred to *improve* the asset and should be "capitalized" or added to its cost. Improvements are defined as those costs that extend the life of the asset, increase the asset's output, or reduce the cost of operating the asset. It is often difficult to decide whether a particular expenditure is a repair to be treated as a period expense or is an improvement to be treated as an asset. The line between maintaining service and improving or extending it is not a distinct one. Some expenditures seem to meet the criteria to be either a repair expense or an improvement cost. There is frequent disagreement between Internal Revenue Service and taxpayers, as well as among accountants, over this question in specific situations.

PLANT ASSETS AND DEPRECIATION: FUNDAMENTAL CONCEPTS

Plant Assets

The terms *plant assets* and *fixed assets* are often used interchangeably. They refer to long-lived assets used in the operations of trading, service, and manufacturing enterprises, and include land, buildings, machinery, and equipment. The ordinary usage of the terms *plant assets* and *fixed assets* often does not adequately encompass the class of long-lived assets that includes all land, buildings, machinery, and equipment. *Plant assets* is sometimes used too narrowly to mean only items in a factory or plant. *Fixed assets* is sometimes used too narrowly to mean only items such as land and buildings that are immovable and tend to have very long service lives.

Most plant assets except land can be kept intact and in usable operating condition for more than a year, but eventually they must be retired from service. The central purpose of the depreciation accounting process is to allocate the cost of these assets to the periods of their use in a reasonable and orderly fashion.

Depreciation

Through a process of evolution in accounting terminology, the use of the term *depreciation* is restricted to the expiration of the cost of plant assets. Although in popular speech *depreciation* is often associated with a decline in market value of any kind of property, its accounting usage is more restricted in two ways; (1) in accounting, depreciation refers to the expiration of cost (or other basis) of an asset which is unlikely to coincide with its decline in market value and (2) depreciation has been restricted to expiration of plant assets and special terms have been developed in accounting usage for the decline in recorded costs of assets other than plant assets. As was suggested earlier, *depletion* refers to the allocation of costs of wasting assets, or natural resources, over time. The general term *amortization* is used for the process of allocating the costs of intangibles over time. On the other hand, merchandise and materials may become shopworn or obsolete, but the accounting recognition of this fact is described as an "inventory adjustment" rather than as depreciation.

It is useful to think of the cost of an asset with a limited life as the price paid for a series of future services—a purchase of so many hours or other units of service. When deciding to purchase a building or machine, the purchaser need not make elaborate calculations to arrive at the present value of a series of precisely appraised future benefits, but the purchaser must at least roughly approximate those procedures. It would be irrational to purchase an asset if the present value of the services expected to be received from it were known to be less than the required investment.

The investment in a depreciating asset is the price paid for a series of future services. The asset account may well be considered as a prepayment, similar in many respects to prepaid rent or insurance—a payment in advance for services to be received. As the asset is used in each accounting period, an appropriate portion of the investment in the asset is treated as the cost of the service received and is treated as an expense of the period or as part of the cost of goods produced during the period.

The Causes of Depreciation

The causes of depreciation are the causes of decline in an asset's service-rendering potential and of its ultimate retirement. Unless the asset must eventually be retired from its planned use, there is no depreciation. The services or benefits provided by land do not ordinarily diminish over time, so land is not depreciated. Many factors lead to the retirement of assets from service, but the causes of decline in service potential can be classified as either *physical* or *functional*. The physical factors include such things as ordinary wear and tear from use, chemical action such as rust or electrolysis, and the effects of wind and rain. The most important functional or nonphysical cause is *obsolescence*. Inventions, for example, may result in new equipment, the use of which reduces the unit cost of production to the point where continued operation of the old asset is not economical, even though it may be relatively unimpaired physically. Retail stores often replace display cases and storefronts long before they are worn out in order to keep the appearance of the store as attractive as their competitors'. Changed economic conditions may also become functional causes of depreciation, such as when an old airport becomes inadequate and must be abandoned, and a new, larger one is built to meet the requirements of heavier traffic, or when an increase in the cost of gasoline causes a reduction in demand for automobile products, which results in a reduced scale of operations in automobile manufacturing.

Identifying the specific causes of depreciation is not essential for considering the fundamental problem of its measurement. It is enough to know that almost any physical asset will eventually have to be retired from service and that in some cases the retirement will become necessary at a time when physical deterioration is negligible. The specific causes do become important, however, when the attempt is made to estimate the useful life of an asset.

Depreciation as a Decline in Value

Depreciation is frequently used in ordinary conversation to mean a decline in value. Such an interpretation may be fundamentally sound when applied to the entire service life of a plant asset—there certainly is a decline in the value of an asset from the time it is acquired until it is retired from service. However, a decline in asset values is an unsatisfactory description of the charge made to the operations of each accounting period. One incorrect inference from such a description is that if, in a given period of time, there has been an increase in the value of an asset, such as an increase arising from increasing prices for the asset, then there has been no depreciation during that period. Rather, there have been two partially offsetting processes: (1) a holding gain on the asset, which usually is not recognized in historical cost-based accounting, and (2) depreciation of the asset's historical cost. As the previous chapter indicated, a holding gain is an increase in the market price of an asset since the time the asset was acquired or last revalued.

Further, the word *value* has so many uses and connotations that it is not a serviceable term for a definition. (The noun *value* should seldom be used in accounting without a qualifying adjective.) If depreciation is defined as a decline in value and the undepreciated balance of an asset account as a "present" value, it is usually necessary to explain that under generally accepted accounting principles, it is value to the going concern based on historical cost, not on selling price, not on second-hand value, nor on replacement cost. The word *value* is not entirely inappropriate in describing an element of depreciation, but it is not helpful in isolating its essence.

Summary of Depreciation Concepts

Depreciation is a process of cost allocation, not one of valuation. This chapter discusses the problems of *allocating* assets' costs to the periods of benefits. A depreciation problem will exist whenever (1) capital is invested in services to be rendered by a plant asset, and (2) at some reasonably predictable date in the future the asset will have to be retired from service with a residual value less than its cost because of a decline in service potential. The problem is to interpret and account satisfactorily for this diminution of the investment in the asset.

Note especially that replacing the asset is *not* essential to the existence of depreciation. Depreciation is the expiration or disappearance of investment from the time the plant asset is put into use until the time it is retired from service. Whether or not the asset is replaced is completely independent of the amount or treatment of its depreciation.

DEPRECIATION ACCOUNTING PROBLEMS

There are three principal accounting problems in allocating the cost of an asset over time:

1 Determining the depreciation basis of the asset
2 Estimating its useful service life
3 Deciding on the pattern of expiration of services over the useful service life.

Calculating the Periodic Charge

Determining the amount of the periodic charge for depreciation is not an exact process. The cost of the plant asset is a *joint cost* of the several benefited periods. That is, each of the periods of the asset's use benefits from its services. There is usually no logically correct way to allocate a joint cost. The depreciation process seeks to assign reasonable periodic charges that reflect a careful and systematic method of calculation.

Whenever it is feasible to do so, depreciation should be computed for individual items such as a single building, machine, or truck. Where many similar items are in use and each one has a relatively small cost, individual calculations may be impracticable and the depreciation charge is usually calculated for the group as a whole. Furniture and fixtures, tools, and telephone poles are examples of assets that are usually depreciated in groups. Group depreciation techniques are treated in advanced financial accounting courses. The basic principles of depreciating individual items discussed here apply in a similar manner, however, to group depreciation situations.

Depreciation Basis of Plant Assets

Depreciation charges have traditionally been based on the acquisition cost of the asset less (except for declining-balance methods described later) the estimated residual value—the amount to be received when the asset is retired from service. As inflation has become recognized as a major economic problem, there has been increasing recognition that basing depreciation charges on acquisition costs will not in most cases charge to expense amounts sufficient to maintain the productive capacity of the business. Basing depreciation on acquisition costs will enable a business to provide for maintenance of its financial position measured in dollars but not of its physical productive capacity in periods of rising prices.

In recent years, the Securities and Exchange Commission has required major corporations to disclose "the estimated current replacement cost . . . of productive capacity . . . and depreciation based on replacement cost . . ."[1] as supplemental information, but the formal financial statements retain acquisition cost as the basis for depreciation calculations.

Estimating Residual Value   Depreciation charges are based on the difference between acquisition cost and the asset's estimated *salvage value* or *net residual value*. Estimates of residual value are necessary for making the depreciation calculation. (The terms *salvage value* and *net residual value* refer to estimated proceeds on disposition of an asset less all removal and selling costs. Salvage value must be an estimate at any time before the asset is retired. Hence, before retirement, the terms *salvage value* and *estimated salvage value* are synonymous.)

For buildings, common practice assumes a zero salvage value. This treatment rests on the assumption that the cost to be incurred in tearing down the building will approximate the sales value of the scrap materials recovered. For other assets, however, the salvage value may be substantial, and should be estimated and taken into account in making the periodic depreciation charge. This is particularly true where it is planned to retire an asset while it still has substantial value. For example, a car rental firm will replace its automobiles at a time when other owners can use the cars for several years more. The rental firm will be able to realize a substantial part of acquisition cost from the sale of used cars. Past experience usually forms the best basis for estimating salvage value.

Estimates of salvage value are necessarily subjective. Disputes over estimated salvage value have led to many disagreements between Internal Revenue Service agents and taxpayers. Partly to reduce such controversy, the Internal Revenue Code was amended to provide that, starting in 1962, salvage value of up to 10 percent of the cost of assets such as machinery and equipment may be ignored in depreciation calculations for tax purposes. The Internal Revenue Code was amended again in 1971 to provide that salvage value may be ignored entirely in calculating depreciation if a procedure known in the Code as the *asset depreciation range system* is used. The asset may not be depreciated below its estimated salvage value, however. The same rule is frequently followed in making calculations for financial records. The entire salvage value is to be taken into account in calculating depreciation in problems in this text unless explicit contrary instructions are given.

Estimating Service Life

The second factor in the depreciation calculation is the estimated economic service life of the asset. In making the estimate, both the physical and the functional causes of depreciation must be taken into account. Experience with similar assets, corrected for

[1]   *Accounting Series Release 190,* Securities and Exchange Commission, 1976.

differences in the planned intensity of use or alterations in maintenance policy, is usually the best guide for this estimate.

In 1962, the Internal Revenue Service published guidelines of suggested useful lives. The guidelines provide estimated useful lives based on categories of assets by broad classes. Examples of guideline lives are as follows:

Warehouses . . . .   60 years
Factory Buildings . . . .   45 years
Land Improvements . . . .   20 years
Office Furniture, Fixtures, Machines, and Equipment . . . .   10 years
Heavy Trucks . . . .   6 years
Light Trucks . . . .   4 years
Automobiles . . . .   3 years

In 1971, the Internal Revenue Service ruled that the guideline lives need not be strictly followed. Rather, the IRS said that taxpayers may use a life anywhere in the range from 80 percent to 120 percent of the guideline life. Such ranges are called *asset depreciation ranges.*

Despite the abundance of data from experience, estimation of service lives is the most difficult task in the entire depreciation calculation. Making proper allowances for obsolescence is particularly difficult because obsolescence results for the most part from forces external to the firm. Unless the estimator possesses prophetic powers, it is likely that the estimates will prove to be incorrect. For this reason, it is wise to reconsider the estimates of useful service life of important assets or groups of assets every few years.

Pattern of Expiration of Services

Once the cost has been determined and both salvage value and service life have been estimated, the total of depreciation charges for the whole life of the asset has been determined. There then remains the problem of selecting the pattern for allocating those charges to the specific years of the life. There are five basic patterns for such allocations. They are labeled E, A, S, D, and N in Figure 9.1.

If salvage value is assumed to be zero, then, of course, the salvage value line coincides with the horizontal axis and the entire cost will be depreciated.

The patterns are discussed in more detail in the next section. A represents *accelerated* depreciation; S, *uniform* or *straight-line* depreciation; D, *decelerated* depreciation. (Understanding the terms "accelerated" and "decelerated" is easier if you compare the depreciation charges in the early years to straight-line depreciation.) Patterns A and S are much more commonly used than D. Pattern E, of course, represents immediate expensing of the item. All costs are charged to the period when the cost is incurred. This pattern is discussed further in the section on intangibles. Pattern N represents the situation, such as for land, where there are no periodic amortization charges. The asset is shown on the books at acquisition cost until it is sold or otherwise retired.

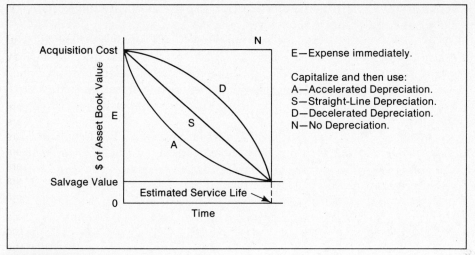

FIGURE 9.1
Patterns of Depreciation:
Book Value Over Life of Asset

DEPRECIATION METHODS

All depreciation methods should aim to allocate, reasonably and systematically, the cost of the asset minus its estimated salvage value, to the periods in which it is used. The methods discussed here are as follows:

1. Straight-line (time) method (Pattern S)
2. Production or use (straight-line use) method
3. Declining-balance methods (Pattern A)
4. Sum-of-the-years'-digits method (Pattern A).

When a depreciable asset is acquired or retired during an accounting period, depreciation should be calculated only for that portion of the period during which the asset is used.

The Straight-Line (Time) Method

The allocation method that is used most commonly for financial reporting is known as the straight-line method. It was used almost exclusively until 1954, when the income tax laws were revised to recognize other depreciation methods for general use. Under the straight-line method, the cost of the asset, less any estimated salvage value, is divided by the number of years of its expected life in order to arrive at the annual depreciation:

$$\text{Annual Depreciation} = \frac{\text{Cost Less Estimated Salvage Value}}{\text{Estimated Life in Years}}.$$

For example, if a machine costs $12,000, has an estimated salvage value of $1,000, and has an expected useful life of 5 years, the annual depreciation will be $2,200 [= ($12,000 − $1,000)/5]. Occasionally, instead of a positive salvage value, the cost of removal exceeds the gross proceeds on disposition. This excess of removal costs over gross proceeds should be added to the cost of the asset in making the calculation. Thus, if a building is constructed for $37,000, and it is estimated that it will cost $5,000 to remove it at the end of 25 years, the annual depreciation would be $1,680 [= ($37,000 + $5,000)/25].

A common practice, especially when the salvage value is assumed to be zero, is to apply an appropriate percentage, known as the depreciation rate, to the *acquisition cost* in order to calculate the annual charge. The rate is chosen so that it will charge the entire acquisition cost off over the estimated life. A rate of 10 percent will write off the cost of an asset in 10 years, a rate of 25 percent in 4 years, and so on. The machine referred to in the preceding paragraph would be depreciated annually at the rate of 20 percent of acquisition cost less salvage value for 5 years.

Production or Use (Straight-Line Use) Method

Although the straight-line (time) method is widely used, it is justifiable only because it frequently corresponds roughly to the amount of use that can be made of the asset and because it requires only simple arithmetic. Many assets are not, however, used uniformly over time. Manufacturing plants often have seasonal variations in operation so that certain machines may be used 24 hours a day at one time and 8 hours or less a day at another time of year. Trucks are not likely to receive the same amount of use in each month or year of their lives. The straight-line (time) method of depreciation may, then, result in an illogical depreciation charge for such assets.

When the rate of usage varies from period to period and when the total usage of an asset over its life can be estimated reliably, a depreciation charge based on actual usage during the period may be justified. For example, depreciation of a truck for a period could be based on the ratio of miles driven during the period to total miles expected to be driven over the truck's life. The depreciation cost per unit (mile) of use is

$$\text{Depreciation Cost per Unit} = \frac{\text{Cost Less Estimated Salvage Value}}{\text{Estimated Number of Units}}.$$

The arithmetic of the calculation is simple, but it is necessary to keep a special record of the units of operation of each asset or of the number of units produced. If a truck that costs $9,000 and has an estimated salvage value of $600 is expected to be driven 100,000 miles before it is retired from service, then the depreciation per mile is $.084 [= ($9,000 − $600)/100,000]. Then, if the truck is operated 1,000 miles in a given month, the depreciation charge for the month is 1,000 × $.084 = $84.

Accelerated Depreciation

The efficiency and earning power of many plant assets decline as the assets grow older. Cutting tools lose some of their precision; printing presses are shut down more frequently for repairs; rentals in an old office building are lower than those in its gleaming new neighbor. These examples show the tendency of some assets to provide more and better services in the early years of their lives while requiring increasing amounts of maintenance as they grow older. Where this is the case, methods that recognize progressively smaller depreciation charges in successive periods may be justified. Such methods are referred to as *accelerated depreciation* methods because the depreciation charges in the early years of the asset's life are larger than in later years. Accelerated depreciation leads to a pattern such as A in Figure 9.1.

For convenience, the depreciation charges for a year, however they are determined, are allocated on a straight-line basis to periods *within* the year.

Declining-Balance Methods

The *declining-balance method* is one accelerated depreciation method. In this method, the depreciation charge is calculated by multiplying the *net book value* of the asset (cost less accumulated depreciation) at the start of each period by a fixed rate. The estimated salvage value is not subtracted from the cost in making the depreciation calculation, as is the case with other depreciation methods. Since the net book value declines from period to period, the result is a declining periodic charge for depreciation throughout the life of the asset.[2] The rate most commonly used is the maximum one permitted for income tax purposes, which ordinarily is twice the straight-line rate. When this rate is used, the method is called the *double-declining-balance* method. Thus, for example, an asset with an estimated 10-year life would be depreciated at a rate of 20 percent ($= \frac{1}{10} \times 2$) per year of the book value at the start of the year. To take another example, if a machine costing $5,000 is purchased on January 1, 1979, and it is estimated to have a 5-year life, a 40 percent ($= \frac{1}{5} \times 2$) rate would be used. The depreciation charges would be calculated as shown in Exhibit 9.1.

The undepreciated cost as of December 31, 1983, as shown in Exhibit 9.1, is $389 ($= \$648 - \$259$). This amount is unlikely to equal the salvage value at that time. The problem is usually anticipated and solved by adjusting the depreciation charge in one or more of the later years. Under income tax rules, the asset cannot be depreciated below salvage value. If the salvage value is large, the asset is likely to be depreciated to that value before the end of the estimated service life and the last period(s) will have no depreciation charges. If the salvage value is small, the firm can switch

---

[2] Under the declining-balance method, as strictly applied, the fixed depreciation rate used is one that will charge the cost less salvage value of the asset over its service life. The formula for computing the rate is

$$\text{Depreciation Rate} = 1 - \sqrt[n]{\frac{s}{c}} = 1 - \left(\frac{s}{c}\right)^{1/n}.$$

In this formula n = estimated periods of service life, s = estimated salvage value, and c = cost.

Estimates of salvage value have a profound effect on the rate. Unless a positive salvage value is assumed, the rate is 100 percent—that is, all depreciation is charged in the first period. For an asset costing $10,000, with an estimated life of 5 years, the depreciation rate is 40 percent per period if salvage value is $778, but it is 60 percent if salvage value is $102.

The effect of small changes in salvage value on the rate and the seeming mathematical complexity of the formula have resulted in widespread use of approximations or rules of thumb instead of the formula.

EXHIBIT 9.1
Double-Declining-Balance
Depreciation
Asset with 5-Year Life

Year	Acquisition Cost (1)	Accumulated Depreciation as of Jan. 1 (2)	Net Book Value as of Jan. 1 (1) − (2) (3)	Depreciation Rate (4)	Depreciation Charge for the Year = (3) × (4) (5)
1979	$5,000	$ 0	$5,000	.40	$2,000
1980	5,000	2,000	3,000	.40	1,200
1981	5,000	3,200	1,800	.40	720
1982[a]	5,000	3,920	1,080[a]	.40	432
1983	5,000	4,352	648	.40	259
1984	5,000	4,611	389	—	—

[a] If the asset had a zero salvage value, the firm would switch to straight-line write-off of the remaining balance over the remaining life, or $540 (= $1,080/2) a year for the last 2 years.

in the last years of asset life to writing off the undepreciated cost minus salvage value in straight-line fashion.

Refer again to Exhibit 9.1. If the asset had an estimated salvage value of $200, the depreciation charges in 1982 and 1983 could be $440 a year (net book value at January 1, 1982 of $1,080 less the estimated salvage value of $200 divided by the 2 years of remaining life). In general, the switch to the straight-line method for the remaining life is made when the switch will produce a greater depreciation charge than the one resulting from continued application of the double-declining-balance method. For assets with zero scrap value, this ordinarily occurs in the period following the midpoint of the service life.

Sum-of-the-Years'-Digits Method

The other accelerated depreciation method mentioned in the Internal Revenue Code is the *sum-of-the-years'-digits method.* Under this method, the depreciation charge is determined by applying a fraction, which diminishes from year to year, to the cost less estimated salvage value of the asset. The numerator of the fraction is the number of periods of remaining life at the beginning of the year for which the depreciation calculation is being made. The denominator is the sum of all such numbers, one for each year of estimated service life; if the service life is n years, the denominator for the sum-of-the-years'-digits method[3] is $1 + 2 + \cdots + n$.

The method is illustrated by again considering an asset costing $5,000 purchased January 1, 1979, which has an estimated service life of 5 years and an estimated salvage

[3]   A useful formula for summing the numbers 1 through n is $1 + 2 + \cdots + n = n(n + 1)/2$.

EXHIBIT 9.2
Sum-of-the-Years'-Digits Depreciation
Asset with 5-Year Life, $5,000 Cost,
and $200 Estimated Salvage Value

Year	Acquisition Cost Less Salvage Value (1)	Remaining Life in Years (2)	Fraction = (2)/15 (3)	Depreciation Charge for the Year = (3) × (1) (4)
1979	$4,800	5	5/15	$1,600
1980	4,800	4	4/15	1,280
1981	4,800	3	3/15	960
1982	4,800	2	2/15	640
1983	4,800	1	1/15	320
				$4,800

value of $200. The sum of the years' digits[4] is 15 (= 1 + 2 + 3 + 4 + 5). The depreciation charges are calculated in Exhibit 9.2.

Compound Interest Methods

Compound interest methods are not widely used in financial accounting, but they are theoretically sound for many management decisions. For plant assets producing equal annual net inflows of cash, compound interest depreciation leads to a pattern like D in Figure 9.1. Compound interest methods are not illustrated in this text.

Factors to Consider in Choosing the Depreciation Method

To the individual firm, depreciation is a factor in the determination of income reported on the financial statements as well as a deduction from otherwise taxable income on tax returns. The firm need not choose the same depreciation method for both financial and tax reporting purposes. If it chooses different methods for the two purposes, the difference between income on the financial statements and taxable income requires a reconciliation in the financial statements. This reconciliation leads to a liability for deferred taxes which is discussed in the next chapter.

Financial Reporting The goal in financial reporting for long-lived assets is to seek a statement of income that realistically measures the expiration of these assets. The only difficulty is that no one knows, in any satisfactory sense, just what portion of the service potential of a long-lived asset expires in any one period. The cost of the plant asset is a joint cost of the several periods of use and there is no logical way of allocating joint costs. All that can be said is that financial statements should report depreciation

---

[4] That is, according to the formula given in the previous footnote: 1 + 2 + 3 + 4 + 5 = 5 × 6/2 = 15.

charges based on reasonable estimates of asset expirations so that the goal of fair presentation can more nearly be achieved. The firm's selection from alternative accounting principles, including the choice of depreciation methods, is discussed more fully in Chapter 13.

Tax Reporting We are relatively confident about the depreciation method to be used for tax purposes. It seems clear that the goal of the firm should be to maximize the present value of the reductions in tax payments from claiming depreciation. When tax rates remain constant over time and there is a flat tax rate (for example, all income taxed at a 48 percent rate), this goal can usually be achieved by maximizing the present value of the depreciation deductions from otherwise taxable income. That is, for tax purposes the asset should be written off as quickly as possible. Of course, a firm can deduct only the acquisition cost, less salvage value, from otherwise taxable income over the life of the asset. Earlier deductions are, however, worth more than later ones because a dollar saved today is worth more than a dollar saved tomorrow.

Congress has presented business firms with several permissible alternatives to follow in determining the amount of depreciation to be deducted each year. The firm can choose double-declining-balance, sum-of-the-years'-digits, straight-line, or various combinations of these methods. It seems clear to us that the firm should choose that alternative which meets the general goal of paying the least amount of tax, as late as possible, within the law. (This goal is sometimes called the *least and latest rule*. Accelerated depreciation has been allowed for income tax reporting only since 1954. This fact accounts for disclosures like that of International Corporation on page 582, where we are told that accelerated depreciation has been used since 1954.)

We can put this more strongly by saying that management has an affirmative obligation in a competitive economy to carry on operations so as to minimize all costs —that is, to minimize the present value of those costs over the long run. Failure to minimize costs hinders the attempt of the competitive market economy to allocate resources efficiently. Management's obligation to reduce costs applies to taxes as well as to other costs, and, in most circumstances, the present value of taxes is minimized by taking depreciation as rapidly as is legally possible. It is clear that either the double-declining-balance or the sum-of-the-years'-digits method will give a more rapid rate of charge-off than the straight-line method. However, the choice between the two accelerated methods depends on the specific circumstances of the firm. In general, the method that will maximize the present value of the depreciation charges is to start with the double-declining-balance method and to switch to the sum-of-the-years'-digits method sometime during the asset's life. There are, however, some limitations on the kinds of changes in methods a firm can make for income tax purposes. The intricacies of the optimal depreciation method are beyond the scope of an introductory accounting course.[5] All problems in this text that require an accelerated depreciation method will specify which method is to be used.

---

[5] For a complete analysis of these problems, see Clyde P. Stickney and Jeffrey B. Wallace, "A Guide to Increasing the Maximum Available Depreciation Deduction Under the ADR System," *Taxation for Accountants,* July 1975, pp. 42–48; and *The Class Life (ADR) System,* Tucson: Lawyers & Judges Publishing Company, 1977.

Accounting for Periodic Depreciation

The debit made in the entry to record periodic depreciation is usually either to an expense account or to a production cost account. In a manufacturing concern, the depreciation of factory buildings and equipment is a production cost, a part of the work-in-process and finished product cost. Depreciation on sales equipment is a selling expense. Depreciation on office equipment is a general or administrative expense. The matching credit for periodic depreciation could logically be made directly to the asset account affected, such as buildings or equipment. Although such an entry is sometimes made, it is customary to credit a special contra-asset account so that the acquisition cost of the asset will be left undisturbed and the total amount written off through depreciation can be readily observed. The effect, however, is precisely the same as a direct credit to the asset account. We have used Accumulated Depreciation as the title of the account to be credited.

The entry to record periodic depreciation of office facilities, a period expense, is

```
Depreciation Expense .............................................     1,500
    Accumulated Depreciation  ........................................           1,500
```

The entry to record periodic depreciation of manufacturing facilities, a product cost, is

```
Work-in-Process Inventory .........................................     1,500
    Accumulated Depreciation  ........................................           1,500
```

The Depreciation Expense account is closed at the end of the accounting period as a part of the regular closing-entry procedure. The Work-in-Process Inventory account is an asset. Product costs, such as depreciation on manufacturing facilities, are accumulated in the Work-in-Process account until the goods being produced are completed and transferred to Finished Goods Inventory. The Accumulated Depreciation account remains open at the end of the period and is shown on the balance sheet as a deduction from the asset account to which it refers. The balance in the Accumulated Depreciation account usually represents the total charges to accounting periods prior to the balance sheet date for the depreciation on assets currently in use. The difference between the balance of the asset account and the balance of its accumulated depreciation account (with possibly an adjustment for salvage value) represents the amount that will presumably be charged to future accounting periods. This difference is called the *book value* of the asset.

In preparing a statement of changes in financial position, the periodic depreciation charge is an addback in the "operations" section, since it represents an expense (or production cost) that does not use funds but instead uses a noncurrent asset.

Changes in Periodic Depreciation

The original depreciation schedule for a particular asset may require changing. The original or previous estimate of useful life (and possibly of salvage value as well) may have been incorrect as judged in the light of new information. To change the depreciation plan because of previous misestimates of useful life or salvage value is a relatively common and desirable accounting practice.

Misestimates of the useful life of an asset may become apparent at any time during its life. It is usually possible to improve the degree of accuracy of the estimates as the time of retirement approaches. If it appears that the misestimate will be relatively minor, an adjustment usually is not made. If the misestimate appears to be material, corrective action must be taken if the effect of the previous estimation error is to be kept at a minimum. The generally accepted procedure for handling this problem is to make no adjustment for the past misestimate, but to spread the remaining undepreciated balance less the revised estimate of salvage value over the new estimate of remaining service life of the asset. We feel that a more logical procedure would be to make an adjustment of past periods' earnings for the misestimate of the past periods, and use the revised rate of depreciation for the remaining portion of the life of the asset. Such an adjustment is not permitted under generally accepted accounting principles, however.[6]

To illustrate the accounting for changes in periodic depreciation, assume the following facts. An office machine was purchased on January 1, 1974, for $9,200. It was estimated that the machine would be operated for 10 years with a salvage value of $200. On December 31, 1979, before the books are closed for the year, it is decided that, in light of the evidence presently available, a total useful life of 15 years with the same salvage estimate of $200 would be a more reasonable estimate. The depreciation charge recorded for each of the years from 1974 through 1978 under the straight-line method would have been $900 [= ($9,200 − $200/10].

If the revised estimate of service life were ignored, the original annual depreciation charge of $900 would be continued through 1983. The years 1984 to 1988 would receive no charge to operations for the use of the machine. The Accumulated Depreciation account would remain undisturbed for those years until the machine was retired from service. Thus, during the last 5 years that the machine was in service, no charge for depreciation would be made.

The accepted procedure for recognizing this substantial increase in service life is to revise the future depreciation so that the correct total will presumably be accumulated in the Accumulated Depreciation account at the end of the revised service life. In our example, the total amount of acquisition cost yet to be depreciated before the 1979 adjustments is $4,500 [= ($9,200 − $200) − $4,500]. The new estimate of the *remaining* life is 10 years, so the new annual depreciation charge is $450 (= $4,500/10). The only change in the accounting procedure is to substitute the new amount of $450 for the former annual depreciation of $900. The depreciation entry on December 31, 1979, and each year thereafter would be

Depreciation Expense 450
   Accumulated Depreciation 450
To record depreciation for 1979 on revised basis.

The revised depreciation path is illustrated in Figure 9.2

---

[6] *APB Opinion No. 20*, 1971, and *FASB Statement No. 16*, 1977.

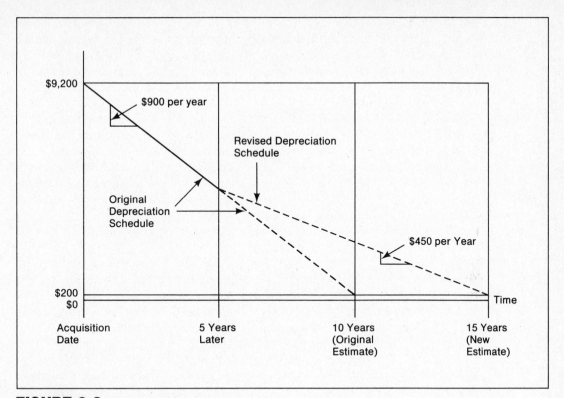

FIGURE 9.2
Illustration of Revised Depreciation
Schedule. Asset's Service Life
Estimate Is Increased from 10 to
15 Years in Year 5. The Straight-
Line Method Is Used. Asset Cost
$9,200 and Has Estimated Salvage
Value of $200.

DEPRECIATION AND REPAIRS

Depreciation is not the only cost of using a depreciating asset. There will almost always be some repair and maintenance costs during the life of the asset. The repair policy adopted by the business will often affect the depreciation rate. If, for example, machinery, trucks, and other plant assets are checked frequently and repaired as soon as any difficulty develops, such assets will have a longer useful life, and therefore, a lower depreciation rate than otherwise. The more commonly used estimates of service life and depreciation rates assume that normal repairs will be made during the life of an asset.

Although some major parts of an asset may have shorter lives than the asset as a whole, it is frequently impracticable to account for them with separate depreciation accounts. Thus, the cost of a replacement set of tires is usually charged to repairs expense, although it would be possible to treat the tires as a separate asset subject to depreciation. It may be useful, though, to disaggregate assets for the purposes of depreciation. For example, using single machines instead of a group of machines, or dealing with engines in aircraft separately from the rest of the asset, may be a practicable and logical procedure.

Repairs must be distinguished from improvements and from rehabilitation. *Repairs* are the small adjustments and replacements of parts whose effect does not extend estimated service life materially or otherwise increase productive capacity. *Improvements* involve adding a part or installing a new part that is substantially better than the old one. The benefit from the improvement will be received for a significant time over the future, but the total useful life of the asset will not ordinarily be extended. *Rehabilitation* involves major construction so that the asset can provide a broader range of services or so that the life of the asset is extended considerably beyond the originally estimated date of retirement.

For example, the replacement of shingles that have blown off a roof would be treated as a repair. The replacement of a shingled roof with a metal roof, or the construction of an addition to the building, would be an improvement. The reconstruction of the interior, the construction of a new front, or the reinforcement of the foundation would in most cases come under the definition of rehabilitation.

Repairs are charged to expense as expenditures are made. Improvements are customarily debited to the asset account or, less frequently and without much justification, to the Accumulated Depreciation account. Rehabilitations are merely extensive improvements. They are normally treated in the same way as improvements even though a rehabilitation may extend the life of an asset. Rehabilitation could logically be viewed, however, as a replacement of the old asset and entries made just as though the old asset were retired from service and a new one acquired. In any case, the accounting for improvements and rehabilitations results in a net debit to the asset account. The total depreciation for the remaining life of the original asset is increased accordingly.

RETIREMENT OF ASSETS

When an asset is retired from service, the cost of the asset and the related amount of accumulated depreciation must be removed from the books. As part of this entry, the amount received from the sale or trade-in and any difference between that amount and book value must be recorded. The difference between the proceeds received on retirement and book value is a gain (if positive) or a loss (if negative). Before making the entry to write off the asset and its accumulated depreciation, an entry should be made to bring the depreciation up to date; that is, the depreciation that has occurred between the start of the current accounting period and the date of disposition must be recorded.

To illustrate the retirement of an asset, assume that sales equipment which cost $5,000, was expected to last 4 years, and had an estimated salvage value of $200 is depreciated on a straight-line basis. Depreciation has been recorded for 2 years, and the equipment is sold at mid-year in the third year. The depreciation from the start of the accounting period to the date of sale of $600 [= $\frac{1}{2} \times$ ($5,000 − $200)/4] is recorded:

Depreciation Expense 600
  Accumulated Depreciation 600
To record depreciation charges up to the date of sale.

The book value of the asset is now its cost less $2\frac{1}{2}$ years of straight-line depreciation of $100 per month or $2,000 (= $5,000 − $3,000). The entry to record the retirement of the assets depends on the amount of the selling price.

1 Suppose that the equipment were sold for $2,000 cash. The entry to record the sale would be

Cash 2,000
Accumulated Depreciation 3,000
  Equipment 5,000

2 Suppose that the equipment were sold for $2,300 cash. The entry to record the sale would be

Cash 2,300
Accumulated Depreciation 3,000
  Equipment 5,000
  Gain on Retirement of Equipment 300

3 Suppose that the equipment were sold for $1,500. The entry to record the sale would be

Cash 1,500
Accumulated Depreciation 3,000
Loss on Retirement of Equipment 500
  Equipment 5,000

Retirement Entries in the Statement of Changes in Financial Position The cash received from the disposition of a plant asset is a nonoperating source of funds. It is shown on the funds statement as a nonoperating source, "Proceeds from Disposition of Noncurrent Assets," see page 174 for an illustration. The Loss on Retirement of Equipment is an item that reduces net income but that does not use funds. Thus, in deriving funds from operations, the amount of the loss is an addback in determining funds from operations. Its presentation is similar to that for depreciation expense.

If there is a Gain on Retirement of Equipment, two alternative treatments are possible and are found in practice. One shows the entire proceeds from disposition of the asset as a nonoperating source of funds and thus requires treating the Gain on Retirement as a subtraction in determining funds from operations. The subtraction would be classified under the general heading of revenues not producing funds from operations, since the funds produced are shown under the heading of proceeds from disposition of plant assets. The alternative treatment would show only the book value of the asset disposed of as a nonoperating source of funds and would include the gain in funds from operations (that is, there would be no subtraction in the operating section). We prefer the first approach and follow it throughout this book.

Trade-in Transactions

Instead of selling the asset when it is retired from service, it is far more common for the asset to be traded in on a new unit. This is a particularly common practice for automobiles. The trade-in transaction can best be viewed as a sale of the old asset followed by a purchase of the new asset. The accounting for trade-in transactions depends on the data available about the value of the asset traded in and the cost of the new asset. The cash-equivalent cost of the new asset acquired is the important information for recording all trade-in transactions.

If the fair market value of the used asset traded in can be determined, that amount plus the cash given up determines the valuation of the new asset. Assume in the preceding illustration that the used equipment had a fair market value of $1,300 and was traded in on a new piece of equipment, along with an additional $5,500 of cash. The entries, using a two-step approach, would be

Accumulated Depreciation	3,000	
Trade-in Allowance	1,300	
Loss on Disposition of Equipment	700	
Equipment		5,000

To record disposition of old equipment; plug for loss.

Equipment	6,800	
Trade-in Allowance		1,300
Cash		5,500

To record acquisition of new equipment; plug for cost of new equipment.

The entries shown above would not be affected by information about the list price of the new equipment. Valuation of the used asset in established second-hand markets almost always offers more reliable information than quoted list prices. However, if a reliable valuation of the used asset is not available, then list price will determine the valuation of the new asset and, indirectly, of the gain or loss on disposition of the old asset. If the list price of the new equipment in the preceding example was $7,000 and there was no reliable information on the second-hand value of the old equipment, the entries would be

Equipment	7,000	
Cash		5,500
Trade-in Allowance		1,500

To record acquisition at list price; plug for trade-in allowance.

Accumulated Depreciation	3,000	
Trade-in Allowance	1,500	
Loss on Disposition of Equipment	500	
Equipment		5,000

To record disposition of old equipment. Loss is determined by list price of new equipment.

The income tax regulations do not permit the recognition of a gain or loss on the trade-in of an old asset in acquiring a new, similar asset. Instead, the cost of the new asset is assumed to be the book value of the used asset plus the cash paid. In the illustration used in this section, the entries would be

Accumulated Depreciation	3,000	
Trade-in Allowance	2,000	
Equipment		5,000

To record disposition of old equipment at book value.

Equipment	7,500	
Cash		5,500
Trade-in Allowance		2,000

To record acquisition of new equipment. Cost of new equipment is a plug.

The recording of all three methods has been illustrated with a two-step approach. The two entries could be combined into one, removing the need for a Trade-in Allowance account.

The same analysis and same type of entries would be made if there were a gain on disposition. The one exception in generally accepted accounting principles to the concept that the cash-equivalent price of the new asset is recorded occurs where this would result in a gain from the trade-in of a *similar* asset. In that case, no gain is recognized and the new asset is recorded at the book value of the old asset plus the cash paid in the trade-in transaction.[7]

THE INVESTMENT TAX CREDIT

In order to stimulate investment in machinery and equipment, Congress has passed tax laws that permit the purchaser of machinery and equipment to claim a credit based on new investment. The credit is applied to reduce the purchaser's income tax liability to the federal government. The rate of the credit and the property eligible for the credit have varied through the years as Congress has amended the tax laws. In the examples in this section, we will assume a 10-percent tax credit on all equipment purchases.[8]

If a firm buys $900,000 of equipment with an estimated service life of 10 years this year, it will receive a $90,000 (= .10 × $900,000) investment tax credit. If its income tax liability shown on the tax return before the investment tax credit is $600,000, the following entry would be made:

---

[7] In the highly unlikely situation where cash is received by the party making the trade-in, some gain is recognized; *APB Opinion No. 29,* 1973. (See *trade-in transaction* in the Glossary at the back of the book.)
[8] The investment credit provisions are much more complex. The eligibility of property for the credit depends on its service life. One-third of the cost of equipment with an estimated service life of 3 but less than 5 years is eligible, whereas two-thirds of the cost of equipment with an estimated service life of 5 but less than 7 years is eligible. Only if the estimated service life is 7 years or more is the entire cost of the asset fully eligible for the investment tax credit. The credit may not exceed a stated percentage (recently 50 percent) of the tax liability with appropriate carrybacks and carryforwards.

| Income Tax Expense | 600,000 | |
| Income Tax Payable | | 600,000 |

To record income taxes before the investment tax credit.

There are two generally accepted methods of recording the investment tax credit—the flow-through method and the deferral method.[9] Under the flow-through method, the entire investment credit for the year is recorded as a reduction in income tax expense of the year. (It all flows through to income this year.) The entry would be

| Income Tax Payable | 90,000 | |
| Income Tax Expense | | 90,000 |

To record the investment credit (= .10 × $900,000) for the year.

If the deferral approach is used, the reduction in income tax expense is spread over the years of the service life of the equipment acquired. The entire investment credit reduces the amount of income taxes payable in the year of acquisition, even though the reductions in income tax expense are spread over the years of service life. In the example, the entry in the year of acquisition, using the deferral method, would be

Income Tax Payable	90,000	
Income Tax Expense		9,000
Deferred Investment Credit		81,000

Part ($9,000) of investment credit reduces expense in first year. The remaining portion will reduce expense in later years.

The Deferred Investment Credit account appears on the balance sheet among the noncurrent equities. In each of the nine following years, the following entry would be made:

| Deferred Investment Credit | 9,000 | |
| Income Tax Expense | | 9,000 |

To amortize the deferred investment credit. Recorded income tax expense is reduced by $9,000 in each year 2 through 10.

Income tax expense is reduced by the full amount of the investment credit under both methods, but over different time periods.

If the deferral approach is used, the credit to income tax expense includes not only a part of this year's investment credit but also portions of the investment credit relating to earlier years that are still being amortized. For a firm in equilibrium (and assuming no recent change in the tax law with regard to the investment credit), income tax expense and net income will be the same under the flow-through and deferral approaches. For a growing firm, the flow-through method produces higher reported net income.

If the deferral method is used, income tax expense for a growing firm will be greater than taxes paid or taxes currently payable. This excess represents an expense that does not use funds. It thus results in an addback in the operating section of the statement of changes in financial position.

---

[9] *APB Opinion No. 4*, 1964. Problem **31** at the end of this chapter explores the theoretical considerations one ought to consider in choosing the methods in practice.

WASTING ASSETS AND DEPLETION

The costs of finding natural resources and preparing to extract them from the earth should be capitalized and amortized. Amortization of wasting assets, or natural resources, is called *depletion.* The depletion method most often used is the *units-of-production* method. For example, if $4.5 million in costs are incurred to discover an oil well that contains an estimated 1.5 million barrels of oil, then the costs of $4.5 million would be amortized (depleted) at the rate of $3 ($= \$4,500,000/1,500,000$) for each barrel of oil removed from the well. The major accounting problem of extractive industries stems from the uncertainty of the benefits from exploratory efforts.

Percentage Depletion Allowances

In some special circumstances, the tax laws permit computation of depletion for measuring taxable income as a percentage of the revenues secured from the sale of the minerals each year. The total of depletion charges over the life of the asset is not limited to costs incurred if this method, known as *percentage depletion,* is used. In financial accounting, depletion allocates the cost of natural resources to the periods when the resources are used. The percentage depletion allowances are a device instituted by the Congress to make some companies' search for natural resources more attractive than it otherwise would be. The effect of percentage depletion is to allow some firms to deduct on income tax returns over the life of the asset amounts larger than the total of costs incurred. Financial statement expense over the life of the asset must be equal to the acquisition cost of the asset in a historical-cost system.

INTANGIBLE ASSETS AND AMORTIZATION

Assets can provide future benefits without having physical form. Such assets are called *intangibles.* Examples are research costs, advertising costs, patents, trade secrets, know-how, trademarks, and copyrights. The first problem with intangibles is to decide whether the expenditures have future benefits and can be quantified with a sufficient degree of precision so that they should be "capitalized" (set up as assets) and amortized over time, or whether they have no future benefits and thus are expenses of the period in which the costs are incurred. In this latter case, the immediate expensing of the asset's cost is represented by Pattern E in Figure 9.1. The second problem to solve is how to amortize the costs if they have been capitalized. Amortization of capitalized intangibles is usually recorded using the straight-line method, but other methods can be used if they seem appropriate. This section discusses some common intangibles and the issues involved in deciding whether to expense or to capitalize their costs.

Research and Development

One common intangible cost is that for research and development (R&D). This type of cost is incurred for various reasons. Perhaps the firm seeks to develop a technological or marketing advance in order to have an edge on competition. Or it might wish to explore possible applications of existing technology to design a new product or improve an old one. Other research may be undertaken in response to a government contract, in preparing for bids on potential contracts, or in pursuit of "discoveries," with no specific product in mind. Whatever the reason, practically all research costs will yield their benefits, if any, in future periods. Herein lies the accounting issue: to expense research and development costs immediately when they are incurred, or to capitalize and amortize them over future periods.

Generally accepted accounting principles[10] require immediate expensing of research and development costs. (Note 6 of the financial statements of International Corporation on page 586 illustrates the required disclosures.) This requirement is based on arguments that the future benefits from most R&D efforts are too uncertain to warrant capitalization, and that writing them off as soon as possible is more conservative. Nevertheless, others feel that there must be future benefits in many cases or else R&D efforts would not be pursued. Theoretically, R&D costs should be matched with the benefits produced by the R&D expenditures through the capitalization procedure with amortization over the benefited periods.

If R&D costs were to be capitalized, there would be a number of problems. The first would be to determine and analyze R&D costs. Direct costs for each research project would have to be segregated for management control purposes. General R&D overhead costs could either be expensed in total, or spread to specific projects and treated just as the rest of the specific project costs are treated. The second problem would be deciding which projects should be capitalized. Where it is obvious that no foreseeable benefits are forthcoming from a certain line of research, its costs should be expensed. Costs of projects that result in future benefits should be capitalized. A third accounting problem would be to determine the period over which capitalized R&D costs should be amortized. Usually, the life span of benefits is uncertain, and the benefits are unevenly distributed over the years. As a consequence, it would usually be necessary to select an arbitrary time period, such as 5 years, over which to amortize the costs.

Patents

A patent is a right obtained from the federal government to exclude others from the benefits from an invention. The legal life of patent protection may be as long as 17 years, although the economic life of the patent may be considerably less. The accounting for patent costs depends on whether the patent was purchased from another party or developed internally. If the former, the purchase price is capitalized. If the latter, the total cost of product development and patent application is expensed as required for all R&D costs. Purchased patent costs are usually amortized over the shorter of: (1) the remaining legal life, or (2) its estimated economic life. If for some reason the patent becomes worthless, the remaining capitalized cost is recognized immediately as an expense of that period.

---

[10] *FASB Statement No. 2,* 1974.

Goodwill

Goodwill is an intangible asset that will be mentioned here only briefly. A more detailed discussion follows in Chapter 12. Goodwill arises from the purchase of one company or operating unit by another company and is measured as the difference between the amount paid for the acquired company as a whole and the sum of the current value of its individual assets and net of its liabilities. Thus, goodwill will appear in the financial statements of the company making the acquisition. Under present practice, goodwill acquired is amortized over a time period not longer than 40 years. It is generally not recognized by a company that develops the goodwill itself, even though large expenditures for advertising and other publicity may be made annually. All such expenditures are charged to expense as incurred. Note 13 of the International Corporation on page 589 illustrates the typical disclosure for goodwill.

SUMMARY

Although there are three major classes of long-lived operating assets—plant assets, wasting assets (natural resources), and intangibles—the major accounting problems for each class are the same: (1) determine the cost of the asset to be capitalized as an asset, (2) estimate the total period of benefit or the amount of expected benefits, and (3) assign the cost among the benefited periods or units of benefit in a systematic and reasonable fashion.

We have focused our attention on depreciable plant assets and their depreciation. For these assets, the cost figure to be charged off is frequently reduced by salvage value. The period (or number of units) of benefit is determined by judgment based on experience or by relying on guidelines set down by the Internal Revenue Service. The pattern of depreciation charges over the asset's life is usually based on some conventional method—the most common methods in practice are straight-line, double-declining-balance, and sum-of-the-years'-digits.

If the asset is retired before the end of the estimated service life for an amount different from its book value, a gain or loss will be recognized. If the asset is traded in on another asset, a gain or loss may or may not be recognized depending on the terms of the transaction.

Intangibles such as trademarks, copyrights, patents, and computer programs are the most valuable resources owned by some firms. The accounting treatment of purchased intangibles is the same as for tangible assets. For intangibles developed by a firm, accounting requires the immediate expensing of the developmental costs. This accounting drastically alters the look of some financial statements. The firms most likely to be affected are service, rather than manufacturing, companies.

QUESTIONS AND PROBLEMS

1 Review the meaning of the following concepts or terms discussed in this chapter.
   a Amortization.
   b Plant assets and depreciation.

    c Wasting assets and depletion.

    d Percentage depletion allowance.

    e Intangibles.

    f Capitalize.

    g Improvements.

    h Repairs.

    i Maintenance.

    j Joint cost.

    k Value.

    l Residual or salvage value.

   m Service or depreciable life.

    n Asset depreciation range.

    o Straight-line (time and use) methods.

    p Accelerated depreciation methods.

    q Declining- and double-declining-balance methods.

    r Sum-of-the-years'-digits method.

    s Book value.

    t Treatment of changes in estimates of useful lives and residual values of long-lived assets.

    u Trade-in transaction.

    v Research and development.

   w Goodwill.

    x Investment credit.

    y Flow-through method.

    z Deferral method.

2 a "Accounting for depreciating assets would be greatly simplified if accounting periods were only long enough or the life of the assets short enough." What is the point of the quotation?

    b "The major purpose of depreciation accounting is to provide funds for the replacement of assets as they wear out." Do you agree? Explain.

3 "Showing both acquisition cost and accumulated depreciation amounts separately provides a rough indication of the relative age of the firm's long-lived assets."

    a Assume that the Abril Company acquired an asset with a depreciable cost of $100,000 several years ago. Accumulated depreciation as of December 31, recorded on a straight-line basis, is $60,000. The depreciation charge for the year is $10,000. What is the asset's depreciable life? How old is the asset?

    b Assume straight-line depreciation. Devise a formula that, given the depreciation charge for the year and the asset's accumulated depreciation, can be used to determine the age of the asset.

4 For each of the following expenditures or acquisitions, indicate the type of account debited. Classify the accounts as asset other than product cost, product cost (Work-in-Process Inventory), or expense. If the account debited is an asset account, then specify whether it is current or noncurrent.

    a $150 for repairs of office machines.

    b $1,500 for emergency repairs to an office machine.

    c $250 for maintenance of delivery trucks.

    d $5,000 for a machine acquired in return for a 3-year note.

    e $4,200 for research and development staff salaries.

   f $3,100 for newspaper ads.

   g $6,400 for wages of factory workers engaged in production.

   h $3,500 for wages of factory workers engaged in installing equipment.

   i $2,500 for salaries of office work force.

   j $1,000 for legal fees in acquiring an ore deposit.

   k $1,200 for a 1-year insurance policy beginning next month.

   l $1,800 for U.S. Treasury Notes, to be sold to pay the next installment due on income taxes.

   m $4,000 for royalty payment on a patent used in manufacturing.

   n $10,000 for purchase of a trademark.

   o $100 filing fee for copyright registration application.

5 Refer to the Simplified Funds Statement for a Period in Exhibit 5.15 or page 174. Ten of the lines in the statement are numbered. Line (2) should be expanded to say "Additions for Expenses and Other Changes Against Income Not Using Funds," and line (3) should be expanded to say "Subtractions for Revenues and other Credits to Income Not Producing Funds from Operations." Ignore the other lines in responding to the questions below.

   Assume that the accounting cycle is complete for the period and that all of the financial statements have been prepared. Then, it is discovered that a transaction has been overlooked. That transaction is recorded in the accounts and all of the financial statements are corrected. Define *funds* as *working capital*. For each of the following transactions, indicate which of the numbered lines of the funds statement is affected and by how much. Ignore income tax effects.

   a A machine that cost $10,000 and that has $7,000 of accumulated depreciation is sold for $4,000 cash.

   b A machine that cost $10,000 and that has $7,000 of accumulated depreciation is sold for $2,000 cash.

   c A machine that cost $10,000 and that has $7,000 of accumulated depreciation is traded in on a new machine. The new machine has a cash price of $12,000. A trade-in allowance for the old machine of $4,000 is given, so that $8,000 cash is paid.

   d A fire destroys a warehouse. The loss is uninsured. The warehouse cost $80,000 and at the time of the fire had accumulated depreciation of $30,000.

   e Refer to the facts of part **d**. Inventory costing $70,000 was also destroyed. The loss was uninsured.

6 Refer to the instructions in the preceding question. Follow the instructions for the following transactions or events relating to the investment credit. During the year, qualifying assets with a 10-year depreciable life are acquired, and investment credits of $10,000 are realized.

   a The flow-through method of accounting is used. Record the effects for the year the assets are acquired.

   b The flow-through method of accounting is used. Record the effects for the year after the assets are acquired.

   c The deferral method is used. Record the effects for the year the assets are acquired.

   d The deferral method is used. Record the effects for the year after the assets are acquired.

7 In 1971 the Internal Revenue Code was amended to provide for depreciable lives for tax purposes from 20 percent less of the guideline lives previously established to 20 percent more of the guideline lives. The Secretary of the Treasury announced that depreciable lives had been extended by 40 percent. A noted accountant remarked that the government could have allowed a range of choices that was extended by 100 percent (from 20 percent less to 80 percent more) with the same effects on tax collections as the 40 percent range. What did the accountant mean?

8 On April 30, 1979, the Tico Wholesale Company acquired a new machine with a fair market value of $14,000. The seller agreed to accept the company's old machine, $7,000 in cash, and a 12-percent, 1-year note for $4,000 in payment.

The old machine was purchased on January 1, 1974, for $10,000. It was estimated that the old machine would be useful for 8 years, after which it would have a salvage value of $400. It is estimated that the new machine will have a service life of 10 years and a salvage value of $800.

Assuming that the Tico Company uses the straight-line method of depreciation and closes its books annually on December 31, give the entries that were made in 1979.

9 On July 1, 1956, a building and site were purchased for $96,000 by The Hub, a retail clothing store. Of this amount, $40,000 was allocated to the land and the remainder to the building. The building is depreciated on a straight-line basis.

On July 1, 1978 (no additions or retirements having been recorded in the meanwhile), the net book value of the building was $25,200. On March 31, 1979, the building and site were sold for $60,000. The fair market value of the land was $50,000 on this date.

The firm closes its books annually at June 30. Give the entries required on March 31, 1979. (Hint: First compute what the annual depreciation charges must be, based on the facts given.)

10 Journalize the following transactions:
   (1) A piece of office equipment is purchased for $850 cash.
   (2) Depreciation for 1 year of $85 is recorded.
   (3) The equipment is sold for $400. At the time of the sale, the Accumulated Depreciation shows a balance of $425. Depreciation of $85 for the year of the sale has not yet been recorded.

11 Give the journal entries for the following selected transactions of the Eagle Manufacturing Company. The company uses the straight-line method of calculating depreciation and closes its books annually on December 31.
   (1) A machine is purchased on November 1, 1976, for $30,000. It is estimated that it will be used for 10 years and that it will have a salvage value of $600 at the end of that time. Give the journal entry for the depreciation at December 31, 1976.
   (2) Record the depreciation for the year ending December 31, 1977.
   (3) In August, 1982, it is decided that the machine will probably be used for a total of 12 years and that its scrap value will be $400. Record the depreciation for the year ending December 31, 1982.
   (4) The machine is sold for $1,000 on March 31, 1987. Record the entries of that date, assuming that depreciation is recorded as indicated in **(3)**.

12 The Alexander Company acquired three used machine tools for a total price of $49,000. Costs to transport the machine tools from the seller to Alexander Company's factory were $1,000. The machine tools were renovated, installed, and put to use in manufacturing the firm's products. The costs of renovation and installation were as follows:

	Machine Tool A	Machine Tool B	Machine Tool C
Renovation Costs	$1,700	$800	$950
Installation Costs	300	550	250

The machine tools have the following estimated remaining lives: tool A—4 years; tool B—10 years; tool C—6 years.

a Assume that each machine tool is capitalized in a separate asset account and that the remaining life of each machine tool is used as the basis for allocating the joint costs of acquisition. Compute the depreciable cost of each of the three machine tools.

b Present journal entries to record depreciation charges for years 1, 5, and 8, given the assumption in part **a**. Use the straight-line method.

c Assume that the three machine tools are treated as one composite asset in the accounts. If management decides to depreciate the entire cost of the composite asset on a straight-line basis over 10 years, what is the depreciation charge for each year?

d Which treatment, **a** or **c,** should management of the Alexander Company probably prefer for tax purposes and why?

13 On March 1, 1979, one of the buildings owned by the Metropolitan Storage Company was destroyed by fire. The cost of the building was $100,000; the balance in the Accumulated Depreciation account at January 1, 1979, was $38,125. A service life of 40 years with a zero salvage value had been estimated for the building. The company uses the straight-line method. The building was not insured.

a Give the journal entries made at March 1.

b If there have been no alterations in the service life estimate, when was the building acquired?

14 Give correcting entries for the following situations. In each case, the firm uses the straight-line method of depreciation and closes its books annually on December 31. Recognize all gains and losses currently.

a A cash register was purchased for $300 on January 1, 1974. It was depreciated at a rate of 10 percent. On June 30, 1979, it was sold for $200 and a new cash register was acquired for $500. The bookkeeper made the following entry to record the transaction:

Store Equipment	300	
Cash in Bank		300

b A used truck was acquired in May 1979 for $4,000. Its cost when new was $6,000, and the bookkeeper made the following entry to record the purchase:

Truck	6,000	
Accumulated Depreciation		2,000
Cash		4,000

c A testing mechanism was purchased on April 1, 1977, for $600. It was depreciated at a 10-percent annual rate. On June 30, 1979, it was stolen. The loss was not insured, and the bookkeeper made the following entry:

Theft Loss	600	
Testing Mechanism		600

15 The Grogan Manufacturing Company started business on January 1, 1977. At that time it acquired machine A for $20,000, payment being made by check.

Due to an expansion in the volume of business, machine B, costing $25,000, was acquired on September 30, 1978. A check for $15,000 was issued, with the balance to be paid in annual installments of $2,000 plus interest at the rate of 6 percent on the unpaid balance. The first installment is due on September 30, 1979.

On June 30, 1979, machine A was sold for $13,000 and a larger model, machine C, was acquired for $30,000.

All installments are paid on time.

All machines have an estimated life of 10 years with an estimated salvage value equal to 10 percent of acquisition cost. The company closes its books on December 31. The straight-line method is used.

Prepare dated journal entries to record all transactions through December 31, 1979, including year-end adjustments but excluding closing entries.

16 The Chisholm Manufacturing Company purchased a plot of land for $50,000 as a plant site. There was a small office building on the plot, conservatively appraised at $8,000, which the company will continue to use with some modification and renovation. The company had plans drawn for a factory and received bids for its construction. It rejected all bids and decided to construct the plant itself. Below are listed additional items that management feels should be included in plant asset accounts.

(1) Materials and supplies	$250,000
(2) Excavation	12,000
(3) Labor on construction	138,000
(4) Cost of remodeling old building into office building	9,000
(5) Interest on money borrowed by Chisholm	5,000
(6) Interest on Chisholm's own money used	13,000
(7) Cash discounts on materials purchased	6,000
(8) Supervision by management	10,000
(9) Compensation insurance premiums	8,000
(10) Payment of claim for injuries not covered by insurance	3,000
(11) Clerical and other expenses of construction	8,000
(12) Paving of streets and sidewalks	4,000
(13) Architect's plans and specifications	3,000
(14) Legal costs of conveying land	2,000
(15) Legal costs of injury claim	1,000
(16) Income credited to Retained Earnings account, being the difference between the foregoing cost and the lowest contractor's bid	15,000

Show in detail the items to be included in the following accounts: Land, Factory Building, Office Building, and Site Improvements. Explain why you excluded any items that you did not include in the four accounts.

17 Calculate the depreciation charge for the first and second years of the asset's life in the following cases.

Asset	Cost	Estimated Salvage Value	Life (Years)	Depreciation Method
a. Blast Furnace	$800,000	$25,000	20	Double-Declining-Balance
b. Hotel	500,000	50,000	45	Straight-Line
c. Typewriter	400	40	8	Sum-of-the-Years'-Digits
d. Tractor	6,000	500	10	Double-Declining-Balance
e. Ferris Wheel	7,600	400	12	Straight-Line
f. Delivery Truck	5,500	1,300	6	Sum-of-the-Years'-Digits

18 On January 1, 1979, the Central Production Company acquired a new turret lathe for $36,000. It was estimated to have a useful life of 4 years and no salvage value. The company closes its books annually on December 31. Indicate the amount of the depreciation charge for each of the 4 years under:

a The straight-line method.

b The declining-balance method at twice the straight-line rate.

c The sum-of-the-years'-digits method.

d Assume now that the lathe was acquired on April 1, 1979. Indicate the amount of the depreciation charge for each of the years 1979–1983, using the sum-of-the-years'-digits method. (Hint: Depreciation charges for a year, however they are determined, are allocated on a straight-line basis to periods *within* a year.)

19 Give the annual or unit depreciation charge in the following cases. The firm uses straight-line (time and use) methods.

Asset	Cost	Estimated Salvage Value	Estimated Life
a. Adding Machine	$ 400	$ 40	12 Years
b. Taxicab	5,000	100	100,000 Miles
c. Building	37,000	1,000	18 Years
d. Desk	280	30	20 Years
e. Aircraft Engine	25,000	500	2,000 Flying Hours
f. Bakery Oven	6,800	350	16 Years
g. Display Counter	2,000	400	12 Years

20 A machine is acquired for $8,900. It is expected to last 8 years and to be operated for 25,000 hours during that time. It is estimated that its salvage value will be $1,700 at the end of that time. Calculate the depreciation charge for each of the first 3 years using:

a The straight-line (time) method.

b The sum-of-the-years'-digits method.

c The declining-balance method using a 25-percent rate (the maximum rate allowed).

d The units-of-production method. Operating times are as follows: first year, 3,500 hours; second year, 2,000 hours; third year, 5,000 hours.

21 The Slowpoke Shipping Company buys a new truck for $10,000 on January 1, 1978. It is estimated that it will last 6 years and have a salvage value of $1,000. Early in 1980, it is determined that the truck will last only an additional 2 years, or 4 years in total. The company closes its books on December 31. Present a table showing the depreciation charges for each year from 1978 to 1981 and give the adjusting entry made in 1980. Follow the instructions for each of the following methods.

a The straight-line method.

b The sum-of-the-years'-digits method.

c The declining-balance method with depreciation at twice the straight-line rate. The remaining undepreciated cost less salvage value is to be written off in the last year.

22 The Linder Manufacturing Company acquires a new machine for $7,200 on July 1, 1975. It is estimated that it will have a service life of 6 years and then have a salvage value of $900. The company closes its books annually on June 30.

a Compute the depreciation charges for each year of the asset's life assuming the use of:

(1) The straight-line method.

(2) The sum-of-the-years'-digits method.

(3) The declining-balance method, with a rate twice the straight-line rate.

b If the machine were sold for $700 on October 30, 1980, give the journal entries that would be made on that date under each of the methods in part **a**.

23 The Twombly Company purchased a new automobile in May 1975. The automobile cost $8,800. It was estimated that the automobile would be driven for 100,000 miles before being traded in and that its salvage value at that time would be $800.

Odometer readings are as follows:

December 31, 1977 12,000
December 31, 1978 50,000
December 31, 1979 82,000
June 16, 1980 98,000

On June 16, 1980, the automobile was traded in for a new one with a list price of $10,000. The old automobile had a fair market value of $800, but the dealer allowed $1,500 on it toward the list price of the new one. The balance of the purchase price was paid by check.

a Determine the depreciation charges for each year through 1979 using a "production" or "use" method.

b Record the entries for June 16, 1980, assuming that the list price of the new automobile is unreliable whereas the fair market value of the old is reliable.

c Record the entries for June 16, 1980, assuming that there were no reliable estimates for the fair market value of the old automobile.

24 Refer to the data in Problem **13** at the end of Chapter 5 on page 176 for the Harris Company. Assume in the Supplementary Information, item **(2)**, that the proceeds of sale of the equipment amount to $400, rather than $1,000. As a result, net income is reduced from $17,000 to $16,400 and dividends are reduced from $10,000 to $9,400. All other items remain unchanged. Prepare a statement of changes in financial position for the year 1979 defining funds as working capital.

25 Refer to the data in Problem **13** at the end of Chapter 5 on page 176 for the Harris Company. Assume in the Supplementary Information, item **(2)**, that the proceeds of sale of the equipment amount to $3,000, rather than $1,000. As a result, net income is increased from $17,000 to $19,000 and dividends are increased from $10,000 to $12,000. All other items remain unchanged. Prepare a statement of changes in financial position for the year 1979 defining funds as working capital.

26 The balance sheet of Woolf's Department Store shows a building with an original cost of $800,000 and accumulated depreciation of $660,000. The building is being depreciated on a straight-line basis over 40 years. The remaining depreciable life of the building is 7 years. On January 2 of the current year, an expenditure of $28,000 was made on the street-level displays of the store. Indicate the accounting for the current year if the expenditure of $28,000 was made under each of the following circumstances. Each of these cases is to be considered independently of the others, except where noted. Ignore income tax effects.

a Management decided that improved displays would make the store's merchandise seem sufficiently more attractive that the displays are a worthwhile investment.

b A violent hailstorm on New Year's Day had destroyed the display windows previously installed. There was no insurance coverage for this sort of destruction. New windows are installed that are physically identical to the old windows. The old windows had a book value of $28,000 at the time of the storm.

c Vandals had destroyed the display windows on New Year's Day. There was no insurance coverage for this sort of destruction. New windows are installed that are physically identical to the old windows. The old windows had a book value of $28,000 at the time of the destruction.

d The old displays contained windows that were constructed of nonshatterproof glass. Management had previously considered replacing its old nonshatterproof windows with new ones, but had decided that there was no benefit to the firm in doing so. New shatter-proof windows are installed because a new law was passed requiring that all stores must have shatterproof windows on the street level. The alternative to installing the new windows was to shut down the store.

e Management had previously considered replacing its old, nonshatterproof windows with new ones, but decided that the new windows would produce future benefits of only $7,000 and so were not a worthwhile investment. However, a new law (see part **d**) now requires them to do so and the new windows are installed.

27 In each of the following situations, compute the amounts of revenue, gain, expense, and loss to be shown on the income statement for the year and the amount of asset to be shown on the balance sheet as of the end of the year. Show the journal entry or entries required, and provide reasons for your decisions. Straight-line amortization is used. The reporting period is the calendar year. The situations are independent of each other, except where noted.

a Because of a new fire code, a department store must install additional fire escapes on its building. The fire escapes are acquired for $28,000 cash on January 1. The building is expected to be demolished 7 years from the date the fire escapes were installed.

b Many years ago, a firm acquired shares of stock in the General Electric Company for $100,000. On December 31, the firm acquired a building with an appraised value of $1 million. The company paid for the building by giving up its shares in the General Electric Company at a time when equivalent shares traded on the New York Stock Exchange for $1,050,000.

c Same data as part **b**, except that the shares of stock represent ownership in Small Timers, Inc., whose shares are traded on a regional stock exchange. The last transaction in shares of Small Timers, Inc., occurred on December 27. Using the prices of the most recent trades, the shares of stock of Small Timers, Inc., given in exchange for the building have a market value of $1,050,000.

d A company decides that it can save $3,500 a year for at least a decade by switching from small panel trucks to larger delivery vans. To do so requires remodeling costs of $18,000 for various garages. The first fleet of delivery vans will last for 5 years, and the garages will last for 20 years. The garages are remodeled on January 1.

e A company drills for oil. It sinks 10 holes during the year at a cost of $1 million each. Nine of the holes are dry, but the tenth is a gusher. By the end of the year, the oil known to be recoverable from the gusher has a net realizable value of $40 million. No oil was extracted during the year.

f A company manufactures aircraft. During the current year, all sales were to the government under defense contracts. The company spent $400,000 on institutional advertising to keep its name before the business community. It expects to resume sales of small jet planes to corporate buyers in 2 years.

g A company runs a large laboratory that has, over the years, found marketable ideas and products worth tens of millions of dollars. On average, the successful products have a life of 10 years. Expenditures for the laboratory this year were $1,500,000.

28 In each of the following situations, compute the amounts of revenue, gain, expense, and loss to be shown on the income statement for the year, as well as the amount of asset to be shown on the balance sheet as of the end of the year. Show the journal entry or entries required, and provide reasons for your decisions. Straight-line amortization is used. The reporting period is the calendar year. The situations are independent of each other, except where noted.

a A textile manufacturer gives $250,000 to the Textile Engineering Department of a local university for basic research in fibers. The results of the research, if any, will belong to the general public.

b A film producer incurred costs of $12 million during the year to produce a movie for television. A television network paid the film producer $10 million during the year for the rights to show the film once. The contract with the network specifies that the film will be shown during the summer of the next accounting period, and that the network will pay the producer another $5 million at the time of that showing.

c Same data as in part **b,** but the network has the additional option to show the film still a third time 2 years from now for an additional fee of $5 million, payable only if the option is exercised.

d The same film producer mentioned above incurred costs of $3 million to produce an *avant garde* film. No network has yet purchased rights to show the film. In the past, the producer has generally not recovered all of the costs of such speculative films.

e On January 1, an automobile company incurs costs of $6 million for specialized machine tools necessary for producing a new model automobile. Such tools last for 6 years, on average, but the new model automobile is expected to be produced for only 3 years.

f A company wishes to acquire a 5-acre site for a new warehouse. The land it wants is part of a 10-acre site that the owner insists be purchased as a whole for $18,000. The company purchases the land, spends $2,000 in legal fees for rights to divide the site into two 5-acre plots, and immediately offers half of the land for resale. The two best offers are

(1) $12,000 for the east half, and
(2) $13,000 for the west half.

The company sells the east half.

g The same data as in part **f,** except the two best offers are

(1) $5,000 for the east half, and
(2) $12,000 for the west half.
The company sells the west half.

29 The Libby Company has income tax expense before any investment credits of $100,000 each year. At the start of the first year, it acquires an asset with a depreciable life of 4 years. Assume that the asset qualifies for an investment credit of $4,000.

   a Record income taxes and the entries related to the investment credit for the 4 years of the asset's life using the flow-through method.

   b Record entries related to income taxes and the investment credit for the 4 years of the asset's life using the deferral method.

30 Refer to the data in the preceding problem for the Libby Company. Assume that each year the Libby Equilibrium Company acquires an asset with a depreciable life of 4 years. Each year the asset acquired qualifies for an investment credit of $4,000 and income tax expense before any investment credits is $100,000.

   a Record entries related to income taxes and the investment credit for each of the first 5 years using the flow-through method.

   b Record entries related to income taxes and the investment credit for each of the first 5 years using the deferral method.

   c Assuming that Libby Equilibrium Company's income taxes, asset acquisitions, and investment credits continue in the following years as in the first 4 years, describe the effects on the financial statements of the two methods of accounting for the investment credit.

   d Assume the same data as in part **c,** but that the new asset's cost increases by 10 percent each year and that the amount of the investment credit earned increases by 10 percent each year. Describe the effects on the financial statements of the two methods of accounting for the investment credit.

31 Three companies have each recently made investments in equipment designed to save fuel. The equipment purchased by each company costs $100,000 and has a 10-year service life. In all three cases, the company was entitled to a $10,000 investment tax credit when it purchased the asset during the current year. The income taxes otherwise payable of all three companies were reduced by $10,000 during the current year. In all three companies management had made careful studies of the costs and benefits of acquiring the new equipment.

   Management of Company A decided that the equipment purchased would provide operating cost savings with a present value of $150,000. The company is delighted to acquire the asset.

   Management of Company B decided that the equipment it purchased would provide operating cost savings with a present value of $90,000. The equipment was worth acquiring only because of the investment credit.

   Management of Company C decided that the equipment it purchased provided operating cost savings with a present value of $94,000. The equipment was acquired only because the investment credit made the investment worthwhile.

   a Discuss the considerations management of each of these companies might give to accounting for the investment credit.

   b What can you conclude from this question about the "right" method of accounting for the investment credit?

32 The Consumer Products Company has $300,000 of total assets. The Consumer Products Company has been earning $45,000 per year and generating $45,000 per year of cash flow from operations. Each year the Consumer Products Company distributes its earnings by paying cash of $45,000 to owners. Management of the Consumer Products Company believes that a new advertising campaign now will lead to increased sales over the next 4 years. The anticipated net cash flows of the project are as follows:

Beginning of Year	Net Cash (Outflow) Inflow
1	($24,000)
2, 3, and 4	10,000 each year

Assume that the advertising campaign is undertaken, that cash flows are as planned, and that the Consumer Products Company makes payments to owners of $45,000 at the end of the first year and $47,000 at the end of each of the next 3 years. Assume that there are no interest expenses in any year. Ignore any income tax effects.

a Compute net income and the all-capital earnings rate of the Consumer Products Company for each of the 4 years, assuming that advertising expenditures are expensed as they occur. Use the year-end balance of total assets in the denominator of the all-capital earnings rate.

b Compute net income and the all-capital earnings rate of the Consumer Products Company for each year of the project, assuming that advertising costs are capitalized and then amortized on a straight-line basis over the last 3 years. Use the year-end balance of total assets in the denominator of the all-capital earnings rate.

c How well has the management of the Consumer Products Company carried out its responsibility to its owners? On what basis do you make this judgment? Which method of accounting seems to reflect performance more adequately?

33 In 1979 Epstein Company acquired the assets of Falk Company. The assets of Falk Company included various intangibles. Discuss the accounting for the acquisition in 1979 and in later years for each of the items described below.

a Registration of the trademark Thyrom® for thyristors expires in 3 years. Epstein Company thought that the trademark had a fair market value of $60,000. It expects to continue making and selling Thyrom thyristors indefinitely.

b The design patent covering the ornamentation of the containers for displaying Thyrom thyristors expires in 5 years. The Epstein Company thought that the design patent had a fair market value of $20,000 and expects to continue making the containers indefinitely.

c An unpatented trade secret on a special material used in manufacturing thyristors was viewed as having a fair market value of $250,000.

d Refer to the trade secret in part c. Suppose that in 1980 a competitor discovers the trade secret, but does not disclose the secret to other competitors. How should the plans for accounting be changed?

e During 1979, the Epstein Company produced a sales promotion film, *Using Thyristors for Fun and Profit,* at a cost of $25,000. The film is licensed to purchasers of thyristors for use in training their employees and customers. The film is copyrighted.

34 Equilibrium Company plans to spend $30,000 at the beginning of each of the next several years advertising the Company's brand names and trademarks. As a result of the advertising expenditure for a given year, aftertax income (not counting advertising expense) is expected to increase by $12,000 a year for 3 years, including the year of the expenditure itself. Equilibrium Company has other aftertax income of $10,000 per year. The controller of Equilibrium Company wonders what the effect on the financial statements will be of following one of two accounting policies with respect to advertising expenditures:

(1) Expensing the advertising costs in the year of expenditures.

(2) Capitalizing the advertising costs and amortizing them over 3 years, including the year of the expenditure itself.

Assume that the Company does spend $30,000 at the beginning of each of 4 years and that the planned increase in income occurs. Ignore income tax effects.

a   Prepare a 4-year condensed summary of net income assuming that policy (1) is followed and advertising costs are expensed as incurred.

b   Prepare a 4-year condensed summary of net income assuming that policy (2) is followed and advertising costs are capitalized and amortized over 3 years. Compute also the amount of Deferred Advertising Costs (asset) to be shown on the balance sheet at the end of each of the four years.

c   In what sense is policy (1) a conservative policy?

d   What will be the effect on net income and on the balance sheet if Equilibrium Company continues to spend $30,000 each year and the effects on aftertax income continue as in the first 4 years?

CHAPTER 10
LIABILITIES

This chapter and the next examine the accounting concepts and procedures for the right-hand side of the balance sheet, which shows the sources of a firm's financing. Business capital comes from two sources: owners and nonowners. Owners' equity is the subject of Chapter 11. This chapter discusses capital provided to a business by nonowners. Banks or creditors providing debt on a long-term basis are aware of their role as providers of capital, but suppliers, employees, and customers usually do not think of themselves as contributing to a firm's capital, even though they do. The obligations that a business incurs to these nonowning contributors of capital are called liabilities.

A thorough understanding of long-term liabilities requires some knowledge of compound interest and present-value computations. In these computations, payments made at different times are made comparable by taking into account the interest that cash can earn over time. Appendix B at the back of the book introduces the computations. Although Appendix B can be omitted without losing continuity with the rest of the book, much of the discussion in this chapter will be easier to follow if you understand the concepts, if not the procedures, of present-value analysis.

BASIC CONCEPTS OF LIABILITIES

A useful working definition of a liability is a legal obligation to make a payment of a definite (or reasonably certain) amount on a definite (or reasonably certain) future date (or dates) in return for a current benefit or for a benefit received in the past. There are four operable constraints on an obligation before it is recognized as a liability: legality, certainty of amount, certainty of due date, and receipt of past or current benefit. Most of the liabilities discussed in this chapter meet all four criteria. If an item is called a *liability* but does not meet all four criteria, then this fact is noted in the discussion.

To be shown as a liability, an obligation *need not yet be legally due for payment.* For example, a borrower will show Notes Payable as a liability even though there is no legal obligation to pay cash to the lender for 2 years.

In *historical*-cost accounting, liabilities are shown on the balance sheet as the present value of payments to be made in the future.[1] The interest rate used in computing the present-value amount throughout the life of a liability is the interest rate that specific borrower was required to pay at the time the liability was initially incurred. That is, the *historical* interest rate is used.

Liabilities are generally classified on the balance sheet as *current* or *noncurrent.* The criterion used for dividing current from noncurrent liabilities is the length of time that will elapse before payment must be made. The dividing line between the two is usually 1 year. We occasionally use a third classification for liabilities of indeterminate term called *indeterminate-term liabilities.*

Example 1   Miller Corporation's employees have earned wages and salaries that will not be paid until the next payday, 2 weeks after the end of the current accounting period. Miller Corporation's suppliers are owed substantial amounts for goods sold to Miller Corporation, but these debts are not due for 10 to 30 days after the end of the period. Miller Corporation owes the federal and state governments for taxes, but the payments are not due until the 15th of next month. Each of these items meets the four criteria to be a liability and is due within 1 year. Thus, they are shown as current liabilities under titles such as Wages Payable, Salaries Payable, Accounts Payable, and Taxes Payable.

Example 2   When Miller Corporation sells television sets, it promises under warranty to repair or replace any faulty parts or faulty sets within 1 year after sale. This obligation meets the four criteria of a liability. There is a legal obligation. The amount is not known with certainty, but Miller Corporation has had sufficient experience with its own television sets to be able to estimate with a reasonable degree of precision what the expected costs of repairs or replacements will be. The repairs or replacements will occur within a time span, 1 year, known with reasonable precision. Miller Corporation will thus show Estimated Liability for Warranty Payments on its balance sheet.

Example 3   Miller Corporation signs a firm contract to supply certain goods to a customer within the next 6 months. In this case, there is a legal obligation, definite time, and definite amount (of goods, if not cash), but there has been no past or current benefit received by Miller Corporation. Thus no liability is shown. (Chapter 2 pointed out that accounting does not recognize assets or liabilities in events where there is no mutual performance. Without some mutual performance, there is no current or past benefit.)

---

[1]   As we mentioned in Chapter 2, most current liabilities are stated as the amount payable because the difference between the amount ultimately payable and its present value is immaterial.

Example 4   Same facts as Example 3 except that the customer has made a $10,000 cash deposit on signing the order. Here Miller Corporation has received a current benefit, $10,000 in cash. It will show a liability called Advances from Customers to the extent of that receipt.

Example 5   Miller Corporation has signed a 3-year, noncancelable lease with the IBM Corporation to make payments of $3,000 per month for the use of a computer system. There is a legal liability, a definite amount due at definite times, and a current benefit—a computer system has been received. Thus Miller Corporation should show a liability called Present Value of Future Payments Under Capital Leases on its balance sheet.

Example 6   Miller Corporation is defendant in a class-action lawsuit alleging damages of $10 million. The lawsuit was filed by customers who claim to have been injured by misleading advertising of Miller Corporation's television sets. Lawyers retained by the Corporation think that there is an adequate defense to the charges. Since there is no legal obligation to make a payment of an estimatable amount at a known time, there is no liability. The notes to the financial statements will disclose the existence of the lawsuit, but no liability will be shown on the balance sheet.

Example 7   Miller Corporation has signed a contract promising to employ its president for the next 5 years and to pay the president a salary of $250,000 per year. The salary is to be increased in future years at the same rate as the Consumer Price Index, published by the U.S. Government, increases. There is a legal obligation on the part of Miller Corporation to make payments (although the president may quit at any time without penalty). The payments are of reasonably certain amounts and are to be made at definite times. At the time the contract is signed, no current or past benefit has been received, at least according to generally accepted accounting principles. Therefore, no long-term liability is shown on the balance sheet. A liability will, of course, arise as the president's salary is earned.

CURRENT LIABILITIES

Current liabilities are normally those due within 1 year. They include accounts payable to creditors, payroll accruals, short-term notes payable, taxes payable, and a few others. Current liabilities are continually discharged and replaced with new ones in the course of business operations.

   These obligations will not be paid for several weeks or months after the current balance sheet date. Their present value is therefore less than the amount that will be paid. Nevertheless, these items are shown at the full amount to be paid, because the difference is usually so small that separate accounting for the discount and subsequent interest expense is judged not worth the trouble.

Accounts Payable to Creditors

Companies seldom pay for goods and services when received. Payment is usually deferred until a bill is received from the supplier. Even then, the bill might not be paid immediately, but instead, accumulated with other bills until a specified time of the month when all bills are paid. Since explicit interest is not paid on these accounts, management tries to obtain as much capital as possible from its creditors by delaying payment as long as possible. Failure to pay creditors according to schedule can, however, lead to poor credit ratings and to restrictions on future credit.

Payroll Items

Deductions are taken from an employee's gross pay to cover federal income taxes, payroll (FICA[2] or social security) taxes, medical plans, pension plans, insurance plans, and other items. The accounting for these deductions is relatively simple, although time-consuming. Instead of showing the gross pay as being entirely payable to employees, the employer shows the net, or "take-home," pay as being payable to employees, and deductions, or withholdings, as being payable to the various recipients. For example, gross wages of $2,000 in a merchandising firm might be shown as follows:

Wage Expense	2,000	
Wages Payable		1,460
Federal Withholding Taxes Payable		240
State Withholding Taxes Payable		80
Payroll Taxes Payable		160
Medical Plan Payable		20
Pension Plan Payable		30
Insurance Plan Payable		10

In addition, the employer is required to pay a FICA tax for each worker. Assuming in this example that the labor contract requires the employer also to match the medical and pension plan contributions of the workers, and those contributions are judged to be a component of wage expense, the additional journal entry would be

Wage Expense	210	
Payroll Taxes Payable		160
Medical Plan Payable		20
Pension Plan Payable		30

---

[2] FICA is the Federal Insurance Contribution Act. The actual deduction depends on several factors and has steadily increased over time. For the purpose of illustrations and problems in this text, it will be assumed that the employee's and employer's shares of the tax are each calculated at 8 percent of the first $20,000 of gross income for each employee.

Short-Term Notes and Interest Payable

Businesses obtain interim financing for less than a year from banks or other creditors in return for a short-term note called a *note payable*. Such notes are discussed in Chapter 7 from the point of view of the lender, or note holder. The treatment of these notes by the borrower is the mirror image of the treatment by the lender. Where the lender records an asset, the borrower records a liability. When the lender records interest receivable and revenue, the borrower records interest payable and expense.

Income Taxes Payable

The corporation is the only major form of business organization on which a separate federal income tax is levied. An income tax must be paid each year by corporations on their taxable income from business activities. In contrast, business entities organized as partnerships or sole proprietorships do not pay income taxes. Instead, the income of the business entity is taxed to the individual partners or sole proprietor. Each partner or sole proprietor adds his or her share of business income to income from all other (nonbusiness) sources in preparing individual income tax returns.

The details of the income tax on corporations are subject to change. The rates and schedules of payments mentioned below should not be taken as an indication of the exact procedure in force at any particular time, but rather as an indication of the type of accounting procedures that are involved.[3] The accounting for state and local income taxes follows the same general pattern as that for federal income taxes, except for rates and dates of payment.

Corporations must make an estimate of the amount of taxes that will be due for the year and make quarterly payments equal to one-fourth of the estimated tax. This is frequently described as "pay-as-you-go" taxation. For a corporation on a calendar-year basis, and using 1979 as an example, 25 percent of the estimated tax for 1979 must be paid by April 15, 1979, 50 percent by June 15, 1979, 75 percent by September 15, 1979, and the entire estimated tax for 1979 must be paid by December 15, 1979.

The estimated income and, hence, the estimated tax may change as the year passes. The corporation must report such changed estimates quarterly. The amount of the quarterly payment is revised to reflect the new estimated tax and takes into account the cumulative payments made during previous quarters of the year. The final income tax return for the year is due by March 15, 1980. Any difference between the actual tax liability for 1979 and the cumulative tax payments during 1979 must be paid, one-half by March 15, 1980, and one-half by June 15, 1980. The law provides for penalties if the amount estimated is substantially less than the actual tax liability.

If income statements are prepared more often than quarterly, or if the end of the reporting period does not coincide with the tax payment period, it is necessary to estimate the income tax for the reporting period so that a more accurate measurement can be made of the net income for the period. Monthly or other short-period

---

[3]   The discussion in this section is based on the law and regulations in effect January 1, 1979. Most corporate income is taxed at a rate of 48 percent. Throughout the remainder of the text, an income tax rate of 40 percent is used in almost all illustrations for ease of calculation.

estimates of the tax are likely to be far from dependable, because there are various special provisions in the tax law. During the first few quarters of the year, it is not clear how many of the special provisions the corporation will ultimately be able to use. All that can be done is to set up the best possible estimate of tax in the light of earnings of the year to date and the prospects for the remainder of the year.

Deferred Performance Liabilities

Another current liability arises from advance payments by customers for goods or services. This liability, unlike the preceding ones, is discharged by delivering goods or services, rather than by paying cash. This liability represents "unearned" and, therefore, unrecognized, revenue; that is, cash is received before the goods or services are furnished to the customer.

An example of this type of liability is the advance sale of theater tickets, say, for $200. Upon the sale, the following entry is made:

```
Cash ............................................................  200
    Liability for Advance Sales ...............................       200
Tickets are sold for cash, but there is no revenue until service is rendered.
```

These deferred performance obligations qualify as liabilities. After the theater performance, or after the tickets have expired, revenue is recognized and the liability is removed:

```
Liability for Advance Sales ....................................  200
    Performance Revenue ......................................        200
Service has been rendered and revenue is recognized.
```

Deferred performance liabilities also arise in connection with the sale of magazine subscriptions, transportation tickets, and service contracts.

A related type of deferred performance liability arises when a firm provides a warranty for free service or repairs for some period after the sale. At the time of sale, the firm can only estimate the likely amount of warranty liability. If sales during the accounting period were $28,000, and the firm estimated that an amount equal to 4 percent of the sales revenue will eventually be used to satisfy warranty claims, the entry is

```
Accounts Receivable ...........................................  28,000
Warranty Expense .............................................   1,120
    Sales ....................................................        28,000
    Estimated Warranty Liability .............................         1,120
To record sales and estimated payment to be made for warranties on items sold.
```

Note that this entry recognizes the warranty expense in the period when revenue is recognized, even though the repairs may be made in a later period. Thus, warranty expense is matched with associated revenues. Because the expense is recognized, the liability is created. In this case, neither the amount nor the due date of the liability is definite, but they are "reasonably certain." FASB Statement No. 5 (1975) allows the accrual of the expense and related warranty liability only when the amounts can be "reasonably estimated."

As expenditures of, say, $175 are made next period for repairs under the warranty, the entry is

Estimated Warranty Liability   175
   Cash (or other assets consumed for repairs)   175
Repairs made. No expense is recognized now; all expense was recognized on
date of sale.

With experience, the firm will adjust the percentage of sales it charges to Warranty Expense. Its goal is to achieve a credit balance in the Estimated Warranty Liability account at each balance sheet date that reasonably estimates the actual cost of repairs to be made under warranties outstanding at that time.

LONG-TERM LIABILITIES

The principal long-term liabilities are mortgages, bonds, and leases. The significant differences between long-term and short-term, or current, liabilities are that: (1) interest on long-term liabilities is ordinarily paid at regular intervals during the life of a long-term obligation, whereas interest on short-term debt is usually paid in a lump sum at maturity; (2a) the principal of long-term obligations is often paid back in installments, or (2b) special funds are accumulated by the borrower for retiring long-term liabilities.

Accounting for all long-term liabilities generally follows the same procedures. Those procedures are outlined next. We illustrate their application to the various long-term liabilities throughout the rest of this chapter.

Procedures for Recording Long-Term Liabilities

The present value of all payments to be made is recorded as the initial liability. Historical-cost accounting uses the market interest rate at the time the liability is recorded in three ways. First, at the time of initial recording, it is used to compute the present value of the payments to be made. Second, it is used to compute the amount of interest expense throughout the life of the liability. Third, it can be used at any time to compute the present value of the remaining payments to be shown on the balance sheet.[4] A portion of each cash payment represents interest expense. Any excess of cash payment over interest expense is used to reduce the liability itself (often called the *principal*). If a given payment is not sufficient to discharge the entire interest expense that has accrued since the last payment date, then the liability principal is increased by the amount of the deficiency.

Retirement of long-term liabilities can occur in several ways, but the process is the

---

[4]   This last use does *not* result from a required calculation. Normally, the remaining balance in a noncurrent liability account (including its adjunct or contra accounts) is correct if the initial amount recorded is correct and if interest expense has been recorded in the fashion described in the text.

same. The net amount shown on the books for the obligation is debited, the asset given up in return (usually cash) is credited, and any difference is recognized as a gain or loss on retirement of the debt.

MORTGAGES

A mortgage is a contract in which the lender is awarded legal title to certain property of the borrower, with the provision that the title reverts to the borrower when the loan is repaid in full. (In a few states, the lender merely acquires a lien on the borrower's property rather than legal title to it.) The mortgaged property is security for the loan. The customary terminology designates the lender as the "mortgagee" and the borrower as the "mortgagor."[5]

As long as the mortgagor meets the obligations under the mortgage agreement, the mortgagee does not have the ordinary rights of an owner to possess and use the property. If the mortgagor defaults on either the principal or interest payments, the mortgagee can usually arrange to have the property sold for his or her benefit through a process called *foreclosure*. The mortgagee has first rights to the proceeds from the foreclosure sale for satisfying any unpaid claim. If there is an excess, it is paid to the mortgagor. If the proceeds are insufficient to pay the remaining loan, the lender becomes an unsecured creditor of the borrower for the unpaid balance.

Accounting for Mortgages

Some of the more common problems in accounting for mortgages are presented in the following illustration.

On October 1, 1979, the Midwestern Products Company borrows $30,000 for 5 years from the Home Savings and Finance Company to obtain funds for additional working capital. As security, Midwestern Products Company gives Home Savings and Finance Company title to several parcels of land that it owns and that are on its books at a cost of $50,000. The interest rate is 8 percent per year compounded semiannually, with payments due on April 1 and October 1. Midwestern agrees to make 10 equal payments of $3,700 each over the 5 years of the mortgage so that when the last payment is made on October 1, 1984, the loan and all interest will have been paid. The Midwestern Products Company closes its books annually on December 31. (The derivation of the semiannual payment of $3,700 is shown in Example 10 in Appendix B at the end of the book.)

The entries from the time the mortgage is issued through December 31, 1980, are as follows:

10/1/79	Cash	30,000	
	Mortgage Payable		30,000
	Loan obtained from Home Savings and Finance Company for 5 years at 8 percent compounded semiannually.		

---

[5] When you borrow money to finance your loan purchase, you give the bank a mortgage, not vice versa.

12/31/79	Interest Expense	600	
	Interest Payable		600
	Adjusting entry: Interest expense on mortgage from 10/1/79 to 12/31/79 (.08 $\times$ \$30,000 $\times$ $\frac{3}{12}$).		
4/1/80	Interest Expense	600	
	Interest Payable	600	
	Mortgage Payable	2,500	
	Cash		3,700
	Cash payment made requires an entry. Interest expense on mortgage from 1/1/80 to 4/1/80, payment of 6 months' interest, and reduction of loan by the difference, \$3,700 − \$1,200 = \$2,500.		
10/1/80	Interest Expense	1,100	
	Mortgage Payable	2,600	
	Cash		3,700
	Cash payment made requires an entry. Payment of interest for the period 4/1/80 to 10/1/80. Interest expense for the period is \$1,100 [= .08 $\times$ (\$30,000 − \$2,500) $\times$ $\frac{1}{2}$]. The loan is reduced by the difference, \$3,700 − \$1,100 = \$2,600.		
12/31/80	Interest Expense	498	
	Interest Payable		498
	Adjusting entry: Interest expense from 10/1/80 to 12/31/80 [.08 $\times$ (\$30,000 − \$2,500 − \$2,600) $\times$ $\frac{3}{12}$].		

Exhibit 10.1 presents an "amortization schedule" for this mortgage. It shows the allocation of each \$3,700 payment between interest and repayment of principal. (The last payment, \$3,685 in this case, often differs slightly from the others because of the cumulative effect of rounding errors.) At the top of the exhibit is the journal entry made each 6-month period. Amortization schedules indicate both the numbers that are recorded each period and the amount of the outstanding loan at the end of each period.

BONDS

Mortgages or notes are used whenever the funds being borrowed can be obtained from a small number of sources. When large amounts are needed, the firm may have to borrow from the general investing public through the use of a bond issue. Bonds are used primarily by corporations and governmental units. The distinctive features of a bond issue are as follows:

1 A *bond indenture,* or agreement, is drawn up which shows in detail the terms of the loan and the rights and duties of the borrower and other parties to the contract.
2 *Bond certificates* are used. Engraved certificates are prepared, each one representing a portion of the total loan. The usual minimum denomination in business practice is \$1,000, although smaller denominations are occasionally used. Government bonds are issued in denominations as small as \$25.
3 If property is pledged as security for the loan (as in a mortgage bond), then a *trustee* is named to hold title to the property serving as security. The trustee acts as the representative of the bondholders and is usually a bank or trust company.

EXHIBIT 10.1
Amortization Schedule for $30,000 Mortgage, Repaid in 10 Semiannual Installments of $3,700, Interest Rate of 8 Percent, Compounded Semiannually

SEMIANNUAL JOURNAL ENTRY

Dr. Interest Expense . . . .   Amount in Column (3)
Dr. Mortgage Payable . . . .   Amount in Column (5)
  Cr. Cash . . . .   Amount in Column (4)

6-Month Period (1)	Mortgage Principal Start of Period (2)	Interest Expense for Period (3)	Payment (4)	Portion of Payment Reducing Principal (5)	Mortgage Principal End of Period (6)
0					$30,000
1	$30,000	$1,200	$3,700	$2,500	27,500
2	27,500	1,100	3,700	2,600	24,900
3	24,900	996	3,700	2,704	22,196
4	22,196	888	3,700	2,812	19,384
5	19,384	775	3,700	2,925	16,459
6	16,459	658	3,700	3,042	13,417
7	13,417	537	3,700	3,163	10,254
8	10,254	410	3,700	3,290	6,964
9	6,964	279	3,700	3,421	3,543
10	3,543	142	3,685	3,543	0

Column (2) = Column (6) from Previous Period
Column (3) = .04 × Column (2)
Column (4)   Given, except row 10 where it is the amount such that Column (4) = Column (2) + Column (3)
Column (5) = Column (4) − Column (3)
Column (6) = Column (2) − Column (5)

4 An agent is appointed, usually a bank or trust company, to act as *registrar* and *disbursing agent*. The borrower deposits interest and principal payments with the disbursing agent, who distributes the funds to the bondholders.

5 Most bonds are *coupon bonds*. Coupons are attached to the bond certificate covering the interest payments throughout the life of the bond. When a coupon comes due, the bondholder cuts it off and deposits it with a bank. The bank sends the coupon through the bank clearing system to the disbursing agent for payment, which is deposited in the bondholder's account at the bank.

6 Bonds are frequently *registered as to principal,* which means that the holder's name appears on the bond certificate and on the records of the registrar. Sometimes both the principal and interest of bonds are registered, in which case the interest payments are mailed directly to the bondholder and coupons are not used. Registered

bonds are easily replaced if lost, but the transfer from one holder to another is cumbersome. Unregistered bonds may be transferred merely by delivery, whereas registered bonds have to be assigned formally from one holder to another.

7 The entire bond issue is usually issued by the borrower to an investment banking firm, or to a group of investment bankers known as a *syndicate,* which takes over the responsibility of reselling the bonds to the investing public. Members of the syndicate usually bear the risks and rewards of interest-rate fluctuations during the period while the bonds are being sold to the public.

Types of Bonds

Mortgage bonds carry a mortgage on real estate as security for the repayment of the loan. *Collateral trust bonds* are usually secured by stocks and bonds of other corporations. The most common type of corporate bond, except in the railroad and public utility industries, is the *debenture bond.* This type carries no special security or collateral; instead, it is issued on the general credit of the business. To give added protection to the bondholders, provisions are usually included in the bond indenture that limit the amount of subsequent long-term debt that can be incurred. *Convertible bonds* are debentures that the holder can exchange, possibly after some specific period of time has elapsed, for a specific number of shares of capital stock.

Almost all bonds provide for the payment of interest at regular intervals, usually semiannually. The amount of interest is typically expressed as a percentage of the principal. For example, an 8-percent, 10-year semiannual coupon bond with face or principal amount of $1,000 promises to pay $40 every 6 months. The first payment generally occurs 6 months after the bond issue date, until a total of 20 payments are made. At the time of the final $40 coupon payment, the $1,000 principal is also due. The coupon rate is 8 percent in this case. The principal amount of a bond is its face, or par value. The terms *face value* and *par value* are used synonymously in this context. In general, the par amount multiplied by the coupon rate equals the amount of cash paid per *year,* whether in quarterly, semiannual, or annual installation. By far the majority of corporate bonds provide for semiannual coupon payments. A bond can be issued and subsequently traded in the marketplace below par, at par, or above par.

Proceeds of a Bond Issue

The amount received by the borrower may be more or less than the par value of the bonds issued. The difference arises primarily because there is a difference between the coupon rate printed on the bond certificates and the interest rate the market requires the firm to pay to borrow under the circumstances. If the coupon rate is less than the rate the market, in aggregate, requires the firm to pay, then the bonds will sell for less than par. The difference between par and selling price is called the *discount* on the bond. If the coupon rate is larger than the rate the market requires, then the bonds will sell above par. The difference between selling price and par is called the *premium* on the bond.

The presence of a discount or premium in and of itself indicates nothing about the credit standing of the borrower. A firm with a credit standing that would enable it to borrow funds at $7\frac{1}{4}$ percent might issue 7-percent bonds that would sell at a discount, whereas another firm with a lower credit standing that would require it to pay $7\frac{3}{4}$ percent on loans might issue bonds at 8 percent that would sell at a premium.

The following illustrations cover the calculations of the proceeds of a bond issue when the market interest rate is equal to, more than, and less than the coupon rate.

Issued at Par The Macaulay Corporation issues $100,000 face value of 8-percent semiannual coupon debenture bonds. The bonds are dated July 1, 1979, and are due July 1, 1989. Coupons are dated July 1 and January 1. The coupon payments promised at each interest payment date total $4,000. Assuming that the issue was taken by L. Fisher and Company, investment bankers, on July 1, 1979, at a rate to yield 8 percent compounded semiannually, the calculation of the proceeds to Macaulay would be as follows. (The present-value calculations are explained in Appendix B at the back of the book.)

(a) Present value of $100,000 to be paid at the end of 10 years . . . . $ 45,639
    (Appendix Table 2 at the back of the book shows the present value of
    $1 to be received in 20 periods at 4 percent per period to be $.45639;
    $100,000 × .45639 = $45,639).

(b) Present value of $4,000 to be paid each 6 months for 10 years   54,361
    (Appendix Table 4 shows the present value of an ordinary annuity of
    $1 per period for 20 periods discounted at 4 percent to be $13.59033;
    $4,000 × 13.59033 = $54,361.)

Total Proceeds $100,000

The issue price would be stated as 100 (that is, 100 percent of par), which implies that the market rate was 8 percent compounded semiannually, the same as the coupon rate.

Issued at Discount Assuming that the bonds were issued at a price to yield 9 percent compounded semiannually, the calculation of the proceeds would be as follows. Why it is that "8-percent" bonds can be issued to yield 9 percent is discussed below on page 372. (The tables at the back of the book do *not* include columns for $4\frac{1}{2}$ percent.)

(a) Present value of $100,000 to be paid at the end of 10 years . . . . $ 41,464
    (Present value of $1 to be received in 20 periods at $4\frac{1}{2}$ percent per period
    is $0.41464; $100,000 × 0.41464 = $41,464.)

(b) Present value of $4,000 to be paid each 6 months for 10 years   52,032
    (Present value of an ordinary annuity of $1 per period for 20 periods,
    discounted at $4\frac{1}{2}$ percent per period = $13.00794; $4,000 × 13.00794 =
    $52,032.)

Total Proceeds . . . . $ 93,496

If the issue price were stated on a conventional pricing basis in the market at 93.50 (93.50 percent of par), the issuing price would be $93,500. This amount implies a market yield of slightly less than 9 percent compounded semiannually.

Issued at Premium   Assuming that the bonds were issued at a price to yield 7 percent compounded semiannually, the calculation of the proceeds would be as follows. (The tables at the back of the book do not include columns for $3\frac{1}{2}$ percent.)

(a) Present value of $100,000 to be paid at the end of 10 years . . . . $ 50,257
      (Present value of $1 to be received in 20 periods at $3\frac{1}{2}$ percent per period
      is $0.50257; $100,000 × 0.50257 = $50,257.)

(b) Present value of $4,000 to be paid each 6 months for 10 years   56,850
      (Present value of an ordinary annuity at $1 per period for 20 periods,
      discounted at $3\frac{1}{2}$ percent per period = $14.2124; $4,000 × 14.2124 =
      $56,850.)

Total Proceeds $107,107

If the issue price were stated on a conventional pricing basis in the market at 107.11 (107.11 percent of par), the issuing price would be $107.110.[6] This price would imply a market yield of slightly less than 7 percent compounded semiannually.

Bond Tables

Fortunately, these tedious calculations need not be made every time a bond issue is analyzed. Special bond tables have been prepared to show the results of calculations like those just described. Examples of such tables are included in the tables at the back of the book. Table 5 shows for 6-percent, semiannual coupon bonds the price as a percent of par for various market interest rates (yields) and years to maturity. Table 6 shows market rates and implied prices for 8-percent, semiannual coupon bonds. (Some modern electronic calculators are capable of making the calculations represented by these tables in a few seconds.)

The percentages of par shown in these tables represent the present value of the bond indicated. Since the factors are expressed as a percent of par, they have to be multiplied by 10 to find the price of a $1,000 bond. If you have never used bond tables before now, turn to Table 6 on page 629 and find in the 10-year column the three different prices for the three different market yields used in the preceding example. Notice further that a bond will sell at par if and only if it has a market yield equal to its coupon rate.

These tables are useful whether a bond is being issued by a corporation or resold later by an investor. The approach to determining the market price will be the same in either case, although the years to maturity will be less than the original term of the

------

[6]   In many contexts, bond prices are quoted in dollars plus thirty-seconds of a dollar. A bond selling for about 107.107 percent of par would be quoted at $107\frac{3}{32}$, which would be written as 107.3. In order to read published bond prices, you must know whether the information after the "decimal" point refers to fractions expressed in one-hundredths or in thirty-seconds. (If you are reading published bond prices and see any number larger than 31 after the decimal point then you can be sure that one-hundredths are being used. If you see many prices, but none of the numbers shown after the point is larger than 31, then you can be reasonably sure that thirty-seconds are being used.) In this book, we use decimal fractions, that is, one-hundredths.

bond when it is resold. The following generalizations can be made regarding bond prices:

1 When the market rate equals the coupon rate, the market price will equal par.
2 When the market rate is greater than the coupon rate, the market price will be less than par.
3 When the market rate is less than the coupon rate, the market price will be greater than par.

Accounting for Bonds Issued at Par

The following illustration covers the more common problems associated with bonds issued at par.

We use the data presented in the previous sections for the Macaulay Corporation, where the bonds were issued at par and we assume that the books are closed semi-annually on June 30 and December 31. The entry at the time of issue would be

7/1/79	Cash	100,000	
	Debenture Bonds Payable		100,000
	$100,000 of 8-percent, 10-year bonds issued at par.		

The entries for interest would be made at the end of the accounting period and on the interest payment dates. Entries through January 2, 1980, would be

12/31/79	Interest Expense	4,000	
	Interest Payable		4,000
1/2/80	Interest Payable	4,000	
	Cash		4,000
	To record payment of 6 months' interest.		

Bond Issued Between Interest Payment Dates   The actual date that a bond is issued seldom coincides with one of the payment dates. Assuming these same bonds were actually brought to market on August 1, rather than July 1, and were issued at par, the purchaser of the bond would be expected to pay Macaulay Corporation for one month's interest in advance. After all, on the first coupon Macaulay Corporation promises a full $40, for 6 months' interest, but would have had the use of the borrowed funds for only 5 months. The purchasers of the bonds would pay $100,000 plus 1 month's interest of $667 ($= .08 \times \$100,000 \times \frac{1}{12}$) and would get the $667 back when the first coupons are redeemed. The journal entries made by Macaulay Corporation, the issuer, would be

8/1/79	Cash	100,667	
	Bonds Payable		100,000
	Interest Payable		667
	To record issue of bonds at par between interest payment dates. The purchasers pay an amount equal to interest for the first month but will get it back when the first coupons are redeemed.		

| 12/31/79 | Interest Expense | 3,333 | |
| | Interest Payable | | 3,333 |

Accrual of interest for 5 months = .08 × $100,000 × $\frac{5}{12}$. The Interest Payable account now has a credit balance of $4,000 (= $667 + $3,333).

| 1/2/80 | Interest Payable | 4,000 | |
| | Cash | | 4,000 |

To record payment of 6 months' interest.

Note that interest expense in 1979 amounts to only $3,333, even though the first coupons total $4,000. After the first coupon payment date, the accounting will be identical for bonds originally issued on an interest payment date or between interest payment dates.

Accounting for Bonds Issued at a Discount

The following illustration covers the more common problems associated with bonds issued at a discount.

Assume the data presented for the Macaulay Corporation where the bonds were issued for $93,500 to yield approximately 9 percent compounded semiannually and the books are closed on June 30 and December 31. The entry at the time of issue would be

7/1/79	Cash	93,500	
	Discount on Debenture Bonds Payable	6,500	
	Debenture Bonds Payable		100,000

$100,000 of 8-percent, 10-year bonds issued at a discount.

The discount is primarily an indication that 8 percent is not a sufficiently high rate of interest for the bonds to bring their face value in the open market. Because the market requires approximately 9 percent compounded semiannually, Macaulay actually acquires the use of only $93,500. Macaulay agrees to pay to bondholders the face value of $100,000 when the bond matures as well as the 20 semiannual payments of $4,000 each. The difference between the par value and the amount of proceeds, $6,500, represents additional interest which will be paid as a part of the face value at maturity. Thus the total interest that must be charged to the periods during which the loan is outstanding is $86,500 (periodic payments totaling $80,000 plus the $6,500 included in the principal payment at maturity). Two acceptable methods of allocating the total interest of $86,500 to the periods of the loan are the effective-interest method and the straight-line method.

Interest Expense Under the Effective-Interest Method

Interest payable each period is equal to the coupon interest rate multiplied by the principal or face amount of the liability. Interest expense each period under the effective-interest method is equal to the market rate at the time the bonds were originally issued multiplied by the amount of the bond liability shown on the books at the beginning of the interest period. When bonds are initially issued at a discount, the amount of interest expense will exceed the coupon payment at each payment date. In the example, on the first interest payment date the interest expense is $93,500 × .045 = $4,207.50. Only $4,000 will be paid in cash at that time. The remaining $207.50 will be added to the principal amount of the liability shown in the balance sheet. In this way, the Discount on Debenture Bonds Payable account will be reduced by $207.50 from $6,500 to $6,292.50. The amount of effective liability for the next 6-month period is $93,707.50 (= $93,500.00 + $207.50). In the second 6-month period, interest expense will be computed on a new, larger financial amount. Interest will exceed that of the first 6-month period: $93,707.50 × .09 × $\frac{6}{12}$ = $4,216.84. Interest expense increases each period as the amount effectively borrowed increases.

The periodic interest expense recorded in the accounting records must include both the coupon payment and an expense representing an allocation of an appropriate part of the discount. This process of allocating the discount as extra interest expense over the life of the bond is called *amortization*. An amortization schedule like the one shown in Exhibit 10.2, which assumes an annual market yield of 9 percent with interest compounded and payable semiannually, would be prepared.

The interest expense for a period, shown in column 3, is determined by multiplying the net liability at the start of the period (column 2) by the market rate on the bond issue *at the time of issue*. Since the market yield at issue is 9 percent compounded semiannually, the market rate for the 6-month period is $4\frac{1}{2}$ percent. The net liability (column 7) is increased at the end of each 6-month period by the amount of discount amortization for the period.

The interest-related entries through June 30, 1980, would be as follows:

12/31/79	Interest Expense	4,207.50	
	Discount on Debenture Bonds Payable		207.50
	Interest Payable		4,000.00
	To record accrual of interest and amortization of discount for 6 months.		
1/2/80	Interest Payable	4,000.00	
	Cash		4,000.00
	To record payment of interest for 6 months.		
6/30/80	Interest Expense	4,216.84	
	Discount on Debenture Bonds Payable		216.84
	Interest Payable		4,000.00
	To record accrual of interest and amortization of discount for the second 6 months.		

The series of entries will continue with an increasing amount of amortization each 6-month period until the entire discount is amortized by the maturity date, July 1, 1989. Exhibit 10.2 shows interest expense in column 3 and the credit to the Discount account in column 5 for each of the entries. This method is often called the "effective-interest method" of accounting for bond discount.

The Discount on Debenture Bonds Payable account is a contra-liability account, since the discount represents additional interest that will be paid as part of the face value at maturity. The Discount on Debenture Bonds Payable should be shown on

EXHIBIT 10.2
Effective-Interest Discount Amortization Schedule for $100,000 of 8-Percent, 10-Year Bonds Issued for 93.5 Percent of Par to Yield 9 Percent, Interest Payable Semiannually

SEMIANNUAL JOURNAL ENTRY

Dr. Interest Expense . . . . Amount in Column (3)
  Cr. Cash . . . . Amount in Column (4)
  Cr. Discount on Debenture Bonds Payable . . . . . Amount in Column (5)

Period (6-month intervals) (1)	Liability at Start of Period (2)	Effective Interest: 4½ Percent per Period (3)	Coupon Rate: 4 Percent of Par (4)	Discount Amortization (5)	End of Period	
					Unamortized Discount (6)	Net Liability (7)
0					$6,500.00	$ 93,500.00
1	$93,500.00	$ 4,207.50	$ 4,000.00	$ 207.50	6,292.50	93,707.50
2	93,707.50	4,216.84	4,000.00	216.84	6,075.66	93,924.34
3	93,924.34	4,226.60	4,000.00	226.60	5,849.06	94,150.94
4	94,150.94	4,236.79	4,000.00	236.79	5,612.27	94,387.73
(calculations continued for 20 periods)						
20	99,521.53	4,478.47	4,000.00	478.47	0	100,000.00
Total		$86,500.00	$80,000.00	$6,500.00		

Column (2) = Column (7) from Previous Period
Column (3) = .045 × Column (2)
Column (4) Given
Column (5) = Column (3) − Column (4)
Column (6) = Column (6) from Previous Period − Column (5) of This Period
Column (7) = Column (2) + Column (5)
      = $100,000.00 − Column (6)

the balance sheet as a deduction from the liability account, Debenture Bonds Payable. The balance sheet for December 31, 1979, would show

Debenture Bonds Payable $100,000.00
  Less: Discount on Debenture Bonds Payable 6,292.50 $93,707.50

Interest Expense Under the Straight-Line Method

The amortization of bond discount by the effective-interest method results from using a constant interest rate over the life of the bond issue, 4.5 percent per 6 months in the example. Since the amount of the principal liability increases each period, the amount of interest expense increases each period. Some accountants find the calculations of the effective-interest method too tedious and too hard to understand. They often use the *straight-line method* of amortizing bond discount. In the straight-line method, the *amount* of interest expense is constant each period; since the amount of the principal liability increases, the implied interest rate decreases.

Under the straight-line method, the amount of discount to be amortized each 6 months is the total discount to be amortized over the life of the bond divided by the number of half-years of the bond's life. In this illustration, the semiannual straight-line amortization of bond discount is $325 (= $6,500/20) per 6 months until the discount is fully amortized at the maturity date.

The entries to record the interest expense through January 2, 1980, would be

12/31/79	Interest Expense	4,325	
	Interest Payable		4,000
	Discount on Debenture Bonds Payable		325
	To record the accrual of interest and amortization of discount for 6 months.		
1/2/80	Interest Payable	4,000	
	Cash in Bank		4,000
	To record payment at 6 months' interest.		

Similar entries would be made every 6 months throughout the life of the bond issue.

Preferred Method of Amortizing Bond Discount

In practice, many (even most) companies use the straight-line method of amortizing bond discount. Most of the accountants working in these companies were trained in the era preceding inexpensive calculating devices. They act as though the calculations required by the effective-interest method are too tedious to be done regularly. The effective-interest method may appear more difficult, but it is based on the same concepts and procedures used for mortgages, explained earlier in the chapter, and for leases, to be explained later.

Amortization of Bond Discount in the Statement of Changes in Financial Position

The amortization of discount requires special treatment in the statement of changes in financial position. Assuming that the straight-line method of amortizing bond discount is used, interest expense reported for the first 6 months is $4,325: $4,000 in coupon payments and $325 in discount amortization. Notice that only $4,000 of working capital was used for the expense. There was an increase in Interest Payable of $4,000 followed by discharge of that current liability with cash payment. The remainder of the interest expense, $325, is an increase in the net noncurrent liability, Debenture Bonds Payable less Discount on Debenture Bonds Payable. Consequently, there must be an *addback* to net income in determining "funds provided by operations" in the statement of changes in financial position. The amount of the addback is the amount of the expense that did not use working capital, $325.

Accounting for Bonds Issued at a Premium

The following illustration covers the more common problems associated with bonds issued at a premium.

Assume now that, for whatever reason (such as the company's fine credit standing), the marketplace requires a return of only 7 percent from investments in Macaulay Corporation bonds. If Macaulay Corporation promises to pay $80 interest each year for every bond issued (in the form of 8-percent coupons), then the marketplace is willing to pay more than $1,000 for the bond. (The marketplace is, after all, willing to pay $1,000 for a bond of Macaulay Corporation promising only $70 per year.) It will pay enough more so that the total cash payments by Macaulay Corporation, $40 per 6-month period plus $1,000 paid in 10 years, will exactly equal a 7-percent rate on the original price paid for the bond. The earlier calculation showed that amount to be approximately $1,071. See page 372.

We assume that Macaulay Corporation issues $100,000 of par-value 8-percent semiannual coupon bonds to mature in 10 years. It receives $107,100. The books are closed on June 30 and December 31 of each year. The entry at the time of issue would be

7/1/79	Cash	107,100	
	Debenture Bonds Payable		100,000
	Premium on Debenture Bonds Payable		7,100
	$100,000 of 8-percent, 10-year bonds issued at a premium. The premium is recorded in a separate liability-adjunct account.		

The extra $7,100 received by Macaulay Corporation at the time of issue represents an extra amount that the market is willing to lend in return for being paid $80 per year rather than $70 per year per bond. Since the market required only $70 per year, but is being paid $80 per year, a portion of each coupon payment represents a return of the principal amount lent to Macaulay Corporation. Macaulay Corporation borrowed $107,100. Observe that interest for the first 6-month period under the effective interest method is only $3,748.50 (= .035 × $107,100). Macaulay Corporation pays $4,000 in cash at the end of the first 6-month period. The difference, $251.50 (= $4,000.00 − $3,748.50), is a partial return of principal to the lenders.

When the bonds are issued at a premium, an amortization schedule such as the one shown in Exhibit 10.3 is prepared. The total premium amortization (sum of the partial principal repayments) over the life of the bond issue will be exactly $7,100. The journal entries made on December 31, 1979, to recognize interest expense and on January 2, 1980, to record the interest payment would be

12/31/79	Interest Expense	3,748.50	
	Premium on Debenture Bonds Payable	251.50	
	Interest Payable		4,000.00
	To record the accrual of interest and amortization of premium for 6 months.		
1/2/80	Interest Payable	4,000.00	
	Cash		4,000.00
	To record payment of 6 months' interest.		

Entries similar to these but with different amounts will continue until July 1, 1989, when the bond premium will be completely amortized and the face value of the bonds will be paid.

EXHIBIT 10.3
**Effective-Interest Premium
Amortization Schedule
for $100,000 of 8-Percent,
10-Year Bonds Issued for 107.1
Percent of Par to Yield 7 Percent,
Interest Payable Semiannually**

SEMIANNUAL JOURNAL ENTRY

Dr. Interest Expense . . . .   Amount in Column (3)
Dr. Premium on Debenture Bonds Payable . . . . .   Amount in Column (5)
  Cr. Cash . . . .   Amount in Column (4)

| Period (6-month Intervals) (1) | Liability at Start of Period (2) | Effective Interest 3½ Percent per Period (3) | Coupon Rate: 4 Percent of Par (4) | Premium Amortization (5) | End of Period | |
					Unamortized Premium (6)	Net Liability (7)
0					$7,100.00	$107,100.00
1	$107,100.00	$ 3,748.50	$ 4,000.00	$ 251,50	6,848.50	106.848.50
2	106,848.50	3,739.70	4,000.00	260.30	6,588.20	106,588.20
3	106,588.20	3,730.59	4,000.00	269.41	6,318.79	106,318.79
4	106,318.79	3,721.16	4,000.00	278.84	6,039.95	106,039.95

(calculations continued for 20 periods)

20	100,483.09	3,516.91	4,000.00	483.09	0	100,000.00
Total		$72,900.00	$80,000.00	$7,100.00		

Column (2) = Column (7) from Previous Period
Column (3) = .035 × Column (2)
Column (4)   Given
Column (5) = Column (4) − Column (3)
Column (6) = Column (6) from Previous Period − Column (5) of This Period
Column (7) = Column (2) − Column (5)
        = $100,000.00 + Column (6)

The Premium on Debenture Bonds Payable account, like the parallel Discount account when the market rate exceeds the coupon rate, represents an adjustment in the amount of borrowing. When premium is amortized, either at an interest-payment date or at the end of an accounting period, the journal entry shows that interest expense is *less* than the amount of cash paid out for redemption of coupons.

The interest expense on the loan each period is the effective interest rate at time of issue, 3.5 percent per 6-month period in the example, multiplied by the amount of the principal borrowed each period. The amount of interest expense declines from period to period. Because $4,000 cash is paid each period, the amount of principal repaid must therefore *increase* from period to period.

The Premium on Bonds Payable account is an adjunct to, or an addition to, the liability account, Debenture Bonds Payable.

Straight-Line Amortization of Bond Premium   As in the case of discount amortization, a straight-line method could be used. In the straight-line method, the amount of premium amortization recorded each period will be constant. (In the example, the total premium to be amortized over 20 six-month periods is $7,100. The amount to be amortized each 6-month period is $355 (= $7,100/20). The entry each 6 months is

Interest Expense	3,645	
Premium on Debenture Bonds Payable	355	
Cash		4,000

Since the principal amount borrowed each period declines, this results in showing an ever-declining interest *rate*. In the effective-interest method, the interest rate is constant and the dollar amount of premium amortization increases.

Amortization of Bond Premium in the Statement of Changes in Financial Position

When the amount of expense is less than the amount of cash that is paid for that expense, there must be an adjustment on the funds statement. More funds are used for the semiannual payment than are reported as interest expense. Thus, in deriving funds provided from operations, the amount of premium amortization might be *subtracted* from net income. This is the procedure we prefer. Alternatively, because the extra funds were used as a reduction of the effective liability, the amount of premium amortization might be shown as an "other" use of funds (debt retirement) below funds provided by operations.

Bond Retirement

Many bonds remain outstanding until the stated maturity date. The company pays the final coupon, $4,000 in the Macaulay example, and the face amount, $100,000 in the example, on the stated maturity date. The journal entry would depend on the original issue terms. Only the retirement of the original issue at par is illustrated here. (The entry recognizing expense and payment is shown as one for convenience.)

7/1/89	Interest Expense	4,000	
	Debenture Bonds Payable	100,000	
	Cash		104,000

Retirement at maturity of bonds originally issued along with payment for final coupons and recognition of interest expense.

Retirement Before Maturity It is not unusual for a firm to enter the marketplace and to purchase its own bonds before maturity. Interest rates constantly change. Assume that Macaulay Corporation originally issued its bonds at par to yield 8 percent compounded semiannually. Assume that 5 years later, on July 1, 1984, interest rates in the marketplace have increased so that the market then requires a 10-percent interest rate to be paid by Macaulay Corporation. Refer to Table 6 at the back of the book, 5-year column, 10-percent row, where you will see that 8-percent bonds with 5 years until maturity will sell in the marketplace for 92.2783 percent of par if the current interest rate is 10 percent compounded semiannually.

The marketplace is not constrained by the principles of historical-cost accounting. Even though Macaulay Corporation continues to show the Debenture Bonds Payable on the balance sheet at $100,000, the marketplace puts a price of only $92,278 on the entire bond issue. From the point of view of the marketplace, these bonds are the same as bonds issued on July 1, 1984, at an effective yield of 10 percent and so carry a discount of $7,722 (= $100,000 − $92,278).

If Macaulay Corporation goes out into the marketplace on July 1, 1984, to purchase, say, $10,000 of par value of its own bonds, it would have to pay only $9,228 (= .92278 × $10,000) for those bonds. The journal entries it would make at the time of purchase are

7/1/84	Interest Payable	4,000	
	Cash		4,000
	To record redemption of coupons, as usual.		
	Debenture Bonds Payable	10,000	
	Cash		9,228
	Gain on Retirement of Bonds		772
	To record purchase of bonds for less than the current amount shown in the accounting records.		

The adjustment to give equal debits and credits in the second journal entry is recorded as a gain. The gain arises because the firm is able to retire a liability recorded at one amount, $10,000, for a cash payment, $9,228, which is less than that amount. This gain actually occurred as interest rates increased between 1979 and 1984. In historical-cost accounting, the gain is reported only when realized—in the period of bond retirement. This phenomenon is analogous to a firm's purchasing marketable securities, holding those securities as prices increase, selling the securities in a subsequent year, and reporting all the gain in the year of sale. It is caused by the historical-cost accounting convention of recording amounts at historical cost and not recording increases in wealth until those increases are realized in arm's-length transactions with outsiders.

During the 1970s, interest rates jumped upward from their levels in the 1960s. Many companies had issued bonds at prices near par with coupon rates of only 3 or 4 percent per year in the 1960s. When interest rates in the 1970s jumped to 10 or 12 percent per year, these bonds sold in the marketplace for substantial discounts. Many companies went into the marketplace and repurchased their own bonds, recording substantial gains in the process. (In one year Pan American World Airlines was able to report profits after 7 consecutive years of losses. Pan Am had gains on bond retirement that year in excess of the entire amount of net income.)

Since there is no alternative in historical-cost accounting to showing a gain (or loss) on bond retirement (the debits must equal the credits) and since the FASB is reluctant to let companies manage their own reported income by repurchasing bonds, it has required that all gains and losses on bond retirements be reported in the income statement as *extraordinary* items.[7]

Special Provisions for Bond Retirement

Serial Bonds   If the issuing firm is required to make a special provision for retiring the bond issue, the details of that requirement will be spelled out in the bond indenture. There are two major types of retirement provisions. One provides that certain portions of the principal amount will come due on a succession of maturity dates; the bonds of such issues are known as *serial bonds*. (The bonds considered so far in this chapter are not serial bonds.)

Sinking-Fund Bonds   The other major type of retirement provision stipulates that the firm must accumulate a fund of cash or other assets that will be used to pay the bonds when the maturity date arrives or to reacquire and retire portions of the bond issue from time to time. Funds of this type are commonly known as *sinking funds,* although *bond-retirement funds* would be a more descriptive term. The sinking fund is usually held by the trustee of the bond issue. It is shown on the balance sheet as a noncurrent asset in the "Investments" section.

Refunded Bonds   Some bond issues make no provision for installment repayment or for accumulating sinking funds for the payment of the bonds when they come due. Such bonds are usually well protected with property held by the trustees as security or by the high credit standing of the issuer. Under these circumstances, the entire bond liability may be paid at maturity out of cash in the bank at that time. Quite commonly, however, this procedure is not followed. Instead the bond issue is *refunded*—a new set of bonds is issued to obtain the funds to retire the old ones when they come due.

Callable Bonds   A common provision gives the issuing company the right to retire portions of the bond issue before maturity if it so desires, but does not require it do so. In order to facilitate such reacquisition and retirement of a part of the bond issue, the bond indenture usually provides that the bonds shall be *callable*. That is, the issuing company will have the right to reacquire its bonds at prices specified in the bond indenture. The *call price* is usually set a few percentage points above the par value and declines as the maturity date approaches. Because the call provision may be exercised by the issuing company at a time when the market rate of interest is less than the coupon rate, callable bonds usually are sold in the marketplace for something less than otherwise similar, but noncallable, bonds.

Assume, for example, that a firm had issued 8-percent semiannual coupon bonds

---

[7]   Financial Accounting Standards Board, *Statement of Financial Accounting Standards No. 4,* 1975.

at par, but market interest rates and the firm's credit standing at a later date would currently allow it to borrow at 6 percent. The firm would be paying more to borrow the face value than it would have to pay if the bonds were issued currently. If $100,000 par value bonds issued at par are called at 105, the entry, in addition to the one to record the accrued interest expense, would be

Debenture Bonds Payable	100,000	
Loss on Retirement of Bonds	5,000	
Cash		105,000
Bonds called and retired.		

This loss, like the analogous gain, recognized on bond retirement must be classified as an extraordinary item in the income statement.

If the bonds were originally issued at a discount (or premium), then the appropriate portion of the unamortized discount (or premium) must also be retired when the bonds are called or otherwise retired. Suppose that $100,000 par value bonds were issued at a premium several years ago and that the unamortized premium is now $3,500. If $10,000 par value bonds are called at 105, the entry to record the retirement would be

Bonds Payable	10,000	
Premium on Bonds Payable	350	
Loss on Retirement of Bonds	150	
Cash		10,500
Partial retirement of bonds originally issued at a premium. The Loss is an extraordinary item.		

The market rate of interest a firm must pay depends on two factors: the general level of interest rates and its own creditworthiness. If the market rate of interest has risen since bonds were issued (or the firm's credit rating has declined), the bonds will sell in the market at less than issue price. A firm that wanted to retire such bonds would not *call* them, because the call price is typically greater than the issue price. Instead the firm would purchase its bonds in the open market and realize a gain on the retirement of bonds.

CONTRACTS AND LONG-TERM NOTES

Real estate is often purchased on a *land contract*. Equipment is frequently acquired on the installment plan, and the liability is called an *equipment contract*. Payments on such contracts are usually made monthly. Sometimes an explicit interest rate is provided in the contract, whereas in other cases so-called *carrying charges* are added to the purchase price, and the total is divided over a certain number of months without any specific charge being indicated for interest. A common arrangement, particularly in the case of real estate, is to have a regular monthly payment which is applied first to interest accrued since the last payment, with the balance of the payment reducing the principal.

When there is no explicit mention of interest on such a long-term contract or note, generally accepted accounting principles require that the liability be shown at its present value.[8] The difference between the present value and the face value of the liability represents the interest to be paid over the period of the loan. It is shown as a discount that is treated much the same as the discount on bonds payable. The discount is amortized over the life of the liability as periodic interest expense is recognized.

There are two acceptable ways to determine the present value of the liability. The first is to use the market value of the assets acquired. For example, if equipment that has a list price of $12,000 but can be bought for $10,500 cash is purchased in return for a single-payment note with face amount $13,500 payable in 3 years, then the implied interest rate is about $8\frac{3}{4}$ percent per year. (That is, $1.0875^3 \times \$10,500$ is approximately equal to $13,500.) The journal entry would be

Equipment	10,500	
Discount on Long-Term Note Payable	3,000	
Long-Term Note Payable		13,500

To record purchase of equipment with known cash price. Discount is inferred from known cash price of equipment.

At the end of each accounting period that intervenes between the acquisition of the equipment and repayment of the note, journal entries would be made to recognize interest expense. Assume that the first accounting period ends 6 months after the note is issued and that the second accounting period ends 1 year later, 18 months after the original issue. The entries would be

(1) Interest Expense	459	
Discount on Long-Term Note Payable		459

Entry made 6 months after issue of note. Interest is .0875 $\times$ $10,500 $\times$ 6/12. The amount is not paid in cash but is added to the principal amount of the liability by a reduction in the amount of the Discount. The entry to the Discount account is a credit. Liabilities increase with credits, whether the amount is credited directly to the liability or to its contra.

(2) Interest Expense	959	
Discount on Long-Term Notes Payable		959

Entry made 1 year after entry above, $1\frac{1}{2}$ years after issue of note. Interest assuming annual compounding is .0875 $\times$ ($10,500 + $459).

The discount would be completely amortized at the time of the single payment of $13,500. $3,000 of that amount would represent interest accumulated on the note since its issue.

If undeveloped land had been purchased with the same 3-year note, the firm might not be able to establish the current market value of the asset acquired. The firm would then use the interest rate it would have to pay for a similar loan in the open market to find the present value of the note. This is the second acceptable method for quantifying the amount of the liability. Suppose that the market rate for notes such as the one above is 8 percent compounded annually, rather than $8\frac{3}{4}$ percent. The present

---

[8]   *APB Opinion No. 21*, 1971.

value at 8 percent per year of the $13,500 note due in 3 years is $10,717 (= $13,500 × .79383; see Example 4 in Appendix B at the end of the book). The entry to record the purchase of land and payment with the note would be

Land	10,717	
Discount on Long-Term Note Payable	2,783	
Long-Term Note Payable		13,500
To record purchase of land. Cost of land is inferred from known interest rate.		

A note that is the long-term liability of the borrower is a long-term asset of the lender. Generally accepted accounting principles require the lender to show the asset in the Long-Term Note Receivable account at its present value. The rate at which the lender discounts the note should in theory be the same as that used by the borrower, but in practice the two rates often differ.

LEASES

Many firms acquire rights to use assets through long-term noncancelable leases. A company might, for example, agree to lease an airplane for 15 years, or a building for 40 years, promising to pay a fixed periodic fee for the duration of the lease. Promising to make an irrevocable series of lease payments commits the firm just as surely as a bond indenture or mortgage, and the accounting is similar.

Here we examine the accounting for long-term, noncancelable leases, how the accounting treatments for short-term and long-term leases differ, and the effects on the financial statements of both treatments.

Suppose that the Myers Company wants to acquire a minicomputer that has a 3-year life and costs $30,000, and assume that Myers Company can borrow money for 3 years at 8 percent per year. The computer manufacturer is willing to sell the equipment for $30,000 or to lease it for 3 years. Myers Company is responsible for property taxes, maintenance, and repairs of the computer whether leased or purchased.

Assume that the lease is signed on January 1, 1979, and that payments on the lease are due on December 31, 1979, 1980, and 1981. In practice, lease payments are usually made in advance, but the computations in the example are simpler if we assume payments at the end of the year. Compound-interest computations show that each lease payment must be $11,641. (The present value of $1 paid at the end of this year and each of the next 2 years is $2.5771 when the interest rate is 8 percent per year. See Table 4 at the end of the book. Since the lease payments must have present value of $30,000, each payment must be $30,000/2.5771 = $11,641.)

Operating-Lease Method

In an *operating lease,* the owner, or lessor, merely transfers the rights to use the property to the lessee for specified periods of time. The telephone company leases telephones by the month, and car rental companies lease cars by the day or week on an operating basis. If the Myers Company lease is cancelable and Myers Company can stop making payments and return the computer at any time, then the lease is an operating lease. No entry would be made on January 1, 1979, when the lease is signed, and the following entry would be made on each of the dates December 31, 1979, 1980, and 1981:

```
Rent Expense ....................................................    11,641
  Cash ..........................................................             11,641
To recognize annual expense of leasing computer.
```

Capital-Lease Method

If this lease is noncancelable, then the lease arrangement would be viewed as a form of borrowing to purchase the computer. It would be accounted for as a capital lease.[9] This treatment recognizes the signing of the lease as the simultaneous acquisition of a long-term asset, called a *leasehold,* and the incurring of a long-term liability for lease payments. At the time the lease is signed, both the leasehold and the liability are recorded on the books at the present value of the liability, $30,000 in the example.

The entry made at the time Myers Company signed its 3-year noncancelable lease would be

```
Asset—Computer Leasehold .........................................    30,000
  Liability—Present Value of Lease Obligations .........................             30,000
To recognize acquisition of asset and the related liability.
```

At the end of the year, two separate entries must be made. The leasehold is a long-term asset and, like most long-term assets, it must be amortized over its useful life. The first entry made at the end of each year recognizes the amortization of the leasehold asset. Assuming that Myers Company uses straight-line amortization of its leasehold, the entry made at the end of 1979, 1980, and 1981 would be

```
Amortization Expense (on Computer Leasehold) .......................    10,000
  Asset—Computer Leasehold ........................................             10,000
```

(An alternative treatment would be to credit a contra-asset account, Accumulated Amortization of Computer Leasehold.) The second entry made at the end of each year recognizes the lease payment, which is part payment of interest on the liability and part reduction in the liability itself. The entries made at the end of each of the 3 years would be

```
December 31, 1979:
Interest Expense ..................................................    2,400
Liability—Present Value of Lease Obligations .........................    9,241
  Cash ..........................................................             11,641
To recognize lease payment, interest on liability for year (.08 × $30,000 = $2,400)
and the plug for reduction in the liability. The present value of the liability after
this entry is $20,759 = $30,000 − $9,241.
```

---

[9] Financial Accounting Standards Board, *Statement of Financial Accounting Standards No. 13,* 1976.

December 31, 1980:

Interest Expense	1,661	
Liability—Present Value of Lease Obligations	9,980	
Cash		11,641

To recognize lease payment, interest on liability for year (.08 × $20,759 = $1,661)
and the plug for reduction in the liability. The present value of the liability after
this entry is $10,779 = $20,759 − $9,980.

December 31, 1981:

Interest Expense	862	
Liability—Present Value of Lease Obligations	10,779	
Cash		11,641

To recognize lease payment, interest on liability for year (.08 × $10,779 = $862)
and the plug for reduction in the liability. The present value of the liability after
this entry is zero (= $10,779 − $10,779).

Exhibit 10.4 shows the amortization schedule for this lease. Note that its form is
exactly the same as in the mortgage amortization schedule shown in Exhibit 10.1.

EXHIBIT 10.4
Amortization Schedule for $30,000 Lease Liability, Repaid in Three Annual Installments of $11,641 Each, Interest Rate 8 Percent, Compounded Annually

---

ANNUAL JOURNAL ENTRY

Dr. Interest Expense	Amount in Column (3)
Dr. Liability—Present Value	
of Lease Obligations	Amount in Column (5)
Cr. Cash	Amount in Column (4)

Year (1)	Lease Liability Start of Year (2)	Interest Expense for Year (3)	Payment (4)	Portion of Payment Reducing Lease Liability (5)	Lease Liability End of Year (6)
0					$30,000
1	$30,000	$2,400	$11,641	$ 9,241	20,759
2	20,759	1,661	$11,641	9,980	10,779
3	10,779	862	$11,641	10,779	0

Column (2) = Column (6), Previous Period
Column (3) = .08 × Column (2)
Column (4)　　Given
Column (5) = Column (4) − Column (3)
Column (6) = Column (2) − Column (5)

Both of these schedules use the effective-interest method of computing interest each period.[10]

Notice that, in the capital-lease method, the total expense over the 3 years is $34,923, consisting of $30,000 (= $10,000 + $10,000 + $10,000) for amortization expense and $4,923 (= $2,400 + $1,661 + $862) for interest expense. This is exactly the same as the total expense recognized under the operating-lease method described above. The difference between the operating-lease method and the capital method is the *timing* of the expense recognition and the entries in income statement and balance sheet accounts. The capital-lease method recognizes both the asset, leasehold, and the liability, and also recognizes expense sooner than does the operating-lease method, as summarized in Exhibit 10.5

EXHIBIT 10.5
Comparison of Expense Recognized Under Operating and Capital-Lease Methods

	Expense Recognized Each Year Under	
Year	Operating-Lease Method	Financing-Lease Method
1979	$11,641	$12,400 (= $10,000 + $2,400)
1980	11,641	11,661 (= 10,000 + 1,661)
1981	11,641	10,862 (= 10,000 + 862)
Total	$34,923[a]	$34,923 (= $30,000[b] + $4,923[c])

[a] Rent expense.
[b] Amortization expense.
[c] Interest expense.

Criteria for Choosing the Accounting Method   In this simple example, expense under the capital-lease method is only slightly larger than expense under the operating-lease method in the first year. In more realistic cases where the lease extends over 20 years, the expense in the first year under the capital-lease method may be 25 percent larger than under the operating-lease method.

---

[10] Constructing the last row of an amortization schedule is just as easy as the first. Consider that the final cash payment must discharge the remaining principal and interest on that principal for the last period. That is,

Final Cash Payment = Principal Repayment + (Interest on Principal Repayment)
Final Cash Payment = Principal Repayment (1 + Interest Rate)
Principal Repayment = Final Cash Payment/(1 + Interest Rate).

In the example in Exhibit 10.4, the final cash payment is $11,641 and the interest rate is 8 percent. Thus, the final principal repayment is $10,779 (= $11,641/1.08) and the interest expense for the last period can be computed in either of two ways as $862 (= .08 × $10,779 = $11,641 − $10,779).

Most firms prefer to use the operating-lease method whenever they can for two reasons:

1 The reported income is higher in the early years than it would be under the capital-lease method, and
2 There is no need to show an account, Present Value of the Lease Obligations, as a liability on the balance sheet. Thus, the debt-equity ratio is not significantly affected under the operating-lease method.

The FASB has established relatively stringent requirements for accounting for long-term noncancelable leases. A lease must be accounted for as a capital lease if it meets any one of four conditions.[11] The most stringent of these conditions compares the contractual lease payments discounted at an "appropriate" market interest rate with 90 percent of the fair market value of the asset at the time the lease is signed. (The interest rate must be appropriate given the creditworthiness of the lessee.) When the present value of lease payments exceeds 90 percent of the fair market value, then the capital lease method must be used. The major risks and rewards of ownership have been transferred from the lessor (landlord) to the lessee. Thus the lessee has in economic substance acquired an asset and agreed to pay for it under a long-term contract, to be recognized as a liability. Another criterion is that the capital-lease method must be used if the lease covers 75 percent or more of the asset's expected economic life.

DEFERRED INCOME TAXES

As we have indicated at various points in this book, there are some areas where there are alternative generally accepted accounting principles. The tax laws and regulations similarly allow a choice of alternative treatments for the same event. One example is in the calculation of depreciation charges. Both generally accepted accounting principles and the tax law allow the firm to choose from among straight-line, sum-of-the-years'-digits, and double-declining-balance methods of depreciation.

In selecting among alternative methods for tax purposes, management often tries to minimize the present value of the firm's tax liabilities for a given set of operating results. The principles of income tax management are summarized conveniently by the expression, "Pay the least amount of tax, as late as possible, within the law." This is sometimes known as the *least and latest* rule. It is difficult to generalize about which of the alternative accounting principles management selects, or should select, for financial reporting. This question is discussed more fully in Chapters 9 and 13.

Suppose that, for whatever reasons it deems appropriate, management decides to use straight-line depreciation for a given plant asset for financial reporting. Suppose, further, that management has calculated that the present value of taxes paid will be smallest if the sum-of-the-years'-digits method is used for tax purposes. The firm is allowed to use straight-line for financial reporting and sum-of-the-years'-digits for taxes. The firm will thereby show a higher pretax income in its financial reports than in its tax return in the early years of the asset's life. This is permissible, but the firm

---

[11] Financial Accounting Standards Board, *Statement of Financial Accounting Standards No. 13,* 1976, paragraph 7.

must report as income tax expense in its income statement the amount of taxes that would have resulted had it used the straight-line method for tax reporting.[12] The difference between the actual tax payment that results from using the accelerated method and the tax payment that *would have* resulted had it used the straight-line method for tax reporting is credited to a Deferred Income Tax Liability account.

Illustration

The problems of deferred income taxes can perhaps be best understood by examining an example. Assume that Drake, Inc., pays income taxes at the rate of 40 percent of taxable income. Suppose that Drake purchased a plant asset for $150,000 that has a 5-year life and an estimated salvage value of zero. Suppose further that this asset produces an excess of revenues over operating expenses (other than depreciation) of $44,000 a year. That is, after paying for the costs of running and maintaining the asset, the firm enjoys a $44,000-per-year excess of revenue over expenses (except depreciation). Drake uses straight-line depreciation for financial reporting and the sum-of-the-years'-digits method for calculating its taxes. Thus, in the first year the new plant asset is used, depreciation on the financial records will be $30,000 (= $150,000/5) and on the tax return will be $50,000 (= $150,000 × 5/15). Suppose that in addition to the $44,000 from the plant asset, other pretax income for each year is $80,000. Exhibit 10.6 summarizes the computation of taxes for financial reporting and for tax purposes.

EXHIBIT 10.6
Deferred Income Tax
Computations for Drake, Inc.

FIRST YEAR	Financial Reports	Tax Return
Other Pretax Income	$80,000	$ 80,000
Excess of Revenues over Expenses (Except Depreciation) from Plant Asset	44,000	44,000
Depreciation	(30,000)	(50,000)
Income Before Taxes	$94,000	$ 74,000
Income Tax Expense (at 40 percent)	$37,600	
Income Tax Currently Payable (at 40 percent)		$ 29,600
FIFTH YEAR		
Other Pretax Income	$80,000	$ 80,000
Excess of Revenues over Expenses (Except Depreciation) from Plant Asset	44,000	44,000
Depreciation	(30,000)	(10,000)
Income Before Taxes	$94,000	$114,000
Income Tax Expense (at 40 percent)	$37,600	
Income Tax Currently Payable (at 40 percent)		$ 45,600

---

[12] *APB Opinion No. 11*, 1967.

Notice that by using the accelerated method on its tax return, Drake, Inc., has income taxes payable in the first year of $29,600 and income taxes payable in the fifth year of $45,600. If Drake, Inc., did not recognize a deferred tax liability, it would show $16,000 smaller expense (= $29,600 − $45,600) in the first year than in the fifth. Consequently, it would show $16,000 larger net income in the first year than in the fifth. In this case the difference in income would result solely from the "borrowing" of income tax deductions in the first year from later years (as we demonstrate below in Exhibit 10.7).

Generally accepted accounting principles are uncomfortable with the notion that in such a situation, income would decline for 5 years on the financial statements. The reason for the decline is predictable during the first year because it is caused by a difference in the depreciation methods used in financial statements and the tax return. The tax reduction in the first year, relative to the fifth, is a difference that will reverse with the mere passage of time. Generally accepted accounting principles prefer that the reported income be the same in each year because pretax income on the financial statements is the same each year. The appropriate accounting matches income tax expense and pretax book income rather than income tax expense and taxable income.

Generally accepted accounting principles require that income tax expense under these conditions be computed as though straight-line depreciation were used on the tax return. Under such an assumption, income tax expense would be $37,600 each year. Since only $29,600 is payable in the first year, the following entry would be made:

Income Tax Expense	37,600	
Income Tax Payable		29,600
Deferred Income Tax Liability		8,000

First year income tax entry; expense is larger than cash payment; liability is created.

Notice that $8,000 of tax expense did not use working capital, so that an addback to net income is required in the statement of changes in financial position in deriving "funds provided by operations." The $8,000 of expense merely increases the noncurrent liability for deferred income taxes. The statement of changes in financial position of International Corporation, in Exhibit A.3 on page 581, illustrates the addback to net income for deferred taxes in arriving at working capital provided by operations.

If only one asset is considered, the $8,000 tax not paid, but credited to the Deferred Income Tax Liability account, is not forgiven by the government. Instead, these payments are merely delayed. So far as this one asset is concerned, the taxes will be paid in the fifth year. The bottom panel of Exhibit 10.6 shows the computation of Income Taxes Payable in the fifth year to be $45,600. Since the financial statements will have Income Tax Expense computed under the assumption that straight-line depreciation is used on the tax return, the reported Income Tax Expense will remain $37,600. Since the actual tax payment must be $45,600, however, the journal entry to recognize the income tax expense for the fifth year is

Income Tax Expense	37,600	
Deferred Income Tax Liability	8,000	
Income Tax Payable		45,600

Fifth-year income tax entry; expense is less than cash payment; liability is discharged.

EXHIBIT 10.7
Summary of Deferred Income Tax Liability Account for Drake, Inc.

ANNUAL JOURNAL ENTRY

Dr. Income Tax Expense	Amount in Column (5)	
or { Dr. Deferred Income Tax Liability	Amount in Column (9)	
Cr. Deferred Income Tax Liability	Amount in Column (10)	
Cr. Income Taxes Payable	Amount in Column (8)	

		Financial Statements			Tax Returns			Deferred Income Tax Liability Account		
Year (1)	Income Before Depreciation and Tax Expenses (2)	Depreciation Expense (3)	Pretax Income (4)	Tax Expense (5)[a]	Depreciation Deduction (6)[b]	Pretax Income (7)[c]	Taxes Payable (8)[d]	Debit (9)	Credit (10)	Credit Balance at Year-End (11)
1	$124,000	$ 30,000	$ 94,000	$ 37,600	$ 50,000	$ 74,000	$ 29,600		$8,000	$ 8,000
2	124,000	30,000	94,000	37,600	40,000	84,000	33,600		4,000	12,000
3	124,000	30,000	94,000	37,600	30,000	94,000	37,600	—	—	12,000
4	124,000	30,000	94,000	37,600	20,000	104,000	41,600	$4,000		8,000
5	124,000	30,000	94,000	37,600	10,000	114,000	45,600	8,000		0
		$150,000	$470,000	$188,000	$150,000	$470,000	$188,000			

[a] 40 × $94,000.
[b] ($170,000 − $20,000) × t/15, where t = 5, 4, 3, 2, 1 for the years, in order.
[c] $124,000 − (6).
[d] (7) × .40.

More working capital ($45,600) is used than the amount of the expense ($37,600) reported in the income statement. Consequently, there must be a subtraction of $8,000 in the statement of changes in financial position to derive "working capital provided by operations."

Exhibit 10.7 shows a summary of the entries in Drake's Deferred Income Tax Liability account for the 5 years during which it uses the plant asset. Observe that the total tax expense shown on the financial statements over the asset's life is the same as the total taxes payable, but that the accelerated method used on the tax returns defers payment and thus leads to a lower present value of taxes paid.

Timing Differences and Permanent Differences

In general, the deferred income tax liability arises from differences in timing between financial reporting of revenues and expenses and tax reporting of these items. The following list shows some of the ways in which the timing differences can arise.

1 Depreciation for tax purposes is different from that shown in the financial records in a given period either because different depreciation methods or different asset lives, or both, are used for the two purposes.
2 Income from credit sales is recognized in the financial records in the year of sale, but recognized for tax purposes in the year when cash is collected from customers.
3 Income from long-term construction projects is recognized in financial records on the percentage-of-completion basis but on tax returns under the completed-contract basis.

Some differences between reported income and taxable income will never reverse. These include items of revenue that are never taxed or expenses that are never deductible in computing income taxes payable. An example is interest revenue on tax-exempt municipal bonds held as asset. Such tax-exempt interest is part of reported income but not of taxable income. Differences between reported income and taxable income that can never reverse are called *permanent differences.* Permanent differences do not require recognition of deferred income taxes.

Income Tax Accounting Summarized   Income taxes payable computed on the tax return are based on accounting principles selected by the firm, generally to minimize the present value of the cash burden for income taxes. Income tax expense shown in the financial statements is computed from a measure of taxable income determined using the financial statement's accounting principles for timing differences, rather than the tax return's accounting principles. The excess of income tax expense over income taxes payable, if any, is credited to the Deferred Income Taxes balance sheet account. The excess of income taxes payable over income tax expense, if any, is debited to the Deferred Income Taxes balance sheet account. If the Deferred Income Taxes account has a credit balance, then it appears on the balance sheet among the equities, usually as a liability. If the Deferred Income Taxes account has a debit balance, then it appears on the balance sheet among the assets.

Disclosure of Deferred Income Taxes in Financial Statements

Generally accepted accounting principles require the firm to recognize the deferred income tax expense. The account credited when the deferred income tax expense is recognized has a special nature which Accounting Principles Board Opinion No. 11 says is a "deferred credit" and not a liability.[13] Since we feel that the right-hand side of the balance sheet logically contains only liabilities and owners' equity items, we classify the Deferred Income Tax Liability as an *indeterminate-term liability*.

Notes to financial statements contain a wealth of information about income taxes. Among the items of information included is the amount of deferred tax expense for the year caused by each of the several important timing differences. This disclosure is illustrated on page 585 (in Appendix A) for International Corporation.

Typically, the financial statements do not disclose the amount of deductions claimed on the tax return. The information in the notes about deferred taxes can be used to deduce many of them. For example, the financial statements of Drake, Inc., for the first year in our example show depreciation expense of $30,000. The notes disclose both that the deferred tax expense caused by depreciation timing differences is $8,000 and that the income tax rate is 40 percent of pretax income. From these data, we can deduce that depreciation claimed on the tax return exceeded depreciation expense on the financial statements by $20,000 (= $8,000/.40). Thus, depreciation claimed on the tax return must have been $50,000 (= $30,000 + $20,000).

Weaknesses of the Accounting for Deferred Income Taxes

As the example for Drake, Inc., shows, if the deferred income tax liability arises from the depreciation of one asset, it will eventually be paid. But the tax law, by granting the general use of accelerated depreciation methods, has in effect offered an interest-free loan to certain firms. These firms are the going concerns who choose to use the accelerated method on the tax return but who believe that the straight-line method properly reflects depreciation and so use it in financial reporting.

Benefits Ignored   The first weakness of deferred tax accounting is that the benefit of accepting the government's interest-free loan is not explicitly reported in the conventional financial statements. Note that the income statements of Drake, Inc., would look exactly the same as in Exhibit 10.6 if it were to use straight-line depreciation on the tax return. (In fact, Income Tax Expense on Drake's financial statement is computed making the assumption that straight-line depreciation is used on the tax return.) Taxes paid later are less burdensome than taxes paid sooner. The conventional financial statements of most firms fail to recognize this fact of economic life.

Payments Deferred Indefinitely   In reality, a going concern using accelerated depreciation on the tax return may be able to defer payment of the so-called liability indefinitely. If the firm continues to acquire depreciable assets each year (in dollar amounts

---

[13] *APB Opinion No. 11*, 1967.

no less than it acquired in the preceding year), then in every year Income Taxes Payable will *be less than or equal to* Income Tax Expense computed as generally accepted accounting principles require. In no year will there be a debit entry to the Deferred Income Tax account on the balance sheet. Tax payments will exceed tax expense (as in years 4 and 5 of the Drake example) only when the firm stops acquiring new assets while it continues to earn taxable income. This points to two more weaknesses in deferred tax accounting.

The second weakness of deferred tax accounting is that the amount shown on the balance sheet is not a legal obligation (to the federal government or to anyone else). The government levies taxes on taxable income as shown on the tax return and only as it is earned. It does not automatically levy a tax because depreciation deductions decline. The government does not suggest to Drake, Inc., in year 1 that the firm will also be profitable in year 5 and that it has in year 1 a liability for $8,000 due in year 5.

The third weakness of deferred tax accounting is that it seems inapplicable to most going concerns. It is difficult to visualize a firm that actually shrinks in size (as is required for the income taxes payable to exceed income tax expense) and at the same time remains profitable. Most shrinking firms owe no taxes because they fail to earn taxable income. (Refer to the financial statements of W. T. Grant Company on pages 231–234. The deferred tax is probably not going to be paid, and if it is, the time when payment is finally made is not certain.[14]

Uncertain Amount   Still another, but less important, weakness of deferred tax accounting is that if the firm does find at some future date that it has income taxes payable larger than income tax expense, it is unlikely that the tax rate on the income will be the same as the rate at the time the deferred tax expense was originally computed. Tax rates change periodically. Even if the amount does eventually come due, it is not an amount that is currently known with reasonable certainty.

Thus, the deferred income taxes reported on the balance sheet clearly does not have the four attributes of liabilities. It lacks three of them—legal obligation, relative certainty of amount, and relative certainty of payment date. Moreover, unlike long-term

---

[14] Whether timing differences actually reverse remains a controversial question among accounting writers. A majority agree with generally accepted accounting principles on the matter of computing and recognizing deferred income taxes. They argue that the reasons offered against recognizing deferred income tax liabilities also support a conclusion that Accounts Payable are not liabilities either. After all, accounts payable are never paid off in the aggregate for a going concern; in fact, the amount of Accounts Payable usually grows over time.

The critical difference between accounts payable and income taxes, however, is that income taxes are levied on the income of a firm as a whole. Losses or deductions from one project can offset gains or income from another. The government does not tax a firm asset by asset. If a firm shrinks and becomes bankrupt, having no taxable income, then the government does not ask for income tax payments; creditors (those who are due to be paid for the Accounts Payable) will be entitled to payment (or partial payment) from the remaining assets as the firm winds down its business. Accounts Payable do have significance as liabilities even though they may increase year after year. There has been empirical work on this issue of whether there are any, many, or few firms that find taxes payable exceeding tax expense because of reversals of depreciation timing differences. The interested reader can refer to the interchange in the *Journal of Accountancy,* April 1977, pages 53–59, where we and others engage in a debate over some actual data. We think the data show that in an examination of 3,100 companies over 19 years (nearly 60,000 company-years), there are about 700 cases (slightly over 1 percent) of a firm remaining profitable while its depreciable assets shrink in size for the year.

liabilities, this amount is not shown at its present value using a historical market interest rate. It is, after all, conceivable that a given firm might be able to estimate that at some future date it would have income taxes payable larger than income tax expense. In those cases, recognition of a deferred tax liability would be appropriate, but the amount should be shown at its present value, not at the full amount to be paid, say, 5 years in the future.

PENSIONS

Most firms have pension plans that provide for payments to be made to retired former employees. The obligations that employers have to their former employees, in general, meet the four criteria to be shown as a liability. Nevertheless, in most cases, the present value of most corporate pension obligations is merely disclosed in notes to the financial statements, rather than being shown directly in the balance sheet. The accounting problems for pensions are sufficiently complex that they are discussed in Appendix 10.1 to this chapter.

LIABILITIES AS A FORM OF LONG-TERM FINANCING

A firm seeking new equity capital has essentially two choices. It can issue shares to new owners, decreasing the proportionate share of current owners. All of the risks and rewards of ownership then become more widespread. Or it can raise capital by issuing long-term debt. Chapter 6 discusses some of the advantages and disadvantages to using one form of long-term equity versus the other. The potential rewards to financial leverage (using long-term debt instead of issuing additional shares) are great. If the firm can borrow funds for, say, a fixed 8-percent rate and invest them in projects that earn 20 percent, then the owners of common shares will enjoy substantially greater income. The potential rewards of leverage are, however, offset by the increased riskiness of the firm to the owners.

Large amounts of long-term debt imply large amounts of fixed interest charges that must be met each period if the firm is to remain solvent. If the firm cannot meet its required debt-service payments (whether for bonds, mortgages, leases, or pensions), owners will find their investments much less valuable than before. Whether a given firm should use debt financing or ownership equity and whether it even makes a difference (in the long run when all factors are considered) which form is used are questions beyond the scope of financial accounting. These issues are discussed in corporate finance books.

Several commonly used financial statement ratios use liabilities or expenses related to liabilities in the numerator or denominator (for example, interest-coverage ratios and debt-to-equity ratios). Consequently, it is important that readers of financial statements understand what items should be considered to be the liabilities of a firm. As is apparent from the earlier discussion, we think that certain deferred tax items ought not to be considered liabilities and that certain pension items, detailed in Appendix 10.1, which are not, should be. Several of the problems at the end of this chapter explore the effects of reclassifying these items for some real companies.

CONTINGENT LIABILITIES—POTENTIAL OBLIGATIONS

One of the criteria used by the accountant to recognize a liability is that there be a legal obligation. The world of business and law is full of uncertainties. At any given time a firm may find itself potentially liable for events that have occurred in the past. This so-called contingent liability is, in fact, not an accounting liability. It is not currently a legal obligation but a potential future obligation. It arises from an event that has occurred in the past but whose outcome is not now known. Whether or not the item becomes a liability, and how large a liability it will become, depends on a future event, such as the outcome of a lawsuit.

Suppose that the company is sued for damages in a formal court proceeding for an accident involving a customer who was visiting the company. The suit is not scheduled for trial until after the close of the accounting period. If the company's lawyers and auditors agree that the outcome is likely to be favorable for the company or that, if unfavorable, the amount of the damage settlement will not be large, then no liability will be recognized on the balance sheet. The notes to the financial statements must disclose, however, significant contingent liabilities.

The FASB has said that an estimated loss from a contingency should be recognized in the accounts only if both of the following conditions are met:[15]

(a) Information available prior to the issuance of the financial statements indicates that it is probable that an asset had been impaired or that a liability had been incurred. . . .

(b) The amount of the loss can be reasonably estimated.

The number of situations that would meet both of these tests seems likely to be small. One example suggested by the FASB Statement is a toy manufacturer who has sold products for which a safety hazard has been discovered. The toy manufacturer thinks it likely that liabilities have been incurred. Test (b) above would be met if experience or other information enabled the manufacturer to make a reasonable estimate of the loss. The journal entry would be

```
Loss on Damage Claim  ..........................................  50,000
   Estimated Liability for Damages  ...................................          50,000
To recognize estimated liability for expected damage arising from safety hazard
of toys sold.
```

The debit in the above entry is to a loss account (presented among other expenses on the income statement), and the credit is to an estimated liability which should be treated as a current liability, similar to the Estimated Warranty Liability account, on the balance sheet. In practice, an account with the title "Estimated Liability for Damages" would seldom, if ever, appear in published financial statements, since it would be perceived as an admission of guilt. Such an admission is likely to adversely

---

[15] Financial Accounting Standards Board, *Statement of Financial Accounting Standards No. 5*, 1975.

affect the outcome of the lawsuit. The liability account would be combined with others for financial statement presentation.

The term *contingent liability* is used only when the item is not recognized in the accounts but, rather, in the footnotes. (Notes receivable sold *with* recourse, described in Chapter 7, are another example of a contingent liability.) A recent annual report of General Motors illustrates the disclosure of contingent liabilities as follows.

> ### Note 15. Contingent Liabilities
> There are various claims and pending actions against the Corporation and its subsidiaries in respect of taxes, product liability, alleged patent infringements, warranties, alleged air pollution, and other matters arising out of the conduct of the business. Certain of these actions purport to be class actions, seeking damages in very large amounts. The amounts of liability on these claims and actions at . . . [year-end] were not determinable but, in the opinion of management, the ultimate liability resulting will not materially affect the consolidated financial position or results of operations of the Corporation and its consolidated subsidiaries.

SUMMARY

Liabilities generally are legal obligations of definite or reasonably certain amounts due at definite or reasonably certain times incurred in return for current or past benefits. Some obligations of the firm do not meet all these criteria but are, nevertheless, treated as liabilities. An example of such a liability is that for deferred income taxes. We suggest that deferred income taxes be viewed as a liability of indeterminate term. Often, obligations under pension plans meet the criteria to be liabilities but are not accounted for as liabilities.

Accounting for long-term liabilities is accomplished by recording these obligations at their present value at the date the obligation is incurred and then showing the change in that present value as the maturity date of the obligation approaches. In historical-cost accounting, the interest rate used throughout the life of the liability is the appropriate market rate at the time the liability was originally incurred. Retirement of long-term liabilities can be brought about in a variety of ways, but in each case, the process is the same. The net obligation is offset against what is given in return, usually cash, with gain or loss on retirement recognized as appropriate.

APPENDIX 10.1
Accounting for Pension Plans

There are almost as many different kinds of pension plans as there are employers who have them. The basic variables of a pension plan are

1 Its requirement for contributions by employers and employees,

2 The kind of promise made by the employer,
3 Vesting provisions,
4 Funding provisions, and
5 Treatment of prior service costs.

Each of these variables is discussed in turn.

Under a *noncontributory* plan, the employee makes no explicit contribution to the pension; only the employer contributes. Under a *contributory* plan both the employee and the employer contribute, but they do not necessarily contribute equal amounts. Employees retain a claim to their explicit contributions under virtually all plans. The employee's rights to the employer's contributions are determined by the *vesting* provisions. The following discussion concerns noncontributory plans or, if the plan is contributory, only the employer's contributions.

A pension plan may be fully vested or partially vested. Under a *fully vested* plan, the employee's rights to pension benefits purchased with the employer's contributions cannot be taken away from the employee. (These benefits are partially insured by an agency of the federal government.) If the rights are not vested, the employee will lose rights to the employer's contributions if he or she leaves the company before retirement. Under *partially vested* (or "graded vesting") plans, rights vest gradually. For example, an employee in the fifth year of work might have no vested rights, but by the time he or she has been employed for 15 years, all rights will be vested. The nature of vesting provisions will influence the expected present value of the pension liabilities generated during an accounting period. If employees leave their jobs, then their rights, and therefore the employer's liabilities, are less if only partially vested than when the rights are fully vested.

A pension plan may be *fully funded* or *partially funded.* Under a fully funded plan, the employer sets aside cash, or pays cash to an outside trustee such as an insurance company, equal to the present value of all expected pension liabilities. Partially funded plans do not have cash available in an amount equal to the present value of all pension obligations. Federal pension law (Employee Retirement Income Security Act—ERISA) mandates certain minimum funding requirements for corporate pension plans.

EMPLOYER PROMISES

Employers make essentially two different kinds of pension promises to employees:

1 Some employers make promises about the amounts to be contributed to the pension plan without specifying the benefits to be received by retired employees (defined-contribution plans).
2 Most employers make promises about the amount each employee will receive during retirement without specifying the amounts the employer will contribute to the plan (defined-benefit plans).

Defined-Contribution Plan

The first type is called a *defined-contribution plan* (or *money-purchase plan*). In such a plan, the employer promises to contribute an amount determined by formula to each employee's pension account. Zenith Radio Corporation, for example, promises to contribute between 6 and 12 percent of income before the contribution (the exact amount depending on some other factors) to the pension plan each year. An employee's share in the company's pension fund depends on his or her annual compensation. Another employer might agree to contribute an amount equal to 5 percent of an employee's salary to a pension fund. Subject to reasonable investment risks, the funds are managed to produce as large a series of payments as is possible during the employee's retirement. No specific promises are made to employees about the amount of the eventual pension. Inputs are defined; total outputs depend on investment performance.

The accounting for defined-contribution plans is particularly simple. If the employer contributes $55,000 to a trustee to be managed for the employee's retirement benefits, the journal entry under generally accepted accounting principles would be

Pension Expense	55,000	
Cash		55,000

Defined-Benefit Plan

Under a *defined-benefit plan,* the employer promises the employee a series of payments at retirement based on a formula. The typical formula takes into account the employee's length of service and average earnings. For example, the employer might promise to pay on retirement an annual pension equal to 30 percent of the average annual salary earned during working years for an employee who has been employed for 5 years. The percentage might increase to 31 percent for 6 years of service, and so on, so that an employee with 30 years of service would get a pension equal to 55 percent of his or her average salary during the working years. The employer must set aside funds currently to fulfill these promises. Outputs are defined; the required inputs must be estimated and depend on factors such as mortality, inflation, investment performance, and future wages.

The rate of return to be earned by the pension funds and the employee's average earnings over his or her working life can be estimated. Thus the accounting for defined-benefit pension plans must take the estimates into account and must be able to cope with misestimates as they become apparent.

Most corporate pension plans are defined-benefit plans. The Federal Pension Act of 1974 (ERISA) makes defined-contribution plans relatively more attractive than they had been previously. The number of defined-contribution plans is increasing, but they still remain a minority. Some employees prefer a defined-benefit plan because it reduces the employee's risk of planning for retirement. Employers tend to prefer defined-contribution plans because of the reduced uncertainty of expenses. The plan used in any given firm is likely to be the result of labor-management negotiations.

GENERALLY ACCEPTED ACCOUNTING PRINCIPLES FOR DEFINED-BENEFIT PLANS

Current Service Benefits—Normal Costs

Generally accepted accounting principles[16] require the corporate employer to show as a cost of the period the present value of the pension liabilities generated during the period under defined-benefit plans. The expense for pensions earned during a given period is called the *normal cost* of that period. Federal law (ERISA) requires that the liabilities generated during the period for normal costs be funded immediately. For example, if actuarial calculations show the expected present value of pension obligations arising from labor services for the year to be $45,000, the entry to recognize the expense is[17]

Pension Expense (Current Service)	45,000	
Pension Liability		45,000
To recognize pension expense for current service and related liability.		

When the pension plan is funded, the entry, assuming that $45,000 is paid to an independent trustee, is

Pension Liability	45,000	
Cash		45,000
To fund pension liability.		

Since federal law requires most companies to fund pension expense for current service in the same year that it is recognized, most companies show no Pension Liability account for current service on their balance sheets. In these cases, the effect of the two entries shown above is often recorded in a single entry:

Pension Expense (Current Service)	45,000	
Cash		45,000
To recognize pension expense for current service and its immediate funding.		

Prior-Service Benefits

When a pension plan is adopted, current employees will usually receive retroactive benefits for services rendered before the plan's adoption. Moreover, from time to time the pension plan may be made more generous; that is, the benefits promised to employees during retirement may be "sweetened." At the time the plan is made more generous, there will usually be retroactive benefits that are given to employees who have been working for several years. Consequently, at any given time, the total expected present value of benefits arising from employees' services may include amounts

---

[16] *APB Opinion No. 8,* November 1966.
[17] If the wages of the workers involved were debited to product cost accounts (such as Work-in-Process Inventory, see Chapter 4), then the pension costs would be product costs, not period expenses.

relating to services rendered during past accounting periods. This amount is called *prior-service cost.*[18]

The present value of the unfunded obligation for prior-service costs is not recognized as a liability in the accounting records, but its amount must be disclosed in the notes to the financial statements.

The obligation for prior-service costs must be amortized and funded, much like a mortgage. To amortize a mortgage, equal periodic payments are made. Part of each payment represents interest on the outstanding loan and part represents repayments of the loan principal. (As time passes and the loan is gradually paid off, a smaller fraction of each payment represents interest and a larger fraction represents payment of principal.) Prior-service costs are similarly amortized and funded with a series of periodic payments.

Generally accepted accounting principles and federal law permit amortization and funding of prior-service costs over a time span chosen by the individual firm, subject to minimum and maximum limitations.

At a minimum, the firm must amortize and fund prior-service costs over 30 or 40 years, depending on the circumstances. That is, the firm must make a series of no more than 30 or 40 annual payments that have a present value equal to the amount of the original prior-service costs. The resulting amounts are the smallest annual payments that can be made for prior-service costs.

The maximum rate at which a firm may amortize prior-service costs under generally accepted accounting principles has been somewhat less than the maximum rate allowed under federal pension law. The issues are beyond the scope of this discussion, but in all cases the prior-service costs must be amortized over a period of 10 years or *more.*

If prior-service costs of $100,000 are to be amortized and funded over 30 years using a discount rate of 6 percent, then the annual expense and funding payment for prior-service costs would be $7,265.[19] The journal entry to recognize the expense would be

```
Pension Expense (Prior Service) ........................................    7,265
    Pension Liability .................................................              7,265
To recognize pension expense for prior-service cost of $100,000 being amortized
and funded over 30 years.
```

The above entry recognizes the pension expense. Its effect is to remove the obligation for pension payments from the footnotes, where it is not recognized as a liability, and to transfer the obligation to the balance sheet where it is shown as an actual liability. When the revenue and expense accounts for the period are closed, the Pension Expense account is closed to income, reducing it, and then to the Retained Earnings

---

[18] The term *past-service cost* also arises in corporate pension accounting. *Past-service cost* at a given time refers to that portion of the benefits granted retroactively at the time of the plan's inception that have not yet been recognized at the given time. Past-service cost is a part of prior-service cost. We shall not use the term *past-service cost* in subsequent discussion. We shall refer to *prior-service cost* even when there have been no "sweetenings" of the plan, since in that case, prior-service cost is exactly equal to past-service cost.

[19] The present value of a $1 annuity for 30 years discounted at 6 percent per year is $13.7648; $100,000/ $13.7648 = $7,265.

account, reducing it. The overall balance sheet effect of this entry is to recognize an increase in a liability and a decrease in owners' equity.

Most corporate pension plans provide for funding of pension liabilities as they are recognized. Thus the corporation making the journal entry just above is likely to make a funding payment of cash of $7,265 to a pension fund and to make the following journal entry:

```
Pension Liability ................................................  7,265
    Cash .......................................................           7,265
To fund liability.
```

Note that the entries recognizing the liability and then funding it could be combined as follows:

```
Pension Expense (Prior Service) ....................................  7,265
    Cash .......................................................           7,265
To recognize and fund pension expense for prior-service costs of $100,000 being
amortized and funded over 30 years.
```

From the point of view of accrual accounting, the funding via cash payment is not required. All accrual accounting requires is that the obligation for both normal costs and prior-service costs be recognized as expenses and recognized as liabilities on a systematic basis. As the obligation is funded, the liability is reduced.

Shortcomings in Generally Accepted Accounting Principles for Prior-Service Costs in Corporate Pension Plans

Recall that a liability is a legal obligation to make a reasonably definite payment at a reasonably definite time in return for a past or current benefit. The obligation to employees for benefits based on prior service meets this definition. The timing of payments is reasonably certain because of specified retirement ages and accurate actuarial estimates of length of life. The amounts of payments are reasonably definite. Actuaries can estimate mortality (both before and after retirement) as well as wage rates. The legal obligation is usually present because of federal law. Thus when a pension plan is brought into existence with retroactive benefits promised for past service or when a plan is sweetened with the sweetenings applying retroactively for prior service, then a liability has been created. Generally accepted accounting principles recognize the amount, but allow it to be merely disclosed in the footnotes as an obligation until amortized, rather than shown in the balance sheet as a liability.

SUMMARY OF CORPORATE PENSION ACCOUNTING

Total corporate pension expense for a period under a defined-benefit plan is made up of the sum of the charge for current-service benefits earned during the period plus the charge for amortization of (including interest on) the prior-service obligation. The generally accepted accounting principle is that obligations for prior-service costs are not recognized as liabilities until an entry is made debiting Pension Expense.

Generally accepted accounting principles tolerate a wide range of treatment for pensions. Certain minimum disclosures should be made. The notes to the balance sheet must disclose:

1 The amount of unfunded prior-service costs, if there are any, and the time over which they are being funded,
2 The amount of vested but funded benefits, almost always an amount less than (1), and
3 Actuarial methods used and the impact of vesting provisions on the expected present value of liabilities.

The required disclosure is illustrated in Note 4 on page 584 in Appendix A at the back of the book for the International Corporation.

The kinds of promises the employer makes as well as the funding and vesting provisions are, of course, matters negotiated between employers and employees, subject to laws passed by the Congress.

QUESTIONS AND PROBLEMS

1 Review the meaning of the following concepts or terms discussed in this chapter.
  a Liability.
  b FICA.
  c Contingent liability and estimated liability.
  d Mortgage, mortgagee, mortgagor.
  e Bond indenture.
  f Coupon bond.
  g Debenture bond.
  h Convertible bond.
  i Discount from and premium over par value of bond.
  j Yield or effective rate on bond.
  k Bond tables.
  l Amortization of bond discount or premium using the straight-line and effective-interest methods.
  m Sinking fund.
  n Serial bonds.
  o Bond refunding.
  p Call price.
  q Capital lease.
  r Operating lease.
  s Deferred income tax expense and liability.
  t Timing difference.
  u Permanent difference.

2 Review the meaning of the following concepts or terms discussed in Appendix 10.1 to this chapter.
  a Pension plan.
  b Defined-benefit plan.
  c Defined-contribution plan.

    d Money-purchase plan.
    e Contributory versus noncontributory plan.
    f Fully funded versus partially funded plan.
    g Fully vested versus partially vested benefits.
    h Normal costs.
    i Past-service cost.
    j Prior-service cost.

3 What factors determine the amount of money a firm actually receives when it offers a bond issue to the market?

4 **a** Why do non-interest-bearing notes have a smaller value at time of issue than at time of maturity?
    b A call premium is the difference between the call price of a bond and its par value. What is the purpose of such a premium?

5 What are the relative advantages and disadvantages of the straight-line method versus the effective-interest method of bond discount (or premium) amortization?

6 **a** Under what circumstances may a deferred tax liability arise? If a firm is growing, what does this imply about when the liability is likely to be paid?
    b How should the deferred income tax liability be treated by an analyst who wishes to study the debt-equity ratio of a business?

7 In what sense is the expense from a lease independent of the method of accounting for it by the lessee?

8 For each of the following items, indicate:

    (1) Does the item meet all of the criteria of the accountant's usual definition of a liability?
    (2) Is the item shown as a liability?
    (3) If the item is recognized as a liability, how is the amount of the liability determined?

    a Interest accrued but not paid on a note.
    b Advances from customers for goods and services to be delivered later.
    c Firm orders from customers for goods and services to be delivered later.
    d Mortgages payable.
    e Bonds payable.
    f Product warranties.
    g Fifteen-year cancelable lease on an office building.
    h Twenty-year noncancelable lease on a factory building.
    i Deferred income taxes.
    j Damages the company must pay if a pending lawsuit is lost.
    k Cost of restoring strip mining sites after mining operations are completed.
    l Obligation to pay pensions under defined-benefit formula for labor services during current year.
    m Obligation to pay pensions under defined-benefit formula for labor services provided before the start of the plan.

9 Anderson Company sells appliances, all for cash. All acquisitions of appliances during a year are debited to the Merchandise Inventory account. The company provides warranties on all its products, guaranteeing to make repairs within 1 year of the date of sale as required for any of its appliances that break down. The company has many years of experience with its products and warranties.

The schedule shown in Exhibit 10.8 contains trial balances for the Anderson Company at the ends of 1979 and 1980. The trial balances for the end of 1979 are the Adjusted Preclosing Trial Balance (after all adjusting entries have been properly made) and the final Postclosing Trial Balance. The trial balance shown for the end of 1980 is taken before any adjusting entries of any kind, although entries have been made to the Estimated Liability for Warranty Repairs account during the year 1980 as repairs have been made. Anderson Company closes its books once each year.

EXHIBIT 10.8
Anderson Company
(Problem 9)

TRIAL BALANCE—END OF 1979	Adjusted Preclosing		Postclosing	
	Dr.	**Cr.**	**Dr.**	**Cr.**
Estimated Liability for Warranty Repairs		$ 3,000		$ 3,000
Merchandise Inventory	$ 100,000		$100,000	
Sales		800,000		
Warranty Expense	18,000			
All Other Accounts	882,000	197,000	110,000	207,000
Totals	$1,000,000	$1,000,000	$210,000	$210,000

TRIAL BALANCE—END OF 1980	Unadjusted Trial Balance	
	Dr.	**Cr.**
Estimated Liability for Warranty Repairs	$ 14,000	
Merchandise Inventory	820,000	
Sales		$1,000,000
Warranty Expense	—	—
All Other Accounts	266,000	100,000
Totals	$1,100,000	$1,100,000

At the end of 1980, the management of Anderson Company analyzes the appliances sold within the preceding 12 months. All appliances in the hands of customers that are still covered by warranty are classified as follows: those sold on or before June 30 (more than 6 months old), those sold after June 30, but on or before November 30 (more than 1 month, but less than 6 months old), and those sold on or after December 1. One-half of one percent of the appliances sold more than 6 months ago are estimated to require repair, 5 percent of the appliances sold 1 to 6 months before the end of the year are estimated to require repair, and 8 percent of the appliances sold within the last month are assumed to require repair. From this analysis, management estimated that $5,000 of repairs still would have to be made in 1981 on the appliances sold in 1980. Ending inventory on December 31, 1980, is $120,000.

a   What were the total acquisitions of merchandise inventory during 1980?

b   What is the cost of goods sold for 1980?

c What was the dollar amount of repairs made during the year 1980?

d What is the Warranty Expense for 1980?

e Give journal entries for repairs made during 1980, for the warranty expense for 1980, and for cost of goods sold for 1980.

10 Refer to the Simplified Funds Statement for a Period in Exhibit 5.15 on page 174. Ten of the lines in the statement are numbered. Line (2) should be expanded to say "Additions for Expenses and Other Changes Against Income Not Using Funds," and line (3) should be expanded to say "Subtractions for Revenues and other Credits to Income Not Producing Funds from Operations." Ignore the other lines in responding to the questions below.

Assume that the accounting cycle is complete for the period and that all of the financial statements have been prepared. Then it is discovered that a transaction has been over-looked. That transaction is recorded in the accounts and all of the financial statements are corrected. Define *funds* as *working capital.* For each of the following transactions, indicate which of the numbered lines of the funds statement is affected and by how much. Ignore income tax effects except where taxes are explicitly mentioned.

a Bonds are issued for $100,000 cash.

b Bonds with a fair market value of $100,000 are issued for a building.

c Bonds with a book value of $100,000 are retired for $90,000 cash.

d Bonds with a book value of $100,000 are called for $105,000 cash and retired.

e Interest expense on bonds is recorded using the effective-interest method. The bonds have a face value of $100,000 and a current book value of $90,000. The coupon rate is 8 percent, paid semiannually, and the bonds were originally issued to yield 10 percent, compounded semiannually.

f Interest expense on bonds is recorded using the effective-interest method. The bonds have a face value of $100,000 and a book value of $105,000. The coupon rate is 8 percent, paid semiannually, and the bonds were originally issued to yield 6 percent, compounded semiannually.

g Depreciation claimed on the tax return exceeds depreciation expense on the financial statements by $10,000. The income tax rate is 40 percent. An entry is made recording deferred income taxes.

h Warranty costs claimed on the tax return are less than warranty expense on the financial statements by $5,000. The income tax rate is 40 percent. An entry is made recording deferred income taxes. Estimated Warranty Liability is a current liability.

i Expense of $25,000 and payment of $35,000 on a financing lease is recognized. The expense consists of $20,000 amortization and $5,000 interest.

j Normal pension costs of $30,000 are recognized and funded.

k Prior-service pension costs are amortized to expense in the amount of $20,000 and $15,000 of this amount funded with a cash payment.

11 If a company borrows $1,000,000 by issuing, at par, 20-year, 8-percent bonds with semi-annual coupons, the total interest expense over the life of the issue is $1,600,000 (= 20 × .08 × $1,000,000). If a company undertakes a 20-year financing lease or mortgage with an implicit borrowing rate of 8 percent, the annual lease payments are $1,000,000/9.81815 = $101,852. (See Table 4 at the end of the book, 20-period row, 8-percent column.) The total lease payments are $2,037,040 (= 20 × $101,852), and the total interest expense over the life of the lease or mortgage is $1,037,040 (= $2,037,040 − $1,000,000). Why are the amounts of interest expense different for these two means of borrowing for the same length of time at identical interest rates?

12 On December 1, 1979, the Percival Company obtained a 90-day loan for $12,600 from the Twin City State Bank at an annual interest rate of 10 percent. On the maturity date the note was renewed for another 30 days, with a check being issued to the bank for the accrued interest. The Percival Company closes its books annually at December 31.

a Present entries on the books of the Percival Company to record the issue of the note, the year-end adjustment, the renewal of the note, and the payment of cash at maturity of the renewed note.

b Present entries at maturity date of the original note for the following variations in the settlement of the note of the Percival Company.

(1) The original note is paid at maturity.

(2) The note is renewed for 30 days; the new note bears interest at 12 percent per annum. Interest on the old note was not paid at maturity.

13 The Myrtle Lunch sells coupon books that patrons may use later to purchase meals. Each coupon book sells for $17 and has a face value of $20. That is, each book can be used to purchase meals with menu prices of $20. On July 1, redeemable unused coupons with face value of $1,500 were outstanding. During July, 250 coupon books were sold; during August, 100; during September, 100. Cash receipts exclusive of coupons were $1,200 in July, $1,300 in August, and $1,250 in September. Coupons with a face value of $2,700 were redeemed by patrons during the 3 months.

a If the Myrtle Lunch had a net income of $500 for the quarter ending September 30, how large were expenses?

b What effect, if any, do the July, August, and September coupon sales and redemptions have on the right-hand side of the September 30 balance sheet?

14 The Jones Company sells service contracts to repair copiers at $300 per year. When the contract is signed, the $300 fee is collected and the Service Contract Fees Received in Advance account is credited. Revenues on contracts are recognized on a quarterly basis during the year in which the coverage is in effect. On January 1, 1,000 service contracts were outstanding. Of these, 500 expired at the end of the first quarter, 300 at the end of the second quarter, 150 at the end of the third quarter, and 50 at the end of the fourth quarter. Sales and service during the year came to these amounts (assume that all sales occurred at the beginning of the quarter):

	Sales of Contracts	Service Expenses
First Quarter	$120,000 (400 contracts)	$50,000
Second Quarter	240,000 (800 contracts)	60,000
Third Quarter	90,000 (300 contracts)	45,000
Fourth Quarter	60,000 (200 contracts)	55,000

a Prepare journal entries for the first three quarters of the year for the Jones Company. Assume that quarterly reports are prepared on March 31, June 30, and September 30.

b What is the balance in the Service Contract Fees Received in Advance account on December 31?

15 The Holmes Sales Company sells a building lot to Ruth Watson on September 1, 1979, for $27,000. The down payment is $3,000, and minimum payments of $265 a month are to be made on the contract. Interest at the rate of 12 percent per annum on the unpaid balance is deducted from each payment, and the balance is applied on the principal. Payments are made as follows: October 1, $265; November 1, $265; December 1, $600; January 2, $265.

Prepare a schedule showing payments, interest and principal, and remaining liability at each of these dates. Round amounts to the nearest dollar.

16 Lynne Michals secures a mortgage loan of $56,000 from the Oakley National Bank. The terms of the mortgage require monthly payments of $830. The interest rate to be applied to the unpaid balance is 9 percent per year.

Calculate the distribution of payments for the first 4 months between principal and interest and present the new balance figures. Prepare a table showing payments, interest and principal, and remaining liability at each of these dates. Round amounts to the nearest dollar.

17 On June 1, the Southern Oil Company purchases a warehouse from F. S. Brandon for $60,000, of which $10,000 is assigned to the land and $50,000 to the building. There is a mortgage on the property payable to the Dixie National Bank, which, together with the accrued interest, will be assumed by the purchaser. The balance due on the mortgage is $24,000. The mortgage provides that interest at the rate of 10 percent per annum on the unpaid balance, and $2,000 of the principal will be paid on April 1 and October 1 of each year. A 10-year second mortgage for $15,000 is issued to F. S. Brandon; it bears interest at the rate of 12 percent per annum, payable on June 1 and December 1. A check is drawn to complete the purchase.

Prepare journal entries for the Southern Oil Company for June 1, October 1, and December 1, which closes its books once a year on December 31.

18 On September 1, 1979, Howell Stores, Inc., issues 20-year, first mortgage bonds with a face value of $1,000,000. The proceeds of the issue are $1,060,000. The bonds bear interest at the rate of 8 percent per annum, payable semiannually at March 1 and September 1. Howell Stores, Inc., closes its books annually at December 31. (Round amounts to the nearest dollar.)

a Present dated journal entries related to the bonds from September 1, 1979, through September 1, 1980, inclusive. Assume that Howell Stores, Inc., uses the straight-line method to amortize the bond premium.

b Repeat instructions for part **a,** but assume that the company uses an effective-interest method. The effective-interest rate to be used is 7.4 percent, compounded semiannually. (Round amounts to the nearest dollar.)

19 On May 1, 1979, the Oliver Company acquired $1,000,000 par value of bonds of the Bret Company for $1,395,000 plus accrued interest. Costs of acquisition amounted to an additional $5,000. The bonds bear interest at 9 percent payable on March 31 and September 30 and mature on March 31, 1989. Use straight-line amortization of premium.

a Present journal entries on the books of the Oliver Company from May 1, 1979, through March 31, 1980, inclusive. Assume that the books are closed annually on December 31.

b Present the journal entry (or entries) for the sale of the bonds on July 1, 1982, at 103.5 plus accrued interest.

20 In 1979, the Central Power Company issued $2 million bonds in two series, A and B. Each series had face amount of $1 million and was issued at prices to yield 7 percent. Issue A contained semiannual 6-percent coupons. Issue B contained 8-percent semiannual coupons. In 1980, Central Power issued series C, with face amount of $1 million. This issue contained 8-percent semiannual coupons; the effective yield at time of issue was 8.6 percent. Issues A, B, and C all mature 30 years from issue date.

Answer the following questions for issue A. Round amounts to the nearest dollar.
a What is the issuing price of the bonds?
b Make the journal entry for the date of bond issue.
c Using the effective-interest method, show the journal entries made on the first semi-annual interest payment date.
d Repeat part **c** for the second and third payment dates.
e Show the semiannual entry if straight-line amortization of discount (or premium) is used.

21 Refer to the data in Problem **20.** Work the problem for issue B.

22 Refer to the data in Problem **20.** Work the problem for issue C.

23 Assume that Federal Department Stores, Incorporated, is about to sign four separate leases for stores in four separate shopping centers. Each of the stores would cost $10 million if purchased outright and has an economic life of 20 years. Assume that the company currently must pay interest at the rate of 10 percent per year on long-term, secured borrowing. The lease payments are to be made at the end of each year in all four cases.

Based on the information given here, decide whether each of the four leases requires accounting as operating leases or as capital leases. Give your reasoning.

	Lease Term	Annual Lease Payment
a. Seaview Mall	16 years	$1,100,000
b. Normandale Center	16 years	1,215,000
c. Eastbrook Haven	12 years	1,250,000
d. Palos Parkview	12 years	1,395,000

24 Assume that the Trans Western Airlines Company is about to sign a lease for 15 years to acquire the use of a new airplane. The interest rate used to compute the lease payments, which are to be made annually at the end of each year, is 12 percent per year. At the start of the lease, the present value of the lease payments is to be $30 million.
a Verify that the annual lease payment is $4,404,730.
b Assuming that the lease is accounted for as an operating lease, compute:
  (i) Total rent expense over 15 years.
  (ii) Rent expense for the first year.
  (iii) Rent expense for the fifteenth year.
c Assuming that the lease is accounted for as a capital lease, and that amortization is straight-line, compute:
  (i) Total expense related to using the asset over 15 years.
  (ii) Expense relating to using the asset in the first year.
  (iii) Expense relating to using the asset in the fifteenth year. (Hint: Refer to footnote 10, p. 386, where the method of deriving the last row of an amortization table is given.)
d Which method of accounting for the lease, operating or capital, is Trans Western Airlines Company likely to prefer for its financial statements and why?
e Assume that the airplane's fair value in the hands of the lessor is $30 million. What is the largest annual lease payment that Trans Western Airlines Company could make to the lessor for 15 years without disqualifying the lease from operating lease treatment in financial statements?

25 (This problem should not be attempted until the previous one has been worked.) Refer to the data in the preceding problem.

    a Which method of accounting for the lease is Trans Western Airlines Company likely to prefer for tax purposes and why?

    b Assuming that the operating-lease method is used on the tax returns and the capital-lease method is used on the financial statements, will income taxes payable exceed income tax expense in the first year or vice versa? By how much, if the income tax rate is 40 percent and there are no other timing differences?

    c Repeat part **b** for the fifteenth year.

26 The Carom Company plans to acquire, as of January 1, 1980, a computerized cash register system that costs $100,000 and that has a 5-year life and no salvage value. The company is considering two plans for acquiring the system.

    (1) Outright purchase. To finance the purchase, $100,000 of par-value 10-percent semi-annual coupon bonds will be issued January 1, 1980, at par.

    (2) Lease. The lease requires five annual payments to be made on December 31, 1980, 1981, 1982, 1983, and 1984. The lease payments are such that they have a present value of $100,000 on January 1, 1980, when discounted at 10 percent per year.

Straight-line amortization methods will be used for all depreciation and amortization computations.

    a Verify that the amount of the required lease payment is $26,380 by constructing an amortization schedule for the five payments. Note that there will be a $2 rounding error in the fifth year. Nevertheless, you may treat each payment as being $26,380 in the rest of the problem.

    b What balance sheet amounts will be affected if plan **(1)** is selected? If plan **(2)** is selected, the lease is cancelable, and the operating-lease treatment is used? If plan **(2)** is selected, the lease is noncancelable, and the financing-lease treatment is used?

    c What will be the total depreciation and interest expenses for the 5 years under plan **(1)**?

    d What will be the total expenses for the 5 years under plan **(2)** if the lease is accounted for as an operating lease? As a financing lease?

    e Why are the answers in part **d** the same? Why are the answers in part **c** different from those in part **d**?

    f What will be the total expenses for the first year, 1980, under plan **(1)**? Under plan **(2)** accounted for as an operating lease? Under plan **(2)** accounted for as a financing lease?

    g Repeat part **f** for the fifth year, 1984.

27 The Pennsylvania Steel Company files its income tax returns on a calendar-year basis and issues financial statements quarterly as of March 31, June 30, and so on.

    Assume that the applicable income tax rates and rules for 1979 are as follows:

    (1) Effective tax rates are 20 percent of the first $25,000 of taxable income, 22 percent of the next $25,000, and 48 percent of all taxable income in excess of $50,000.

    (2) Corporations must pay estimated taxes during the year. For a corporation on a calendar-year basis, 25 percent of the estimated tax payment for the year 1979 must be paid by April 15, 1979; 50 percent of the estimated tax payment for the year must have been paid by June 15, 1979; 75 percent of the estimated tax payment for the year must have been paid by September 15, 1979; and, all of the estimated tax payment for the year must have been paid by December 15, 1979.

(3) Any tax due when the tax return is filed in 1980 must be paid, one-half by March 15, 1980, and one-half by June 15, 1980.

The following data are applicable to the company's 1979 income tax.

1979

March 31 It is estimated that total taxable income for the year 1979 will be about $1.5 million. The first quarter's financial statements are prepared.

April 15 The first payment on estimated taxes is made.

June 15 It is now estimated that total taxable income for the year will be about $1.7 million. The second payment on estimated taxes is made.

June 30 The second quarter's financial statements are prepared.

Sept. 15 It is now estimated that total taxable income for the year will be about $1.6 million. The third payment on estimated taxes is made.

Sept. 30 The third quarter's financial statements are prepared.

Dec. 15 It is now estimated that total taxable income for the year will be about $1.75 million. The fourth payment on estimated taxes is made.

Dec. 31 Income for the year is $1,775,000. Financial statements for the year are prepared.

1980

March 15 The first payment of the balance of 1979 taxes is made.

June 15 The second payment of 1979 tax balance is made.

a Prepare schedules showing
  (i) For tax returns: estimated taxes for year, cumulative payments due and payment made for April 15, June 15, September 15, and December 15, 1979, as well as for March 15 and June 15, 1980.
  (ii) For financial statements: tax expenses for the quarterly reports and annual report.
b Record the transactions related to 1979 income taxes in journal entry form.
c Present the T-accounts for Cash, Prepaid Income Taxes (if necessary), Income Tax Payable, and Income Tax Expense.

28 Refer to the data in Exhibit 3.4 on page 82 showing income over a 5-year period under various methods of revenue and income recognition. Use the methods of accounting indicated below for financial statements and for tax returns. Assume an income tax rate of 40 percent. Compute income tax expense, income taxes payable, and deferred income taxes for each period. Put this information into journal entry form.
a Use the percentage of completion method on the financial statements and the completed contract method on the tax return.
b Use the cost-recovery-first method on the financial statements and the installment method on the tax return.

29 Refer to the data in Problem **34** at the end of Chapter 3 for the Acme Construction Company. Use the methods of accounting indicated below for financial statements and for tax returns. Assume an income tax rate of 40 percent. Compute income tax expense, income taxes payable, and deferred income taxes for each year. Put this information into journal entry form for each year.
a Use the percentage-of-completion method on the financial statements and the completed-contract method on the tax return.
b Use the cost-recovery-first method on the financial statements and the installment method on the tax return.

30 The following events are recorded on the books of the K. Schipper Company during a recent year.

(1) Machinery costing $100,000 is acquired. Estimated service life is 5 years with no salvage value.

(2) Installment sales of $800,000 are made; cost of goods sold is $600,000. During the year, $500,000 of this amount is collected.

(3) The estimated future warranty liability on sales is charged to warranty expense for the year and amounts to $100,000. Actual expenditures for warranty repairs under the agreements during the year total $25,000. Tax regulations require that deductions from revenues for warranty expense cannot exceed actual expenditures for that purpose.

(4) Outlays for research and development are $50,000. Management estimates that benefits of this R&D outlay will accrue to the company over a 5-year period.

Recall the "least and latest rule," and make the unrealistic assumption that only these four events occurred during the year. Compute the income before taxes, tax liabilities, and income after taxes for the K. Schipper Company. If there is a difference between tax expense and tax currently payable, indicate how this difference is recorded. Assume a tax rate of 40 percent. Use straight-line depreciation and completed-sales revenue recognition for financial reports. Use the sum-of-the-years'-digits method of depreciation and cash-collection revenue recognition for tax purposes.

31 Equilibrium Company adopted a program of purchasing a new machine each year. It uses the sum-of-the-years'-digits method of depreciation on its income tax return and straight-line depreciation on its financial statements. Each machine costs $15,000 installed and has a depreciable life of 5 years.

a Calculate depreciation for each of the first 7 years in accordance with the sum-of-the-years'-digits method of depreciation.

b Calculate depreciation for each year in accordance with the straight-line method of depreciation.

c Calculate annual difference in depreciation calculated in parts **a** and **b**.

d Calculate annual increase or decrease in the Deferred Income Tax Liability account. Assume a 40-percent tax rate and straight-line depreciation in financial reports.

e Calculate year-end balances for the Deferred Income Tax Liability account.

f If Equilibrium Company continues to follow its policy of buying a new machine every year, what will happen to the balance in the Deferred Income Tax Liability account?

32 The Strawcab Company owns one depreciable asset. The asset originally had a depreciable life of 6 years. It is 4 years old at the end of the current year. It had an estimated salvage value of $4,000 when new. This estimate has not changed. The company uses sum-of-the-years'-digits depreciation on its tax return and straight-line depreciation on its financial statements. The company's income tax rate is 40 percent of pretax taxable income. The footnotes to the financial statements indicate that the only cause of timing differences between the financial statements and tax returns is depreciation and that the income tax expense differs from income taxes payable by $1,200.

a Which is larger this year, income taxes payable or income tax expense, and by how much?

b What is the acquisition cost of the asset?

c Assume the same general facts as above except the asset had an original depreciable life of 8 years, is 2 years old at the end of the current year, and has an estimated salvage value of $2,000. The difference between income tax expense and income taxes payable this year was reported to be $1,600. Repeat parts **a** and **b**.

33 The numbers in this problem are hypothetical, but the size relation between them is adapted from recent financial statements of Sears, Roebuck & Co. The purpose of this problem is to demonstrate the effects of deferred income tax accounting in a retailing operation.

Sears reports income on a charge account sale in the tax year when the sale is made, but reports the income on the tax return in the year when the cash is collected from the customer. Every Christmas season, Sears makes hundreds of millions of dollars of sales that are not collected until the next tax year. Each year, the Christmas sales exceed the previous year's Christmas sales. The tax on these sales is not paid until the next year, but Sears must report the tax on the current year's income statement. In recent years, the amount of the deferred tax expense for these charge sales alone has been larger than 10 percent of Sears' entire aftertax net income. The balance sheet amount of Sears' deferred tax liability for charge sales alone is of the order of $1 billion and has never declined. That $1 billion would be part of its Retained Earnings account if Sears were not required to report deferred income taxes on those charge sales. Retained Earnings would be about 20 percent larger.

Sears will have to pay its deferred taxes for charge sales only when its dollar sales shrink in amount while it remains profitable. This is unlikely ever to happen. When W. T. Grant, another large retailer, went bankrupt in the mid-1970s, it had a large credit balance in its deferred tax account that disappeared in one year. But not a single penny was paid to the government for deferred taxes.

Assume (for parts **a–d**) that Rosenwald Stores makes all of its sales on account, that the physical amount sold remains constant each year, and that prices are stable from year to year. Of those sales, five-sixths are collected in the year of sale and one-sixth is collected in the next year. The financial statements of Rosenwald Stores in each year are shown in Exhibit 10.9. Rosenwald Stores has been using the sales basis of revenue recognition on its tax returns, so that there have been no timing differences. In 1980, Rosenwald Stores, following the rule of least and latest, switches to the installment method of revenue recognition on its income tax returns. Its tax returns for 1980 differ from tax returns for all subsequent years. These tax returns are also shown in Exhibit 10.9. The income tax rate is 40 percent.

a Prepare a journal entry that recognizes income tax expense and income taxes payable for each of the years before 1980.

b Prepare a journal entry that recognizes income tax expense and income taxes payable for 1980.

c Prepare a journal entry that recognizes income tax expense and income taxes payable for each year after 1980.

d What will happen in subsequent years to the Deferred Income Tax Credits account created in 1980?

e Now, assume that because of expanding physical volume of sales and general inflation, all pretax figures on the financial statements grow at the rate of 10 percent per year. What will happen to the balance in the Deferred Income Tax Credits account?

f Return to the steady-state, stable-price environment of parts **a–d.** Now assume that in a later year, say 1990, Rosenwald Stores declares bankruptcy. (This is not representative of Sears, Roebuck & Co., but other retailers have gone bankrupt.) In 1990, collections of all sales made in 1989 are completed, but sales for 1990 fall to $40,000 all of which are collected in 1990. Cost of Goods Sold is $24,000 and All Other Expenses Except Taxes fall to $30,000. Prepare a schedule computing income taxes payable and an income statement for 1990.

g What conclusions can you draw from this exercise about deferred income tax accounting? If you can find them, obtain financial statements for a recent year for Sears, Roebuck & Co. What is the current balance in the Deferred Tax account for installment sales? What

EXHIBIT 10.9
Rosenwald Stores
(Problem 33)

**INCOME STATEMENT EACH YEAR
(ALSO TAX RETURN PRIOR TO 1980)**

Sales	$120,000
Cost of Goods Sold	$ 72,000
All Other Expenses Except Income Taxes	36,000
Total	$108,000
Pretax Income	$ 12,000
Income Tax Expense at 40 Percent	4,800
Net Income	$ 7,200

INCOME TAX RETURN	**1980**	**Subsequent Years**
Collections on Sales Made in Current Year	$100,000	$100,000
Collections on Sales Made in Previous Year	–	20,000
Total Revenue	$100,000	$120,000
Costs of Goods Sold and Collected for in Current Year	$ 60,000	$ 60,000
Costs of Goods Sold in Previous Year and Collected for This Year	–	12,000
All Other Expenses Except Income Taxes	36,000	36,000
Total Deductions	$ 96,000	$108,000
Taxable Income	$ 4,000	$ 12,000
Income Taxes Payable at 40 Percent	$ 1,600	$ 4,800

fraction of shareholders' equity does this represent? By what percentage would Sears' income increase if deferred tax expense from installment sales were not deducted in computing net income? Discuss.

34 The Hicks Company is adopting a pension plan. Two plans are being considered. Both of the proposed pension plans are defined-benefit plans. The benefits actually paid to a given retired ex-employee who actually qualifies for benefits are to be the same for whichever of the two proposed plans is adopted.
  a Who, the employee or The Hicks Company, is more likely to bear the risks and rewards of fluctuating market returns on funds invested to pay the pensions?
  In each of the parts below, explain which of the two plans is likely to be less costly from the standpoint of The Hicks Company and why. If the costs are likely to be the same in both of the plans, then explain why.
  b Contributory plan or noncontributory plan.
  c Plan with benefits fully vested in 5 years or plan with benefits fully vested in 10 years.
  d Fully funded plan or partially funded plan.
  e Plan that amortizes prior-service costs over 20 years or plan that amortizes prior-service costs over 30 years.

35 On January 1, 1979, Kayco Company instituted a pension plan. The past-(prior)service cost — the present value of the past-service benefits awarded to current employees — is $1,200,000. The present value of the benefits earned by employees during both 1979 and 1980 is $700,000 at the end of each of those years. Kayco Company designates the Retirement Insurance Company as the trustee of the pension plan and deposits all funding payments with the insurance company at the end of each year. Interest on unfunded liabilities is accrued at a rate of 4 percent per year. Kayco Company plans to fund an amount each year equal to the pension expense recognized for the year.

Show the journal entries that Kayco Company would make on December 31, 1979 and 1980, for its pension plan and related expenses under the following two assumptions.
  a Prior-(past)service cost is amortized over 10 years.
  b Prior-(past)service cost is amortized over 30 years.
  c What is the present value on January 1, 1979, of the cash outlays related to prior-service costs under each of the assumptions above, if the outlays are discounted at 4 percent per year? At 8 percent per year?

36 (This problem should not be attempted until the previous one has been worked.) Refer to the prior-service cost data for Kayco Company presented in the preceding problem. Assume that prior-service cost is amortized over 10 years, that all expenses are funded as recognized, and that interest on the unfunded amount of prior-service cost accrues at the rate of 4 percent per year.
  a What amount of unfunded obligation for prior-service cost would be disclosed in the footnotes to Kayco Company's financial statements issued for December 31, 1979?
  b What amount of unfunded obligation for prior-service cost would be disclosed in the footnotes to Kayco Company's financial statements issued for December 31, 1980?

37 Refer to Note 5 of the financial statements of International Corporation shown in Appendix A on pages 584–586.
  a What is the combined marginal federal, state, and local income tax rate that International Corporation appeared to pay in 19X1? That is, if International Corporation were to earn another $1, how much of that $1 would be paid in income taxes to federal, state, and local governments?
In the remainder of this problem, assume that the marginal income tax rate is 40 percent of pretax income.
  b By how much did depreciation claimed on the tax return exceed depreciation expense reported in the financial statements for the year 19X1?
  c International Corporation uses the percentage-of-completion method of income recognition on certain long-term contracts but the installment method on tax returns. In one of the years 19X0 and 19X1, income from the percentage-of-completion method exceeded income under the installment method. In the other year the direction was reversed. Which is which? How can you tell?
  d Warranty costs are not deductible on the tax return until actual repairs or replacements are made. Estimated warranty expenses are shown in the financial statements whenever they can be computed with a reasonable degree of precision. Did warranty expense on the financial statements exceed deductions for warranty costs on the tax return or vice versa in 19X1? How can you tell? By how much?

CHAPTER 11
OWNERS' EQUITY

The economic resources of a firm come essentially from two major sources. Non-owners provide funds to a firm; the sources of these funds are shown on the balance sheet as *liabilities,* which were discussed in Chapter 10. Owners provide funds; the sources of these funds are shown on the balance sheet as *owners' equity.* This chapter discusses owners' equity.

The accounting equation states

$$\text{Assets} = \text{Liabilities} + \text{Owners' Equity}$$

or

$$\text{Assets} - \text{Liabilities} = \text{Owners' Equity}.$$

Many readers of financial statements think of owners' equity as being calculated from the excess of assets over liabilities. Double-entry record keeping, however, provides for the continuous, independent calculation of owners' equity.

Our emphasis in this chapter is on the corporation. Appendix 11.1 of this chapter introduces partnership accounting. The corporation is a widely used form of business organization in the United States for at least three reasons:

1 The corporate form provides the owner, or stockholder, with limited liability. That is, should the corporation become insolvent, creditors' claims are limited to the assets of the corporate entity. The assets of the individual owners are not subject to the claims of the corporation's creditors. On the other hand, creditors of partnerships and sole proprietorships have a claim on both the owners' personal and business assets in settlement of such firms' debts.
2 The corporate form facilitates the raising of large amounts of funds through the issue of shares of capital stock by the corporation. The general public can acquire the shares in varying amounts. Individual investments can range from a few dollars to hundreds of millions of dollars.
3 The corporate form makes transfer of ownership interests relatively easy, because individual shares can be sold by current owners to others without interfering with

the ongoing operations of the business. The continuity of the management and of operations is not affected by these ongoing changes in ownership.

This chapter discusses three separate kinds of problems in accounting for owners' equity in corporations: the accounting for capital contributed by owners, the accounting for income earned by the firm which may be retained or distributed to owners, and other changes in owners' equity accounts. Appendix 11.1 discusses the treatment of capital contributions as well as the determination and distribution of earnings in partnerships.

CAPITAL CONTRIBUTIONS: CORPORATIONS

The corporation is viewed in the law as a legal entity separate from its owners. Capital contributions are made by individuals or other entities under a contract between themselves and the corporation.[1] Because those who contribute capital funds are usually issued certificates for shares of stock, they are known as "stockholders" or "shareholders." The rights and obligations of a shareholder are determined by:

1 The corporation laws of the state in which incorporation takes place.
2 The articles of incorporation or *charter.* This is the agreement between the firm and the state in which the business is incorporated. The enterprise is granted the privilege of operating as a corporation for certain stated purposes and of obtaining its capital through the issue of shares of stock.
3 The bylaws of the corporation. Bylaws are adopted by the board of directors and act as the rules and regulations under which the internal affairs of the corporation are conducted.
4 The stock contract. Each type of capital stock has its own provisions as to such matters as voting, sharing in earnings, distribution of earnings, and sharing in assets in case of dissolution.

Some "closely held" corporations have a small number of shareholders and operate much the same as a partnership. The few people involved agree to the amount of capital to be contributed, elect each other to be members of the board of directors and officials of the firm, and agree on policies regarding dividends and salaries. They may restrict the transfer of shares to outsiders, and may even become liable for debts of the corporation by endorsing its notes and bonds.

In the case of large, widely owned corporations, the effect of the separate legal entity of the corporation becomes more pronounced. Officials and directors may own little or no stock in the corporation. Actual control is likely to be in the hands of a few individuals or a group who own or control enough shares to elect a majority of the board of directors. Most "minority" shareholders think of their stock holdings merely as investments, and they participate little, if at all, in the conduct of the affairs of the

---

[1] In accounting for owners' equity, the term *contribution* almost never means a gift; capital given to the corporation as a gift is specifically called *donated capital.*

corporation. The shareholders assume no obligation for the debts of the business. Shares of stock change hands at the will of the shareholders, and the record may not show the change for some time after it has occurred. The record of who owns shares is usually kept by a bank or trust company.

Issue of Shares of Stock

The accounting for the initial issue of shares of stock is normally a routine matter. The usual entry, where the shares are issued for cash, is

Cash 1,250,000
  Capital Stock 1,250,000
Issue of shares of capital stock.

In addition to exchanges for cash, stock is sometimes issued in exchange for property, for personal services rendered, or in settlement of a liability. The form of the entry in these cases is the same as the one illustrated above, but the debit will be made to the accounts for property or services received or the liability settled. The amount for the entry should be the fair market value of the product, property, or services received, or, if this amount is not reasonably determinable, the fair market value of the stock issued.[2]

Classes of Shares

Corporations are often authorized to issue more than one class of shares, each representing ownership in the business. Most shares issued are either *common* or *preferred*. Occasionally, there may be several classes of common or preferred shares. Each share of stock has the same rights and privileges as every other share of the same class. All corporations must have at least one class of shares. They are usually called "common shares," but they may be designated by another name, such as class A shares. Preferred shares may, but need not be, issued by a corporation.

  Common shares have the claim to earnings of the corporation after commitments to preferred shareholders have been satisfied. Frequently, common shares are the only voting shares of the company. In the event of corporate dissolution, all of the proceeds of asset disposition, after settling the claims of creditors and required distributions to preferred shareholders, are distributable to the common shareholders.

  Preferred stock is granted special privileges. Although these features vary considerably from issue to issue, a preferred share usually entitles its holder to dividends at a certain rate, which must be paid before dividends can be paid to common shareholders. Sometimes, though, these dividends may be postponed or omitted, according to the provisions of the issue. If the preferred dividends are *cumulative,* then all current and previously postponed dividends must be paid before any dividends on common shares can be paid.

---

[2] *APB Opinion No. 29,* 1973.

Most preferred shares issued by corporations in recent years have been *callable*. Callable preferred shares may be reacquired by the corporation at a specified price, which may vary according to a predetermined time schedule. Callability is commonly thought to be for the benefit of the corporation. If sufficient financing is otherwise available, especially if that alternative financing is available at a lower cost than the rate previously fixed for the preferred shares, a corporation may wish to reduce the relatively fixed commitment of preferred dividends (as compared to common). It can do so by calling the preferred shares. The corporation has the option to call the shares. This option is valuable to the corporation but makes the shares less attractive to potential owners. Other things being equal, noncallable shares will be issued for a higher price than will callable shares. Thus, the degree to which the corporation benefits by making shares callable is not clearcut.

Preferred shares with a conversion feature have become increasingly popular. Convertible preferred shares may be converted into a specified amount of common shares at specified times by their owner. The conversion privilege may appear advantageous to both the individual shareholder and the corporation. The preferred shareholder enjoys the security of a relatively assured dividend as long as the shares are held. The shareholder also has the opportunity to realize capital appreciation by converting the shares into common stock if the market price of the common shares rises sufficiently. Because of this feature, the change in the market price of convertible preferred shares will often parallel changes in the market price of the common shares.

The firm may also benefit from the conversion option. By including it in the issue, the company is usually able to specify a lower dividend rate on the preferred than otherwise would have been required to issue the shares for a given price.

A major consideration in the issue of preferred shares is that dividends are not deductible in calculating taxable income. However, bond interest is deductible. Thus, the aftertax cost of borrowing may be less than the aftertax cost of issuing preferred shares, even though the interest rate is higher than the preferred stock dividend rate.

Separate accounts are used for each class of shares. On the balance sheet, each class of shares is shown separately, many times with a short description of the major features of the shares. Customarily, preferred shares are listed before common shares on the balance sheet.

Par Value and No-Par Shares

Shares of capital stock often have a *par,* or nominal, value per share specified in the articles of incorporation and printed on the face of the stock certificates. The par value of common stock has some legal significance but little economic significance. For legal reasons, accountants separate par value from other contributed capital amounts. Shares assigned a certain par value will almost always sell on the stock market at a price different from par. Also, *the book value of a share of common stock*—the total common shareholders' equity divided by the number of shares outstanding—is almost always greater than the par value of the shares, in part because retained earnings are usually positive. The par value rarely denotes the worth of the shares, except perhaps at the date of original issue. Readers of financial statements can usually assume merely that the par value of all common shares is the minimum investment that has been made by the shareholders in the corporation. Par value of preferred stock is more meaningful. The dividend rate specified in the preferred stock contract (for example, 8 percent) is almost always based on par value. Any preference as to assets in liquidation that preferred stockholders may have is usually related to the par value of the preferred shares.

Although preferred shares usually have a par value, common shares without a par value are widely used. When no-par-value shares are issued, there need be no problem of assigning a nominal value to the shares issued, because the amount actually contributed can be credited directly to the capital stock account. However, customary practice assigns a *stated* value to the no-par shares, which has much the same effect as assigning the shares a par value. Some state corporation laws require the directors to assign a stated value to each no-par share. The stated value can usually be changed from time to time at the discretion of the directors.

Contributions in Excess of Par or Stated Value

One awkward convention in accounting is that the capital stock account is usually credited with the par or stated value of the shares issued. Shares are usually issued for amounts greater than par. For example, individuals who purchase newly issued shares from the corporation some years after the corporation began operations normally pay a higher price per share to compensate current stockholders for the additional capital that has been accumulated by the retention of earnings in the business. The excess of issue proceeds over par (or stated) value is credited to an account called Additional Paid-in Capital. The title Capital Contributed in Excess of Par (Stated) Value is probably a more appropriate one, but is too cumbersome to be used extensively. Sometimes the title used is Premium on Capital Stock.

The entries to record additional paid-in capital involve nothing new. If par-value shares are used, the credit to the Additional Paid-in Capital account is always the difference between the amount received and the par value of the shares issued to the stockholders. For shares with no par value, the additional paid-in capital is the excess of the amount received over the stated value. Thus, the entry to record the issue of 100 shares of no-par-value stock, with a stated value of $1 per share, for $10,000, would be the same as the entry to record the issuance of a like number of $1 par-value shares for the same proceeds:

Cash	10,000	
Capital Stock—Stated (or Par) Value		100
Additional Paid-in Capital		9,900

Issue of shares for amount greater than stated (or par) value.

Since shares ordinarily have no maturity date, the Additional Paid-in Capital, or Premium on Capital Stock account, remains on the books indefinitely as a partial measure of contributions by stockholders. This account differs from Premium on Bonds, considered in Chapter 10, in two respects. Premium on Capital Stock appears in the stockholders' equity section of the balance sheet, whereas Premium on Bonds is shown in the liability section; Premium on Capital Stock is not amortized, whereas Premium on Bonds is amortized over the life of the bonds to which the premium relates.

Treasury Shares

Shares of stock reacquired by the issuing corporation are called *treasury stock* or *treasury shares*. Treasury shares may be acquired for a variety of purposes. The firm may reacquire its own shares for later distribution under stock option plans or for stock dividends. (Stock option plans and stock dividends are discussed later in this chapter.) The firm may also consider treasury shares a worthwhile use for idle funds. Treasury shares are not entitled to dividends nor to vote, since they are not considered to be "outstanding" shares for these purposes.

When common shares are reacquired, a Treasury Shares—Common account is debited with the total amount paid to reacquire the shares.

Treasury Shares—Common	11,000	
Cash		11,000

$11,000 paid to reacquire 1,000 shares of $5-par-value common stock.

If the treasury shares are later reissued by the corporation, Cash is debited with the amount received and the Treasury Shares account credited. It is unlikely, of course, that the reissue price will precisely equal the amount paid to acquire the treasury shares. Generally accepted accounting principles do not permit a company to recognize any "gain" or "loss" to be included in net income on its dealings in treasury shares. If the reissue price is greater than the acquisition price, the Additional Paid-in Capital account is credited to make the entry balance. Assuming that the 1,000 shares reacquired in the entry illustrated above were reissued for $14,000, the entry would be

Cash	14,000	
Treasury Shares—Common		11,000
Additional Paid-in Capital		3,000

Reissue of 1,000 shares of treasury stock at a price greater than acquisition cost.

If the reissue price is less than the amount paid, the debit to make the entry balance is usually to Additional Paid-in Capital, as long as there is a sufficient credit balance in that account. If there is not, the additional balancing debit is made directly to Retained Earnings. This debit represents an income distribution, not an expense or loss.

The Treasury Shares account is a contra to owners' equity. A recent balance sheet of the General Electric Company illustrates this disclosure:

Shareholders' Equity (Dollar Amounts in Millions)

Preferred Stock ($1 par value; 2,000,000 shares authorized; none issued)	—
Common Stock ($2.50 par value; 251,500,000 shares authorized; 230,368,572 shares issued)	$ 575.9
Amounts Received for Stock in Excess of Par Value	618.3
Retained Earnings	4,251.2
Total	$5,445.4
Deduct Common Stock Held in Treasury	(192.5)
Total Share Owners' Equity	$5,252.9

RETENTION OF EARNINGS: CORPORATIONS

After a new business has established itself and is profitable, it usually generates additional owners' equity from undistributed earnings. These undistributed earnings are the accumulated periodic net income that remains after dividends have been declared. Retention of earnings increases owners' or shareholders' equity and often provides the main source of capital for expansion.

Net Income and Cash Position

One misconception about net income is that it represents a fund of cash available for distributions or expenditures. Earnings from operations usually involve cash at some stage—goods are sold to customers, the cash is collected, more goods are acquired, bills are paid, more sales are made, and so on—but assets generated by earnings do not remain in the form of cash. Only under most unrealistic conditions, with net plant and equipment, inventories, receivables, and liabilities remaining at constant figures, would it be reasonable to presume that the earnings, or net income, resulted in a corresponding increase in cash during the period. The statement of changes in financial position shows how the funds provided by operations and other sources are used during a period. An interesting paradox is that for many businesses an increased net income is frequently associated with decreased cash, whereas contraction of net income may be accompanied by an increase in cash. In the first stages of a business decline, cash may start to build up from the liquidation of inventories and receivables that have not been replaced, as well as from postponing replacement or expansion of plant. When conditions improve, inventories and receivables are expanded, new plant acquired, and a cash shortage may develop.

A well-managed firm keeps its cash at a reasonable minimum. If cash starts to accumulate, the firm may pay some obligations, increase its inventory, buy more equipment, declare dividends, or use the funds in some other way. This process of cash management goes on continuously. Thus, there is no way of determining how the retention of earnings is reflected in the individual asset and liability accounts at any particular time. The only certain statement that can be made about the effect of an increase in retained earnings is that it results in increased *net assets* (that is, an increase in the excess of all assets over all liabilities).

Cash Dividends

The shareholders of a corporation do not directly control distributions of corporate net income. State laws and corporation bylaws almost always delegate the authority to declare dividends to the board of directors. When a dividend is declared, the entry is

Retained Earnings	150,000	
Dividends Payable		150,000

To record declaration of dividends. (Sometimes an account called Dividends or Dividends Declared would be debited. The Dividends account is a temporary income distribution account and is closed to Retained Earnings at the end of the period.)

Once the board of directors declares a dividend, the dividend becomes a legal liability of the corporation. Dividends Payable is shown as a current liability on the balance sheet if the dividends have not been paid at the end of the accounting period. When the dividends are paid, the entry is

```
Dividends Payable .............................................   150,000
   Cash ......................................................            150,000
```

Stock Dividends

The previous section has indicated that through the retention of earnings there may be a substantial increase in the amount of shareholders' equity that is more or less permanently committed to the business. To indicate such a permanent commitment of reinvested earnings, a *stock dividend* may be issued. When a stock dividend is issued, shareholders receive additional shares of stock in proportion to their existing holdings without making any additional contributions. If a 20-percent stock dividend is issued, each shareholder receives one additional share for every five shares held before the dividend. In the accounts, a stock dividend requires a transfer from retained earnings to the contributed capital accounts. Generally accepted accounting principles require that the amount transferred from retained earnings be equal to the market value of the shares issued. For example, the directors of a corporation may decide to issue a stock dividend of 10,000 additional shares of common stock with a par value of $10 per share at a time when the market price of a share is $38. The entry would be

```
Retained Earnings .............................................   380,000
   Common Stock—Par ..........................................            100,000
   Additional Paid-in Capital .................................            280,000
Declaration of a stock dividend—recorded using market price of shares to
quantify the amounts.
```

The most significant internal effect of the stock dividend is to relabel a portion of the retained earnings that had been legally available for dividend declarations as a more permanent form of owners' equity. A stock dividend formalizes the fact that some of the funds represented by past earnings have been used for plant expansion, to replace assets at higher price levels, or to retire bonds or other debt and are therefore unavailable for cash dividends.

Shareholders should not celebrate upon receiving a stock dividend. If the shares are of the same type as those held before, each shareholder's proportionate interest in the capital of the corporation and proportionate voting power have not changed. The book value per common share (total common shareholders' equity divided by number of common shares outstanding) will have decreased, but the total book value of each shareholder's interest will remain unchanged, since a proportionately larger number of shares will be held. The market value per share should decline, but, all else being equal, the total market value of the shareholders' holdings will not change. Shareholders cannot dispose of the additional shares without affecting their proportionate interests in the corporation. To describe such a distribution of shares as a "dividend" is, therefore, misleading but is, nevertheless, generally accepted terminology.

If the shareholder receives shares of a different class from those held before, the situation may be slightly different. For example, if a corporation has preferred shares outstanding and issues preferred shares to common shareholders as a stock dividend, then the position of the common shareholders is altered in relation to that of the previous preferred shareholders.

The distribution of shares of stock issued by another, unrelated corporation to stockholders as a dividend is not a stock dividend. It is described as a *dividend in kind* or a *property dividend*. Another dividend in kind would be a systematic distribution of a corporation's products to its shareholders. Such dividends are accounted for just like cash dividends, except that when the dividend is paid, the asset given up, rather than cash, is credited.

DIVIDEND POLICY

The directors, in considering whether or not to declare cash dividends, must conclude both (1) that the declaration of a dividend is legal and (2) that it would be financially expedient.

Statutory Restrictions on Dividends

State corporation laws impose certain restrictions on the directors' freedom to declare dividends. These restrictions are designed primarily to protect creditors, who otherwise might be in a precarious position because neither shareholders nor directors are liable for debts of the corporation.

Generally, the laws provide that dividends "may not be paid out of capital" but must be "paid out of earnings." The interpretation of this rule varies among jurisdictions. "Capital" is sometimes defined to be equal to the total amount paid in by shareholders. In some jurisdictions, however, "capital" is defined to be the amount shown in the Capital Stock account so that the amount in the Additional Paid-in Capital account may be used for certain kinds of dividend declarations. In other states, the corporation must indicate a certain amount of stated capital below which shareholders' equity may not be reduced through dividend declarations. This stated capital amount may be less than the total paid-in capital. In some jurisdictions, dividends may be declared out of the earnings of the current period even though there is an accumulated deficit from previous periods. There are other specialized features and variations among the state statutes.

For most companies, these legal restrictions have little influence on the accounting for stockholders' equity, net income, and dividends. A balance sheet does not spell out all the legal niceties of amounts available for dividends, but it ought to disclose information necessary for the user to apply the legal rules of the state in which the business is incorporated. For example, state statutes can provide that "treasury shares may be acquired only with retained earnings." If shares of stock are reacquired by the issuing corporation under these circumstances, then the amount of this restriction on dividends should be indicated by a footnote to the balance sheet.[3]

Contractual Restrictions on Dividends

Contracts with bondholders, preferred stockholders, and lessors often place restrictions on dividend payments and thereby compel the retention of earnings. For example, a recent balance sheet of the Caterpillar Tractor Company contains the following footnote:

> There are varying restrictions on the payment of cash dividends under the indentures relating to the long-term debt. . . . [U]nder the terms of the most restrictive indenture, approximately $695 million of "profit employed in the business" [retained earnings of $1.8 billion] was not available for the payment of dividends.

Bond contracts often provide that the retirement of the obligation shall be made "out of earnings." Such a provision involves curtailing dividends so that the necessary deposits or payments plus any dividends will not exceed the amount of net income for the period. The policy does not in any sense use up earnings. The result is merely to force the shareholders to increase their investment in the business by restricting the amount of dividends that might otherwise be made available to them.

Dividends and Corporate Financial Policy

Dividends are seldom declared up to the limit of the amount legally available for distribution. Some of the reasons why the directors may decide to allow the retained earnings to increase as a matter of corporate financial policy are as follows:

1 The earnings may not be reflected in a corresponding increase of available cash.
2 A restriction of dividends in prosperous years may permit the continued payment of dividends in poor years.
3 Funds may be needed for expansion of plant and equipment.
4 It may be considered desirable to reduce the amount of indebtedness rather than declare all or most of the net income in dividends.

Earnings Are Not Cash   Earlier we emphasized that net earnings do not represent a fund of available cash. Although there are ample earnings, the directors might decide that cash could not be spared for dividends equal to the net income of the period. Such factors as a maturing bank loan, an increase in the replacement cost of merchandise, or the need for new machinery could easily consume all available cash in spite of substantial profits. The statement of changes in financial position, intro-

---

[3]   *APB Opinion No. 6*, 1965.

duced in Chapter 5, helps the reader understand how earnings, and other sources of funds, have been used during the year.

Equalization of Dividends   Many shareholders of corporations want to receive a regular minimum cash return. In order to accommodate such shareholders and in order to create a general impression of stability of the corporation, directors commonly attempt to declare a regular dividend. They try to maintain the regular dividend through good years and bad. When earnings and financial policy permit, they may declare "extra" dividends.

The legal requirements for declaring regular dividends can be met by retaining part of the income over several periods to build up a balance in retained earnings. Such a policy, however, does not mean that a fund of cash will always be available for the regular dividends. Managing cash is a specialized problem of corporate finance; cash for dividends must be anticipated just as well as cash for the purchase of equipment, the retirement of debts, and so on. Borrowing from the bank to pay the regular dividend is not objectionable provided that the corporation's financial condition justifies the increase in liabilities that results.

Financing Expansion   Many corporations have financed substantial increases in their receivables, inventories, or plant and equipment without issuing bonds or additional shares of stock. Funds provided by operations that are not paid out as dividends may be used to acquire additional assets such as plant facilities. Increased retained earnings cannot be associated with any particular item or group of items in the balance sheet, but it can be correct to say that expansion is, as a matter of policy, financed through the retention of earnings. From the corporation's standpoint, the overall financial result is much the same as if a substantial amount of cash had been distributed as dividends and an equal amount of cash had been obtained through issuing additional shares of stock. It has, however, saved the trouble and cost of finding buyers and issuing the additional stock certificates.

Shareholders who want to maintain their proportion of ownership in a growing firm will prefer a policy that restricts dividends in order to finance expansion. If dividends are declared, such shareholders will use the funds received to acquire an equivalent amount of the new shares issued to finance the expansion. These shareholders will be saved transaction costs and will be able to defer individual income taxes. If the corporation pays dividends, the shareholders must pay income taxes on the receipts before they can be reinvested. If the funds are reinvested directly by the corporation, there is a deferral of, and possibly a saving in, personal income taxes.

Other shareholders may want a steady flow of cash and are unable, for contractual or psychological reasons, to sell a portion of their shares to raise cash if regular dividends are not declared. Such shareholders will resent being forced to reinvest in the corporation when expansion is financed through the retention of earnings. They may attempt to force the board of directors to adopt a more liberal dividend policy or change their investment to corporations that have more liberal dividend policies.

The degree to which expansion should be financed through retention of earnings is basically a problem of managerial finance, not accounting. Recent research in finance suggests that, within wide limits, what a firm does makes little difference so long as it tends to follow the same policy over time. Shareholders who want earnings reinvested can invest in shares of firms that finance expansion with earnings, whereas others who want a flow of cash can invest in shares of firms that pay out most of their net income in dividends.

Voluntary Reduction of Indebtedness   Contractual arrangements for reducing long-term debt may impose legal restrictions on the directors' dividend-paying powers. Even when there is no contractual obligation to do so, the directors may decide to reduce the amount of the liabilities and use the funds provided by operations for this purpose, rather than paying dividends.

OTHER CHANGES IN OWNERS' EQUITY ACCOUNTS

Stock Splits

Stock splits (or, more technically, *split-ups*) are similar to a stock dividend. Additional shares of stock are issued to shareholders in proportion to existing holdings. No additional assets are brought into the firm. In a stock split, the par or stated value of all the stock in the issued class is reduced in proportion to the additional shares issued. A corporation may, for example, have 1,000 shares of $100-par-value stock outstanding, and, by a stock split, exchange those shares for 2,000 shares of $50-par-value stock (a two-for-one split), or 4,000 shares of $25-par-value stock (a four-for-one split), or any number of shares of no-par stock. If the shares outstanding have no par or stated value, then the shareholders are merely issued additional stock certificates.

A stock split generally does not require a journal entry. The amount of retained earnings is not reduced. The amount shown in the capital stock account is merely represented by a larger number of shares. Of course, the additional number of shares held by each stockholder must be recorded in the subsidiary capital stock ledger.

It is customary to limit stock dividends to a maximum of 20 or 25 percent (that is, one share for every five or four shares held). Distributions in a greater ratio (for example, one share for every two shares held) are treated as stock splits.

A stock split (or a stock dividend) usually reduces the market value per share, all other factors remaining constant, in inverse proportion to the split (or dividend). Thus a two-for-one split could be expected to result in a 50-percent reduction in the market price per share. Stock splits have, therefore, usually been used to keep the market price per share from rising to a price level unacceptable to management. For example, the board of directors might think that a market price of $30 to $40 is an effective trading range for its stock. This is purely a subjective estimate, and is almost never supported by convincing evidence. If the share prices have risen to $60 in the market, then the board of directors may declare a two-for-one split. The only certain result of stock splits and dividends is increased record-keeping costs. Stock splits and stock dividends are seldom used by corporations whose stocks are not currently or soon to be traded on a stock exchange or in a public over-the-counter market.

Stock Options

Stock options are often a part of employee compensation plans. Under such plans, employees are granted an option to purchase shares in their company. Stock options present two kinds of accounting problems: (1) recording the granting of the option and (2) recording its exercise or lapse.

Granting the Option The generally accepted accounting treatment[4] for options usually results in no entry being made at the time the options are granted. The *exercise price of an option* is the price the option holder will have to pay to acquire the share. If the exercise price is equal to the market price at the date the option is granted, then granting of the option is not viewed as resulting in compensation to the employee or expense to the employer and no entry is made.

Exercise or Lapse When the option is exercised, the conventional entry treats the transaction simply as an issue of shares at the option price.

Cash	35,000	
Common Shares—Par		5,000
Additional Paid-in Capital		30,000

To record issue of 1,000 shares of $5-par-value stock upon exercise of options and receipt of $35,000 cash.

If the option lapses or expires without being exercised, no entry is required.

Disclosure of Options Generally accepted accounting principles require that the terms of options granted, outstanding, and exercised during a period be disclosed in text or notes accompanying the financial statements. For example, Note 17 to the financial statements of International Corporation on page 590 in Appendix A discloses data on stock options. The note explains that each of the options outstanding is exercisable at the market prices at the date of the grant. Thus International Corporation recognized no compensation expense for these options.

Stock Appreciation Rights

Because of changes in the income tax laws and because of lackluster performance of the stock market in recent years, many executives have found stock option plans less attractive as a form of compensation than before. Corporations have in many cases substituted stock appreciation rights for stock options. A *stock appreciation right* is a promise made to an employee to pay cash to that employee at a future date. The amount is the difference between the market price of a certain number of shares on a given future date and the market price of those shares on the date the rights are granted. The granting of stock appreciation rights is a form of compensation, but generally accepted accounting principles do not allow any recognition of the event in

---

[4] *APB Opinion No. 25*, 1972.

the financial statements. Only when the cash is paid to the employee in a later year is an entry made. The entry would be

```
Compensation Expense .............................................  10,000
   Cash ........................................................           10,000
Payment of $10,000 to an employee under plan granting stock appreciation
rights.
```

Stock Rights and Warrants

Opportunities to buy shares of stock may be granted through *stock rights.* Although stock rights are similar to stock options, there are some differences. Stock options are granted to employees, are nontransferable, and are a form of compensation. In contrast, stock rights are granted to current shareholders, are usually transferable, and can be traded in public markets. Stock rights are ordinarily associated with attempts to raise new capital for the firm from current shareholders.

A *stock warrant* is the name often used for the certificate issued by a corporation containing the rights granted to shareholders. The terms *warrant* and *rights* are sometimes used interchangeably in this context. In addition, stock warrants, which permit their owners to purchase shares of stock, are often sold directly to the public or may be combined with a bond issue or a preferred stock issue as a "bonus" to facilitate the issue of these other securities.

Stock rights entitle the owner to purchase shares at a specified price. They are generally exercisable for only a limited period, but occasionally are good indefinitely. Journal entries are not necessary when stock rights are granted to current shareholders. When the rights are exercised, the entry is like the one to record the issue of new shares at the price paid.

Stock warrants issued to the general investing public or used as a "bonus" with other security issues also are exercisable for a limited period in most cases. When the corporation issues directly to the public warrants containing rights to purchase 10,000 shares for $20 each and receives $15,000 cash for the warrants, the entry would be

```
Cash ........................................................  15,000
   Common Stock Warrants .........................................           15,000
To record issue of warrants to the public. The Common Stock Warrants account
would normally be included with Additional Paid-in Capital for balance sheet
presentation.
```

When the rights contained in these warrants are exercised and 10,000 shares of $5-par-value common stock are issued in exchange for the warrants and $200,000, the entry would be

```
Cash ........................................................  200,000
Common Stock Warrants .........................................   15,000
   Common Stock—Par Value ........................................            50,000
   Additional Paid-in Capital .....................................           165,000
To record the issue of 10,000 shares for $200,000 cash and the redemption
of warrants. (The amount originally received for the warrants is transferred
to Additional Paid-in Capital.)
```

If the warrants expire without having been exercised, the entry would be

Common Stock Warrants   15,000
    Additional Paid-in Capital   15,000
To record expiration of common stock warrants and the transfer to permanent
contributed capital.

Convertible Bonds

Convertible bonds are typically semiannual coupon bonds like the ones discussed
in Chapter 10 but with one added feature. The holder of the bond can *convert* or "trade
in" the bond into shares of capital stock. The number of shares to be received when
the bond is converted into stock, the dates when conversion can occur, and other
details are specified in the bond indenture. Convertible bonds are usually callable.

    Investors often find convertible bonds attractive. The owner is promised a regular
interest payment. In addition, should the company business be so successful that its
share prices rise on the stock market, then the holder of the bond can convert the
investment from debt into equity. The creditor has become an owner and can share
in the good fortune of the company.[5] Of course, an investor does not get something
for nothing. Because of the potential participation in the earnings of the company
once the bonds are converted into common shares, an investor in the bonds must
accept a lower interest rate than would be received if the bonds were not convertible
into stock. From the company's point of view, convertible bonds allow borrowing at
lower rates of interest than is required on ordinary debt, but the company must promise to give up an equity interest if the bonds are converted. The purchaser of the convertible bond is paying something for the option to acquire common stock later. Thus,
a portion of the proceeds from the issue of convertible bonds actually represents a
form of capital contribution even though it is not so recorded.

Issue of Convertible Bonds   Suppose, for example, that the Johnson Company's
credit rating would allow it to issue $100,000 of ordinary 10-year, 11-percent semi-
annual coupon bonds at par. The firm prefers to issue convertible bonds with a lower
coupon rate. Assume that Johnson Company issues at par $100,000 of 10-year, 8-
percent semiannual coupon bonds, but each $1,000 bond is convertible into 50 shares
of Johnson Company $5-par-value common stock. (The entire issue is convertible
into 5,000 shares.) Appendix Table 6 (for 8-percent coupon bonds) indicates that 8-
percent, 10-year semiannual (nonconvertible) coupon bonds sell for about 82 percent
of par when the market rate of interest is 11 percent. Thus, if the 8-percent convertible
bonds can be issued at par, then the conversion feature must be worth 18 percent of
par. Then 18 percent of the proceeds from the bond issue is actually a capital contribution by the bond buyers for the right to acquire common stock later. The logical
entry to record the issue of these 8-percent convertible bonds at par would be

---

[5]   In recent years the brokerage commission fees on convertible bonds have often been less than those
for comparable dollar amounts of investments in the underlying common shares.

Cash	100,000	
Discount on Convertible Bonds	18,000	
Convertible Bonds Payable		100,000
Additional Paid-in Capital		18,000

Issue of 8-percent semiannual coupon convertible bonds at a time when ordinary 8-percent bonds could be issued for 82 percent of par.

Notice that the determination of the amounts for this entry requires that we know
what the proceeds would be of an issue of nonconvertible bonds that are otherwise
similar to the convertible bonds. Because auditors are often unable to ascertain this
information in a reasonably objective manner, generally acceptable accounting principles do not allow the logical journal entry above. Instead, the following, simpler
entry is required:[6]

Cash	100,000	
Convertible Bonds Payable		100,000

Issue of convertible bonds at par.

This entry effectively treats convertible bonds just like ordinary, nonconvertible
bonds and records the value of the conversion feature at zero. (Generally accepted
accounting principles do recognize the potential issue of common stock implied by
the conversion feature in the calculations of earnings-per-share figures.)

Conversion of Bonds   To carry the illustration further, assume that the common
stock of the Johnson Company increases in the market to $30 a share so that one $1,000
bond, which is convertible into 50 shares of stock, can be converted into stock with a
market value of $1,500. If the entire convertible bond issue were converted into com-
mon stock at this time, then 5,000 shares of $5-par-value stock would be issued on
conversion.

    The usual entry to record the conversion of bonds into stock ignores current market
prices in the interest of simplicity and merely shows the swap of stocks for bonds at
their book value.

Convertible Bonds Payable	100,000	
Common Stock—$5 Par		25,000
Additional Paid-in Capital		75,000

To record conversion of 100 convertible bonds with book value of $100,000
into 5,000 shares of $5-par-value stock.

An allowable alternative treatment recognizes that market prices provide information
useful in quantifying the market value of the shares issued. Under the alternative
treatment, when the market price of a share is $30 and the fair market value of the
5,000 shares issued on conversion is $150,000, then the journal entry made would be

---

[6]   *APB Opinion No. 14,* 1969. The Accounting Principles Board stated that, in reaching its conclusions,
less weight was given to the practical difficulties than to some other considerations, spelled out in the
Opinion. We concur with the dissent to this Opinion expressed by several members of the Board.

Convertible Bonds Payable	100,000	
Loss on Conversion of Bonds	50,000	
Common Stock—$5 Par		25,000
Additional Paid-in Capital		125,000

To record conversion of 100 convertible bonds into 5,000 shares of $5-par-value stock at a time when the market price of a share is $30.

The alternative entry is the equivalent of the following two entries:

Cash	150,000	
Common Stock—$5 Par		25,000
Additional Paid-in Capital		125,000

To record issue of 5,000 shares of $5-par-value stock at $30 per share.

Convertible Bonds Payable	100,000	
Loss on Retirement of Bonds	50,000	
Cash		150,000

Retirement by purchase for $150,000 of 100 convertible bonds carried on the books at $100,000.

Earnings per Share

Chapter 6 explained that earnings per share of common stock is conventionally calculated by dividing net income attributable to the common stockholders by the weighted-average number of shares of common stock outstanding during the period. When a firm has outstanding securities that, if exchanged for common stock, would decrease earnings per share as conventionally calculated, then the earnings-per-share calculations become somewhat more complicated. Stock options, stock rights, warrants, and convertible bonds all have the potential of reducing earnings per share and must be taken into account in calculating earnings per share. To review the concepts involved, refer to the discussion in Chapter 6 and to the following terms in the Glossary at the back of the book: *potentially dilutive, common stock equivalent, primary earnings per share,* and *fully diluted earnings per share.*

Retained Earnings Adjustments

Nearly all items that cause the total of retained earnings to change during a period result from transactions reported in the income statement for that period. The only common exception to this general rule—dividend declarations—has been mentioned throughout the book. Dividend declarations are income distributions that reduce the balance in the Retained Earnings account but that do not affect the determination of net income. There are two other exceptions to the general rule that changes in retained earnings arise from transactions reported in the income statement. These are *corrections of errors* and *prior-period adjustments* for items significant enough that they are not reported as part of, or "buried in," the current year's income statement.

Errors result from such actions as miscounting inventories, arithmetic mistakes, and misapplications of accounting principles. Such errors, if they are material, are

EXHIBIT 11.1
Michigan Company
Consolidated Statement of
Shareholders' Equity
(in millions of dollars)

Line Number[a]		Capital Stock		Capital Account in Excess of Par Value of Shares	Earnings Retained for Use in the Business	Total Share-holders' Equity
		Shares	Amount			
	Balance, January 1, 1979	101.5	$253.7	$379.5	$5,328.1	$5,961.3
(1)	Net Income				906.5	906.5
(2)	Cash Dividends				(317.1)	(317.1)
(3)	Common Stock Issued Under Certain					
	Employee Stock Plans	0.2	0.5	9.9		10.4
(4)	Conversion of Debentures			0.6		0.6
(5)	Capital Stock Retired	(2.5)	(6.2)	(9.5)	(140.9)	(156.6)
	Balance, December 31, 1979	99.2	248.0	$380.5	$5,776.6	$6,405.1
(1)	Net Income				360.9	360.9
(2)	Cash Dividends				(298.1)	(298.1)
(3)	Common Stock Issued Under Certain					
	Employee Stock Plans	0.1	0.2	1.8		2.0
(4)	Conversion of Debentures			1.4		1.4
(5)	Capital Stock Retired	(5.7)	(14.2)	(21.8)	(194.0)	(230.0)
	Balance, December 31, 1980	93.6	$234.0	$361.9	$5,645.4	$6,241.3

[a] This caption and the line numbers do not appear on the original statement. The line numbers correspond to the journal entries in the paragraphs that follow.

corrected with debits or credits to the Retained Earnings account. If, for example, merchandise inventory is discovered to be $10,000 less than was reported at the end of the previous period, and the amount is material, then the following entry (ignoring income tax effects) would be made this period:

Retained Earnings   10,000
   Merchandise Inventory   10,000
Correction of inventory error.

Since FASB *Statement No. 16* was issued in 1977, prior-period adjustments are even rarer than they were before. There is only one transaction that qualifies for prior-period adjustment. It is esoteric and we do not discuss it here.[7]

DISCLOSURE OF CHANGES IN OWNERS' EQUITY

The changes in all owners' equity accounts must be explained in the annual reports to stockholders.[8] As previous chapters have pointed out, the reconciliation of retained earnings may appear in the balance sheet, in a statement of income and retained earnings, or in a separate statement. The financial statements of International Corporation in Appendix A show the reconciliation of retained earnings at the bottom of the combined statement of income and retained earnings (Exhibit A.1, on page 579) and the causes of all other changes in owners' equity accounts in a separate schedule in Note 18 on page 590.

A recent annual report contained the Consolidated Statement of Shareholders' Equity reproduced as Exhibit 11.1 for the Michigan Company. The 2-year comparative statement shows separate columns for capital stock at par, capital contributed in excess of par value, retained earnings (Earnings Retained for Use in the Business), and total shareholders' equity. The statement shows opening balances, net income, cash dividends, stock issued under employee option plans, capital stock retired, and capital stock issued on conversion of convertible bonds. The company made no prior-period adjustments during the 2 years reported on in Exhibit 11.1.

Journal Entries for Changes in Owners' Equity

To review the accounting for owners' equity, we reconstruct the journal entries made which resulted in the changes in owners' equity disclosed in Exhibit 11.1. The amounts in the entries below represent millions of dollars, and the journal entries are numbered in the same way as the lines in Exhibit 11.1 to which the entries apply.

---

[7] For the sake of completeness we shall state that a prior-period adjustment is recorded only when a firm receives an income tax benefit associated with using an operating loss carryforward of a subsidiary acquired in a purchase.

[8] *APB Opinion No. 12*, 1967.

	(Millions of Dollars)			
	1979		**1980**	
(1) Income Summary	906.5		360.9	
Earnings Retained for Use in Business		906.5		360.9
Net income for the year, recorded assuming that an Income Summary account is used. This entry in effect closes all temporary revenue and expense accounts with the credit balance being reported as income for the year.				
(2) Earnings Retained for Use in Business	317.1		298.1	
Cash (or Dividends Payable)		317.1		298.1
Cash dividends declared.				
(3) Cash	10.4		2.0	
Capital Stock		0.5		0.2
Capital Account in Excess of Par Value of Stock . . .		9.9		1.8
Common stock issued under certain employee stock plans.				
(4) Convertible Debentures (Bonds)	X + 0.6		Y + 1.4	
Treasury Stock		X		Y
Capital Account in Excess of Par Value of Stock . . .		0.6		1.4
Common stock issued on conversion of convertible debentures (bonds). The shares "issued" on conversion were shares reissued from a block of treasury shares. Thus, the par value of these shares is already shown in the capital stock account and does not appear in Exhibit 11.1. X and Y represent the cost to the Michigan Company of the treasury shares at the time of acquisition. Data to determine these amounts are not given.				
(5) Capital Stock	6.2		14.2	
Capital Account in Excess of Par Value of Stock	9.5		21.8	
Earnings Retained for Use in the Business	140.9		194.0	
Cash		156.6		230.0
Retirement of capital stock acquired for cash. When shares are acquired for the treasury, the debit is usually to a Treasury Stock account, shown as a contra to all of shareholders' equity. In this case, the shares are "retired," so that the specific amounts for Capital Account in Excess of Par Value and Earnings Retained for Use in the Business corresponding to these shares are identified. The debits are to these accounts and to the Capital Stock account, rather than to a single contra account.				

Changes in Owners' Equity Reported in the Statement of Changes in Financial Position

The transactions affecting owners' equity are generally reported in the statement of changes in financial position. Exhibit 11.2 presents the statement of changes in financial position for Michigan Company corresponding to Exhibit 11.1. The lines of the statement of changes in financial position that are affected by the owners' equity trans-

EXHIBIT 11.2
Michigan Company
Consolidated Statement of
Changes in Financial Position
(in millions of dollars)

Line Number[a]		1979	1980
	Working Capital, January 1	$1,684.5	$1,660.5
	Additions to Working Capital		
	From operations		
(1)	Net Income	$ 906.5	$ 360.9
	Depreciation	485.1	530.8
	Amortization of special tools	463.1	392.7
	Deferred income taxes and investment		
	tax credits	113.2	120.3
	Other	58.0	(44.0)
	Total from operations	$2,025.9	$1,360.7
	Issuance of long-term debt	186.7	578.4
	Increase in minority interests in net assets	18.4	14.4
(3 and 4)	Issuance of Common Stock	11.0	3.4
	Total additions	$2,242.0	$1,956.9
	Dispositions of Working Capital		
(2)	Cash dividends	$ 317.1	$ 298.1
	Net additions to property	1,403.0	1,414.8
(5)	Capital stock purchased	156.6	230.0
(4)	Reductions in long-term debt	203.6	78.7
	Additional investments in unconsolidated		
	subsidiaries and affiliates	120.7	33.2
	Other	65.0	62.3
	Total dispositions	$2,266.0	$2,117.1
	Decrease in Working Capital	$ (24.0)	$ (160.2)
	Working Capital, December 31	$1,660.5	$1,500.3

Changes in the Components of Working Capital	Increase (Decrease) in Working Capital	
Cash and marketable securities	$ (387.0)	$ (476.3)
Receivables	232.0	378.3
Inventories	811.9	660.3
Currently payable and deferred income taxes . . .	125.6	46.0
Accounts payable and accrued liabilities	(419.2)	(395.2)
Debt payable within one year	(439.5)	(447.8)
Other current assets	52.2	74.5
Net Change	$ (24.0)	$ (160.2)

[a] This caption and the line numbers do not appear on the original statement. The line numbers correspond to the journal entries in the text.

actions are identified with the numbers used for the journal entries reconstructed above. The working capital produced by operations shows net income as the first item (1). Dividends are the first use ("disposition") of working capital (2). The proceeds of the common stock issues are shown as a source of ("an addition to") working capital (3 and 4). For entry (4), only the amount credited to Capital Account in Excess of Par Value of Stock is shown on the Issuance of Common Stock and Reductions in Long-Term Debt lines. The exchange of treasury stock for the convertible debt is viewed as an exchange not involving working capital. Finally, the acquisition and retirement of capital stock that was retired are reported in the statement of changes in financial position as a use of working capital (5).

SUMMARY

Accounting for owners' equity in a corporation is based on the premise that there should be a separate account for each source of capital contributed by owners. The sources of capital from shareholders include:

1 Receipts from issues of stock at par or stated value
2 Receipts in excess of par or stated value of stock issues
3 Earnings retentions.

Owners' equity is reduced when the corporation experiences losses from business operations, declares dividends, or acquires treasury stock.

APPENDIX 11.1
Partnerships

A partnership is a contractual arrangement between individuals to share resources and operations in a jointly owned business. The partnership form is generally used by small businesses and groups of professionals such as lawyers, accountants, or doctors. (A partnership need not be "small"; some of the large public accounting partnerships and law firms are multimillion dollar businesses.) The relationships between the partners are governed by the partnership agreement, which is usually a written contract. The partnership contract specifies matters such as division of income, management responsibilities, and procedures to be followed upon dissolution of the partnership or withdrawal of a partner. Partnerships are used as a business form because:

1 They are simple to organize.
2 There are no income taxes on partnership earnings comparable to the corporate income tax. Rather, income is allocated to the individual partners, who include their share of the income as part of their personal taxable income for the year.

The debts of the partnership are the residual responsibility of the general partners. Partnerships may have limited partners who are not personally responsible for partnership debts, but every partnership must have at least one general partner who is fully liable for all debts. The accounting for partnerships is based on the same underlying principles as for the corporation except for the entries that affect owners' equity.

For all practical purposes, a sole proprietorship is accounted for like a partnership with a single partner. Thus, the following discussion applies also to sole proprietorships except that there is no need to separate the interest of the several partners.

CAPITAL CONTRIBUTIONS: PARTNERSHIPS

The amount and the form of the capital contribution of each partner are determined by the partnership agreement. The property contributed may be in the form of cash or other property, or it may be in the form of goodwill—above-normal earnings expected to be derived from the reputation or experience of a particular partner. A separate capital account is opened for each partner. This account is credited with the amount of each partner's original investment and with any additional amounts subsequently invested in the business.

The capital account balances may be increased by the investment of additional funds or by the retention of earnings; they may be decreased by partners' withdrawals or by losses. The understanding between the partners as to the provisions for making additional investments or withdrawing funds should be covered by the partnership agreement. The partners may, for example, agree to keep the ratios of capital accounts constant, which implies that withdrawals by partners must be in proportion to the ownership percentage of each partner.

The amount appearing in each partner's capital account is significant for a number of purposes. Its proportion to the total partners' capital indicates his or her *interest in the capital of the business.* For example, if the total capital is $40,000 and one partner's capital account has a balance of $10,000, then that partner has a one-quarter, or 25-percent interest, in the partnership at that time. The capital balances are often a factor in the distribution of net income, as when profits are distributed in proportion to capital balance or when an "interest" allowance is made on capital balances. In case of dissolution, the balance in the partners' accounts indicates their share in the net assets (assets less liabilities) of the partnership. Any profits or losses incurred in the disposition of the assets would, of course, change the capital account balances.

The legal features of partnerships may require a partner to make additional contributions in order to meet the liabilities of the firm. General partners usually are "jointly and severally" liable for partnership obligations, so that one partner may not only lose his or her entire investment in the enterprise but also may have to pay the obligations of the partnership from personal resources. Such a partner would then try to collect from the other partners their proportionate shares of the obligations.

FORMATION OF A PARTNERSHIP

Accounting for the formation of a partnership is demonstrated in the following illustration.

Lois L. Baker and John A. Stone start business as partners. Each partner is to contribute $20,000 of capital. Baker, who has been in business before, contributes some installment notes receivable from her customers with a face value of $7,000 but valued at $6,000, office equipment worth $3,000, cash of $1,000, and her customer relationships valued at $10,000 as goodwill. Stone's contribution consists of $8,000 cash, office equipment valued at $5,000, an automobile valued at $3,600, and his promissory 8-percent demand note for $3,400. In transactions of this sort, it is necessary for the partners to agree on the valuation that is to be assigned to each asset; this is especially true in the case of goodwill. The entries would be

Installment Notes Receivable	7,000	
Office Equipment	3,000	
Cash	1,000	
Goodwill	10,000	
Allowance for Uncollectible Notes		1,000
L. L. Baker, Capital		20,000
To record contributions of partner Baker.		
Cash	8,000	
Office Equipment	5,000	
Automobile	3,600	
Notes Receivable—Partners	3,400	
J. A. Stone, Capital		20,000
To record contributions of partner Stone.		

The opening balance sheet of the partnership would appear as shown in Exhibit 11.3.

ALLOCATION OF PARTNERSHIP NET INCOME

In a partnership, the change in ownership equity from operations shown in each partner's capital account is determined in two steps: (1) allocating net income of the period among the partners, and (2) deducting partners' drawings during the period.

At the end of each accounting period, the net income of the period is allocated among the partners. The partnership agreement determines the fraction to which each partner is entitled. If the partnership agreement does not specify the sharing arrangements, the Uniform Partnership Act generally provides that profits and losses are to be shared equally.

There are many variations in the arrangements that may be specified by the partnership agreement. The more common types of arrangements for the allocation of profits and losses are as follows:

1 A fixed percentage allocation
2 Allocation in proportion to capital balances
3 Allocation on a combination of bases to reflect various aspects of the partners' contribution of services and capital to the business.

The allocation of net income is usually recorded in the final closing entry. The Income Summary account is debited with an amount that reduces its balance to zero, and each of the partners' capital accounts is credited as appropriate. (If there is a loss for the period, the accounts debited and credited in the previous sentence are, of course, reversed.) The simplest form of net income or loss distribution is the allocation to each

EXHIBIT 11.3
Opening Balance Sheet
for Partnership
Baker & Stone
(Date)

Assets			Liabilities and Capital	
Cash		$ 9,000	L. L. Baker, Capital	$20,000
Installment Notes			J. A. Stone, Capital	20,000
Receivable	$7,000			
Less: Allowance for Un-				
collectible Notes	1,000	6,000		
Notes Receivable—Partners		3,400		
Office Equipment		8,000		
Automobile		3,600		
Goodwill		10,000		
Total Assets		$40,000	Total Liabilities and Capital	$40,000

partner of a fixed fraction or percentage of the total net income or net loss. For example, if there are three partners, each may be entitled to one-third or some other proportion of net income. If the net income of the Baker and Stone partnership for the year is $60,000, and the profits and losses are to be distributed 60 percent to Baker and 40 percent to Stone, the closing entry would be

Income Summary (All Revenue and Expense Accounts in Aggregate)	60,000	
L. L. Baker, Capital		36,000
J. A. Stone, Capital		24,000

Revenue and expense accounts have been closed to an Income Summary account. This entry closes the Income Summary account and allocates income between partners.

PARTNERS' WITHDRAWALS

A partnership may legally adopt any desired policy with regard to the retention or distribution of net income. The withdrawal of assets by the partners is guided only by the wishes of the partners and the provisions of the partnership agreement. These withdrawals seldom present accounting complications, and do not merit extended discussion.

PARTNERS' CAPITAL ACCOUNTS

One capital account for each partner will often be sufficient. It will be credited with the partner's share of the net income as well as with capital contributions and debited with the partner's share of any losses and the amount of any withdrawals. The balance of such an account may be withdrawn at any time, subject to the restrictions imposed by the partners themselves in their partnership agreement.

Although a single capital account for each partner is usually sufficient, a second account, known as a *drawing* or *personal* account, is often used. The drawing account records each partner's withdrawals for personal use and other current charges. The balance in the drawing account at the end of the period is then closed into the capital account.

The monthly entry to record withdrawals of $1,250 by partner Baker might be

L. L. Baker, Drawings	1,250	
Cash		1,250
Entry to record partner Baker's monthly withdrawal.		

At the end of the year the drawing account would have a debit balance of $15,000 ($= 12 \times \$1,250$). If Baker's share of income for the year is $36,000, the combined closing entries for her might be

Income Summary	36,000	
L. L. Baker, Drawings		15,000
L. L. Baker, Capital		21,000
To close temporary account.		

SUMMARY OF PARTNERSHIP ACCOUNTING

In a partnership, capital is either contributed directly by the owners or indirectly through earnings retentions. Since there is no capital stock, there is no need to differentiate contributions by classes of stock or between contributions made at par value and in excess of par value. Rather, the accounting for partnership owners' equity attempts to disclose separately the interest of each partner. Partnership owners' equity is increased by capital contributions and periodic income and is reduced by partners' drawings and losses.

QUESTIONS AND PROBLEMS

1 Review the meaning of the following concepts or terms discussed in this chapter.
   a Corporation.
   b Corporate charter.
   c Corporate bylaws.
   d Capital stock, common stock, preferred stock.
   e Cumulative preferred stock.
   f Callable preferred stock.
   g Convertible preferred stock.
   h Par value.
   i Stated value.
   j Additional paid-in capital.
   k Treasury stock.

    l Earnings are not cash.

    m Convertible bond.

    n Stock dividend.

    o Stock split.

    p Stock option.

    q Stock appreciation right.

    r Stock right.

    s Stock warrant.

    t Correction of error.

    u Prior-period adjustment.

2 Review the meaning of the following concepts or terms discussed in the appendix of this chapter.

    a Partnership.

    b General and limited partners.

    c Drawings.

3 Under what circumstances would you expect par-value stock to be issued at a price in excess of par? What is the entry to record such an issue?

4 A construction corporation is attempting to borrow money on a note secured by some of its property. A bank agrees to accept the note, provided that the president of the corporation will personally endorse it. What is the point of this requirement? Would the bank be likely to require a similar endorsement if the firm were a partnership?

5 "Par value of preferred stock is frequently a significant figure, but par value of common stock possesses little significance." Why may par value of preferred stock be significant? In what way is the par value of common stock with a par value different from the stated value of no-par common stock?

6 What is treasury stock? How is it reported on the balance sheet?

7 A certain corporation retained almost all of its earnings, only rarely paying a cash dividend. When some of the stockholders objected, the reply of the president was: "Why do you want cash dividends? You would just have to go to the trouble of reinvesting them. Where can you possibly find a better investment than our own company?" Comment.

8 Compare the position of a shareholder who receives a cash dividend with that of one who receives a stock dividend.

9 At the annual shareholders' meeting, the president of the Santa Cris Corporation made the following statement: "The net income for the year, after taxes, was $1,096,000. The directors have decided that the corporation can only afford to distribute $500,000 as a cash dividend." Are the two sentences of this statement compatible?

10 The text says that "convertible bonds are usually callable." The call feature is included so that the issuer can force conversion of the bonds. Explain.

11 a Assume that accounting were to require recognition of compensation expense on the date that stock options were granted to an employee. A precise measure of the amount of the compensation expense would not be possible, but various approximations could be made. How might the accountant put a dollar amount on the compensation expense granted through stock options? You may assume that the exercise price is the market price on the date the option is granted.

b Assume that accounting were to require recognition of compensation expense on the date a stock appreciation right were granted to an employee. A precise measure of the amount of the compensation expense would not be possible, but various approximations could be made. How might the accountant put a dollar amount on the compensation expense granted through stock appreciation rights?

12 Indicate whether each of the following statements is true or false and justify your response. Ignore the effects of income taxes.

a Cash dividends reduce the book value per share of capital stock.

b A stock dividend does not affect the Retained Earnings account.

c Investing 50 percent of net income in government bonds has no effect on the amount legally available for dividends.

d Stock dividends reduce the book value per share of capital stock.

e The declaration of a cash dividend does not reduce the amount of the stockholders' equity.

f The distribution of a stock dividend tends to reduce the market value per share of capital stock.

g A stock split generally does not affect the Retained Earnings account.

h A stock-dividend declaration is usually accompanied by a reduction in par or stated value per share.

13 Indicate the effect of each of the following transactions on **(1)** the balance in the Retained Earnings and **(2)** the total stockholders' equity.

a Bonds are issued at a discount.

b A check is written to the Internal Revenue Service for additional income taxes levied on past years' income (no previous entry).

c A stock split is voted by the directors. The par value per share is reduced from $200 to $50 and each shareholder is given four new shares in exchange for each old share.

d The manager is voted a bonus of $3,500 by the directors.

e Notes payable in the face amount of $50,000 are paid by check.

f A dividend in preferred stock is issued to common stockholders (no previous entry).

g Securities held as a long-term investment are sold at book value.

h A building site is donated to the company by the local chamber of commerce.

i A building is sold for less than its book value.

14 Refer to the Simplified Funds Statement for a Period in Exhibit 5.15 on page 174. Ten of the lines in the statement are numbered. Line (2) should be expanded to say "Additions for Expenses and Other Charges Against Income Not Using Funds," and line (3) should be expanded to say "Subtractions for Revenues and other Credits to Income Not Producing Funds from Operations." Ignore the other lines in responding to the questions below.

Assume that the accounting cycle is complete for the period and that all of the financial statements have been prepared. Then it is discovered that a transaction has been overlooked. That transaction is recorded in the accounts and all of the financial statements are corrected. Define *funds* as *working capital*. For each of the following transactions, indicate which of the numbered lines of the funds statement is affected and by how much. Ignore income tax effects.

a Common shares are issued for $100,000.

b Common shares originally issued for $60,000 are repurchased for $75,000 and retired.

c Convertible bonds with a book value of $100,000 and a market value of $250,000 are converted into common shares with a par value of $20,000 and a market value of $250,000.

d Treasury shares acquired for $10,000 are reissued for $15,000.

e A stock dividend is declared. The par value of the shares issued is $10,000 and their market value is $100,000.

f A cash dividend of $50,000 is declared.

g A previously declared cash dividend of $50,000 is paid.

h Stock rights are exercised. The shares have a par value of $10,000 and market value of $25,000 on the date of exercise. The exercise price is $15,000 and $15,000 cash is received.

15 For each of the following transactions, present the journal entries in two-column form. These transactions do not relate to the same set of records.

a The shares of no-par stock of a corporation are selling on the market at $200 a share. In order to bring the market value down to a "more popular" figure, the board of directors votes to issue five shares to stockholders in exchange for each share already held by them. The shares are issued.

b The treasurer of the corporation reports that cash on hand exceeds normal requirements by $200,000. Pending a decision by the board of directors on the final disposition of the funds, investments in marketable securities in the amount of $198,640 are made.

c The net income for the year is $150,000. The directors vote to issue 500 shares of 6-percent, $15-par-value preferred stock as a stock dividend on the 2,500 shares of no-par common stock outstanding. The preferred's market price is $20 a share. The common's market price is $5 a share.

d After the books are closed and the financial statements are issued, it is discovered that an arithmetic error was made in calculating depreciation on equipment for the preceding period. The depreciation charged was $900 too high.

16 The comparative balance sheet of the Forty-Misty Company shows the following data:

	Dec. 31, 1979	Dec. 31, 1980
Common Stock	$1,200,000	$1,320,000
Retained Earnings	460,000	400,000
Total Stockholders' Equity	$1,660,000	$1,720,000

During 1980, common stockholders received $60,000 in cash dividends and $120,000 in stock dividends. A refund on 1978 taxes of $30,000 was received on March 1, 1980, and was credited directly to Retained Earnings. A loss on retirement of plant assets of $5,600 occurred during the year and was charged directly to Retained Earnings.

a What net income is reported for 1980 after the accounting was done as described?

b What net income should actually be reported for 1980? Show your calculations.

17 The comparative balance sheet of the Royal Corporation shows the following information:

	Dec. 31, 1979	Dec. 31, 1980
Preferred Stock (6%)	$ 750,000	$ 600,000
Common Stock	1,400,000	1,540,000
Retained Earnings	324,000	372,000
Total Stockholders' Equity	$2,474,000	$2,512,000

During 1980 stock dividends of $140,000 were issued to common stockholders. In addition, common stockholders received $70,000 in cash dividends; the preferred stockholders received $40,500 in cash dividends. On July 1, 1980, preferred stock with a par value of $150,000 was called at 104; that is, $156,000 was paid to retire the shares. What net income is reported to stockholders for 1980?

18 The Chelex Company began business on January 1. Its balance sheet on December 31 contains the stockholders' equity section shown below.

Chelex Company
Stockholders' Equity
as of December 31

Capital Stock ($10 par value)	$ 50,000
Additional Paid-in Capital	77,000
Retained Earnings	10,000
Less: 300 Shares Held in Treasury	(6,000)
Total Stockholders' Equity	$131,000

During the year, Chelex Company engaged in the following capital stock transactions:

(1) Issued shares for $25 each.
(2) Acquired a block of 500 shares for the treasury in a single transaction.
(3) Reissued some of the treasury shares.

Assuming that these were all the capital stock transactions during the year, answer the following questions:

a How many shares were issued for $25?
b What was the price at which the treasury shares were acquired?
c How many shares were reissued from the block of treasury shares?
d What was the price at which the treasury shares were issued?
e What journal entries must have been made during the year?

19 The Worman Company began business on January 1. Its balance sheet on December 31 contains the stockholders' equity section shown below.

Worman Company
Stockholders' Equity
as of December 31

Capital Stock ($5 par value)	$ 50,000
Additional Paid-in Capital	252,800
Retained Earnings	25,000
Less: 600 Shares Held in Treasury	(16,800)
Total Stockholders' Equity	$311,000

During the year, Worman Company engaged in the following capital stock transactions:

(1) Issued shares for $30 each.
(2) Acquired a block of 1,000 shares for the treasury in a single transaction.
(3) Reissued some of the treasury shares.

Assuming that these were the only capital stock transactions during the year, answer the following questions:
a How many shares were issued for $30 each?
b What was the price at which the treasury shares were acquired?
c How many shares were reissued from the block of treasury shares?
d What was the price at which the treasury shares were reissued?
e What journal entries must have been made during the year?

20 On March 1, Wilma A. Strover, Larry J. Martin, and Roberta R. Dawson form a partnership to conduct a retail business. The partnership agreement provides for the following contributions by the partners:

(1) Wilma A. Strover, who has been conducting a retail business as a sole proprietor, is to turn over all the assets of her business except the cash to the partnership and the partnership is to assume all its liabilities. The store's condensed balance sheet at February 28 showed the following assets and liabilities:

Assets:
Cash, $8,000
Accounts Receivable, $7,600
Merchandise, $30,200
Store Furniture and Fixtures (net), $7,800

Liabilities:
Accounts Payable, $3,800.

The partners agree that an allowance for uncollectible accounts of $1,000 should be set up for the receivables and that the store furniture and fixtures should be valued at $7,000.
(2) Larry J. Martin is to contribute a delivery truck valued at $3,000, his 6-month, 8-percent note for $10,000, and cash of $7,000.
(3) Roberta R. Dawson is to contribute $16,000 in cash and office equipment valued at $4,000.

All capital contributions are made as set forth in the partnership agreement.
a Prepare journal entries for Strover's books to show her investment in the partnership.
b Prepare journal entries for the partners' contributions on the new set of books that is opened for the partnership.
c Present a balance sheet of the partnership on March 1, after the contributions have been made.

21 S. Walter, R. Ron, and K. Kelvin are partners engaged in a retail business under the name of Prosperity Company. Their partnership agreement provides that net income or loss is to be shared in the following manner:
(1) Interest at the rate of 8 percent per annum is to be allowed on the partners' average capital balances during the year.

(2) The following salary allowances are to be provided: Ron $17,000 and Kelvin $14,400. Walter is no longer active in the business and receives no salary allowance.

(3) Any remaining income or loss is to be divided 40 percent to Walter, 35 percent to Ron, and 25 percent to Kelvin.

The partners' capital accounts during the year show the following data:

	S. Walter, Capital					**R. Ron, Capital**			
3/31	2,000	1/ 1	80,000		6/30	2,000	1/ 1	36,000
6/30	2,000				8/31	4,000	4/30	14,000
9/30	2,000				10/31	6,000		

	K. Kelvin, Capital		
1/31	6,000	1/ 1	24,000
10/31	3,000	9/30	4,000

The net income from operations for the year, before deducting any salary or interest allowances, was $54,960.

a   Show the calculation of the partners' average capital balances.

b   Prepare a schedule showing the distribution of net income to the partners.

c   Prepare a schedule of partners' capital accounts for the year.

22 Journalize the following transactions:

a   A cash dividend of $2 a share is declared on the outstanding preferred stock. There are 5,000 shares authorized, 3,000 shares issued, and 100 shares reacquired and held in the treasury.

b   A cash dividend of $1 a share is declared on the no-par common stock of which there are 10,000 shares authorized, 7,000 shares issued, and 1,000 shares reacquired and held in the treasury.

c   The dividend on the preferred stock is paid.

d   The dividend on the common stock is paid.

23 The following events relate to stockholders' equity transactions of the Richardson Copper Company during the first year of its existence. Present journal entries for each of the transactions.

a   January 2. Articles of incorporation are filed with the State Corporation Commission. The authorized capital stock consists of 5,000 shares of $100 par value, preferred stock which offers a 5-percent annual dividend, and 50,000 shares of no-par common stock. The original incorporators are issued 100 shares of common stock at $20 per share; cash is collected for the shares. A stated value of $20 per share is assigned to the common stock.

b   January 6. 1,500 shares of common stock are issued for cash at $20 per share.

c   January 8. 2,800 shares of preferred stock are issued at par.

d   January 9. Certificates for the shares of preferred stock are issued.

e   January 12. The tangible assets and goodwill of Richardson Copper Works, a partnership, are acquired in exchange for 600 shares of preferred stock and 10,000 shares of common stock. The tangible assets acquired are valued as follows: inventories, $40,000; land, $45,000; buildings, $80,000; and equipment, $95,000.

f   July 3. The semiannual dividend on the preferred stock outstanding is declared, payable July 25, to stockholders of record on July 12.

g July 5. Operations for the first 6 months have been profitable, and it is decided to expand. The company issues 20,000 shares of common stock for cash at $23 per share.

h July 25. The preferred stock dividend declared July 3 is paid.

i October 2. The directors declare a dividend of $1 per share on the common stock, payable October 25, to stockholders of record on October 12.

j October 25. The dividend on common stock declared on October 2 is paid.

24 The following data are selected from the records of capital stock and retained earnings of the Wheellock Company. Present journal entries for these transactions.

a July 5, 1979. Articles of incorporation are filed with the secretary of state. The authorized capital stock consists of 1,000 shares of 6-percent preferred stock with a par value of $100 per share and 10,000 shares of no-par common stock.

b July 8, 1979. The company issues 3,000 shares of common stock for cash at $50 per share.

c July 9, 1979. The company issues 6,000 shares of common stock for the assets of the partnership of Wheellock and Wheellock. Their assets are valued as follows: accounts receivable, $30,000; inventories, $60,000; land, $20,000; buildings, $90,000; and equipment, $100,000.

d July 13, 1979. 750 shares of preferred stock are issued at par for cash.

e December 31, 1979. The balance in the Income Summary account after closing all expense and revenue accounts is $200,000. That account is to be closed to the Retained Earnings account.

f January 4, 1980. The regular semiannual dividend on the preferred stock and a dividend of $2 per share on the common stock are declared. The dividends are payable on February 1.

g February 1, 1980. The dividends declared on January 4 are paid.

h July 2, 1980. The regular semiannual dividend on the preferred stock is declared. The dividend is payable on August 1.

i August 1, 1980. The dividend declared on July 2 is paid.

25 Give journal entries for the following transactions.

a Outstanding shares of stock are acquired by the issuing corporation for its treasury at a cost of $500,000.

b Dividends are declared on preferred stock, $120,000.

c A dividend is paid to common stockholders consisting of shares of preferred stock in the same corporation with a par value of $200,000.

d A dividend is paid to common stockholders consisting of shares of no-par common stock in the same corporation. The amount assigned to these shares of stock is $600,000.

e The building is mortgaged for $100,000, and this amount is distributed to the common stockholders as a cash dividend.

26 Give journal entries, if required, for the following transactions, which are unrelated unless otherwise specified:

a The regular quarterly dividend is declared on the 5-percent, $100-par-value preferred stock. There are 10,000 shares authorized, 8,000 shares issued, and 1,600 shares reacquired and held in the treasury.

b The dividend on the preferred stock (see part **a**) is paid.

c A stock dividend of $250,000 of no-par common stock is issued to common stockholders.

d A building replacement fund of $125,000 is created. The fund is to be used to purchase a new building when the present one becomes inadequate.

    e Bonds with $500,000 par value are retired at par out of the sinking fund created for that purpose.

    f The shares of no-par stock of the corporation are selling on the market at $300 a share. In order to bring the market value down to a more popular price and thereby broaden the distribution of its stockholdings, the board of directors votes to issue four extra shares to stockholders for each share already held by them. The shares are issued.

27 The following transactions all relate to the same set of records. Use the straight-line method for amortizing bond discount and premium. Journalize these transactions.

    a The company issues 23,000 shares of common stock (par value, $100 per share) for cash at $105 per share.

    b Twenty-year, 8-percent bonds with $500,000 par value are issued for $492,000.

    c Interest expense on the bond is recognized at the time the first semiannual interest payment is made.

    d The bond indenture requires a sinking fund to be built up to pay the principal of the bonds at maturity. The company deposits $18,600 with the sinking fund trustee.

    e A cash dividend of $2 per share of common stock is declared.

    f At the end of the twentieth year of the life of the bonds, the final semiannual interest payment is made and the bonds are retired. There are sufficient funds in the sinking fund to accomplish the retirement.

    g A fund of $50,000 is created for future expansion.

    h An additional 7,000 shares of common stock are issued for cash at $110 a share.

28 Refer to the schedule reproduced here, which shows employee stock option data for the General Products Company (GP). At December 31, 1980, there were 2.7 million options outstanding to purchase shares at an average of $54 per share. Total stockholders' equity at December 31, 1980, was about $2.5 billion.

General Products Company
Disclosure of Employee
Stock Options

Stock Options	Shares Subject to Option	Average per Share	
		Option Price	Market Price
Balance at December 31, 1978................	2,388,931	$45	$72
Options granted	475,286	77	77
Options exercised........	(297,244)	42	76
Options terminated	(90,062)	45	—
Balance at December 31, 1979	2,476,911	50	83
Options granted	554,965	75	75
Options exercised........	(273,569)	42	74
Options terminated	(58,307)	52	—
Balance at December 31, 1980................	2,700,000	54	77

a If GP were to issue 2.7 million shares in a public offering at the market price per share on December 31, 1980, what would be the proceeds of the issue?

b If GP were to issue 2.7 million shares to employees who exercised all outstanding stock options, what would be the proceeds of the issue?

c Are GP's stockholders better off under **a** or under **b?**

d The text accompanying the stock option data in the GP annual report reads, in part, as follows:

> Option price under these plans is the full market value of General Products common stock on date of grant. Therefore, participants in the plans do not benefit unless the stock's market price rises, thus benefiting all share owners. . . .

GP seems to be saying that stockholders are not harmed by these options, whereas your answers to parts **a** and **b** show stockholders are worse off when options are exercised than when shares are issued to the public. Attempt to reconcile GP's statement with your own analysis in parts **a** and **b**.

29 On January 2, 1976, the Oklahoma Corporation issues $1 million of 20-year, $1,000-par-value, 6-percent semiannual coupon bonds at par. Each $1,000 bond is convertible into 40 shares of $1-par-value common stock. The Oklahoma Corporation's credit rating is such that it would have to issue 8-percent semiannual coupon bonds if the bonds were not convertible and if they were to be issued at par. On January 2, 1980, the bond issue is converted into common stock. The common stock has a market price of $45 a share on January 2, 1980. Present the journal entries made on January 2, 1976 and 1980, under generally accepted accounting principles, to record the issue and conversion of the issue.

30 The net income of the firm of Donald, Marvin, and Patron for the year is $54,000. The partnership agreement provides that the net profits shall be divided in the following manner:

(1) Interest at 8 percent per annum on the average investment of each partner during the year shall be computed and credited to their respective capital accounts.

(2) The partners' capital accounts shall be credited with special salary allowances as follows: Donald, $30,000; Marvin, $20,000; Patron, $10,000.

(3) The balance of the net income or loss shall be divided equally among the respective partners' capital accounts.

The capital accounts of the partners show the following data:

	Donald	Marvin	Patron
Balance, January 1	$20,000	$10,000	$10,000
Withdrawals, June 30	(10,000)	(4,000)	(6,000)
Invested, September 30		4,000	4,000
Balance December 31 Before Distributing Income for the Year	$10,000	$10,000	$ 8,000

Calculate and present in a schedule the division of the net income among the three partners. Neither partners' salary allowances nor interest on capital contributions is treated as expenses in the determination of net income.

31 Gordon and Ginn are partners with capital balances of $90,000 and $120,000, respectively, on January 1. Their partnership agreement provides:

(1) Salaries are to be allowed to Gordon, $15,000 per year; to Ginn, $14,000 per year.
(2) Each partner is to be credited with an interest allowance at the rate of 8 percent per annum on his capital balance at the beginning of the year.
(3) The balance of profits or losses is to be distributed 60 percent to Gordon and 40 percent to Ginn.

During the year, both partners drew their full salary allowances. What would the balances in the partners' capital accounts be at December 31, under the following alternative conditions? Assume that net income figures are calculated before salary and interest allowances are deducted.
a Net income during the year was $30,000.
b Net income during the year was $70,000.
c Net income during the year was $120,000.

32 In May 1976, the Skelton Company issued 100,000 shares of no-par, convertible preferred stock for $50 a share. The shares promised a dividend of $4. All shares were issued for cash. These shares were convertible into common stock (par value, $1 a share) at a rate of 5 shares of common stock for each share of preferred. The preferred shares were issued when the prime interest rate was 5 percent, and they are not regarded as equivalent to common shares in the calculation of earnings per share.

The company's earnings increased sharply during the next 2 years, and during January 1980 all shares of preferred were converted into common shares. One million common shares were outstanding before conversion of the shares. If the conversion had not taken place, the net income to common for the year 1980 would have been $2,000,000. Other data are as follows:

Market Prices:	**May 1976**	**January 1980**
Skelton Common Stock	$10	$ 20
Skelton $3.50 Preferred Stock	50	100
Book Value per Skelton Common Share (before conversion to preferred)	14	16

a Prepare journal entries to record the issuance and conversion of the preferred stock.
b Ignore the preferred shares in computing earnings per common share before conversion of the shares. What was the effect of the conversion on book values and on earnings per common share?
c Did the conversion of the preferred shares into common stock lead to a dilution of the common shareholders' equity? Explain your reasoning.

33 After several years of rapid expansion, the Spero Company approached the State National Bank for a $1 million loan. The bank was willing to lend the money at an interest rate of 10 percent per year. Spero Company then approached an individual investor who was willing to provide the same funds for only 8 percent per year provided that the Spero Company gave the investor an option to purchase 20,000 shares of Spero Company $5-par-value common stock for $20 per share at any time within 5 years of the initial date of the loan.

Spero weighed both opportunities and decided to borrow from the investor. At the time of the loan, the common shares had a market price of $15 per share. Five years after the initial date of the loan, the investor exercised the option and purchased 20,000 shares for $20 each. At that time, the market price of the common shares was $45 each.

a Did the use of the "detachable warrants" (the technical name for the option granted to the investor) reduce the Spero Company's cost of borrowing?

b How should the loan and annual interest payments of $80,000 be recorded in the books of the Spero Company to reflect the economic reality of the transaction.

c How might the exercise of the warrants (and the purchase of the 20,000 shares) be recorded?

d Did exercise of the option dilute the owners' equity of the other shareholders on the date the option was exercised?

e What disclosures during the life of the loan do you think appropriate? Why?

34 The stockholders' equity section of the balance sheet of the Conte Corporation at December 31 is shown below.

Stockholders' Equity

Common Stock—$10 Par Value, 500,000 Shares Authorized and	
100,000 Shares Outstanding	$1,000,000
Additional Paid-in Capital	500,000
Retained Earnings	2,000,000
Total Stockholders' Equity	$3,500,000

a Determine the total book value and the book value per common share as of December 31.

b For each of the following transactions or events, give the appropriate journal entry and determine the total book value and the book value per common share of the Conte Corporation after the transaction. The transactions and events are independent of each other, except where noted.

(1) A 10-percent stock dividend is declared when the market price of Conte Corporation's common stock is $50 per share.

(2) A two-for-one stock split is declared and the par value of the common stock is reduced from $10 to $5 per share. The new shares are issued immediately.

(3) Ten thousand shares of Conte Corporation's common stock are purchased on the open market for $50 per share and held as treasury stock.

(4) Ten thousand shares of Conte Corporation's common stock are purchased on the open market for $30 per share and held as treasury stock.

(5) The shares acquired in (3) are sold for $60 per share.

(6) The shares acquired in (3) are sold for $40 per share.

(7) The shares acquired in (3) are sold for $30 per share.

(8) Options to acquire 10,000 shares of Conte Corporation stock are exercised by officers for $20 per share.

(9) Same as (8), except that the exercise price is $40 per share.

(10) Convertible bonds with a book value of $300,000 and a market value of $340,000 are exchanged for 10,000 shares of common stock having a market value of $34 per share. No gain or loss is recognized on the conversion of bonds.

(11) Same as (10), except that gain or loss is recognized on the conversion of bonds into stock. Ignore income tax effects.

c Using the results from b, summarize the transactions and events that result in a reduction in

(1) total book value

(2) book value per share.

35 Refer to the financial statements for International Corporation in Appendix A, Note 17 and Note 18, starting on page 590.

    a Note 17 presents information on stock options. Reconstruct journal entries for the events summarized in Note 17 that occurred during 19X1 that require accounting recognition.

    b Note 18 presents information on all changes in contributed capital accounts. Reconstruct journal entries for the events summarized in Note 18 that occurred during 19X1 that require accounting recognition.

    c Identify which of the entries, if any, in part **b** were already accounted for by the entries made in part **a**.

36 Repeat the instructions in the preceding question for 19X0.

37 (Case introducing earnings per share calculations for companies with a complicated capital structure.) The Layton Ball Corporation has a relatively complicated capital structure. In addition to common shares, it has issued stock options, warrants, and convertible bonds. Exhibit 11.4 summarizes some pertinent information about these items. Net income for the year 1979 is $9,500, and the income tax rate used in computing income tax expense is 40 percent of pretax income.

EXHIBIT 11.4
Layton Ball Corporation
Information on Capital Structure
for Earnings-per-Share Calculation
(Problem 37)

Assume the following data about the capital structure and
    earnings for the Layton Ball Corporation for the year 1979:

Number of Common Shares Outstanding Throughout 1979	2,500 shares
Market Price per Common Share Throughout 1979	$25
Options Outstanding During 1979:	
Number of Shares Issuable on Exercise of Options	1,000 shares
Exercise Price per Share	$15
Warranty Outstanding During 1979:	
Number of Shares Issuable on Exercise of Warrants	2,000 shares
Exercise Price per Share	$30
Convertible Bonds Outstanding (Issued in December 1968)	
Number	100 bonds
Proceeds per Bond at Time of Issue (= par value)	$1,000
Shares of Common Issuable on Conversion (per bond)	10 shares
Coupon Rate (per year)	$4\frac{1}{6}$%

---

    a First, ignore all items of capital except for the common shares. Calculate earnings per common share.

    b In past years, employees have been issued options to purchase shares of stock. Exhibit 11.4 indicates that the price of the common stock throughout 1979 was $25, but that the stock options could be exercised at any time for $15 each. The holder of an option is allowed to surrender it along with $15 cash and receive one share in return. Thus the number of shares would be increased, which would decrease the earnings-per-share figure. The company would, however, have more cash. We could assume that the company would use the cash to go out and buy outstanding shares for the treasury, which would reduce the number of shares outstanding and increase earnings per share. Assume that the holders of warrants were to tender their warrants along with $15 each to purchase shares. Assume that the company would use the cash to purchase shares for the treasury at a price of $25 each. Compute a new earnings-per-share figure. (Treasury shares are *not* counted in the denominator of the earnings-per-share calculation.)

c Exhibit 11.4 indicates that there are also warrants outstanding in the hands of the public. Anyone who owns such a warrant is allowed to turn in that warrant along with $30 cash and to purchase one share. If the warrants are exercised then there would be more shares outstanding, which would reduce earnings per share. The company would, however, have more cash, which it could use to purchase shares for the treasury, reducing the number of shares outstanding. Assume that all holders of warrants were to exercise them. Assume that the company were to use the cash to purchase outstanding shares for the treasury. Compute a new earnings-per-share figure. (Ignore the information about options and the calculations in part **b** at this point.)

d There are convertible bonds outstanding. A holder of a convertible bond is entitled to trade that bond in for 10 shares. If a bond is converted, the number of shares would increase, which would tend to reduce earnings per share. On the other hand, the company would not have to pay interest and thus would have no interest expense on the bond because it would no longer be outstanding. This would tend to increase income and earnings per share. Assume that all holders of convertible bonds were to convert their bonds into shares. Compute a new net income figure (do not forget income tax effects on income of the interest saved) and a new earnings per share figure. (Ignore the information about options and warrants and the calculations in parts **b** and **c** at this point.)

e Now consider all the above calculations. Which sets of assumptions from parts **b, c,** and **d** would lead to the lowest possible earnings per share when they are all made simultaneously? Compute a new earnings per share under the most restrictive set of assumptions about reductions in earnings per share.

f Accountants publish several earnings-per-share figures for companies with complicated capital structures and complicated events during the year. *The Wall Street Journal,* however, publishes only one figure in its daily columns (where it reports the price-earnings ratio—the price of a share of stock divided by its earnings per share). Which of the figures computed above for earnings per share do you think would be reported by *The Wall Street Journal* as *the* earnings-per-share figure?

CHAPTER 12
INVESTMENTS IN CORPORATE SECURITIES

For a variety of reasons, corporations often acquire the capital stock of other corporations. For example, a corporation may hold excess cash, and its management may think that an investment in another corporation is the most profitable use that can be made of the excess funds. Relatively short-term investments of excess cash in corporate securities are usually classified as Marketable Securities and are shown in the Current Assets section of the balance sheet. Chapter 7 discusses the accounting for marketable securities.

A corporation may acquire another corporation's stock to gain control of the acquired company's operations or to make easier the integration of separate operations. These investments, which have a more long-term purpose, are typically classified on the asset side of the balance sheet in a separate section called "Investments."

The method of accounting for long-term investments depends primarily on the percentage of the voting stock that one corporation owns of another. If the acquiring company owns less than 20 percent of the stock of the acquired company, it generally accounts for its investment by the *lower-of-cost-or-market method*. If it owns from 20 or more, up to 50 percent or less of the acquired company, it generally must use the *equity method*. If the acquiring company owns more than 50 percent of the stock of the acquired company, the *consolidation method* is usually used in reports to stockholders, but the equity method may be used under special circumstances. The three methods are discussed in the following sections.

Throughout this chapter, we call the acquiring corporation P for *purchaser* or for *parent*, depending on the context, whereas S stands for *seller* or for *subsidiary*.

MINORITY INVESTMENTS

When a firm owns less than 50 percent of the voting shares of another company, the firm is called a *minority* investor. Investors account for minority investments using one of two methods, depending on the fraction of shares owned. These two methods are the *lower-of-cost-or-market method* and the *equity method*.

Lower-of-Cost-or-Market Method

When a corporation, P, holds less than 20 percent of the stock of another corporation, S, P will use the lower-of-cost-or-market method to account for its investment under current generally accepted accounting principles. Chapter 7 presented this method of accounting for marketable securities. The accounting for long-term investments closely parallels the accounting for marketable securities. There are only two important differences. First, marketable securities are current assets, whereas investments are noncurrent assets. Second, the amounts of unrealized losses (and any subsequent gains) from changes in market prices of the *portfolio* of marketable equity securities, during the time the securities are held, do not appear in the income statement. Instead, they are debited (losses) or credited (gains) directly to an owners' equity account on the balance sheet.[1]

Suppose that P acquires 1,000 shares of S for $40,000. This is P's only investment in an equity security, so the single investment is its "portfolio" for purposes of applying the lower-of-cost-or-market method. The entry to record the acquisition would be

Investment in Equity Securities	40,000	
Cash		40,000
Acquisition of equity shares as investment.		

If the purpose of the purchase were merely a short-term investment to use idle cash, the debit would be to Marketable Securities.

If, while P holds this stock, S declares a dividend of $2 per share, P would make the following entry:

Dividends Receivable	2,000	
Dividend Revenue		2,000
Dividend declared on shares held as an investment.		

When the dividend is collected, P will debit Cash and credit Dividends Receivable.

If, at the end of the period, the market value of the investment has dropped to $30,000, the journal entry would be

Unrealized Loss on Investment in Equity Securities	10,000	
Allowance for Excess of Cost of Investment in Equity Securities over Market Value		10,000
Entry to write investment down to market value.		

The credit is to a contra account, known as a *valuation account*. In this regard, the entry is like the ones discussed in Chapter 7 for marketable equity securities treated as current assets. The Unrealized Loss account does not appear on the income statement for the period, but appears in the owners' equity section of the balance sheet as an amount reducing owners' equity. (Unlike the Treasury Stock account, it is not

---

[1] Financial Accounting Standards Board, *Statement of Financial Accounting Standards No. 13,* 1976.

typically shown as a contra to all of owners' equity, but is shown with the other components of owners' equity as a negative number.)

If, at the end of the next period, the market value of the investment has increased to $36,000, the entry would be

```
Allowance for Excess of Cost of Investment in Equity Securities
over Market Value  ..................................................  6,000
    Unrealized Loss on Investment in Equity Securities  ......................          6,000
To write the investment up to current market value.
```

This entry does not affect reported income for the period. The Unrealized Loss on Investment account is a balance sheet account, not an income statement account. The Allowance account can never have a debit balance. That is, once the market value has recovered to original cost, no additional debits to the Allowance account are permitted. The investment will continue to be shown at original cost.

When the investment is sold, or otherwise disposed of, a realized gain or loss is recognized in an amount equal to the difference between selling price and the *original cost* (not current book value) of the securities. Assume that the investment is sold at the end of the third period for $39,000. Then the holding loss during the time the investment is held is $1,000 (= $40,000 − $39,000). The entire loss is recognized in the period when the investment is sold:

```
Cash  ..........................................................  39,000
Realized Loss on Investment in Equity Securities........................   1,000
    Investment in Equity Securities  .....................................          40,000
To recognize sale of investments at a loss.
```

Since this was P's only investment in marketable equity securities, an entry must also be made at the end of the period to eliminate amounts in the Allowance account and in the Unrealized Loss account:

```
Allowance for Excess of Cost of Investment in Equity Securities
over Market Value  ................................................  4,000
    Unrealized Loss on Investment in Equity Securities  ......................          4,000
At the end of the period, the Allowance account has a credit balance of $4,000; this
entry removes the Allowance account and the Unrealized Loss account from the
balance sheet.
```

Suppose that the investment were sold for $42,000. The investment would be

```
Cash  ..........................................................  42,000
    Investment in Equity Securities  .....................................          40,000
    Realized Gain on Investment in Equity Securities ........................           2,000
To recognize sale of investments at a gain.
Allowance for Excess of Cost of Investment in Equity Securities
over Market Value  ................................................  4,000
    Unrealized Loss on Investment in Equity Securities  ......................          4,000
To close the Allowance account and the Unrealized Loss account, since there
are no equity securities at the end of the period.
```

To summarize, when Company P accounts for its long-term investment in Company S using the lower-of-cost-or-market method:

1 Company P reports as income each period its share of the dividends declared by Company S.
2 Company P reports on the balance sheet the lower-of-cost-or-market value of the shares in Company S.
   a Declines in market value below cost are debited directly to an owners' equity account such as "Unrealized Losses on Investments" and credited to an asset contra account.
   b Subsequent increases in price up to, but not exceeding, the original cost of the investment are debited to the asset contra and credited to the balance sheet account for unrealized losses.
3 Company P recognizes gains or losses on the income statement from holding the stock of Company S only at the time the shares are sold. The gain or loss is the difference between selling price and original cost.

Equity Method: Rationale

Under the lower-of-cost-or-market method, P recognizes income or loss on the income statement only when it becomes entitled to receive a dividend or sells all or part of the investment. Suppose, as often happens, that S follows a policy of financing its own growing operations through retention of earnings and consistently declares dividends substantially less than its net income. The market price of S's shares may increase. Under the lower-of-cost-or-market method, P will continue to show the investment at original cost and P's income from the investment will be only the modest dividends it receives. If P holds a substantial fraction of the shares of S, then P can influence the dividend policy of S. Under these conditions, the lower-of-cost-or-market method may not reasonably reflect the earnings of S generated under P's control. The equity method is designed to provide a better measure of P's earnings and its assets for investments where it can control the operations of S because of substantial holdings.

When Company P can exercise significant influence over operating and financial policies of Company S, generally accepted accounting principles require that the investment by P in S be reported using the *equity method.*[2] To determine when significant influence can be exercised involves judgment. For the sake of objectivity, generally accepted accounting principles presume that P can influence S and should use the equity method when P owns 20 percent or more of the common stock of S, but not more than 50 percent of it. It may be required even when less than 20 percent is owned, but in those cases management and accountants must agree on whether or not Company P exercises significant influence over Company S. (The equity method is also required when more than 50 percent of the shares are owned and consolidated statements are not issued.)

---

[2] *APB Opinion No. 18,* 1971.

Equity Method: Procedures

Under the equity method, the initial purchase of an investment is recorded at cost, the same as under the lower-of-cost-or-market method. Company P treats as income (or revenue) each period its proportionate share of the periodic earnings, not the dividends, of Company S. Dividends declared by S are then treated by P as a reduction in its Investment in S.

Suppose that P acquires 30 percent of the outstanding shares of S for $600,000. The entry to record the acquisition would be

(1) Investment in S	600,000	
Cash		600,000
Investment made in 30 percent of Company S.		

Between the time of the acquisition and the end of P's next accounting period, S reports income of $80,000. P, using the equity method, would record

(2) Investment in S	24,000	
Revenue from Investments		24,000
To record 30 percent of income earned by investee accounted for using the equity method. Revenue account title often used in practice is Equity in Income of Unconsolidated Affiliates.		

If S declares a dividend of $30,000 to holders of common stock, P would be entitled to receive $9,000 and would record

(3) Dividends Receivable	9,000	
Investment in S		9,000
To record dividends receivable from investee accounted for using the equity method and the resulting reduction in the investment account.		

Notice that the credit is to the Investment in S account. P records income earned by S as an *increase* in investment. The dividend becomes a return of capital or a *decrease* in investment.

Suppose that S subsequently reports earnings of $100,000 and also declares dividends of $40,000. P's entries would be

(4) Investment in S	30,000	
Revenue from Investments		30,000
(5) Dividends Receivable	12,000	
Investment in S		12,000
To record revenue and dividends from investee, accounted for using equity method.		

P's Investment in S account now has a balance of $633,000 as follows:

Investment in S

(1) 600,000	9,000 (3)
(2) 24,000	12,000 (5)
(4) 30,000	
Bal. 633,000	

If P now sells one-fourth of its shares for $152,000, P's entry to record the sale would be

(6) Cash	152,000	
Loss on Sale of Investment in S	6,250	
Investment in S		158,250
($\frac{1}{4}$ × $633,000 = $158,250.)		

The equity method as described above is simple enough to use. To make financial reports using the equity method more realistic, generally accepted accounting principles require some modification of the entries under certain circumstances.[3]

Even though S does not declare all of its earnings in dividends, P reports its proportionate share of S's earnings as income. But this income to P is not currently taxable. Consequently, there will sometimes be an entry in the deferred tax account. Determination of the amount of the deferred tax charge presents issues too complex for this introductory text.

An additional complication in using the equity method arises when the acquisition cost of P's shares exceeds P's proportionate share of the book value of the net assets (= assets minus liabilities), or stockholders' equity of S, at the date of acquisition. For example, assume that P acquires 25 percent of the stock of S for $400,000 when the total stockholders' equity of S is $1 million. The excess of P's cost over book value acquired is $150,000 (= $400,000 − .25 × $1,000,000) and is called *goodwill*. Goodwill must be amortized over a period not greater than forty years.[4] Accounting for goodwill, including its amortization, is discussed later in this chapter.

On the balance sheet, an investment accounted for on the equity method is shown in the Investments section. The amount shown will generally be equal to the acquisition cost of the shares plus P's share of S's undistributed earnings since the date the shares were acquired. On the income statement, P shows its share of S's income as a revenue each period. (The financial statements of the investee, S, are not affected by the accounting method used by the investor, P.)

Minority Investments in the Statement of Changes in Financial Position

When Company P uses the lower-of-cost-or-market method to account for its investment in Company S, all dividend revenues recognized in determining net income also produce working capital. No adjustment to net income is required in determining Funds Provided by Operations.

Accounting for investments using the equity method, however, requires an adjustment to net income to determine Funds Provided by Operations. Suppose that Company P prepares its financial statements at the end of a year during which transactions (1)–(5), above, occurred. P's revenue from its investment in S is $54,000. This amount is the sum of the revenue recognized in transactions (2) and (4). P's income (ignoring

---

[3] *APB Opinion No. 18*, 1971.
[4] *APB Opinion No. 17*, 1970.

income tax effects) increased $54,000 because of its investment. However, P's working capital increased by only $21,000 [transactions (3) and (5)] as a result of S's dividend declarations. Consequently, there must be a *subtraction* from net income of $33,000 (= $54,000 − $21,000) in determining Funds Provided by Operations, to show that working capital did not increase by as much as the amount of revenue recognized under the equity method.

In preparing P's statement of changes in financial position using the T-account method, the following change in a noncurrent asset account would have to be explained:

Investment in S

Bal. 0	
Bal. 633,000	

The entries to explain this debit change of $633,000 would be

Investment in S	600,000	
Working Capital (Use—Acquisition of Investment)		600,000
To recognize use of funds for an investment in a noncurrent asset.		
Investment in S	33,000	
Working Capital (Subtraction—Undistributed Income		
Under Equity Method)		33,000
To recognize that working capital was not increased by the full amount of revenue recognized under the equity method.		

Keep in mind that these two entries are not formally made in the accounting records, but are made only in the work sheet used for preparing the statement of changes in financial position.

Minority Investments Illustrated

Exhibits A.1, A.2, and A.3 (on pages 579–581) show the income statement, balance sheet, and statement of changes in financial position of the International Corporation. The balance sheet, Exhibit A.2, shows investments of approximately $289 million as of year-end 19X1.

The income statement for 19X1 shows income of $14,513,000 from the investments accounted for on the equity method as "Equity in Income (Loss) from Nonconsolidated Subsidiaries and Affiliated Companies." This income did not produce working capital because the subsidiaries and affiliated companies did not declare dividends. Thus, the funds statement, Exhibit A.3, shows a subtraction of $14,513,000 in deriving "Working Capital Provided by Continuing Operations." For the year 19X0, the nonconsolidated subsidiaries and affiliates had losses of $32,285,000. The parent's equity in these losses is shown on the income statement as an amount reducing net income. On the funds statement in Exhibit A.3, the amount is added back in deriving funds provided by operations because it did not use working capital. Instead, this loss reduced a noncurrent asset account, Investments.

MAJORITY INVESTMENTS

When a firm owns more than 50 percent of the voting stock of another company, the firm is called the *majority* investor, or *parent*. In most cases, the financial statements of the majority-owned *subsidiary* are combined, or *consolidated,* with those of the parent. In some instances, however, consolidated financial statements are not prepared. Instead, the investment is reported using the equity method. Whether consolidated statements are prepared or the equity method is used depends on the consolidation policy of the firm, which is discussed later in this section.

Reasons for Legally Separate Corporations

There are many reasons why a business firm prefers to operate as a group of legally separate companies, rather than as a single legal company. From the standpoint of the parent company, the more important reasons for maintaining legally separate subsidiary companies include the following:

1   To reduce the financial risk. Separate corporations may be used for mining raw materials, transporting them to a manufacturing plant, producing the product, and selling the finished product to the public. If any one part of the total process proves to be unprofitable or inefficient, the corporation performing the particular step can be dissolved or sold and the required goods or services purchased from other sources without seriously interfering with the operations of other corporations in the group. Losses from insolvency will fall only on the owners and creditors of the one subsidiary corporation.
2   To meet more effectively the requirements of state corporation laws and tax legislation. If an organization does business in a number of states, it is often faced with overlapping and inconsistent taxation, regulations, and requirements. It may be more economical to organize separate corporations to conduct the operations in the various states.
3   To expand with a minimum of capital investment. A firm may absorb another company by acquiring a controlling interest in its voting stock. The result may be accomplished with a substantially smaller capital investment, as well as with less difficulty and inconvenience, than if a new plant had been constructed or a complete merger were arranged.

Purpose of Consolidated Statements

For a variety of reasons, then, a single economic entity may exist in the form of several legally separate companies. (The General Electric Company, for example, consists of about 150 separate legal companies.) Consolidated financial statements present the results of operations, financial position, and changes in financial position of an affiliated group of corporations under the control of a parent essentially as if the group of corporations were a single entity. The parent and each subsidiary corporation are legally separate entities, but they operate as one centrally controlled *economic entity*. Consolidated financial statements generally provide more useful information to the stockholders of the parent corporation than would separate financial statements of the parent and each subsidiary.

Consolidated financial statements also generally provide more useful information than does using the equity method. The parent, because of its voting interest, can effectively control the use of the subsidiary's assets. Consolidation of the individual assets and equities of both the parent and the subsidiary provides a more realistic picture of the operations and financial position of the single economic entity.

In a legal sense, consolidated statements merely supplement, and do not replace, the separate statements of the individual corporations, although it is common practice to present only the consolidated statements in published annual reports.

Consolidation Policy

Consolidated financial statements are generally prepared when all of the following three criteria are met:

1 The parent owns more than 50 percent of the voting stock of the subsidiary.
2 There are no important restrictions on the ability of the parent to exercise control of the subsidiary.
3 The asset and equity structure of the subsidiary is not significantly different from that of the parent.

Ownership of more than 50 percent of the subsidiary's voting stock implies an ability to exert control over the activities of the subsidiary. For example, the parent can control the subsidiary's corporate policies and dividend declarations. There may be situations, however, where control of the subsidiary's activities cannot be carried out effectively, despite the ownership of a majority of the voting stock. For example, the subsidiary may be located in a foreign country that has severely restricted the withdrawal of funds from that country. Or the subsidiary may be in bankruptcy and under the control of a court-appointed group of trustees. In these cases, the financial statements of the subsidiary probably will not be consolidated with those of the parent. When the parent owns more than 50 percent of the shares and can exercise control, but consolidated statements are not prepared, then the equity method must be used.

If the asset and equity structure of the subsidiary is significantly different from that of the parent, the subsidiary's financial statements are frequently not consolidated with those of the parent and the equity method is used. For example, a consolidated statement might not be prepared if the parent is a manufacturing concern with heavy investments in property, plant, and equipment, whereas the subsidiary is a finance or insurance company with large holdings of cash, receivables, and marketable securities. The presentation of consolidated financial statements of corporations with significantly different asset and equity structures is sometimes thought to submerge potentially important information about the individual corporations. This is particularly true when the assets of the subsidiary are not, by law, fully available for use by the parent, such as when the subsidiary is a bank or an insurance company.

Example 1   American Telephone and Telegraph Company (AT&T) conducts its activities through many subsidiaries organized under the laws of various states (for example, Southern New England Telephone Company, Southern Bell, Pacific Telephone and Telegraph). AT&T owns all, or a significant percentage, of the common shares of each of these subsidiaries. It can therefore exert control over the activities of the subsidiaries much the same as if the subsidiaries were branches or divisions. AT&T often raises capital in the debt and equity markets and distributes it to the subsidiaries. In evaluating the operations and financial position of AT&T, it is more useful to consider all of the assets under its control, not just those of the parent, many of whose assets are investments. Consolidated statements are also easier to comprehend than separate statements for each of its many operating subsidiaries. AT&T also owns Western Electric, the manufacturer of most of AT&T's telephone equipment. Since Western Electric is a manufacturing company whereas most of the other subsidiaries operate telephone systems, AT&T chooses not to consolidate Western Electric, but to use the equity method for it.

Example 2   General Motors, General Electric, and Westinghouse, among others, have wholly owned finance subsidiaries. These subsidiaries make many of their loans to customers who wish to purchase the products of the parent company. The financial statements of these subsidiaries are not consolidated with those of the parent company. The assets of these subsidiaries are largely receivables. It is argued that statement readers might be misled as to the relative liquidity of these firms if consolidated statements were prepared and the assets of the parent, largely noncurrent manufacturing plant and equipment, were combined with the more liquid assets of the finance subsidiary.

Example 3   Sears, Roebuck & Co. and J. C. Penney Company are large retailers. Each has organized a separate subsidiary to finance customers' purchases and another separate subsidiary to sell insurance. Sears consolidates the finance subsidiary, but not the insurance subsidiary. Penney's consolidates neither, but uses the equity method for both.

Example 4   A major mining corporation owns a mining subsidiary in South America. The government of the country enforces stringent control over cash payments outside the country. The company is not able to control the use of all the assets, despite the ownership of a majority of the voting shares. Therefore, it does not prepare consolidated statements with the subsidiary.

Disclosure of Consolidation Policy   The summary of significant accounting principles in financial statements includes a statement about the consolidation policy of the parent. If a significant majority-owned subsidiary is not consolidated, then its financial statements are often included in the notes to the financial statements. For example, Note 1 on page 582 for the International Corporation indicates that all significant majority-owned subsidiaries are consolidated with the exception of its finance company and its real estate development company. For these, the equity method is required and used. The financial statements of the finance company are themselves presented in Note 11 on pages 587–588.

Understanding Consolidated Statements

The remainder of this section discusses the following four concepts essential for understanding published consolidated statements:

1 The need for intercompany eliminations
2 The meaning of consolidated income and retained earnings
3 The nature of the minority interest
4 The consolidated statement of changes in financial position.

Need for Intercompany Eliminations The items on consolidated statements are little more than the sum of the items on the financial statements of the corporations being consolidated. Consolidated statements are intended to reflect the results that would be achieved if the affiliated group of companies were a single company. The amounts resulting from a summation of the accounts of the companies being consolidated must therefore be adjusted to eliminate double counting and intercompany transactions.

For example, a parent may lend funds to its subsidiary. If the separate balance sheets were merely added together, those funds would be counted twice: once as the notes receivable on the parent's books and again as the cash or other assets on the subsidiary's books. Consolidated balance sheets eliminate intercompany transactions that would not be reported for a single, integrated enterprise. Thus, the note receivable of the parent and the note payable of the subsidiary are eliminated in preparing the consolidated balance sheet.

To take a more complex example, the parent's balance sheet shows an asset, Investment in Subsidiary. The subsidiary's balance sheet shows its individual assets. If the two balance sheets were merely added together, the sum would show both the parent's investment in the subsidiary's assets and the assets themselves. The parent's balance sheet item, Investment in Subsidiary, must therefore be eliminated from the sum of the balance sheets. Because the consolidated balance sheet must maintain the accounting equation, corresponding eliminations must be made on the right-hand side as well.

To understand the eliminations from the right-hand side of the balance sheet, recall that the right-hand side shows the sources of the firm's financing. The subsidiary is financed by creditors (liabilities) and by owners (shareholders' equity). Assume that the parent owns 100 percent of the subsidiary's voting shares. Then the assets on the consolidated balance sheet of the single economic entity are financed by the creditors of both companies and by the parent's shareholders. That is, the equities of the consolidated entity are the liabilities of both companies but the shareholders' equity of the parent alone. If the shareholders' equity accounts of the subsidiary were added to those of the parent, then the financing from the parent's shareholders would be counted twice (once on the parent's books and once on the subsidiary's books). Hence, when the parent's investment account is eliminated from the sum of the two companies' assets, the accounting equation is maintained by eliminating the shareholders' equity accounts of the subsidiary.

Similarly, certain intercompany transactions must be eliminated from the sum of income statement accounts so that the operating performance of the consolidated entity can be meaningfully presented. For example, if a manufacturing parent sells goods to a subsidiary which, in turn, sells the goods to the public, then the sum of individual income statements would double-count sales and costs of goods sold. Suppose that the parent sells to the subsidiary but that the subsidiary has not yet sold the goods to the public. The parent will have recorded profits on the sale, but from the standpoint of the overall economic entity, no profits for shareholders have actually been realized because the items are still in the inventory of the overall economic entity. Consequently, profits from the parent's sales to subsidiaries that have not been realized by subsequent sales to outsiders are eliminated from consolidated net income and balance sheet amounts. The consolidated income statement attempts to show sales, expenses, and net income figures that report the results of operations of the group of companies as though it were a single company.

Consolidated Income and Retained Earnings The amount of consolidated net income for a period is the same as the amount that would be reported if the parent company used the equity method of accounting for the intercorporate investment. That is, consolidated net income is equal to

$$\begin{array}{l} \text{Parent Company's} \\ \text{Net Income} \end{array} + \begin{array}{l} \text{Parent's Share of Sub-} \\ \text{sidiary's Net Income} \end{array} - \begin{array}{l} \text{Profit (or Plus Loss) on} \\ \text{Intercompany Transactions.} \end{array}$$

The principal difference between the consolidated income statement and the income statement where the subsidiary is accounted for under the equity method is the components of income presented. When a consolidated income statement is prepared, the individual revenues and expenses of the subsidiary (less intercompany adjustments) are combined with those of the parent. When the equity method is used for an unconsolidated subsidiary, the parent's share of the subsidiary's net income minus gain (or plus loss) on intercompany transactions is shown on a single line of the income statement with a title such as "Equity in Earnings (Loss) of Unconsolidated Subsidiary." (See, for example, the income statement of International Corporation in Exhibit A.1, page 579. That income statement is a consolidated income statement. The company has, however, "subsidiaries and affiliates" that are not consolidated but are accounted for with the equity method.)

The amount shown on the consolidated balance sheet for retained earnings is likewise the amount that would be reported if the parent company used the equity method of accounting for the intercorporate investment. That is, consolidated retained earnings is equal to

$$\begin{array}{l} \text{Parent's} \\ \text{Retained} \\ \text{Earnings} \end{array} + \begin{array}{l} \text{Parent's Share of the Change} \\ \text{in Subsidiary's Retained} \\ \text{Earnings Since Acquisition} \end{array} - \begin{array}{l} \text{Profit (or Plus Loss)} \\ \text{on Intercompany} \\ \text{Transactions.} \end{array}$$

If the parent actually used the equity method of accounting for the investment on its books, the second and third terms above would already be included in the parent's retained earnings. In this case, consolidated retained earnings equals the parent's retained earnings. The parent may, however, merely record the investment at cost on its own, single-company books if it intends to publish consolidated statements. Recall that the investment account is eliminated in preparing consolidated statements so on its own books the parent can account in any convenient way for a subsidiary to be consolidated in published financial statements. Some parent companies use the equity method, whereas others merely record the investment at cost and record dividends as revenue. If the parent records the investment at cost, then the parent's share of the subsidiary's retained earnings since acquisition less any profit on intercompany transactions must be combined with the parent's retained earnings in preparing the consolidated balance sheet. The mechanics of the required adjustments are discussed later.

Minority Interest in Consolidated Subsidiary   In many cases, the parent will not own 100 percent of the voting stock of a consolidated subsidiary. The owners of the remaining shares of voting stock are called *minority shareholders,* or the *minority interest.*[5] These shareholders continue to have a proportionate interest in the net assets (= total assets minus total liabilities) of the subsidiary as shown on the subsidiary's separate corporate records. They also have a proportionate interest in the earnings of the subsidiary.

An issue in the generally accepted accounting principles for consolidated statements is whether the statements should show only the parent's share of the assets and equities of the subsidiary or whether they should show all of the subsidiary's assets and equities along with the minority interests in them. The generally accepted accounting principle is to show all of the assets and equities of the subsidiary, since the parent, with its controlling voting interest, can effectively direct the use of all the assets and liabilities, not merely an amount equal to the parent's percentage of ownership. The consolidated balance sheet and income statement in these instances must, however, disclose the interest of the minority shareholders in the subsidiary that has been consolidated.

The amount of the minority interest shown on the balance sheet is generally the result of multiplying the common stockholders' equity of the subsidiary by the minority's percentage of ownership. For example, if the common shareholders' equity (or assets minus liabilities) of a consolidated subsidiary totals $500,000 and the minority owns 20 percent of the common stock, then the minority interest shown on the consolidated balance sheet is $100,000 (= .20 × $500,000).

The minority interest is typically presented among the equities on the consolidated balance sheet between the liabilities and shareholders' equity. See, for example, the International Corporation consolidated balance sheet in Exhibit A.2 on page 580. Note that "Minority Interest" is shown among the liabilities but is not clearly labeled as one. This presentation is typical of many published financial statements. We think that the right-hand side of the balance sheet should contain only liabilities and owners' equity items, so that the minority interest should be classified as one or the other. The minority interest does not meet the criteria to be a liability discussed in Chapter 10,

---

[5] Do not confuse this minority interest in a consolidated subsidiary with a firm's own minority investments, discussed earlier. The minority *interest* belongs to others outside the parent and its economic entity. The parent's minority *investments* are merely those for which the parent owns less than 50 percent of the shares.

because there is no maturity date. The minority interest might be classified as an indeterminate-term liability, much the same as deferred taxes.

The amount of the minority interest in the subsidiary's income shown on the consolidated income statement is generally the result of multiplying the *subsidiary's* net income by the minority's percentage of ownership. The consolidated income is allocated to show the portions applicable to the parent company and the portion of the subsidiary's income applicable to the minority interest. Refer again to International Corporation's consolidated income statement shown in Exhibit A.1. Notice the deduction of $2,452,000 for the "Minority Interest in Net Income of Consolidated Subsidiaries" before the consolidated net income figure. The consolidated net income includes only that portion of net income of subsidiary companies allocable to the shareholders of International Corporation. Typically, the minority interest in the subsidiary's income is shown as a deduction in calculating consolidated net income.

Statement of Changes in Financial Position   The consolidated statement of changes in financial position is constructed from the consolidated balance sheet, income statement, and supplementary information in the same way as explained in Chapter 5 for a single company. Two items may appear in the consolidated statement, however, that do not usually appear on single-company funds statements.

The first item in consolidated funds statements that does not appear in single-company statements is the addback to net income for the minority interest in earnings. As we pointed out in the discussion of minority interest above, International Corporation shows a deduction of $2,452,000 for the minority's share of earnings before the final net income figure in Exhibit A.1. This deduction did not require the use of any working capital. Consequently, there must be an addback to derive "Working Capital Provided by Continuing Operations" in the consolidated statement of changes in financial position. International Corporation shows the addback of $2,452,000 in its statement of changes in financial position, Exhibit A.3, as "Minority Interest in Net Income of Consolidated Subsidiaries."

Second, the amortization of goodwill may appear in consolidated income statements. Goodwill was introduced in Chapter 9, and is explained in more detail later in this chapter. Just like other amortization charges, amortization of goodwill causes a reduction in reported net income without using any working capital. Therefore, there must be an addback to net income in the amount of that amortization in order to derive the amount of working capital provided by operations. Often, however, as in the case of the consolidated statement of changes in financial position of International Corporation shown in Exhibit A.3, the amount of this amortization is so small that it does not warrant separate disclosure and is included with "Other" items.

Limitations of Consolidated Statements

The consolidated statements do not replace those of individual corporations; rather, they supplement those statements and aid in their interpretation. Creditors must rely on the resources of one corporation and may be misled if forced to rely entirely on a consolidated statement that combines the data of a company in good financial condition with those of one verging on insolvency. Dividends can legally be declared only from the retained earnings of one corporation. Where the parent company does not own all of the shares of the subsidiary, the outside or minority stockholders can judge the dividend constraints, both legal and financial, only by an inspection of the subsidiary's statements.

In the best of all possible worlds, parent corporations would report on their own and their subsidiaries' operations in both single-company and consolidated statements. Generally accepted accounting principles do not require the publication of both single-company and consolidated reports. Only the consolidated report need be published. Few U.S. corporations publish separate financial statements for both the parent and the subsidiaries as single companies. (In recent years Kimberly Clark Corporation has done so.)

PREPARING CONSOLIDATED FINANCIAL STATEMENTS

This section illustrates the preparation of consolidated financial statements for Company P and Company S. Knowing how to construct consolidated financial statements is not essential for learning how to interpret and to analyze them. Nevertheless, we think it helps.

Data for the Illustration

The single-company financial statements of Company P and Company S are shown in Exhibit 12.1. The following additional information is to be considered in preparing the consolidated financial statements.

1 Company P acquired 100 percent of the outstanding shares of Company S for $650,000 cash on January 1, 1976. At the time of acquisition, the book value of the shareholders' equity of Company S was $650,000 comprised of the following balances.

Company S, January 1, 1976

Capital Stock	$500,000
Retained Earnings	150,000
Total Shareholders' Equity	$650,000

Company P made the following journal entry on its books at the time of acquisition:

Investment in Stock of Company S (at cost)	650,000	
Cash		650,000

2 Company P records its investment in the shares of Company S at their cost. (The equity method need not be used in the parent's single-company accounts when consolidated statements are to be prepared.)
3 At December 31, 1979, $12,000 of Company S's accounts receivable represent amounts payable by Company P.
4 During 1979 Company S sold merchandise to Company P for $40,000. None of that merchandise remains in Company P's inventory as of December 31, 1979.

EXHIBIT 12.1
**Illustrative Data for
Preparation of Consolidated
Financial Statements**

CONDENSED INCOME STATEMENT FOR 1979	Single-Company Statements	
	Company P	Company S
Revenues:		
Sales	$ 900,000	$ 250,000
Dividend Revenue	13,000	—
Total Revenues	$ 913,000	$ 250,000
Expenses:		
Cost of Goods Sold (excluding depreciation)	$ 440,000	$ 80,000
Depreciation Expense	120,000	50,000
Administrative Expenses	80,000	40,000
Income Tax Expense	104,000	32,000
Total Expenses	$ 744,000	$ 202,000
Net Income	$ 169,000	$ 48,000
Dividend Declarations	50,000	13,000
Increase in Retained Earnings for the Year	$ 119,000	$ 35,000

**CONDENSED BALANCE SHEETS
FOR DECEMBER 31, 1979**

	Company P	Company S
Assets:		
Accounts Receivable	$ 200,000	$ 25,000
Investment in Stock of Company S (at cost)	650,000	—
Other Assets	2,150,000	975,000
Total Assets	$3,000,000	$1,000,000
Equities:		
Accounts Payable	$ 75,000	$ 15,000
Other Liabilities	70,000	280,000
Capital Stock	2,500,000	500,000
Retained Earnings	355,000	205,000
Total Equities	$3,000,000	$1,000,000

**CONDENSED (PARTIAL) STATEMENT OF
CHANGES IN FINANCIAL POSITION FOR 1979**

	Company P	Company S
Sources of Working Capital:		
Net Income	$ 169,000	$ 48,000
Add Back Depreciation Expense	120,000	50,000
Total Sources	$ 289,000	$ 98,000
Uses of Working Capital:		
Dividends Declared and Paid	50,000	13,000
Net Increase in Working Capital	$ 239,000	$ 85,000

EXHIBIT 12.2
Work Sheet to Derive Consolidated Financial Statements for Company P and Company S Based on Data in Postclosing Trial Balances and Income Statements

	Company P		Company S		Adjustments and Eliminations		P and S Consolidated	
	Debit	Credit	Debit	Credit	Debit	Credit	Debit	Credit
Trial Balance Accounts								
Accounts Receivable	200,000		25,000			**(3)** 12,000	213,000	
Investment in Stock of Company S	650,000		—		**(1)** 55,000	**(2)** 705,000	—	
Other Assets	2,150,000		975,000				3,125,000	
Total Assets	3,000,000		1,000,000		55,000	717,000	3,338,000	
Accounts Payable		75,000		15,000	**(3)** 12,000			78,000
Other Liabilities		70,000		280,000				350,000
Capital Stock		2,500,000		500,000	**(2)** 500,000			2,500,000
Retained Earnings (Co. P)		355,000				**(1)** 55,000		410,000
Retained Earnings (Co. S)				205,000	**(2)** 205,000			
Total Equities		3,000,000		1,000,000	717,000	55,000		3,338,000
Income Statement and Income Distribution Accounts								
Sales		900,000		250,000	**(4)** 40,000			1,110,000
Dividend Revenue		13,000		—	**(5)** 13,000			—
Total Revenues		913,000		250,000	53,000			1,110,000
Cost of Goods Sold	440,000		80,000			**(4)** 40,000	480,000	
Depreciation Expense	120,000		50,000				170,000	
Administrative Expenses	80,000		40,000				120,000	
Income Taxes	104,000		32,000				136,000	
Total Expenses	744,000		202,000			40,000	906,000	
Net Income	169,000		48,000		53,000	40,000	204,000	
Dividends Declared	50,000		13,000			**(5)** 13,000	50,000	
Addition to Retained Earnings	119,000		35,000				154,000	
Adjustments and Eliminations Totals					825,000	825,000		

Statement Preparation

In preparing consolidated statements for Company P and Company S, the following steps, characteristic of the consolidation procedure, are illustrated.

A. Adjustment of the parent company's Investment account
B. Elimination of the parent company's Investment account
C. Elimination of intercompany receivables and payables
D. Elimination of intercompany sales and purchases
E. Elimination of intercompany dividends.

The preparation of consolidated statements illustrated here starts with the single-company balance sheet accounts (from the postclosing trial balances) and the single-company income statements. These data are shown in the first two pairs of columns in Exhibit 12.2. The last pair of columns in Exhibit 12.2 show the items of the consolidated balance sheet and income statement. The amounts in the last pair of columns are merely the horizontal sum of the other items—Company P items, Company S items, as well as the adjustments and eliminations. The adjusting and eliminating entries are discussed below. The entries are numbered consecutively and correspond to the numbers shown in the adjustments and eliminations column in Exhibit 12.2. Keep in mind that these entries are recorded only on a work sheet used to prepare the consolidated statements—not in the accounting records of either company. There is no "consolidated" set of books.

A. Adjustment of the Parent Company's Investment Account   Because Company P records its Investment in Stock of Company S at cost, the Investment account must first be adjusted for P's share of the undistributed income or losses of the subsidiary arising since the date of acquisition. This adjustment restates the Investment account to what it would be if the equity method were used. The procedure is done in four steps, as follows:

A.1 Determine the retained earnings of the subsidiary applicable to the type of stock held by the parent. In most cases this will be the balance in the Retained Earnings account. In the illustration, the balance in the Retained Earnings account as of December 31, 1979, the date of the consolidated balance sheet, is $205,000.
A.2 Compute the difference between the retained earnings figure found in A.1 and the corresponding retained earnings at the date the stock was acquired by the parent. The difference represents the increase (if positive, decrease if negative) in the subsidiary's retained earnings since acquisition. In the illustration this difference is $55,000 (= $205,000 − $150,000).
A.3 Multiply the change in retained earnings found in A.2 by the percentage of the subsidiary's outstanding stock held by the parent. In the illustration, Company P owns 100 percent of Company S so that the parent's share of the increase in retained earnings is the total increase, $55,000.
A.4 Debit the Investment in Stock of Company S account and credit the Retained Earnings account of the parent with the amount found in A.3.

(1) Investment in Stock of Company S 55,000
    Retained Earnings (Company P)   55,000
    To adjust the amounts on P's books from cost to the amount shown if the
equity method were used. The parent's share of the subsidiary's retained
earnings is added to both the investment and Retained Earnings accounts.

This entry is entered in Exhibit 12.2. Remember that this entry is not made on the books of either company.

Once entry (1) is made, the balance in the Investment in Stock of Company S is the same as it would have been if Company P used the equity method in accounting for its investment in Company S. If Company P were using the equity method, then the preparation of consolidated statements would start with the next step, B.

B. Elimination of Parent Company's Investment Account   Company P purchased the shares of Company S for their book value at the time of acquisition. Now, after the adjustment from step A above, the parent's investment account equals the parent's ownership of the subsidiary's capital stock and retained earnings. Before adding together the single-company balance sheet items to determine consolidated totals, the parent's Investment in Stock of Company S must be eliminated so that the subsidiary's assets and the parent's investment in those assets are not both shown on the consolidated balance sheet.

Aside from the minority interest, if any, the owners' equity of the consolidated entity is provided by the shareholders of the parent. There is no minority interest in this example. Thus, the owners' equity of the subsidiary is provided entirely by financing from the parent. If the owners' equity of the parent and of the subsidiary were merely added together, then equities would be counted twice. When the investment account is eliminated to avoid double counting of assets, the subsidiary's owners' equity accounts corresponding to the parent's investment are eliminated to avoid double counting of the equities. (If there are amounts in the subsidiary's owners' equity accounts in excess of the parent's investment, then there is a minority interest.)

To eliminate the parent's investment account and the subsidiary's owners' equity accounts, debit the subsidiary's Capital Stock (also Additional Paid-in Capital, if any) and Retained Earnings accounts for the parent company's interest. Then credit the Investment account with its balance as adjusted by step A. The entry in Exhibit 12.2 to eliminate Company P's Investment in Stock of Company S is

(2) Capital Stock (Company S) 500,000
    Retained Earnings (Company S) 205,000
      Investment in Stock of Company S   705,000
    To eliminate the adjusted Investment in Stock of Company S account
($650,000 + $55,000) and the Capital Stock and Retained Earnings
accounts of Company S.

C. Elimination of Intercompany Receivables and Payables   A parent may sell goods on account or buy goods on account from a subsidiary and treat the resulting obligation as an account receivable or an account payable. The subsidiary will treat the obligation as an account payable or an account receivable. A parent often makes loans to subsidiaries that appear as Notes Receivable, Investment in Bonds, or Advances to Subsidiary on the parent's books. The subsidiary would show Notes Payable, Bonds Payable, or Advances from Parent on its books. A single company would not show Accounts Receivable and Accounts Payable for departments within the company. These transactions must be eliminated from the consolidated balance sheet so that the resulting statement will appear as that of a single company.

In the illustration, Company S's accounts receivable include $12,000 due it from Company P. The entry to record the elimination of the intercompany receivables and payables in Exhibit 12.2 is

(3) Accounts Payable 12,000
    Accounts Receivable 12,000
    To eliminate intercompany payables and receivables.

This entry completes the adjustments and eliminations for the consolidated balance sheet. The next eliminations are required for the consolidated income statement.

D. Elimination of Intercompany Sales and Purchases Sales between consolidated companies should not be reported in a consolidated income statement, any more than transfers from Work-in-Process Inventory to Finished Goods Inventory should be reported as sales within a single company. During 1979, Company P acquired $40,000 of merchandise inventory from Company S. To eliminate intercompany sales requires a debit to Sales and a credit to Purchases or to Goods Available for Sale. In the illustration we are working with, there are no Purchases or Goods Available for Sale accounts. As part of its regular closing entries, Company P computed its cost of goods sold from the inventory equation:

$$\text{Cost of Goods Sold} = \text{Beginning Inventory} + \text{Purchases} - \text{Ending Inventory}$$
$$= \text{Goods Available for Sale} - \text{Ending Inventory}.$$

Therefore, the offsetting credit to eliminate intercompany sales must be to the Cost of Goods Sold account.

(4) Sales 40,000
    Cost of Goods Sold 40,000
    To eliminate intercompany sales and purchases.

Company S sold goods to Company P and Company P sold the goods outside the consolidated pair of companies. In the absence of the elimination of intercompany sales, these sales would be counted twice. The profits on the sales would be computed properly, but the amount of gross sales and purchases would be inflated. To see that profits are computed properly even without the elimination, assume that the goods cost Company S $30,000 and that Company P sold them for $45,000. In the single-company income statements, Company S profits are $10,000 (= $40,000 − $30,000) as a result of the sale to Company P. Company P profits are $5,000 (= $45,000 − $40,000) as a result of its sales to others. Total profits of the consolidated group from these transactions are $15,000, or Company P's revenue of $45,000 less Company S's cost of $30,000. The elimination of intercompany sales does not change the consolidated sales to outsiders or the consolidated cost of goods sold to outsiders.

If either company holds bonds or long-term notes of the other, then there would be a similar elimination of the "borrower's" interest expense and of the "lender's" interest revenue.

E. Elimination of Intercompany Dividends   From the standpoint of Company S, dividend declarations are income distributions. But since the dividends are paid, or payable, to Company P, they represent merely a transfer of funds from one entity within the consolidated group to another. In consolidated statements, intercompany dividends are eliminated so that income distributions to stockholders of the parent are shown correctly. The entry in Exhibit 12.2 to eliminate intercompany dividends is

(5) Dividend Revenue	13,000	
Dividends Declared		13,000
To eliminate intercompany dividends.		

The adjustments and eliminations for the consolidated balance sheet and income statement are now complete. The last pair of columns in Exhibit 12.2 shows the horizontal sums of each row in the form needed to prepare both the consolidated balance sheet and income statement.

Consolidated Statement of Changes in Financial Position   The consolidated statement of changes in financial position is prepared from consolidated balance sheets for the beginning and end of the period plus additional information from the consolidated income statement. In the illustration, the consolidated statement of changes in financial position is particularly simple. It starts with consolidated net income of $204,000, shows an addback for depreciation expense of $170,000, shows income distributions of $50,000 for dividends, as well as other details of changes in current asset and current liability items.

The illustration, now complete, for Company P and Company S is simpler than typical consolidation problems in several respects. More complex consolidation problems are discussed in Appendix 12.1.

SUMMARY OF ACCOUNTING FOR MINORITY AND MAJORITY INVESTMENTS

Businesses acquire stock in other businesses for a variety of reasons in a variety of ways. The acquisition of stock of another company is generally recorded as follows:

Investment in S	X	
Cash or Other Consideration Given		X

The investment account is recorded at the amount of cash given or the market value of other consideration exchanged.

The accounting for the investment subsequent to acquisition depends on the ownership percentage. The lower-of-cost-or-market method is used when the parent owns less than 20 percent. The equity method is used when the parent owns at least 20 percent but not more than 50 percent of the stock of another company. Consolidated statements are generally prepared when the parent owns more than 50 percent of the voting shares of another company, but the equity method may be used. Exhibit 12.3 summarizes the accounting for investments subsequent to the acquisition.

Under the lower-of-cost-or-market method, income is recognized only when dividends become receivable by the investor.

EXHIBIT 12.3
Effects of Various Methods
of Accounting for Investments
in Corporate Securities

Method of Accounting	Balance Sheet	Income Statement	Statement of Changes in Financial Position
Lower-of-cost-or-market method (generally when ownership percentage is less than 20 percent)	Investment account shown at lower of acquisition cost or current market value as a noncurrent asset. Unrealized losses resulting from decline in market value below cost are credited to an asset contra and debited to an unrealized loss account that is shown as a negative component of owners' equity.	Dividends declared by investee shown as revenue of investor. Gains and losses (from original cost) are reported in income only as realized in arm's-length transactions with outsiders.	Dividends declared by investee included in working capital provided by operations of investor.
Equity method (generally when ownership percentage is at least 20 percent but not more than 50 percent)	Investment account shown at cost plus share of investee's net income less share of investee's dividends since acquisition.	Equity in investee's net income shown as revenue in period that investee earns income.	Equity in investee's undistributed earnings is subtracted from net income to derive working capital provided by operations of investor. Working capital from operations is thus increased only by the amount of dividend declarations.
Consolidation method (generally when ownership percentage is greater than 50 percent)	Investment account is eliminated and replaced with individual assets and liabilities of subsidiary. Minority interest in subsidiary's net assets shown among equities.	Individual revenues and expenses of subsidiary are combined with those of parent. Minority interest in subsidiary's net income shown as a subtraction.	Individual sources and uses of working capital of subsidiary are combined with those of parent. Minority interest in net income is added to net income to obtain working capital provided by operations.

Consolidated statements and the equity method both have the same effect on net income. The parent shows as income its proportional share of the acquired firm's periodic income after acquisition. Income statement amounts of revenues and expenses will be larger under the consolidation method, however, because the revenues and expenses of the acquired company are combined with those of the parent. Balance sheet components will be larger under the consolidation method than under the equity method, since the individual assets and liabilities of the acquired company will be substituted for the investment balance on the parent company's books.

CORPORATION ACQUISITIONS

Firms acquire all, or substantially all, of the common shares of the other companies for a variety of reasons. The examples below illustrate some of the reasons for corporate acquisitions.

Example 1 Standard Electronics Corporation manufactures a variety of devices that it sells throughout the United States. It has decided to expand into Canada. Rather than set up new manufacturing and distribution facilities there, Standard has agreed to combine its operations with those of an established electronics firm already operating in Canada. The two firms will maintain separate legal existences, but will become a single economic entity.

Example 2 A small Midwestern city has been served by three taxicab companies, each with less than a dozen cabs. The three companies have agreed to merge into a single business firm. Because of its size, the new firm will be able to take advantage of quantity discounts offered on purchases of automobiles, gasoline, and other supplies. Moreover, it will be able to purchase and maintain a central radio-operated dispatching facility that none of the three could justify for its own individual operations. The economies of scale permit the three firms to operate more efficiently as one.

Example 3 Acme Construction Company, a builder of office buildings, has previously purchased all of its cement and concrete from three local firms. Acme anticipates a dramatic upturn in the economy and an increase in construction activity. It acquired one of these companies in order to ensure availability of cement and concrete products for its construction work.

Example 4 Sleeptite Motor Inns operates a chain of motels along interstate highways. Management forecasts that increases in the cost of driving will lead to significant reductions in the number of vacationers using motel facilities. In an effort to balance the level of operations, it merged with Downtown Hotels, Incorporated, which owns several hotels, all located in downtown areas or near airports.

Corporate acquisitions are accounted for using either the *purchase method* or the *pooling-of-interests method*. The remainder of this section discusses the differing implications of the two methods of accounting for the combination, both at the time of acquisition and later, when consolidated statements are prepared.

Purchase Method—Central Concepts

The purchase method follows normal historical-cost accounting principles for recording acquisitions of assets and issuances of stock. Three particular principles are central to the purchase method.

First, assets acquired under historical costing are recorded at their cost. Cost is generally the amount of cash given in exchange for the asset acquired. If a firm acquires a building for $100,000, the entry is

Building	100,000	
Cash		100,000

Second, cost is measured by the fair market value of any noncash consideration given in exchange for an asset acquired. If a firm gives 5,000 shares of its $2-par-value common stock for a building and the common stock currently sells for $20 a share, the cash-equivalent value of the shares given is $100,000 (= 5,000 shares $\times$ $20 per share). The entry is

Building	100,000	
Common Stock—$2 Par Value		10,000
Additional Paid-in Capital		90,000
Building acquired for shares with current market value of $100,000.		

Third, when more than one asset is acquired in a single transaction, the total cost must be allocated to each of the assets acquired according to their market value. (Such an acquisition of several assets in a single transaction is sometimes called a *basket purchase*.) Assume the preceding transaction involved the acquisition of land with a market value of $25,000 and of a building with a market value of $75,000. The entry is

Land	25,000	
Building	75,000	
Common Stock—$2 Par Value		10,000
Additional Paid-in Capital		90,000

The purchase method may require two extensions of the historical-cost model. In most business combinations, the amount of the consideration given by the acquiring company exceeds the sum of the market values of the identifiable assets acquired. This excess generally represents items not shown in the balance sheet such as a good reputation with customers, a well-trained labor force, superior managerial talent, or the fruits of internal research and development efforts. The excess is caused by the failure in accounting to record all future benefits as assets and the requirement that assets be shown at cost, not current value. Under the purchase method, the excess of cost over the fair market value of the identifiable net assets acquired is called "goodwill."

Assume that the preceding transaction involved the acquisition of land with a market value of $25,000 and a building having a market value of $75,000, and that these were the only assets of the firm acquired. Now assume that 6,000 (rather than 5,000 as before) shares are required to persuade the previous owner to sell. The value of the shares given up is $120,000 (= 6,000 shares $\times$ $20 per share). The market value of the identifiable assets acquired is $100,000 (= $25,000 + $75,000). The goodwill is $20,000 (= $120,000 − $100,000). The entry would be

Land	25,000	
Building	75,000	
Goodwill	20,000	
Common Stock—$2 Par Value		12,000
Additional Paid-in Capital		108,000

$120,000 of shares given for a firm with assets having market value of $100,000.

The valuations assigned to the land and building by the purchaser are their current fair market values. The valuations shown on the books of the seller will rarely, if ever, reflect current fair market value. Thus, they are not useful for establishing the valuation on the books of the purchaser.

The second extension of the historical-cost model occurs when liabilities of an acquired company are assumed by the acquiring company. The liabilities assumed will be stated at the present value of the future cash payments at the date of acquisition. The payments are discounted at a *current* rate of interest appropriate for the risk of the borrowing company. This present value is the current market value of the liabilities. Assume in the preceding transaction that liabilities having a present value of $20,000 were assumed by the acquiring company but still 6,000 shares were given up. The entry would be

Land	25,000	
Building	75,000	
Goodwill	40,000	
Liabilities		20,000
Common Stock—$2 Par Value		12,000
Additional Paid-in Capital		108,000

$120,000 of shares given for a firm with assets having current value of $100,000 and liabilities having current value of $20,000.

These three central components of the purchase method are summarized as follows:

1 Consistent with the historical-cost model, assets acquired are recorded at their cost on the acquisition date.
2 Cost is equal to the amount of cash given plus the market value of any noncash consideration exchanged.
3 The aggregate acquisition cost amount is allocated to all identifiable assets acquired (less liabilities assumed) based on the fair market values of each. Any excess of acquisition cost over the market values of the identifiable net assets acquired is considered goodwill.[6]

---

[6] In cases where the market value of the consideration given is less than the market values of net identifiable assets acquired, Accounting Principles Board *Opinion No. 16* (1970) provides that the "values otherwise assignable to noncurrent assets acquired (except long-term investments in marketable securities) should be reduced by a proportionate part of the excess to determine assigned values."

Example—Merger   To illustrate the application of the purchase method, consider the balance sheet amounts for P Company and S Company shown in Exhibit 12.4.

P Company and S Company have agreed to merge. P Company will give 40,000 shares of its $5 par-value common stock for all of the outstanding common shares of S Company. The S Company shares will then be canceled and S Company will be legally dissolved. The current market price of P Company stock is $20 per share. The market value of the shares given is $800,000 (= 40,000 shares × $20 per share). Company P makes the following entry to record the acquisition of the S Company shares:

Current Assets	250,000	
Fixed Assets—Net	600,000	
Patent	50,000	
Goodwill	70,000	
Current Liabilities		80,000
Long-Term Liabilities		90,000
Common Stock—$5 Par Value		200,000
Additional Paid-in Capital		600,000

Exhibit 12.5 shows the effects of recording the merger on the books of P Company. Note the following aspects of the purchase method:

1   All assets are recorded on P Company's books at their cost. P Company gave consideration for the patent and goodwill and these assets are therefore recorded, even though they did not appear on the records of S Company. (Recall from Chapter 9 that costs incurred for internally developed patents are expensed.)

2   The book value of P Company, after the merger, exceeds the sum of the book values of P Company and S Company before the merger. This is caused by the fact that the recorded assets and liabilities of S Company were restated to current market values and the patent and goodwill were recognized.

3   The goodwill arising from a purchase is a long-lived asset, and generally accepted accounting principles require that this asset be amortized over a period of no more than 40 years.[7] Some theorists disagree with this treatment and argue that goodwill ought never to be recognized. Others disagree in the opposite direction; they contend that the future benefits can have an indefinite life, and therefore that amortization is not appropriate in all cases. (Goodwill arising from the purchase of an interest in another company accounted for on the equity method must similarly be amortized over a period not to exceed 40 years.[8] If less than 100 percent of the subsidiary's stock is acquired, the goodwill recognized is calculated as the acquisition price minus the product of the fraction of the outstanding stock acquired times

---

[7]   *APB Opinion No. 17*, 1970.
[8]   *APB Opinion No. 18*, 1971.

EXHIBIT 12.4
Illustration Data for P Company and S Company

Assets	P Company Book Value	S Company Book Value	S Company Market Value
Current Assets[a]	$ 500,000	$200,000	$250,000
Property, Plant, and Equipment (net)[a]	2,000,000	500,000	600,000
Patent	0	0	50,000
Total Assets	$2,500,000	$700,000	
Equities			
Current Liabilities[a]	$ 300,000	$ 80,000	$ 80,000
Long-Term Liabilities	400,000	100,000	90,000
Common Stock—$5 Par Value	1,000,000	100,000	—
Additional Paid-in Capital	200,000	200,000	—
Retained Earnings	600,000	220,000	—
Total Equities	$2,500,000	$700,000	

[a] Individual assets and liabilities have been aggregated to simplify the illustration.

the fair market value of the recorded net assets. Note 13 to the International Corporation annual report (page 589) states:

> Other Assets include goodwill of $80 million in 19X2 and $88 million in 19X1. Goodwill acquired prior to November 1, 1970, is not being amortized. Goodwill of $14.2 million at December 31, 19X1, and $15.1 million at December 31, 19X0, resulting from business combinations subsequent to November, 1, 1970, remained to be amortized over the estimated period to be benefited, not to exceed 40 years.

Example—Acquisition of Shares   Assume that P Company merely acquires all of the common shares of S Company but does not execute a merger. P Company's entry to record the acquisition of shares is

Investment in S Company	800,000	
Common Stock—$5 Par Value		200,000
Additional Paid-in Capital		600,000
Shares of S Company acquired in purchase.		

Since S Company continues as a separate legal entity, it is inappropriate for P Company to record the individual assets and liabilities of S Company on its books. The postacquisition accounts of P Company will appear as shown in Exhibit 12.6. In order for the individual assets and liabilities of S Company to appear with those for P Company, consolidated financial statements must be prepared, as described earlier.

EXHIBIT 12.5
**Effects on P Company's Books
of Recording the Merger
of S Company Under the
Purchase Method**

	Acquisition and Merger			
Assets	Before Merger	Debit	Credit	After Merger
Current Assets	$ 500,000	$250,000		$ 750,000
Fixed Assets (net)	2,000,000	600,000		2,600,000
Patent	0	50,000		50,000
Goodwill	0	70,000		70,000
Total Assets	$2,500,000			$3,470,000
Equities				
Current Liabilities	$ 300,000		$ 80,000	$ 380,000
Long-Term Liabilities	400,000		90,000	490,000
Common Stock—$5 Par Value	1,000,000		200,000	1,200,000
Additional Paid-in Capital	200,000		600,000	800,000
Retained Earnings	600,000			600,000
Total Adjustments		$970,000	$970,000	
Total Equities	$2,500,000			$3,470,000

EXHIBIT 12.6
**Effects on P Company's Books
of Recording the Acquisition
of S Company's Common Shares**

	P Company Before Acquisition	Acquisition		P Company After Acquisition
Assets		Debit	Credit	
Current Assets	$ 500,000			$ 500,000
Investment in S Company	0	$800,000		800,000
Fixed Assets (net)	2,000,000			2,000,000
Total Assets	$2,500,000			$3,300,000
Equities				
Current Liabilities	$ 300,000			$ 300,000
Long-Term Liabilities	400,000			400,000
Common Stock—$5 Par Value . .	1,000,000		$200,000	1,200,000
Additional Paid-in Capital	200,000		600,000	800,000
Retained Earnings	600,000			600,000
Total Adjustments		$800,000	$800,000	
Total Equities	$2,500,000			$3,300,000

Pooling of Interests—Central Concepts

The key elements of the pooling concept are as follows:

1 In a pooling of interests, the *form* in which the entities conduct their operations has changed (that is, a new combined firm replaces the previously separate firms) but the *substance* has not—each business entity has the same assets and liabilities and carries out the same business activities as before.

2 In order for there to be only a change in form, rather than in substance, the combination must be executed by the *exchange* of common shares for common shares. If some other form of consideration is involved, then there would be a shift in the relative equity interests of the two companies. A change in substance would then occur.

3 Since no acquisition has taken place, no new basis of accounting arises. The book values of the assets and liabilities of the former companies are carried over to the new combined company.

APB Opinion No. 16 describes the pooling-of-interests method as follows:

> The pooling of interest method accounts for a business combination as the uniting of the ownership interests of two or more companies by exchange of equity securities. No acquisition is recognized because the combination is accomplished without disbursing resources of the constituents.
>
> Ownership interests continue and the former bases of accounting are retained. The recorded assets and liabilities of the constituents are carried forward to the combined corporation at their recorded (book value) amounts. Income of the combined corporation includes income of the constituents for the entire fiscal period in which the combination occurs. The reported income of the constituents for prior periods is combined and restated as income of the combined corporation. . . .
>
> Those who support the pooling of interest method believe that a business combination effected by issuing common stock is different from a purchase in that no corporate assets are disbursed to stockholders and the net assets of the issuing corporation are enlarged by the net assets of the corporation whose stockholders accept common stock of the combined corporation. There is no newly invested capital nor have the owners withdrawn assets from the group since the stock of a corporation is not one of its assets. Accordingly, the net assets of the constituents remain intact but combined; the stockholder groups remain intact but combined. Aggregate income is not changed since the total resources are not changed. Consequently, the historical costs and earnings of the separate corporations are appropriately combined. In a business combination effected by exchanging stock, groups of stockholders combine their resources, talents, and risks to form a new entity to carry on in combination the previous businesses and to continue their earnings streams. The sharing of risks by the constituent stockholder groups is an important element in a business combination effected by exchanging stock. By pooling equity interests, each group continues to maintain risk elements of its former investment and they mutually exchange risk and benefits.

The pooling-of-interests concept is somewhat unusual in accounting because current market values are ignored in the accounting for a negotiated trade.[9] The pooling-of-interests method has been, and continues to be, controversial. Before evaluating the pooling concept, however, let us first consider how business combinations are recorded under the pooling-of-interests method.

Illustration of the Pooling-of-Interests Method

The balance sheet data for S Company and P Company, as presented in Exhibit 12.4, will be used to illustrate the pooling-of-interests method.

P Company exchanges 40,000 shares of its common stock for all of the outstanding common shares of S Company. The S Company shares will then be canceled and S Company will be legally dissolved. The current market price of the P Company is $20. The entry to record the acquisition of the S Company shares is

Current Assets	200,000	
Fixed Assets (Net)	500,000	
Current Liabilities		80,000
Long-Term Liabilities		100,000
Common Stock—$5 Par Value		200,000
Additional Paid-in Capital		100,000
Retained Earnings		220,000

EXHIBIT 12.7
Effects on P Company's Books of Recording the Merger of S Company Under the Pooling-of-Interests Method

	Combination and Merger			
Assets	**Before Merger**	**Debit**	**Credit**	**After Merger**
Current Assets	$ 500,000	$200,000		$ 700,000
Fixed Assets (net)	2,000,000	500,000		2,500,000
Total Assets	$2,500,000			$3,200,000
Equities				
Current Liabilities	$ 300,000		$ 80,000	$ 380,000
Long-Term Liabilities	400,000		100,000	500,000
Common Stock—$5 Par Value	1,000,000		200,000	1,200,000
Additional Paid-in Capital	200,000		100,000	300,000
Retained Earnings	600,000		220,000	820,000
Total Adjustments		$700,000	$700,000	
Total Equities	$2,500,000			$3,200,000

[9] Parallel concepts are used only in certain trade-in transactions.

EXHIBIT 12.8
Illustration of the Effects of the Purchase and Pooling-of-Interests Methods on Net Income

	Before Combination		Combined Operations After Merger	
	P Company	**S Company**	**Purchase**	**Pooling of Interests**
Sales	$2,000,000 +	$400,000 =	$2,400,000	$2,400,000
Cost of Goods Sold	(1,200,000) +	(200,000) =	(1,400,000)	(1,400,000)
Selling and Administrative Expenses	(300,000) +	(50,000) =	(350,000)	(350,000)
Additional Cost of Goods Sold			(50,000)	—
Additional Depreciation Expense ($100,000/10 years)			(10,000)	—
Patent Amortization Expense ($50,000/10 years)			(5,000)	—
Goodwill Amortization Expense ($70,000/40 years)			(1,750)	—
Net Income Before Taxes	$ 500,000	$150,000	$ 583,250	$ 650,000
Income Taxes at 40 Percent	(200,000)	(60,000)	(260,000)[a]	(260,000)
Net Income	$ 300,000	$ 90,000	$ 323,250	$ 390,000
Total Assets on Merger Date			$3,470,000	$3,200,000
All Capital Earnings Rate (Based on Totals on Merger Date)			9.3%	12.2%
Total Owners' Equity (Based on Merger Date)			$2,600,000	$2,320,000
Rate of Return on Owners' Equity (Based on Merger Date)			12.4%	16.8%

[a] See discussion of income tax expense in the text.

From the standpoint of the combined firm, the shares of P Company merely replace the shares of S Company. S Company contributed capital is shown on its books at $300,000 (= $100,000 + $200,000). The shares issued by P Company are stated at this amount. The $300,000 is allocated to common stock and additional paid-in capital of P Company based on the par value of the shares issued. (That is, 40,000 shares × $5 par value = $200,000. This amount is allocated to common stock at par value. The remainder is allocated to Additional Paid-in Capital.)

Exhibit 12.7 shows the effects of recording the merger on the books of P Company. Note the following aspects of the pooling-of-interests method:

1 The amounts for the individual assets and liabilities after the merger are merely the sum of the amounts for each firm before the merger.

2 The total contributed capital after the merger ($1,200,000 + $300,000) is equal to the sum of the contributed capital accounts of the two companies before the merger.

3 Retained earnings after the merger is the sum of the retained earnings of the two firms before the merger.

Effect of Purchase and Pooling of Interests on Net Income

The asset amounts recorded under the purchase method in Exhibit 12.5 exceed the corresponding amounts under the pooling-of-interests method in Exhibit 12.7. Such an excess usually occurs. The market values of assets acquired usually exceed their book values. What are the effects of these two methods of recording the business combination on net income of subsequent years?

Net income under the purchase method will be lower than under pooling. The higher amounts for inventory, buildings, and equipment recorded in a purchase lead to larger amounts for cost of goods sold and depreciation. In addition, any previously unrecorded assets that are recognized in a purchase, such as patents and goodwill, must be amortized. The extra amortization expense after a purchase lowers the income as compared to that after a pooling.

To illustrate the effects of these methods on net income subsequent to the combination, assume that the $50,000 excess of market value over book value of S Company's current assets is attributable to an undervaluation of inventory. A FIFO cost-flow assumption is made. The fixed assets and patents have a 10-year life remaining on the date of the combination. The goodwill is to be amortized over 40 years, the longest period allowed in generally accepted accounting principles.[10] The straight-line method of depreciation (for fixed assets) and amortization (for patents) is to be used.

Exhibit 12.8 shows the calculation of net income for the first year after the merger assuming that the levels of income for the two firms before the merger are maintained afterwards. We assume that there are no savings in operating costs as a result of merging the two firms.

---

[10] *APB Opinion No. 17*, 1970.

The pretax net income under the pooling method of $650,000 is higher than under the purchase method, since the additional cost of goods sold, depreciation, and amortization expense are not recognized after a pooling. Coupling this higher net income with the lower book value of assets and owners' equity under pooling leads to significant differences in the rates of return on both assets and owners' equity.

A Note on Income Taxes   Income tax expense under the purchase method is usually the same as under pooling. This reflects the fact that in most cases a business combination involving a stock issuance is treated as a nontaxable exchange *for tax purposes* (a "pooling of interests") regardless of how it is treated for financial reporting. If this is the case, cost of goods sold, depreciation, and amortization expense will be limited to the acquisition-cost amounts to S Company. Thus, the additional expenses will not be deductible in determining taxable income. Since these represent permanent differences, rather than timing differences, no deferred income tax provision is required.

Purchase or Pooling?

When a merger occurs, the companies do not have a choice of using either the purchase or the pooling method. Rather, the facts of each merger will determine which method is required under the circumstances.[11] In our opinion, pooling-of-interests accounting is seldom justified. Nearly every business combination results from arm's-length negotiations between independent parties. A fair-market exchange has occurred. Given a choice, most firms would prefer to treat business combinations as a pooling of interests rather than as a purchase because of the favorable effects on earnings and rates of return.

Managing Earnings   Pooling of interests not only keeps reported income from decreasing after the merger, it may also allow management of the pooled companies to manage the reported earnings in an arbitrary way. Suppose, as has happened, that Company P merges with an old, established firm, Company F, which has produced commercial movie films. These films were made in the 1940s and 1950s and were amortized so that by 1970 the book value of these films is zero or close to zero. But the market value of the films is much larger than zero, because television stations find that old movies please their audiences. If Company P purchases Company F, then the old films will be shown on the consolidated balance sheet at the films' current fair market value. If Company P merges with Company F using the pooling-of-interests method, the films will be shown on the consolidated balance sheet at their near-zero book values. Then, when Company P wants to bolster reported earnings for the year, all it need do is sell some old movies to a television network, and a handsome gain can be reported. Actually, of course, the owners of Company F enjoyed this gain when their stock was "sold to" (or exchanged with) Company P for current asset values, not the obsolete book values.

---

[11] *APB Opinion No. 16.* A merger will not qualify for a pooling of interests unless the "acquiring" firm acquires 90 percent or more of the voting shares of the "acquired" firm. Several other conditions must be met before the merger will be considered a pooling of interests.

Those who defend pooling-of-interests accounting argue that the management of the pooled enterprise has no more opportunity to manage earnings than did the management of Company F before the pooling. Management of Company F can sell old movies any time it chooses and then report handsome gains. The fault lies ultimately in the historical-cost basis of accounting, which recognizes gains only when there has been a market transaction. Defenders of pooling argue that there is no reason to penalize the management of a merged company relative to the management of an established company with many assets undervalued on its books. Opponents of pooling reply that it was the management of Company F that earned the holding gains, whereas the management of Company P will be able to report them as realized gains under pooling.

ACCOUNTING FOR FOREIGN INVESTMENTS

In order to carry on operations in a foreign country, a company may establish a division, branch, or a corporation in a foreign country, or it may acquire the capital stock of an existing foreign company. Generally accepted accounting principles require special techniques for reporting assets and liabilities carried on the books in foreign currencies and for reporting the results of operations carried on in foreign countries.[12] The two major problems in accounting for foreign subsidiaries are discussed briefly below. These problems are as follows:

1 Should the operations and the assets and liabilities of the foreign unit be consolidated with the parent company's statements?
2 How should the amounts of assets, liabilities, revenues, and expenses originally expressed in foreign currencies be translated into dollars?

Consolidating Foreign Operations

In general, a parent consolidates a subsidiary when the parent exercises control over the subsidiary and the nature of the subsidiary's assets and equity structure is not substantially different from that of the parent. These criteria apply to foreign subsidiaries as well. Most U.S. companies consolidate their foreign operations. In recent years, about half of the 600 companies surveyed in *Accounting Trends and Techniques*[13] had foreign subsidiaries. More than two-thirds of these companies consolidated their foreign subsidiaries, and that portion has been growing steadily.

When assets are held in a foreign country, however, there may exist conditions that inhibit the exercise of effective control over the subsidiary. Foreign governments may restrict the use of assets or the flow of capital and currency across international borders. When there is sufficient uncertainty about the parent's ability to control foreign opera-

---

[12] Financial Accounting Standards Board, *Statements of Financial Accounting Standards No. 1,* 1973, and *No. 8,* 1975.
[13] Annual publication of the American Institute of Certified Public Accountants; see description in Chapter 1.

tions, the foreign unit's net assets and results of operations should not be consolidated in the parent's statements. Rather, the equity method would be used.

In some cases, earnings of foreign units operating under severe restrictions on operations or on currency flows may not be reported by the parent until cash has been transferred between countries.

Currency Translation

Accounting seeks to report assets, liabilities, and the results of operations using a single, common measurement unit. The measurement unit used by U.S. corporations is, of course, the U.S. dollar. Once the decision has been made to combine foreign operations with domestic operations in the financial statements, a decision must be made as to how to translate foreign currency amounts into dollars so that items can be meaningfully added together.

The translation of foreign currency items into dollars is accomplished by multiplying the foreign currency amount by an exchange rate. An *exchange rate* indicates the number of currency units of one currency (for example, U.S. dollars) that is equivalent to, or could be exchanged for, one unit of another currency (for example, a French franc or a German mark). If we lived in a world of fixed, unchanging exchange rates, where there was never any doubt about the number of dollars required to purchase a given amount of foreign currency or vice versa, there would be no problem. All foreign currency amounts could be translated into dollars by using a multiplier that is constant over time for a given currency. But, of course, exchange rates do vary. The major problem in accounting for foreign units arises because the exchange rate between foreign currencies and the dollar can vary substantially over time. The exchange rate between the dollar and the German mark or the Japanese yen has varied by as much as 25 percent within a single year. Exchange rates between the dollar and some South American currencies have varied even more.

Once we recognize that exchange rates can vary, a problem arises in accounting for the gains and losses in dollars that occur just because of exchange rate fluctuations, independent of any operating results. Suppose, for example, that a U.S. company converts $36,000 into 20,000 British pounds at a time when the exchange rate is £1 = $1.80. Assume that the £20,000 are merely deposited in a checking account in London. One year later, assume that the exchange rate has changed so that £1 is worth only $1.60, and that the U.S. company converts its pounds back into dollars. The U.S. company would receive only $32,000 (= £20,000 × $1.60/£). The U.S. company would have suffered a *foreign exchange loss* of $4,000 (= $36,000 − $32,000). To make the example more realistic, suppose that a foreign subsidiary makes sales on account for £20,000 at a time when the exchange rate is £1 = $1.80 and collects cash after the pound has fallen to $1.60. Some recognition will have to be given to the difference in the dollar value of the revenue at the time of sale and the dollar value of the cash collected at the later date.

In translating foreign currency amounts into dollars, there are basically two different rates that can be used. The exchange rate used can be either the historical rate—the rate in effect at the time of a given transaction—or the current rate—the rate in effect as of the date of the financial statements. Generally accepted accounting principles favor the use of the current rate for all *monetary items,* and the historical rate for all other items.

A *monetary item* in foreign currency analysis is any asset or liability requiring settlement in specific amounts of foreign currency. Examples include payables and receivables denominated in foreign currencies, whether current or noncurrent, as well as amounts of foreign cash. Monetary items are translated into dollars using the exchange rate in effect as of the date of the financial statements.

Nonmonetary items include all other accounts—that is, all of the balance sheet accounts that are not specifically monetary items, as well as all revenue and expense accounts recorded in foreign currencies. Nonmonetary items are translated at the rate in effect at the time of the transaction that brought the item onto the books.

These two general procedures imply, for example, that the translated dollar amount of a bond denominated in a foreign currency will vary from one financial statement date to another as the exchange rate varies, but the cost of a foreign plant asset will always be reported on the parent's books in dollars at the exchange rate applicable to the time of acquisition. All depreciation charges are then based on historical costs translated into dollars at historical rates.

Controversy Surrounding GAAP for Foreign Currency Transactions

Since FASB *Statement No. 8* was issued in 1975, managements of many U.S. corporations have complained about it. Two major points cause the disagreement with GAAP.

Inventory Is Translated at Historical Rates Under FASB *Statement No. 8,* items of inventory and cost of goods sold are translated at the historical rate in effect on the date the inventory was acquired. Prior to FASB *Statement No. 8,* many companies translated inventory at the exchange rate in effect at the end of the period and translated cost of goods sold at the rate in effect at the time of sale. These companies complain that selling prices are changed as price levels in a country change and that price levels in a country are reflected in exchange rate changes. Thus, they argue, inventory is really a monetary item. The required accounting sometimes reports income or loss in periods when inventory is held, rather than in periods when goods are sold.

Long-Term Debt Is Translated at Current Rates Under FASB *Statement No. 8,* long-term debt is translated at current rates (similar to short-term monetary items). Any changes in the dollar value of the debt are reported as part of current income. Prior to FASB *Statement No. 8,* many companies translated long-term debt at historical rates. Others translated long-term debt at current rates but deferred recognizing the gain or loss in the income statement. Instead, the companies carried the resulting gains and losses to the balance sheet and gradually amortized them to income over time. These companies complain that the long-term debt was used to raise funds that were in turn used to acquire noncurrent assets. The noncurrent assets are translated on the balance sheet at historical rates and are amortized on the income statement (expensed) at historical rates. These companies argue that it is misleading to require that exchange-rate fluctuations on debt used to finance noncurrent assets flow through income each year as exchange rates vary.

Much of the controversy involves elements too advanced for discussion here, but we can state that in our opinion the controversy results from the requirements of historical-cost accounting. If assets were shown on financial statements at some measure of current value, then changes in these values would be recorded from period to period. Moreover, all items in translated financial statements would be shown at current values translated at current exchange rates. There would be much less fluctuation in income caused merely by fluctuating exchange rates.

SUMMARY

Accounting for the acquisition of an investment and subsequent events depends on both the amount of stock involved and the manner of acquisition.

Figure 12.1 summarizes the various aspects of accounting for investments in corporate securities. The lower-of-cost-or-market method is used when the parent owns less than 20 percent of the stock of another company. The equity method is used when the parent owns at least 20 percent but not more than 50 percent. Consolidated statements are generally prepared, but the equity method may be used when the parent owns more than 50 percent of the voting shares of another company.

Recording an acquisition as a pooling of interests, rather than as a purchase, produces different results in the consolidated income statement and balance sheet. Under pooling, assets and equities will generally be shown at lower values on the balance sheet, and the income statement will generally report a higher net income.

Investments in foreign operations are accounted for in much the same way as domestic ones. Foreign investments raise the problems of accounting for fluctuating exchange rates and the resulting gains or losses from these fluctuations.

APPENDIX 12.1
Some Complexities in Consolidation

The illustrations in Exhibits 12.1 and 12.2 were simplified. This appendix considers two situations encountered in consolidated statements not illustrated in the chapter. These are

1 Acquisition price of subsidiary exceeds book value acquired.
2 Less than 100 percent of the subsidiary's stock is acquired, resulting in a minority interest.

Refer to the data in Exhibits 12.1 and 12.2 and to steps A—E listed on p. 470.

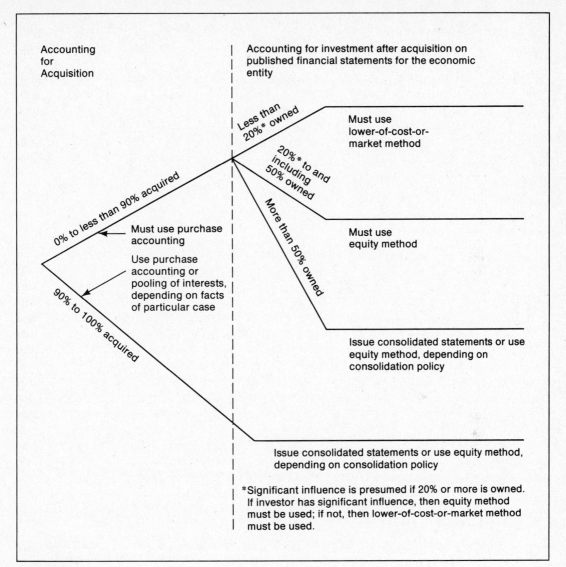

FIGURE 12.1
**Summary of Accounting
for Investments**

ACQUISITION PRICE EXCEEDS BOOK VALUE ACQUIRED

Suppose that Company P had paid $700,000, rather than $650,000, for its 100-percent investment in Company S. After step B and entry (2), the parent's Investment account would still have a debit balance of $50,000. This $50,000 represents the price paid for

Company S's assets in excess of their book value, for goodwill, or for both. Assume that $25,000 represents the price paid for buildings, machinery, and equipment in excess of the depreciated cost shown on Company S's books, $5,000 represents the price paid for land in excess of the cost shown on Company S's books, and $20,000 represents the price paid for goodwill. To complete the elimination of the parent's Investment in Stock of Company S, the following entry is required:

```
(6) Buildings, Machinery, and Equipment ...........................    25,000
       Land ......................................................     5,000
       Goodwill ..................................................    20,000
          Investment in Stock of Company S ........................            50,000
    To complete elimination of parent's Investment account recognizing in-
    creased valuation of the consolidated assets.
```

The consolidated balance sheet will show the building, machinery, and equipment accounts with larger balances than the sum of the single-company accounts. Goodwill, which does not appear in the single-company accounts, will be shown on the consolidated statement. The plant assets, except land, and the goodwill must be amortized, so there will be an adjusting entry to recognize the extra amortization charges on the past and current consolidated income statements. Assume that depreciable plant assets are to be amortized over a 10-years' remaining life and that goodwill is to be amortized over 40 years, both on a straight-line basis. Company P purchased Company S on January 1, 1976, so that the worksheet entry to recognize the 3 years of accumulated amortization up to January 1, 1979, would be

```
(7) Retained Earnings .............................................    9,000
       Accumulated Depreciation ......................................            7,500
       Goodwill ..................................................             1,500
    To recognize 3 years of depreciation on plant assets with a remaining 10-year
    life, $7,500 (= 3 × $25,000/10), and 3 years of amortization of goodwill, which
    is assumed to have a 40-year life, $1,500 (= 3 × $20,000/40), from 1/1/76
    to 1/1/79.
```

The entries to recognize the additional amortization charges for the year of 1979 would be

```
(8) Depreciation Expense ..........................................    2,500
       Accumulated Depreciation ......................................            2,500
    Depreciation for 1979 on incremental value of plant assets.

    Amortization of Goodwill (Expense) ..................................    500
       Goodwill ..................................................              500
    Amortization of goodwill for 1979.
```

When the temporary revenue and expense accounts are closed from the consolidated income summary to the consolidated balance sheet, the debit amounts in entry (8) would be effectively debited to consolidated retained earnings. The December 31, 1979, consolidated balance sheet, ignoring income tax effects, would show $12,000 (= $9,000 + $2,500 + $500) smaller Retained Earnings as a result of entries (7), (8), and the related closing entries.

The consolidated statement of changes in financial position would show addbacks for these extra amortization charges of $3,000 for 1979, which use no working capital.

RECOGNIZING MINORITY INTEREST

Now assume that Company P acquired 90 percent of the stock of Company S for a price equal to the book value of 90 percent of Company S's net assets. If Company P purchased only 90 percent of the stock of Company S for its book value of $585,000 (= .90 × $650,000), then the minority shareholders in Company S have a claim on 10 percent of its stockholders' equity. Entry (1) from Exhibit 12.2 would become:

(1a) Investment in Stock of Company S 49,500
     Retained Earnings (Company P)   49,500
     To adjust P's books from the cost to the equity method (.90 × $55,000).

Entry (2) in Exhibit 12.2 eliminates 100 percent of Company S's stockholders' equity. Under the new conditions, it would eliminate only 90 percent and would become:

(2a) Capital Stock (Company S) 450,000
     Retained Earnings (Company S) 184,500
     Investment in Stock of Company S   634,500
     To eliminate the adjusted Investment in Stock of Company S account
     [.90 × ($650,000 + $55,000)] and 90 percent of the capital stock and
     retained earnings of Company S.

The remaining balances in Company S's stockholders' equity accounts are the minority interest. The logical entries to recognize the minority interest would be

(2b) Capital Stock (Company S) 50,000
     Minority Interest in Company S Capital Stock   50,000
     To recognize the 10-percent minority interest in the capital stock of
     Company S.
     Retained Earnings (Company S) 20,500
     Minority Interest in Company S Retained Earnings   20,500
     To recognize the 10-percent minority interest in the retained earnings of
     Company S.

Then the consolidated balance sheet would show separately the minority interest in capital stock and retained earnings. In practice, however, the credit entries in (2b) are seldom made that way. Instead, they are combined to show a single account, Minority Interest, which does not disclose its components. The usual entry to recognize minority interest is

(2c) Capital Stock (Company S) 50,000
     Retained Earnings (Company S) 20,500
     Minority Interest in Company S   70,500
     To recognize the 10-percent minority interest in the stockholders' equity
     of Company S.

The entry to eliminate intercompany receivables and payables is not affected by the existence of a minority interest. The entry would be the same as the one shown in entry (3).

The eliminations of intercompany sales and purchases can be somewhat more complicated when there are unrealized profits on intercompany transactions and a minority interest exists. In our example, we assume that Company P has sold all of the items it purchased from Company S, so there is no special problem and the entry to eliminate intercompany sales and purchases is the same as the one shown in entry (4).

When no minority interest exists, we eliminate all $13,000 of the intercompany dividends, because in a consolidated entity they are the equivalent of cash transfers between divisions of a single company. When a minority interest does exist, all of the subsidiary's dividends are also eliminated, but cash of $1,300 (= .10 × $13,000) is distributed outside the consolidated entity to the minority shareholders. This distribution of cash to the minority shareholders reduces the minority interest. The entry to eliminate the subsidiary's dividends would be

(5a) Dividend Revenue	11,700	
Minority Interest	1,300	
Dividends Declared		13,000

To eliminate intercompany dividends ($11,700 is 90 percent of Company S's dividends and represents all of Company P's dividend revenue from Company S) and to show dividends declared on minority stock as a reduction in the minority interest.

Income Statement

The consolidated income statement shows a deduction of $4,800 (= .10 × $48,000) for the minority interest in S's earnings of the year in determining the net income of $199,200 (= $204,000 − $4,800) to the stockholders of Company P. The dividends declared by the consolidated entity consist of $51,300 (Company P's dividends of $50,000 and Company S's dividends of $1,300 declared on the stock owned by the minority interest).

Funds Statement

The consolidated statement of changes in financial position starts with the net income of $199,200 to stockholders of Company P. Amounts are added back for the minority interest in S's undistributed earnings for the year of $3,500 (= $4,800 − $1,300) and for depreciation ($170,000), neither of which uses working capital. The only use of working capital shown is the $50,000 of dividends declared by the parent. The net increase in working capital for the year is $372,700, exactly $1,300 less than when there was no minority interest. This $1,300 difference represents the funds distributed outside the consolidated entity in the form of dividends declared on S's shares owned by the minority interest.

QUESTIONS AND PROBLEMS

1 Review the meaning of the following concepts or terms discussed in this chapter.
  a Minority investment.
  b Minority interest.
  c Majority investment.
  d Marketable securities versus long-term investments.
  e Lower-of-cost-or-market method.
  f Equity method.
  g Parent.
  h Subsidiary.
  i Consolidated statements.
  j Purchase method.
  k Goodwill.
  l Pooling-of-interests method.
  m Adjustments and eliminations in consolidated work sheet.
  n Intercompany transactions.
  o Managing earnings.
  p Monetary items.
  q Nonmonetary items.
  r Exchange rate.

2 The following item appears on a consolidated balance sheet: Minority Interest in Subsidiary Companies. What does it represent?

3 A consolidated balance sheet does not include an item of "goodwill." What are the possible explanations? Consider stock acquired on the market after the subsidiary had been in existence for several years.

4 a Why is it impossible to determine from a consolidated balance sheet the amount of retained earnings legally available for dividends, either for the parent company or for the subsidiary company?
  b Indicate some of the types of eliminations that may be necessary in the preparation of a consolidated income statement.

5 Why is the equity method sometimes called a *one-line consolidation*?

6 Company P acquires 100 percent of the stock of Company S at a time when Company S has negative retained earnings, that is, a deficit. P pays more for S than the book value of S's owners' equity. How can this happen?

7 The Annoppers Copper Corporation has, for many years, consolidated the financial position and results of operations of its South American copper mining facility. During the last year, the government of the country in which the mine is located has expropriated the plants of two other U.S. corporations. These two other companies were engaged in manufacturing operations. Should the Annoppers Copper Corporation continue to consolidate the financial statements of its South American facility in its statements issued to stockholders?

8 The exchange rate used in translating accounts from foreign-based books to domestic financial statements can be either the historical exchange rate (the exchange rate in effect when the assets were acquired, liabilities were incurred, common stock was issued, or revenues were recognized) or the current exchange rate (the exchange rate on the date of the balance sheet). Indicate which of these two exchange rates would be used for each of the following accounts.

a Cash (Swiss francs).

b Accounts Payable (in yen).

c Investment in German Government Bonds.

d Bonds Payable (in French francs).

e Sales Revenue.

f Interest Revenue.

g Merchandise Inventory.

h Equipment.

i Accumulated Depreciation—Equipment.

9 Refer to the items **a–i** in the preceding question. Which of these accounts are "monetary items"?

10 In consolidated statements where the initial acquisition is accounted for with the purchase method, the assets of the acquired firm are revalued to current costs. In consolidated statements where the initial acquisition is accounted for with the pooling-of-interests method, no assets are revalued.

a What would be the effect on consolidated statements if the assets of both acquiring and acquired firms were revalued to current market values?

b What would be the logic to consolidations based on revalued assets for both firms?

11 Refer to the Simplified Funds Statement for a Period in Exhibit 5.15 on page 174. Ten of the lines in the statement are numbered. Line (2) should be expanded to say "Additions for Expenses and Other Charges Against Income Not Using Funds," and line (3) should be expanded to say "Subtractions for Revenue and Other Credits to Income Not Producing Funds from Operations." Ignore the other lines in responding to the questions below.

Assume that the accounting cycle is complete for the period and that all of the financial statements have been prepared. Then it is discovered that a transaction has been overlooked. That transaction is recorded in the accounts, and all of the financial statements are corrected. Define *funds* as *working capital*. For each of the following transactions or events, indicate which of the numbered lines of the funds statement is affected and by how much. Ignore income tax effects.

a An affiliate accounted for on the equity method earns $10,000 and declares dividends of $4,000.

b An affiliate accounted for on the equity method reports a loss for the year of $5,000.

c Minority interest in income of a consolidated subsidiary is recognized in the amount of $20,000.

d Minority interest in the losses of a consolidated subsidiary is recognized in the amount of $8,000.

e A 100-percent-owned consolidated subsidiary sold merchandise to the parent company for $10,000. The subsidiary's cost of the goods sold was $6,000. The parent sold the merchandise for $12,000. An elimination of the intercompany transaction is made.

f The *investment* in the portfolio of equity securities accounted for with the lower-of-cost-or-market method is written down from $10,000 to $8,000.

g A dividend of $7,000 is declared on shares held as an *investment* and accounted for with the lower-of-cost-or-market method.

h The market value of the portfolio of equity securities accounted for as *current assets* (Marketable Securities) is $5,000 less than the net amount shown for the same portfolio on the balance sheet at the end of the previous accounting period. The amount in the allowance contra to the Marketable Securities account is changed.

i The market value of the portfolio of marketable equity securities in the preceding part **g** increases $3,000 by the end of the next accounting period. The amount in the allowance contra to the Marketable Securities account is changed.

12 On January 1, Buyer Company acquired common stock of X Company. At the time of acquisition, the book value and fair market value of X Company's net assets were $100,000. During the year, X Company earned $25,000 and declared dividends of $20,000. How much income would Buyer Company report for the year from its investment under the assumption that Buyer Company:

a Paid $15,000 for 15 percent of the common stock and uses the lower-of-cost-or-market method for its investment in X Company?

b Paid $20,000 for 15 percent of the common stock and uses the lower-of-cost-or-market method for its investment in X Company?

c Paid $30,000 for 30 percent of the common stock and uses the equity method to account for its investment in X Company?

d Paid $40,000 for 30 percent of the common stock and uses the equity method to account for its investment in X Company? Give the maximum income that Buyer Company can report from the investment.

13 The CAR Corporation manufactures computers in the United States. It owns 75 percent of the voting stock of Charles of Canada, 80 percent of the voting stock of Alexandre de France (in France), and 90 percent of the voting stock of R Credit Corporation (a finance company). The CAR Corporation prepares consolidated financial statements consolidating Charles of Canada, using the equity method for R Credit Corporation, and using the lower-of-cost-or-market method for its investment in Alexandre de France. Data from the annual reports of these companies are given below.

	Percentage Owned	Net Income	Dividends	Accounting Method
CAR Corporation Consolidated	—	$1,000,000	$ 70,000	—
Charles of Canada	75%	100,000	40,000	Consolidated
Alexandre de France	80	80,000	50,000	Cost
R Credit Corporation	90	120,000	100,000	Equity

a Which, if any, of the companies is incorrectly accounted for by CAR according to generally accepted accounting principles?

Assuming the accounting for the three subsidiaries shown above to be correct, answer the following questions.

b How much of the net income reported by CAR Corporation Consolidated is attributable to the operations of the three subsidiaries?

c What is the amount of the minority interest shown on the income statement and how does it affect net income of CAR Corporation Consolidated?

d If all three subsidiaries had been consolidated, what would have been the net income of CAR Corporation Consolidated?

e If all three subsidiaries had been consolidated, what would be the minority interest shown on the income statement?

14 During the current year, Buyer Corporation purchased machinery for $20,000, its fair market value, from its wholly owned subsidiary. The machinery had been carried on the books of the subsidiary at a cost of $30,000 and had accumulated depreciation of $16,000. What net book values for this machinery would be shown on:

a Buyer Corporation's single-company books?

b Consolidated balance sheet for Buyer and its subsidiary?

c What adjustments would have to be made on the consolidated income statement because of this intercompany transaction?

15 Company P owns 70 percent of a consolidated subsidiary, Company S. During the year, Company P's sales to Company S amounted to $50,000. The cost of those sales was $35,000. The following data are taken from the two companies' income statements:

	Company P	Company S
Sales	$120,000	$250,000
Cost of Goods Sold	70,000	150,000

a Compute consolidated sales and consolidated cost of goods sold for the year assuming that Company S sold all the goods purchased from Company P.

b Compare the consolidated gross margin on sales to the sum of the gross margins of the separate companies.

16 The Roe Company purchased 80 percent of the stock of the Danver Company on January 2 at book value, $480,000. The total capital stock of the Danver Company at that date was $450,000, and the retained earnings balance was $150,000. During the year, the "net income to stockholders" of the Danver Company was $90,000; dividends declared were $36,000. Present adjusting and eliminating entries that would be necessary in the preparation of the December 31 consolidated balance sheet, assuming that Roe Company uses the cost method on its single-company books to account for its investment in Danver Company.

17 A parent company owns shares in one other company. It has owned them since the other company was formed. The parent company alone has retained earnings of $100,000. The consolidated balance sheet shows no goodwill and retained earnings of $160,000. Consider each of the following questions independently of the others.

a If the parent owns 80 percent of its consolidated subsidiary, what are the retained earnings of the subsidiary?

b If the subsidiary has retained earnings of $96,000, what fraction of the subsidiary does the parent own?

c If the subsidiary had not been consolidated but instead had been accounted for by the equity method, how much revenue in excess of dividends received would the parent have recognized from the investment?

18 Lesala Corporation purchased most of the capital stock of its subsidiary in 1977. The subsidiary earned $1 million in 1979 but declared no dividends. The following is an excerpt from Lesala Corporation's financial statements issued for 1979:

Lesala Corporation
Consolidated Statement of
Changes in Financial Position
For the Year 1979

Sources of Working Capital:

Consolidated Net Income		$3,000,000
Addback Charges Not Requiring Working Capital:		
Depreciation of Plant	$150,000	
Amortization of Goodwill Arising from Acquisition of		
Consolidated Subsidiary	10,000	
Minority Interest in Earnings of Consolidated		
Subsidiary	200,000	360,000
Total Working Capital from Operations		$3,360,000

---

a What percentage of the consolidated subsidiary does Lesala Corporation own?

b Goodwill arising from the acquisition of the consolidated subsidiary is being amortized using the straight-line method to show the minimum charges allowed by generally accepted accounting principles. What was the excess of the subsidiary's market value as a going concern over the market value of the actual assets shown on its books as of the date of acquisition? Assume that the acquisition occurred on January 1, 1977.

19 The Hart Company acquired control of the Keller Company on January 2, 1979, by purchasing 80 percent of its outstanding stock for $700,000. The entire excess of cost over book value acquired is attributed to goodwill, which is amortized over 40 years. The stockholders' equity accounts of the Keller Company appeared as follows on January 2, 1979, and December 31, 1979:

	Jan. 2, 1979	Dec. 31, 1979
Capital Stock	$600,000	$600,000
Retained Earnings	200,000	420,000

The accounts receivable of the Hart Company at December 31, 1979, include $4,500 which is due it from the Keller Company. Hart Company carries its investment in Keller Company on its single-company books at cost. Present journal entries for the following adjustments and eliminations in the December 31, 1979, work sheet for the preparation of the consolidated balance sheet:

a The adjustment of the Investment in Keller Company account at December 31, 1979.

b The elimination of the Investment in Keller Company account.

c The amortization of goodwill.

d The elimination of intercompany obligations.

e The determination of the minority interest.

20 Miller Company and Gordon Company merge in a pooling of interests. Miller Company issues 12,500 shares with market value of $150,000 for 100 percent of Gordon's shares, which have a book value of $125,000. Data for the two companies before the merger are shown below.

	Miller Company	Gordon Company
Common Stock (at par)	$100,000	$ 20,000
Additional Paid-in Capital	50,000	30,000
Retained Earnings	200,000	75,000
Stockholders' Equity	$350,000	$125,000

Construct the pooled stockholders' equity accounts. Assume that Miller Company's stock has a par value per share of

a $4.
b $6.
c $10.
d $12.

21 Marmee Company and Small Enterprises agree to merge at a time when the balance sheets of the two companies are as shown below.

	Marmee Company	Small Enterprises
Assets	$700,000	$312,000
Liabilities	$150,000	$100,000
Common Stock ($1 par)	160,000	64,000
Additional Paid-in Capital	120,000	34,000
Retained Earnings	270,000	114,000
Total Equities	$700,000	$312,000

Marmee issues 50,000 shares with market value of $800,000 to the owners of Small in return for their 64,000 shares, which represent equity of $212,000 (= $312,000 of assets − $100,000 of liabilities). The excess of Marmee's cost ($800,000) over the book value of Small's assets acquired ($212,000) results from Small's book value of assets being $448,000 less than their current value and from $140,000 of goodwill ($800,000 − $212,000 = $448,000 + $140,000).

Prepare consolidated balance sheets as of the merger date, assuming that the merger is treated as a

a Purchase.
b Pooling of interests.

22 Refer to the data in the preceding problem. Partial single-company income statements for Marmee Company and Small Enterprises are shown below for the first year after the merger.

	Marmee Company	Small Enterprises
Sales	$2,000,000	$1,500,000
Other Revenues	50,000	10,000
Total Revenues	$2,050,000	$1,510,000
Expenses Except Income Taxes	1,700,000	1,300,000
Pretax Income	$ 350,000	$ 210,000

Make the following assumptions:

(1) The income tax rate for the consolidated firm is 40 percent.

(2) Where necessary, the extra asset costs that must be recognized in the consolidated statement are amortized over 5 years, and the goodwill is amortized over 40 years.

(3) Amortization of asset costs and goodwill arising from the purchase are not deductible from taxable income in calculations for tax returns.

(4) Small Enterprises declared no dividends.

Prepare consolidated income statements and consolidated earnings per share for the first year following the merger. Assume that the merger is treated as a

a Purchase.

b Pooling of interests.

23 Sealco Enterprises published the consolidated income statement for the year that is shown below.

Sealco Enterprises
Consolidated Income Statement
for the Year

Revenues:

Sales	$1,000,000
Equity in Earnings of Unconsolidated Affiliate	40,000
Total Revenues	$1,040,000

Expenses:

Cost of Goods Sold (Excluding Depreciation)		$ 650,000
Administrative Expenses		100,000
Depreciation Expense		115,000
Amortization of Goodwill		5,000
Income Tax Expenses:		
Currently Payable	$42,000	
Deferred	10,000	52,000
Total Expenses		$ 922,000
Income of the Consolidated Group		$ 118,000
Less Minority Interest in Earnings of Consolidated Subsidiary		30,000
Net Income to Shareholders		$ 88,000

The unconsolidated affiliate retained 20 percent of its earnings of $100,000 during the year, having paid out the rest as dividends. The consolidated subsidiary earned $200,000 during the year and declared no dividends.

a What percentage of the unconsolidated affiliate does Sealco Enterprises own?

b What dividends did Sealco Enterprises receive from the unconsolidated affiliate during the year?

c What percentage of the consolidated subsidiary does Sealco Enterprises own?

d Prepare the "working capital provided by operations" section of the Sealco Enterprises Consolidated Statement of Changes in Financial Position for the year assuming that

  (i) The statement starts with net income to shareholders;

  (ii) The statement shows only revenues and expenses that involve working capital.

24 The condensed balance sheets of the Ely Company and the Sims Company at December 31 are as follows:

ASSETS	Ely Company	Sims Company
Cash	$ 60,000	$ 5,000
Receivables	120,000	15,000
Investment in Sims Company Stock (cost)	80,000	—
Other Assets	540,000	100,000
	$800,000	$120,000
LIABILITIES AND STOCKHOLDERS' EQUITY		
Current Liabilities	$250,000	$ 30,000
Capital Stock	400,000	50,000
Retained Earnings	150,000	40,000
	$800,000	$120,000

The receivables of the Ely Company and the liabilities of the Sims Company contain an advance from the Ely Company to the Sims Company of $5,500.

The Ely Company acquired 85 percent of the capital stock of the Sims Company on the market at January 2 of this year for $80,000. At that date, the balance in the Retained Earnings account of the Sims Company was $30,000. Amortize goodwill, if any, over 40 years.

Prepare journal entries for the adjustments and eliminations on the December 31 consolidated work sheet to:

a Adjust the Investment in the Sims Company account.
b Eliminate the Investment in the Sims Company account.
c Amortize goodwill.
d Eliminate intercompany obligations.
e Determine the minority interest.
f Prepare a work sheet for the consolidated balance sheet.

25 The Little Company is a subsidiary of the Butler Company carried at cost on the single-company books of the Butler Company.

a Present journal entries for the following selected transactions. Record the set of entries on the books of the Little Company separately from the set of entries on the books of the Butler Company.

  (1) On January 2, the Butler Company acquired on the market, for cash, 80 percent of all the capital stock of the Little Company. The outlay was $325,000. The total contributed capital of the stock outstanding was $300,000; the retained earnings balance was $80,000. The excess of cost over book value acquired is all attributed to goodwill.

  (2) The Little Company purchased materials from the Butler Company at the latter's cost, $23,000.

  (3) The Little Company obtained an advance of $9,000 from the Butler Company. The funds were deposited in the bank.

  (4) The Little Company paid $19,000 on the purchases in **(2)** above.

  (5) The Little Company repaid $7,500 of the loan received from the Butler Company in **(3)** above.

(6) The Little Company declared and paid a dividend of $24,000 during the year.

(7) The "net income to stockholders" of the Little Company for the year was $40,000. Present only the entry to close the Income Summary account.

b Prepare the adjustment and elimination entries which would be necessary in the preparation of the December 31 consolidated balance sheet, recognizing the effects of only the above transactions. Amortize goodwill over 40 years.

26 The condensed balance sheets of Companies R and S on December 31, 1979, are as follows

ASSETS	Company R	Company S
Cash	$ 18,000	$ 13,000
Accounts and Notes Receivable	90,000	25,000
Dividends Receivable	–	–
Inventories	220,000	125,000
Investment in Stock of Company S (cost)	300,000	–
Plant Assets	300,000	212,000
Total Assets	$928,000	$375,000
LIABILITIES AND STOCKHOLDERS' EQUITY		
Accounts and Notes Payable	$ 55,000	$ 17,000
Dividends Payable	–	12,500
Other Liabilities	143,000	11,000
Capital Stock	600,000	250,000
Capital Contributed in Excess of Stated Value	–	50,000
Retained Earnings	130,000	34,500
Total Liabilities and Stockholders' Equity	$928,000	$375,000

Additional information:

Company R owns 90 percent of the capital stock of Company S. The stock of Company S was acquired on January 1, 1978, when Company S's retained earnings amounted to $20,000.

Company R has not recorded its share of the dividend declared by Company S.

Company R holds a note issued by Company S in the amount of $8,200.

Excess of cost over book value acquired is all attributable to goodwill, to be amortized over 40 years.

a Present adjustment and elimination journal entries for a consolidated work sheet.

b Prepare a work sheet for a consolidated balance sheet.

27 Company A owns 51 percent of the voting stock of Company B. Company B owns 51 percent of the voting stock of Company C. Company C owns 51 percent of the voting stock of Company D. Company D owns 51 percent of the voting stock of Company E. Notice that Company A effectively controls Companies B, C, D, and E. Company A decides that it wishes to control Company Z. Company Z has $30 million of assets and $22 million of liabilities. Company Z's outstanding voting stock sells in the market place for $10 million. Suppose that Company A acquires control of Company Z by having Company E purchase 51 percent of the voting stock of Company Z for $5.1 million. Company E "raises" the cash needed to acquire voting control of Company Z by not declaring dividends that would otherwise be declared. Companies D, C, and B ordinarily add to their dividend declarations the amounts received in dividends from their own investments.

What cash receipt does the management of Company A forgo by having Company E purchase the stock of Company Z in this fashion? Ignore income tax effects.

28 The following balance sheets show current data for Quarta Company alone and for Quarta Company consolidated with its subsidiary:

ASSETS	Quarta	Quarta Consolidated
Current Assets	$220,000	$365,000
Plant	79,000	147,000
Investment in Subsidiary (cost)	152,000	—
	$451,000	$512,000

EQUITIES		
Liabilities	$ 78,000	$145,000
Minority Interest	—	29,200
Capital Stock	320,000	320,000
Retained Earnings	53,000	17,800
	$451,000	$512,000

Several years ago, Quarta purchased 80 percent of the subsidiary for its book value. Quarta accounts for the investment using the cost method. The subsidiary issued $100,000 of capital stock at the time of its incorporation and has not changed that amount over the years. Assume that there are no intercompany transactions.

a What would be the current balance in Quarta's Investment account had it accounted for the subsidiary using the equity rather than the cost method? (It is possible to answer this question without the calculations called for below. If you cannot, then do the other parts and come back to this one.)

b Reconstruct the subsidiary's current balance sheet.

c What was the balance in the subsidiary's retained earnings account at the time that it was purchased by Quarta?

d What is the current stockholders' equity in the subsidiary?

e Prepare a balance sheet for Quarta Company assuming that it used the equity method to account for the investment in the subsidiary.

29 General Products (G.P.) Company manufactures heavy-duty industrial equipment and consumer durable goods. In order to enable its customers to make convenient credit arrangements, G. P. Company organized General Products Credit Corporation several years ago. G. P. Credit Corporation is 100 percent owned by G. P. Company. G. P. Company accounts for its investment in G. P. Credit Corporation using the *equity method.* G. P. owns shares of many other companies, and consolidates several of them in its financial statements. Refer to the comparative balance sheets and income statements for the two companies in Exhibits 12.9 and 12.10.

a Given that G. P. Company accounted for its investment in G. P. Credit Corporation on the equity method, identify for 1980, the components of G. P. Company's income that are attributable to the Credit Corporation's dividends and earnings.

b Assume that G. P. Company had accounted for its investment in the Credit Corporation using the *cost method.*

(i) Show the components of G. P. Company's income from the Credit Corporation and compute how much larger or smaller G. P. Company's income would have been for 1980 than was reported.

EXHIBIT 12.9
General Products Company and Consolidated Affiliates
(Problems, 29, 30, 31)

	(In Millions of $) December 31		
BALANCE SHEET	**1980**	**1979**	**1978**
Investment in G. P. Credit Corporation	$ 260.0	$ 231.9	$ 190.0
Other Assets	7,141.8	6,655.9	6,008.5
Total Assets	$7,401.8	$6,887.8	$6,198.5
Total Liabilities	$4,317.2	$4,086.0	$3,644.9
Shareholders' Equity	3,084.6	2,801.8	2,553.6
Total Equities	$7,401.8	$6,887.8	$6,198.5

	For the Year		
INCOME STATEMENT	**1980**	**1979**	**1978**
Sales	$10,387.6	$9,546.4	$8,813.6
Equity in Net Earnings of Credit Corporation ...	41.1	30.9	19.9
Total Revenues	$10,428.7	$9,577.3	$8,833.5
Expenses	(9,898.7)	(9,105.5)	(8,505.0)
Net Income	$ 530.0	$ 471.8	$ 328.5

EXHIBIT 12.10
General Products Credit Corporation
(Problems 29, 30, 31)

	(In Millions of $) December 31		
BALANCE SHEET	**1980**	**1979**	**1978**
Total Assets	$2,789.5	$2,358.7	$2,157.0
Total Liabilities	$2,529.5	$2,216.8	$1,967.0
Capital Stock	$ 110.0	$ 90.0	$ 55.0
Retained Earnings	150.0	141.9	135.0
Stockholders' Equity	$ 260.0	$ 231.9	$ 190.0
Total Equities	$2,789.5	$2,358.7	$2,157.0

	For the Year		
STATEMENT OF INCOME AND RETAINED EARNINGS	**1980**	**1979**	**1978**
Revenues	$ 319.8	$ 280.0	$ 247.5
Less: Expenses	278.7	249.1	227.6
Net Income	$ 41.1	$ 30.9	$ 19.9
Less: Dividends	33.0	24.0	15.0
Earnings Retained for Year	$ 8.1	$ 6.9	$ 4.9
Retained Earnings at January 1	141.9	135.0	130.1
Retained Earnings at December 31	$ 150.0	$ 141.9	$ 135.0

(ii) Identify any G. P. Company balance sheet accounts that would have different balances, and calculate the differences from what is shown in the actual statements and what would be shown had the alternative treatment been used.

c Assume that G. P. Company had accounted for its investment in the Credit Corporation by *consolidating* it. Perform the same computations as required in **(i)** and **(ii)** of part **b** above for 1980. Notice that when a 100-percent-owned affiliate accounted for with the equity method is consolidated the effect on balance sheet totals and subtotals can be summarized as follows:

(1) Total owners' equity on the parent's books remains unchanged.

(2) Total liabilities on the parent's books increases by the amount of the affiliate's total liabilities (assuming no intercompany receivables and payables).

(3) Total assets on the parent's books increases net by an amount equal to the affiliate's liabilities. (All of the affiliate's assets are put onto the parent's books, but the parent's investment in the affiliate, an amount equal to the affiliate's owners' equity, is removed. The net effect is to increase assets by the amount of the affiliate's total assets − parent's owners' equity = affiliate's liabilities.)

d Compute the following ratios for G. P. from the annual report as published for 1980. (Refer to Exhibit 6.10 if you have forgotten how to compute these ratios.)

 (i) Rate of return on total capital. (Insufficient information is given to allow an addback to the numerator for interest payments net of tax effects; ignore that adjustment to net income which is ordinarily required. Use the year-end balance of total assets for the year's average.)

 (ii) Debt-equity ratio.

e For 1980, compute the two ratios required in part **d,** assuming that G. P. had consolidated the Credit Corporation, rather than accounting for it with the equity method. Use the information derived in part **c.**

f Compare the results in parts **d** and **e.** What conclusions can you draw from this exercise about comparing financial ratios for companies consolidating their subsidiaries with those of companies that do not?

30 Repeat Problem **29** for 1979.

31 Repeat Problem **29** for 1978.

32 Company P and Company S decide to combine operations. Management estimates that the combination will save $50,000 a year in expenses of running the combined businesses. Columns (1) and (2) in Exhibit 12.11 show abbreviated single-company financial statements for Company P and Company S before combination. Company S has 20,000 shares of stock outstanding that sell for $84 per share in the market. The market value of Company S as a going concern is, then, $1,680,000. As shown in column (3), S's stockholders have $1,230,000 of equity not recorded on the books. Of this $1,230,000, $400,000 is determined to be attributable to undervalued noncurrent assets and $830,000 is assigned to goodwill. Company P has 100,000 shares outstanding, which have a $5 par value and sell for $42 each in the market. Ignore income taxes throughout this problem.

a *Purchase.* Assume that Company P purchases Company S to combine their operations. Company P issues (sells) 40,000 additional shares on the market for $42 each, or $1,680,000 in total, and uses the proceeds to purchase all shares of Company S for $84

EXHIBIT 12.11
Consolidated Statements Comparing Purchase and Pooling-of-Interests Methods
(Problem 32)

BALANCE SHEETS	Historical Cost		Company S Shown at Current Values	Companies P & S Consolidated at Date of Acquisition	
	P (1)	S (2)	(3)	Purchase (4)	Pooling of Interests (5)
Assets					
Current Assets	$1,500,000	$450,000	$ 450,000	$1,950,000	$1,950,000
Long-Term Assets Less					
Accumulated Depreciation	1,700,000	450,000	850,000	?	?
Goodwill	—	—	830,000	?	—
Total Assets	$3,200,000	$900,000	$2,130,000	$5,330,000	$4,100,000
Equities					
Liabilities	$1,300,000	$450,000	$ 450,000	$1,750,000	$1,750,000
Common Stock ($5 par)	500,000	100,000	100,000	?	?
Additional Paid-in Capital	200,000	150,000	150,000	?	?
Retained Earnings	1,200,000	200,000	200,000	?	?
Unrecorded Equity at Current					
Valuation	—	—	1,230,000		—
Total Liabilities and					
Stockholders' Equity	$3,200,000	$900,000	$2,130,000	$5,330,000	$4,100,000

INCOME STATEMENTS (IGNORING INCOME TAXES)	Actual			Projected	
Precombination Income	$ 300,000	$160,000		$ 460,000	$ 460,000
from Combination					
Cost Savings (Projected)	—	—		50,000	50,000
Extra Depreciation Expense	—	—		?	—
Amortization of Goodwill	—	—		?	—
Net Income	$ 300,000	$160,000		$ 409,250	$ 510,000
Number of Common Shares					
Outstanding	100,000	20,000		?	?
Earnings Per Share	$3.00	$8.00		?	?
All-Capital Earnings Rate (Using					
Balances at Merger Date)				?	?
Rate of Return on Owners'					
Equity (Using Balances at					
Merger Date)				?	?

Assumptions: (1) Company S has 20,000 shares outstanding that sell for $84 each in the market.
(2) Company P's shares sell for $42 each in the market. Company P issues 40,000 shares for the purpose of acquiring Company S.

each. (Each share of Company S is, in effect, "sold" for two shares of Company P.) Company P has acquired 100 percent of the shares of Company S and now owns Company S. Company P's acquisition of Company S would be accounted for as a purchase. Company P decides to amortize the revalued asset costs over 5 years and to amortize the goodwill over 40 years. Complete column (4) to show the effects of purchase accounting.

b *Pooling of Interests.* Assume that Company P issued the 40,000 shares of stock directly to the owners of Company S in return for their shares. The merger is treated as a pooling of interests. Complete column (5) to show the effects of pooling accounting.

33 This problem illustrates the impact that consolidation policy can have on financial statements and financial statement analysis. Sears, Roebuck & Co. and J. C. Penney Company are large retailers who have similar operations. Both companies have organized financing subsidiaries. Each subsidiary borrows funds in credit markets and lends the funds to customers who purchase goods or services from the retailers. Each subsidiary is 100-percent owned by its parent company. Sears consolidates its financing subsidiary (Sears, Roebuck Acceptance Corp.) in published financial statements. Penney's uses the equity method for its financing subsidiary (J. C. Penney Financial Corporation) and shows the separate financial statements of the financing subsidiary in notes to the published financial statements.

In this problem we focus on the debt ratio, because the effects are easy to illustrate. Other ratios could be used as well. Throughout this text, we have defined the debt-equity ratio as

$$\text{Debt-Equity Ratio} = \frac{\text{Total Liabilities}}{\text{Total Equities}}.$$

Many financial analysts prefer to use a form of the debt ratio such as

$$\text{Debt Ratio} = \frac{\text{Total } \textit{Long-Term} \text{ Debt}}{\text{Total Shareholders' Equity}}.$$

Such analysts feel that this version of the debt ratio focuses more attention on the risk of companies being analyzed. (The notion is that the percentage of current liabilities to total equities is to a large degree determined by the nature of the business and that so long as current assets are as large as current liabilities, the percentage of current liabilities in total equities is not important.)

The accompanying Exhibit 12.12 shows pertinent data for both Sears and Penney's from recent financial statements. Both versions of the debt ratio mentioned above are presented. The data for Sears are taken directly from the financial statements. For Penney's, the exhibit shows data from the published balance sheet in column (1), data from the statements of the financing subsidiary in column (2), and presents a column for Penney's hypothetical financial statements assuming consolidation of the financing subsidiary. Column (3) represents the accounting for Penney's that is analogous to Sears' accounting.

a Complete column (3) for Penney's. (The ratios shown are correct; you can check your work from them.) You may find the summary in part **c** of Problem **29** above to be useful.

b As measured by the debt ratios (and ignoring other factors—see Problem **15** in Chapter 13), which company appears to be the more risky? Which company do you think is more risky and why?

c Assume that the managements of Penney's and Sears are both considering additional long-term financing to raise funds. Managements of both companies are concerned about how the marketplace will react to new debt financing on the one hand or new common share issues on the other. How are financial analysts who are concerned with

EXHIBIT 12.12
(All Dollar Amounts in Millions)
(Problem 33)

	J. C. Penney Company			Sears, Roebuck & Co.
	Financial Statements as Issued (1)	Financing Subsidiary Statements as Shown in Notes (2)	Hypothetical Financial Statements if Subsidiary Were Consolidated (3)	Financial Statements as Issued (4)
Total Assets	$3,483.8	$1,458.1	?	$12,711.5
Total Liabilities	1,567.2	1,078.9	?	6,774.6
Long-Term Debt	355.5	517.0	?	1,563.5
Shareholders' Equity	1,916.6	379.2	?	5,936.9
Debt-Equity Ratio (Total Liabilities/Total Equities)	45.0%	72.3%	58.0%	53.3%
Long-Term Debt/Shareholders' Equity	18.5%	136.3%	45.5%	26.3%

risk (as measured in part by debt ratios) likely to react to these two companies? How are managements of the two companies likely to react in making their financing decisions if they anticipate the reaction of financial analysts?

PART FOUR
SYNTHESIS

CHAPTER 13
SIGNIFICANCE AND IMPLICATIONS OF ALTERNATIVE ACCOUNTING PRINCIPLES

The independent accountant expresses an unqualified opinion on a firm's financial statements by stating that the statements were prepared in accordance with "generally accepted accounting principles." In previous chapters, we have described and illustrated most of the important accounting principles currently employed in preparing financial statements. In this chapter, we focus on the following questions:

1 What criteria should a firm employ in selecting its accounting principles from among those that are considered "generally acceptable"?
2 What are the effects of using alternative accounting principles on the principal financial statements?
3 What are the effects of using alternative accounting principles on investors' decisions to invest their capital resources?

One who understands the significance and implications of alternative generally accepted accounting principles is a more effective reader and interpreter of published financial statements. Throughout this chapter, we use the terms *accounting principles*, *methods*, and *procedures* interchangeably.

SUMMARY OF GENERALLY ACCEPTED ACCOUNTING PRINCIPLES

A list of major currently acceptable accounting principles, most of which have been discussed in previous chapters, is presented in this section. These accounting principles might be classified into three broad groups based on the flexibility permitted to firms in selecting alternative methods of accounting for a specific item. In some instances, the firm has wide flexibility in choosing among alternative methods, such as in the selection of depreciation methods. In other instances, the specific conditions associated with a transaction or event dictate the method of accounting that must be used. For example, the method of accounting for investments in the common stock of other firms depends on the ownership percentage. The use of the purchase or pooling-of-interests methods of accounting for corporate acquisitions depends, among other factors, on the form of the consideration given by the acquiring firm. In a third category are instances where the firm has wide flexibility in selecting accounting principles for purposes of preparing its income tax return but limited flexibility in selecting methods for its financial statements. For example, a retail merchandising firm selling goods or services on an installment basis is permitted to use the installment basis of recognizing revenue in its tax return but generally cannot use this method in its financial statements. Although a list of major currently acceptable accounting principles is given below, it should be remembered that a particular firm does not have wide flexibility in selecting its accounting methods in all instances.

Revenue Recognition   Revenue may be recognized at the time goods are sold or services are rendered, as is typically done under the accrual basis of accounting, at the time cash is collected (installment basis), or as production progresses (percentage-of-completion method for long-term contracts).

Uncollectible Accounts   A provision for uncollectible accounts can be made in the period when revenue is recognized (allowance method) or, if the amount of uncollectibles is not material, in the period when specific accounts are determined to be uncollectible (direct write-off method).

Inventories   Inventories can be valued on one of several bases: acquisition cost, lower of acquisition cost or market, standard cost, and, in the case of some by-products and precious minerals, net realizable value. When the cost of the specific goods sold cannot be, or is not, determined, a cost-flow assumption must be made. The cost-flow assumption may be FIFO, LIFO, or weighted average, although LIFO must be used for financial reports if it is used for income tax returns.

Investments in Securities   Investments in the common stock securities of other firms are accounted for using either the lower-of-cost-or-market method or the equity method, or else consolidated statements are prepared. The method employed depends primarily on the percentage of outstanding shares that are held.

Machinery, Equipment, and Other Depreciable Assets   These fixed assets may be depreciated using the straight-line, double-declining-balance, sum-of-the-years'-digits, or units-of-production method. Estimates of service lives of similar assets may differ among firms.

Intangible Resources Development Cost   The costs incurred in creating intangible resources, such as a well-trained labor force or a good reputation among customers, can be treated as an expense in the year the costs are incurred, or capitalized and amortized over some period of years. Research and development costs, however, must be recognized as an expense in the year in which the costs are incurred.

Corporate Acquisitions and Goodwill   Corporate acquisitions may be accounted for using the purchase method or the pooling-of-interests method, depending on the type of consideration given by the acquiring company, the percentage of outstanding common stock acquired, and other factors. Any goodwill purchased in such acquisitions subsequent to October 31, 1970, must be amortized. The length of the amortization period may differ among similar firms, but in no case may it exceed 40 years.

Leases   Rights to the use of property acquired under lease may be set up as an asset and subsequently amortized (capital-lease method), or no recognition can be given to the lease except at the time that lease payments are made or due each period (operating-lease method). Likewise, the lessor can set up the rights to receive future lease payments as a receivable at the inception of the lease (capital-lease method), or no recognition can be given to the lease except to the extent that lease payments are received or due each period (operating-lease method). Whether the capital- or operating-lease method is used depends on such factors as the life of the lease relative to the life of the leased asset, the present value of the lease payments relative to the market value of the leased property, and other factors. The facts of each lease agreement determine which method must be used. The same method will be used for any one lease by both the lessor and the lessee.

Premium or Discount on Receivables and Payables   Premium or discount on receivables and payables is amortized using the effective-interest method, although the straight-line method can be used if the results are not materially different.

Investment Tax Credits   A credit, or reduction, in income taxes is permitted for investments in certain depreciable assets, such as equipment, furniture, automobiles, and similar property. The credit is currently 10 percent of the cost of the property, although the rate has been changed several times by Congress. The credit reduces the amount of income tax that the firm must pay in the year the assets are acquired. For financial reporting purposes, the firm can recognize the credit as an immediate reduction in income tax expense (flow-through method), or the credit can be deferred and amortized over the life of the property that gave rise to the credit (deferral method).

The preceding list of alternative acceptable accounting principles is not intended to be exhaustive. Also, it should be remembered that a firm does not always have a choice in the methods which can be used. The factors that a firm might consider in selecting its accounting principles are discussed next.

THE FIRM'S DECISION TO SELECT ACCOUNTING PRINCIPLES

The methods of accounting used for income tax and financial reporting purposes generally do not have to be the same. (An exception is the requirement that if LIFO is used for income tax purposes, it must also be used for financial reporting.) Since the firm might pursue different objectives for financial and tax reporting, we discuss separately the selection of accounting principles for the two types of reports.

Financial Reporting Purposes

Accurate Presentation   One of the criteria that might be used in assessing the usefulness of accounting information is *accuracy in presentation* of the underlying events and transactions. This criterion might be used by the firm as a basis for selecting its methods of accounting. For example, assets have been defined as resources having future service potential and expenses as a measurement of the services consumed during the period. In applying the accuracy criterion, the firm would select the inventory cost-flow assumption and depreciation method that most accurately measured the pattern of services consumed during the period and the amount of services still available at the end of the period. As a basis for selecting accounting methods, this approach has at least one serious limitation. The notions of service potential and services consumed are seldom observable and therefore difficult to measure. Without this information, it is virtually impossible to determine which accounting principles lead to the most accurate presentation of the underlying events. This criterion might serve as a normative criterion toward which the development and selection of accounting principles should be directed.

Fair Presentation   The standard, unqualified opinion of the independent accountant indicates that the financial statements "present fairly the results of operations, financial position, and changes in financial position" for the period. *Fair presentation* might also be used, and supposedly is used, as the reporting objective in choosing accounting methods. The fair presentation criterion suffers from the same limitation as the criterion of accurate presentation. Since flows of past and future benefits are difficult to measure, there are likely to be differences of opinion regarding which accounting principles provide a fair presentation for a particular firm. The independent accountant's opinion that the statements "present fairly . . . in conformity with generally accepted accounting principles" in effect means that a "fair presentation" results, by definition, so long as the methods used are in the list of those currently deemed acceptable. "Present fairly" is, then, merely a statement that the accounting methods used are generally accepted and appropriate in the circumstances.

Conservatism   In choosing among alternative, generally acceptable, methods, the firm might select the set that provides the most conservative measure of net income. Considering the uncertainties involved in measuring benefits received as revenues and services consumed as expenses, others have suggested that a conservative measure of earnings should be provided, thereby reducing the possibility of unwarranted optimism by users of financial statements. As a criterion for selecting accounting principles, *conservatism* implies that methods should be chosen that minimize cumulative reported earnings. That is, expenses should be recognized as quickly as possible, and the recognition of revenue should be postponed as long as possible. This reporting objective would lead to selecting the double-declining-balance or sum-of-the-years'-digits depreciation method, selecting the LIFO cost-flow assumption if periods of rising prices are anticipated, and expensing of intangible development costs in the year incurred.

The rationale for conservatism as a reporting objective has been challenged. Over the whole life of the firm, income is equal to cash receipts minus cash expenditures. Thus, to the extent that net income of earlier periods is smaller, earnings of later periods must be larger. The "later" periods when income must be larger may, however, be many periods later, sometimes even the last period of the firm's existence. Also, it is conceivable that some statement users may be misled by earnings reports based on conservative reporting principles. Consider, for example, an investor who sells shares because he or she feels that the firm is not operating in a sufficiently profitable manner with the resources available, when earnings reported in a less conservative manner would not have induced the sale. Or consider the potential investors who do not purchase securities because they are misled by the published "conservative" statement of earnings.

Profit Maximization   A reporting objective having the opposite effects to conservatism might be employed in selecting among alternative generally accepted accounting principles. Somewhat loosely termed *reported profit maximization*,[1] this criterion suggests the selection of accounting methods that maximize cumulative reported earnings. That is, revenue should be recognized as quickly as possible, and the recognition of expense should be postponed as long as possible. For example, the straight-line method of depreciation would be used and, when periods of rising prices were anticipated, the FIFO cost-flow assumption would be selected. The use of profit maximization as a reporting objective is an extension of the notion that the firm is in business to generate profits and the firm should present as favorable a report on performance as possible within currently acceptable accounting methods. Profit maximization is subject to a similar, but mirror-image, criticism as the use of conservatism as a reporting objective. Reporting income earlier under the profit maximization criterion must mean that smaller income will be reported sometime later.

Income Smoothing   A final reporting objective that might be used in selecting accounting principles is referred to as *income smoothing*. This criterion suggests the selection of accounting methods that result in the smoothest earnings trend over time. As discussed later in this chapter, empirical research has shown that a relationship exists between changes in earnings and changes in stock prices. Advocates of income smoothing suggest that if a company can minimize fluctuations in earnings, then the perceived risk of investing in shares of its stock will be reduced and fluctuations in its stock price will be minimized. Note that this reporting criterion suggests that net income, not revenues and expenses individually, is the object of smoothing. As a result, the firm must consider the total pattern of its operations before selecting the appropriate accounting methods. For example, the straight-line method of depreciation may provide the smoothest amount of depreciation expense on a machine over its life. If, however, the productivity of the machine declines with age so that revenues decrease in later years, net income using the straight-line method may not provide the smoothest net income stream. In this case, perhaps the double-declining-balance or sum-of-the-years'-digits method should be used.

---

[1]   The concept of profit maximization as a reporting objective is not the same as the profit-maximization dictum of microeconomics.

Summary   The principal message of this section is that accurate and fair presentation, although perhaps desirable reporting objectives, are not operational goals in selecting accounting principles. As a result, firms are free to select from among the methods included in the set of generally acceptable accounting principles, using whatever reporting criterion they choose.

Where does this flexibility permitted in selecting accounting principles leave the user of financial statements? Accounting Principles Board *Opinion No. 22*[2] requires firms to disclose the accounting principles employed in preparing financial statements, either in a separate statement or as a note to the principal statements. An example of such disclosure for International Corporation is presented in Note 1 to the financial statements in Appendix A. The effect of alternative accounting principles on investment decisions is discussed later in the chapter.

Income Tax Reporting Purposes

In selecting accounting procedures for income tax purposes, the corporation's objective should be to select those methods that minimize the present value of the stream of income tax payments. The operational rule, sometimes called the *least and latest rule,* is to pay the least amount of taxes as late as possible within the law. The desirability of this rule was discussed at somewhat greater length in Chapters 9 and 10. The least and latest rule generally translates into a policy of recognizing expenses as quickly as possible and postponing the recognition of revenue as long as possible. This policy might be altered somewhat if income tax rates are expected to change, if the firm had losses in earlier years, or if the firm is a sole proprietorship or partnership where earnings of the firm are subject to graduated income tax rates of the owners.

The desire to recognize expenses as quickly as possible suggests the adoption of the LIFO inventory cost-flow assumption, accelerated depreciation methods (either double-declining-balance or sum-of-the-years'-digits), and immediate expensing of research and development, advertising, and similar costs. Using the installment basis of recognizing revenue is generally desirable for income tax purposes where permitted by the Internal Revenue Code and Regulations, since it results in postponing the recognition of revenue and the resulting income tax payments until cash is collected.

AN ILLUSTRATION OF THE EFFECTS OF ALTERNATIVE ACCOUNTING PRINCIPLES ON A SET OF FINANCIAL STATEMENTS

In this section, we illustrate the effects of using different accounting principles on a set of financial statements. The illustration has been constructed so that the accounting principles employed create significant differences in the financial statements. Therefore, inferences should not be drawn about the usual magnitude of the effects of alternative methods from this example.

---

[2]   *APB Opinion No. 22,* 1972.

The Scenario

On January 1, 1979, two corporations are formed to operate merchandising businesses. The two firms are alike in all respects except for their methods of accounting. Conservative Company chooses the accounting principles that will minimize its reported net income. High Flyer Company chooses the accounting principles that will maximize its reported net income. The following events occur during 1979.

1 Both corporations issue 2 million shares of $10 par value stock on January 1, 1979, for $20 million cash.
2 Both firms acquire equipment on January 1, 1979, for $14 million cash. The equipment is estimated to have a 10-year life and zero salvage value.
3 Both firms make the following purchases of merchandise inventory:

Date	Units Purchased	Unit Price	Cost of Purchases
January 1	170,000	@ $60	$10,200,000
May 1................................	190,000	@ $63	11,970,000
September 1	200,000	@ $66	13,200,000
Total	560,000		$35,370,000

4 During the year, both firms sell 420,000 units at an average price of $100 each. All sales are made for cash.
5 During the year, both firms have selling, general, and administrative expenses, excluding depreciation, of $7.3 million.

Accounting Principles Employed

The methods of accounting used by each firm in preparing its financial statements are described below.

Inventory Cost-Flow Assumption   Conservative Company makes a LIFO cost-flow assumption, whereas High Flyer Company makes a FIFO assumption. The method chosen by each firm is used for both its financial reports and income tax returns. Since the beginning inventory is zero, the cost of goods available for sale by each firm is equal to the purchases during the year of $35,370,00. Both firms have 140,000 units in ending inventory. Conservative Company therefore reports a cost of goods sold of $26,970,000 [= $35,370,000 − ($140,000 × $60)], whereas High Flyer Company reports a cost of goods sold of $26,130,000 [= $35,370,000 − (140,000 × $66)]. Income tax regulations require a firm to use LIFO in its financial reports if it uses LIFO for its tax return. High Flyer Company desires not to use LIFO in its financial reports and therefore forgoes the tax savings opportunities from using it for tax purposes.

Depreciation   Conservative Company decides to depreciate its equipment using the double-declining-balance method both on its tax return and in its financial statements. High Flyer Company decides to use the straight-line method in reporting income to stockholders but the double-declining-balance method in its tax return. Conservative Company therefore reports depreciation expense of $2.8 million (= $2 \times \frac{1}{10} \times \$14,000,000$), whereas High Flyer Company reports depreciation expense of $1.4 million (= $\frac{1}{10} \times \$14,000,000$) to stockholders and $2.8 million on its tax return.

Investment Tax Credit   Since both firms purchased long-term, depreciable equipment costing $14 million, each is entitled to a tax reduction or credit of $1.4 million (= .10 × $14,000,000) in the taxes otherwise payable for 1979. On its financial statements to stockholders, Conservative Company chooses to report the benefits of the tax reduction over the 10-year life of the equipment that gave rise to the tax reduction (deferral method), while High Flyer Company reports the entire benefit of the tax reduction in determining net income reported to stockholders (flow-through method) for 1979.

Comparative Income Statements

Exhibit 13.1 presents comparative income statements for Conservative Company and High Flyer Company for the year ending December 31, 1979. Because Conservative Company reports the same revenues and expenses on both its financial statements

---

EXHIBIT 13.1
Comparative Income Statements
Based on Different
Accounting Principles
For the Year Ending
December 31, 1979
(dollar amounts shown in
thousands except for per-share
amounts)

	Conservative Company		High Flyer Company	
	Financial Statement	Tax Return	Financial Statement	Tax Return
Sales Revenue	$42,000.0	$42,000.0	$42,000.0	$42,000.0
Expenses:				
Cost of Goods Sold	$26,970.0	$26,970.0	$26,130.0	$26,130.0
Depreciation on Equipment	2,800.0	2,800.0	1,400.0[b]	2,800.0[b]
Other Selling, General, and Administrative	7,300.0	7,300.0	7,300.0	7,300.0
Expenses Before Income Taxes	$37,070.0	$37,070.0	$34,830.0	$36,230.0
Net Income Before Income Taxes	$ 4,930.0	$ 4,930.0	$ 7,170.0	$ 5,770.0
Income Tax Expense[a]	2,212.9		2,028.1	
Net Income	$ 2,717.1		$ 5,141.9	
Earnings per Share (2,000,000 Shares Outstanding)	$1.36		$2.57	

[a] Computation of Income Tax Expense:				
Income Before Taxes	$ 4,930.0	$ 4,930.0	$ 7,170.0	$ 5,770.0
Income Tax on Current Income (20 percent of first $25,000, 22 percent of the next $25,000, plus 48 percent of remainder)	$ 2,352.9	$ 2,352.9	$ 3,428.1	$ 2,756.1
Less: Tax Credit for Investment in Equipment	140.0	1,400.0	1,400.0	1,400.0
Income Tax Expense	$ 2,212.9		$ 2,028.1	
Income Tax Currently Payable		$ 952.9		$ 1,356.1
Deferred Investment Tax Credit ($1,400 − $140)	$ 1,260.0			
[b] Income Taxes Deferred by Timing Differences for Depreciation [.48 × ($2,800 − $1,400)]			$ 672.0	

and income tax return, its taxable income is the same as reported income before taxes. High Flyer Company reports larger deductions from revenues on the income tax return than it reports to shareholders. The difference for depreciation on equipment is viewed as a timing difference. A portion of the income tax expense shown on the income statement of High Flyer Company is not payable currently, and therefore a deferred tax liability will appear on the balance sheet. In this illustration, net income and earnings per share of High Flyer Company are almost double the amounts shown for Conservative Company.

Comparative Balance Sheets

Exhibit 13.2 presents comparative balance sheets for Conservative Company and High Flyer Company as of December 31, 1979. The individual asset accounts as well as total assets of Conservative Company are stated at lower amounts than those of High Flyer Company. The only real difference between the economic positions of each company is the amount of cash. The difference in the amount of cash is attributable to the payment of different amounts of income taxes by the two firms. Note that Conservative Company has more cash because it paid smaller income taxes. We would argue that it is better off than High Flyer Company.

The differences in the amounts at which the remaining assets are stated are attributable to the different accounting methods used by the two companies. The amounts shown for merchandise inventory and equipment net of depreciation of Conservative Company are smaller than the corresponding amounts for High Flyer Company

EXHIBIT 13.2
Comparative Balance Sheets
Based on Alternative
Accounting Principles
December 31, 1979

	(Amounts Shown in Thousands)	
ASSETS	**Conservative Company**	**High Flyer Company**
Cash	$ 4,377.1	$ 3,973.9
Merchandise Inventory	8,400.0	9,240.0
Equipment (at acquisition cost)	14,000.0	14,000.0
Less: Accumulated Depreciation	(2,800.0)	(1,400.0)
Total Assets	$23,977.1	$25,813.9
EQUITIES		
Deferred Investment Tax Credits	$ 1,260.0	—
Deferred Income Taxes	—	$ 672.0
Common Shares	20,000.0	20,000.0
Retained Earnings	2,717.1	5,141.9
Total Equities	$23,977.1	$25,813.9

because a larger portion of the costs incurred during the period by Conservative Company has been recognized as an expense.

In the equities portion of the balance sheet, Conservative Company shows deferred investment tax credits, reflecting its decision to recognize the current reduction in income taxes payable as an element of income over the life of the property. Each year $140,000 (= $1,400,000/10) will be amortized and shown as a reduction in income tax expense. (Income taxes *payable* in future years are not affected.) High Flyer Company used the flow-through method and recognized the full $1.4 million of tax savings in the determination of net income for 1979. High Flyer Company also reports deferred income taxes on the balance sheet resulting from differences in the timing of depreciation on equipment in the financial statements and income tax return.

Note the effect of using alternative accounting principles on the ratio, rate of return on total assets. Conservative Company reports a smaller amount of net income and also a smaller amount of total assets. One might expect the rate of return on total assets of the two firms to approximate each other more closely than either net income or total assets individually. Significant differences in the ratio for the two firms are still observable, however. The rate of return on total assets of Conservative Company is 12.4 percent [= $2,717,100/($20,000,000 + $23,977,100/2)] and of High Flyer Company is 22.4 percent [= $5,141,900/($20,000,000 + $25,813,900/2)].

Comparative Statements of Changes in Financial Position

Exhibit 13.3 presents comparative statements of changes in financial position for Conservative Company and High Flyer Company. The amount of working capital provided by operations of High Flyer Company is larger than for Conservative Company. The difference is more than accounted for by the difference in inventory cost-flow assumptions employed. High Flyer Company, using FIFO, reported a smaller amount for cost of goods sold and thereby used a smaller amount of working capital in generating revenues. The remaining difference between the amounts reported as working capital provided by operations of the two firms is attributable to the differing amount of income taxes paid. Unlike the income statement and balance sheet, the accounting principles that create differences between the amounts of working capital provided by operations and in the increases or decreases in working capital for the year are only those principles affecting working capital accounts (for example, inventory valuation method and cost-flow assumption, treatment of uncollectible accounts). The effects of using different accounting principles for nonworking capital accounts are eliminated from this statement through the process of adding and subtracting amounts to net income to obtain working capital provided by operations. The use of alternative accounting principles generally creates smaller differences in the amounts of working capital provided by operations than in the amounts reported as net income.

Moral of the Illustration

In order to interpret published financial statements, you must be aware of which accounting principles from the set of alternative generally accepted accounting principles are used. When reports of several companies are compared, the amounts shown

EXHIBIT 13.3
Comparative Statements of Changes
in Financial Position
For the Year Ending
December 31, 1979

	(Amounts Shown in Thousands)	
	Conservative Company	High Flyer Company
Sources of Working Capital:		
Net Income	$ 2,717.1	$ 5,141.9
Add Depreciation Expense Not Using Working Capital	2,800.0	1,400.0
Add Excess of Investment Tax Credit Reducing Current Taxes Payable Over Credit Recognized in Determining Net Income ($1,400 − $140)	1,260.0	—
Add Portion of Income Tax Expense Not Payable Currently	—	672.0
Working Capital Provided by Operations	$ 6,777.1	$ 7,213.9
Issuance of Common Shares	20,000.0	20,000.0
Total Sources of Working Capital . . .	$26,777.1	$27,213.9
Uses of Working Capital:		
Purchase of Equipment	14,000.0	14,000.0
Increase in Working Capital	$12,777.1	$13,213.9
Analysis of Increases in Working Capital:		
Cash	$ 4,377.1	$ 3,973.9
Merchandise Inventory	8,400.0	9,240.0
Increase in Working Capital	$12,777.1	$13,213.9

should be adjusted where possible for the different accounting methods used. The techniques for making some of these adjustments were illustrated in previous chapters (for example, LIFO to FIFO cost-flow assumption, equity method to consolidated statements). The notes to the financial statements will disclose the accounting methods used, but not necessarily the data required to make appropriate adjustments.

ASSESSING THE EFFECTS OF ALTERNATIVE ACCOUNTING PRINCIPLES ON INVESTMENT DECISIONS

In previous sections of this chapter, emphasis has been given to the flexibility that firms have in selecting accounting procedures and to the possible effects of using different accounting procedures on the financial statements. We now focus briefly on a related and important question: Do investors accept financial statement information as presented, or do they somehow filter out all or most of the differences in the financial statements of various firms resulting from differences in the methods of accounting employed? Assume first that investors accept financial statement information in the form presented without adjustments for the methods of accounting used. Then two firms otherwise identical except for the accounting procedures employed might receive a disproportionate amount of capital funds. Thus, the use of alternative accounting principles could lead to a misallocation of resources in the economy. On the other hand, assume that investors make adjustments for the different accounting procedures in analyzing the financial statements of various firms. Then perhaps the concern over the variety of acceptable accounting principles is excessive. If investors do make such adjustments, then increased disclosure of the procedures followed may be more important than greater uniformity in accounting principles.

The question as to the effect of alternative accounting principles on investment decisions has been the subject of extensive debate among public accountants, academicians, personnel in government agencies, and financial statement users.

Those who believe that investors can be misled point to examples where the market prices of particular firms' shares of stock have decreased dramatically after the effects of using specific accounting procedures have been carefully analyzed and reported in the financial press.[3] In these examples it is often difficult, however, to determine if the price change is attributable to the disclosure of the effects of using particular accounting procedures or to other, more temporary factors affecting the specific firm, its industry, or all firms in the economy. Also, it is difficult to generalize on the effects of using alternative accounting principles on investment decisions from isolated and anecdotal examples.

An expanding number of empirical research studies, on the other hand, have provided support for the view that investors at the aggregate market level are rarely misled by the accounting methods employed. This research has developed from the theory and empirical evidence that the stock market is efficient, in the sense that market prices adjust quickly and in an unbiased manner to new information.[4] Unlike the examples supporting the view that investors are misled, these empirical studies have been based on data for a large number of firms spanning long time periods. Also, an effort is made in these studies to control for the effects of economy-wide and industry effects on market price changes.

Several studies have shown that changes in earnings and changes in market prices are associated and, therefore, indicate that information contained in the financial statements is used by investors in making their resource allocation decisions.[5] Several

---

[3] For several examples, see Abraham J. Briloff, *More Debits Than Credits* (New York: Harper & Row, 1976).

[4] See Eugene F. Fama, "Efficient Capital Markets: A Review of Theory and Empirical Work," *Journal of Finance*, May 1970, pp. 383–417.

[5] See, for example, Ray Ball and Philip Brown, "An Empirical Evaluation of Accounting Income Numbers," *Journal of Accounting Research*, Autumn 1968, pp. 159–173; William H. Beaver, "The Information Content of Annual Earnings Announcements," *Empirical Research in Accounting: Selected Studies, 1968*, Supplement to Vol. 6, *Journal of Accounting Research*, pp. 67–92; Robert G. May, "The Influence of Quarterly Earnings Announcements on Investor Decisions as Reflected in Common Stock Price Changes," *Empirical Research in Accounting: Selected Studies, 1971*, Supplement to Vol. 9, *Journal of Accounting Research*, pp. 119–163.

studies have examined the effects of *changes* in the methods of accounting on market prices. Changes in accounting methods that have no real or economic effects have been shown to have little influence on market prices.[6] A third group of studies looked at *differences* in the methods of accounting across firms to assess the effects on investment decisions. The results of this last group of studies have been mixed, with several studies supporting the position that investors are misled and several studies supporting the position that they are not misled.[7] The methodology employed in most studies in this third group has been extensively criticized, so the full implications are not clear, at least to us.

Research into the question regarding the effects of alternative accounting principles on investment decisions has not progressed sufficiently for any consensus to have been reached. We have briefly described some of the research that has been conducted to emphasize an important point. It is not obvious, as it might first appear, that the current flexibility permitted firms in selecting accounting principles necessarily misleads investors and results in a misallocation of resources. In fact, there is an impressive and growing amount of evidence to the contrary.[8]

DEVELOPMENT OF PRINCIPLES IN ACCOUNTING

In Chapter 1, we indicated that the development of "generally accepted accounting principles" is essentially a political process. Various persons or groups have power or authority in the decision process, including Congress and the Securities and Exchange Commission, the courts, professional accounting organizations and their members, and financial statement users. Although Congress has the ultimate authority to specify acceptable accounting methods, it has delegated that authority in almost all cases to the Securities and Exchange Commission. The Commission has indicated that it will generally accept the pronouncements of the Financial Accounting Standards Board on accounting principles. The role of the private sector versus the public sector in setting accounting principles and regulating professional accounting practice continues, however, to be the subject of extensive debate.

---

[6] See, for example, Ray Ball, "Changes in Accounting Techniques and Stock Prices," *Empirical Research in Accounting: Selected Studies, 1972,* Supplement to Vol. 10, *Journal of Accounting Research,* pp. 1–38; Robert S. Kaplan and Richard Roll, "Investor Evaluation of Accounting Information: Some Empirical Evidence," *Journal of Business,* April 1972, pp. 225–257; Shyam Sunder, "Relationships Between Accounting Changes and Stock Prices: Problems of Measurement and Some Empirical Evidence," *Empirical Research in Accounting: Selected Studies, 1973,* Supplement to Vol. 11, *Journal of Accounting Research,* pp. 1–45.

[7] See, for example, Robert E. Jensen, "An Experimental Design for Study of Effects of Accounting Variations in Decision Making," *Journal of Accounting Research,* Autumn 1966, pp. 224–238; Thomas R. Dyckman, "On the Investment Decision," *The Accounting Review,* April 1964, pp. 285–295; John L. O'Donnell, "Relationships Between Reported Earnings and Stock Prices in the Electric Utility Industry," *The Accounting Review,* January 1965, pp. 135–143.

[8] For a description of the theoretical framework and a summary of the empirical work behind this position, see Nicholas J. Gonedes and Nicholas Dopuch, "Capital Market Equilibrium, Information-Production, and Selecting Accounting Techniques: Theoretical Framework and Review of Empirical Work," *Studies on Financial Accounting Objectives: 1974,* Supplement to Vol. 12, *Journal of Accounting Research,* pp. 48–129; and Robert S. Kaplan, "Information Content of Financial Accounting Numbers: A Survey of Empirical Evidence," in *Symposium of Impact of Accounting Research in Financial Accounting and Disclosure on Accounting Practice,* ed. by T. Keller and R. Abdel-khalik, Duke University, 1978.

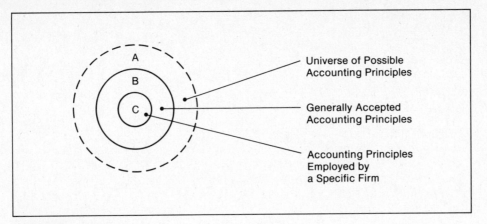

FIGURE 13.1
Structure of Accounting
Principles

SUMMARY

The structure of accounting principles might be depicted as shown in Figure 13.1 The *universe* of possible accounting principles is encircled by a dashed line because of the difficulty in determining the relative size, or boundaries, of circle A. The process of specifying the principles designated as *generally acceptable* (the subset of principles from circle A represented by circle B) is political in nature. Congress and the Securities and Exchange Commission have the legal authority to make the selection, but most of the responsibility for doing so has, in effect, been delegated to the Financial Accounting Standards Board. The individual firm's selection of accounting principles (the subset of principles from circle B represented by circle C) might be based on a criterion of accurate or fair presentation. However, since benefits received and services consumed are seldom observable events and are therefore difficult to measure, consensus on which generally accepted accounting principles provide an accurate or fair presentation is difficult to obtain. This chapter suggests that a firm might pursue a specific reporting objective, such as conservatism, profit maximization, or income smoothing, in selecting its accounting principles.

Before we can know whether circle B should be widened or narrowed, we must learn whether investors accept financial statement information as presented or whether investors make adjustments to recognize the effects of using alternative accounting principles. This question has been and continues to be the subject of extensive research.

QUESTIONS AND PROBLEMS

1 Review the meaning of the following concepts or terms discussed in this chapter.
  a Generally accepted accounting principles.
  b Accurate presentation.

    c Fair presentation.

    d Conservatism.

    e Profit maximization.

    f Income smoothing.

    g Least and latest rule.

    h Statement of accounting policies.

    i Development of accounting principles is a political process.

2 Indicate the generally accepted accounting principle, or method, described in each of the following statements. Indicate your reasoning.

    a This inventory cost-flow assumption results in reporting the largest net income during periods of rising prices.

    b This method of accounting for uncollectible accounts recognizes the implied income reduction in the period of sale.

    c This method of accounting for long-term investments in the securities of unconsolidated subsidiaries or other corporations usually requires an adjustment to net income to determine working capital provided by operations in the statement of changes in financial position.

    d This method of accounting for long-term leases by the lessee gives rise to a noncurrent liability.

    e The presence of goodwill expense on the income statement indicates that a corporate acquisition has been accounted for using this method.

    f This inventory cost-flow assumption results in approximately the same balance sheet amount as the FIFO flow assumption.

    g This method of amortizing bond premium or discount provides a uniform annual rate of interest revenue or expense over the life of the bond.

    h During periods of rising prices, this inventory valuation basis produces approximately the same results as the acquisition-cost valuation basis.

    i When specific customers' accounts are deemed uncollectible and written off, this method of accounting results in a decrease in the current ratio.

    j This method of depreciation generally provides the largest amounts of depreciation expense during the first several years of an asset's life.

    k This method of accounting for intercorporate investments in securities can result in a decrease in the investor's total stockholders' equity without affecting retained earnings.

    l The method of recognizing income from long-term contracts generally results in the least fluctuation in earnings over several periods.

    m When specific customers' accounts are deemed uncollectible and are written off, this method of accounting has no effect on working capital.

    n When used in determining taxable income, this inventory cost-flow, assumption must also be used in determining net income reported to stockholders.

    o Under this method of accounting for long-term leases of equipment by the lessor, an amount for depreciation expense on the leased equipment will appear on the income statement.

    p This method of amortizing bond premium or discount provides a uniform annual amount of interest revenue or expense over the life of the bonds.

3 Indicate the accounting principle, or procedure, apparently being used to record each of the following independent transactions. Indicate your reasoning.

a Losses from Uncollectible Accounts   X
   Accounts Receivable   X

b Cash   X
   Dividend Income   X

c Income Taxes Payable—Current   X
   Deferred Investment Tax Credits   X

d Unrealized Loss from Price Declines in Marketable Securities   X
   Allowance to Reduce Marketable Securities to Market   X

e Goodwill Amortization Expense   X
   Goodwill   X

f Cash   X
   Investment in Unconsolidated Subsidiary   X
   Dividend declared and received from unconsolidated subsidiary

g Sales, Uncollectible Accounts Adjustment   X
   Allowance for Uncollectible Accounts   X

4 Indicate the accounting principle, or procedure, apparently being used to record each of the following independent transactions. Give your reasoning.

a Rent Expense (for Lease Contract)   X
   Cash   X

b Advertising Expense   X
   Deferred Advertising Costs   X

c Investment in Unconsolidated Subsidiary   X
   Equity in Earnings of Unconsolidated Subsidiary   X

d Allowance for Uncollectible Accounts   X
   Accounts Receivable   X

e Loss from Price Decline of Inventories   X
   Merchandise Inventories   X

f Income Taxes Payable—Current   X
   Income Tax Expense (from Investment Credit)   X

g Liability under Long-Term Lease   X
   Interest Expense   X
   Cash   X

5 Indicate the accounting principle that provides the most conservative measure of earnings in each of the following cases.

a FIFO, LIFO, or weighted-average cost-flow assumption for inventories during periods of rising prices.

b FIFO, LIFO, or weighted-average cost-flow assumption for inventories during periods of declining prices.

c Cost or equity method of accounting for long-term investments in the securities of unconsolidated subsidiaries where dividends declared by the subsidiary are less than its earnings.

d Sum-of-the-years'-digits or straight-line depreciation method during the first one-third of an asset's life.

e Sum-of-the-years-digits or straight-line depreciation method during the last one-third of an asset's life.

f Deferral or flow-through method of accounting for the investment tax credit in the year qualifying assets are acquired.

    g The valuation of inventories at acquisition cost or lower of cost or market.

    h Cost or equity method of accounting for long-term investments in the securities of unconsolidated subsidiaries where the investee realizes net losses and does not pay dividends.

    i Purchase or pooling-of-interests method of accounting for corporate acquisitions where the market value of the consideration given by the acquiring company exceeds the book value of the acquired company's net assets.

    j Effective-interest or straight-line method of amortizing bond premium in the first year that bonds are outstanding.

    k Effective-interest or straight-line method of amortizing bond discount in the first year that bonds are outstanding.

6 South Company and North Company incur $50,000 of advertising costs each year. South Company expenses these costs immediately, whereas North Company capitalizes the costs and amortizes them over 5 years.

    a Determine the amount of advertising expense and deferred advertising costs each firm would report beginning in the first year that advertising costs are incurred and continuing for 6 years.

    b For this part, assume that the amount of advertising costs incurred by each firm increases by $10,000 each year. Repeat part **a.**

    c Comment on the differences noted in parts **a** and **b**.

7 On January 1, 1979, two corporations are formed to operate merchandising businesses. The firms are alike in all respects except for their methods of accounting. Ruzicka Company chooses the accounting principles that will minimize its reported net income. Murphy Company chooses the accounting principles that will maximize its reported net income but, where different procedures are permitted, will use accounting methods that minimize its taxable income. The following events occur during 1979.

    (1) Both companies issue 500,000 shares of $1 par-value common shares for $6 per share on January 2, 1979.

    (2) Both firms acquire equipment on January 2, 1979, for $1,650,000 cash. The equipment is estimated to have a 10-year life and zero salvage value. An investment tax credit of 10 percent is applicable to this equipment.

    (3) Both firms engage in extensive sales promotion activities during 1979, incurring costs of $400,000.

    (4) The two firms make the following purchases of merchandise inventory.

Date	Units Purchased	Unit Price	Cost of Purchases
January 2	50,000	$6.00	$ 300,000
April 1	60,000	6.20	372,000
August 15	40,000	6.25	250,000
November 30	50,000	6.50	325,000
Total	200,000		$1,247,000

    (5) During the year both firms sell 140,000 units at an average price of $15 each.

    (6) Selling, general, and administrative expenses during the year other than advertising total $100,000.

The Ruzicka Company uses the following accounting methods (for both book and tax purposes): LIFO inventory cost-flow assumption, sum-of-the-years'-digits depreciation method, immediate expensing of the costs of sales promotion, and the deferral method of accounting for the investment credit.

The Murphy Company uses the following accounting methods: FIFO inventory cost-flow assumption for both book and tax purposes, the straight-line depreciation method for book and the double-declining-balance method for tax purposes, capitalization and amortization of the costs of the sales promotion campaign over 4 years for book and immediate expensing for tax purposes, and the flow-through method of accounting for the investment credit.

a Prepare comparative income statements for the two firms for the year 1979. Include separate computations of income tax expense. The income tax rate is 20 percent of the first $25,000 of taxable income, 22 percent of the next $25,000, and 48 percent of the remainder.

b Prepare comparative balance sheets for the two firms as of December 31, 1979. Both firms have $1 million of outstanding accounts receivable on this date and a single current liability for income taxes payable for the year.

c Prepare comparative statements of changes in financial position for the two firms for the year 1979.

8 The Langston Corporation is formed on January 2, 1979, with the issuance at par of 100,000 shares of $10-par-value common stock for cash. During 1979, the following transactions occur.

(1) The assets of the Dee's Department Store are acquired on January 2, 1979, for $800,000 cash. The market values of the identifiable assets received are as follows: accounts receivable, $200,000; merchandise inventory, $400,000 (200,000 units); store equipment, $150,000. The acquisition is accounted for as a purchase.

(2) Merchandise inventory is purchased during 1979 as follows:

Date	Units Purchased	Unit Price	Cost of Purchase
April 1	30,000	$2.10	$ 63,000
August 1	20,000	2.20	44,000
October 1	50,000	2.40	120,000
Total	100,000		$227,000

(3) During the year, 210,000 units are sold at an average price of $3.20.

(4) Extensive training programs are held during the year to acquaint previous employees of Dee's Department Store with the merchandising policies and procedures of Langston Corporation. The costs incurred in the training programs total $50,000.

(5) Selling, general, and administrative costs incurred and recognized as an expense during 1979 are $80,000.

(6) The store equipment is estimated to have a 5-year useful life and zero salvage value.

(7) The income tax rate is 20 percent of the first $25,000 of taxable income, 22 percent of the next $25,000, and 48 percent of the remainder. Goodwill arising from a corporate acquisition is not deductible in determining taxable income. Ignore investment tax credit provisions in this problem.

The management of Langston Corporation is uncertain about the accounting methods that should be used in preparing its financial statements. The choice has been narrowed to two sets of accounting methods, and you have been asked to determine net income for 1979 using each set.

   a Set A consists of the following accounting methods (for book and tax purposes): LIFO inventory cost-flow assumption, double-declining-balance depreciation method, immediate expensing of the costs of the training program, amortization of goodwill over 10 years.

   b Set B consists of the following accounting methods: FIFO inventory-costing assumption, straight-line depreciation for book and double-declining-balance for tax purposes, capitalization and amortization of the costs of the training program over 5 years for book and immediate expensing for tax purposes, amortization of goodwill over 40 years.

9 Refer to Problem **8.** Determine working capital provided by operations under both set A and set B accounting principles. Prepare a separate analysis explaining the difference in the amount of working capital provided by operations under set A and set B.

10 Net income of Miller Corporation for the year ending December 31, 1979, is $600,000 based on the accounting methods actually used by the firm. You have been asked to determine the amount of net income that would have been reported under several alternative accounting methods. The income tax rate is 40 percent, and the same accounting methods are used for financial reporting and income tax purposes unless otherwise indicated. Each of the following questions should be considered independently.

   a Miller Corporation acquired a machine costing $300,000 on January 1, 1979. The machine was depreciated during 1979 using the straight-line method based on a 5-year useful life and zero salvage value. What would net income have been if the sum-of-the-years'-digits depreciation method had been used? Ignore the investment tax credit.

   b Miller Corporation obtained an investment tax credit of $10,000 on the machine acquired in part **a.** It accounted for the investment credit using the flow-through method. What would net income have been if the deferral method had been used? In responding to this question, assume that the machine was depreciated using the straight-line method based on a 5-year life and zero salvage value. Also assume that this is the first year that investment tax credits have been realized by Miller Corporation.

   c Miller Corporation used the lower-of-cost-or-market method of accounting for its 18-percent investment in the common shares of General Tools Corporation. During 1979, General Tools Corporation earned $200,000 and paid dividends of $50,000. The market value of General Tools Corporation was the same at the end of 1979 as it was at the beginning of 1979. What would net income have been during 1979 if Miller Corporation continued to account for the investment under the lower-of-cost-or-market method for income tax purposes but used the equity method for financial reporting purposes?

   d Miller Corporation used the FIFO inventory cost-flow assumption. Under FIFO, the January 1, 1979, inventory was $300,000 and the December 31, 1979, inventory was $320,000. Under LIFO, the January 1, 1979, inventory would have been $240,000 and the December 31, 1979, inventory would have been $230,000. What would net income have been if the LIFO inventory costing assumption had been used?

11 Refer to Problem **25** in Chapter 6. Illinois Corporation and Ohio Corporation are in an industry that experienced a 10-percent increase in prices during 1979. Illinois Corporation uses the LIFO inventory cost-flow assumption and straight-line depreciation method. Ohio Corporation uses the FIFO inventory cost-flow assumption and the double-declining-balance depreciation method. Reassess the relative profitability and liquidity of the two firms in light of the information concerning their accounting procedures.

12 The income statement of Garrett Corporation for 1979 appears below.

**Garrett Corporation
Income Statement
for the Year Ended
December 31, 1979**

Revenues:

Sales	$5,000,000
Interest	100,000
Dividends (Note 1)	60,000
Equity in Earnings of Unconsolidated Affiliate (Note 2)	300,000
Recovery of Loss on Valuation of Marketable Equity Securities	30,000
Total Revenue	$5,490,000
Expenses:	
Cost of Goods Sold (Note 3)	$3,000,000
Selling and Administrative (Note 3)	800,000
Interest	200,000
Total Expenses	$4,000,000
Income Before Income Taxes	$1,490,000
Income Tax Expense (Note 4)	700,000
Income Before Minority Interest	$ 790,000
Less Minority Interest in Earnings of Consolidated Subsidiary	160,000
Net Income	$ 630,000

Note 1: Garrett Corporation owns 10 percent of the outstanding common shares of Williams Corporation. During 1979, Williams Corporation earned $2,000,000 and declared dividends of $600,000.

Note 2: Garrett Corporation owns 30 percent of the outstanding common shares of Knowles Corporation. During 1979, Knowles Corporation earned $1,000,000 and declared dividends of $400,000.

Note 3: Depreciation charges of $200,000 and $100,000 are included in Cost of Goods Sold and Selling and Administrative Expenses respectively.

Note 4: Income Tax Expense is composed of the following:

Current	$500,000
Deferred	200,000
Total	$700,000

Current income tax expense has been reduced by $40,000 for amortization of deferred investment tax credits. The investment credit realized during 1979 and added to the Deferred Investment Tax Credit account on the balance sheet is $60,000.

Determine the amount of working capital provided by operations for Garrett Corporation during 1979. Your analysis should begin with net income of $630,000.

13 The following data are taken from the adjusted trial balances of the Hickory Merchandising Company as of December 31, 1978 and 1979. The brackets indicate amounts to be found in the solution of the problem.

	December 31, 1978		December 31, 1979	
Accounts Payable		$ 97,320		$ 98,715
Accounts Receivable—Net	$ 580,335		$ 617,530	
Accrued Expenses and Withholdings Payable		99,800		99,700
Administrative Expense Control	449,160		447,260	
Bonds Payable (6%)		300,000		300,000
Cash	114,080		149,485	
Common Stock		100,000		[ ]
Cost of Goods Sold	3,207,840		3,220,390	
Depreciation Expense	45,710		48,825	
Discount on Bonds	25,000		[ ]	
Dividends on Common Shares— Cash and Stock	50,000		[ ]	
Dividends on Preferred Shares—Cash . . .	6,000		6,000	
Dividends Payable		–		[ ]
Federal and State Income Tax Expense	104,975		122,675	
Federal and State Income Taxes Payable		104,975		111,675
Gain on Sale of Plant		–		[ ]
Interest Expense on Notes	2,900		3,100	
Interest Expense on Bonds	20,000		[ ]	
Interest and Dividend Revenue		16,010		18,070
Inventories	616,120		633,690	
Investments in Subsidiaries	162,000		162,000	
Notes Payable		51,500		53,400
Notes Receivable	65,600		68,400	
Plant and Equipment—Net	391,880		[ ]	
Preferred Stock		100,000		100,000
Premium on Common Stock		700,000		[ ]
Prepaid Insurance	8,240		7,640	
Retained Earnings		[ ]		[ ]
Royalties Revenue		37,020		44,285
Sales		4,552,320		4,605,275
Selling Expenses	642,530		656,230	
	$6,492,370	$6,492,370	$6,762,860	$6,762,860

Additional data:

(1) Preferred shares: 6 percent, cumulative, $100 par value, 2,000 shares authorized.

(2) Common shares: $1 par value, 150,000 shares authorized.

(3) On January 10, 1979, a 10-percent stock dividend was declared on common stock, issuable in common stock. The market price per share was $10 and the dividend was capitalized at $10 per share.

(4) On March 31 and September 30, 1979, dividends of 25 cents per share were declared. The dividends were payable on April 20 and October 20, 1979, respectively. On December 31, 1979, an extra dividend of 12½ cents per share was declared payable on January 20, 1980. Note that all dividends, in cash and in shares, have been debited to Income Distribution accounts, not to Retained Earnings.

(5) Plant and equipment items having a cost of $39,240 and accumulated depreciation of $32,570 were retired and sold for $15,000. Acquisitions during 1979 amounted to $71,500.

(6) The bonds were issued on June 30, 1961, and mature on June 30, 1991. All bonds issued remain outstanding; straight-line amortization is used.

a Prepare a well-organized comparative statement of income and retained earnings.
b Prepare a well-organized comparative balance sheet.
c Prepare a well-organized statement of changes in financial position.

14 The following data are taken from the records of the Barr Sales Company:

	December 31	
	1979 Adjusted Trial Balance	**1978 Postclosing Trial Balance**
Accounts Payable—Merchandise	$ 8,400	$ 9,160
Accounts Receivable	25,100	25,900
Accumulated Depreciation	4,600	5,600
Allowance for Uncollectible Accounts	400	430
Cash	27,802	21,810
Common Stock ($10 par value)	55,000	50,000
Cost of Goods Sold	155,000	
Deposits by Customers	420	
Depreciation	1,000	
Dividends on Common Shares (both in cash and in shares)	8,125	
Dividends Payable	2,750	2,500
Federal Income Tax Expense	3,600	
Federal Income Tax Payable	3,600	2,400
Furniture and Fixtures	21,000	20,000
Gain on Sale of Land	1,500	
Installment Contracts Payable	2,000	
Interest Expense on Mortgage	482	
Interest Revenue on Investments	500	
Interest Payable on Mortgage	50	
Interest Receivable	50	30
Investments	14,000	15,000
Loss on Sale of Investments	300	
Merchandise Inventory	33,450	31,150
Mortgage Payable (5%)	10,000	10,000
Other Expenses	26,293	
Premium on Common Shares	4,500	4,000
Premium on Mortgage Payable	122	140
Prepaid Rent	300	
Rent Expense	3,600	
Retained Earnings	28,860	28,860
Sales	210,000	
Sales Commissions	12,400	
Sales Commissions Payable	600	800
Sales, Uncollectible Accounts Adjustment	800	

Additional information:

(1) During the year the company retired fully depreciated fixtures that had cost $2,000. These were the only dispositions of furniture and fixtures.

(2) Furniture and fixtures acquired on May 10, 1979, were financed one-third down, one-third due May 10, 1980, and one-third due May 10, 1981.

(3) On December 9, 1979, the company sold a parcel of land that it had purchased on January 14, 1979, at a cost of $8,000.

(4) On June 15, 1979, the company purchased additional investments at a cost of $3,200. This was the only acquisition during the year. All investments are shown at cost, since market value exceeds cost.

(5) Merchandise was delivered during the year on customers' deposits in the amount of $1,200. All other deliveries were on account.

(6) On January 2, 1979, the board of directors declared a 5-percent stock dividend. The dividend was capitalized at $11 per share.

(7) On June 20, 1979, and December 20, 1979, the board of directors declared the regular semiannual cash dividends of $0.50 per share.

(8) On June 30, 1979, the company issued 250 shares of stock for cash.

(9) Note that all dividends, both in cash and in shares, were debited to the Income Distribution account, Dividends on Common Shares, not to Retained Earning.

a Prepare a well-organized statement of income and retained earnings for 1979.
b Prepare a well-organized comparative balance sheet.
c Prepare a well-organized statement of changes in financial position for 1979.

15 Two conventional calculations of the debt-equity ratio were introduced in Chapter 6. In this problem we focus on the following definition:

$$\text{Debt Ratio} = \frac{\text{Total Long-Term External Financing}}{\text{Owners' Equity}}.$$

Many analysts use this ratio to assess the risk in the financial structure of a corporation. The higher the debt-equity ratio, other things being equal, the greater the risk. Most analysts construct ratios from the conventional, historical-cost financial statements without adjustment. This problem illustrates how the assessment of the relative risk of companies can change as more sophisticated analysis of the financial statements is undertaken. In this problem, various adjustments to the conventional financial statements are made and new versions of the debt-equity ratio are compared.

The problem may be worked all at once at the end of the course as a review, or it may be worked part by part as the various topics in the course are covered. Each part contains guidance as to when in the course the reader should be ready to work that part.

Data for four companies are presented in Exhibit 13.4. The methods are illustrated with the data for International Corporation (from Appendix A). The reader is to prepare answers for the three other companies. All data are taken from the financial statements of the various companies for the same year. All dollar amounts are in millions. Income tax effects are ignored, except where noted.

a (After Chapter 6.) Compute the debt ratio for each of the companies. Include deferred income taxes with long-term financing in the numerator. For International Corporation the debt ratio is

EXHIBIT 13.4
(Dollar Amounts in Millions)
(Problem 15)

	International Corporation	Eastman Kodak	General Motors	Zenith
1. Long-Term Debt	$ 723.7	$ 152.4	$ 1,668.7	$ 50.0
2. Deferred Tax Credits (Balance Sheet)	171.0[a]	144.0	472.5	18.3
3. Owners' Equity	2,001.7	4,026.3	14,385.2	292.4
4. Excess of Current (FIFO) Cost over LIFO Cost of Ending Inventory	370.0	330.3	299.5	9.2
5. Unrecognized Pension Cost (Unamortized Prior-Service Costs or Unfunded Vested Costs, if Larger)	508.0	520.0	3,000.0[b]	None
6. Long-Term Debt of Financing Subsidiary	340.0	None	6,509.2[b]	None

[a] Includes $53.6 million of current liabilities for deferred taxes.
[b] Excludes $2 billion of unfunded pension obligations of subsidiary.

$$\frac{\$723.7 + \$171.0 - \$53.6}{\$2,001.7} = \frac{\$723.7 + \$117.4}{\$2,001.7}$$

$$= \frac{\$841.1}{\$2,001.7}$$

$$= 42.0\%.$$

Which companies appear to be significantly different from the others in terms of financial structure and risk? Discuss.

b (After Chapter 8.) Chapter 8 pointed out that LIFO companies show old, out-of-date inventory amounts on their balance sheets. The LIFO cost-flow assumption has the effect of understating total assets and understating owners' equity. (Owners' equity is understated because the unrealized holding gains on the inventory are not included in the balance sheet.) We can make the financial statements more realistic by adjusting them with the following entry, which ignores income tax effects:

Inventory	370.0	
Owners' Equity		370.0

$370.0 million is the amount shown in International Corporation's notes as the excess of current cost, or FIFO cost, over the balance sheet amount of ending inventory.

The debt-equity ratio for International Corporation after making this inventory adjustment is

$$\frac{\$723.7 + \$117.4}{\$2,001.7 + \$370.0} = \frac{\$841.1}{\$2,371.7} = 35.5\%.$$

Compute the debt ratio for each of the companies and the percentage change in the ratio from part **a** for each of the firms. On which companies did this adjustment have the most impact?

c (After Chapter 10.) Chapter 10 suggests that certain items shown as liabilities should not be, whereas certain other items not shown as liabilities should be. These two "errors" do not necessarily cancel each other out.

(i) First, note that in most cases Deferred Income Taxes are not likely even to be paid and ought, in our opinion, to be reclassified as owners' equity. We can reflect this reclassification in the financial statements by making the following entry:

Deferred Current Income Taxes (Balance Sheet)	53.6	
Deferred Noncurrent Income Taxes (Balance Sheet)	117.4	
Owners' Equity		171.0

$171.0 million = ($53.6 + $117.4) is the amount shown on International Corporation's balance sheet for current and long-term deferred income taxes.

Observe that International Corporation has both current and long-term deferred taxes. Since the numerator of the debt ratio includes only long-term financing, only the long-term deferred taxes of $117.4 million were previously counted in the numerator and should be taken out now. Our reasoning about deferred taxes implies that *all* deferred taxes, whether current or long-term, should be added back to owners' equity. (Most current deferred taxes arise from installment sales. See Problem **33** in Chapter 10.) The denominator shows the addition of *all* deferred taxes. None of the other three companies illustrated here has current deferred taxes reported on the balance sheet. This complication, therefore, does not arise in the computations for the other three companies.

    Case-by-case analysis might be required in practice to find out if some of the companies' timing differences are likely to reverse in the foreseeable future. Our analysis of these companies' items does not reveal any such significant potential reversals.

    If the adjustment for deferred taxes alone is made, the debt ratio for International Corporation is

$$\frac{\$723.7}{\$2,001.7 + \$117.4 + \$53.6} = \frac{\$723.7}{\$2,172.7} = 33.3\%.$$

If both the deferred tax adjustment and the inventory adjustment are made, International Corporation's debt ratio is

$$\frac{\$723.7}{\$2,001.7 + \$117.4 + \$53.6 + \$370.0} = \frac{\$723.7}{\$2,542.7} = 28.5\%.$$

(ii) The unrecognized prior-service cost for pension plans meets all of the criteria to be a (long-term) liability, but is not shown as such. The amount is merely disclosed in the notes. To bring this number onto the balance sheet, the financial statements are adjusted with the following entry, which ignores income tax effects:

Owners' Equity	508.0	
Pension Liability		508.0

$508 million is the amount shown in International Corporation's notes to the financial statements for unamortized prior-service costs.

After adjusting for the pension liability only, International Corporation's debt-equity ratio is

$$\frac{\$723.7 + \$117.4 + \$508.0}{\$2,001.7 - \$508.0} = \frac{\$1,349.1}{\$1,493.7} = 90.3\%.$$

If all adjustments in parts **a, b,** and **c** are made, International Corporation's debt-equity ratio is

$$\frac{\$723.7 + \$508.0}{\$2,001.7 - \$508.0 + \$370.0 + \$117.4 + \$53.6} = \frac{\$1,231.7}{\$2,034.7} = 60.5\%.$$

Make the adjustments suggested above and recompute the debt ratio for each of the other three companies. Compute the ratios on a cumulative and noncumulative basis; that is, compute the debt ratio after making each individual adjustment to the ratios computed in part **a,** and then after taking all the adjustments together, compute the percentage change in the ratio for each company. On which of the companies did each of these adjustments have the most impact?

d (After Chapter 12.) Chapter 12 illustrated that various companies use different consolidation policies with respect to a wholly owned subsidiary engaged in the financing of customer purchases of the company's goods. For example (see Chapter 12, Problem 33), Sears consolidates its financial subsidiary, but J. C. Penney does not. To make comparisons of debt ratios more valid, the same consolidation policy should be used for all companies. The following entry has the effect of consolidating an unconsolidated, but 100-percent-owned subsidiary:

Assets of Subsidiary	1,143.9	
Investment of Parent in Subsidiary		151.8
Liabilities of Subsidiary		992.1

See Note 11 of International Corporation's financial statements. $1,143.9 million represents the total amount of the subsidiary's assets; $151.8 million represents International Corporation's investment in the subsidiary (which is equal to the subsidiary's total owners' equity); $992.1 million represents the subsidiary's total liabilities.

Once this entry is made, there may be another entry eliminating intercompany receivables and payables, if any. These eliminating entries are immaterial, and their effect has been taken into account in showing the data above.

For purposes of this problem, we are interested in examining the effect of bringing the financing subsidiary's long-term liabilities onto the parent company's balance sheet. The effect of the preceding entry on long-term liabilities can be accomplished with the following entry:

Assets	340.0	
Long-Term Liabilities		340.0

$340.0 million represents the amount of International Corporation's financing subsidiary's total long-term liabilities.

After consolidating International Corporation's financing subsidiary, the debt ratio becomes

$$\frac{\$723.7 + \$117.0 + \$340.0}{\$2,001.7} = \frac{\$1,180.7}{\$2,001.7} = 60.0\%.$$

If all adjustments to International Corporation's balance sheet are taken into account, the debt ratio is

$$\frac{\$723.7 + \$340.0 + \$508.0}{\$2,001.7 - \$508.0 + \$370.0 + \$119.4 + \$53.6} = \frac{\$1,571.7}{\$2,034.7} = 77.2\%.$$

Make the adjustments suggested here for General Motors, the only company of the three that does not consolidate its financing subsidiary. Recompute the debt ratio for this company both cumulatively and noncumulatively. Calculate the percentage change in the debt ratio. Comment on any apparent changes in the debt ratio from those computed in parts **a, b,** and **c.**

e   What can you infer from this exercise about the debt ratio computed from published financial statements?

16 The principal objective of this book has been to help you develop a sufficient understanding of the accounting process that generates financial statements for external users so that the resulting statements can then be (1) interpreted, (2) analyzed, and (3) evaluated. This problem has been designed partly as a review of the material covered in the book and partly as a means of assessing your progress toward this objective. A partial set of financial statements of Calmes Corporation for 1979, including consolidated comparative balance sheets at December 31, 1978 and 1979, and a consolidated statement of income and retained earnings for the year 1979 is presented on the following pages. A series of discussion questions and short problems relating to the financial statements of Calmes Corporation are then presented. It is suggested that you study the financial statements before responding to these questions and problems.

Part I—Financial Statement Interpretation

For each of the accounts or items listed below and appearing on the consolidated balance sheets and income statement of the Calmes Corporation, describe **(1)** the nature of the account or item (that is, the transaction or conditions that resulted in its recognition) and **(2)** the valuation method used in determining its amount. Respond in descriptive terms rather than using specific numbers from the financial statements of the Calmes Corporation. The first one is provided as an example.

a   Accumulated Costs Under Contracts in Progress in Excess of Progress Billings—
The Calmes Corporation is providing services of some type to specific customers under contract. All costs incurred under the contracts are accumulated in this current asset account. When customers are billed periodically for a portion of the contract price, this account is credited. The account therefore reflects the excess of costs incurred to date on uncompleted contracts over the amounts billed to customers. Since the account does not include any income or profit from the contracts (that is, "accumulated costs"), the firm is apparently using the completed-contract rather than the percentage-of-completion method of recognizing revenues.

b   Investment in Calmes Finance Corporation.

Calmes Corporation
Consolidated Statement of Income
and Retained Earnings
for the Year
Ended December 31, 1979

Revenues

Sales		$6,000,000
Less Estimated Uncollectible Accounts		60,000
Net Sales		$5,940,000
Gain on Sale of Machinery and Equipment		100,000
Income from Completed Contracts		960,000
Equity in Earnings of Unconsolidated Subsidiaries and Affiliates:		
Calmes Finance Corporation	$900,000	
Richardson Company	50,000	
Anthony Company	50,000	
		1,000,000
Total Revenues		$8,000,000

Expenses

Cost of Goods Sold	$2,500,000
Employee Payroll	1,500,000
Depreciation of Plant and Equipment and Amortization of Leased Property Rights	500,000
Amortization of Intangibles	100,000
Interest	300,000
General Corporate	100,000
Income Taxes—Current	700,000
Income Taxes—Deferred	100,000
Total Expenses	$5,800,000
Net Income Before Minority Interest	$2,200,000
Minority Interest in Earnings	200,000
Net Income	$2,000,000
Less: Dividends on Preferred Shares	60,000
Dividends on Common Shares	840,000
Increase in Retained Earnings	$1,100,000
Retained Earnings, January 1, 1979	1,400,000
Retained Earnings, December 31, 1979	$2,500,000
Primary Earnings per Common Share (based on 1,000,000 average shares outstanding)	$1.94
Fully Diluted Earnings per Share (assuming conversion of preferred stock)	$1.25

c   Property Rights Acquired Under Lease.
d   Goodwill.
e   Rent Received in Advance.
f   Discount on Bonds Payable.
g   Deferred Income Taxes (Balance Sheet).
h   Minority Interest in Subsidiary (Balance Sheet).
i   Treasury Stock.
j   Estimated Uncollectible Accounts (Income Statement).

Calmes Corporation
Consolidated Balance Sheets
December 31

ASSETS	1979	1978
Current Assets		
Cash	$ 50,000	$ 100,000
Marketable Securities at Lower of Cost or Market (market value, $160,000)	150,000	—
Accounts Receivable (net of estimated uncollectibles of $80,000 in 1979 and $50,000 in 1978)	300,000	250,000
Merchandise Inventory	700,000	600,000
Accumulated Costs Under Contracts in Process in Excess of Progress Billings	200,000	150,000
Prepayments	100,000	100,000
Total Current Assets	$ 1,500,000	$1,200,000
Investments (at equity)		
Calmes Finance Corporation (100% owned)	$ 2,000,000	$1,100,000
Richardson Company (50% owned)	500,000	450,000
Anthony Company (25% owned)	100,000	50,000
Total Investments	$ 2,600,000	$1,600,000
Property, Plant, and Equipment		
Land	$ 250,000	$ 200,000
Building	2,000,000	2,000,000
Machinery and Equipment	4,000,000	3,650,000
Property Rights Acquired Under Lease	750,000	750,000
Total	$ 7,000,000	$6,600,000
Less Accumulated Depreciation and Amortization	(2,000,000)	(1,900,000)
Total Property, Plant, and Equipment	$ 5,000,000	$4,700,000
Intangibles (at net book value)		
Patent	$ 200,000	$ 250,000
Goodwill	700,000	750,000
Total Intangibles	$ 900,000	$1,000,000
Total Assets	$10,000,000	$8,500,000

LIABILITIES AND SHAREHOLDERS' EQUITY

Current Liabilities	1979	1978
Notes Payable	$ 250,000	$ 200,000
Accounts Payable	350,000	330,000
Salaries Payable	150,000	120,000
Income Taxes Payable	200,000	150,000
Rent Received in Advance	50,000	—
Other Current Liabilities	200,000	100,000
Total Current Liabilities	$ 1,200,000	$ 900,000

Long-Term Debt

Bonds Payable (net of discount of $176,000 in 1979 and $200,000 in 1978)	$ 1,824,000	$1,800,000
Equipment Mortgage Indebtedness	176,000	650,000
Capitalized Lease Obligations	500,000	550,000
Total Long-Term Debt	$ 2,500,000	$3,000,000
Deferred Income Taxes	$ 800,000	$ 700,000
Minority Interest in Subsidiary	$ 500,000	$ 300,000

Shareholders' Equity

Convertible Preferred Stock	$ 1,000,000	$1,000,000
Common Stock	1,000,000	1,000,000
Additional Paid-in Capital	1,000,000	900,000
Retained Earnings	2,500,000	1,400,000
Total	$ 5,500,000	$4,300,000
Less Cost of Treasury Shares	(500,000)	(700,000)
Total Shareholders' Equity	$ 5,000,000	$3,600,000
Total Liabilities and Shareholders' Equity	$10,000,000	$8,500,000

Additional Information:

(1) Machinery and equipment costing $500,000 and with a book value of $100,000 were sold for cash during 1979.
(2) The only transaction affecting common or preferred stocks during 1979 was the sale of treasury stock.

Part II—Financial Statement Analysis

a Determine the amount of specific customers' accounts written off as uncollectible during 1979, assuming that there were no recoveries during 1979 of accounts written off in years prior to 1979.
b The Calmes Corporation used the LIFO cost-flow assumption in determining its cost of goods sold and beginning and ending merchandise inventory amounts. If the FIFO cost-flow assumption had been used, the beginning inventory would have been $900,000 and the ending inventory would have been $850,000. Determine the actual gross profit (net sales less cost of goods sold) of the Calmes Corporation for 1979 under LIFO and the corresponding amount of gross profit if FIFO had been used (ignore income tax effects). Calmes Corporation used the periodic inventory method.
c Refer to part b. What can be said about the quantity of merchandise inventory at the beginning and end of 1979 and the direction of price changes during 1979? Explain.
d The Calmes Corporation accounts for its three intercorporate investments in unconsolidated subsidiaries under the equity method. The shares in each of these companies were acquired at book value at the time of acquisition. What were the total dividends declared by these three companies during 1979? How can you tell?
e The Calmes Corporation accounts for its three intercorporate investments in unconsolidated subsidiaries under the equity method. The shares in each of these companies

were acquired at book value at the time of acquisition. Give the journal entry (entries) that was (were) made during 1979 in applying the equity method.

f The building was acquired on January 1, 1978. It was estimated to have a 40-year useful life and zero salvage value at that time. Determine the amount of depreciation expense on this building for 1979 assuming that the double-declining-balance method is used.

g Machinery and equipment costing $500,000 and with a book value of $100,000 were sold for cash during 1979. Give the journal entry to record the disposition.

h The bonds payable carry 6-percent annual coupons. Interest is paid on December 31 of each year. Give the journal entry made on December 31, 1979, to recognize interest expense for 1979 and to amortize the bond discount, assuming that Calmes Corporation uses the effective-interest method of amortizing the bond discount.

i Refer to part **h.** What was the effective or market interest rate on these bonds on the date they were issued? Explain.

j The only timing difference between net income and taxable income during 1979 was in the amount of depreciation expense. If the income tax rate was 40 percent, determine the difference between the depreciation deduction reported on the tax return and the depreciation expense reported on the income statement.

k Give the journal entry that explains the change in the treasury shares account assuming that there were no other transactions affecting common or preferred shares during 1979.

l Calmes Corporation has only one consolidated subsidiary. Was the acquisition of this consolidated subsidiary accounted for as a purchase or as a pooling of interests? How can you tell?

m If the original amount of the patent acquired was $500,000 and the patent is being amortized on a straight-line basis, when was the patent acquired?

n The stock of the Anthony Company was acquired on December 31, 1978. If the same amount of stock in the Anthony Company were held during the year, but the amount represented only *15 percent* ownership of the Anthony Company, how would the financial statements have differed? Disregard income tax effects.

o During 1979, Calmes paid $85,000 to the lessor of property represented on the balance sheet by "Property Rights Acquired Under Lease." Property rights acquired under lease have a 10-year life and are being amortized on a straight-line basis. What was the total expense reported by Calmes Corporation during 1979 from using the leased property?

p How would the financial statements have differed if the Calmes Corporation accounted for marketable securities on the lower-of-cost-or-market basis and the market value of these securities had been $130,000 instead of $160,000 at the end of 1979? Disregard income tax effects.

q If the Minority Interest in Subsidiary represents a 20-percent interest in Calmes Corporation's only consolidated subsidiary, what was the *total* amount of dividends declared by this subsidiary during 1979? How can you tell?

r Refer to the earnings-per-share amounts in the income statement of Calmes Corporation. How many shares of common stock would be issued if all of the outstanding shares of preferred stock were converted into common stock?

s Insert the missing items of information numbered **(1)–(17)** in the following statement of changes in financial position of the Calmes Corporation. Be sure to include both descriptions of the missing items and their amounts. Provide supporting calculations for each of the missing items in the statement. You may assume that there is no discount or premium on the Equipment Mortgage Indebtedness (See the Exhibit on page 541.)

t As indicated in the statement of changes in financial position, working capital provided by operations of Calmes Corporation during 1979 was $1,824,000. Convert this figure to cash flow provided by operations.

u On January 2, 1980, the Calmes Corporation requested its bank to grant a 6-month loan for $300,000. If approved, the loan would be granted on January 10, 1980. As the bank's senior credit analyst, you have been asked to assess the liquidity of the Calmes Corporation and present a memorandum summarizing your conclusions. Include any ratios and any other information from the financial statements which you feel are relevant. Also include a summary of information not disclosed in the financial statements that you feel the loan officer should consider before making a final decision.

Calmes Corporation
Statement of Changes in Financial
Position for the Year Ended
December 31, 1979

Sources of Working Capital
Operations
(3) _____ . . . . $ _____
Add Back Expenses and Deductions Not
Using Working Capital for Operations:
(4) _____ . . . . _____
(5) _____ . . . . _____
(6) _____ . . . . _____
(7) _____ . . . . _____
(8) _____ . . . . _____
Subtract Revenues and Additions Not
Providing Working Capital for Operations:
(9) _____ . . . . (_____)
(10) _____ . . . . (_____)
Working Capital Provided by Operations $1,824,000
Other Sources of Working Capital:
(11) _____ . . . . _____
(12) _____ . . . . _____
Total Sources of Working Capital . . . . (2) $ _____

Uses of Working Capital
(13) _____ . . . . $ _____
(14) _____ . . . . _____
(15) _____ . . . . _____
(16) _____ . . . . _____
(17) _____ . . . . _____
Total Uses of Working Capital $2,324,000

Net Change in Working Capital . . . . (1) $ _____

Part III—Financial Statement Evaluation

a The treasurer of the Calmes Corporation recently remarked, "The value or worth of our company on December 31, 1979, is $5,000,000, as measured by total stockholders' equity." Describe briefly at least three reasons why the difference between recorded total assets and recorded total liabilities on the balance sheet does not represent the firm's value or worth.

b The accounting profession has been criticized for permitting several "generally accepted accounting principles" for the same or similar transactions. What are the major arguments for (1) narrowing the range of acceptable accounting methods and (2) continuing the present system of permitting business firms some degree of flexibility in selecting their accounting methods?

17 Presented below are a set of financial statements for Kaplan Corporation, including an income statement and statement of changes in financial position for 1979 and a comparative balance sheet on December 31, 1978 and 1979. Following the financial statements is a series of notes providing additional information on certain items in the financial statements. Questions about the financial statements follow the notes. We suggest that you carefully study the statements and notes before attempting to respond to the questions.

Kaplan Corporation
Income Statement
for the Year 1979
(Amounts in Thousands)

Revenues:

Sales	$12,000
Less Sales, Uncollectible Accounts Adjustment	120
Net Sales	$11,880
Equity in Earnings of Unconsolidated Affiliates	300
Dividend Revenue	20
Gain on Sale of Marketable Securities	30
Total Revenues	$12,230

Expenses:

Cost of Goods Sold	$ 7,200
Selling and Administrative	2,569
Loss on Sale of Equipment	80
Unrealized Loss from Price Decline of Marketable Equity Securities	20
Interest (Notes 7 and 8)	561
Total Expenses	$10,430
Net Income Before Income Taxes and Minority Interest	$ 1,800
Income Tax Expense	720
Net Income Before Minority Interest	$ 1,080
Minority Interest in Earnings of Heimann Corporation	40
Net Income	$ 1,040

Kaplan Corporation
Balance Sheets
December 31, 1978 and 1979
(Amounts in Thousands)

ASSETS	December 31, 1978	December 31, 1979
Current Assets:		
Cash	$ 1,470	$ 2,739
Marketable Securities (Note 2)	450	550
Accounts Receivable (net; Note 3)	2,300	2,850
Inventories (Note 4)	2,590	3,110
Prepayments	800	970
Total Current Assets	$ 7,610	$10,219
Investments (Note 5):		
Investment in Maher Corporation		
(10 percent)	$ 200	$ 185
Investment in Johnson Corporation		
(30 percent)	310	410
Investment in Burton Credit Corporation		
(100 percent)	800	930
Total Investments	$ 1,310	$ 1,525
Property, Plant, and Equipment:		
Land.................................	$ 400	$ 500
Buildings	800	940
Equipment	3,300	3,800
Total Cost...........................	$ 4,500	$ 5,240
Less Accumulated Depreciation	(1,200)	(930)
Net Property, Plant, and Equipment	$ 3,300	$ 4,310
Goodwill (Note 6)......................	90	80
Total Assets	$12,310	$16,134

LIABILITIES AND SHAREHOLDERS' EQUITY

	December 31, 1978	December 31, 1979
Current Liabilities:		
Note Payable (Note 7)	$ —	$ 1,000
Accounts Payable	1,070	2,425
Salaries Payable	800	600
Interest Payable	300	400
Income Taxes Payable	250	375
Total Current Liabilities	$ 2,420	$ 4,800
Long-Term Liabilities:		
Bonds Payable (Note 8)	$ 6,209	$ 6,209
Deferred Income Taxes	820	940
Total Long-Term Liabilities	$ 7,029	$ 7,149
Minority Interest	$ 180	$ 214

Shareholders' Equity:

Common Shares ($10 par value)	$ 500	$ 600
Additional Paid-in Capital	800	1,205
Unrealized Loss on Valuation of Investments	(25)	(40)
Retained Earnings	1,436	2,226
Total	$ 2,711	$ 3,991
Less Treasury Shares (at cost)	(30)	(20)
Total Shareholders' Equity	$ 2,681	$ 3,971
Total Liabilities and Shareholders' Equity . . .	$12,310	$16,134

**Kaplan Corporation
Statement of Changes
in Financial Position
For the Year 1979
(Amounts in Thousands)**

Sources of Working Capital:

Operations:

Net Income	$1,040	
Plus Expenses and Losses Not Using Working Capital:		
Depreciation	560	
Deferred Taxes	120	
Loss on Sale of Equipment	80	
Minority Interest in Net Income	40	
Amortization of Discount on Bonds	28	
Amortization of Goodwill	10	
Less Revenues and Gains Not Providing Working Capital:		
Equity in Earnings of Affiliates and Subsidiaries in Excess of Dividends Received	(180)	
Amortization of Premium on Bonds	(28)	
Working Capital Provided by Operations		$1,670
Equipment Sold		150
Common Shares Issued		500
Treasury Shares Sold		15
Total Sources		$2,335

Uses of Working Capital:

Dividends	$ 256
Investments in Securities (Johnson Corporation)	50
Acquisition of Land	100
Acquisition of Building	300
Acquisition of Equipment	1,400
Total Uses	$2,106
Net Change in Working Capital	$ 229

ANALYSIS OF CHANGES IN WORKING CAPITAL ACCOUNTS

Increases in Working Capital:

Cash	$1,269
Marketable Securities	100
Accounts Receivable	550
Inventories	520
Prepayments	170
Salaries Payable	200
Total Increases	$2,809

Decreases in Working Capital:

Notes Payable	$1,000
Accounts Payable	1,355
Interest Payable	100
Income Taxes Payable	125
Total Decreases	$2,580
Net Change in Working Capital	$ 229

Note 1: Summary of Accounting Policies

Basis of Consolidation The financial statements of Kaplan Corporation are consolidated with Heimann Corporation, an 80-percent-owned subsidiary acquired on January 2, 1978, in a transaction accounted for using the purchase method.

Marketable Securities Marketable securities are stated at the lower of acquisition cost or market.

Accounts Receivable Uncollectible accounts of customers are accounted for using the allowance method.

Inventories Inventories are determined using a last-in, first-out (LIFO) cost-flow assumption.

Investments Investments of less than 20 percent of the outstanding common stock of other companies are accounted for using the lower-of-cost-or-market method. Investments of greater than or equal to 20 percent of the outstanding common stock of unconsolidated affiliates and subsidiaries are accounted for using the equity method.

Buildings and Equipment Depreciation for financial reporting purposes is calculated using the straight-line method. For income tax purposes, the sum-of-the years'-digits method is used.

Goodwill Goodwill arising from corporate acquisitions is amortized over a period of 10 years.

Bond Discount and Premium Discount and premium on bonds payable are amortized using the effective interest method.

Deferred Income Taxes Deferred income taxes are provided for timing differences between book income and taxable income.

Investment Tax Credit The investment tax credit is accounted for using the flow-through method.

Note 2: Marketable securities are shown net of an allowance for market price declines below acquisition cost of $50,000 on December 31, 1978, and $70,000 on December 31, 1979.

Note 3: Accounts receivable are shown net of an allowance for uncollectible accounts of $200,000 on December 31, 1978, and $250,000 on December 31, 1979.

Note 4: Inventories consist of the following:

	December 31, 1978	December 31, 1979
Raw Materials	$ 330,000	$ 380,000
Work in Process	. 460,000	530,000
Finished Goods	1,800,000	2,200,000
Total	$2,590,000	$3,110,000

The current cost of inventories exceeded the amounts determined on a LIFO basis by $420,000 on December 31, 1978, and $730,000 on December 31, 1979.

Note 5: Condensed financial statements for Burton Credit Corporation, a wholly owned, unconsolidated subsidiary, are shown below.

Burton Credit Corporation
(Amounts in Thousands)

BALANCE SHEET	December 31, 1978	December 31, 1979
Cash and Marketable Securities	$ 760	$ 840
Accounts Receivable (net)	6,590	7,400
Other Assets	1,050	1,260
Total Assets	$8,400	$9,500
Notes Payable Due Within 1 Year	$3,900	$4,300
Long-Term Note Payable	2,620	3,100
Other Liabilities	1,080	1,170
Common Stock	100	100
Additional Paid-in Capital	300	300
Retained Earnings	400	530
Total Equities	$8,400	$9,500

STATEMENT OF INCOME AND RETAINED EARNINGS	1979
Revenues	$680
Expenses	520
Net Income	$160
Less Dividends	(30)
Retained Earnings, December 31, 1978	400
Retained Earnings, December 31, 1979	$530

Note 6: On January 2, 1978, Kaplan Corporation acquired 80 percent of the outstanding common shares of Heimann Corporation by issuing 20,000 shares of Kaplan Corporation common stock. The Kaplan Corporation shares were selling on January 2, 1978, for $40 a share. Any difference between the acquisition price and the book value of the net assets acquired was considered goodwill and is being amortized over a period of 10 years from the date of acquisition.

Note 7: The note payable included under current liabilities is a 1-year note due on January 2, 1980. The note requires annual interest payments on December 31 of each year.

Note 8: Bonds payable are the following:

	December 31, 1978	December 31, 1979
4%, $2,000,000 bonds due December 31, 1984, with interest payable semiannually	$1,800,920	$1,829,390
10%, $3,000,000 bonds due December 31, 1988, with interest payable semiannually ..	3,407,720	3,379,790
8%, $1,000,000 bonds due on December 31, 1994, with interest payable semiannually ..	1,000,000	1,000,000
Total	$8,208,640	$6,209,180

a Marketable securities costing $180,000 were sold during 1979. Determine the price at which these securities were sold.

b Refer to part **a.** Determine the cost of marketable securities purchased during 1979.

c What was the amount of specific customers' accounts written off as uncollectible during 1979?

d Assume that all sales are made on account. Determine the amount of cash collected from customers during the year.

e Determine the cost of units completed and transferred to the finished-goods storeroom during 1979.

f Direct labor and overhead costs incurred in manufacturing during the year totaled $4,500. Determine the cost of raw materials purchased during 1979.

g Assume that the amounts disclosed in Note 4 for the current cost of inventories represent the amounts that would be obtained from using a first-in, first-out (FIFO) cost-flow assumption. What would cost of goods sold have been if FIFO rather than LIFO had been used?

h Prepare an analysis that explains the causes of the changes in each of the three intercorporate investment accounts.

i Assume that Burton Credit Corporation had been consolidated with Kaplan Corporation instead of being treated as an unconsolidated subsidiary. Prepare a condensed consolidated balance sheet on December 31, 1979, and a condensed consolidated income statement for 1979 for Kaplan Corporation and Burton Credit Corporation.

j Prepare an analysis that explains the change in each of the following four accounts during 1979: Land, Building, Equipment, and Accumulated Depreciation.

k Give the journal entry made on Kaplan Corporation's books on January 2, 1978, when it acquired Heimann Corporation.

l Determine the book value of the net assets of Heimann Corporation on January 2, 1978.

m Determine the total amount of dividends declared by Heimann Corporation during 1979.

n Give the entry made at the end of 1979 to eliminate the Investment in Heimann Corporation's account as part of the process of preparing consolidated financial statements assuming that Kaplan Corporation had used the cost method to account for the investment during 1978 and 1979.

o The 4-percent bonds payable were initially priced to yield 6 percent compounded semiannually. The 10-percent bonds were initially priced to yield 8 percent compounded semiannually. Using the apporpriate present value tables at the back of the book, demonstrate that $1,800,920 and $3,407,720 (see Note 8) were the correct valuations of these two bond issues on December 31, 1978.

p Calculate the amount of interest expense and any amortization of discount or premium for 1979 on each of the three long-term bond issues (see Note 8).

q Determine the amount of interest actually paid during 1979.

r Determine the amount of income taxes actually paid during 1979.

s On July 1, 1979, Kaplan Corporation sold 10,000 shares of its common stock on the open market for $50 a share. Prepare an analysis explaining the change during 1979 in each of the following accounts: Common Share, Additional Paid-in Capital, Retained Earnings, Treasury Shares.

18 In the 1960s, Chrysler switched its inventory cost-flow assumption from FIFO to LIFO. It was the only one of the big-three auto makers to do so at that time. By 1970, Chrysler's inventories had grown and prices of its acquisitions for inventory had increased so much that it had saved over $50 million in income taxes by using LIFO. Then, in the 1970s, Chrysler switched from LIFO back to FIFO. To comply with government tax regulations on inventory accounting, Chrysler paid to the government all of the taxes that it had saved from using LIFO over the entire time it had used LIFO. Chrysler paid the federal government over $50 million for the privilege of switching from LIFO back to FIFO.

Investigation of why Chrysler would send the government $50 million for the privilege of switching back to FIFO suggests that Chrysler was in danger of violating a covenant in some of its bond indentures with respect to the debt-equity ratio. If the debt-equity ratio fell below a critical value, certain bonds would become due immediately that otherwise would not mature for a decade or more.

Under what conditions would a company not want its old bonds suddenly to come due for immediate payment? Explain. Under what conditions would switching from LIFO to FIFO and incurring an immediate $50 million liability improve Chrysler's position? Explain. What is the purpose of bond indentures such as the one Chrysler had agreed to? Were the bondholders made better off by Chrysler's actions? Discuss.

CHAPTER 14
CURRENT ISSUES IN FINANCIAL REPORTING

Financial accounting and reporting are in a state of continual evolution and development. Current issues are researched and debated; then, official pronouncements are issued. New issues emerge as business practices and conditions change. Some appreciation can be obtained of the ever-changing nature of financial accounting by considering the titles of some of the Statements issued by the Financial Accounting Standards Board in recent years.

Statement No. 2: "Accounting for Research and Development Costs" (1975)
Statement No. 8: "Accounting for the Translation of Foreign Currency Transactions and Foreign Financial Statements" (1975)
Statement No. 12: "Accounting for Certain Marketable Securities" (1975)
Statement No. 13: "Accounting for Leases" (1976)
Statement No. 19: "Financial Accounting and Reporting by Oil and Gas Producing Companies" (1977)
Statement No. 21: "Suspension of the Reporting of Earnings per Share and Segment Information by Nonpublic Enterprises" (1978).

Most of these reporting issues have been discussed in previous chapters. In this chapter, we focus on four additional topics currently being discussed and debated:

1 Line-of-business or segment reporting
2 Interim-period reporting
3 General purchasing power accounting
4 Development of a conceptual framework.

LINE-OF-BUSINESS OR SEGMENT REPORTING

A growing number of conglomerate firms have segments (that is, divisions) operating in widely different industries. Investors want information concerning the performance and financial position of individual segments. Generally accepted accounting principles[1] require the disclosure of certain information about the important segments of a firm in its annual report. Note 21 to the financial statements of International Corporation in Appendix A (page 592) illustrates the required disclosures. Although an official pronouncement on segment reporting has been issued, certain aspects of the topic continue to be controversial and warrant consideration as a current issue.

Purpose of Segment Reports

Segment reports are intended to provide more useful information for assessing a firm's operating performance and financial position than is possible with consolidated financial statements alone. Most large publicly held firms operate in numerous product and geographical markets. The returns and risks from operating in these markets can differ substantially. Consolidated financial statements tend to obscure these differences; segment reports attempt to highlight them.

Measurement Issues

FASB *Statement No. 14* prescribes that revenue, income, and asset information be reported for each major segment of a firm. Questions arise as to the identification of a firm's segments and to the measurement of segment revenues, expenses, and assets.

Identifying Segments   The segments of a firm might be defined in terms of products, geographical markets, types of customers (for example, government, industry, consumers), or other groupings. If the objective of segment reporting is to permit comparisons of profitability and financial position among similar segments of different firms, it is desirable that a reasonably uniform segment classification system be used. If the objective of segment reporting is to permit analysis of changes in profitability and financial position of different parts of a particular firm over time, then the need for a uniform segment classification system is not as great. In this case, it is more important that each firm select the segment classification scheme that provides the most useful information about its particular activities.

FASB *Statement No. 14* requires that segments be defined in three broad ways: (1) by type of products, (2) by geographic location of markets (domestic versus foreign), and (3) by type of major customers. Not all firms are required to report on all three types of segments; *Statement No. 14* spells out the conditions under which reports for each type of segment are required. The segment report of International Corporation in Appendix A uses both type of products and geographical location of markets as bases for defining segments. By granting firms some flexibility in the way their segments are defined, the Financial Accounting Standards Board has adopted the view that comparisons of performance for segments of a particular firm over time are more important than comparisons of performance among similar segments of different firms at a given time.

---

[1]   Financial Accounting Standards Board, *Statement of Financial Accounting Standards No. 14*, 1976.

Measuring Segment Revenues If all of a segment's sales are to unaffiliated customers, there are few revenue measurement problems beyond those discussed in Chapter 3. Many segments, however, sell or transfer a portion of their output to other segments within the firm. Semifinished products are transferred from one manufacturing division to another. Products are manufactured domestically and then transferred to sales divisions in foreign countries. From the viewpoint of the firm as a whole, these intersegment transfers do not give rise to revenues until the products are sold to outsiders. (As Chapter 12 points out, such intersegment sales must be eliminated in consolidated financial statements.) Two questions that must be addressed in preparing a segment report are as follows:

1 Should revenues reported for a segment include sales to unaffiliated customers only, or should they also include intersegment sales?
2 If intersegment sales are included in segment revenues, what transfer price should be used?

FASB *Statement No. 14* requires that intersegment sales be included in segment revenues but disclosed separately from sales to unaffiliated customers. It also requires that the total of revenues for all segments together be reconciled with revenues reported in the consolidated income statement. Appendix A provides an example of such disclosure by International Corporation.

Measuring the segment revenues arising from intersegment sales requires setting a selling, or transfer, price of the goods sold. Among the transfer prices commonly used are (1) cost to the selling segment, (2) cost to the selling segment plus a markup for profit, (3) outside market price for similar products, and (4) a price negotiated by the managers of the segments involved in the transfer. The amount reported as segment revenues depends on which transfer price is used. There are advantages and disadvantages to each of these transfer prices. The issues are discussed in managerial accounting texts. FASB *Statement No. 14* permits firms to choose any transfer pricing scheme desired as long as the method is disclosed and used consistently. Note 21 for International Corporation in Appendix A indicates that its transfer prices are based on outside market prices for comparable products.

Measuring Segment Expenses Three types of expenses must be considered in preparing a segment report: (1) direct segment expenses; (2) indirect but assignable segment expenses; and (3) indirect and nonassignable central corporate expenses. The first category includes expenses incurred by or directly traceable to a particular segment. Examples include materials and labor costs of a manufacturing division or salaries and commissions of a sales unit. There is little question that direct segment expenses should be deducted in determining segment income. The second category includes expenses incurred jointly by several segments but that can be assigned to individual segments on some more or less reasonable basis. Examples include depreciation, taxes, and insurance on shared production facilities and operating expenses for a shared computer facility. These expenses are generally included among segment expenses if reasonable allocation bases can be established. The third category includes expenses that are joint or shared by all segments of a firm and for which a reasonable allocation base cannot be established. Examples include the salary of the corporation president and operating expenses of the corporate headquarters.

FASB *Statement No. 14* prescribes that expenses in the first two categories be deducted in determining segment operating profit. Central corporate expenses, interest expense, income tax expense, and several similar items are not assigned to segments. Instead, they are treated as items reconciling the sum of all segments' operating profit with consolidated net income. The required disclosure is shown for International Corporation in Appendix A.

Measuring Segment Assets   The assets of a firm must be disclosed by segments. The assets fall into the same three categories as expenses: (1) direct segment assets; (2) indirect but assignable segment assets; and (3) indirect and nonassignable central corporate assets. Questions similar to those discussed for expenses apply in the case of assets. FASB *Statement No. 14* requires that assets in the first two categories be included in segment assets, but that those in the third group be excluded and reported as items reconciling the sum of segment totals to consolidated totals.

Reporting Issues

FASB *Statement No. 14* requires that revenues, operating profit, and assets be reported for each segment. A full set of financial statements for each segment is not currently required. The major danger of analyzing segment reports results from their failure to allocate some assets and expenses to any segment. Ratio analysis of the type illustrated in Chapter 6 can give somewhat misleading results when applied to segment data.

Perhaps the most important information not currently disclosed is the effect of each segment's operations on the liquidity of the firm. A segment may show low operating profit but actually, because of large depreciation charges, be generating significant amounts of funds for the firm. On the other hand, segments may show good operating profit results but, because of capital expenditures necessary for growth, require large amounts of corporate funds. As the usefulness of segment reports becomes more widely appreciated, perhaps additional segment information, including sources and uses of funds by segments, will be provided.

INTERIM-PERIOD REPORTING

Most publicly held corporations issue condensed financial statements more often than once a year. Such financial reports issued at regular intervals during the company's annual accounting period are called *interim reports.* Interim reports are most often issued quarterly.

Several pronouncements have already been issued on interim reporting. APB *Opinion No. 28* described some of the procedures to be followed in preparing interim period income statements. ASR No. 177 of the Securities and Exchange Commission requires that companies disclose certain income statement information for the last eight quarters in their annual reports. An example of such disclosures appears in Note 22 for International Corporation on page 593. This topic remains controversial, however, because certain important issues have not been settled. These issues are discussed next.

Purpose of Interim Reports

There is as yet no consensus as to the purpose of interim reports. Some adopt the view that the interim report is a report on performance during a self-contained time period whose income is independent of other interim periods during the year. Others adopt the view that the purpose of the interim report is to help users predict net income for the year. The accounting for certain revenues and expenses is critically affected, as we discuss next, by which of these two purposes the interim report is intended to serve.

Measurement Issues

Two important measurement issues in interim reporting concern annually determined items and seasonality.

Annually Determined Items   There are several revenue and expense items that are not determinable until the end of the year but whose amounts affect measurement of revenues and expenses for interim periods. For example, the effective tax rate for calculating income tax expense depends on the types and amounts of income generated during the entire year. The amount of executive bonuses may depend on the amount of net income for the year. Cost of goods sold under a LIFO cost-flow assumption depends on whether or not inventory layers liquidated during the year will be replenished before the end of the year. Earnings per share, based on the average number of shares outstanding, is affected by issues or redemptions of stock during subsequent quarters of the year.

Official pronouncements on these accounting problems have taken inconsistent positions with respect to the purpose of the interim report. For example, the effective tax rate expected for the entire year is to be used in computing income tax expense for interim periods. If a liquidated LIFO layer is expected to be replenished by the end of the year, then it should not be treated as liquidated in calculating cost of goods sold for interim periods. These positions suggest that the purpose of the interim report is to help in predicting annual net income. On the other hand, earnings per share for each interim period should be based on the average number of shares outstanding during that period independent of significant changes in the number of shares during later periods. This position suggests that the purpose of the interim report is to provide a report on performance for a self-contained time period.

Seasonality   Perhaps the most difficult problems involved in preparing and interpreting interim reports arise for businesses that have seasonal trends in revenues. Professional sports teams, vacation resorts, and most department stores, for example, sell their goods and services at a nonuniform rate throughout the year. Many operating costs are nevertheless incurred at a relatively uniform rate throughout the year. Examples include rent, property taxes, insurance, and most salaries. The accounting question is how these operating costs are to be assigned to each of the quarters during the year. Suppose that a summer resort generates 80 percent of its revenues during the third quarter of the year. Should the interim report for the first quarter of the year, January through March, which shows little or no revenue, show one-fourth of the year's property taxes, insurance, and similar costs and thereby report a loss? Alternatively, should the interim report for the third quarter, which shows 80 percent of the year's revenues, show 80 percent of the year's costs as expenses and thereby report 80 percent of the anticipated net income for the year? The official position states:[2]

> Costs and expenses other than product costs should be charged to income in interim periods as incurred, or be allocated among interim periods on the basis of an estimate of time expired, benefit received, or activity associated with the period.

Given the official pronouncement, it would appear that firms are permitted to allocate expenses among quarters in any manner that seems appropriate to them.

Reporting Issues

Most interim reports issued during the early 1970s included condensed income statement data only (for example, sales or net income). Since that time, firms have been providing increasing amounts of information in the interim report. It is not uncommon to find condensed income statements, balance sheets, and statements of changes in financial position. Thus far, there has been only limited discussion of interim reporting as it relates to the balance sheet and statement of changes in financial position, particularly with respect to the effect on these statements of measurement biases in determining interim-period net income.

Most interim reports are not audited by the independent accountant but are merely subject to a limited review. Auditors are reluctant to express an opinion on interim reports because of the numerous subjective measurements and arbitrary allocations that must be made. There are pressures being exerted, however, to have some form of attestation (certification) of interim reports. Before such attestation can take place, additional consideration must be given to the purpose of interim reports and the associated accounting and reporting problems.

GENERAL PURCHASING POWER ACCOUNTING

The conventional accounting model rests on the assumption that a *common* or *uniform measuring unit* is used in recording the results of transactions and events in the accounts. That is, the measuring unit (the dollar) applied in recording the acquisition

---

[2] *APB Opinion No. 28,* paragraph 15.

of a machine costing $10,000 five years ago is assumed to be the same measuring unit applied in recording the purchase of merchandise inventory one week ago for $10,000. Only by using a common measuring unit over time can the amounts assigned to individual assets and equities be meaningfully summed to obtain measures of total assets and total equities. It would not make sense, for example, to add together $10,000 and £10,000. Likewise, only by using a common measuring unit can the portion of the acquisition cost of various assets reported as expenses of the current period (cost of goods sold, depreciation expense) be meaningfully matched with revenues recognized during the period.

In debates as to whether or not the uniform measuring unit assumption in accounting is valid, the most frequent criticism focuses on changes in the dollar's *general purchasing power*. Since 1945, the general purchasing power of the dollar has decreased at a rate of approximately 4 percent per year. In some years the rate of inflation decreased the dollar's general purchasing power by more than 10 percent in a single year. Many critics therefore question if the uniform measuring unit assumption in accounting is valid in light of these dramatic changes in the purchasing power of the dollar.

In this section we describe a procedure for accounting for changes in the general purchasing power of the dollar. There have been various proposals in this country and abroad that restatements of financial statements to recognize general purchasing power changes be required, but the proposals have not been adopted.

The Restatement Procedure
for Changes in General Purchasing Power

The objective of the general purchasing power restatement procedure is to obtain a common monetary measuring unit by stating all amounts in dollars of uniform general purchasing power. The purchasing power of the dollar on the date of the most recent balance sheet is usually recommended as the unit of measurement for all financial statements with this objective. General price level indices, such as the Gross National Product Implicit Price Deflator or the Consumer Price Index, are used to measure the general purchasing power of the dollar on various dates. The general approach is to convert the number of dollars received or expended at various price levels to an equivalent number of dollars in terms of the price level on the date of the financial statements.

For example, assume that two parcels of land are held on December 31, 1979, at which time an index of the general price level is 155. Tract A was acquired during 1961 for $100,000, when the general price index was 100. Tract B was acquired for $100,000 during 1964, when the general price index was 106. The acquisition cost of these parcels of land would be restated from 1961 and 1964 dollars to an equivalent number of 1979 dollars as shown in Exhibit 14.1.

The sacrifice in general purchasing power made during 1961 when Tract A was acquired for $100,000 is equivalent to sacrificing $155,000 (= 155/100 × $100,000) in general purchasing power on December 31, 1979. Likewise, the sacrifice in general purchasing power made during 1964 when Tract B was acquired for $100,000 is

EXHIBIT 14.1
Illustration of General Purchasing
Power Restatement Procedure
for Land

Item	Conventionally Reported Acquisition Cost	Conversion	General Purchasing Power Restated Acquisition Cost
Tract A	$100,000	155/100	$155,000
Tract B	$100,000	155/106	$146,226

equivalent to sacrificing $146,226 (= 155/106 × $100,000) in general purchasing power on December 31, 1979. The restated amounts in Exhibit 14.1 use a measuring unit of uniform general purchasing power.

Two important aspects of the general price level restatement procedure can be noted in Exhibit 14.1. First, *the procedure does not represent a departure from the use of acquisition cost* as the principal valuation method in preparing financial statements. As is illustrated later, the restatements to a common dollar basis are made to the items reported in the conventional financial statements. Second, the amounts shown for general price level restated acquisition cost *do not reflect the current values* of these two parcels of land. The market prices of the land could have changed in an entirely different direction and pattern from that of the general price level change. The focus of the general purchasing power restatement procedure is on making the measuring unit used in acquisition cost-based accounting systems more comparable over time and not on reflecting current values of individual assets and equities.

Restatement of Monetary and Nonmonetary Items

An important distinction is made in the general purchasing power restatement procedure between monetary items and nonmonetary items, a distinction that was also made in Chapter 12 in the discussion of foreign currency translation.

A *monetary item* is a claim receivable or payable in a specified number of dollars regardless of changes in the general purchasing power of the dollar.[3] Examples of monetary items are cash; accounts, notes, and interest receivable; accounts, notes,

---

[3] For purposes of translating foreign financial statement items into dollars, a monetary item was defined in Chapter 12 as a claim receivable or payable in a specified number of units of foreign currency regardless of changes in the exchange rate. The principal difference between the two definitions of monetary items relates to receivables or payables of the foreign unit denominated in dollars. Such items are nonmonetary for purposes of foreign currency translation and monetary for purposes of general price level accounting.

and interest payable; income taxes payable; and bonds. In preparing a general purchasing power restated balance sheet, the valuation of monetary items at the number of dollars due on the date of the balance sheet automatically states them in terms of the general purchasing power of the dollar at that time. No restatement is therefore necessary, and the conventionally reported and restated amounts are the same. For example, assume that a firm has $30,000 of cash on hand on December 31, 1979. On the conventionally prepared balance sheet, this item would be stated at $30,000, the amount of cash on hand. On the general price level restated balance sheet, this item would also be reported at $30,000, representing $30,000 of December 31, 1979, general purchasing power. Since monetary items are receivable or payable in a specified number of dollars rather than in terms of a given amount of general purchasing power, holding monetary items over time while the general purchasing power of the dollar changes gives rise to *monetary gains and losses.*

During a period of inflation, a holder of monetary assets loses general purchasing power. For example, a firm with outstanding accounts receivable incurs a monetary loss, since the dollars at the date of sale are worth more in terms of general purchasing power than the dollars received when the account is collected. Likewise, a holder of monetary liabilities gains in general purchasing power during periods of inflation, since the dollars required to repay the debt represent less purchasing power than the dollars originally borrowed. The gain or loss from holding monetary items is reported as an element of general price level restated net income but is not included in conventionally reported net income.

A *nonmonetary item* is an asset or equity that does not represent a claim to or for a specified number of dollars. That is, if an item is not a monetary item, then it must be nonmonetary. Examples of nonmonetary items are inventory, land, buildings, equipment, capital stock, revenues, and expenses. In conventionally prepared financial statements, nonmonetary items are stated in terms of varying amounts of general purchasing power depending on the date the nonmonetary assets were acquired and nonmonetary equities arose. As illustrated in Exhibit 14.1 with the two parcels of land, the conventionally reported amounts of these items must be restated to an equivalent number of dollars as of the date of the balance sheet. The amount of this restatement does not represent a gain or loss to be included in net income, but merely an adjustment of the measuring unit from historical dollars to dollars of constant purchasing power.

Illustration of the Restatement Procedure

On January 1, 1979, The Aliber Corporation was formed to operate a retail business. A general price index (GPI) on this date was 100. During 1979, the general purchasing power of the dollar declined (prices increased), resulting in a GPI on December 31, 1979, of 110. The Aliber Corporation engaged in the illustrative transactions listed below during the year (income tax effects are ignored). Notice that each transaction is dated, that the value of the GPI on the date of the transaction is shown, and that all accounts are marked as monetary (M) or nonmonetary (N) in the accompanying journal entry.

January 1, 1979: GPI = 100. The Aliber Corporation is formed with the issuance of 500 shares of $10 par value common stock for $7,500 cash.

(1) Cash (M)	7,500	
Common Stock (N)		5,000
Additional Paid-in Capital (N)		2,500

January 1, 1979: GPI = 100. A store building is rented for 1 year with 12 months' rent of $600 paid in advance.

(2) Rent Expense (N)	600	
Cash (M)		600

January 1, 1979: GPI = 100. Store equipment is purchased for $500 cash. The equipment has a 5-year life and is to be depreciated on a straight-line basis.

(3) Store Equipment (N)	500	
Cash (M)		500

April 1, 1979: GPI = 103. Merchandise inventory is purchased for $6,000 cash.

(4) Merchandise Inventory (N)	6,000	
Cash (M)		6,000

July 1, 1979: GPI = 105. Merchandise inventory purchased on April 1, 1979, for $5,000 is sold for $8,000 cash.

(5) Cash (M)	8,000	
Sales Revenue (N)		8,000
(6) Cost of Goods Sold (N)	5,000	
Merchandise Inventory (N)		5,000

October 1, 1979: GPI = 108. Salaries for the year ending December 31, 1979, of $800 are paid in cash.

(7) Salaries Expense (N)	800	
Cash (M)		800

December 31, 1979: GPI = 110. Depreciation expense for the year is recorded.

(8) Depreciation Expense (N)	100	
Accumulated Depreciation (N)		100

December 31, 1979: GPI = 110. The revenue and expense accounts are closed and the financial statements are prepared.

(9) Sales Revenue (N)	8,000	
Cost of Goods Sold (N)		5,000
Rent Expense (N)		600
Salaries Expense (N)		800
Depreciation Expense (N)		100
Retained Earnings (N)		1,500

Both the conventional and the general purchasing power restated balance sheet as of December 31, 1979, as well as the income statement for the year 1979 are presented in Exhibit 14.2.

Notice that cash is the only monetary item appearing on the balance sheet. Since this account is already stated in terms of December 31, 1979, dollars, it is extended in the general purchasing power balance sheet at the same amount as is reported in the conventional balance sheet. The merchandise inventory, store equipment, and accumulated depreciation accounts are nonmonetary items. The conversion restates the acquisition cost of these items to an equivalent number of December 31, 1979, dollars. The common stock and additional paid-in capital accounts are also nonmonetary, and are restated in a manner similar to the merchandise inventory and store equipment. General purchasing power restated retained earnings is the amount necessary to equate general price level restated total assets and total equities. As shown in Exhibit 14.2, this amount can be determined independently by restating net income and calculating the monetary gain or loss.

Revenue and expense accounts are nonmonetary, and must be restated. The approach, as with other nonmonetary accounts, is to convert each item from the price level when revenues were generated and costs were incurred to an equivalent number of December 31, 1979, dollars. Particular notice should be taken of the restatement of cost of goods sold and depreciation expense. The price index when the inventory

EXHIBIT 14.2
Restatement of the Financial Statements of The Aliber Corporation for Changes in General Purchasing Power

BALANCE SHEET AS OF DECEMBER 31, 1979 Assets:	Historical Dollars	(Date for Denominator of Conversion Factor)	×	Conversion Factor: Price Index Values for Conversion[a]	=	Common Dollars
Cash	$7,600	(12/31/79)	×	110/110	=	$7,600
Merchandise Inventory	1,000	(04/01/79)	×	110/103	=	1,070
Store Equipment	500	(01/01/79)	×	110/100	=	550
Less: Accumulated Depreciation	(100)	(01/01/79)	×	110/100	=	(110)
Total Assets	$9,000					$9,110
Equities:						
Common Stock	$5,000	(01/01/79)	×	110/100	=	$5,500
Additional Paid-In Capital	2,500	(01/01/79)	×	110/100	=	2,750
Retained Earnings	1,500	(see Income Statement)				860
Total Equities	$9,000					$9,110

INCOME STATEMENT FOR 1979						
Sales Revenue	$8,000	(07/01/79)	×	110/105	=	$8,400
Less Expenses:						
Cost of Goods Sold	$5,000	(04/01/79)	×	110/103	=	$5,350
Rent Expense	600	(01/01/79)	×	110/100	=	660
Salaries Expense	800	(10/01/79)	×	110/108	=	816
Depreciation Expense	100	(01/01/79)	×	110/100	=	110
Total Expenses	$6,500					$6,936
Net Income in Historical Dollars	$1,500					

Income Before Monetary Gain or Loss	$1,464
Monetary Gain or (Loss) (see computations below)	(604)
Net Income in Common Dollars	$ 860

COMPUTATION OF THE MONETARY GAIN OR LOSS FOR 1979

Monetary Items in Historical Dollars (Monetary transactions expressed in the general purchasing power of the dollar at the time of the transaction)		Price Index Values for × Conversion[a] =	Implied Common-Dollar Amounts (Monetary transactions expressed in an equivalent number of December 31, 1979, dollars)	
(1) 7,500		× 110/100 =	(1) 8,250	
	600 (2)	× 110/100 =		660 (2)
	500 (3)	× 110/100 =		550 (3)
	6,000 (4)	× 110/103 =		6,420 (4)
(5) 8,000		× 110/105 =	(5) 8,400	
	800 (7)	× 110/108 =		816 (7)

			Implied Common-Dollar Amount Balance	$8,204
✓ Balance 7,600		× 110/110 =	Actual Dollar Balance	7,600
			Monetary Loss ...	$ 604

[a] In these calculations, conversion factors are rounded to two decimal places. Thus, 110/103 = 1.07; 110/105 = 1.05; 110/108 = 1.02.

items and store equipment were originally acquired is used, and not the price index when the inventory items were sold and depreciation expense was recorded. The transaction giving rise to the valuation of merchandise inventory and cost of goods sold occurred on April 1, 1979, when the price index was 103. Likewise, the transaction giving rise to the valuation of the store equipment and depreciation expense occurred on January 1, 1979, when the price index was 100. These dollars amounts must therefore be restated.

A "two-T-account" approach, as shown at the bottom of Exhibit 14.2, is used in calculating the monetary gain or loss. The T-account at the left presents the effects of the various transactions during the period on the monetary accounts. To simplify the example, we have assumed that all monetary transactions affect cash directly, so there are no accounts receivable or monetary liabilities. The numbers in parentheses refer to the journal entries presented earlier in this section. The actual balance in the monetary account (cash in this illustration) on December 31, 1979, is $7,600. The middle column presents the conversion of each monetary transaction from the general price level when the transaction occurred during the year to the general price level on December 31, 1979. The T-account at the right shows the number of December 31, 1979, dollars that are equivalent to the general purchasing power received or expended when the monetary transactions took place. The balance in this second T-account serves as a standard, or criterion, for determining the nature and amount of the monetary gain or loss. If the general purchasing power of the dollar amounts of monetary items received and expended during 1979 had been maintained during the period, the monetary accounts would have a balance of $8,204 at year-end. The actual balance in the monetary account is only $7,600, so a monetary loss of $604 is recognized. During periods of inflation, holders of net monetary assets recognize monetary losses, and holders of net monetary liabilities report monetary gains. During deflationary periods, the opposite results occur.

The general purchasing power restatement procedure for the balance sheet and income statement can be summarized as follows:

1. The balance sheet at the end of the period is segregated into monetary and non-monetary accounts. Monetary accounts, claims receivable or payable in a specified number of dollars regardless of changes in the general price level, are already expressed in terms of the desired general purchasing power; they are therefore extended in the restated balance sheet as the same amounts as reported in the conventional balance sheet. The remaining balance sheet accounts, except retained earnings, are restated from the general price level when the assets were acquired or capital stock was issued to an equivalent number of year-end dollars. General purchasing power adjusted retained earnings at the end of the period is the amount necessary to equate restated total assets and restated total equities.

2. The amount determined in step 1 as restated retained earnings is reconciled or "proved" by restating all transactions affecting retained earnings during the period. For a firm in its first year of operations, as illustrated for The Aliber Corporation, this reconciliation generally involves restating the revenue and expense accounts and calculating the monetary gain or loss. After the first year of operations, the balance in retained earnings at the beginning of the period must also be restated. This amount is determined by repeating step 1 for the balance sheet at the beginning of the period but stating each item in terms of the purchasing power of the dollar at the end of the period. This latter step is necessary in any case when comparative balance sheets are presented.

Exhibit 14.3 presents the Statement of Changes in Financial Position of The Aliber Corporation before and after restatement for general price level changes. The principal difference between the statements is in the amount of working capital provided by operations. The general price level restated amount for working capital provided by operations of $970 includes the monetary loss recognized during the year on current monetary accounts. As was the case with the conventional statement discussed in Chapter 5, the general price level restated statement of changes in financial position is most easily prepared after the restated balance sheet and income statement have been prepared.

In practice, a firm would not restate every transaction using the price index in effect on the day of the transaction. At the present time, general price indices are prepared only on monthly and quarterly bases. Also, since there usually are thousands of transactions during the year, gathering data on price indices and restating each transaction would be expensive. Instead, various averaging techniques are used. For example, sales for the year might be restated using the average price index for the year. Firms experiencing seasonal sales patterns during the year might use the index for each month or quarter. Our illustration effectively uses an averaging technique by assuming that all sales occur on July 1. Averaging of price indices is also effectively employed under our assumption in the example that all inventory is acquired on April 1, and all salaries are accrued and paid on October 1. In practice, inventory and labor services are acquired at many different times during the year. Average price indices

EXHIBIT 14.3
**Restatement of the
Statement of Changes in
Financial Position for
The Aliber Corporation**

Sources of Working Capital:	Historical Dollars	Conversion Factor[a]	Common Dollars
Net Income	$1,500	See Income Statement	$ 860
Add Back Depreciation Expense Not Using Working Capital	100	110/100	110
Working Capital Provided by Operations	$1,600		$ 970
Issue of Common Stock	7,500	110/100	8,250
Total Sources of Working Capital	$9,100		$9,220
Uses of Working Capital:			
Purchase of Store Equipment	500	110/100	550
Increase in Working Capital	$8,600		$8,670

ANALYSIS OF INCREASES (DECREASES) IN WORKING CAPITAL ACCOUNTS			
Cash	$7,600	110/110	$7,600
Merchandise Inventory	1,000	110/103	1,070
Increase in Working Capital	$8,600		$8,670

[a] See note a to Exhibit 14.2 for rounding of conversion factors.

for the period are used, however, in restating these financial statement items for changes in general purchasing power.

This illustration has been deliberately kept simple to demonstrate the basic mechanics of the general purchasing power restatement procedure. More extensive treatment of the procedure is beyond the scope of this text. In the next section, the major arguments for and against general purchasing power restated financial statements are presented.

Assessment of General Purchasing Power Restated Financial Statements

The Case for Restatement Proponents of restating financial statements for changes in general purchasing power argue that the annual rate of inflation in the United States is large. They argue that it is now so large that the historical dollar cannot serve as a common monetary measuring unit. When the measured annual rate of inflation averaged between 2 and 3 percent, as was the case during the 1950s and early 1960s, the violation of the common monetary measuring unit assumption was considered tolerable. Most assets, other than land and buildings, were not held for a sufficiently long period of time for the cumulative changing general purchasing power of the dollar to distort seriously the conventional measures of earnings and financial position. With an average rate of inflation now substantially higher than had been experienced earlier, serious distortions in accounting measurements can occur over periods of just a few years.

A second argument favoring restatement concerns the objective nature of general purchasing power restated financial statements. The same valuation methods are used as in the conventional financial statements. The general price indices used are prepared by governmental agencies and are widely available. The restated financial statements, therefore, are as objective, or verifiable, and hence are as easily audited as the conventional statements.

A third argument favoring restatement involves the usefulness of the information on the monetary gain or loss. This gain or loss is in many ways the most meaningful of the adjustments for changes in general purchasing power. The interest expense in the conventional financial statements is the reported cost of borrowing in historical dollars. The amount of the expense depends on the interest rate negotiated between the borrower and the lender at the time of the loan. That interest rate, in turn, depends in part on the lender's and borrower's anticipations about the rate of inflation during the term of the loan.

The lender asks a higher interest rate when inflation is expected to occur during the term of a loan because lenders are aware that they will be repaid with dollars of smaller general purchasing power than were loaned. Borrowers are willing to pay a larger interest rate in times of anticipated inflation because they expect to repay the loan with "cheaper" dollars.

The borrower's conventional income statement shows an interest expense that reflects the inflation expected both by the borrower and by the lender. The higher the anticipated inflation, the higher the interest expense. The gain from being in a net monetary liability position during a period of rising general prices is in large measure an offset to the reported interest expense. It reflects the reduction in the reported cost of borrowing caused by the general inflation that reduces the value of the dollars to be repaid. Both the borrower and the lender may have expected this reduction.

Whether the borrower or lender benefited at the expense of the other depends on the amount of *un*anticipated inflation during the term of the loan. If the actual rate of inflation during the term of the loan is greater than that anticipated at the time the loan was made, then the borrower benefits at the expense of the lender. The dollars actually repaid have smaller general purchasing power than both parties expected. (Actual inflation rates appear to have been larger during the first half of the 1970s than had been expected, so borrowers benefited at the expense of lenders.) If the actual rate of price increase is less than that expected at the time the loan was made, then the lender benefits at the expense of the borrower.

The Case Against Restatement   Critics of restatement argue that the monetary gain or loss reported is of limited usefulness because the price index used to calculate the gain or loss covers too wide a variety of goods and services. Of more importance, it is suggested, is the firm's success or failure in maintaining the purchasing power of its capital for the types of goods and services it normally acquires (that is, merchandise inventory, land, plant, equipment). These items are given relatively little weight in the general price indices, which place heavy weight on the prices of consumer goods and services.

A second argument advanced by critics of restatement concerns the possibly significant measurement biases in the general price indices employed. The general price indices have been criticized for (1) failing to filter out properly the portion of price changes attributable to changes in the quality or other aspects of goods and services; (2) using posted prices for some goods and services (particularly industrial goods) rather than the actual invoice prices, which may include discounts and other price reductions; and (3) failing to update the goods and services included in the market basket on a sufficiently frequent basis, with the result that the price indices do not adequately reflect the items currently being purchased.

Critics of restatement also argue that financial statement users do not understand financial statements restated for changes in general purchasing power. They argue that an extensive educational effort will be required before the statements can be used in investment decisions. An illustration of the misunderstanding concerning general price level statements is the belief by some persons that the general price level restated amounts for nonmonetary assets, particularly land, buildings, and equipment, represent the current values of these individual assets.

Critics of restatement also point out that several surveys of financial analysts, bankers, and other potential users of the restated accounting reports have indicated that a large proportion of these individuals would not find the statements particularly useful. Some observers thus doubt that financial statement users would find general price level adjusted statements helpful in their decisions even after an extensive educational program.

The Impact of Restatement on Reported Income   One means of assessing the desirability of restatement is to determine if the earnings results would be significantly different from those conventionally reported. During periods of rising prices, one important factor causing restated net income to be *less* than conventional net income is the upward restatement of depreciation expense for cumulative inflation since the long-term assets were acquired. A larger difference between conventional and restated earnings would be expected for manufacturing and merchandising firms than for firms in service industries. The most important factor causing restated net income to be *larger* than conventional net income is the monetary gain recognized from outstanding long-term debt during periods of inflation. Highly levered firms, those with high debt ratios such as public utilities, would probably report significant monetary gains. In assessing the impact of restatement on net income of a particular firm, attention should center on the types and relative age of various assets and the extent to which long-term debt is used as a source of capital.[4]

---

[4]   If prices are rising steadily through time, then eventually net income reported in statements restated for changes in general purchasing power must be less than the net income reported in the conventional statements whose measurements are made in dollars of varying purchasing power. The time when the restated income becomes less can, however, be arbitrarily far into the future. This issue is addressed by George S. Staubus in "The Effects of Price-Level Restatements on Earnings," *The Accounting Review*, Vol. LI, No. 3 (July 1976), pp. 574–589.

DEVELOPMENT OF FINANCIAL STATEMENT OBJECTIVES

We indicated in previous chapters that the development of generally accepted accounting principles is essentially a political process. Various individuals and groups express their opinions on the most appropriate ways of accounting for events. An official rule-making body (such as the Financial Accounting Standards Board or the Securities and Exchange Commission) weighs the various views and then issues an official pronouncement.

One of the criticisms of this process is that each issue tends to get considered in isolation. The number of issues continually under consideration is large. Thus, there has been insufficient time for developing a comprehensive theory of financial accounting or for insuring that the rationale for various official positions is internally consistent and logical.

In recent years there have been several efforts to identify the objectives of financial statements.[5] The hope is that such a set of objectives can be used as a basis for deciding particular accounting issues and establishing acceptable accounting principles. The most recent effort in setting financial statement objectives has been by the Financial Accounting Standards Board. Its conclusions regarding objectives are summarized below.[6]

> Financial reporting should provide information that is useful to present and potential investors and creditors in making rational investment and credit decisions. The information should be comprehensible to those who have a reasonable understanding of business and economic activities and are willing to study the information with reasonable diligence. . . .

> Financial reporting should provide information to help investors and creditors assess the amounts, timing, and uncertainty of prospective cash receipts from dividends or interest and from the proceeds from the sale, redemption, or maturity of securities or loans. The prospects for those cash receipts are affected by (a) an enterprise's ability to obtain enough cash to meet its obligations when due and its other cash operating needs, to reinvest in earning resources and activities, and to pay cash dividends and (b) perceptions of investors and creditors generally about that ability, which affect market prices of the enterprise's securities. Thus, financial reporting should provide information to help investors and creditors assess the amounts, timing, and uncertainty of prospective net cash inflows to the related enterprise. . . .

> Financial reporting should provide information about the economic resources of an enterprise, its obligations to transfer resources to other enterprises, and changes in its resources and obligations. . . .

It is, of course, too early to judge (1) if establishing objectives first and then deciding specific reporting questions based on the objectives is a process that will work any better than the current issue-by-issue approach, and (2) if the specific objectives sum-

---

[5] *APB Statement No. 4*, 1970; Study Group on the Objectives of Financial Statements, AICPA, 1973.
[6] FASB, *Statement of Financial Accounting Concepts No. 1*, 1978.

marized above will prove sufficiently operational for formulating accounting policy or whether another set will have to be developed. The objectives quoted above place greater emphasis on a firm's cash-generating ability than did previous official pronouncements. It should be recognized that the setting of objectives for financial statements, like the setting of acceptable accounting principles, is itself a political process.

SUMMARY

Because financial accounting and reporting are continually in a state of evolution and development, accounting knowledge can become out of date rapidly. We have attempted in this book to identify the most important concepts underlying financial accounting. With this conceptual base, you should be able to make appropriate applications of the concepts as new issues arise. To maintain the effectiveness of your conceptual basis, it is important that you use it frequently. We have found the most effective ways of doing this are to read one or more financial periodicals regularly and to study the annual reports of several firms carefully.

QUESTIONS AND PROBLEMS

1 Review the meaning of the following concepts or terms discussed in this chapter.
   a Segment report.
   b Transfer price.
   c Direct segment expenses.
   d Indirect but assignable segment expenses.
   e Central corporate expenses.
   f Interim report.
   g Common monetary measuring unit assumption.
   h General price level changes.
   i General price index.
   j General purchasing power of the dollar.
   k Monetary item.
   l Nonmonetary item.
   m Monetary gain versus loss.
   n Financial statement objective.

2 Consolidated financial statements essentially represent an aggregation of the financial statements of a parent company and its subsidiaries. Segment reports represent a disaggregation of financial statement information for various units or divisions of the firm. Explain the apparent paradox of aggregating financial information and then disaggregating it.

3 What is the purpose of interim earnings reports? Are there any problems unique to interim reports that are not encountered in preparing annual earnings reports?

4 The accounting problems associated with changing prices have been described as *general* and *specific*. Explain.

5 Distinguish between the pair of terms listed in each of the following cases.
  a General price index and general price level.
  b General price index and general purchasing power of the dollar.
  c General price index and specific price index.

6 "Financial statements prepared under the conventional accounting model reflect dollars of mixed purchasing power." Explain the meaning of this statement in relation to the balance sheet, income statement, and statement of changes in financial position.

7 When general price level restated financial statements are prepared, under what conditions will a firm recognize:
  a A monetary gain?
  b A monetary loss?

8 For which types of asset and equity structures would you expect:
  a Significant differences between earnings as conventionally reported and as restated for general price level changes?
  b Insignificant differences between the two earnings measures?

9 Why is there no nonmonetary gain or loss in general price level restated financial statements?

10 In financial statements prepared under the conventional accounting model, some items are stated in terms of the current general purchasing power of the dollar whereas other items are stated in terms of the general purchasing power of the dollar during prior periods. Give several examples of each type.

11 Indicate whether each of the following accounts is a monetary item (M) or a nonmonetary item (N). State any assumptions you feel are necessary.
  a Certificate of Deposit.
  b Land.
  c Investment in U.S. Treasury Bills.
  d Deferred Income Taxes.
  e Notes Receivable.
  f Bonds Payable.
  g Patents.
  h Common Stock.
  i Investment in Unconsolidated Subsidiaries.
  j Allowance for Uncollectible Accounts.

12 Each of the following describes the contents of interim reports or a policy used by a company in preparing its interim reports. On the basis of this information, does it appear that the company is (1) treating the interim period as a self-contained accounting period, or (2) treating the interim period as an integral part of the annual period and reporting in such a way that valid inferences about annual net income can be made?
  a A department store makes 40 percent of its sales in the months of October through December and allocates 40 percent of the annual depreciation charge on the store building to that quarter.
  b Payroll taxes are levied on the first $15,000 of the salary earned by an individual during the year. Many of the company's employees earn more than $15,000 per year. The

company reports payroll tax expense for employees in interim reports as the salaries are earned and the liability to the government arises.

c The income tax expense was computed as 22 percent of the income before taxes in the first quarter's interim report and 48 percent of the income before taxes in the third quarter's interim report.

d An appliance manufacturer sells most of its television sets in the second half of the year. The company pays bonuses to executives based on income before taxes for the year. The amount of executive bonuses shown as expenses on each of the four quarterly reports for the year is the same.

e A cereal company reports that income for the quarter is 60 percent larger than for the comparable quarter of the preceding year. The increase is attributable to a reduction in advertising expenditures this quarter, relative to expenditures in the corresponding quarter last year. The company expects its advertising expense for this year to be about the same as for last year.

13 Brown Tax Services, Incorporated, provides income tax preparation services to its customers. Fee revenues are highly seasonal during the four quarters of the calendar year and occur in the following percentages:

Quarter	Percentage
First (1/1–3/31)	60%
Second (4/1–6/30)	20%
Third (7/1–9/30)	10%
Fourth (10/1–12/31)	10%

The following operating costs were anticipated and actually incurred evenly throughout the year ended December 31, 1979:

Salaries	$250,000
Rent	125,000
Insurance	25,000
Total	$400,000

During the first quarter of 1979, fee revenues totaled $360,000.

a Determine net income for the first quarter assuming that operating costs are assigned equally to each of the four quarters during the year.

b Determine net income for the first quarter assuming that operating costs are assigned to each quarter in proportion to the percentage of the anticipated year's revenues recognized during each quarter.

c If the pattern of fee revenues during 1979 occurs as anticipated (that is, .60, .20, .10, .10), what is the anticipated net income for the year?

d Which of the interim earnings measures determined in parts **a** and **b** will lead to the more accurate prediction of the annual net income calculated in part **c**?

14 St. Nicholas Tailors rents out a single Santa Claus costume for the months of November and December each year. Its transactions are as follows:

(1) The company commences business on January 1, 1979.

(2) June 1, 1979. One Santa Claus costume is purchased for $100. The costume will last for 10 annual rental periods and is depreciated on a straight-line basis. The costume has a zero estimated salvage value. The company takes a full year of depreciation in the first year.

(3) The costume is rented for the months of November and December 1979 for $70, total.

(4) January 2, 1980. Cleaning costs of $5 are incurred for the costume, which has been returned to St. Nicholas Tailors.

(5) The costume is stored for the months of January through October 1980 at a cost of $2 per month.

(6) The costume is rented for the months of November and December 1980 for $70, total.

(7) The books are closed annually on December 31. Income taxes are to be paid at the rate of 20 percent of the first $5 of taxable income and 40 percent of the rest.

Income statements for the years 1979 and 1980 are shown below.

St. Nicholas Tailors
Income Statements
for the Years 1979 and 1980

	1979	1980
Revenues	$70	$70
Expenses:		
Storage Costs	$ 0	$20
Depreciation	10	10
Cleaning Costs	0	5
Income Taxes	23	13
Total Expenses	$33	$48
Net Income	$37	$22

---

a Prepare interim quarterly reports for March 31, June 30, September 30, and December 31, 1979.

b Prepare interim quarterly reports for March 31, June 30, September 30, and December 31, 1980.

15 Southside Development Corporation acquired a parcel of land on July 1, 1978, for $50,000. The tract was sold on July 1, 1979, for $38,000.

An index of the general price level on various dates is determined to be as follows:

July 1, 1978: 100;
December 31, 1978: 115;
July 1, 1979: 125;
December 31, 1979: 140.

a Determine the amount of gain or loss recognized during 1979 relating to this property under the acquisition-cost valuation method assuming that changes in the general purchasing power of the dollar are ignored.

b Restate the gain or loss recognized during 1979 on the sale of the tract to the general price level on December 31, 1979.

16 Jones Manufacturing Corporation depreciates its machinery using the straight-line method over a 10-year life with zero estimated salvage value. A full year's depreciation is taken in the year of acquisition and none in the year of disposal. Acquisitions, which took place evenly over the appropriate years, were as follows: 1977, $500,000; 1978, $100,000; 1979, $200,000. An index of the average general price level during 1977 was 120, during 1978 was 160, and during 1979 was 180. The general price index on December 31, 1979, is 200.

  a Determine the amount of depreciation expense for 1979 and the book value of the machinery on December 31, 1979, using the acquisition-cost valuation method as conventionally reported.

  b Repeat part **a,** using the acquisition-cost valuation method restated for general price level changes. Round conversion factors used to two decimal places (for example, $200/120 = 1.67$).

17 The Whitley Hardware Store had a net monetary asset position of $200,000 on January 1, 1979, at which time an index of the general price level was 100. Transactions during 1979 and associated indices of the general price level (GPI) are listed below.

  (1) Purchases, all on account, totaled $300,000 (GPI = 120).
  (2) Sales, all on account, totaled $500,000 (GPI = 120).
  (3) Collections from customers for sales on account, $350,000 (GPI = 125).
  (4) Payments to suppliers for purchases on account, $200,000 (GPI = 125).
  (5) Declaration of a $100,000 dividend, payable during January 1980 (GPI = 150). The general price index on December 31, 1979, is 150.

  a Using the two-T-account approach, determine the amount of the monetary gain or loss for 1979.

  b Repeat part **a,** assuming a net monetary liability position of $200,000 on January 1, 1979.

18 On January 1, 1979, the Robert Pratt family had $1,200 in its checking account and $5,000 in a savings account. The unpaid balance on the mortgage on their home totaled $20,000, whereas unpaid bills relating to purchases during December 1978 amounted to $1,000. An index of the general price level on January 1, 1979, was 150. During 1979, the following transactions occurred (general price index is shown in parentheses):

  (1) Robert Pratt's take-home salary during 1979 was $15,000 (average GPI = 160).
  (2) The unpaid bills of $1,000 on January 1, 1979, were paid (GPI = 152).
  (3) Principal repayments of $2,500 were made during 1979 on the home mortgage loan (average GPI = 160).
  (4) Food, clothing, interest, and other costs incurred by the family during 1979 totaled $10,100, of which $9,300 were paid in cash (average GPI = 160).
  (5) Interest earned and added to the savings account totaled $250 (average GPI = 160).
  (6) In addition to the interest earned in **(5),** $2,500 was transferred from the checking to the savings account during 1979 (GPI = 158). The general price index on December 31, 1979, is 170.

Using the two-T-account approach, determine the monetary gain or loss for the family during 1979. Round conversion factors used to two decimal places ($170/150 = 1.13$).

19 The financial statements of the Hargrave Corporation for 1979, its first year of operations, are presented on pages 573 and 574.

**Hargrave Corporation
Balance Sheet
December 31, 1979**

ASSETS

Cash	$ 50,000
Accounts Receivable	180,000
Merchandise Inventory	300,000
Store Equipment	300,000
Less Accumulated Depreciation	(30,000)
Total Assets	$800,000

EQUITIES

Accounts Payable	$ 50,000
Common Stock	500,000
Additional Paid-in Capital	100,000
Retained Earnings	150,000
Total Equities	$800,000

**Hargrave Corporation
Income Statement
For the Year 1979**

Sales Revenue	$500,000

Less Expenses:

Cost of Goods Sold	$250,000
Depreciation Expense	30,000
Selling and Administrative Expenses	70,000
Total Expenses	$350,000
Net Income	$150,000

**Hargrave Corporation
Statement of Changes
in Financial Position
For the Year 1979**

Sources of Working Capital:

Net Income	$150,000	
Add Back Depreciation Expense Not Using Working Capital	30,000	
Working Capital Provided by Operations	$180,000	
Issuance of Common Stock	600,000	
Total Sources of Working Capital		$780,000

Uses of Working Capital:

Purchase of Store Equipment	300,000
Net Increase in Working Capital	$480,000

ANALYSIS OF INCREASES (DECREASES) IN WORKING CAPITAL

Cash	$ 50,000
Accounts Receivable	180,000
Merchandise Inventory	300,000
Accounts Payable	(50,000)
Net Increase in Working Capital	**$480,000**

Indices of the general price level on various dates were as follows (round conversion factors to two decimal places; for example, 200/180 = 1.11).

(1) On January 1, 1979, when common stock was issued	160
(2) When store equipment was acquired	165
(3) When merchandise inventory was acquired	170
(4) When sales were made	180
(5) When selling and administrative costs were incurred	175
(6) On December 31, 1979	200

  a Restate the balance sheet on December 31, 1979, to the general purchasing power of the dollar on December 31, 1979.

  b Restate the income statement for the year 1979 to the general purchasing power of the dollar on December 31, 1979. Include a separate calculation of the monetary gain or loss.

  c Restate the statement of changes in financial position for the year 1979 to the general purchasing power of the dollar on December 31, 1979.

20 The financial statements of the Hargrave Corporation (see Problem **19**) for 1980, its second year of operations, are presented below.

Hargrave Corporation
Balance Sheet
December 31, 1980

ASSETS

Cash	$ 90,000
Accounts Receivable	190,000
Merchandise Inventory (based on FIFO)	450,000
Store Equipment	400,000
Accumulated Depreciation	(70,000)
Total Assets	$1,060,000

EQUITIES

Accounts Payable	$ 70,000
Mortgage Payable	90,000
Common Stock	500,000
Additional Paid-in Capital	100,000
Retained Earnings	300,000
Total Equities	$1,060,000

**Hargrave Corporation
Income Statement
For the Year 1980**

Sales Revenue	$750,000

Less Expenses:

Cost of Goods Sold	$400,000
Depreciation Expense	40,000
Selling and Administrative Expenses	110,000
Total Expenses	$550,000
Net Income	$200,000

**Hargrave Corporation
Statement of Changes
in Financial Position
For the Year 1980**

Sources of Working Capital:

Net Income	$200,000	
Add Back Depreciation Expense		
Not Using Working Capital	40,000	
Working Capital Provided by Operations	$240,000	
Mortgage Liability Assumed in Acquiring		
Store Equipment	100,000	
Total Sources of Working Capital		$340,000

Uses of Working Capital:

Dividends Paid	$ 50,000	
Mortgage Liability Partial Payment	10,000	
Store Equipment Acquired	100,000	
Total Uses of Working Capital		160,000
Net Increase in Working Capital		$180,000

ANALYSIS OF INCREASES (DECREASES) IN WORKING CAPITAL

Cash	$ 40,000
Accounts Receivable	10,000
Merchandise Inventory	150,000
Accounts Payable	(20,000)
Net Increase in Working Capital	$180,000

Additional Information Store equipment costing $100,000 was acquired during the year. The acquisition was financed by long-term borrowing, with the equipment serving as collateral. The equipment is depreciated using the straight-line method over a 10-year life with zero estimated salvage value. A full year's depreciation is taken in the year of acquisition.

Indices of the general price level on various dates were as follows (round conversion factors to two decimal places; for example, $225/200 = 1.13$).

(1) On January 1, 1980 200
(2) When store equipment was acquired 202
(3) When merchandise inventory was acquired 204
(4) When sales were made 215
(5) When selling and administrative costs were incurred 212
(6) When mortgage payments were made 225
(7) When dividend was declared and paid 225
(8) On December 31, 1980 225

a Restate the balance sheet on December 31, 1980, to the general purchasing power of the dollar on December 31, 1980.

b Restate the income statement for the year ending December 31, 1980, to the general purchasing power of the dollar on December 31, 1980. Include a separate calculation of the monetary gain or loss.

c Prepare an analysis of changes in retained earnings for the year ending December 31, 1980, before and after restatement for changes in the general purchasing power of the dollar. The January 1, 1980, balance in retained earnings, restated to the general purchasing power of the dollar on December 31, 1980, is $120,600.

21 The Whitmyer Corporation was formed on January 1, 1979, to conduct an office rental business. Listed below are various transactions and other events of the firm during 1979. An index of the general price level at the time of each transaction is also shown.

(1) January 1, 1979 (GPI = 100): Capital stock is issued for $1,000,000.

(2) January 2, 1979 (GPI = 100): Land costing $100,000 and a building costing $1,500,000 are acquired. A cash payment of $900,000 is made, with a long-term, 10-percent mortgage assumed for the remainder of the purchase price.

(3) January 2, 1979, to December 1, 1979 (average GPI = 106): Rentals of $300,000 are collected in cash.

(4) January 2, 1979, to December 31, 1979 (average GPI = 106): Operating costs incurred evenly over the year total $60,000, of which $50,000 are paid in cash and the remainder are on account. All of these costs expired during 1979.

(5) January 2, 1979, to December 31, 1979 (average GPI = 106): Interest costs are accrued monthly on the mortgage payable and were paid on December 31, 1979.

(6) December 31, 1979 (GPI = 110): Depreciation on the building is calculated using the straight-line method, a 30-year life, and zero salvage value.

(7) December 31, 1979 (GPI = 110): A cash dividend of $75,000 is declared and paid.

a Set up T-accounts as needed and enter the transactions during the year based on the conventional accounting model.

b Prepare a balance sheet as of December 31, 1979, and an income statement and statement of changes in financial position for 1979 using the conventional accounting model.

c Repeat part **b,** but restate the conventional financial statements for changes in general purchasing power. Round conversion factors to two decimal places (for example, $110/106 = 1.04$).

22 Refer to the segment report of International Corporation in Appendix A. Calculate for each product segment for 19X0 and 19X1:
  a Segment sales to unaffiliated customers as a percentage of combined (or consolidated) segment sales to unaffiliated customers.
  b Segment operating profit as a percentage of segment sales to unaffiliated customers.
  c Segment operating profit as a percentage of identifiable segment assets at the end of each year.
  d What changes can you see in the profitability of the three segments of International Corporation between 19X0 and 19X1?

23 Refer to the segment report of International Corporation in Appendix A. For the domestic and foreign segments, calculate the following amounts for 19X0 and 19X1:
  a Segment sales to unaffiliated customers as a percentage of combined sales to unaffiliated customers.
  b Segment operating profit as a percentage of segment sales to unaffiliated customers.
  c Segment operating profit as a percentage of identifiable segment assets at the end of each year.
  d What changes can you see in the profitability of these two segments of International Corporation between 19X0 and 19X1?

APPENDIX A

CORPORATE FINANCIAL STATEMENTS ILLUSTRATED AND ANNOTATED

This appendix illustrates current financial reporting with a comprehensive set of corporate financial statements prepared in accordance with generally accepted accounting principles.

The financial statements are those of the International Corporation (IC), a fictitious company. These statements are, however, adapted from the actual statements of a well-known, major company in the United States that has worldwide operations. We have omitted some materials from that company's annual report because of its specialized nature; we have added some material to illustrate significant financial reporting on matters not applicable to the actual company.

This appendix is organized into four exhibits, as follows:

Exhibit A.1. International Corporation Consolidated Statements of Income and Retained Earnings
Exhibit A.2. International Corporation Consolidated Balance Sheet
Exhibit A.3. International Corporation Consolidated Statement of Changes in Financial Position
Exhibit A.4. International Corporation Notes to Financial Statements.

First, we have presented the exhibits that comprise the financial statements. Then we have included our own notes and comments related to the items in the financial statements. Our comments are numbered to correspond with the note numbers used by International Corporation in Exhibit A.4.

The financial statements of International Corporation begin on the following page. Our commentary begins on page 595.

EXHIBIT A.1
International Corporation
Consolidated Statements of
Income and Retained Earnings
(Dollar Amounts in Thousands)

Income Statement	Year Ended December 31, 19X1	Year Ended December 31, 19X0
Revenues:		
Sales (net of estimated uncollectibles—Note 8)	$5,862,747	$5,798,513
Equity in income (loss) from nonconsolidated subsidiaries		
and affiliated companies (Note 3)	14,513	(32,285)
Other revenues	51,348	71,890
	5,928,608	5,838,118
Expenses:		
Cost of goods sold	4,647,161	4,669,745
Selling, administration, and general	801,283	727,426
Depreciation	128,828	123,518
Interest	76,425	111,261
Income taxes (Note 5)	93,835	63,970
Minority interest in net income of consolidated subsidiaries	2,452	3,261
	5,749,984	5,699,181
Income from continuing operations	178,624	138,937
Discontinued operations (Note 2):		
Loss from operations of discontinued businesses		
(net of taxes of $35,274)	—	(39,805)
Loss on disposal of discontinued businesses		
(net of taxes of $10,000 in 19X1 and $42,000 in 19X0)	(13,400)	(71,000)
Net income	$ 165,224	$ 28,132
Earnings per common share:		
Continuing operations	$2.04	$1.57
Discontinued operations:		
Loss from operations	—	(.45)
Loss on disposal	(.15)	(.81)
Net income per common share	$1.89	$ .31

Retained Earnings	Year Ended December 31, 19X1	Year Ended December 31, 19X0
Retained earnings at beginning of year	$1,162,556	$1,220,914
Plus:		
Net income	165,224	28,132
Less:		
Dividends paid on preferred stock	(895)	(1,158)
Dividends paid on common stock	(84,544)	(85,332)
Retained earnings at end of year	$1,242,341	$1,162,556

The financial information in the notes is an integral part of these financial statements.

EXHIBIT A.2
International Corporation
Consolidated Balance Sheet
(Dollar Amounts in Thousands)

Assets	At December 31, 19X1	At December 31, 19X0
Current assets:		
Cash	117,984	98,906
Marketable securities (Note 7)	256,600	38,900
Customer receivables (Note 8)	1,142,267	1,247,121
Inventories (Note 9)	1,040,571	1,072,963
Costs of uncompleted contracts in excess of related billings (Note 10)	172,473	197,205
Prepaid and other current assets	110,729	184,417
Total current assets	2,840,624	2,839,512
Investments (Note 11)	289,188	226,209
Estimated realizable value— discontinued businesses (Note 2)	95,543	202,442
Plant and equipment, net (Note 12)	1,380,680	1,298,576
Other assets (Note 13)	260,251	246,879
Total assets	$4,866,286	$4,813,618

Liabilities and Shareholders' Equity		
Current liabilities:		
Short-term loans and current portion of long-term debt (Notes 14 and 15)	$ 131,754	$ 236,063
Accounts payable—trade	361,310	392,835
Accrued payrolls and payroll deductions	201,143	180,473
Income taxes currently payable	50,248	47,172
Deferred current income taxes	53,597	31,146
Estimated future liabilities—discontinued businesses	32,178	46,394
Billings on uncompleted contracts in excess of related costs (Note 10)	739,480	511,814
Other current liabilities	453,711	382,122
Total current liabilities	2,023,421	1,828,019
Noncurrent liabilities	52,255	62,360
Deferred noncurrent income taxes	117,449	97,270
Debentures and other debt (Notes 16 and 19)	610,242	843,123
Total noncurrent liabilities	779,946	1,002,753
Minority interest	61,227	58,775
Shareholders' equity (Notes 17 and 18):		
Cumulative preferred stock	16,593	30,482
Common stock	277,108	277,108
Capital in excess of par value	490,697	480,896
Retained earnings	1,242,341	1,162,556
Less: Treasury stock, at cost	(25,047)	(26,971)
Total stockholders' equity	2,001,692	1,924,071
Total liabilities and stockholders' equity	$4,866,286	$4,813,618

The financial information in the notes is an integral part of these financial statements.

EXHIBIT A.3
International Corporation
Consolidated Statement of Changes in Financial Position
(Dollar Amounts in Thousands)

Changes in Financial Position	Year Ended December 31, 19X1	Year Ended December 31, 19X0
Working capital provided:		
Net income from continuing operations	$ 178,624	$138,937
Add (subtract) income charges (credits) not affecting working capital:		
Depreciation	128,828	123,518
Deferred income taxes	20,179	21,222
Minority interest in net income of consolidated subsidiaries	2,452	3,261
Equity in losses (income) of nonconsolidated subsidiaries and affiliated companies	(14,513)	32,285
Working capital provided by continuing operations	315,570	319,223
Losses applicable to discontinued operations	(13,400)	(110,805)
Add (deduct) income charges (credits) not affecting working capital:		
Depreciation	—	10,143
Deferred income taxes	—	(4,907)
Loss on disposal (less $46,394 current estimated future costs in 19X0)	—	24,606
Working capital absorbed by discontinued operations	(13,400)	(80,963)
Other sources:		
Realization of estimated value—discontinued businesses	125,925	—
Increase in debentures and other debt	44,974	219,747
Issuance of common stock to employees	18,743	25,467
Sale of long-term investments	17,000	—
Total other sources	206,642	245,214
Total resources provided	508,812	483,474
Working capital applied:		
Expenditures for new and improved facilities	187,517	356,653
Dividend payments	85,439	86,490
Reduction in debentures and other debt	277,855	48,351
Purchase of long-term investments	106,679	40,479
Acquisition of common stock for treasury	14,242	39,442
Purchase of preferred stock for cancellation	6,944	—
Other—net	24,426	6,119
Total resources applied	703,102	577,534
Net change in working capital	$(194,290)	$(94,060)

Analysis of Changes in Working Capital

Increase (decrease) in working capital:		
Cash and marketable securities	$ 236,778	$ 8,517
Customer receivables	(104,854)	(61,111)
Inventories and costs of uncompleted contracts in excess of related billings	(57,124)	(69,818)
Prepaid and other current assets	(73,688)	(1,929)
Short-term loans and current portion of long-term debt	104,309	239,238
Accounts payable—trade	31,525	12,472
Income taxes (including deferred income taxes)	(25,527)	80,873
Estimated future costs—discontinued businesses	14,216	(46,394)
Billings on uncompleted contracts in excess of related costs	(227,666)	(155,739)
All other current liabilities	(92,259)	(100,169)
Net change in working capital	$(194,290)	$(94,060)

EXHIBIT A.4
International Corporation
Notes to Financial Statements

Note 1—Summary of Significant Accounting Policies
The major accounting principles and policies followed by International are presented to assist the reader in evaluating the consolidated financial statements and other data in this report.

Principles of Consolidation: The financial statements include the consolidation of all significant wholly and majority owned subsidiaries except International Credit Company and Suburban Development Corporation. The equity method of accounting is followed for nonconsolidated subsidiaries and for investments in significant affiliates (20 to 50 percent owned).

The assets and liabilities of non-U.S. subsidiaries are translated at current exchange rates except that plant and equipment are translated at rates in effect at dates of acquisition. Income and expense amounts, except depreciation, are translated at rates prevailing during the year. Translation adjustments in the consolidated financial statements are not material.

Sales are recorded as products are shipped on substantially all contracts. All sales are made on account. The percentage-of-completion method is used only for certain orders with durations generally in excess of 5 years and for certain construction projects where this method of accounting is consistent with industry practices. In accordance with these practices, Long-Term Contracts in Process are stated at cost plus estimated profits recognized to date. Costs related to long-term contracts are also accumulated in Inventories, Recoverable Engineering and Development Costs (Government Contracts), and Progress Payments to Subcontractors. In accordance with terms of the particular contracts, progress payments are obtained from customers. The amounts of long-term contracts do not exceed realizable value.

Inventories: The cost of the inventories of the consolidated companies is determined principally by the LIFO method. Inventories not on LIFO are valued at current standard costs, which approximate actual or average cost. The elements of cost included in inventories are direct labor, direct material, and factory overhead.

Pension Plans cover substantially all employes of the Corporation. Benefits under the plans are being funded by the pension trust method. It is the policy of the Corporation to fund each year the amount actuarially determined to be necessary to provide benefits earned during the year and to amortize prior-service liability over a period of 30 years.

Depreciation on plant and equipment acquired since January 1, 1968, is provided by the straight-line method based on guideline lives. Plant and equipment acquired prior to that date is depreciated using accelerated methods. Accelerated depreciation methods using guideline lives, giving effect to the class life system for assets acquired since 1970, are used for federal income tax purposes.

Deferred Income Taxes are provided for timing differences between financial and tax reporting, principally related to long-term contracts in process, depreciation, certain leasing transactions by International Credit Company, and loss on discontinued operations. Timing differences for long-term contracts result from the use of the percentage-of-completion method for financial reporting and the completed-contract method for income tax reporting.

Deferred federal income taxes are not provided on the undistributed earnings of certain subsidiaries when such earnings have been indefinitely reinvested.

The Investment Credit on all qualified assets is recorded under the flow-through method of accounting as a reduction of the current provision for federal income taxes except for investment credit on assets leased to others by the International Credit Company. Investment credit on such leased assets is deferred and amortized over the terms of the respective leases.

Note 2—Discontinued operations: During 19X0, decisions were reached to dispose of two major business segments, the trade book publication business and the mail order book club business.

The Corporation agreed to sell the publication business to East Consolidated Industries, Inc. (ECI), in exchange for cash and securities, resulting in provisions for losses on disposal in 19X0 of $55 million (net of income tax savings of $30 million).

The initial phase of the transaction included the sale of the domestic trade book business and the trade book business of International Canada Ltd., a majority-owned subsidiary. The transaction for the domestic business is essentially complete. Sale of the International Canada portion to ECI initially was denied due to a Canadian government ruling regarding non-Canadian investment. ECI has filed a second application and the Canadian government is expected to make a decision regarding this sale in early 19X2. International is continuing negotiations with ECI for sale of its trade book operations in three other countries. No additional provisions for disposal cost are considered necessary.

During 19X0, the Corporation sold the member list and inventories of the International Book Club. The remaining portion of the mail order book club business was to have been phased out during 19X1. A provision for disposal costs of $16 million (net of income tax savings of $12 million) was charged against income in 19X0. A comprehensive review and analysis of the progression of the phase-out resulted in an additional provision for losses on disposal of $13 million (net of income tax savings of $10 million) against income in 19X1. This additional provision was required due to extended time needed to complete successive stages of the planned phase-out, higher than anticipated costs of inventory disposal, excessive returns of books, and lower than anticipated collection of outstanding receivables.

Estimated Realizable Value—Discontinued Businesses includes the assets and liabilities to be disposed. These amounts consist primarily of the net assets of the book publishing subsidiaries outside the United States.

Note 3—Equity in Income (Loss) from Nonconsolidated Subsidiaries and Affiliated Companies includes pretax losses of Suburban Development Corporation (SDC) amounting to $25.9 million and $40.8 million for the years ended December 31, 19X1 and 19X0, respectively. During 19X0, the total SDC short-term debt guaranteed by International in the amount of $85 million was repaid with funds provided by the parent company.

Note 4—Pension expense was $66.2 million in 19X1 and $75.2 million in 19X0. No changes in actuarial assumptions were made in either year. Unfunded prior-service liability at December 31, 19X0 was estimated at $587 million, of which $444 million represented unfunded vested benefits. Based on the latest actuarial valuation, which recognizes the increased pension liabilities resulting from wage and salary improvements and increases for retirees effective July 1, 19X1, unfunded prior-service liability approximates $616 million, of which $508 million represents unfunded vested benefits at December 31, 19X1.

For purposes of determining unfunded prior-service liability, fixed-income securities were valued at cost and common stock assets were valued by assuming a long-range yield (capital appreciation and dividends) of 8 percent. The long-range-yield method minimizes the impact of short-term market fluctuations. As a result, the carrying value of common stock assets may, as at present, exceed the market value.

Statement of Changes in Pension Assets (Dollar Amounts in Thousands)	Year Ended December 31, 19X1	Year Ended December 31, 19X0
Book value—beginning of year—at cost	$877,418	$851,580
Additions:		
Company contributions	66,231	68,750
Employee contributions	11,712	10,689
Income from investments	35,794	34,693
Net gain (loss) from disposal of assets	3,617	(27,648)
	117,354	86,484
Deductions:		
Benefit payments	71,634	59,908
Fees, asset transfers, etc.	2,253	738
Book value—end of year—at cost	$920,885	$877,418
Market value	$904,007	$973,453

The divestment of the domestic publication business provided for the assumption of the related pension liability by East Consolidated Industries, Inc., and the transfer of the proportionate share of pension fund assets.

Various pension arrangements, which are normally supplementary to required government plans, are in effect for most non-U.S. subsidiary companies.

Note 5—Income tax expense for financial reporting was reduced by investment tax credits of $12.9 million in 19X1 and $9.9 million in 19X0. In addition, investment tax credit of $4.7 million has been deferred at the end of 19X1 by International Credit Company and remains to be amortized.

Income Taxes (Dollar Amounts in Thousands)	Year Ended December 31, 19X1	Year Ended December 31, 19X0
Continuing operations:		
Currently payable:		
Federal	$45,918	$ 69,044
State	5,275	6,851
Non-U.S.	37,252	29,451
	88,445	105,346
Deferred:		
Federal	4,276	(39,693)
State	884	(4,175)
Non-U.S.	230	2,492
	5,390	(41,376)
Total income tax expense caused by continuing operations	93,835	63,970
Discontinued operations:		
Currently payable	(48,615)	(37,974)
Deferred	38,376	(39,347)
Total income tax expense caused by discontinued operations	(10,239)	(77,321)
Total income tax expense	$83,596	$(13,351)

Deferred tax expense results from timing differences in the recognition of revenue and expense for tax and financial statement purposes. The source of these differences for the years 19X1 and 19X0 and the tax effect of each follows:

Income Taxes Deferred (Dollar Amounts in Thousands)	Year Ended December 31, 19X1	Year Ended December 31, 19X0
Excess of tax over book depreciation	$21,312	$ 26,530
Difference between financial and tax reporting on long-term contracts in process	13,232	(40,988)
Provisions for warranties	(29,154)	(26,918)
	5,390	(41,376)
Losses recorded in prior years on discontinued operations currently deductible for tax purposes	38,376	(39,347)
Total	$43,766	$(80,723)

Deferred federal income taxes have not been provided on cumulative undistributed earnings of $275 million from certain subsidiaries which have been reinvested for an indefinite period.

The federal income tax returns of the Corporation and its wholly owned subsidiaries are settled through December 31, 1972, and it is believed that adequate provisions for taxes have been made through the current year, December 31, 19X1.

The reconciliation between the federal statutory tax rate and the International effective consolidated tax rate for 19X1 and 19X0 is as follows:

Effective Consolidated Tax Rate (Dollar Amounts in Thousands)	Year Ended Dec. 31, 19X1		Year Ended Dec. 31, 19X0	
	Amount	Effective Rate	Amount	Effective Rate
Tax expense if based on federal statutory tax rate applied to income before taxes of continuing operations	$131,957	48.0%	$ 98,961	48.0%
Increases (reductions) in taxes resulting from:				
Income of U.S. subsidiaries exempt from tax or subject to tax at reduced rates	(31,011)	(11.3)	(26,744)	(13.0)
Investment tax credit	(12,931)	(4.7)	(9,895)	(4.8)
State and local income taxes less reduction in federal income tax	3,203	1.1	1,392	.7
Miscellaneous items	2,617	1.0	256	.1
Total—continuing operations	93,835	34.1%	63,970	31.0%
Tax applicable to discontinued operations	(10,239)		(77,321)	
Income taxes (reduction)	$ 83,596		$(13,351)	

U.S. subsidiaries exempt from tax are U.S. possessions companies, and subsidiaries subject to reduced income tax rates include a Domestic International Sales Corporation (DISC) and a Western Hemisphere Trade Corporation.

Note 6—Research and development costs of $135 million were incurred in each of the years 19X1 and 19X0. The costs were expensed during their respective years of incurrence in accord with Statement of Financial Accounting Standards No. 2.

Note 7—Marketable securities at December 31 of $256.6 million in 19X1 and $38.9 million in 19X0 are recorded at cost, which is less than market value of $260 million on December 31, 19X1, and $40 million on December 31, 19X0.

Note 8—Customer receivables are net of allowances for uncollectible accounts of $15 million for 19X1 and $18 million for 19X0. A provision for estimated uncollectibles of $60 million was made during 19X1 and is subtracted from sales revenue in the income statement.

Note 9—Inventories

Inventories (Dollar Amounts in Thousands)	At December 31, 19X1	At December 31, 19X0
Inventories—valued principally on LIFO method	$1,159,280	$1,158,856
Recoverable engineering and development costs (government contracts)	67,562	56,017
Long-term contracts in process	1,171,225	961,230
Progress payments to subcontractors	502,166	468,617
	2,900,233	2,644,720
Less: Costs related to contracts with progress billing terms	1,859,662	1,571,757
Total	$1,040,571	$1,072,963

The replacement cost over the cost of inventories valued on the LIFO basis was approximately $370 million at December 31, 19X1 and $340 million at December 31, 19X0. During 19X1, some inventory quantities valued on the LIFO basis were reduced. This reduction resulted in a liquidation of LIFO inventory quantities carried at lower costs prevailing in prior years as compared with the cost of 19X1 purchases, the effect of which increased net income by approximately $10 million.

Note 10—Progress billings have increased due to the extension of progress payments to a wider range of products and work delayed at the request of customers. A contract-by-contract analysis of contracts with progress billing terms reflects an excess of progress billings over costs included in inventory as shown in the table that follows.

Costs of Uncompleted Contracts In Excess of Related Billings (Dollar Amounts in Thousands)	At December 31, 19X1	At December 31, 19X0
Costs included in inventory	$ 702,725	$ 694,579
Progress billings on contracts	530,252	497,374
Excess of costs	$ 172,473	$ 197,205

Billings on Uncompleted Contracts In Excess of Related Costs (Dollar Amounts in Thousands)	At December 31, 19X1	At December 31, 19X0
Progress billings on contracts	$1,896,417	$1,388,992
Costs included in inventory	1,156,937	877,178
Excess of progress billings	$ 739,480	$ 511,814

Costs included in inventory do not include certain costs expended on behalf of customers which are charged to income currently.

Note 11—Investments include International Credit Company and other significant unconsolidated affiliates, valued at cost plus equity in undistributed earnings since acquisition. Condensed financial statements of the Credit Company are shown on the next page.

International Corporation operations outside the United States contributed to consolidated totals approximately 21 percent of revenues and 16 percent of income from continuing operations in 19X1 and 20 percent of revenues and 27 percent of income from continuing operations in 19X0. These same operations represent approximately 22 percent of assets and 30 percent of liabilities in 19X1 and 23 percent of assets and 29 percent of liabilities in 19X0. In addition, the Corporation exports products to overseas customers. These sales contributed approximately 8 percent and 7 percent to revenues of 19X1 and 19X0, respectively.

International Credit Company
Condensed Consolidated Financial Statements
(Dollar Amounts in Thousands)

Balance Sheet	At December 31, 19X1	At December 31, 19X0
Cash	$ 20,779	$ 11,514
Receivables, less unearned finance charges and allowance for losses	1,110,138	1,123,769
Investments and other assets	13,029	38,572
Total assets	$1,143,946	$1,173,855
Short-term notes payable and other liabilities	$ 652,119	$ 670,049
Long-term senior debt	270,000	280,000
Subordinated debt	70,000	83,400
Total liabilities	992,119	1,033,449
Capital	59,500	59,500
Retained earnings	92,327	80,906
Total liabilities and stockholders' equity	$1,143,946	$1,173,855

Statement of Income	Year Ended December 31, 19X1	Year Ended December 31, 19X0
Total earned income	$ 141,683	$ 147,874
Less:		
Operating expense	34,339	31,711
Provision for losses on receivables	16,615	8,560
Interest	67,288	89,051
Income taxes	12,020	10,026
Net income	$ 11,421	$ 8,526

Statement of Changes in Financial Position	Year Ended December 31, 19X1	Year Ended December 31, 19X0
Financial resources provided by:		
Net income	$ 11,421	$ 8,526
Sale of investments	26,478	—
Increases in accrued interest, accounts payable and other liabilities	16,514	3,586
Increase (decrease) in long-term debt	(23,400)	111,600
Other—net	5,959	(1,717)
	$ 36,972	$ 121,995
Financial resources were used for:		
Increase (decrease) in receivables, net of unearned finance charges and provision for losses	$ (26,309)	$ 95,586
Receivables written off	12,678	6,807
Decrease in short-term notes payable	48,705	8,336
Increase in investments	1,898	11,266
	$ 36,972	$ 121,995

Note 12—Plant and Equipment

Plant and Equipment, at Cost (Dollar Amounts in Thousands)	At December 31, 19X1	At December 31, 19X0
Land and buildings	$ 753,803	$ 727,155
Machinery and equipment	1,660,559	1,563,651
Construction in progress	130,202	90,208
	2,544,564	2,381,014
Less: accumulated depreciation	1,163,884	1,082,438
Total	$1,380,680	$1,298,576

Note 13—Other assets include goodwill of $80 million in 19X1 and $88 million in 19X0. Goodwill acquired prior to November 1, 1970, is not being amortized. Goodwill of $14.2 million at December 31, 19X1, and $15.1 million at December 31, 19X0, resulting from business combinations subsequent to November 1, 1970, remained to be amortized over the estimated period to be benefited, not to exceed 40 years.

Note 14—Short-term loans amounted to $99 million on December 31, 19X1, and $187 million on December 31, 19X0. The maximum amounts of borrowings outstanding were $239 million in 19X1 and $566 million in 19X0. The average aggregate short-term borrowings outstanding during 19X1 totaled $203 million at a 10.7-percent approximate weighted-average interest rate.

Short-term credit arrangements include $65 million master notes under which the Corporation may borrow at the 180-day commercial paper rate, domestic bank lines of credit totaling $100 million at the prime commercial rate, and $277 million of credit available to subsidiaries, principally outside the United States, at the most favorable local rates. Of these lines, $309 million was unused at December 31, 19X1.

Note 15—Compensating balance arrangements without contractual withdrawal restrictions exist under the $100 million open bank lines of credit. Similar arrangements exist with banks that provide $55 million of credit lines for the International Credit Company. These arrangements provided for balances ranging from 10 to 25 percent of the line of credit to assure future credit availability and for loans outstanding. The average balance of corporate funds identified during the year for compensating balance purposes was not material.

Note 16—Debentures and Other Debt

Debentures and Other Debt (Dollar Amounts in Thousands)	Interest Rates	Year of Maturity	Amount At December 31, 19X1	At December 31, 19X0
Debentures	$3\frac{1}{2}$%	19Y3	$ 75,000	$ 90,000
Debentures	$5\frac{3}{8}$%	19Y8	145,193	160,000
Debentures	$8\frac{5}{8}$%	19Z1	71,372	100,000
Other Debt	Various	Various	318,677	493,123
Total			$610,242	$843,123

The $8\frac{5}{8}$ percent indenture requires sinking-fund deposits of $10 million annually beginning in 19X2. Sinking-fund deposits of $15 million annually until maturity and $8 million annually until maturity are being provided under the terms of the $3\frac{1}{2}$ percent and the $5\frac{3}{8}$ percent indentures, respectively.

Other debt includes the present value of capitalized lease obligations. See Note 19. Other debt also includes $142 million of borrowings outside the United States with an average rate of 7.6 percent and $13 million in notes convertible into the Corporation's common stock.

Long-term debt maturing in each of the following years is 19X2—$33 million; 19X3—$54 million; 19X4—$65 million; 19X5—$42 million; 19X6—$42 million.

Note 17—Stock Options

	19X1		19X0	
Stock Options	Shares	Average Price per Share	Shares	Average Price per Share
Outstanding at beginning of year	743,200	$22.37	593,806	$31.30
Granted	223,400	17.73	402,700	12.96
Exercised	(12,200)	13.00	—	—
Terminated	(359,800)	32.40	(253,306)	28.35
Outstanding at end of year	594,600	$14.75	743,200	$22.37
Exercisable at end of year	371,200	$12.95	340,500	$33.50

On April 24, 19X0, the stockholders of the Corporation approved the 19X0 Stock Option Plan, which provides for granting of options to purchase 1.2 million shares of common stock at a minimum of 100 percent of market value at the date of grant. The 19X0 Plan authorizes qualified stock options, nonqualified stock options, or combinations of both. The terms of the options are substantially the same except that nonqualified options for terms up to 10 years may be granted. The Plan provides for a limit on options granted to any one employee of 50,000 shares; the options may not be exercised for one year after the date of grant, and the period during which options may be granted expires on March 31, 19X5.

Note 18—International Corporation
Consolidated Statement of Contributed Capital

Consolidated Statement of Contributed Capital (Dollar Amounts in Thousands)	Cumulative Preferred Stock	Common Stock	Capital In Excess of Par Value	Treasury Stock at Cost
Balance at January 1, 19X0	$30,482	$277,108	$491,856	$(24,223)
3,106,300 shares acquired for treasury				(39,442)
1,863,140 treasury shares delivered under employee stock and savings and investment plans			(10,813)	5,880
18,500 treasury shares issued for a business acquired				345
Other—net			(147)	469
Balance at December 31, 19X0	30,482	277,108	480,896	(26,971)

Consolidated Statement of Contributed Capital (Dollar Amounts in Thousands)	Cumulative Preferred Stock	Common Stock	Capital In Excess of Par Value	Treasury Stock at Cost
138,892 shares of Cumulative Preferred Stock purchased for cancellation	(13,889)		6,945	
1,029,100 shares acquired for treasury				(14,242)
1,400,993 treasury shares delivered under stock option, employee stock and savings and investment plans			3,122	15,621
Other—net			(266)	545
Balance at December 31, 19X1	$16,593	$277,108	$490,697	$(25,047)

Cumulative preferred stock, par value $100, authorized 235,954 shares at December 31, 19X1, and 374,846 shares at December 31, 19X0; 3.80 percent Series B, issued and outstanding 165,928 shares at December 31, 19X1, and 304,820 shares at December 31, 19X0.

Common stock, par value $3.125; authorized 120,000,000 shares at December 31, 19X1 and 19X0; issued (including treasury shares) 88,674,610 shares at December 31, 19X1 and 19X0.

Common stock held in treasury amounted to 1,596,722 shares at December 31, 19X1, and 2,008,717 shares at December 31, 19X0.

Treasury shares are used to supply stock for the various plans under which common stock is distributed to employees.

Note 19—Lease payments for rentals under noncancelable capital leases amounted to $66 million in 19X1 and $60 million in 19X0. Minimum annual lease payments, primarily for rentals of land, buildings, and computers, under noncancelable leases having an original term of more than 1 year are $47 million in 19X2, $37 million in 19X3, $33 million in 19X4, $29 million in 19X5, and $16 million in 19X6. The average minimum annual rentals for the next three succeeding 5-year periods after 19X6 are $11 million for the first 5 years, $5 million in the second 5 years, and $1 million in the third 5 years. The total rentals for years ending after that is approximately $4 million.

Capital leases have been recorded as long-term debt included with "Debentures and other debt" and the related property rights amortized under the straight-line method. The present value of these capital leases (7 percent weighted-average interest rate) on December 31, 19X1, is $350 million and was $360 million on December 31, 19X0.

Note 20—Contingent Liabilities: At December 31, 19X1, the Corporation was guarantor of customers' notes sold to bank and other liabilities aggregating $232 million.

There are various claims and pending actions against International Corporation and its subsidiaries in respect of commercial matters, including warranties and product liability, governmental regulations including environmental and safety matters, civil rights, patent matters, taxes and other matters arising out of the conduct of the business. Certain of these actions purport to be class actions, seeking damages in very large amounts. The amounts of liability on these claims and actions at December 31, 19X1, were not determinable but, in the opinion of the management, the ultimate liability resulting will not materially affect the consolidated financial position or results of operations of International Corporation and its consolidated subsidiaries.

Note 21—Presented below is selected financial information about the major segments of International Corporation. The segment amounts are reconciled to the amounts shown in the consolidated statements.
(Dollar Amounts in Thousands)

19X0	Power Systems	Industry Products	Broadcasting	Adjustments and Eliminations	Consolidated
Sales to unaffiliated customers...	$2,046,980	$2,240,670	$1,510,863	—	$5,798,513
Intersegment sales	94,630	92,747	—	$(187,377)	—
Total segment revenues	$2,141,610	$2,333,417	$1,510,863	$(187,377)	$5,798,513
Operating profit	$ 131,329	$ 140,005	$ 69,572	$ (17,673)	$ 323,233
Equity in net loss of nonconsolidated subsidiaries and affiliated companies					(32,285)
Central corporate revenues					71,890
Central corporate expenses					(48,670)
Interest expense					(111,261)
Income tax expense					(63,970)
Loss from discontinued operations ...					(110,805)
Net income					$28,132
Identifiable assets at December 31, 19X0	$1,463,220	$1,367,426	$981,977	$(68,430)	$3,744,193
Investment in net assets of unconsolidated and affiliated companies					226,209
Corporate assets					843,216
Total assets					$4,813,618

19X1	Power Systems	Industry Products	Broadcasting	Adjustments and Eliminations	Consolidated
Sales to unaffiliated customers...	$2,194,237	$2,286,871	$1,381,639	—	$5,862,747
Intersegment sales	98,465	97,775	—	$(196,240)	—
Total segment revenues	$2,292,702	$2,384,646	$1,381,639	$(196,240)	$5,862,747
Operating profit	$ 140,430	$ 159,473	$ 56,430	$ (18,420)	$ 337,913
Equity in net income of nonconsolidated subsidiaries and affiliated companies					14,513
Central corporate revenues					51,348
Central corporate expenses					(54,890)
Interest expense					(76,425)
Income tax expense					(93,835)
Loss from discontinued operations ...					(13,400)
Net income					$ 165,224
Identifiable assets at December 31, 19X1	$1,469,862	$1,369,433	$947,833	$ (66,460)	$3,720,668
Investment in net assets of unconsolidated and affiliated companies					289,188
Corporate assets					856,430
Total assets					$4,866,286

The amounts shown for segment revenues, operating profit, and assets can be reclassified in terms of geographical location as follows:
(Dollar Amounts in Thousands)

19X0	Domestic	Foreign	Adjustments and Eliminations	Consolidated
Sales to unaffiliated customers	$3,643,985	$2,154,528	—	$5,798,513
Intersegment sales	78,940	47,490	$(126,430)	—
Total segment revenues	$3,722,925	$2,202,018	$(126,430)	$5,798,513
Operating profit.............................	$ 160,748	$ 176,160	$ (13,675)	$ 323,233
Identifiable assets on December 31, 19X0	$2,146,340	$1,640,293	$ (42,440)	$3,744,193

19X1	Domestic	Foreign	Adjustments and Eliminations	Consolidated
Sales to unaffiliated customers	$3,655,460	$2,207,287	—	$5,862,747
Intersegment sales	84,870	53,605	$(138,475)	—
Total segment revenues	$3,740,330	$2,260,892	$(138,475)	$5,862,747
Operating profit.............................	$ 156,185	$ 195,288	$ (14,560)	$ 337,913
Identifiable assets on December 31, 19X1	$2,076,344	$1,685,094	$ (40,770)	$3,720,668

Intersegment sales prices (called transfer prices) are based on external market prices for similar goods. Expenses deducted in determining segment operating profit include direct segment expenses plus indirect expenses that can be assigned, or allocated, on a reasonable basis. Central corporate expenses, interest expense, and income tax expense are not subtracted in determining segment operating profit.

Note 22—(Unaudited) Presented below is selected quarterly financial information for 19X0 and 19X1. These quarterly data are subject to limited review by independent public accountants.

(Dollar Amounts in Thousands)	First	Second	Quarter Third	Fourth	Total Year
Sales:					
19X0	$1,320,142	$1,433,246	$1,470,623	$1,574,502	$5,798,513
19X1	1,323,180	1,434,802	1,446,340	1,658,425	5,862,747
Earnings:					
Continuing operations,					
19X0	29,203	32,743	42,478	34,513	138,937
19X1	33,043	41,580	50,012	53,989	178,624
Discontinued operations,					
19X0	—	—	—	(110,805)	(110,805)
19X1	—	—	(13,400)	—	(13,400)
Net income					
19X0	29,203	32,743	42,478	(76,292)	28,132
19X1	33,043	41,580	36,612	53,989	165,224

(Dollar Amounts in Thousands)	First	Second	Third	Fourth	Total Year
			Quarter		
Earnings per common share:					
Continuing operations,					
19X0	$0.33	$0.37	$0.48	$0.39	$1.57
19X1	.38	.47	.57	.62	2.04
Discontinued operations,					
19X0	—	—	—	(1.26)	(1.26)
19X1	—	—	(.15)	—	(.15)
Net income,					
19X0	.33	.37	.48	(.87)	.31
19X1	.38	.47	.42	.62	1.89
Dividends per common share:					
19X0	$0.243	$0.243	$0.243	$0.243	$0.972
19X1	.243	.243	.243	.243	.972
Common stock prices per share:					
19X0—High	$15	$26	$18\frac{3}{4}$	$13\frac{5}{8}$	$26
Low	$11\frac{1}{2}$	$12\frac{7}{8}$	$9\frac{7}{8}$	8	8
19X1—High	$15\frac{1}{2}$	$19\frac{1}{4}$	20	$14\frac{1}{8}$	20
Low	$9\frac{3}{4}$	$13\frac{1}{4}$	$12\frac{7}{8}$	$10\frac{3}{4}$	$9\frac{3}{4}$

Note 23—Replacement Cost Data (Unaudited): The Corporation's Annual Report to the Securities and Exchange Commission on Form 10-K for the year ended December 31, 19X1, contains estimated replacement costs for inventories, property and equipment, properties leased under capital leases, and the effect of these costs on cost of goods sold and depreciation expenses.

These data indicate that replacement costs of inventories, property and equipment, and leased properties as of December 31, 19X1, are substantially larger than historical-cost amounts reported in the accompanying consolidated financial statements. Since the Corporation uses the LIFO cost-flow assumption for most of its inventories, the replacement cost of goods sold is not substantially different from the historical cost of goods sold. Depreciation and amortization expenses calculated on a replacement-cost basis is larger than historical amounts.

Shareholders who wish to obtain the replacement-cost data should request a copy of the Form 10-K from the Office of Shareholder Relations of the Corporation.

Report of Independent Accountants

To the Board of Directors and Stockholders of
International Corporation

We have examined the statement of financial position of International Corporation and consolidated subsidiaries as of December 31, 19X0 and 19X1, and the related statements of current and retained earnings and changes in financial position for the years then ended. Our examination was made in accordance with generally accepted auditing standards, and accordingly included such tests of the accounting records and such other auditing procedures as we considered necessary in the circumstances.

In our opinion, the aforementioned financial statements present fairly the financial position of International Corporation and consolidated subsidiaries at December 31, 19X0 and 19X1, and the results of their operations and the changes in their financial position for the years then ended, in conformity with generally accepted accounting principles applied on a consistent basis.

Stuckey Wells & Co.

5836 South Greenwood Avenue
Chicago, Illinois 60637

February 11, 19X2

AUTHORS' COMMENTS

Note 1: Summary of Significant Accounting Policies

The first note to published financial statements is the "Summary of Significant Accounting Policies" as required by APB *Opinion No. 22* (1972). The requirement and purposes of this summary are described in Chapter 13, starting on page 517.

Consolidation Policies   The consolidation policy of International Corporation (IC), an industrial company, is fairly standard—all majority-owned subsidiaries are consolidated except for those engaged in financial operations and real estate development. The equity method is used for the nonconsolidated affiliates. The issues involved in deciding whether or not to consolidate are discussed in Chapter 12, starting on page 462. Our own view is that financial statements are more useful if all majority-owned companies are consolidated, but the presentation in Note 11 of Exhibit A.4 allows us to make the required adjustment for the major subsidiary reported on the equity method.

Revenue Recognition   IC uses the completed-sales method in recognizing revenue and the completed-contract method for long-term construction contracts, except for certain contracts extending over 5 years or more, where the percentage-of-completion method is used.

Cost-Flow Assumption for Inventories   IC uses a LIFO cost-flow assumption for inventories, choosing to report lower income and to reduce current income taxes payable in times of rising prices. See Note 9 below.

Pensions   See our Note 4 below.

Depreciation   Most industrial companies use the straight-line depreciation method for financial statements and accelerated methods for tax reporting. This leads to the accounting for deferred income taxes, discussed below in Note 5.

Deferred Income Taxes   APB *Opinion No. 11* (1967) requires an adjustment of income tax expense for differences between financial income and taxable income that are viewed as temporary. See Note 5 below. Income reported in the consolidated income statement earned by subsidiaries that do not plan to declare dividends in the indefinite future is not currently taxable to the parent, and this difference between financial and taxable income is treated as if permanent. Thus, no deferred taxes need be provided for this income.

Investment Credit   The investment credit provides a reduction in income taxes otherwise payable when a company purchases qualifying long-term assets. The accounting possibilities of this benefit are discussed in Chapter 9, starting on page 341. IC uses the flow-through method (increasing current income over what it would be if the deferral method were used) for its investment credits, whereas its nonconsolidated subsidiary uses the deferral method.

Note 2: Discontinued Operations

APB *Opinion No. 30* (1973) requires that the effects on income from segments that have been discontinued (or are expected to be discontinued) be reported separately in the financial statements. See the discussion in Chapter 3 on page 83.

Note 3: Operations of Nonconsolidated Subsidiaries

IC uses the equity method for two nonconsolidated subsidiaries. The effects on income for both of these subsidiaries are shown on one line in the income statement. The note provides more information on the operations of one subsidiary, Suburban Development Corporation, which engages in real estate development.

Note 4: Pensions

APB *Opinion No. 8* (1966) and the SEC require disclosures of current expense for pension plans and the present value of current commitments made to employees for retirement plans. The funds that IC has contributed to pay the pensions are in a separate pension trust. The changes in the amounts in that trust fund are shown in a separate schedule reported by IC. These pension assets are not included in the consolidated balance sheet totals.

Note 5: Income Taxes

The first schedule in IC's Note 5 starts with the amount of income taxes currently payable because of continuing operations. Next are the amounts of currently reported income tax expense for which no taxes are currently payable. These deferred taxes are caused by differences viewed as temporary between pretax income reported on the financial statements and pretax income reported on the tax return. Finally, as required by APB *Opinion No. 30,* the schedule shows separately the income tax effects of discontinued operations. The bottom line of this first schedule shows the total income tax expense reported in the income statement, Exhibit A.1. Notice that in 19X0, IC showed a loss from discontinued operations on the financial statements and negative income tax expense. On the tax returns, however, the pretax income from both continuing and discontinued operations was positive and there was $105.3 million of income taxes payable that year.

The second schedule in IC's Note 5, showing the causes of the various deferred tax items, is required by the SEC. First, depreciation claimed on the tax return because of the use of accelerated methods exceeded the amount of depreciation charges on the income statement where the straight-line method is used. If the marginal tax rate is 48 percent, then the excess of tax over financial statement depreciation in 19X1 must have been $21,312,000/.48 = $44,400,000. Even though 19X0 taxes payable were larger than tax expense because of reversals of total timing differences, the net effect of accelerated depreciation on the tax return was to reduce taxes currently payable by $21.3 million.

The next timing difference originates in the method of revenue recognition. IC uses the percentage-of-completion method for some contracts in its financial statements, but, attempting to minimize the present value of its tax burden, uses the completed-contract method on the tax return. In 19X1, the financial statements report larger revenues on these long-term contracts than does the tax return. In 19X0, the situation was just the opposite.

The expected costs of warranties is deducted from income on the financial statements in the year the product is sold, but for tax purposes the cost of warranties is a deduction only when actual repairs or replacements are made. Thus from warranties alone, financial statement income is less than taxable income. This is viewed as a timing difference leading to prepaid income taxes, an asset.

The third schedule in Note 5, like the second, is required by the SEC. This schedule helps us understand why it is that a company with a marginal tax rate of 48 percent (the legal rate) usually reports income tax expense different from 48 percent, between 30 and 35 percent in the case of IC. Most of the difference arises because of permanent differences—financial statement revenue never subject to tax, such as foreign income exempt from taxes, or taxed at lower rates, such as corporate dividends received. See the discussion in Chapter 10, starting on page 390.

International Corporation is not unusual in having unsettled tax returns outstanding for almost a decade, since 1972. The Internal Revenue Service typically takes over 10 years to settle with U.S. Steel about its annual tax return.

Note 6: Research and Development

FASB *Statement of Financial Accounting Standards No. 2* (1974) requires the expensing of all costs for research and development except those that are contractually reimbursable. It is clear that companies would not engage in R&D projects year after year unless they expected some future benefits from the R&D. If there are future benefits, then we conclude that they should be reported as assets on the balance sheet. The FASB does not agree. See the discussion in Chapter 9, starting on page 344.

Note 7: Marketable Securities

Statement of Financial Accounting Standards No. 12 (1975) requires that marketable equity securities be shown at the lower of cost or market and that the portfolios of such securities classified as a current asset be accounted for separately, and in a different way, from the portfolio of such securities classified as a noncurrent asset. Chapter 7 discusses some of the details. IC classifies all its securities as current assets and the market value at the two year-ends is immaterially different from cost, so the disclosure is relatively simple.

Note 8: Customer Receivables

APB *Opinion No. 10* (1966) and FASB *Statement of Financial Accounting Standards No. 5* (1975) effectively require companies to use the allowance method, rather than the direct write-off method, of accounting for the effects of receivables that are expected to be uncollectible. This note discloses the estimated uncollectible amounts subtracted from gross customer receivables in arriving at the net balance sheet amount.

Note 9: Inventories

The SEC requires that companies using a LIFO cost-flow assumption report in notes to the financial statements the current value of beginning and ending inventories. Under LIFO, earliest purchases, usually made at lower prices, remain in balance sheet inventory amounts. (Last-in, first-out for goods sold means the same thing as first-in, still-here for ending inventory; LIFO = FISH.) The discussion in Chapter 8, starting on page 292, illustrates how to calculate the approximate effects on income of IC's using the LIFO cost-flow assumption rather than FIFO. Pretax income would have been about \$30 (= \$370 − \$340) million larger had IC used a FIFO flow assumption. The Internal Revenue Service will not allow taxpayers using LIFO to report the hypothetical effect on income of using FIFO, but the SEC requires disclosure sufficient for us to be able to calculate it. Exhibit 8.3, page 293, illustrates the difference between LIFO and FIFO assumptions on reported income.

Note 10: Costs and Billings of Uncompleted Contracts

As Note 1 indicates, IC uses the completed-contract method of revenue recognition for many long-term contracts. (The indication comes from the statement that the percentage-of-completion method is used *only* for certain contracts.) The information given here relates to contracts accounted for on the completed-contract method. The intricacies of that method are beyond the scope of this text, but a brief discussion follows.

As assets are put into production on a long-term contract and liabilities (such as for wages) are incurred, the following journal entry is made:

Temporary Account A (or Construction in Process)   X
    Assets Used or Liabilities Incurred   X
To record work on contract.

As payments are due to be made to the company according to the terms of the contract, but before the contract is completed, the following entry is made:

Accounts Receivable . . . .   Y
    Temporary Account A (or Progress Billings) . . . .   Y
To record amount due from customers.

At the end of the period, Temporary Account A will have a debit balance if X is greater than Y or a credit balance if Y is greater than X. If there is a debit balance, then the balance $X - Y$ is reported as an asset, Excess of Costs (over progress billings for uncompleted contracts). If the progress billings exceed the costs incurred, then the credit balance in Temporary Account A is $Y - X$ and is reported as a current liability with the title Excess of Progress Billings (over related costs for uncompleted contracts).

The contracts with debit balances in Temporary Account A must be reported separately from those with credit balances in accordance with *Accounting Research Bulletin No. 45* (1955). Since IC has some contracts with billings in excess of costs and others with costs in excess of billings, both the liability and the asset are shown in the balance sheet.

Note 11: Investments in Nonconsolidated Subsidiaries

The operations of the International Credit Company are sufficiently different in nature from those of IC that IC chooses not to consolidate but to use the equity method of accounting for this subsidiary. See the discussion in Chapter 12, starting on page 462.

Condensed financial statements for the Credit Company are shown in IC's Note 11 (Exhibit A.4). If the Credit Company were consolidated, then all the assets, $1,144 million at the end of 19X1, would be added in with IC's assets and all of the liabilities, $992 million, would be added in with IC's liabilities. IC's consolidated balance sheet would be kept in balance by reducing the Investment account ($289.2 million shown in Exhibit A.2) by the current carrying amount of the investment in the Credit Company, $152 (= $1,144 − $992) million. Thus balance sheet asset and liability totals would both increase by $992 million. IC's consolidated net income would not be affected, but certain important ratios, such as the all-capital earnings rate and the debt-equity ratio, would be reduced.

For a discussion of the effects of the equity method on the statement of changes in financial position, Exhibit A.3, see Chapter 12, page 459.

Note 12: Plant and Equipment

The schedule shown in IC's Note 12 gives details of plant and equipment accounts that might otherwise appear on the balance sheet. Construction in Progress is plant and equipment that is being added by IC, but that is not yet complete and functioning.

Note 13: Goodwill from Business Combinations and Subsidiaries

APB *Opinion No. 17* (1970) requires that goodwill acquired (the excess of cost of a purchased subsidiary over the fair value of the net assets acquired) after October 31, 1970, must be amortized over a period not to exceed 40 years. See the discussion in Chapter 12, starting on page 477. Goodwill acquired before November 1, 1970, need not be amortized.

IC does not own 100 percent of all of its consolidated subsidiaries. This we can determine from the existence of the account, Minority Interest, on IC's consolidated balance sheet and the deduction for minority interest in net income of consolidated subsidiaries on IC's income statement. See Chapter 12, page 466, for a discussion of the minority interest.

Notes 14, 15, and 16: Debt Financing

The three notes on borrowings enable the reader to assess the maturity structure of the outstanding debt and the components of current interest expense. Note 14 presents short-term debt; Note 15, required by the SEC, presents information concerning compensating balances; Note 16 presents intermediate-term debt maturities and long-term debt obligations. Compensating balances (see the Glossary) are sometimes required by lending banks. The effect of a required compensating balance is to increase the effective interest rate. The SEC deems it important that financial statement readers be able to approximate the true interest rate on borrowings, not just the quoted rate, and thus requires this disclosure.

Note 17: Stock Option Plans

Accounting Research Bulletin No. 43 (1953) requires the disclosure of the details of stock option plans and of the currently outstanding options. At the end of 19X1, the market price of a share of IC common stock was about $20.00. The average price of the 371,200 options exercisable at the end of 19X1 was about $13.00. Thus, if all the options were exercised, the present owners' equity would be diluted approximately $2.6 million [= ($20 − $13) × 371,200 shares] in comparison to the issue of new shares at the current market price.

Note 18: Owners' Capital Accounts

APB *Opinion No. 12* (1966) requires the disclosure of all changes in owners' equity accounts. IC shows the sources of the changes in the retained earnings account in a statement just below the income statement, Exhibit A.1. The schedule shown in Note 18 shows the sources of the changes in the other owners' equity accounts.

Note 19: Leases

Chapter 10, starting on page 384, explains the issues in accounting for long-term noncancelable leases. The first paragraph of IC's Note 19 includes the disclosure on payment commitments that is required by APB *Opinion No. 31* (1973).

Note 20: Contingent Liabilities

Contingent liabilities, in contrast with estimated liabilities (see Glossary), are not shown in the financial statements according to FASB *Statement of Financial Accounting Standards No. 5* (1975). The causes of uncertainty and the possibility of future losses should be disclosed in the notes, as IC does in Note 20.

Note 21: Segment Report

FASB *Statement of Financial Accounting Standards No. 14* requires the disclosure of revenue, operating profit, and identifiable assets for major segments of a firm. International Corporation uses both industry and geographical location (domestic versus foreign) as the bases for identifying segments. Note the types of items that reconcile the sum of segment operating profit with consolidated net income.

Note 22: Interim Reporting

These quarterly disclosures are required by SEC *Accounting Series Release No. 177*. Note that sales do not show a particularly strong seasonal pattern but quarterly net income varies significantly during the year. The information in the note is not audited.

Note 23: Replacement-Cost Disclosures

SEC *Accounting Series Release No. 190* requires mention of replacement-cost disclosures. Most companies merely refer to them in the annual report and include the details only in their Form 10-K (filed with the SEC).

Report of Independent Accountants

The auditor's report attached by the accounting firm of Stuckey Wells & Co. is an unqualified ("clean") opinion. A qualified opinion would be shown if, for example, the company changed accounting principles during the year, such as from FIFO to LIFO (an "except for" qualification as to consistency).

QUESTIONS AND PROBLEMS

1 Review the meaning of the following concepts or terms discussed in the Appendix.
  a Consolidated financial statements.
  b Discontinued operations.

c Deferred income tax debit.
d LIFO = FISH.
e Progress billings.
f Excess of costs over progress billings for uncompleted contracts.
g Excess of progress billings over related costs for uncompleted contracts.
h Compensating balance.
i Qualified opinion.

2 Assume that all sales of International Corporation for the year 19X1 were made on account. How much cash was collected from customers?

3 What dividends were declared during 19X1 by IC's nonconsolidated subsidiaries accounted for with the equity method?

4 Assuming a marginal tax rate of 48 percent, by what amount did the depreciation charge claimed on the tax return for 19X0 differ from the depreciation expense reported on the financial statements for 19X0?

5 Assuming a marginal tax rate of 48 percent, by what amount did revenues from long-term contracts in process reported on the income statement differ from the amount reported on the tax return for 19X1?

6 IC's research and development costs have averaged $135 million per year for the past 10 years and have been expensed as incurred. How would the financial statements at December 31, 19X1, differ if those costs had instead been capitalized and amortized over a 5-year period using the straight-line method? Ignore income tax effects.

7 What would be the effect on pretax income for 19X1 if IC's marketable securities had a market value of $240 million on December 31, 19X1?

8 Refer to IC's Note 9. Explain why the decline in inventory quantities during 19X1 caused income to increase.

9 Compute both the all-capital earnings rate for IC during 19X1 and the debt-equity ratio on December 31, 19X1, using the year-end balance sheet totals assuming:
a The financial statements as shown in Exhibit A.1–A.4.
b The International Credit Company had been consolidated, rather than accounted for with the equity method. (Assume that IC organized the Credit Company and has been its sole owner since organization, so that the book values shown for the Credit Company are those properly carried by IC in its investment account.)

10 If IC borrowed $100 million from its banks at a rate of 8 percent per year, but was required to maintain a compensating balance of 20 percent, how much was IC actually able to borrow and at what rate?

APPENDIX B
COMPOUND INTEREST CONCEPTS AND APPLICATIONS

Money is a scarce resource, which its owner can use to command other resources. Like owners of other scarce resources, owners of money can permit others (borrowers) to rent the use of their money for a period of time. Payment for the use of money differs little from other rental payments, such as those made to a landlord for the use of property or to a car rental agency for the use of a car. Payment for the use of money is called *interest*. Accounting is concerned with interest because it must record transactions where the use of money is bought and sold.

Accountants and managers are concerned with interest calculations for another, equally important, reason. Expenditures for an asset most often do not occur at the same time as the receipts for services produced by that asset. Money received sooner is more valuable than money received later. The difference in timing can affect whether or not acquiring an asset is profitable. Amounts of money received at different times are different commodities. Managers use interest calculations to make amounts of money to be paid or received at different times comparable. For example, an analyst might compare two amounts to be received at two different times by using interest calculations to find the equivalent value of one amount at the time the other is due.

Contracts involving a series of money payments over time, such as bonds, mortgages, notes, and leases, are evaluated by finding the *present value* of the stream of payments. The present value of a stream of payments is a single amount of money at the present time that is the economic equivalent of the entire stream.

COMPOUND INTEREST CONCEPTS

The quotation of interest "cost" is typically specified as a percentage of the amount borrowed per unit of time. Examples are 6 percent per year and 1 percent per month. Another example occurs in the context of discounts on purchases. The terms of sale "2/10, net/30" is equivalent to 2 percent for 20 days because if the discount is not taken, payment can be delayed and the money can be used for up to an extra 20 (= 30 − 10) days.

The amount borrowed or loaned is called the *principal*. To *compound* interest means that the amount of interest earned during a period is added to the principal and the principal for the next interest period is larger.

For example, if you deposit $1,000 in a savings account that pays compound interest at the rate of 6 percent per year, you will earn $60 by the end of 1 year. If you do not withdraw the $60, then $1,060 will be earning interest during the second year. During the second year your principal of $1,060 will earn $63.60 interest, $60 on the initial deposit of $1,000 and $3.60 on the $60 earned the first year. By the end of the second year, you will have $1,123.60.

When only the original principal earns interest during the entire life of the loan, the interest due at the time the loan is repaid is called *simple* interest. Simple interest is computed as the principal multiplied by the rate multiplied by the elapsed time. In the example where you deposited $1,000 in the bank at 6 percent interest, "simple interest" would require that you leave the $60 on deposit during the second period. Interest earnings for the second period are computed only on the original $1,000. Ordinarily, the use of simple interest calculations arises in a slightly different way. If you borrow $10,000 at a rate of 12 percent per year, but compute interest for any month as $100 (= $10,000 × .12 × $\frac{1}{12}$), then you are using a simple interest calculation.

The "force," or effect of compound interest is more substantial than many people realize. For example, compounded annually at 6 percent, money "doubles itself" in less than 12 years. Put another way, if you invest $49.70 in a savings account that pays 6 percent compounded annually, you will have $100 in 12 years. If the Indians who sold Manhattan Island for $24 in May 1626 had been able to invest that principal at 8 percent compounded annually, the principal would have grown to $16 *trillion* by May 1980, 354 years later. The rate of interest affects the amount of accumulation more than you might expect. If the investment earned 6 percent rather than 8 percent, the $24 would have grown to $22 *billion* in 354 years; if the rate were 4 percent, the $24 would have grown to a mere $26 *million*.

At simple interest of 6 percent per year, the Indians' $24 would have grown to only $534 in 354 years, $24 of principal and $510 of simple interest (= $24 × .06 × 354). Nearly all economic calculations involve compound interest.

Problems involving compound interest generally fall into two groups with respect to time: First, there are the problems for which we want to know the future value of money invested or loaned today; second, there are the problems for which we want to know the present value, or today's value, of money to be received or paid at later dates.

FUTURE VALUE

When $1.00 is invested today at 6 percent compounded annually, it will grow to $1.06000 at the end of 1 year, $1.12360 at the end of 2 years, $1.19102 at the end of 3 years, and so on according to the formula

$$F_n = P(1 + r)^n$$

where

F_n represents the accumulation or future value,
P represents the one-time investment today,
r is the interest rate per period, and
n is the number of periods from today.

The amount F_n is the future value of the present payment, P, compounded at r percent per period for n periods. Table 1, on page 624, shows the future values of $P = \$1$ for various numbers of periods and for various interest rates. Extracts from that table are shown here in Table B.1.

TABLE B.1
(Excerpt from Table 1)
Future Value of $1 at 6 Percent and 8 Percent per Period
$F_n = (1 + r)^n$

Number of Periods = n	Rate = r	
	6%	8%
1	1.06000	1.08000
2	1.12360	1.16640
3	1.19102	1.25971
10	1.79085	2.15892
20	3.20714	4.66096

Example Problems in Determining Future Value

Example 1 How much will $1,000 deposited today at 6 percent compounded annually be worth 10 years from now?

One dollar deposited today at 6 percent will grow to $1.79085; therefore $1,000 will grow to $1,000$(1.06)^{10}$ = $1,000 \times 1.79085 = $1,790.85.

Example 2 Macaulay Corporation deposits $10,000 in an expansion fund today. The fund will earn 8 percent per year. How much will the $10,000 grow to in 20 years if the entire fund and all interest earned on it is left on deposit in the fund?

One dollar deposited today at 8 percent will grow to $2.15892 in 20 years. Therefore, $10,000 will grow to $21,589 (= $10,000 \times 2.15892) in 20 years.

PRESENT VALUE

The preceding section developed the tools for computing the future value, F_n, of a sum of money, P, deposited or invested today. P is known; F_n is calculated. This section deals with the problems of calculating how much principal, P, has to be invested today in order to have a specified amount, F_n, at the end of n periods. The future amount, F_n, the interest rate, r, and the number of periods, n, are known; P is to be found. In order to have \$1 one year from today when interest is earned at 6 percent, P of \$.94340 must be invested today. That is, $F_1 = P(1.06)^1$ or \$1 = \$.94340 × 1.06. Because $F_n = P(1 + r)^n$, dividing both sides of the equation by $(1 + r)^n$ yields

$$\frac{F_n}{(1 + r)^n} = P$$

or

$$P = \frac{F_n}{(1 + r)^n} = F_n(1 + r)^{-n}.$$

Present-Value Terminology

The number $(1 + r)^{-n}$ is the present value of \$1 to be received after n periods when interest is earned at r percent per period. The term *discount* is used in this context as follows: The *discounted* present value of \$1 to be received n periods in the future is $(1 + r)^{-n}$ when the *discount* rate is r percent per period for n periods. The number r is the discount *rate* and the number $(1 + r)^{-n}$ is the discount *factor* for n periods. A discount factor $(1 + r)^{-n}$ is merely the reciprocal, or inverse, of a number, $(1 + r)^n$, in Table B.1. Therefore, tables of discount factors are not necessary for present-value calculations if tables of future values are at hand. But present-value calculations are so frequently needed, and division is so onerous, that tables of discount factors are as widely available as tables of future values. Portions of Table 2 (on page 625), which shows discount factors or, equivalently, present values of \$1 for various interest (or discount) rates for various numbers of periods, are shown in Table B.2.

TABLE B.2
(Excerpt from Table 2)
Present Value of \$1 at 6 Percent
and 8 Percent per Period
$P = F_n(1 + r)^{-n}$

Number of Periods = n	Rate = r	
	6%	8%
1	.94340	.92593
2	.89000	.85734
3	.83962	.79383
10	.55839	.46319
20	.31180	.21455

Example Problems in Determining Present Values

Example 3   What is the present value of $1 due 10 years from now if the interest (equivalently, the discount) rate r is 6 percent per year?

From Table B.2, 6-percent column, 10-period row, the present value of $1 to be received 10 periods hence at 6 percent is $.55839.

Example 4   (This example is used in Chapter 10 on page 382.) You issue a non-interest-bearing note that promises to pay $13,500 3 years from today in exchange for undeveloped land. How much is that promise worth today if the discount rate is 8 percent per period?

One dollar received 3 years hence discounted at 8 percent has a present value of $.79383. Thus, the promise is worth $13,500 × .79383 = $10,717.

CHANGING THE COMPOUNDING PERIOD: NOMINAL AND EFFECTIVE RATES

"Twelve percent, compounded annually" is the price for a loan; this means that interest is added to or *converted* into principal once a year at the rate of 12 percent. Often, however, the price for a loan states that compounding is to take place more than once a year. A savings bank may advertise that it pays 6 percent, compounded quarterly. This means that at the end of each quarter the bank credits savings accounts with interest calculated at the rate 1.5 percent (= 6 percent/4). The interest payment can be withdrawn or left on deposit to earn more interest.

If $10,000 is invested today at 12 percent compounded annually, its future value 1 year later is $11,200. If the rate of interest is stated as 12 percent compounded semi-annually, then 6 percent interest is added to the principal every 6 months. At the end of the first 6 months, $10,000 will have grown to $10,600, so that the accumulation will be $10,600 × 1.06 = $11,236 by the end of the year. Notice that 12 percent compounded *semiannually* is equivalent to 12.36 percent compounded *annually*.

Suppose that the price is quoted as 12 percent, compounded quarterly. Then an additional 3 percent of the principal will be added to, or converted into, principal every 3 months. By the end of the year, $10,000 will grow to $10,000 × $(1.03)^4$ = $10,000 × 1.12551 = $11,255. Twelve percent compounded quarterly is equivalent to 12.55 percent compounded annually. If 12 percent is compounded monthly, then $1 will grow to $1 × $(1.01)^{12}$ = $1.12683 and $10,000 will grow to $11,268. Thus, 12 percent compounded monthly is equivalent to 12.68 percent compounded annually.

For a given *nominal* rate, such as the 12 percent in the examples above, the more often interest is compounded or converted into principal, the higher the *effective* rate of interest paid. If a nominal rate, r, is compounded m times per year, then the effective rate is $(1 + r/m)^m - 1$.

In practice, to solve problems that require computation of interest quoted at a nominal rate of r percent per period compounded m times per period for n periods, merely use the tables for rate r/m and $m \times n$ periods. For example, 12 percent compounded quarterly for 7 years is equivalent to the rate found in the interest tables for $r = 12/4 = 3$ percent for $m \times n = 4 \times 7 = 28$ periods.

Some savings banks advertise that they compound interest daily or even continuously. The mathematics of calculus provides a mechanism for finding the effective rate when interest is compounded continuously. We shall not go into details but merely state that if interest is compounded continuously at nominal rate r per year, then the effective annual rate is $e^r - 1$, where e is the base of the natural logarithms. Tables of values of e^r are widely available.[1] Six percent per year compounded continuously is equivalent to 6.1837 percent compounded annually; 12 percent per year compounded continuously is equivalent to 12.75 percent compounded annually. Do not confuse the compounding period with the payment period. Some banks, for example, compound interest daily but pay interest quarterly. You can be sure that such banks do not employ clerks or even computers to calculate interest every day. They merely use tables to derive an equivalent effective rate to apply at the end of each quarter.

Sample Problems in Changing the Compounding Period

Example 5   What is the future value 5 years hence of $600 invested at 8 percent compounded quarterly?

Eight percent compounded four times per year for 5 years is equivalent to 2 percent per period compounded for 20 periods. Table 1 shows the value of $F_{20} = (1.02)^{20}$ to be 1.48595. Six hundred dollars, then, would grow to $600 \times 1.48595 = \$891.57$.

Example 6   How much money must be invested today at 6 percent compounded semiannually in order to have $1,000 four years from today?

Six percent compounded two times a year for 4 years is equivalent to 3 percent per period compounded for 8 periods. The *present* value, Table 2, of $1 received 8 periods hence at 3 percent per period is $.78941. That is, $.78941 invested today for 8 periods at an interest rate of 3 percent per period will grow to $1. To have $1,000 in 8 periods (4 years), $789.41 (= $1,000 \times \$.78941$) must be invested today.

Example 7   If prices increased at the rate of 6 percent during each of two consecutive 6-month periods, how much did prices increase during the entire year?

If a price index is 100.00 at the start of the year, it will be $100.00 \times (1.06)^2 = 112.36$ at the end of the year. The price change for the entire year is $(112.36/100.00) - 1 = 12.36$ percent.

---

[1]   See, for example, Sidney Davidson and Roman L. Weil (eds.), *Handbook of Modern Accounting*, 2nd ed. (New York: McGraw-Hill Book Company, 1977), chap. 8, Exhibit 1.

ANNUITIES

An *annuity* is a series of equal payments made at the beginning or end of equal periods of time. Examples of annuities include monthly rental payments, semiannual corporate bond coupon (or interest) payments, and annual payments to a retired employee under a pension plan. Armed with an understanding of the tables for future and present values, you can solve any annuity problem. Annuities arise so often, however, and their solution is so tedious without special tables that annuity problems warrant special study and the use of special tables.

Terminology for Annuities

The terminology used for annuities can be confusing because not all writers use the same terms. Definitions of the terms used in this text follow.

An annuity whose payments occur at the *end* of each period is called an *ordinary annuity* or an *annuity in arrears*. Corporate bond coupon payments are usually paid in arrears or, equivalently, the first payment does not occur until after the bond has been outstanding for 6 months.

An annuity whose payments occur at the *beginning* of each period is called an *annuity due* or an *annuity in advance*. Rent is usually paid in advance, so that a series of rental payments is an annuity due.

A *deferred* annuity is one whose first payment is at some time later than the end of the first period.

Annuities can be paid forever. Such annuities are called *perpetuities*. Bonds that promise payments forever are called *consols*. The British and Canadian governments have, from time to time, issued consols. A perpetuity can be in arrears or in advance. The only difference between the two is the timing of the first payment.

Annuities can be confusing. Their study is made easier with a *time line* such as the one shown below.

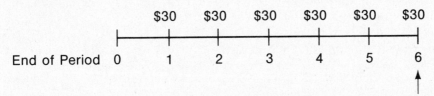

A time line marks the end of each period, numbers the period, shows the payments to be received or paid, and shows the time at which the annuity is valued. The time line just pictured represents an ordinary annuity (in arrears) for six periods of $30 to be valued at the end of period 6. The end of period 0 is "now." The first payment is to be received one period from now.

Ordinary Annuities (Annuities in Arrears)

The future values of ordinary annuities are shown in the back of the book in Table 3, portions of which are reproduced in Table B.3.

TABLE B.3 (Excerpt from Table 3)
Future Value of an Ordinary
Annuity of $1 per Period
at 6 Percent and 8 Percent

$$F_A = \frac{[(1 + r)^n - 1]}{r}$$

Number of Periods = n	Rate = r	
	6%	8%
1	1.00000	1.00000
2	2.06000	2.08000
3	3.18360	3.24640
5	5.63709	5.86660
10	13.18079	14.48656
20	36.78559	45.76196

Consider an ordinary annuity for three periods at 6 percent. The time line for the future value of such an annuity is

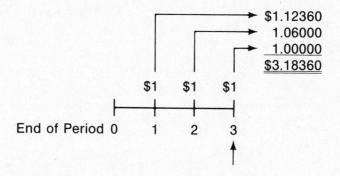

The $1 received at the end of the first period earns interest for two periods, so it is worth $1.12360 at the end of period 3. (See Table B.1.) The $1 received at the end of the second period grows to $1.06 by the end of period 3, and the $1 received at the end of period 3 is, of course, worth $1 at the end of period 3. The entire annuity is worth $3.18360 at the end of period 3. This is the amount shown in Table B.3 for the future value of an ordinary annuity for three periods at 6 percent. The mathematical expression for the future value, F_A, of an annuity of A per period compounded at r percent per period for n periods is

$$F_A = \frac{A[(1 + r)^n - 1]}{r}.$$

The present values of ordinary annuities are shown on page 627, in Table 4, portions of which are reproduced in Table B.4.

TABLE B.4 (Excerpt from Table 4)
Present Value of an Ordinary Annuity of $1 per Period at 6 Percent and 8 Percent

$$P_A = \frac{[1 - (1 + r)^{-n}]}{r}$$

Number of Periods = n	Rate = r	
	6%	**8%**
1	.94340	.92593
2	1.83339	1.78326
3	2.67301	2.57710
5	4.21236	3.99271
10	7.36009	6.71008
20	11.46992	9.81815

The time line for the present value of an ordinary annuity of $1 per period for three periods, discounted at 6 percent, is

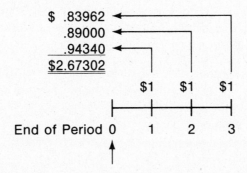

The $1 to be received at the end of period 1 has a present value of $.94340, the $1 to be received at the end of period 2 has a present value of $.89000, and the dollar to be received at the end of the third period has a present value of $.83962. Each of these numbers comes from Table B.2. The present value of the annuity is the sum of these individual present values, $2.67302, shown in Table B.4 as 2.67301 (our calculation differs because of roundings).

The present value of an ordinary annuity for n periods is the sum of the present value of $1 received 1 period from now plus the present value of $1 received two periods from now, and so on until we add on the present value of $1 received n periods from now. The mathematical expression for the present value, P_A, of an annuity of A per period, for n periods, compounded at r percent per period, is

$$P_A = \frac{A[1 - (1 + r)^{-n}]}{r}.$$

Sample Problems Involving Ordinary Annuities

Example 8   What is the present value of an annuity in arrears of $40 to be received every 6 months for 10 years if interest is 8 percent compounded semiannually? (If an 8-percent semiannual coupon bond with face value of $1,000 to mature in 10 years is issued at par, then this example computes the present value at the time of issue of all the coupon payments.)

Eight percent compounded semiannually for 10 years is equivalent to 4 percent per period compounded for 20 periods. From Table 4, 4-percent column and 20-payment row, $1 received at the end of each period has a present value of $13.59033. So the $40 semiannual annuity has a present value of $40 × 13.59033 = $543.61.

Example 9   Parents are accumulating a fund to send their child to college. The parents will invest a fixed amount at the end of each calendar quarter for the next 10 years. The funds will accumulate in a savings certificate that promises to pay 6 percent compounded quarterly. What amount must be invested to accumulate a fund of $12,000?

The effective interest rate is $1\frac{1}{2}$ percent (= 6 percent per year/4 quarters per year) per period for 40 (= 4 × 10) periods. Table 3, 40-period row, $1\frac{1}{2}$ percent column shows that a quarterly investment of $1 compounded at $1\frac{1}{2}$ percent per period will grow to $54.26789 in 40 periods. The parents want a fund of $12,000, so they must invest $221 (= $12,000/54.26789) in the fund.

Example 10   (Midwestern Products Company mortgage example from Chapter 10.) A company borrows $30,000 for 5 years from a savings and loan association. The interest rate is 8 percent compounded semiannually. The company agrees to repay the loan in equal semiannual installments for 5 years. The first payment is to be made 6 months from now. What is the amount of the required semiannual payment?

The present values of annuities are shown in Table 4. If $1 is paid each period for 10 periods and the discount rate is 4 percent per period, then the present value of the annuity (Table 4, 10-period row, 4-percent column) is $8.11090. The entire stream of payments must have a present value of $30,000 on the date the loan begins. The amount of each monthly payment must be $3,699 (= $30,000/8.11090). Note that the example in Chapter 10 uses a semiannual payment of $3,700, but that the last payment is less than $3,700. If you have not already done so, turn to page 367 to study the "amortization table" in Exhibit 10.1, constructed to show how these payments actually discharge both principal and interest.

Example 11   (Myers Company lease example from Chapter 10.) A company signs a lease acquiring the right to use property for 3 years. Lease payments are to be made annually at the end of this and each of the next 2 years. The discount rate is 8 percent per year. What is the amount of the annual lease payment?

The present value of $1 paid annually in arrears for 3 years is $2.57710 when the payments are discounted at the rate of 8 percent per year. (See Table 4, 3-period row,

8-percent column.) If the series of three payments is to have present value of $30,000 when the lease is signed, then each payment must be $11,461 (= $30,000/2.57710). Exhibit 10.4 on page 385 shows the amortization schedule for this loan.

Example 12 (Pension expenses for prior service costs under defined benefit plan from Appendix 10.1 of Chapter 10.) A company is obligated to make annual payments to a pension fund at the ends of the next 30 years. The present value of those payments is to be $100,000. What must the annual payment be if the fund earns interest at the rate of 6 percent per year?

The present value of $1 paid at the ends of the next 30 periods is $13.76483 if the discount rate is 6 percent per period. (See Table 4, 30-period row, 6-percent column.) If the present value of the entire payment stream is to be $100,000, then the annual payment in arrears must be $7,625 (= $100,000/13.76483).

Example 13 Mr. Mason is 62 years old. He wishes to invest equal amounts on his sixty-third, sixty-fourth, and sixty-fifth birthdays so that starting on his sixty-sixth birthday he can withdraw $5,000 on each birthday for 10 years. His investments will earn 8 percent per year. How much should be invested on the sixty-third through sixty-fifth birthdays?

The time line for this problem is

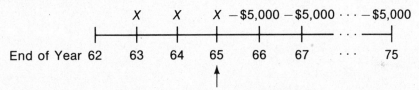

For each $1 that Mr. Mason invests on his sixty-third, sixty-fourth, and sixty-fifth birthdays, he will have $3.24640 (see Table 3, for 3-period row, 8-percent column) on his sixty-fifth birthday. On his sixty-fifth birthday Mr. Mason needs to have ac- cumulated an amount large enough to fund a 10-year, $5,000 annuity. A 10-year, $1 ordinary annuity has a present value of $6.71008 (Table 4, 10-periods row, 8-percent column). Mr. Mason then needs on his sixty-fifth birthday an accumulation of $33,550 (= $5,000 × 6.71008). Because each $1 deposited on the sixty-third through sixty-fifth birthdays grows to $3.24640, Mr. Mason must deposit $10,335 (= $33,550/ 3.24640) on each of the sixty-third through sixty-fifth birthdays to accumulate $33,550.

Example 14 Two parents are accumulating a fund to send their child to college. The parents will invest a fixed amount in a savings certificate at the end of each calendar quarter starting on March 30, 1980. The savings certificate earns 6 percent com- pounded quarterly. Starting March 30, 1986, the parents will withdraw $1,000 at the end of each calendar quarter for 4 years to use to pay bills.

The parents expect to make payments through the end of 1989 (for a total of 10 years and 40 payments). How much must be paid into the fund quarterly for 10 years so that $1,000 can be withdrawn quarterly for the last 4 years?

614

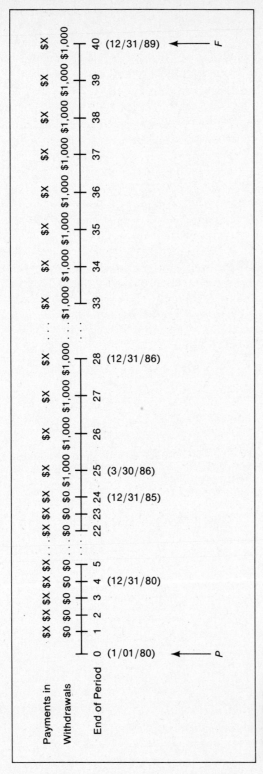

FIGURE B.1
Time Line for Example 14

Figure B.1 shows the time line for this problem. The payments into the fund are called $X and are to be found. There are 40 of them. The withdrawals from the fund are to be $1,000 per period, starting on March 30, 1986. There are to be 16 withdrawals altogether. On December 31, 1989, the last withdrawal is made. The future value of all withdrawals at that time, labeled F in the graph, is $17,932 (= $1,000 × 17.93237; see Table 3, 16-period row, 1½-percent column). Thus the stream of payments $X must have a future value at point F of $17,932. A quarterly payment of $1 will grow to $54.26789. (See Example 9 above; or refer to Table 3, 40-period row, 1½-percent column where the factor is 54.26789.) Thus the required payment must be $330 (= $17,932/54.26789).

Now we examine this problem in terms of present values. (This is somewhat more difficult but still is a reasonable way to attack the problem.) From the standpoint of January 1, 1980, labeled P in the time line, the present value of each $1 paid into the fund is $29.91585; (see Table 4, 40-period row, 1½-percent column). The present value of $1,000 withdrawn each period for 40 periods is thus $29,916. But there are no withdrawals for the first 24 periods. The present value of $1 per period for 24 periods discounted at a rate of 1½ percent per period is $20.03041. The present value of a stream of 24 payments of $1,000 each is $20,030. Therefore, the present value on of a stream of 24 payments of $1,000 each is $20,030. Therefore, the present value on January 1, 1980, of the actual withdrawals for the final 16 periods is $9,876 (= $29,916 − $20,030). Recall that the present value of the payments into the fund is $29.91585 for each dollar of payment. The required payment into the fund is $330 (= $9,876/29.91585).

PERPETUITIES

A periodic payment to be received forever is called a *perpetuity*. Future values of perpetuities are undefined. If $1 is to be received at the end of every period and the discount rate is r percent, then the present value of the perpetuity is $1/r$. This expression can be derived with algebra or by observing what happens in the expression for the present value of an ordinary annuity of A per payment as n, the number of payments, approaches infinity:

$$P_A = \frac{A[1 - (1 + r)^{-n}]}{r}.$$

As n approaches infinity, $(1 + r)^{-n}$ approaches zero, so that P_A approaches $A(1/r)$. If the first payment of the perpetuity occurs now, the present value is $A[1 + 1/r]$.

Examples of Perpetuities

Example 15 The Canadian government offers to pay $30 every 6 months forever in the form of a perpetual bond. What is that bond worth if the discount rate is 8 percent compounded semiannually?

Eight percent compounded semiannually is equivalent to 4 percent per 6-month period. If the first payment occurs 6 months from now, the present value is $30/.04 = $750. If the first payment occurs today, the present value is $30 + $750 = $780.

Example 16   Every 2 years, Ms. Young gives $10,000 to the University to provide a scholarship for an entering student in a 2-year business administration course. If the University earns 6 percent per year on its investments, how much must Ms. Young give to the University to provide such a scholarship every 2 years forever, starting 2 years hence?

A perpetuity in arrears assumes one payment at the end of each period. Here, the period is 2 years; 6 percent compounded once a year over 2 years is equivalent to a rate of $(1.06)^2 - 1 = .12360$ or 12.36 percent compounded once per 2-year period. Consequently, the present value of the perpetuity paid in arrears every 2 years is $80,906 $(= \$10,000/.12360)$. A gift of $80,906 will be sufficient to provide a $10,000 scholarship forever. A gift of $90,906 $(= \$80,906 + \$10,000)$ is required if the first scholarship is to be awarded now.

COMBINATIONS OF CASH FLOWS

Financial instruments may combine annuities and single payments. Bonds typically pay a specified sum every 6 months and a single, lump-sum payment along with the final periodic payment. Here is a simple example: The Macaulay Corporation promises to pay $40 every 6 months for 10 years, the first payment to occur 6 months from now, and an additional $1,000, ten years from now. If payments are discounted at 8 percent, compounded semiannually, then the $1,000 single payment has a present value of $1,000 $\times$ .45639 = $456.39 (Table 2, 20 periods, 4 percent) and the present value of the annuity is $40 $\times$ 13.59033 = $543.61 (Table 4, 20 periods, 4 percent). The sum of the two components is $1,000. (This is a $1,000 par-value, 10-year bond with 8-percent semiannual coupons issued at par to yield 8 percent compounded semiannually. See also page 369 in Chapter 10.)

LIFE-CONTINGENT ANNUITIES

The annuities discussed above all last for a certain or specified number of payments. Such annuities are sometimes called *certain annuities* to distinguish them from *contingent annuities,* for which the number of payments depends on an event to occur at an uncertain date. For example, businesses often want to know the cost of an annuity (pension) that will be paid only so long as the annuitant (retired employee) lives. Such annuities are called *life-contingent* or *life annuities.* Some texts show an incorrect calculation for the cost of a life annuity. The details of life-annuity calculations are beyond the scope of this text, but an unrealistic, hypothetical example is shown below so that our readers will be properly warned about the subtleties of life annuities.

Mr. Caplan is 65 years old today, and he has an unusual disease. He will die either $1\frac{1}{2}$ years from today or $10\frac{1}{2}$ years from today. Mr. Caplan has no family, and his employer wishes to purchase an ordinary life annuity for Mr. Caplan that will pay him $10,000 on his sixty-sixth birthday and $10,000 on every birthday thereafter on which Mr. Caplan is still alive. Funds invested in the annuity will earn 10 percent per year. How much should Mr. Caplan's life annuity cost?

The Wrong Calculation   Mr. Caplan's life expectancy is 6 years: one-half chance of his living $1\frac{1}{2}$ years plus one-half chance of his living $10\frac{1}{2}$ years. The employer expects that six payments will be made to Mr. Caplan. The present value of an ordinary annuity of $1 for 6 years at 10 percent is $4.35526 (Table 4). Therefore the annuity will cost $43,553.

The Right Calculation   Mr. Caplan will receive one payment for certain. The present value of that payment of $10,000 at 10 percent is $9,091 (Table 2). Mr. Caplan will receive nine further payments if he survives the critical second year. Those nine payments have present value $52,355; which is equal to the present value of a nine-year ordinary annuity that is deferred for 1 year, $61,446 − $9,091 (Table 4). The probability is one-half that Mr. Caplan will survive to receive those nine payments. Thus, their *expected* present value is $26,178 (= .5 × $52,355), and the *expected* present value of the entire life annuity is $9,091 + $26,178 = $35,269.

Mr. Caplan's life annuity, calculated correctly, costs only 81 percent as much as is found by the incorrect calculation. Actuaries for insurance companies use mortality tables to estimate probabilities of an annuitant's receiving each payment and, from those data, calculate the expected cost of a life annuity. Different mortality tables have been used for men and women because of the difference in life expectancies.

SUMMARY

Accountants typically use one of four kinds of compound interest calculations: the present or future value of a single payment or of a series of payments. In working annuity problems, you will find drawing a time line helpful in deciding which particular kind of annuity is involved.

QUESTIONS AND PROBLEMS

1 Review the following concepts or terms discussed in this Appendix.
   a Compound interest.
   b Principal.
   c Simple interest.
   d Future value.
   e Present value.
   f Discounted value.
   g Discount factor.
   h Discount rate.
   i Rule of 72.
   j Ordinary annuity (annuity in arrears).

   k Contingent annuity.

   l Perpetuity.

2 Does the present value of a given amount to be paid in 10 years increase or decrease if the interest rate increases? Suppose that the amount were due in 5 years? 20 years? Does the present value of an annuity to be paid for 10 years increase or decrease if the discount rate decreases? Suppose that the annuity were for 5 years? 20 years?

3 Rather than pay you $100 a month for the next 20 years, the person who injured you in an automobile accident is willing to pay a single amount now to settle your claim for injuries. Would you rather an interest rate of 6 percent or 12 percent be used in computing the present value of the lump-sum settlement? Comment or explain.

4 The terms of sale "2/10, net/30" mean that a discount of 2 percent from gross invoice price can be taken if the invoice is paid within 10 days and that otherwise the full amount is due within 30 days.

   a Write an expression for the implied annual rate of interest being offered, if the entire discount is viewed as being interest for funds received sooner rather than later. (Note that 98 percent of the gross invoice price is being borrowed for 20 days.)

   b The tables at the back of the book do not permit the exact evaluation of the expression derived in part **a.** The rate of interest implied is 44.59 percent per year. Use the tables to convince yourself that this astounding (to some) answer must be close to correct.

5 State the rate per period and the number of periods, in each of the following:

   a 12 percent per annum, for 5 years, compounded annually.

   b 12 percent per annum, for 5 years, compounded semiannually.

   c 12 percent per annum, for 5 years, compounded quarterly.

   d 12 percent per annum, for 5 years, compounded monthly.

6 Compute the future value of:

   a $100 invested for 5 years at 4 percent compounded annually.

   b $500 invested for 15 periods at 2 percent compounded once per period.

   c $200 invested for 8 years at 3 percent compounded semiannually.

   d $2,500 invested for 14 years at 8 percent compounded quarterly.

   e $600 invested for 3 years at 12 percent compounded monthly.

7 Compute the present value of:

   a $100 due in 30 years at 4 percent compounded annually.

   b $250 due in 8 years at 8 percent compounded quarterly.

   c $1,000 due in 2 years at 12 percent compounded monthly.

8 Compute the amount (future value) of an ordinary annuity (an annuity in arrears) of:

   a 13 rents of $100 at $1\frac{1}{2}$ percent per period.

   b 8 rents of $850 at 6 percent per period.

   c 28 rents of $400 at 4 percent per period.

9 Mr. Adams has $500 to invest. He wishes to know how much it will amount to if he invests it at

   a 6 percent per year for 21 years.

   b 8 percent per year for 33 years.

10 Ms. Black wishes to have $15,000 at the end of 8 years. How much must she invest today to accomplish this purpose if the interest rate is
a 6 percent per year?
b 8 percent per year?

11 Mr. Case plans to set aside $4,000 each year, the first payment to be made on January 1, 1979, and the last on January 1, 1984. How much will he have accumulated by January 1, 1984, if the interest rate is
a 6 percent per year?
b 8 percent per year?

12 Ms. David wants to have $450,000 on her sixty-fifth birthday. She asks you to tell her how much she must deposit on each birthday from her fifty-eighth to sixty-fifth, inclusive, in order to receive this amount. Assume an interest rate of
a 4 percent per year.
b 6 percent per year.

13 If Mr. Edwards invests $900 on June 1 of each year from 1979 to 1989, inclusive, how much will he have accumulated on June 1, 1990 (note that 1 year elapses after last payment) if the interest rate is
a 5 percent per year?
b 10 percent per year?

14 Mr. Frank has $145,000 with which he purchases an annuity on February 1, 1979. The annuity consists of six annual payments, the first to be made on February 1, 1980. How much will he receive in each payment? Assume an interest rate of
a 4 percent per year.
b 6 percent per year.

15 In the preceding Questions **6–14,** you have been asked to compute a number. First you must decide what factor from the tables is appropriate and then you use that factor in the appropriate calculation. Notice that the last step could be omitted. You could write an arithmetic expression showing the factor you want to use without actually copying down the number and doing the arithmetic. For example, define the following notation: T(i, p, r) means Table i (1, 2, 3, or 4), row p (periods 1 to 20, 22, 24, . . . , 40, 45, 50, 100), and column r (interest rates from $\frac{1}{2}$ percent up to 20 percent). Thus, T(3, 16, 12) would be the factor in Table 3 for 16 periods and an interest rate of 12 percent per period, which is 42.75328. Using this notation, you can write an expression for any compound interest problem. Any clerk can evaluate the expression.

You can check that you understand this notation by observing that the following are true statements:

T(1, 20, 8) = 4.66096
T(2, 12, 5) = .55684
T(3, 16, 12) = 42.75328
T(4, 10, 20) = 4.19247.

In the following questions, write an expression for the correct answer using the notation introduced here, but do not attempt to evaluate the expression.
a Work the **a** parts of Questions **6–10,** above.
b Work the **b** parts of Questions **11–14,** above.

c   How might the use of this notation make it easier for your instructor to write examination questions on compound interest?

16 Ms. Grady agrees to lease a certain property for 10 years, at the following annual rentals, payable in advance:

years 1 and 2—$1,000 per year.
years 3 to 6—$2,000 per year.
years 7 to 10—$2,500 per year.

What single immediate sum will pay all of these rents if they are discounted at
a   6 percent per year?
b   8 percent per year?
c   10 percent per year?

17 In order to establish a fund that will provide a scholarship of $3,000 a year indefinitely, with the first award to occur now, how much must be deposited if the fund earns:
a   6 percent per period?
b   8 percent per period?

18 Consider the scholarship fund in the preceding question. Suppose that the first scholarship is not to be awarded until 1 year from now. How much should be deposited if the fund earns:
a   6 percent per period?
b   8 percent per period?
Suppose that the first scholarship is not to be awarded until 5 years from now. How much should be deposited if the fund earns:
c   6 percent per year?
d   8 percent per year?

19 The state helps a rural county maintain a bridge and has agreed to pay $6,000 now and every 2 years thereafter forever toward the expenses. The state wishes to discharge its obligation by paying a single sum to the county now in lieu of the payment due and all future payments. How much should the state pay the county if the discount rate is
a   4 percent per year?
b   6 percent per year?

20 An oil-drilling company figures that $300 must be spent for an initial supply of drill bits and that $100 must be spent every month to replace the worn-out bits. What is the present value of the cost of the bits if the company plans to be in business indefinitely and discounts payments at 1 percent per month?

21 If you promise to leave $25,000 on deposit at the Quarter Savings Bank for 4 years, the bank will give you a new car today and your $25,000 back at the end of 4 years. How much are you, in effect, paying today for the car if the bank pays 8 percent interest compounded quarterly (2 percent paid four times per year)?

22 When Mr. Shafer died, his estate after taxes amounted to $300,000. His will provided that Widow Shafer would receive $24,000 per year starting immediately from the principal of the estate and that the balance of the principal would pass to the Shafers' son on Widow Shafer's death. The state law governing this estate provided for a *dower* option. If Widow

Shafer elects the dower option, she renounces the will and can have one-third of the estate in cash now. The remainder will then pass immediately to their son. Widow Shafer wants to maximize the present value of her bequest. Should she take the annuity or elect the dower option if she will receive five payments and discounts payments at:

a 8 percent per year?
b 12 percent per year?

23 Mrs. Heileman occasionally drinks beer. She consumes one case in 20 weeks. She can buy beer in disposable bottles for $6.60 per case or for $6.00 a case of returnable bottles if a $1.50 refundable deposit is paid at the time of purchase. If her discount rate is $\frac{1}{4}$ percent per week, how much in present-value dollars does she save by buying the returnables and thereby losing the use of the $1.50 deposit for 20 weeks?

24 When the General Electric Company first introduced the Lucalox ceramic, screw-in light bulb, the bulb cost $3\frac{1}{2}$ times as much as an ordinary bulb but lasted 5 times as long. An ordinary bulb cost $.50 and lasted about 8 months. If a firm has a discount rate of 12 percent compounded three times a year, how much would it save in present-value dollars by using one Lucalox bulb?

25 The Roberts Dairy Company switched from delivery trucks with regular gasoline engines to ones with diesel engines. The diesel trucks cost $2,000 more than the ordinary gasoline trucks, but $600 per year less to operate. Assume that the operating costs are saved at the end of each month. If Roberts Dairy uses a discount rate of 1 percent per month, approximately how many months, at a minimum, must the diesel trucks remain in service for the switch to save money?

26 On January 1, 19X0, Outergarments, Inc., opened a new textile plant for the production of synthetic fabrics. The plant is on leased land; 20 years remain on the nonrenewable lease.

The cost of the plant was $2 million. Net cash flow to be derived from the project is estimated to be $300,000 per year. The company does not normally invest in such projects unless the anticipated yield is at least 12 percent.

On December 31, 19X0, the company finds cash flows from the plant to be $280,000 for the year. On the same day, farm experts predict cotton production to be unusually low for the next two years. Outergarments estimates the resulting increase in demand for synthetic fabrics to boost cash flows to $350,000 for each of the next 2 years. Subsequent years' estimates remain unchanged. Ignore tax considerations.

a Calculate the present value of the future expected cash flows from the plant when it was opened.

b What is the present value of the plant on January 1, 19X1, after the reestimation of future incomes?

c On January 1, 19X1, the day following the cotton production news release, Overalls Company announces plans to build a synthetic fabrics plant to be opened in 3 years. Outergarments, Inc., keeps its 19X1–19X3 estimates, but reduces the estimated annual cash flows for subsequent years to $200,000. What is the value of the Outergarments' present plant on January 1, 19X1, after the new projections?

d On January 2, 19X1, an investor contacts Outergarments about purchasing a 20-percent share of the plant. If the investor expects to earn at least a 12-percent annual return on the investment, what is the maximum amount that the investor can pay? Assume that the investor and Outergarments, Inc., use the same estimates of annual cash flows.

27 A group of investors has decided to purchase a large herd of beef cattle, to sell cattle as calves are born, and to sell the entire herd after 6 years. They have also agreed that no investment of the syndicate should return less than 10 percent per year. They purchase the cattle on January 1, 19X0, for a price of $1,200,000, and they expect to sell the herd remaining on December 31, 19X5, for the same price. The projected net cash flows from sale of beef during the 6 years is $200,000 per year.

On December 31, 19X0, the syndicate finds that its cash flow from the herd is $210,000. But during December, the herd was stricken with a disease and 20 percent of the cattle died. The syndicate wants to rebuild the herd, and they decide to sell only enough beef to cover expenses until the herd grows to its original size. They anticipate that this process will result in zero cash flow for 19X1, and $200,000 for each of the remaining 4 years.

Ignore tax considerations in your calculations.

a Calculate the present value of the herd to the syndicate at time of purchase.

b If there had been no disease, what would have been the value of the herd on January 1, 19X1? Use only future cash flows for this and subsequent computations.

c What was the value of the herd on January 1, 19X1, after the disease and the decision to rebuild?

d What was the cost to the syndicate of the disease?

e On January 1, 19X1, an investor who has a 25-percent interest in the herd decides to sell out. What is the least amount that the investor should be willing to accept for the 25-percent share? Assume that the investor is looking at alternative investments that would yield 10 percent per year.

COMPOUND INTEREST, ANNUITY, AND BOND TABLES

TABLE 1
Future Value of $1

$$F_n = P(1 \times r)^n$$

r = interest rate; n = number of periods until valuation; P = $1

Periods = n	¼%	½%	⅔%	¾%	1%	1½%	2%	3%	4%	5%	6%	7%	8%	10%	12%	20%
1	1.00250	1.00500	1.00667	1.00750	1.01000	1.01500	1.02000	1.03000	1.04000	1.05000	1.06000	1.07000	1.08000	1.10000	1.12000	1.20000
2	1.00501	1.01003	1.01338	1.01506	1.02010	1.03023	1.04040	1.06090	1.08160	1.10250	1.12360	1.14490	1.16640	1.21000	1.25440	1.44000
3	1.00752	1.01508	1.02013	1.02267	1.03030	1.04568	1.06121	1.09273	1.12486	1.15763	1.19102	1.22504	1.25971	1.33100	1.40493	1.72800
4	1.01004	1.02015	1.02693	1.03034	1.04060	1.06136	1.08243	1.12551	1.16986	1.21551	1.26248	1.31080	1.36049	1.46410	1.57352	2.07360
5	1.01256	1.02525	1.03378	1.03807	1.05101	1.07728	1.10408	1.15927	1.21665	1.27628	1.33823	1.40255	1.46933	1.61051	1.76234	2.48832
6	1.01509	1.03038	1.04067	1.04585	1.06152	1.09344	1.12616	1.19405	1.26532	1.34010	1.41852	1.50073	1.58687	1.77156	1.97382	2.98598
7	1.01763	1.03553	1.04761	1.05370	1.07214	1.10984	1.14869	1.22987	1.31593	1.40710	1.50363	1.60578	1.71382	1.94872	2.21068	3.58318
8	1.02018	1.04071	1.05459	1.06160	1.08286	1.12649	1.17166	1.26677	1.36857	1.47746	1.59385	1.71819	1.85093	2.14359	2.47596	4.29982
9	1.02273	1.04591	1.06163	1.06956	1.09369	1.14339	1.19509	1.30477	1.42331	1.55133	1.68948	1.83846	1.99900	2.35795	2.77308	5.15978
10	1.02528	1.05114	1.06870	1.07758	1.10462	1.16054	1.21899	1.34392	1.48024	1.62889	1.79085	1.96715	2.15892	2.59374	3.10585	6.19174
11	1.02785	1.05640	1.07583	1.08566	1.11567	1.17795	1.24337	1.38423	1.53945	1.71034	1.89830	2.10485	2.33164	2.85312	3.47855	7.43008
12	1.03042	1.06168	1.08300	1.09381	1.12683	1.19562	1.26824	1.42576	1.60103	1.79586	2.01220	2.25219	2.51817	3.13843	3.89598	8.91610
13	1.03299	1.06699	1.09022	1.10201	1.13809	1.21355	1.29361	1.46853	1.66507	1.88565	2.13293	2.40985	2.71962	3.45227	4.36349	10.69932
14	1.03557	1.07232	1.09749	1.11028	1.14947	1.23176	1.31948	1.51259	1.73168	1.97993	2.26090	2.57853	2.93719	3.79750	4.88711	12.83918
15	1.03816	1.07768	1.10480	1.11860	1.16097	1.25023	1.34587	1.55797	1.80094	2.07893	2.39656	2.75903	3.17217	4.17725	5.47357	15.40702
16	1.04076	1.08307	1.11217	1.12699	1.17258	1.26899	1.37279	1.60471	1.87298	2.18287	2.54035	2.95216	3.42594	4.59497	6.13039	18.48843
17	1.04336	1.08849	1.11958	1.13544	1.18430	1.28802	1.40024	1.65285	1.94790	2.29202	2.69277	3.15882	3.70002	5.05447	6.86604	22.18611
18	1.04597	1.09393	1.12705	1.14396	1.19615	1.30734	1.42825	1.70243	2.02582	2.40662	2.85434	3.37993	3.99602	5.55992	7.68997	26.62333
19	1.04858	1.09940	1.13456	1.15254	1.20811	1.32695	1.45681	1.75351	2.10685	2.52695	3.02560	3.61653	4.31570	6.11591	8.61276	31.94800
20	1.05121	1.10490	1.14213	1.16118	1.22019	1.34686	1.48595	1.80611	2.19112	2.65330	3.20714	3.86968	4.66096	6.72750	9.64629	38.33760
22	1.05647	1.11597	1.15740	1.17867	1.24472	1.38756	1.54598	1.91610	2.36992	2.92526	3.60354	4.43040	5.43654	8.14027	12.10031	55.20614
24	1.06176	1.12716	1.17289	1.19641	1.26973	1.42950	1.60844	2.03279	2.56330	3.22510	4.04893	5.07237	6.34118	9.84973	15.17863	79.49685
26	1.06707	1.13846	1.18858	1.21443	1.29526	1.47271	1.67342	2.15659	2.77247	3.55567	4.54938	5.80735	7.39635	11.91818	19.04007	114.4755
28	1.07241	1.14987	1.20448	1.23271	1.32129	1.51722	1.74102	2.28793	2.99870	3.92013	5.11169	6.64884	8.62711	14.42099	23.88387	164.8447
30	1.07778	1.16140	1.22059	1.25127	1.34785	1.56308	1.81136	2.42726	3.24340	4.32194	5.74349	7.61226	10.06266	17.44940	29.95992	237.3763
32	1.08318	1.17304	1.23692	1.27011	1.37494	1.61032	1.88454	2.57508	3.50806	4.76494	6.15339	8.71527	11.73708	21.11378	37.58173	341.8219
34	1.08860	1.18480	1.25347	1.28923	1.40258	1.65068	1.96068	2.73191	3.79432	5.25335	7.25103	9.97811	13.69013	25.54767	47.14252	492.2235
36	1.09405	1.19668	1.27024	1.30865	1.43077	1.70914	2.03989	2.89828	4.10393	5.79182	8.14725	11.42394	15.96817	30.91268	59.13557	708.8019
38	1.09953	1.20868	1.28723	1.32835	1.45953	1.76080	2.12230	3.07478	4.43881	6.38548	9.15425	13.07927	18.62528	37.40434	74.17966	1020.675
40	1.10503	1.22079	1.30445	1.34835	1.48886	1.81402	2.20804	3.26204	4.80102	7.03999	10.28572	14.97446	21.72452	45.25926	93.05097	1469.772
45	1.11892	1.25162	1.34852	1.39968	1.56481	1.95421	2.43785	3.78160	5.84118	8.98501	13.76461	21.00245	31.92045	72.89048	163.9876	3657.262
50	1.13297	1.28323	1.39407	1.45296	1.64463	2.10524	2.69159	4.38391	7.10668	11.46740	18.42015	29.45703	46.90161	117.3909	289.0022	9100.438
100	1.28362	1.64667	1.94343	2.11108	2.70481	4.43205	7.24465	19.21863	50.50495	131.5013	339.3021	867.7163	2199.761	13780.61	83522.27	828×10⁶

TABLE 2
Present Value of $1

$$P = F_n (1 + r)^{-n}$$

r = discount rate; n = number of periods until payment; P = $1

Periods = n	¼%	½%	⅔%	¾%	1%	1½%	2%	3%	4%	5%	6%	7%	8%	10%	12%	20%
1	.99751	.99502	.99338	.99256	.99010	.98522	.98039	.97087	.96154	.95238	.94340	.93458	.92593	.90909	.89286	.83333
2	.99502	.99007	.98680	.98517	.98030	.97066	.96117	.94260	.92456	.90703	.89000	.87344	.85734	.82645	.79719	.69444
3	.99254	.98515	.98026	.97783	.97059	.95632	.94232	.91514	.88900	.86384	.83962	.81630	.79383	.75131	.71178	.57870
4	.99006	.98025	.97377	.97055	.96098	.94218	.92385	.88849	.85480	.82270	.79209	.76290	.73503	.68301	.63552	.48225
5	.98759	.97537	.96732	.96333	.95147	.92826	.90573	.86261	.82193	.78353	.74726	.71299	.68058	.62092	.56743	.40188
6	.98513	.97052	.96092	.95616	.94205	.91454	.88797	.83748	.79031	.74622	.70496	.66634	.63017	.56447	.50663	.33490
7	.98267	.96569	.95455	.94904	.93272	.90103	.87056	.81309	.75992	.71068	.66506	.62275	.58349	.51316	.45235	.27908
8	.98022	.96089	.94823	.94198	.92348	.88771	.85349	.78941	.73069	.67684	.62741	.58201	.54027	.46651	.40388	.23257
9	.97778	.95610	.94195	.93496	.91434	.87459	.83676	.76642	.70259	.64461	.59190	.54393	.50025	.42410	.36061	.19381
10	.97534	.95135	.93571	.92800	.90529	.86167	.82035	.74409	.67556	.61391	.55839	.50835	.46319	.38554	.32197	.16151
11	.97291	.94661	.92952	.92109	.89632	.84893	.80426	.72242	.64958	.58468	.52679	.47509	.42888	.35049	.28748	.13459
12	.97048	.94191	.92336	.91424	.88745	.83639	.78849	.70138	.62460	.55684	.49697	.44401	.39711	.31863	.25668	.11216
13	.96806	.93722	.91725	.90743	.87866	.82403	.77303	.68095	.60057	.53032	.46884	.41496	.36770	.28966	.22917	.09346
14	.96565	.93256	.91117	.90068	.86996	.81185	.75788	.66112	.57748	.50507	.44230	.38782	.34046	.26333	.20462	.07789
15	.96324	.92792	.90514	.89397	.86135	.79985	.74301	.64186	.55526	.48102	.41727	.36245	.31524	.23939	.18270	.06491
16	.96084	.92330	.89914	.88732	.85282	.78803	.72845	.62317	.53391	.45811	.39365	.33873	.29189	.21763	.16312	.05409
17	.95844	.91871	.89319	.88071	.84438	.77639	.71416	.60502	.51337	.43630	.37136	.31657	.27027	.19784	.14564	.04507
18	.95605	.91414	.88727	.87416	.83602	.76491	.70016	.58739	.49363	.41552	.35034	.29586	.25025	.17986	.13004	.03756
19	.95367	.90959	.88140	.86765	.82774	.75361	.68643	.57029	.47464	.39573	.33051	.27651	.23171	.16351	.11611	.03130
20	.95129	.90506	.87556	.86119	.81954	.74247	.67297	.55368	.45639	.37689	.31180	.25842	.21455	.14864	.10367	.02608
22	.94655	.89608	.86400	.84842	.80340	.72069	.64684	.52189	.42196	.34185	.27751	.22571	.18394	.12285	.08264	.01811
24	.94184	.88719	.85260	.83583	.78757	.69954	.62172	.49193	.39012	.31007	.24698	.19715	.15770	.10153	.06588	.01258
26	.93714	.87838	.84134	.82343	.77205	.67902	.59758	.46369	.36069	.28124	.21981	.17220	.13520	.08391	.05252	.00874
28	.93248	.86966	.83023	.81122	.75684	.65910	.57437	.43708	.33348	.25509	.19563	.15040	.11591	.06934	.04187	.00607
30	.92783	.86103	.81927	.79919	.74192	.63976	.55207	.41199	.30832	.23138	.17411	.13137	.09938	.05731	.03338	.00421
32	.92321	.85248	.80846	.78733	.72730	.62099	.53063	.38834	.28506	.20987	.15496	.11474	.08520	.04736	.02661	.00293
34	.91861	.84402	.79779	.77565	.71297	.60277	.51003	.36604	.26355	.19035	.13791	.10022	.07305	.03914	.02121	.00203
36	.91403	.83564	.78725	.76415	.69892	.58509	.49022	.34503	.24367	.17266	.12274	.08754	.06262	.03235	.01691	.00141
38	.90948	.82735	.77686	.75281	.68515	.56792	.47119	.32523	.22529	.15661	.10924	.07646	.05369	.02673	.01348	.00098
40	.90495	.81914	.76661	.74165	.67165	.55126	.45289	.30656	.20829	.14205	.09722	.06678	.04603	.02209	.01075	.00068
45	.89372	.79896	.74156	.71445	.63905	.51171	.41020	.26444	.17120	.11130	.07265	.04761	.03133	.01372	.00610	.00027
50	.88263	.77929	.71732	.68825	.60804	.47500	.37153	.22811	.14071	.08720	.05429	.03395	.02132	.00852	.00346	.00011
100	.77904	.60729	.51455	.47369	.36971	.22563	.13803	.05203	.01980	.00760	.00295	.00115	.00045	.00007	.00001	.00000

TABLE 3
Future Value of Annuity of $1 in Arrears

$$F = \frac{(1+r)^n - 1}{r}$$

r = interest rate; n = number of payments

No. of Payments = n	¼%	½%	⅔%	¾%	1%	1½%	2%	3%	4%	5%	6%	7%	8%	10%	12%	20%
1	1.00000	1.00000	1.00000	1.00000	1.00000	1.00000	1.00000	1.00000	1.00000	1.00000	1.00000	1.00000	1.00000	1.00000	1.00000	1.00000
2	2.00250	2.00500	2.00667	2.00750	2.01000	2.01500	2.02000	2.03000	2.04000	2.05000	2.06000	2.07000	2.08000	2.10000	2.12000	2.20000
3	3.00751	3.01503	3.02004	3.02256	3.03010	3.04523	3.06040	3.09090	3.12160	3.15250	3.18360	3.21490	3.24640	3.31000	3.37440	3.64000
4	4.01503	4.03010	4.04018	4.04523	4.06040	4.09090	4.12161	4.18363	4.24646	4.31013	4.37462	4.43994	4.50611	4.64100	4.77933	5.36800
5	5.02506	5.05025	5.06711	5.07556	5.10101	5.15227	5.20404	5.30914	5.41632	5.52563	5.63709	5.75074	5.86660	6.10510	6.35285	7.44160
6	6.03763	6.07550	6.10089	6.11363	6.15202	6.22955	6.30812	6.46841	6.63298	6.80191	6.97532	7.15329	7.33593	7.71561	8.11519	9.92992
7	7.05272	7.10588	7.14157	7.15948	7.21354	7.32299	7.43428	7.66246	7.89829	8.14201	8.39384	8.65402	8.92280	9.48717	10.08901	12.91590
8	8.07035	8.14141	8.18918	8.21318	8.28567	8.43284	8.58297	8.89234	9.21423	9.54911	9.89747	10.25980	10.63663	11.43589	12.29969	16.49908
9	9.09053	9.18212	9.24377	9.27478	9.36853	9.55933	9.75463	10.15911	10.58280	11.02656	11.49132	11.97799	12.48756	13.57948	14.77566	20.79890
10	10.11325	10.22803	10.30540	10.34434	10.46221	10.70272	10.94972	11.46388	12.00611	12.57789	13.18079	13.81645	14.48656	15.93742	17.54874	25.95868
11	11.13854	11.27917	11.37410	11.42192	11.56683	11.86326	12.16872	12.80780	13.48635	14.20679	14.97164	15.78360	16.64549	18.53117	20.65458	32.15042
12	12.16638	12.33556	12.44993	12.50759	12.68250	13.04121	13.41209	14.19203	15.02581	15.91713	16.86994	17.88845	18.97713	21.38428	24.13313	39.58050
13	13.19680	13.39724	13.53293	13.60139	13.80933	14.23683	14.68033	15.61779	16.62684	17.71298	18.88214	20.14064	21.49530	24.52271	28.02911	48.49660
14	14.22979	14.46423	14.62315	14.70340	14.94742	15.45038	15.97394	17.08632	18.29191	19.59863	21.01507	22.55049	24.21492	27.97498	32.39260	59.19592
15	15.26537	15.53655	15.72063	15.81368	16.09690	16.68214	17.29342	18.59891	20.02359	21.57856	23.27597	25.12902	27.15211	31.77248	37.27971	72.03511
16	16.30353	16.61423	16.82544	16.93228	17.25786	17.93237	18.63929	20.15688	21.82453	23.65749	25.67253	27.88805	30.32428	35.94973	42.75328	87.44213
17	17.34429	17.69730	17.93761	18.05927	18.43044	19.20136	20.01207	21.76159	23.69751	25.84037	28.21288	30.84022	33.75023	40.54470	48.88367	105.9306
18	18.38765	18.78579	19.05719	19.19472	19.61475	20.48938	21.41231	23.41444	25.64541	28.13238	30.90565	33.99903	37.45024	45.59917	55.74971	128.1167
19	19.43362	19.87972	20.18424	20.33868	20.81090	21.79672	22.84056	25.11687	27.67123	30.53900	33.75999	37.37896	41.44626	51.15909	63.43968	154.7400
20	20.48220	20.97912	21.31880	21.49122	22.01900	23.12367	24.29737	26.87037	29.77808	33.06595	36.78559	40.99549	45.76196	57.27500	72.05244	186.6880
22	22.58724	23.19443	23.61066	23.82230	24.47159	25.83758	27.29898	30.53678	34.24797	38.50521	43.39229	49.00574	55.45676	71.40275	92.50258	271.0307
24	24.70282	25.43196	25.93319	26.18847	26.97346	28.63352	30.42186	34.42647	39.08260	44.50200	50.81558	58.17667	66.76476	88.49733	118.1552	392.4842
26	26.82899	27.69191	28.28678	28.59027	29.52563	31.51397	33.67091	38.55304	44.31174	51.11345	59.15638	68.67647	79.95442	109.1818	150.3339	567.3773
28	28.96980	29.97452	30.67187	31.02823	32.12910	34.48148	37.05121	42.93092	49.96758	58.40258	68.52811	80.69769	95.33883	134.2099	190.6989	819.2233
30	31.11331	32.28002	33.08585	33.50290	34.78489	37.53868	40.56808	47.57542	56.08494	66.43885	79.05819	95.33883	113.2832	164.4940	241.3327	1181.881
32	33.27157	34.60862	35.53818	36.01483	37.49407	40.68829	44.22703	52.50276	62.70147	75.29883	90.88978	110.2181	134.2135	201.1378	304.8477	1704.109
34	35.44064	36.96058	38.02026	38.56458	40.25770	43.93309	48.03380	57.73018	69.85791	85.06696	104.1838	128.2588	158.6267	245.4767	384.5210	2456.118
36	37.62056	39.33610	40.53556	41.15272	43.07688	47.27597	51.99437	63.27594	77.59831	95.83632	119.1209	148.9135	187.1022	299.1268	484.4631	3539.009
38	39.81140	41.73545	43.08450	43.77982	45.95272	50.71989	56.11494	69.15945	85.97034	107.7095	135.9042	172.5610	220.3159	364.0434	609.8305	5098.373
40	42.01320	44.15885	45.66754	46.44648	48.88637	54.26789	60.40198	75.40126	95.02552	120.7998	154.7620	199.6351	259.0565	442.5926	767.0914	7343.858
45	47.56606	50.32416	52.27734	53.29011	56.48107	63.61420	71.89271	92.71986	121.0294	159.7002	212.7435	285.7493	386.5056	718.9048	1358.230	18281.31
50	53.18868	56.64516	59.11042	60.39426	64.46318	73.68283	84.57940	112.7969	152.6671	209.3480	290.3359	406.5289	573.7702	1163.909	2400.018	45497.19
100	113.44996	129.33370	141.51445	148.14451	170.4814	228.8030	312.2323	607.2877	1237.624	2610.025	5638.368	12381.66	27484.52	137796.1	696010.5	414×10⁶

Note: To convert from this table to values of an annuity in advance, determine the annuity in arrears above for one more period and subtract 1.00000.

TABLE 4
Present Value of an Annuity of $1 in Arrears

$$P_A = \frac{1-(1+r)^{-n}}{r}$$

r = discount rate; n = number of payments

No. of Payments = n	¼%	½%	⅔%	¾%	1%	1½%	2%	3%	4%	5%	6%	7%	8%	10%	12%	20%
1	0.99751	0.99502	0.99338	0.99256	.99010	.98522	.98039	.97087	.96154	.95238	.94340	.93458	.92593	.90909	.89286	.83333
2	1.99252	1.98510	1.98018	1.97772	1.97040	1.95588	1.94156	1.91347	1.88609	1.85941	1.83339	1.80802	1.78326	1.73554	1.69005	1.52778
3	2.98506	2.97025	2.96044	2.95556	2.94099	2.91220	2.88388	2.82861	2.77509	2.72325	2.67301	2.62432	2.57710	2.48685	2.40183	2.10648
4	3.97512	3.95050	3.93421	3.92611	3.90197	3.85438	3.80773	3.71710	3.62990	3.54595	3.46511	3.38721	3.31213	3.16987	3.03735	2.58873
5	4.96272	4.92587	4.90154	4.88944	4.85343	4.78264	4.71346	4.57971	4.45182	4.32948	4.21236	4.10020	3.99271	3.79079	3.60478	2.99061
6	5.94785	5.89638	5.86245	5.84560	5.79548	5.69719	5.60143	5.41719	5.24212	5.07569	4.91732	4.76654	4.62288	4.35526	4.11141	3.32551
7	6.93052	6.86207	6.81701	6.79464	6.72819	6.59821	6.47199	6.23028	6.00205	5.78637	5.58238	5.38929	5.20637	4.86842	4.56376	3.60459
8	7.91074	7.82296	7.76524	7.73661	7.65168	7.48593	7.32548	7.01969	6.73274	6.46321	6.20979	5.97130	5.74664	5.33493	4.96764	3.83716
9	8.88852	8.77906	8.70719	8.67158	8.56602	8.36052	8.16224	7.78611	7.43533	7.10782	6.80169	6.51523	6.24689	5.75902	5.32825	4.03097
10	9.86386	9.73041	9.64290	9.59958	9.47130	9.22218	8.98259	8.53020	8.11090	7.72173	7.36009	7.02358	6.71008	6.14457	5.65022	4.19247
11	10.83677	10.67703	10.57242	10.52067	10.36763	10.07112	9.78685	9.25262	8.76048	8.30641	7.88687	7.49867	7.13896	6.49506	5.93770	4.32706
12	11.80725	11.61893	11.49578	11.43491	11.25508	10.90751	10.57534	9.95400	9.38507	8.86325	8.38384	7.94269	7.53608	6.81369	6.19437	4.43922
13	12.77532	12.55615	12.41303	12.34235	12.13374	11.73153	11.34837	10.63496	9.98565	9.39357	8.85268	8.35765	7.90378	7.10336	6.42355	4.53268
14	13.74096	13.48871	13.32420	13.24302	13.00370	12.54338	12.10625	11.29607	10.56312	9.89864	9.29498	8.74547	8.24424	7.36669	6.62817	4.61057
15	14.70420	14.41662	14.22934	14.13699	13.86505	13.34323	12.84926	11.93794	11.11839	10.37966	9.71225	9.10791	8.55948	7.60608	6.81086	4.67547
16	15.66504	15.33993	15.12848	15.02431	14.71787	14.13126	13.57771	12.56110	11.65230	10.83777	10.10590	9.44665	8.85137	7.82371	6.97399	4.72956
17	16.62348	16.25863	16.02167	15.90502	15.56225	14.90765	14.29187	13.16612	12.16567	11.27407	10.47726	9.76322	9.12164	8.02155	7.11963	4.77463
18	17.57953	17.17277	16.90894	16.77918	16.39827	15.67256	14.99203	13.75351	12.65930	11.68959	10.82760	10.05909	9.37189	8.20141	7.24967	4.81219
19	18.53320	18.08236	17.79034	17.64683	17.22601	16.42617	15.67846	14.32380	13.13394	12.08532	11.15812	10.33560	9.60360	8.36492	7.36578	4.84350
20	19.48449	18.98742	18.66590	18.50802	18.04555	17.16864	16.35143	14.87747	13.59033	12.46221	11.46992	10.59401	9.81815	8.51356	7.46944	4.86958
22	21.37995	20.78406	20.39967	20.21121	19.66038	18.62082	17.65805	15.93692	14.45112	13.16300	12.04158	11.06124	10.20074	8.77154	7.64465	4.90943
24	23.26598	22.56287	22.11054	21.88915	21.24339	20.03041	18.91393	16.93554	15.24696	13.79864	12.55036	11.46933	10.52876	8.98474	7.78432	4.93710
26	25.14261	24.32402	23.79883	23.54219	22.79520	21.39863	20.12104	17.87684	15.98277	14.37519	13.00317	11.82578	10.80998	9.16095	7.89566	4.95632
28	27.00989	26.06769	25.46484	25.17071	24.31644	22.72672	21.28127	18.76411	16.66306	14.89813	13.40616	12.13711	11.05108	9.30657	7.98442	4.96967
30	28.86787	27.79405	27.10885	26.77508	25.80771	24.01584	22.39646	19.60044	17.29203	15.37245	13.76483	12.40904	11.25778	9.42691	8.05518	4.97894
32	30.71660	29.50328	28.73116	28.35565	27.26959	25.26714	23.46833	20.38877	17.87355	15.80268	14.08404	12.64656	11.43500	9.52638	8.11159	4.98537
34	32.55611	31.19555	30.33205	29.91278	28.70267	26.48173	24.49859	21.13184	18.41120	16.19290	14.36814	12.85401	11.58693	9.60857	8.15656	4.98984
36	34.38647	32.87102	31.91181	31.44681	30.10751	27.66068	25.48884	21.83225	18.90828	16.54685	14.62099	13.03521	11.71719	9.67651	8.19241	4.99295
38	36.20770	34.52985	33.47071	32.95808	31.48466	28.80505	26.44064	22.49246	19.36786	16.86789	14.84602	13.19347	11.82887	9.73265	8.22099	4.99510
40	38.01986	36.17223	35.00903	34.44694	32.83469	29.91585	27.35548	23.11477	19.79277	17.15909	15.04630	13.33171	11.92461	9.77905	8.24378	4.99660
45	42.51088	40.20720	38.76658	38.07318	36.09451	32.55234	29.49016	24.51871	20.72004	17.77407	15.45583	13.60552	12.10840	9.86281	8.28252	4.99863
50	46.94617	44.14279	42.40134	41.56645	39.19612	34.99969	31.42361	25.72976	21.48218	18.25593	15.76186	13.80075	12.23348	9.91481	8.30450	4.99945
100	88.38248	78.54264	72.81686	70.17462	63.02888	51.62470	43.09835	31.59891	24.50500	19.84791	16.61755	14.26925	12.49432	9.99927	8.33323	5.00000

Note: To convert from this table to values of an annuity in advance, determine the annuity in arrears above for one less period and add 1.00000.

TABLE 5
Bond Values in Percent of Par:
6-Percent Semiannual Coupons

$$\text{Bond Value} = 6/r + (100 - 6/r)(1 + r/2)^{-2n}$$
$$r = \text{yield to maturity}; \; n = \text{years to maturity}$$

Market Yield % Per Year Compounded Semiannually	Years to Maturity							
	½	5	10	15	19½	20	30	40
3.0	101.478	113.833	125.753	136.024	144.047	144.874	159.071	169.611
3.5	101.228	111.376	120.941	128.982	135.118	135.743	146.205	153.600
4.0	100.980	108.983	116.351	122.396	126.903	127.355	134.761	139.745
4.5	100.734	106.650	111.973	116.234	119.337	119.645	124.562	127.712
5.0	100.488	104.376	107.795	110.465	112.365	112.551	115.454	117.226
5.1	100.439	103.928	106.982	109.356	111.037	111.202	113.752	115.293
5.2	100.390	103.483	106.177	108.262	109.731	109.874	112.087	113.411
5.3	100.341	103.040	105.380	107.181	108.445	108.568	110.458	111.578
5.4	100.292	102.599	104.590	106.115	107.180	107.283	108.864	109.792
5.5	100.243	102.160	103.807	105.062	105.935	106.019	107.306	108.053
5.6	100.195	101.724	103.031	104.023	104.710	104.776	105.780	106.359
5.7	100.146	101.289	102.263	102.998	103.504	103.553	104.288	104.707
5.8	100.097	100.857	101.502	101.986	102.317	102.349	102.828	103.098
5.9	100.049	100.428	100.747	100.986	101.149	101.165	101.399	101.529
6.0	100	100	100	100	100	100	100	100
6.1	99.9515	99.5746	99.2595	99.0262	98.8685	98.8535	98.6309	98.5088
6.2	99.9030	99.1513	98.5259	98.0650	97.7549	97.7254	97.2907	97.0546
6.3	99.8546	98.7302	97.7990	97.1161	96.6587	96.6153	95.9787	95.6364
6.4	99.8062	98.3112	97.0787	96.1793	95.5796	95.5229	94.6942	94.2529
6.5	99.7579	97.8944	96.3651	95.2545	94.5174	94.4478	93.4365	92.9031
6.6	99.7096	97.4797	95.6580	94.3414	93.4717	93.3899	92.2050	91.5860
6.7	99.6613	97.0670	94.9574	93.4400	92.4423	92.3486	90.9989	90.3007
6.8	99.6132	96.6565	94.2632	92.5501	91.4288	91.3238	89.8178	89.0461
6.9	99.5650	96.2480	93.5753	91.6714	90.4310	90.3152	88.6608	87.8213
7.0	99.5169	95.8417	92.8938	90.8039	89.4487	89.3224	87.5276	86.6255
7.5	99.2771	93.8404	89.5779	86.6281	84.7588	84.5868	82.1966	81.0519
8.0	99.0385	91.8891	86.4097	82.7080	80.4155	80.2072	77.3765	76.0846
8.5	98.8010	89.9864	83.3820	79.0262	76.3899	76.1534	73.0090	71.6412
9.0	98.5646	88.1309	80.4881	75.5666	72.6555	72.3976	69.0430	67.6520

TABLE 6
Bond Values in Percent of Par:
8-Percent Semiannual Coupons

$$\text{Bond Value} = 8/r + (100 - 8/r)\,(1 + r/2)^{-2n}$$
$$r = \text{yield to maturity}; \quad n = \text{years to maturity}$$

Market Yield % Per Year Compounded Semiannually	½	5	10	15	19½	20	30	40
5.0	101.463	113.128	123.384	131.396	137.096	137.654	146.363	151.678
5.5	101.217	110.800	119.034	125.312	129.675	130.098	136.528	140.266
6.0	100.971	108.530	114.877	119.600	122.808	123.115	127.676	130.201
6.5	100.726	106.317	110.905	114.236	116.448	116.656	119.690	121.291
7.0	100.483	104.158	107.106	109.196	110.551	110.678	112.472	113.374
7.1	100.435	103.733	106.367	108.225	109.424	109.536	111.113	111.898
7.2	100.386	103.310	105.634	107.266	108.314	108.411	109.780	110.455
7.3	100.338	102.889	104.908	106.318	107.220	107.303	108.473	109.044
7.4	100.289	102.470	104.188	105.382	106.142	106.212	107.191	107.665
7.5	100.241	102.053	103.474	104.457	105.080	105.138	105.934	106.316
7.6	100.193	101.638	102.767	103.544	104.034	104.079	104.702	104.997
7.7	100.144	101.226	102.066	102.642	103.003	103.036	103.492	103.706
7.8	100.096	100.815	101.371	101.750	101.987	102.009	102.306	102.444
7.9	100.048	100.407	100.683	100.870	100.986	100.997	101.142	101.209
8.0	100	100	100	100	100	100	100	100
8.1	99.9519	99.5955	99.3235	99.1406	99.0279	99.0177	98.8794	98.8170
8.2	99.9039	99.1929	98.6529	98.2916	98.0699	98.0498	97.7798	97.6589
8.3	99.8560	98.7924	97.9882	97.4528	97.1257	97.0962	96.7006	96.5253
8.4	99.8081	98.3938	97.3294	96.6240	96.1951	96.1566	95.6414	95.4152
8.5	99.7602	97.9973	96.6764	95.8052	95.2780	95.2307	94.6018	94.3282
8.6	99.7124	97.6027	96.0291	94.9962	94.3739	94.3183	93.5812	93.2636
8.7	99.6646	97.2100	95.3875	94.1969	93.4829	93.4191	92.5792	92.2208
8.8	99.6169	96.8193	94.7514	93.4071	92.6045	92.5331	91.5955	91.1992
8.9	99.5692	96.4305	94.1210	92.6266	91.7387	91.6598	90.6295	90.1982
9.0	99.5215	96.0436	93.4960	91.8555	90.8851	90.7992	89.6810	89.2173
9.5	99.2840	94.1378	90.4520	88.1347	86.7949	86.6777	85.1858	84.5961
10.0	99.0476	92.2783	87.5378	84.6275	82.9830	82.8409	81.0707	80.4035
10.5	98.8123	90.4639	84.7472	81.3201	79.4271	79.2656	77.2956	76.5876
11.0	98.5782	88.6935	82.0744	78.1994	76.1070	75.9308	73.8252	73.1036

GLOSSARY[1]

AAA. *American Accounting Association.*

Abacus. A scholarly journal containing articles on theoretical aspects of accounting. Published twice a year by the Sydney University Press, Sydney, Australia.

abnormal spoilage. Actual spoilage exceeding that expected to occur under normal operating efficiency. Spoilage that should not occur if operations are normally efficient. Usual practice treats this cost as an *expense* of the period rather than as a *product cost.* Contrast with *normal spoilage.*

aboriginal cost. In public utility accounting, the *acquisition cost* of an asset incurred by the first *entity* devoting that *asset* to public use. Most public utility regulation is based on aboriginal cost. If it were not, then public utilities could exchange assets among themselves at ever-increasing prices in order to raise the rate base and, then, prices based thereon. *Historical cost* only to the first acquirer.

absorption costing. The generally accepted method of *costing* that assigns all types of *manufacturing costs* (direct material and labor as well as fixed and variable overhead) to units produced. Sometimes called "full costing." Contrast with *direct costing.*

accelerated depreciation. Any method of calculating *depreciation* charges where the charges become progressively smaller each period. Examples are *double-declining-balance* and *sum-of-the-years'-digits* methods.

acceptance. A written promise to pay that is equivalent to a promissory *note.*

---

[1] Various words or terms in the definitions are *italicized.* The *italicized* words or terms, or variants of them, are themselves explained in the glossary. The glossary contains some defined terms that are not included in the text. These are included to make the glossary more useful.

account. Any device for accumulating additions and subtractions relating to a single *asset, liability, owners' equity, revenue, expense,* and other items.

account form. The form of *balance sheet* where *assets* are shown on the left and *equities* are shown on the right. Contrast with *report form.*

account payable. A *liability* representing an amount owed to a *creditor,* usually arising from purchase of *merchandise* or materials and supplies; not necessarily due or past due. Normally, a *current* liability.

account receivable. A claim against a *debtor* usually arising from sales or services rendered; not necessarily due or past due. Normally, a *current asset.*

accountancy. The British word for *accounting.* In the United States, it means the theory and practice of accounting.

Accountants' Index. A publication of the *AICPA* that indexes, in detail, the accounting literature of the period.

accountant's opinion. *Auditor's report.*

accountant's report. *Auditor's report.*

accounting. An *information system* conveying information about a specific *entity.* The information is in financial terms and is restricted to information that can be made reasonably precise. The *AICPA* defines accounting as a service activity whose "function is to provide quantitative information, primarily financial in nature, about economic entities that is intended to be useful in making economic decisions."

accounting changes. As defined by *APB Opinion* No. 20, a change in (a) an *accounting principle (*such as a switch from *FIFO* to *LIFO* or from *sum-of-the-years'-digits* to *straight-line depreciation),* (b) an accounting estimate (such as estimated useful lives or salvage value of depreciable assets and estimates of *warranty* costs or *uncollectible accounts*), and (c) the reporting *entity.* Changes of type (a) should be disclosed.

The cumulative effect of the change on *retained earnings* at the start of the period during which the change was made should be included in reported earnings for the period of change. Changes of type (b) should be treated as affecting only the period of change and, if necessary, future periods. The reasons for changes of type (c) should be disclosed and, in statements reporting on operations of the period of the change, the effect of the change on all other periods reported on for comparative purposes should also be shown. In some cases (such as a change from *LIFO* to other inventory *flow assumptions* or in the method of accounting for long-term construction contracts), changes of type (a) are treated like changes of type (c). That is, for these changes all statements shown for prior periods must be restated to show the effect of adopting the change for those periods as well. See *all-inclusive concept* and *accounting errors*.

accounting conventions. Methods or procedures used in accounting. This term tends to be used when the method or procedure has not been given official authoritative sanction by a pronouncement of a group such as the *APB, FASB,* or *SEC.* Contrast with *accounting principles.*

accounting cycle. The sequence of accounting procedures starting with *journal entries* for various transactions and events and ending with the *financial statements* or, perhaps, the *post-closing trial balance.*

accounting entity. See *entity.*

accounting equation. *Assets = Equities. Assets = Liabilities + Owners' Equity.*

accounting errors. Arithmetic errors and misapplications of *accounting principles* in previously published financial statements that are corrected in the current period with direct *debits* or *credits* to *retained earnings.* In this regard, they are treated like *prior-period adjustments,* but, technically, they are not classified by *APB Opinion* No. 9 as prior-period adjustments. See *accounting changes* and contrast with changes in accounting estimates as described there.

accounting event. Any occurrence that is recorded as a transaction in the accounting records.

accounting methods. *Accounting principles.* Procedures for carrying out accounting principles.

accounting period. The time period for which *financial statements* that measure *flows,* such as the *income statement* and the *statement of changes in financial position,* are prepared. Should be clearly identified on the financial statements. See *interim statements.*

accounting policies. *Accounting principles* adopted by a specific *entity.*

accounting principles. The concepts that determine the methods or procedures used in accounting for *transactions* or events reported in the *financial statements.* This term tends to be used when the method or procedure has been given official authoritative sanction by a pronouncement of a group such as the *APB, FASB,* or *SEC.* Contrast with *accounting conventions.*

Accounting Principles Board. See *APB.*

accounting procedures. See *accounting principles,* but usually this term refers to the methods required to implement accounting principles.

accounting rate of return. Income for a period divided by average investment during the period. Based on income rather than discounted cash flows and, hence, is a poor decision-making aid or tool. See *ratio.*

Accounting Research Bulletin (ARB). The name of the official pronouncements of the former *Committee on Accounting Procedure* of the *AICPA.* Fifty-one bulletins were issued between 1939 and 1959. ARB No. 43 summarizes the first forty-two bulletins.

Accounting Research Study. One of a series of studies published by the Director of Research of the *AICPA* "designed to provide professional accountants and others interested in the development of accounting with a discussion and documentation of accounting problems." Fifteen such studies were published between 1961 and 1974. Abbreviated as *ARS.*

The Accounting Review. Scholarly publication of the *American Accounting Association,* which appears four times a year.

Accounting Series Release. See *SEC.*

accounting standards. *Accounting principles.*

Accounting Trends and Techniques. An annual publication of the *AICPA* that surveys the reporting practices of 600 large corporations. It presents tabulations of specific practices, terminology, and disclosures along with illustrations taken from individual annual reports.

accounts receivable turnover. *Net sales* on account for a period divided by the average balance of net accounts receivable. See *ratio.*

accretion. Increase in economic worth through physical change, usually said of a natural resource such as an orchard, caused by natural growth. Contrast with *appreciation.*

accrual. Recognition of an *expense* (or *revenue*) and the related *liability* (or *asset*) that is caused by an *accounting event,* frequently by the passage of time, and that is not signaled by an explicit cash transaction. For example, the recognition of interest expense or revenue (or wages, salaries, or rent) at the end of a period even though no explicit cash transaction is made at that time.

accrual basis of accounting. The method of recognizing *revenues* as *goods* are sold (or delivered) and as *services* are rendered, independent of the time when cash is received. *Expenses* are recognized in the period when the related revenue is recognized independent of the time when cash is paid out. Contrast with the *cash basis of accounting.* See *accrual.*

accrued. Said of a *revenue (expense)* that has been earned (recognized) even though the related *receivable (payable)* is not yet due. This adjective should not be used as part of an account title. Thus, we prefer to use Interest Receivable (Payable) as the account title, rather than Accrued Interest Receivable (Payable). See *matching convention.* See *accrual.*

accrued depreciation. An inferior term for *accumulated depreciation.* See *accrued.*

accrued payable. A *payable* usually resulting from the passage of time. For example, *salaries* and *interest* accrue as time passes. See *accrued.*

accrued receivable. A *receivable* usually resulting from the passage of time. See *accrued.*

accumulated depreciation. A preferred title for the *contra-asset* account that shows the sum of *depreciation* charges on an asset since it was acquired. Other titles used are *allowance for depreciation* (acceptable term) and *reserve for depreciation* (unacceptable term).

accurate presentation. The qualitative accounting objective suggesting that information reported in financial statements should correspond as precisely as possible with the economic effects underlying transactions and events. See *fair presentation* and *full disclosure.*

acid test ratio. Sum of *(cash, current marketable securities, and receivables)* divided by *current liabilities.* Some nonliquid receivables may be excluded from the numerator. Often called the *quick* ratio. See *ratio.*

acquisition cost. Of an *asset,* the net *invoice* price plus all *expenditures* to place and ready the asset for its intended use. The other expenditures might include legal fees, transportation charges, and installation costs.

activity accounting. *Responsibility accounting.*

activity-based depreciation. *Production method of depreciation.*

actual cost (basis). *Acquisition* or *historical cost.* Also contrast with *standard cost.*

actuarial. Usually said of computations or analyses that involve both *compound interest* and probabilities. Sometimes the term is used if only one of the two is involved.

additional paid-in capital. An alternative acceptable title for the *capital contributed in excess of par (or stated) value* account.

adequate disclosure. *Fair presentation* of *financial statements* requires *disclosure* of *material* items. This *auditing standard* does not, however, require publicizing all information detrimental to a company. For example, the company may be threatened with a lawsuit and disclosure might seem to require a *debit* to a *loss* account and a *credit* to an *estimated liability.* But the mere making of this entry might adversely affect the actual outcome of the suit. Such entries need not be made, although impending suits should be disclosed.

adjunct account. An *account* that accumulates additions to another account. For example, Premium on Bonds Payable is adjunct to the liability Bonds Payable; the effective liability is the sum of the two account balances at a given date. Contrast with *contra account.*

adjusted acquisition (historical) cost. Cost adjusted for *general* or *specific price level changes.* See also *book value.*

adjusted bank balance of cash. The *balance* shown on the statement from the bank plus or minus appropriate adjustments, such as for unrecorded deposits or outstanding checks, to reconcile the bank's balance with the correct cash balance. See *adjusted book balance of cash.*

adjusted basis. The *basis* used to compute gain or loss on disposition of an *asset* for tax purposes. Also, see *book value.*

adjusted book balance of cash. The *balance* shown in the firm's account for cash in bank plus or minus appropriate adjustments, such as for *notes* collected by the bank or bank service charges, to reconcile the account balance with the correct cash balance. See *adjusted bank balance of cash.*

adjusted trial balance. *Trial balance* taken after *adjusting entries* but before *closing entries.* Contrast with *pre-* and *post-closing trial balances.* See *unadjusted trial balance* and *work sheet.*

adjusting entry. An entry made at the end of an *accounting period* to record a *transaction* or other *accounting event,* which for some reason has not been recorded or has been improperly recorded during the accounting period. An entry to update the accounts. See *work sheet.*

adjustment. A change in an *account* produced by an *adjusting* entry. Sometimes the term is used to refer to the process of restating *financial statements* for *general price level changes.*

administrative expense. An *expense* related to the enterprise as a whole as contrasted to expenses related to more specific functions such as manufacturing or selling.

admission of partner. Legally, when a new partner joins a *partnership,* a new partnership comes into being. In practice, however, the old accounting records may be kept in use and the accounting entries reflect the manner in which the new partner joined the firm. If the new partner merely purchases the interest of another partner, the only accounting is to change the name for one capital account. If the new partner contributes *assets* and *liabilities* to the partnership, then the new assets must be recognized with debits and the liabilities and other source of capital, with credits. See *bonus method.*

ADR. See *asset depreciation range.*

advances from (by) customers. A preferred term for the *liability* account representing *receipts* of *cash* in advance of delivering the *goods* or rendering the *service* (that will cause *revenue* to be recognized). Sometimes called "deferred revenue" or "deferred income."

advances to affiliates. *Loans* by a parent company to a *subsidiary.* Frequently combined with "investment in subsidiary" as "investments and advances to subsidiary" and shown as a *noncurrent asset* on the parent's *balance sheet.* These advances are eliminated in *consolidated financial statements.*

advances to suppliers. A preferred term for *disbursements* of cash in advance of receiving *assets* or *services.*

adverse opinion. An *auditor's report* stating that the financial statements are not fair or are not in accord with *GAAP.*

affiliated company. Said of a company controlling or controlled by another company.

after closing. *Post closing;* said of a *trial balance* at the end of the period.

after cost. Said of *expenditures* to be made subsequent to *revenue* recognition. For example, *expenditures* for *repairs* under warranty are after costs. Proper recognition of after costs involves a debit to expense at the time of the sale and a credit to an *estimated liability.* When the liability is discharged, the debit is to the estimated liability and the credit is to the assets consumed.

agent. One authorized to transact business, including executing contracts, for another.

aging accounts receivable. The process of classifying *accounts receivable* by the time elapsed since the claim came into existence for the purpose of estimating the amount of uncollectible accounts receivable as of a given date. See *sales, uncollectible accounts adjustment* and *allowance for uncollectibles.*

aging schedule. A listing of *accounts receivable,* classified by age, used in *aging account receivable.*

AICPA. American Institute of Certified Public Accountants. The national organization that represents CPAs. It oversees the writing and grading of the Uniform CPA Examination. Each state, however, sets its own requirements for becoming a CPA in that state. See *certified public accountant.*

all-capital earnings rate. Net *income* plus interest charges, net of tax effects, plus minority interest in income divided by average total assets. Perhaps the single most useful ratio for assessing management's overall operating performance. See *ratio.*

all financial resources. All *assets* less all *liabilities.* Sometimes the *statement of changes in financial position* explains the changes in all financial resources rather than only the changes in *working capital.*

all-inclusive (income) concept. Under this concept, no distinction is drawn between *operating* and *nonoperating revenues* and *expenses;* thus the only entries to retained earnings are for *net income* and *dividends.* Under this concept all income, *gains* and *losses* are reported in the *income statement;* thus, events usually reported as *prior-period adjustments* and as *corrections of errors* are included in net income. This concept in its pure form is not the basis of *GAAP,* but *APB Opinions* No. 9 and 30 move very far in this direction. They do permit retained earnings entries for prior-period adjustments and correction of errors.

allocate. To spread a *cost* from one *account* to several accounts, to several products, or activities, or to several periods.

allocation of income taxes. See *deferred income tax.*

allowance. A balance sheet *contra account* generally used for *receivables* and depreciable assets. See *sales* (or *purchase*) *allowance* for another use of this term.

allowance for funds used during construction. One principle of public utility regulation and rate setting is that customers should pay the full costs of producing the services (e.g., electricity) that they use—nothing more and nothing less. Thus a public utility is even more careful than other businesses to capitalize into an *asset account* the full costs, but no more, of producing a new electric power generating plant. One of the costs of building a new plant is the *interest* cost on money tied up during construction. If *funds* are explicitly borrowed by an ordinary business, the journal entry for interest of $1,000 is typically:

Interest Expense 1,000
   Interest Payable 1,000
Interest expense for the period.

If the firm is a public utility constructing a new plant (or one of a group of ordinary businesses that for whatever reason

follows the same practice in constructing new plants), then another entry would be made:

Construction Work in Progress 750
   Interest Expense 750
Capitalize relevant portion of interest relating to construction work in progress into the asset account.

The cost of the *plant asset* is increased; when the plant is used, *depreciation* is charged; the interest will become an expense through the depreciation process in the later period of use, not currently as the interest is paid. Thus the full cost of the electricity generated during a given period is reported as expense in that period.

But suppose, as is common, that the electric utility does not explicitly borrow the funds, but uses some of its own funds, including funds raised from shares as well as from debt. Even though there is no explicit interest expense, there is the *opportunity cost* of the funds. Put another way, the cost of the plant under construction is not less in an economic sense just because the firm used its own cash, rather than borrow. The public utility using its own funds, on which $750 of interest would be payable if the funds had been explicitly borrowed, will make the following entry:

Construction Work in Progress $750
   Allowance for Funds Used During
     Construction $750
Recognition of interest, an opportunity cost, on own funds used.

The allowance account is a form of *revenue,* to appear on the income statement, and will be closed to Retained Earnings, increasing it. On the *funds statement,* it is an income or revenue item not producing funds and so must be subtracted from net income in deriving *funds provided by operations.*

allowance for uncollectibles (accounts receivable). A *contra* to Accounts Receivable that shows the estimated amount of *accounts receivable* that will not be collected. When such an allowance is used, the actual *write-off* of specific accounts receivable (*debit* allowance, *credit* specific account) does not affect *revenue* or *expense* at the time of the write-off. The revenue reduction is recognized when the allowance is credited; the amount of the credit to the allowance may be based on a percentage of sales on account for a period of time or determined from *aging accounts receivable.* This contra account enables an estimate to be shown of the amount of receivables that will be collected without identifying specific uncollectible accounts. See *allowance method.*

allowance method. A method of attempting to *match* all *expenses* of a transaction with its associated *revenues.* Usually involves a debit to expense and credit to an *estimated liability,* such as for estimated warranty expenditures, or a debit to a revenue (*contra*) account and a credit to an asset (*contra*) account, such as for uncollectible accounts. See *allowance for uncollectibles* for further explanation. When the allowance method is used for *sales discounts,* sales are recorded at *gross invoice* prices (not reduced by the amounts of discounts made available). An estimate of the amount of discounts to be taken is debited to a *revenue contra account* and *credited* to an allowance account, shown contra to *accounts receivable.*

American Accounting Association. An organization primarily for academic accountants, but open to all interested in accounting. See *The Accounting Review.*

American Institute of Certified Public Accountants. See *AICPA.*

American Stock Exchange. AMEX. ASE. A public market where various corporate *securities* are traded.

AMEX. *American Stock Exchange.*

amortization. The general process of *allocating acquisition cost* of assets to either the periods of benefit as *expenses* or to *inventory* accounts as *product costs.* Called *depreciation* for *plant assets, depletion* for *wasting assets* (natural resources), and *amortization* for *intangibles.* Also used for the process of allocating *premium* or *discount* on *bonds* and other *liabilities* to the periods during which the liability is outstanding.

analysis of changes in working capital accounts. The *statement of changes in financial position* explains the causes of the changes in *working capital* during a period. This part of the statement, which may appear in footnotes, shows the net changes in the specific working capital accounts that have been explained in the main section of the statement.

analysis of variances. See *variance analysis.*

annual report. A report for stockholders and other interested parties prepared once a year; includes a *balance sheet,* an *income statement,* a *statement of changes in financial position,* a reconciliation of changes in *owners' equity* accounts, a *summary of significant accounting principles,* other explanatory notes, the *auditor's report,* and, perhaps, comments from management about the year's events. See *10-K* and *financial statements.*

annuitant. One who receives an *annuity.*

annuity. A series of payments, usually made at equally spaced time intervals.

annuity certain. An *annuity* payable for a definite number of periods. Contrast with *contingent annuity.*

annuity due. An *annuity* whose first payment is made at the start of period 1 (or at the end of period 0). Contrast with *annuity in arrears.*

annuity in advance. *An annuity due.*

annuity in arrears. An *ordinary annuity* whose first payment occurs at the end of the first period.

annuity method of depreciation. See *compound interest depreciation.*

antidilutive. Said of a *potentially dilutive security* that will increase *earnings per share* if it is *exercised* or *converted* into common stock. In computing *primary* and *fully diluted earnings per share,* antidilutive securities may not be assumed to be exercised or converted and hence do not affect reported earnings per share in a given period.

APB. Accounting Principles Board of the *AICPA.* It was responsible for setting *accounting principles* from 1959 through 1973, issuing 31 *APB Opinions.* It was superseded by the *FASB.*

APB Opinion. The name given to pronouncements of the APB that make up much of *generally accepted accounting principles;* there are 31 APB Opinions, issued from 1962 through 1973.

APB Statement. The *APB* issued four Statements between 1962 and 1970. The Statements were approved by at least two-thirds of the Board, but they are recommendations, not requirements. For example, Statement No. 3 (1969) suggested the publication of *general price level adjusted statements* but did not require them.

APBs. An abbreviation used for *APB Opinions.*

application of funds. Any transaction that reduces *funds* (however "funds" is defined). A *use of funds.*

applied overhead. *Overhead costs* charged to departments, products, or activities.

appraisal. The process of obtaining a valuation for an *asset* or *liability* that involves expert opinion rather than explicit market transactions.

appraisal method of depreciation. The periodic *depreciation* charge is the difference between the beginning and end-of-period appraised value of the *asset* if that difference is positive. If negative, there is no charge. Not generally accepted.

appreciation. An increase in economic worth caused by rising market prices for an *asset.* Contrast with *accretion.*

appropriated retained earnings. See *retained earnings, appropriated.*

appropriation. In governmental accounting, an *expenditure* authorized for a specified amount, purpose, and time.

ARB. *Accounting Research Bulletin.*

arbitrage. Strictly speaking, the simultaneous purchase in one market and sale in another of a *security* or commodity in hope of making a *profit* on price differences in the different markets. Often this term is loosely used when the item sold is somewhat different from the item purchased; for example, the sale of shares of *common stock* and the simultaneous purchase of a *convertible bond* that is convertible into identical common shares.

arms' length. Said of a transaction negotiated by unrelated parties, each acting in his or her own self interest; the basis for a *fair market value* determination.

arrears. Said of *cumulative preferred stock dividends* that have not been declared up to the current date. See *annuity in arrears* for another context.

ARS. *Accounting Research Study.*

articles of incorporation. Document filed with state authorities by persons forming a corporation. When the document is returned with a certificate of incorporation, it becomes the corporation's *charter.*

articulate. Said of the relationship between any operating statement (for example, *income statement* or *statement of changes in financial position*) and *comparative balance sheets,* where the operating statement explains (or reconciles) the change in some major balance sheet category (for example, *retained earnings* or *working capital*).

ASE. American Stock Exchange.

ASR. *Accounting Series Release.*

assess. To value property for the purpose of property taxation; the assessment is determined by the taxing authority. To levy a charge on the owner of property for improvements thereto, such as for sewers or sidewalks.

asset.   A future benefit or service potential, recognized in accounting only when a transaction has occurred. May be *tangible* or *intangible, short-term* (current) or *long-term* (noncurrent).

asset depreciation range. ADR.   The range of *depreciable lives* allowed by the *Internal Revenue Service* for a specific depreciable *asset.*

asset turnover.   Ratio of net sales to average assets. See *ratio.*

at par.   Said of a *bond* or *preferred stock* issued or selling at its *face amount.*

attachment.   The laying claim to the *assets* of a borrower or debtor by a lender or creditor when the borrower has failed to pay debts on time.

attest.   Rendering of an *opinion* by an auditor that the *financial statements* are fair. This procedure is called the "attest function" of the CPA. See *fair presentation.*

audit.   Systematic inspection of accounting records involving analyses, tests, and *confirmations.* See *internal audit.*

audit committee.   A committee of the board of directors of a *corporation* usually consisting of outside directors who nominate the independent auditors and discuss the auditors' work with them. If the auditors believe certain matters should be brought to the attention of stockholders, the auditors first bring these matters to the attention of the audit committee.

Audit Guides.   See *Industry Audit guides.*

audit program.   The procedures followed by the *auditor* in carrying out the *audit.*

audit trail.   A reference accompanying an *entry,* or *posting,* to an underlying source record or document. A good audit trail is essential for efficiently checking the accuracy of accounting entries. See *cross-reference.*

auditing standards.   A set of 10 standards promulgated by the *AICPA,* including three general standards, three standards of field work, and four standards of reporting. According to the AICPA, these standards "deal with the measures of the quality of the performance and the objectives to be attained," rather than with specific auditing procedures.

auditor.   One who checks the accuracy, fairness, and general acceptability of accounting records and statements and then *attests* to them.

auditor's opinion.   *Auditor's report.*

auditor's report.   The auditor's statement of the work done and an opinion of the *financial statements.* Opinions are usually unqualified ("clean"), but may be *qualified,* or the auditor may disclaim an opinion in the report. Often called the "accountant's report." See *adverse opinion.*

authorized capital stock.   The number of *shares* of stock that can be issued by a corporation; specified by the *articles of incorporation.*

average.   The arithmetic mean of a set of numbers; obtained by summing the items and dividing by the number of items.

average collection period of receivables.   See *ratio.*

average tax rate.   The rate found by dividing *income tax expense* by *net income* before taxes. Contrast with *marginal tax rate, statutory tax rate.*

average-cost flow assumption.   An *inventory flow assumption* where the cost of units is the *weighted average* cost of the beginning inventory and purchases. See *inventory equation.*

avoidable cost.   An *incremental* or *variable cost.* See *programmed cost.*

bad debt.   An *uncollectible account receivable;* see *sales, uncollectible accounts adjustment.*

bad debt expense.   See *sales, uncollectible accounts adjustment.*

bad debt recovery.   Collection, perhaps partial, of a specific account receivable previously written off as uncollectible. If the *allowance method* is used, the *credit* is usually to the *allowance* account. If the direct write-off method is used, the credit is to a *revenue account.*

balance.   The difference between the sum of *debit* entries minus the sum of *credit* entries in an *account.* If positive, the difference is called a debit balance; if negative, a credit balance.

balance sheet.   Statement of financial position that shows *total assets = total liabilities + owners' equity.*

balance sheet account.   An account that can appear on a balance sheet. A *permanent account;* contrast with *temporary account.*

bank balance.   The amount of the balance in a checking account shown on the *bank statement.* Compare with *adjusted bank balance* and see *bank reconciliation schedule.*

bank prime rate.   See *prime rate.*

bank reconciliation schedule.   A schedule that shows how the difference between the book balance of the cash in bank account and the bank's statement can be explained. Takes into account the amount of such items as checks issued that have not cleared or deposits that have not been recorded by the bank as well as errors made by the bank or the firm.

bank statement.   A statement sent by the bank to a checking account customer showing deposits, checks cleared, and service charges for a period, usually one month.

bankrupt.   Said of a company whose *liabilities* exceed its *assets* where a legal petition has been filed and accepted under the bankruptcy law. A bankrupt firm is usually, but need not be, *insolvent.*

basis.   *Acquisition cost,* or some substitute therefor, of an asset used in computing gain or loss on disposition or retirement.

basket purchase.   Purchase of a group of assets for a single price; *costs* must be assigned to each of the assets so that the individual items can be recorded in the *accounts.*

bear.   One who believes that security prices will fall. A "bear market" refers to a time when stock prices are generally declining. Contrast with *bull.*

bearer bond.   See *registered bond* for contrast and definition.

beginning inventory. Valuation of *inventory* on hand at the beginning of the accounting period.

betterment. An *improvement,* usually *capitalized.*

bid. An offer to purchase, or the amount of the offer.

big bath. A *write-off* of a substantial amount of costs previously treated as *assets.* Usually caused when a corporation drops a line of business that required a large investment but that proved to be unprofitable. Sometimes used to describe a situation where a corporation takes a large write-off in one period in order to free later periods of gradual write-offs of those amounts. In this sense it frequently occurs when there is a change in top management.

Big Eight. The eight largest *public accounting* (*CPA*) partnerships; in alphabetical order: Arthur Andersen & Co.; Coopers & Lybrand; Deloitte Haskins & Sells; Ernst & Ernst; Peat, Marwick, Mitchell & Co.; Price Waterhouse & Co.; Touche Ross & Co.; and Arthur Young & Company.

bill. An *invoice* of charges and *terms of sale* for *goods* and *services.* Also, a piece of currency.

bill of materials. A specification of the quantities of *direct materials* expected to be used to produce a given job or quantity of output.

board of directors. The governing body of a corporation elected by the stockholders.

bond. A certificate to show evidence of debt. The *par value* is the *principal* or face amount of the bond payable at maturity. The *coupon rate* is the amount of interest payable in one year divided by the principal amount. Coupon bonds have attached to them coupons that can be redeemed at stated dates for interest payments. Normally, bonds are issued in $1,000 units and carry semiannual coupons.

bond conversion. The act of exchanging *convertible bonds* for *preferred* or *common stock.*

bond discount. From the standpoint of the issuer of a *bond* at the issue date, the excess of the *par value* of a bond over its initial sales price; at later dates the excess of par over the sum of (initial issue price plus the portion of discount already amortized). From the standpoint of a bondholder, the difference between par value and selling price when the bond sells below par.

bond indenture. The contract between an issuer of *bonds* and the bondholders.

bond premium. Exactly parallel to *bond discount* except that the issue price (or current selling price) is higher than *par value.*

bond ratings. Ratings of corporate and *municipal bond* issues by Moody's Investors Service and by Standard & Poor's Corporation, based on the issuer's existing *debt* level, its previous record of payment, the *coupon rate* on the bonds, and the safety of the *assets* or *revenues* that are committed to paying off *principal* and *interest.* Moody's top rating is Aaa; Standard & Poor's is AAA.

bond redemption. Retirement of *bonds.*

bond refunding. To incur *debt,* usually through the issue of new *bonds,* intending to use the proceeds to retire an *outstanding* bond *issue.*

bond sinking fund. See *sinking fund.*

bond table. A table showing the current price of a *bond* as a function of the *coupon rate,* years to *maturity,* and effective *yield to maturity* (or *effective rate*).

bonus. Premium over normal *wage* or *salary,* paid usually for meritorious performance.

bonus method. When a new partner is admitted to a *partnership* and the new partner is to be credited with *capital* in excess proportion to the amount of *tangible* assets he or she contributes, two methods may be used to recognize this excess, say $10,000. First, $10,000 may be transferred from the old partners to the new one. This is the bonus method. Second, goodwill in the amount of $10,000 may be recognized as an asset with the credit to the new partner's capital account. This is the *goodwill method.* (Notice that the new partner's percentage of total ownership is *not* the same under the two methods.) If the new partner is to be credited with capital in smaller proportion than the amount of contribution, then there will be bonus or goodwill for the old partners.

book. As a verb, to record a transaction. As a noun, usually plural, the *journals* and *ledgers.* As an adjective, see *book value.*

book inventory. An *inventory* amount that results, not from physical count, but from the amount of initial inventory plus *invoice* amounts of purchases less invoice amounts of *requisitions* or withdrawals; implies a perpetual method.

book of original entry. A *journal.*

book value. The amount shown in the books or in the *accounts* for any *asset, liability,* or *owners' equity* item. Generally used to refer to the net amount of an asset or group of assets shown in the accounts that record the asset and reductions, such as for *amortization,* in its cost. Of a firm, the excess of total assets over total liabilities. *Net assets.*

book value per share of common stock. Common *stockholders' equity* divided by the number of shares of *common stock outstanding.* See *ratio.*

bookkeeping. The process of analyzing and recording transactions in the accounting records.

boot. The additional money paid or received along with a used item in a trade-in or exchange transaction for another item. See *trade-in transaction.*

borrower. See *loan.*

branch. A sales office or other unit of an enterprise physically separated from the home office of the enterprise but not organized as a legally separate *subsidiary.* The term is rarely used to refer to manufacturing units.

branch accounting. An accounting procedure that enables the financial position and operations of each *branch* to be reported separately but later combined for published statements.

breakeven point. The volume of sales required so that total *revenues* and total *costs* are equal. May be expressed in units (*fixed costs/contribution per unit*) or in sales dollars [selling price per unit × (fixed costs/contribution per unit)].

budget. A financial plan used to estimate the results of future operations. Frequently used to help control future operations.

budgetary accounts. In governmental accounting, the accounts that reflect estimated operations and financial condition, as affected by estimated *revenues, appropriations,* and *encumbrances. Proprietary accounts* record the transactions.

budgetary control. Management of governmental (nongovernmental) unit in accordance with an official (approved) *budget* in order to keep total expenditures within authorized (planned) limits.

budgeted statements. *Pro forma* statements prepared before the event or period occurs.

bull. One who believes that security prices will rise. A "bull market" refers to a time when stock prices are generally rising. Contrast with *bear.*

burden. See *overhead costs.*

business combination. As defined by the *APB* in Opinion No. 16, the bringing together into a single accounting *entity* of two or more incorporated or unincorporated businesses. The *merger* will be accounted for either with the *purchase method* or the *pooling-of-interests method.* See *conglomerate.*

business entity. *Entity. Accounting entity.*

bylaws. The rules adopted by the stockholders of a corporation that specify the general methods for carrying out the functions of the corporation.

by-product. A *joint product* of relatively minor value. Whereas *joint costs* are allocated among joint products, none of the joint costs is typically allocated to byproducts. Rather, the net proceeds from the sale of byproducts is *credited* to the *cost* of the major joint products, thus reducing that joint cost or, less often and less preferably, the proceeds are credited to a *revenue account.*

CA. *Chartered Accountant.*

call premium. See *callable bond.*

call price. See *callable bond.*

callable bond. A *bond* for which the issuer reserves the right to pay a specific amount, the call price, to retire the obligation before *maturity* date. If the issuer agrees to pay more than the *face amount* of the bond when called, the excess of the payment over the face amount is the call premium.

Canadian Institute of Chartered Accountants. The national organization that represents *Chartered Accountants* in Canada.

cancelable lease. See *lease.*

capacity costs. A *fixed cost* incurred to provide a firm with the capability to produce or to sell. Consists of *standby costs* and *enabling costs.* Contrast with *programmed costs.*

capital. *Owners' equity* in a business. Often used, equally correctly, to mean the total assets of a business. Sometimes used to mean *capital assets.*

capital asset. Properly used, a designation for income tax purposes that describes property held by a taxpayer, except *cash,* inventoriable *assets,* goods held primarily for sale, most

depreciable property, *real estate, receivables,* certain *intangibles,* and a few other items. Sometimes this term is imprecisely used to describe *plant* and *equipment,* which are clearly not capital assets under the income tax definition. Often the term is used to refer to an *investment* in *securities.*

capital budget. Plan of proposed outlays for acquiring long-term *assets* and the means of *financing* the acquisition.

capital budgeting. The process of choosing *investment* projects for an enterprise by considering the *present value* of cash flows and deciding how to raise the funds required by the investment.

capital consumption allowance. The term used for *depreciation expense* in national income accounting and the reporting of flows of funds in the economy.

capital contributed in excess of par (or stated) value. A preferred title for the account that shows the amount received by the issuer for *capital stock* in excess of *par (or stated) value.*

capital expenditure (outlay). An *expenditure* to acquire long-term *assets.*

capital gain. The excess of proceeds over *cost,* or other basis, from the sale of a *capital asset* as defined by the Internal Revenue Code. If the capital asset is held more than nine months before sale, then the tax on the gain is computed at a rate lower than is used for other gains and ordinary income.

capital lease. See *financing lease.*

capital loss. A negative capital gain; see *capital gain.*

capital rationing. In a *capital budgeting* context, the imposing of constraints on the amounts of total capital expenditures in each period.

capital stock. The ownership shares of a corporation. Consists of all classes of *common* and *preferred stock.*

capital structure. The composition of a corporation's equities; the relative proportions of *short-term debt, long-term debt,* and *owners' equity.*

capital surplus. An inferior term for *capital contributed in excess of par (or stated) value.*

capitalization of a corporation. A term used by investment analysts to indicate *stockholders' equity* plus *bonds outstanding.*

capitalization of earnings. The process of estimating the economic worth of a firm by computing the *net present value* of the predicted *net income* (not *cash flows*) of the firm for the future.

capitalization rate. An *interest rate* used to convert a series of payments or receipts or earnings into a single *present value.*

capitalize. To record an *expenditure* that may benefit a future period as an *asset* rather than to treat the expenditure as an *expense* of the period of its occurrence. Whether or not expenditures for advertising or for research and development should be capitalized is controversial, but *FASB Statement* No. 2 requires expensing of R&D costs. We believe expenditures should be capitalized if they lead to future benefits and thus meet the criterion to be an asset.

carryback, carryforward, carryover. The use of losses or tax credits in one period to reduce income taxes payable in other periods. There are three common kinds of carrybacks: for net operating losses, for *capital losses,* and for the *investment tax credit.* The first two are applied against taxable income and the third against the actual tax. In general, carrybacks are for three years with the earliest year first. Operating losses and the investment tax credit can be carried forward for 7 years. Corporate capital loss carryforwards are for 5 years. The capital loss for individuals can be carried forward indefinitely.

carrying cost. Costs (such as property taxes and insurance) of holding, or storing, *inventory* from the time of purchase until the time of sale or use.

carrying value (amount). *Book value.*

CASB. Cost Accounting Standards Board. A board of five members authorized by the U.S. Congress to "promulgate cost-accounting standards designed to achieve uniformity and consistency in the cost-accounting principles followed by defense contractors and subcontractors under federal contracts." The *principles* promulgated by the CASB are likely to have considerable weight in practice where the *FASB* has not established a standard.

cash. Currency and coins, negotiable checks, and balances in bank accounts.

cash basis of accounting. In contrast to the *accrual basis of accounting,* a system of accounting in which *revenues* are recognized when *cash* is received and *expenses* are recognized as *disbursements* are made. No attempt is made to *match revenues* and *expenses* in determining *income.* See *modified cash basis.*

cash budget. A schedule of expected cash *receipts* and *disbursements.*

cash collection basis. The *installment method* for recognizing *revenue.* Not to be confused with the *cash basis of accounting.*

cash cycle. The period of time that elapses during which *cash* is converted into *inventories,* inventories are converted into *accounts receivable,* and receivables are converted back into cash. *Earnings cycle.*

cash disbursements journal. A specialized *journal* used to record *expenditures* by *cash* and by *check.* If a *check register* is also used, a cash disbursements journal records only expenditures of currency and coins.

cash discount. A reduction in sales or purchase price allowed for prompt payment.

cash dividend. See *dividend.*

cash equivalent value. A term used to describe the amount for which an *asset* could be sold. *Market value. Fair market price* (*value*).

cash flow. Cash *receipts* minus *disbursements* from a given *asset,* or group of assets, for a given period.

cash flow statement. A statement similar to the typical *statement of changes in financial position* where the flows of cash, rather than of *working capital,* are explained.

cash receipts journal. A specialized *journal* used to record all *receipts* of *cash.*

cash (surrender) value of life insurance. An amount equal, not to the face value of the policy to be paid in event of death, but to the amount that could be realized if the policy were immediately canceled and traded with the insurance company for cash.

cash yield. See *yield.*

cashier's check. A bank's own *check* drawn on itself and signed by the cashier or other authorized official. It is a direct obligation of the bank. Compare with *certified check.*

CCA. Current-cost accounting; *current-value accounting.*

central corporate expenses. General *overhead expenses* incurred in running the corporate headquarters and related supporting activities of a corporation. These expenses are treated as *period expenses.* Contrast with *manufacturing overhead.* A major problem in *line-of-business reporting* is the treatment of these expenses.

certificate. The document that is the physical embodiment of a *bond* or a *share of stock.* A term sometimes used for the *auditor's report.*

certificate of deposit. Federal law constrains the *rate of interest* that banks can pay. Under current law, banks are allowed to pay a higher rate than the one allowed on a *time deposit* if the depositor promises to leave funds on deposit for several months or more. When the bank receives such funds, it issues a certificate of deposit. The depositor can withdraw the funds before maturity if a penalty is paid.

certified check. The *check* of a depositor drawn on a bank on the face of which the bank has inserted the words "accepted" or "certified" with the date and signature of a bank official. The check then becomes an obligation of the bank. Compare with *cashier's check.*

certified financial statement. A financial statement attested to by an independent *auditor* who is a *CPA.*

certified internal auditor. See *CIA.*

certified public accountant (CPA). An accountant who has satisfied the statutory and administrative requirements of his or her jurisdiction to be registered or licensed as a public accountant. In addition to passing the Uniform CPA Examination administered by the *AICPA,* the CPA must meet certain educational, experience, and moral requirements that differ from jurisdiction to jurisdiction. The jurisdictions are the 50 states, the District of Columbia, Guam, Puerto Rico, and the Virgin Islands.

chain discount. A series of *discount* percentages; for example, if a chain discount of 10 and 5 percent is quoted, then the actual, or *invoice,* price is the nominal, or list, price times .90 times .95, or 85.5% of invoice price.

change fund. Coins and currency issued to cashiers, delivery drivers, and so on.

changes, accounting. See *accounting changes.*

changes in financial position. See *statement of changes in financial position.*

charge. As a noun, a *debit* to an account; as a verb, to debit.

charge off. To treat as a *loss* or *expense* an amount originally recorded as an *asset;* usually the term is used when the charge is not in accord with original expectations.

chart of accounts. A list of names and numbers of *accounts* systematically organized.

charter. Document issued by a state government authorizing the creation of a corporation.

chartered accountant (CA). The title used in Australia, Canada, and the United Kingdom for an accountant who has satisfied the requirements of the institute of his or her jurisdiction to be qualified to serve as a *public accountant.* In Canada, each provincial institute or order has the right to administer the examination and set the standards of performance and ethics for Chartered Accountants in its province. For a number of years, however, the provincial organizations have pooled their rights to qualify new members through the Interprovincial Education Committee, and the result is that there are nationally set and graded examinations given in English and French. The pass/fail grade awarded by the Board of Examiners (a subcommittee of the Interprovincial Education Committee) is rarely deviated from.

check. You know what a check is. The Federal Reserve Board defines a check as "a *draft* or order upon a bank or banking house purporting to be drawn upon a deposit of funds for the payment at all events of a certain sum of money to a certain person therein named or to him or his order or to bearer and payable instantly on demand." It must contain the phrase "pay to the order of." The amount shown on the check's face must be clearly readable and it must have the signature of the drawer. Checks need not be dated, although they usually are. The *balance* in the *cash account* is usually reduced when a check is issued, not later when it clears the bank and reduces cash in bank.

check register. A *journal* to record *checks* issued.

CIA. Certified Internal Auditor. One who has satisfied certain requirements of the *Institute of Internal Auditors* including experience, ethics, education, and examinations.

CICA. *Canadian Institute of Chartered Accountants.*

CIF. A term used in contracts along with the name of a given port to indicate that the quoted price includes insurance, handling, and freight charges up to delivery by the seller at the given port.

circulating capital. *Working capital.*

clean opinion. See *auditor's report.*

clean surplus concept. The notion that the only entries to the *retained earnings* account are to record net earnings and dividends. Contrast with *current operating performance concept.* This concept, with minor exceptions, is now controlling in *GAAP.* (See *APB Opinions* Nos. 9 and 30.)

clearing account. An account containing amounts to be transferred to another account(s) before the end of the *accounting period.* Examples are the *income summary* account (whose balance is transferred to retained earnings) and the purchases account (whose balance is transferred to *inventory* or to *cost of goods sold*).

close. As a verb, to transfer the *balance* of a *temporary* or *contra* or *adjunct* account to the main account to which it relates; for example, to transfer *revenue* and *expense* accounts directly, or through the *income summary* account, to an *owner's equity* account, or to transfer *purchase discounts* to purchases.

closed account. An account with equal debits and credits, usually as a result of a closing entry. See *ruling an account.*

closing entries. The entries that accomplish the transfer of balances in temporary accounts to the related balance sheet accounts. See *work sheet.*

closing inventory. *Ending inventory.*

CMA. Certificate in Management Accounting. Awarded by the Institute of Management Accounting of the *National Association of Accountants* to those who pass a set of examinations and meet certain experience and continuing education requirements.

CoCoA. *Continuously contemporary accounting.*

coding of accounts. The numbering of *accounts,* as for a *chart of accounts,* which is particularly necessary for computerized accounting.

coinsurance. Insurance policies that protect against hazards such as fire or water damage often specify that the owner of the property may not collect the full amount of insurance for a loss unless the insurance policy covers at least some specified percentage, usually about 80 percent, of the *replacement cost* of the property. Coinsurance clauses induce the owner to carry full, or nearly full, coverage.

collateral. Assets pledged by a *borrower* that will be given up if the *loan* is not paid.

collectible. Capable of being converted into cash; now, if due; later, otherwise.

commercial paper. *Short-term notes* issued by corporate borrowers.

commission. Remuneration, usually expressed as a percentage, to employees based on an activity rate, such as sales.

Committee on Accounting Procedure. Predecessor of the *APB.* The *AICPA's* principle-promulgating body from 1939 through 1959. Its 51 pronouncements are called *Accounting Research Bulletins.*

common cost. *Cost* resulting from use of *raw materials,* a facility (for example, plant or machines), or a service (for example, fire insurance) that benefits several products or departments and must be allocated to those products or departments. Common costs result when multiple products are produced together although they could be produced separately; joint costs occur when multiple products are of necessity produced together. Many writers use common costs and *joint costs* synonymously. See *joint costs, indirect costs,* and *overhead.*

common monetary measuring unit. For U.S. corporations, the dollar. See also *stable monetary unit assumption.*

common stock. *Stock* representing the class of owners who have residual claims on the assets and earnings of a corporation after all debt and preferred stockholders' claims have been met.

common stock equivalent. A *security* whose primary value arises from its ability to be exchanged for *common shares;* includes *stock options, warrants,* and also *convertible bonds* or *convertible preferred stock* whose cash *yield* for any year within 5 years of issue is less than two-thirds the *prime rate* at the time of issue.

common-dollar accounting. General *price level adjusted accounting.*

common-size statement. A *percentage statement* usually based on total *assets* or *net sales* or *revenues.*

company-wide control. See *control system.*

comparative (financial) statements. Financial statements showing information for the same company for different times, usually two successive years. Nearly all published financial statements are in this form. See the annual report for International Corporation in Appendix A. Contrast with *historical summary.*

compensating balance. When a bank lends funds to a customer, it often requires that the customer keep on deposit in his or her checking account an amount equal to some percentage, say 20 percent, of the loan. The amount required to be left on deposit is the compensating balance. Such amounts effectively increase the *interest rate.* The amounts of such balances must be disclosed in *notes* to the *financial statements.*

completed-contract method. Recognizing *revenues* and *expenses* for a job or order only when it is finished, except that when a loss on the contract is expected, revenues and expenses are recognized in the period when the loss is first forecast.

completed-sales basis. See *sales basis of revenue recognition.*

composite depreciation. *Group depreciation* of dissimilar items.

composite life method. *Group depreciation,* which see, for items of unlike kind. The term may be used when a single item, such as a crane, which consists of separate units with differing service lives, such as the chassis, the motor, the lifting mechanism, and so on, is depreciated as a whole rather than treating each of the components separately.

compound entry. A *journal entry* with more than one *debit* or more than one *credit,* or both. See *trade-in transaction* for an example.

compound interest. *Interest* calculated on *principal* plus previously undistributed interest.

compound interest depreciation. A method designed to hold the *rate of return* on an asset constant. First find the *internal rate of return* on the cash inflows and outflows of the asset. The periodic depreciation charge is the cash flow for the period less the internal rate of return multiplied by the asset's book value at the beginning of the period. When the cash flows from the asset are constant over time, the method is sometimes called the "annuity method" of depreciation.

compounding period. The time period for which *interest* is calculated. At the end of the period, the interest may be paid to the lender or added (that is, converted) to principal for the next interest-earning period, which is usually a year or some portion of a year.

comprehensive budget. *Master budget.*

comptroller. Same meaning and pronunciation as *controller.*

confirmation. A formal memorandum delivered by the customers or suppliers of a company to its independent *auditor* verifying the amounts shown as receivable or payable. The confirmation document is originally sent by the auditor to the customer. If the auditor asks that the document be returned whether the *balance* is correct or incorrect, then it is called a "positive confirmation." If the auditor asks that the document be returned only if there is an error, it is called a "negative confirmation."

conglomerate. *Holding company.* This term is used when the owned companies are in dissimilar lines of business.

conservatism. A *reporting objective* that calls for anticipation of all *losses* and *expenses* but defers recognition of *gains* or *profits* until they are *realized* in *arms'-length* transactions. In the absence of certainty, events are to be reported in a way that tends to minimize current income.

consignee. See *on consignment.*

consignment. See *on consignment.*

consignor. See *on consignment.*

consistency. Treatment of like *transactions* in the same way in consecutive periods so that financial statements will be more comparable than otherwise. The reporting policy implying that procedures, once adopted, should be followed from period to period by a reporting *entity.* See *accounting changes* for the treatment of inconsistencies.

consol. A *bond* that never matures; a *perpetuity* in the form of a bond. Originally issued by Great Britain after the Napoleonic wars to consolidate debt issues of that period. The term arose as an abbreviation for "consolidated annuities."

consolidated financial statements. Statements issued by legally separate companies that show financial position and income as they would appear if the companies were one legal *entity.* Such statements reflect an economic, rather than a legal, concept of the *entity.*

constructive receipt. An item is included in taxable income when the taxpayer can control funds whether or not cash has been received. For example, *interest* added to *principal* in a savings account is deemed to be constructively received.

consumer price index (CPI). A *price index* computed and issued monthly by the Bureau of Labor Statistics of the U.S. Department of Labor. The index attempts to track the price level of a group of goods and services purchased by the average consumer. Contrast with *GNP Implicit Price Deflator.*

contingent annuity. An *annuity* whose number of payments depends on the outcome of an event whose timing is uncertain at the time the annuity is set up; for example, an annuity payable for the life of the *annuitant.* Contrast with *annuity certain.*

contingent issue (securities). Securities issuable to specific individuals upon the occurrence of some event, such as the firm's attaining a specified level of earnings.

contingent liability. A potential *liability;* if a specified event were to occur, such as losing a lawsuit, a liability would be recognized. Until the outcome is known, the contingency is merely disclosed in notes rather than shown in the balance sheet accounts. A *material* contingency may lead to a qualified, *"subject to,"* auditor's opinion.

continuity of operations. The assumption in accounting that the business *entity* will continue to operate long enough for current plans to be carried out. The *going-concern assumption.*

continuous compounding. *Compound interest* where the *compounding period* is every instant of time. See *e* for the computation of the equivalent annual or periodic rate.

continuous inventory method. The *perpetual inventory* method.

continuously contemporary accounting. A name coined by the Australian theorist, Raymond J. Chambers, to indicate a combination of current-value accounting where amounts are general price level adjusted and all current-value measurements are exit values. CoCoA.

contra account. An *account,* such as *accumulated depreciation,* that accumulates subtractions from another account, such as machinery. Contrast with *adjunct account.*

contributed capital. The sum of the balances in *capital stock* accounts plus *capital contributed in excess of par (or stated) value* accounts. Contrast with *donated capital.*

contributed surplus. An inferior term for *capital contributed in excess of par value.*

contribution margin. *Revenue* from *sales* less all variable *expenses.* See *gross margin.*

contribution per unit. Selling price less *variable costs* per unit.

contributory. Said of a *pension plan* where employees, as well as employers, make payments to a pension *fund.* Note that the provisions for *vesting* are applicable to the employer's payments. Whatever the degree of vesting of the employer's payments, the employee typically gets back his or her payments, with interest, in case of death, or other cessation of employment, before retirement.

control (controlling) account. A summary *account* with totals equal to those of entries and balances that appear in individual accounts in a *subsidiary ledger.* Accounts Receivable is a control account backed up with accounts for each customer. The balance in a control account should not be changed unless a corresponding change is made in the subsidiary accounts.

control system. A device for ensuring that actions are carried out according to plan or for safeguarding *assets.* A system for ensuring that actions are carried out according to plan can be designed for a single function within the firm, called "operational control," for autonomous segments within the firm that generally have responsibility for both revenues and costs, called "divisional control," or for activities of the firm as a whole, called "company-wide control." Systems designed for safeguarding *assets* are called "internal control" systems.

controllable cost. A *cost* whose amount can be influenced by the way in which operations are carried out, such as advertising costs. These costs can be *fixed* or *variable.* See *programmed costs* and *managed costs.*

controlled company. A company, a majority of whose voting stock is held by an individual or corporation. Effective control can sometimes be exercised when less than 50 percent of the stock is owned.

controller. The title often used for the chief accountant of an organization. Often spelled *comptroller.*

conversion. The act of exchanging a convertible security for another security.

conversion cost. *Direct labor* costs plus factory *overhead* costs incurred in producing a product. That is, the cost to convert raw materials to finished products. *Manufacturing cost.*

conversion period. *Compounding period.* Period during which a *convertible bond* or *preferred stock* can be converted into *common stock.*

convertible bond. A *bond* that may be converted into a specified number of shares of *capital stock* during the *conversion period.*

convertible preferred stock. *Preferred stock* that may be converted into a specified number of shares of *common stock.*

co-product. A product sharing production facilities with another product. For example, if an apparel manufacturer produces shirts and jeans on the same line, these are co-products. Co-products are distinguished from *joint products* and *by-products* which, by their very nature, must be produced together, such as the various grades of wood produced in a lumber factory.

copyright. Exclusive right granted by the government to an individual author, composer, playwright, and the like for the life of the individual plus 50 years. If the copyright is granted to a firm, then the right extends 75 years after the original publication. The *economic life* of a copyright may be considerably less than the legal life as, for example, the copyright of this book.

corporation. A legal entity authorized by a state to operate under the rules of the entity's *charter.*

correction of errors. See *accounting errors.*

cost. The sacrifice, measured by the *price* paid or required to be paid, to acquire *goods* or *services.* See *acquisition cost* and *replacement cost.* The term "cost" is often used when referring to the valuation of a good or service acquired. When "cost" is used in this sense, a cost is an *asset.* When the benefits of the acquisition (the goods or services acquired) expire, the cost becomes an expense or *loss.* Some writers, however, use cost and expense as synonyms. Contrast with *expense.*

cost accounting. Classifying, summarizing, recording, reporting, and allocating current or predicted *costs.* A subset of *managerial accounting.*

Cost Accounting Standards Board. See *CASB.*

cost center. A unit of activity for which *expenditures* and *expenses* are accumulated.

cost effective. Among alternatives, the one whose benefit, or payoff, divided by cost is highest. Sometimes said of an action whose expected benefits exceed expected costs whether or not there are other alternatives with larger benefit/cost ratios.

cost-flow assumption. See *flow assumption.*

cost flows. Costs passing through various classifications within an entry. See *flow of costs* for a diagram.

cost method (for investments). Accounting for an investment in the *capital stock* of another company where the investment is shown at *acquisition cost,* and only *dividends* declared are treated as *revenue.* Used if less than 20 percent of the voting stock is held by the investor.

cost method (for treasury stock). The method of showing *treasury stock* as a *contra* to all other items of *stockholders' equity* in an amount equal to that paid to reacquire the stock.

cost of capital. The average rate per year a company must pay for its *equities.* In efficient capital markets, the *discount rate* that equates the expected *present value* of all future cash flows to common stockholders with the market value of common stock at a given time.

cost of goods manufactured. The sum of all costs allocated to products completed during a period; includes materials, labor, and *overhead.*

cost of goods purchased. Net purchase price of goods acquired plus costs of storage and delivery to the place where the items can be productively used.

cost of goods sold. Inventoriable *costs* that are expensed because the units are sold; equals beginning inventory plus *cost of goods purchased* or *manufactured* minus *ending inventory.*

cost of sales. Generally refers to *cost of goods sold;* occasionally, to *selling expenses.*

cost or market, whichever is lower. See *lower of cost or market.*

cost principle. The *principle* that requires reporting *assets* at *historical* or *acquisition cost,* less accumulated *amortization.* This principle is based on the assumption that cost is equal to *fair market value* at the date of acquisition and subsequent changes are not likely to be significant.

cost sheet. Statement that shows all the elements comprising the total cost of an item.

costing. The process of determining the cost of activities, products, or services. The British word for *cost accounting.*

cost-recovery-first method. A method of *revenue* recognition that *credits cost* as collections are received until all costs are recovered. Only after costs are completely recovered is *income* recognized. To be used only when the total amount of collections is highly uncertain. Contrast with the *installment method* where *pro rata* portions of all collections are credited both to cost and to income.

cost-to-cost. The *percentage-of-completion method* where the estimate of completion is the ratio of costs incurred to date divided by total costs expected to be incurred for the entire project.

coupon. That portion of a *bond* document redeemable at a specified date for *interest* payments. Its physical form is much like a ticket; each coupon is dated and is deposited at a bank, just like a check, for collection or is mailed to the issuer's agent for collection.

coupon rate. Of a *bond.* the amount of annual coupons divided by par value. Contrast with *effective rate.*

covenant. A promise with legal validity.

CPA. See *certified public accountant.* The *AICPA* suggests that no periods be shown in the abbreviation.

CPI. *Consumer price index.*

CPP. Current purchasing power; usually used as an adjective modifying the word "accounting" to mean the accounting that produces *price level adjusted statements.*

Cr. Abbreviation for *credit.*

credit. As a noun, an entry on the right-hand side of an *account.* As a verb, to make an entry on the right-hand side of an account. Records increases in *liabilities, owners' equity, revenues,* and *gains;* records decreases in *assets* and *expenses.* See *debit and credit conventions.* Also the ability or right to buy or borrow in return for a promise to pay later.

credit loss. The amount of *accounts receivable* that is, or is expected to become, *uncollectible.*

credit memorandum. A document used by a seller to inform a buyer that the buyer's *account receivable* is being credited (reduced) because of *errors, returns,* or *allowances.* Also, the document provided by a bank to a depositor to indicate that the depositor's balance is being increased because of some event other than a deposit, such as the collection by the bank of the depositor's *note receivable.*

creditor. One who lends.

cross-reference (index). A number placed by each *account* in a *journal entry* indicating the *ledger* account to which the entry is posted and placing in the ledger the page number of the journal where the entry was made. Used to link the *debit* and *credit* parts of an entry in the ledger accounts back to the original entry in the journal. See *audit trail.*

cross-section analysis. Analysis of *financial statements* of various firms for a single period of time, as opposed to time series analysis where statements of a given firm are analyzed over several periods of time.

cumulative dividend. Preferred stock *dividends* that, if not paid, accrue as a commitment that must be paid before dividends to common stockholders can be declared.

cumulative preferred stock. *Preferred* stock with *cumulative dividend* rights.

current asset. *Cash* and other *assets* that are expected to be turned into cash, sold, or exchanged within the normal operating cycle of the firm, usually 1 year. Current assets include *cash, marketable securities, receivables, inventory,* and *current prepayments.*

current cost. *Cost* stated in terms of current market prices rather than in terms of *acquisition cost. Current replacement cost.* See *net realizable value, current selling price.*

current fund. In governmental accounting, a synonym for *general fund.*

current funds. *Cash* and other assets readily convertible into cash.

current (gross) margin. See *operating margin (based on replacement costs).*

current liability. A debt or other obligation that must be discharged within a short time, usually the *earnings cycle* or 1 year, normally by expending *current assets.*

current operating performance concept. The notion that reported *income* for a period ought to reflect only ordinary, normal, and recurring operations of that period. A consequence is that *extraordinary* and nonrecurring items are entered directly in the Retained Earnings account. Contrast with *clean surplus concept*. This concept is no longer acceptable. (See *APB Opinions* Nos. 9 and 30.)

current ratio. Sum of *current assets* divided by sum of *current liabilities*. See *ratio*.

current replacement cost. Of an *asset*, the amount currently required to acquire an identical asset (in the same condition and with the same service potential) or an asset capable of rendering the same service at a current *fair market price*. If these two amounts differ, the lower is usually used. See *reproduction cost*.

current selling price. The amount for which an *asset* could be sold as of a given time in an *arms'-length* transaction, rather than in a forced sale.

current-value accounting. The form of accounting where all assets are shown at *current replacement cost (entry value)* or *current selling price* or *net realizable value (exit value)* and all *liabilities* are shown at *present value*. Entry and exit values may be quite different from each other, so there is no general agreement on the precise meaning of current-value accounting.

customers' ledger. The *ledger* that shows accounts receivable of individual customers. It is the *subsidiary ledger* for the *controlling account*, Accounts Receivable.

days of average inventory on hand. See *ratio*.

DDB. *Double-declining-balance depreciation.*

debenture bond. A *bond* not secured with *collateral*.

debit. As a noun, an entry on the left-hand side of an *account*. As a verb, to make an entry on the left-hand side of an account. Records increases in *assets* and *expenses;* records decreases in *liabilities, owners' equity,* and *revenues*. See *debit and credit conventions*.

debit and credit conventions. The equality of the two sides of the *accounting equation* is maintained by recording equal amounts of *debits* and *credits* for each *transaction*. The conventional use of the *T-account* form and the rules for debit and credit in *balance sheet accounts* are summarized as follows.

Any Asset Account

Opening Balance Increase	Decrease
+	−
Dr.	Cr.
Ending Balance	

Any Liability Account

Decrease	Opening Balance Increase
−	+
Dr.	Cr.
	Ending Balance

Any Owners' Equity Account

Decrease	Opening Balance Increase
−	+
Dr.	Cr.
	Ending Balance

Revenue and expense accounts belong to the owner's equity group. The relationship and the rules for debit and credit in these accounts can be expressed as follows.

Owners' Equity

Decrease		Increase	
−		+	
Dr.		Cr.	
Expenses		Revenues	
Dr.	Cr.	Dr.	Cr.
+	−	−	+
*			*

*Normal balance prior to closing.

debit memorandum. A document used by a seller to inform a buyer that the seller is debiting (increasing) the amount of the buyer's *account receivable* because of an error. Also, the document provided by a bank to a depositor to indicate that the depositor's *balance* is being decreased because of some event other than payment for a *check,* such as monthly service charges or the printing of checks.

debt. An amount owed. The general name for *notes, bonds, mortgages,* and the like that are evidence of amounts owed and have definite payment dates.

debt-equity ratio. Total *liabilities* divided by total *equities*. See *ratio*. Sometimes the denominator is merely total *stockholders' equity*. Sometimes the numerator is restricted to long-term *debt*.

debt financing. Raising *funds* by issuing *bonds, mortgages,* or *notes*. Contrast with *equity financing. Leverage.*

debt ratio. *Debt-equity ratio.*

debt service requirement. The amount of cash required for payments of *interest*, current maturities of *principal* on outstanding *debt*, and payments to *sinking funds* (corporations).

debtor. One who borrows.

declaration. Time when a *dividend* is declared by the *board of directors*.

declining-balance depreciation. The method of calculating the periodic *depreciation* charge by multiplying the *book value* at the start of the period by a constant percentage. In pure declining balance depreciation the constant percentage is $1 - \sqrt[n]{s/c}$ where n is the *depreciable life, s* is salvage value, and c is *acquisition cost*. See *double-declining-balance depreciation*.

deep discount bonds. Said of *bonds* selling much below (exactly how much is not clear) *par value*. A term sometimes used when there is a presumption that the *face amount* will not be paid at *maturity*.

defalcation. Embezzlement.

default. Failure to pay *interest* or *principal* on a *debt* when due.

deferral method. See *flow-through method* (of accounting for the *investment tax credit*) for definition and contrast.

deferred annuity. An *annuity* whose first payment is made sometime after the end of the first period.

deferred asset. *Deferred charge.*

deferred charge. *Expenditure* not recognized as an *expense* of the period when made but carried forward as an *asset* to be *written off* in future periods, such as for advance rent payments or insurance premiums.

deferred cost. *Deferred charge.*

deferred credit. Sometimes used to indicate *advances from customers*. Also sometimes used to describe the *deferred income tax liability*.

deferred debit. *Deferred charge.*

deferred expense. *Deferred charge.*

deferred gross margin. *Unrealized gross margin.*

deferred income. *Advances from customers.*

deferred income tax (liability). An *indeterminate-term liability* that arises when the pretax income shown on the tax return is less than what it would have been had the same *accounting principles* been used in tax returns as used for financial reporting. *APB Opinion* No. 11 requires that the firm debit income tax *expense* and credit deferred income tax with the amount of the taxes delayed by using different accounting principles in tax returns from those used in financial reports. See *timing difference* and *permanent difference*. See *installment sales*. If, as a result of timing differences, cumulative taxable income exceeds cumulative reported income before taxes, the deferred income tax account will have a *debit* balance and will be reported as a *deferred charge*.

deferred revenue. Sometimes used to indicate *advances from customers*.

deferred tax. See *deferred income tax*.

deficit. A *debit balance* in the Retained Earnings account; presented on the balance sheet as a *contra* to stockholders' equity.

defined benefit plan. A *pension plan* where the employer promises specific benefits to each eligible employee. The employer's cash contributions and pension expense are adjusted in relation to *actuarial* experience in the eligible employee group and investment performance of the pension *fund*. Sometimes called a "fixed-benefit" pension plan. Contrast with *money purchase plan*.

defined contribution plan. A *money purchase (pension) plan* or other arrangement, based on formula or discretion, where the employer makes cash contributions to eligible individual employee *accounts* under the terms of a written plan document.

deflation. A period of declining general prices.

demand deposit. *Funds* in a *checking account* at a bank.

demand loan. See *term loan* for definition and contrast.

denominator volume. Capacity measured in expected number of units to be produced this period; divided into *budgeted fixed costs* to obtain fixed costs applied per unit of product.

depletion. Exhaustion or *amortization* of a *wasting asset*, or natural resource. Also see *percentage depletion*.

depletion allowance. See *percentage depletion*.

deposit, sinking-fund. Payments made to a *sinking fund*.

deposits in transit. Deposits made by a firm but not yet reflected on the *bank statement*.

depreciable cost. That part of the *cost* of an asset, usually *acquisition cost* less *salvage value*, that is to be charged off over the life of the asset through the process of *depreciation*.

depreciable life. For an *asset*, the time period or units of activity (such as miles driven for a truck) over which *depreciable cost* is to be allocated. For tax returns, depreciable life may be shorter than estimated *service life*.

depreciation. *Amortization* of *plant assets;* the process of allocating the cost of an asset to the periods of benefit—the *depreciable life*. Classified as a *production cost* or a *period expense*, depending on the asset and whether *absorption* or *direct costing* is used. Depreciation methods described in this glossary include the *annuity method, appraisal method, composite method, compound interest method, declining-balance method, double-declining-balance method, production method, replacement method, retirement method, straight-line method, sinking-fund method,* and *sum-of-the-years'-digits method*.

depreciation reserve. An inferior term for *accumulated depreciation*. See *reserve*. Do not confuse with a replacement *fund*.

differential analysis. Analysis of *incremental costs*.

differential cost. *Incremental cost*. If a total cost curve is smooth (in mathematical terms, differentiable), then the curve graphing the derivative of the total cost curve is often said to show differential costs which show the cost increments associated with infinitesimal changes in volume.

dilution. A potential reduction in *earnings per share* or *book value* per share by the potential *conversion* of securities or by the potential exercise of *warrants* or *options*.

dilutive. Said of a *security* that would reduce *earnings per share* if it were exchanged for *common stock*.

dipping into LIFO layers. See *LIFO inventory layer*.

direct cost. Cost of *direct material* and *direct labor* incurred in producing a product. See *prime cost*. In some accounting literature, this term is used to mean the same thing as *variable cost*.

direct costing. The method of allocating costs that assigns only *variable manufacturing costs* to product and treats *fixed manufacturing costs as period* expenses. A better term for this concept is "variable costing."

direct labor (material) cost. Cost of labor (material) applied and assigned directly to a product; contrast with *indirect labor (material)*.

direct posting.   A method of bookkeeping where *entries* are made directly in *ledger accounts*, without the use of a *journal*.

disbursement.   Payment by *cash* or by a *check*. See *expenditure*.

DISC.   Domestic International Sales Corporation. A U.S. *corporation*, usually a *subsidiary*, whose *income* is attributable primarily to exports. *Income* tax on 50 percent of a DISC's income is usually deferred for a long period. Generally, this results in a lower overall corporate tax for the *parent* than would otherwise be incurred.

disclaimer of opinion.   An auditor's report stating that an opinion cannot be given on *financial statements*. Usually results from *material* restrictions on the scope of the audit or from material uncertainties about the *accounts* which cannot be resolved at the time of the audit.

disclosure.   The showing of facts in *financial statements*, *notes* thereto, or the *auditor's report*.

discontinued operations.   See *income from discontinued operations*.

discount.   In the context of *compound interest, bonds,* and *notes,* the difference between *face* or *future value* and *present value* of a payment. In the context of *sales* and *purchases,* a reduction in price granted for prompt payment. See also *chain discount, quantity discount,* and *trade discount*.

discount factor.   The reciprocal of one plus the *discount rate*. If the discount rate is 10 percent per period, the discount factor for three periods is $(1 + 10)^{-3} = 0.75131$.

discount rate.   *Interest rate* used to convert future payments to *present values*.

discounting a note.   See *note receivable discounted* and *factoring*.

discounts lapsed (lost).   The sum of *discounts* offered for prompt payment that were not taken (or allowed) because of expiration of the discount period. See *terms of sale*.

discovery-value accounting.   In exploration for natural resources, there is the problem of what to do with the expenditures for exploration. Suppose that $10 million is spent to drill 10 holes ($1 million each) and that nine of them are dry whereas one is a gusher containing oil with a *net realizable value* of $40 million. Dry-hole, or successful-efforts, accounting would *expense* $9 million and *capitalize* $1 million to be *depleted* as the oil was lifted from the ground. Full costing would expense nothing but capitalize the $10 million of drilling costs to be depleted as the oil is lifted from the single productive well. Discovery-value accounting would capitalize $40 million to be depleted as the oil is lifted, with a $30 million *credit* to *income* or *contributed capital*. *FASB Statement* No. 19 requires successful-efforts accounting.

Discussion Memorandum.   A neutral discussion of all the issues concerning an accounting problem of current concern to the *FASB*. The publication of such a document usually implies that the FASB is considering issuing a *Statement of Financial Accounting Standards* on this particular problem. The discussion memorandum brings together material about the particular problem to facilitate interaction and comment by those interested in the matter. It may lead to an *Exposure Draft*.

dishonored note.   A *promissory note* whose maker does not repay the loan at *maturity* for a *term loan*, or on demand, for a *demand loan*.

disintermediation.   Federal law regulates the maximum *interest rate* that both banks and savings and loan associations can pay for *time deposits*. When free-market interest rates exceed the regulated interest ceiling for such time deposits, some depositors withdraw their funds and invest them elsewhere at a higher interest rate. This process is known as "disintermediation."

distributable income.   The portion of conventional accounting net income that can be distributed to owners (usually in the form of *dividends*) without impairing the physical capacity of the firm to continue operations at current levels. Pretax distributable income is conventional pretax income less the excess of *replacement cost* of goods sold and *depreciation* charges based on the replacement cost of *productive capacity* over cost of goods sold and depreciation on an *acquisition cost basis*. Since *SEC Accounting Series Release* No. 190 became effective, annual reports of large manufacturing and retailing companies disclose information sufficient for calculation of distributable income. Contrast with *sustainable income*. See *inventory profit*.

distribution expense.   *Expense* of selling, advertising, and delivery activities.

dividend.   A distribution of *earnings* to owners of a corporation; it may be paid in cash (cash dividend), with stock (stock dividend), with property, or with other securities (dividend in kind). Dividends, except stock dividends, become a legal liability of the corporation when they are declared. Hence, the owner of stock ordinarily recognizes *revenue* when a dividend, other than a stock dividend, is declared. See also *liquidating dividend* and *stock dividend*.

dividend yield.   *Dividends* declared for the year divided by market price of the stock as of a given time of the year.

dividends in arrears.   Dividends on *cumulative preferred stock* that have not been declared in accordance with the preferred stock contract. Such arrearages must usually be cleared before dividends on *common stock* can be declared.

dividends in kind.   See *dividend*.

divisional control.   See *control system*.

divisional reporting.   *Line-of-business reporting*.

dollar-sign rules.   In presenting accounting statements or schedules, place a dollar sign beside the first figure in each column and beside any figure below a horizontal line drawn under the preceding figure.

dollar-value LIFO method.   A form of *LIFO* inventory accounting with inventory quantities (*layers*) measured in dollar, rather than physical, terms. Adjustments to account for changing prices are made by use of a specific price index appropriate for the kinds of items in the inventory.

Domestic International Sales Corporation.   See *DISC*.

donated capital.   A *stockholders' equity* account credited when contributions, such as land or buildings, are freely given to the company. Do not confuse with *contributed capital*.

double-declining-balance depreciation (DDB).   *Declining-balance depreciation*, which see, where the constant percentage used to multiply by book value in determining the depreciation charge for the year is $2/n$ and n is the *depreciable life* in periods. Maximum declining-balance rate permitted in the *income tax* laws. *Salvage value* is omitted from the depreciable amount. Thus if the asset cost $100 and has a depreciable life of 5 years, the depreciation in the first year would be $40 = 2/5 \times \$100$, in the second would be $24 = 2/5 \times (\$100 - \$40)$, and in the third year would be $14.40 = 2/5 \times (\$100 - \$40 - \$24)$. By the fourth year, the remaining undepreciated cost could be depreciated under the straight-line method at $10.80 = 1/2 \times (\$100 - \$40 - \$24 - \$14.40)$ per year for tax purposes.

double entry. The system of recording transactions that maintains the equality of the accounting equation; each entry results in recording equal amounts of *debits* and *credits.*

double taxation. Corporate income is subject to the corporate income tax and the aftertax income, when distributed to owners, is subject to the personal income tax.

doubtful accounts. *Accounts receivable* estimated to be *uncollectible.*

Dr. The abbreviation for *debit.*

draft. A written order by the first party, called the drawer, instructing a second party, called the drawee (such as a bank), to pay a third party, called the payee. See also *check, cashier's check, certified check, sight draft,* and *trade acceptance.*

drawee. See *draft.*

drawer. See *draft.*

drawing account. A *temporary account* used in *sole proprietorships* and *partnerships* to record payments to owners or partners during a period. At the end of the period, the drawing account is closed by crediting it and debiting the owner's or partner's share of income or, perhaps, his or her capital account.

drawings. Payments made to a *sole proprietor* or to a *partner* during a period. See *drawing account.*

dry-hole accounting. See *discovery value accounting* for definition and contrast.

duality. The axiom of *double-entry* record keeping that every *transaction* is broken down into equal *debit* and *credit* amounts.

dual-transactions assumption (fiction). In presenting the *statement of changes in financial position,* some transactions not involving *working capital* accounts are reported as though working capital was generated and then used. For example, the issue of *capital stock* in return for the *asset,* land, is reported in the statement of changes in financial position as though stock were issued for *cash* and cash were used to acquire land. Other examples of transactions that require the dual-transaction fiction are the issue of a *mortgage* in return for a noncurrent asset and the issue of stock to bondholders in return for their *bonds.*

earned surplus. A term once used, but no longer considered proper, for *retained earnings.*

earnings. *Income,* or sometimes *profit.*

earnings cycle. The period of time that elapses for a given firm, or the series of transactions, during which *cash* is converted into *goods* and *services,* goods and services are sold to customers, and customers pay for their purchases with cash. *Cash cycle.*

earnings per share (of common stock). *Net income* to common stockholders (net income minus *preferred dividends*) divided by the average number of *common shares* outstanding; see also *primary earnings per share* and *fully diluted earnings per share.* See *ratio.*

earnings per share (of preferred stock). *Net income* divided by the average number of *preferred shares* outstanding during the period. This ratio indicates how well the preferred dividends are covered or protected; it does not indicate a legal share of *earnings.* See *ratio.*

earnings, retained. See *retained earnings.*

easement. The acquired right or privilege of one person to use, or have access to, certain property of another. For example, a public utility's right to lay pipes or lines under property of another and to service those facilities.

economic entity. See *entity.*

economic life. The time span over which the benefits of an *asset* are expected to be received. The economic life of a *patent, copyright,* or *franchise* may be less than the legal life. *Service life.*

effective-interest method. A systematic method for amortizing *bond discount* or *premium* that makes the *interest expense* for each period divided by the amount of the net *liability (face amount* minus *discount* or plus *premium)* at the beginning of the period equal to the *yield rate* on the bond at the time of issue. Interest expense for a period is yield rate (at time of issue) multiplied by the net liability at the start of the period. The *amortization* of discount or premium is the *plug* to give equal *debits* and *credits.* (Interest expense is a debit and the amount of coupon payments is a credit.) The bond holder makes a similar calculation.

effective (interest) rate. Of a bond, the *internal rate of return* or *yield to maturity* at the time of issue. Contrast with *coupon rate.* If the bond is issued for a price below *par,* the effective rate is higher than the coupon rate; if it is issued for a price greater than par, then the effective rate is lower than the coupon rate. In the context of *compound interest,* when the *compounding period* on a *loan* is different from 1 year, such as a nominal interest rate of 12 percent compounded monthly, then the single payment that could be made at the end of a year that is economically equivalent to the series of interest payments is larger than an amount equal to the quoted nominal rate multiplied by the *principal.* If 12 percent per year is compounded monthly, the effective interest rate is 12.683 percent. In general, if the nominal rate is r percent per year and is compounded m times per year, then the effective rate is $(1 + r/m)^m - 1$.

efficient market hypothesis. The supposition in finance that securities' prices reflect all available information and react nearly instantaneously and in an unbiased fashion to new information.

eliminations. *Work sheet* entries to prepare *consolidated statements* that are made to avoid duplicating the amounts of *assets, liabilities, owners' equity, revenues,* and *expenses* of the consolidated *entity* when the accounts of the *parent* and *subsidiaries* are summed.

employee stock option. See *stock option.*

Employee Stock Ownership Trust (or Plan). See *ESOT.*

employer, employee payroll taxes. See *payroll taxes.*

enabling costs. A type of *capacity cost* that will stop being incurred if operations are shut down completely but must be incurred in full if operations are carried out at any level. Costs of a security force or of a quality control inspector for an assembly line might be examples. Contrast with *standby costs.*

ending inventory. The *cost* of *inventory* on hand at the end of the *accounting period,* often called "closing inventory." The dollar amount of inventory to be carried to the subsequent period.

endorsee. See *endorser.*

endorsement. See *draft.* The *payee* signs the draft and transfers it to a fourth party, such as the payee's bank.

endorser. The *payee* of a *note* or *draft* signs it, after writing "Pay to the order of X," transfers the note to person X, and presumably receives some benefit, such as cash, in return. The payee who signs over the note is called the endorser and person X is called the endorsee. The endorsee then has the rights of the payee and may in turn become an endorser by endorsing the note to another endorsee.

enterprise. Any business organization, usually defining the accounting *entity.*

entity. A person, *partnership, corporation,* or other organization. The *accounting entity* for which accounting statements are prepared may not be the same as the entity defined by law. For example, a *sole proprietorship* is an accounting entity but the individual's combined business and personal assets are the legal entity in most jurisdictions. Several affiliated corporations may be separate legal entities while *consolidated financial statements* are prepared for the group of companies operating as a single economic entity.

entity theory. The view of the corporation that emphasizes the form of the *accounting equation* that says *assets = equities.* Contrast with *proprietorship theory.* The entity theory is less concerned with a distinct line between *liabilities* and *stockholders' equity* than is the proprietorship theory. Rather, all equities are provided to the corporation by outsiders who merely have claims of differing legal standings. The entity theory implies using a *multiple-step* income statement.

entry value. The current *cost* of acquiring an asset or service at a *fair-market price. Replacement cost.*

EPS. *Earnings per share.*

EPVI. *Excess present value index.*

equalization reserve. An inferior title for the allowance account when the *allowance method* is used for such things as maintenance expenses. Periodically, maintenance *expense* is debited and the allowance is credited. As maintenance *expenditures* are actually incurred, the allowance is debited and cash or the other asset expended is credited.

equities. *Liabilities* plus *owners' equity.*

equity. A claim to *assets;* a source of assets.

equity financing. Raising *funds* by issuance of *capital stock.* Contrast with *debt financing.*

equity method. A method of accounting for an *investment* in the stock of another company in which the proportionate share of the earnings of the other company is debited to the investment account and credited to a *revenue* account as earned. When *dividends* are received, *cash* is debited and the investment account is credited. Used in reporting when the investor owns twenty percent or more of the stock of an unconsolidated company. One of the few instances where revenue is recognized without a change in *working capital.*

equity ratio. *Stockholders' equity* divided by total *assets.* See *ratio.*

ERISA. Employee Retirement Income Security Act of 1974. The federal law that sets *pension plan* requirements.

error accounting. See *accounting errors.*

ESOP. Employee Stock Ownership Plan. See *ESOT.*

ESOT. Employee Stock Ownership Trust. A trust *fund* created by a corporate employer that can provide certain tax benefits to the corporation while providing for employee stock ownership. The corporate employer can contribute up to 25 percent of its payroll per year to the trust. The contributions are *deductions* from otherwise taxable income for federal *income tax* purposes. The assets of the trust must be used for the benefit of employees—for example, to fund death or retirement benefits. The assets of the trust are usually the *common stock,* sometimes nonvoting, of the corporate employer. As an example of the potential *tax shelter,* consider the case of a corporation with $1 million of *debt* outstanding, which it wishes to retire, and an annual payroll of $2 million. The corporation sells $1 million of common stock to the ESOT. The ESOT borrows $1 million with the loan guaranteed by, and therefore a *contingent liability* of, the corporation. The corporation uses the $1 million proceeds of the stock issue to retire its outstanding debt. (The debt of the corporation has been replaced with the debt of the ESOT.) The corporation can contribute $500,000 (= .25 × $2 million payroll) to the ESOT each year and treat the contribution as a deduction for tax purposes. After a little more than 2 years, the ESOT has received sufficient funds to retire its loan. The corporation has effectively repaid its original $1 million debt with pretax dollars. Assuming an income tax rate of 40 percent, it has saved $400,000 (= .40 × $1 million) of aftertax dollars *if* the $500,000 expense for the contribution to the ESOT for the pension benefits of employees would have been made, in one form or another, anyway. Observe that the corporation could use the proceeds ($1 million in the example) of the stock issue to the ESOT for any of several different purposes: financing expansion, replacing plant assets, or acquiring another company.

Basically this same form of pretax dollar financing through pensions is "almost" available with any corporate pension plan, but with one important exception. The trustees of an ordinary pension trust must invest the assets "prudently" and if they do not, they are personally liable to employees. Current judgment about "prudent" investment requires diversification—pension trust assets should be invested in a wide variety of investment opportunities. (Not more than 10 percent of a pension trust's assets can ordinarily be invested in the parent's common stock.) Thus the ordinary pension trust cannot, in practice, invest all, or even most, of its assets in the parent corporation's stock. This constraint does not apply to the investments of an ESOT. All ESOT assets may be invested in the parent company's stock.

The ESOT also provides a means for closely held corporations to achieve wider ownership of shares without *going public*. The laws enabling ESOTs provide for independent professional appraisal of shares not traded in public markets and for transactions between the corporation and the ESOT or between the ESOT and the employees to be based on the appraised values of the shares.

estimated expenses. See *after cost*.

estimated liability. The preferred terminology for estimated costs to be incurred for such uncertain things as repairs under *warranty*. An estimated liability is shown in the *balance sheet*. Contrast with *contingent liability*.

estimated revenue. A term used in governmental accounting to designate revenue expected to accrue during a period whether or not it will be collected during the period. A *budgetary account* usually established at the beginning of the budget period.

estimated salvage value. Synonymous with *salvage value* of an *asset* before its retirement.

estimates, changes in. See *accounting changes*.

except for. Qualification in *auditor's report*, usually caused by a change, approved by the auditor, from one acceptable accounting principle or procedure to another.

excess present value index. *Present value* of future *cash* inflows divided by initial cash outlay.

exchange. The generic term for a transaction (or more technically, a reciprocal transfer) between one entity and another. In another context, the name for a market, such as the New York Stock Exchange.

exchange gain or loss. The phrase used by the *FASB* for *foreign exchange gain or loss*.

exchange rate. The *price* of one country's currency in terms of another country's currency. For example, the British pound might be worth $1.80 at a given time. The exchange rate would be stated as "one pound is worth one dollar and eighty cents" or "one dollar is worth .5556 ($= £1/$1.80$) pounds."

excise tax. Tax on the manufacture, sale, or consumption of a commodity.

ex-dividend. Said of a stock at the time when the declared *dividend* becomes the property of the person who owned the stock on the *record date*. The payment date follows the ex-dividend date.

exemption. A term used for various amounts subtracted from gross income to determine taxable income. Not all such subtractions are called "exemptions." See *tax deduction*.

exercise. When the owner of an *option* or *warrant* purchases the security that the option entitles him or her to purchase, he or she has exercised the option or warrant.

exercise price. See *option*.

exit value. The proceeds that would be received if assets were disposed of in an *arms'-length transaction*. *Current selling price*. *Net realizable value*.

expected value. The mean or arithmetic *average* of a statistical distribution or series of numbers.

expenditure. Payment of *cash*. Virtually synonymous with *disbursement*, except that some use expenditure as a narrower term and exclude from its definition all payments to discharge liabilities.

expense. As a noun, the *cost* of *assets* used up in producing *revenue*. A "gone" asset; an expired cost. Do not confuse with *expenditure* or *disbursement*, which may occur before, when, or after the related expense is recognized. Use the word "cost" to refer to an item that still has service potential and is an asset. Use the word "expense" after the asset's service potential has been used. As a verb, to designate a past or current expenditure as a current expense.

expense account. An *account* to accumulate *expenses;* such accounts are closed at the end of the accounting period. A *temporary owners' equity* account. Also used to describe a listing of expenses by an employee submitted to the employer for reimbursement.

experience rating. A term used in insurance, particularly unemployment insurance, to denote changes from ordinary rates to reflect extraordinarily large or small amounts of claims over time by the insured.

expired cost. An *expense* or a *loss*.

Exposure Draft. A preliminary statement of the *FASB* (or *APB* between 1962 and 1973) that shows the contents of a pronouncement the Board is considering making effective.

external reporting. Reporting to stockholders and the public, as opposed to internal reporting for management's benefit. See *financial accounting* and contrast with *managerial accounting*.

extraordinary item. A *material expense* or *revenue* item characterized both by its unusual nature and infrequency of occurrence that is shown along with its income tax effects separately from ordinary income and *income from discontinued operations* on the *income statement*. A *loss* from an earthquake would probably be classified as an extraordinary item. Gain (or loss) on retirement of *bonds* is treated as an extraordinary item under the terms of *FASB Statement No. 4*.

face amount (value). The nominal amount due at *maturity* from a *bond* or *note* not including contractual interest that may also be due on the same date. The corresponding amount of a stock certificate is best called the *par* or *stated value*, whichever is applicable.

factoring. The process of buying *notes* or *accounts receivable* at a *discount* from the holder to whom the debt is owed; from the holder's point of view, the selling of such notes or accounts. When a single note is involved, the process is called "discounting a note."

factory. Used synonymously with *manufacturing* as an adjective.

factory cost. *Manufacturing cost*.

factory expense. Manufacturing *overhead*. *Expense* is a poor term in this context because the item is a *product cost*.

factory overhead. Usually an item of *manufacturing cost* other than *direct labor* or *direct materials*.

fair-market price (value). Price (value) determined at *arms'-length* between a willing buyer and a willing seller,

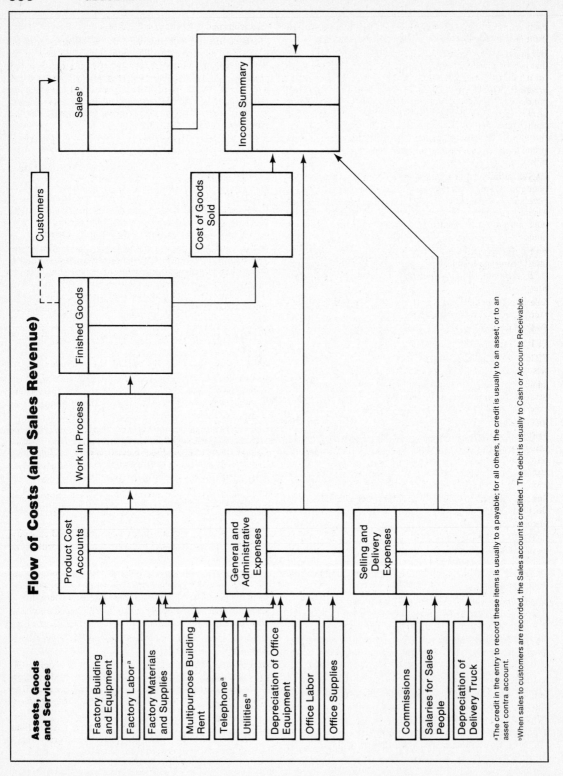

Flow of Costs (and Sales Revenue)

Assets, Goods and Services

Sales[b]

Customers

Income Summary

Finished Goods

Cost of Goods Sold

Work in Process

Product Cost Accounts

General and Administrative Expenses

Selling and Delivery Expenses

Factory Building and Equipment

Factory Labor[a]

Factory Materials and Supplies

Multipurpose Building Rent

Telephone[a]

Utilities[a]

Depreciation of Office Equipment

Office Labor

Office Supplies

Commissions

Salaries for Sales People

Depreciation of Delivery Truck

[a]The credit in the entry to record these items is usually to a payable; for all others, the credit is usually to an asset, or to an asset contra account.

[b]When sales to customers are recorded, the Sales account is credited. The debit is usually to Cash or Accounts Receivable.

each acting rationally in his or her own self-interest. May be estimated in the absence of a monetary transaction.

fair presentation (fairness). When the *auditor's report* says that the *financial statements* "present fairly . . . ," the auditor means that the accounting alternatives used by the entity are all in accordance with *GAAP*. In recent years, however, courts are finding that conformity with *generally accepted accounting principles* may be insufficient grounds for an opinion that the statements are fair. *SAS* No. 5 requires that the auditor judge the accounting principles used "appropriate in the circumstances" before attesting to fair presentation.

FASB. Financial Accounting Standards Board. An independent board responsible, since 1973, for establishing *generally accepted accounting principles.* Its official pronouncements are called "Statements of Financial Accounting Standards" and "Interpretations of Financial Accounting Standards." See *Discussion Memorandum.*

FASB *Interpretation.* An official statement of the *FASB* interpreting the meaning of *Accounting Research Bulletins, APB Opinions,* and *Statements of Financial Accounting Standards.*

federal income tax. *Income tax* levied by the U.S. government on individuals and corporations.

Federal Unemployment Tax Act. See *FUTA.*

FEI. *Financial Executives Institute.*

FICA. Federal Insurance Contributions Act. The law that sets *"Social Security" taxes* and benefits.

fiduciary. Someone responsible for the custody or administration of property belonging to another, such as an executor (of an estate), agent, receiver (in *bankruptcy*), or trustee (of a trust).

FIFO. First-in, first-out; an *inventory-flow assumption* by which *ending inventory* cost is determined from most recent purchases and *cost of goods sold* is determined from oldest purchases including beginning inventory. See *LISH.* Contrast with *LIFO.*

finance. As a verb, to supply with *funds* through the *issue* of stocks, bonds, notes, or mortgages, or through the retention of earnings.

financial accounting. The accounting for *assets, equities, revenues,* and *expenses* of a business. Concerned primarily with the historical reporting of the *financial position* and operations of an *entity* to external users on a regular, periodic basis. Contrast with *managerial accounting.*

Financial Accounting Standards Board. *FASB.*

Financial Executives Institute. An organization of financial executives, such as chief accountants, *controllers,* and treasurers, of large businesses.

financial expense. An *expense* incurred in raising or managing *funds.*

financial position (condition). Statement of the *assets* and *equities* of a firm displayed on the *balance sheet* statement.

financial ratio. See *ratio.*

financial statements. The *balance sheet, income statement, statement of retained earnings, statement of changes in financial position,* statement of changes in *owners' equity accounts,* and *notes* thereto.

financial structure. *Capital structure.*

financing lease. A *lease* treated by the lessee as both the borrowing of funds and the acquisition of an *asset* to be *amortized.* Both the *liability* and the asset are recognized on the balance sheet. Expenses consist of *interest* on the *debt* and *amortization* of the asset. The lessor treats the lease as the sale of the asset in return for a series of future cash receipts. Contrast with *operating lease.* Called a "capital lease" by the *FASB* in *Statement* No. 13.

finished goods. Manufactured product ready for sale; a *current asset (inventory) account.*

firm. Informally, any business entity. (Strictly speaking, a firm is a *partnership.*)

first-in, first-out. See *FIFO.*

fiscal year. A period of 12 consecutive months chosen by a business as the *accounting period* for annual reports. May or may not be a *natural business year* or a calendar year.

FISH. An acronym, conceived by George H. Sorter, for *first-in, still-here.* FISH is the same cost-flow assumption as *LIFO.* Many readers of accounting statements find it easier to think about inventory questions in terms of items still on hand. Think of LIFO in connection with *cost of goods sold* but of FISH in connection with *ending inventory.* See *LISH.*

fixed assets. *Plant assets.*

fixed assets turnover. *Sales* divided by average total *fixed assets.*

fixed-benefit plan. A *defined-benefit (pension) plan.*

fixed budget. A plan that provides for specified amounts of *expenditures* and *receipts* that do not vary with activity levels. Sometimes called a "static budget." Contrast with *flexible budget.*

fixed cost (expense). An *expenditure* or *expense* that does not vary with volume of activity, at least in the short run. See *capacity costs,* which include *enabling costs* and *standby costs,* and *programmed costs* for various subdivisions of fixed costs.

fixed liability. *Long-term* liability.

fixed manufacturing overhead applied. The portion of *fixed manufacturing overhead cost* allocated to units produced during a period.

flexible budget. *Budget* that projects receipts and expenditures as a function of activity levels. Contrast with *fixed budget.*

flexible budget allowance. With respect to manufacturing overhead, the total cost that should have been incurred at the level of activity actually experienced during the period.

float. *Checks* that have been *credited* to the depositor's bank account, but not yet *debited* to the *drawer's* bank account.

flow. The change in the amount of an item over time. Contrast with *stock.*

flow assumption. When a *withdrawal* is made from *inventory,* the cost of the withdrawal must be determined by a flow assumption if *specific identification* of units is not used. The usual flow assumptions are *FIFO, LIFO,* and *weighted-average.*

flow of costs. *Costs* passing through various classifications within an *entity.* See the accompanying diagram for a summary of *product* and *period cost* flows.

flow-through method.   Accounting for the *investment tax credit* to show all income statement benefits of the credit in the year of acquisition, rather than spreading them over the life of the asset acquired, called the "deferral method." The *APB* preferred the deferral method in Opinion No. 2 (1962) but accepted the flow-through method in Opinion No. 4 (1964). Sometimes also used in connection with *depreciation* accounting where *straight-line method* is used for financial reporting and an *accelerated* method for tax reporting. Followers of the flow-through method would not recognize a *deferred tax liability.* APB Opinion No. 11 prohibited the use of the flow-through approach in this connection.

FOB.   Free on board at some location (for example, FOB shipping point; FOB destination); the *invoice* price includes delivery at seller's expense to that location. Title to goods usually passes from seller to buyer at the FOB location.

footing.   Adding a column of figures.

footnotes.   More detailed information than that provided in the *income statement, balance sheet, statement of retained earnings,* and *statement of changes in financial position;* these are considered an integral part of the statements and are covered by the *auditor's report.* Sometimes called "notes."

forecast.   An estimate or projection of costs or revenues or both.

foreign currency.   For *financial statements* prepared in a given currency, any other currency.

foreign exchange gain or loss.   Gain or loss from holding *net* foreign *monetary items* during a period when the *exchange rate* changes.

Form 10-K.   See *10-K.*

franchise.   A privilege granted or sold, such as to use a name or to sell products or services.

free on board.   *FOB.*

freight-in.   The *cost* of freight or shipping in acquiring *inventory,* preferably treated as a part of the cost of *inventory.* Often shown temporarily in an *adjunct account* that is closed at the end of the period with other purchase accounts to the inventory account by the acquirer.

freight-out.   The *cost* of freight or shipping in selling *inventory,* treated by the seller as a selling *expense* in the period of sale.

full costing.   *Absorption costing.* See *discovery-value accounting* for another definition in the context of accounting for natural resources.

full disclosure.   The reporting policy requiring that all significant or *material* information is to be presented in the financial statements. See *fair presentation.*

fully diluted earnings per share.   Smallest *earnings per share* figure on *common stock* that can be obtained by computing an earnings per share for all possible combinations of assumed *exercise* or *conversion* of *potentially dilutive securities.* Must be reported on the *income statement* if it is less than 97 percent of earnings available to common stockholders divided by the average number of common shares outstanding during the period.

fully vested.   Said of a *pension plan* when an employee (or his or her estate) has rights to all the benefits purchased with the employer's contributions to the plan even if the employee is not employed by this employer at the time of retirement.

function.   In governmental accounting, said of a group of related activities for accomplishing a service or regulatory program for which the governmental unit is responsible. In mathematics, a rule for associating a number, called the dependent variable, with another number or numbers, called independent variable(s).

functional classification.   *Income statement* reporting form in which *expenses* are reported by functions, that is, cost of goods sold, administrative expenses, financing expenses, selling expenses; contrast with *natural classification.*

fund.   An *asset* or group of assets set aside for a specific purpose. See also *fund accounting.*

fund accounting.   The accounting for resources, obligations, and *capital* balances, usually of a not-for-profit or governmental *entity,* which have been segregated into *accounts* representing logical groupings based on legal, donor, or administrative restrictions or requirements. The groupings are described as "funds." The accounts of each fund are *self-balancing* and from them a *balance sheet* and an operating statement for each fund can be prepared. See *fund* and *fund balance.*

fund balance.   In governmental accounting context, the excess of assets of a *fund* over its liabilities and reserves; the not-for-profit equivalent of *owners' equity.*

funded.   Said of a *pension plan* or other obligation when *funds* have been set aside for meeting the obligation when it becomes due. The federal law for pension plans requires that all *normal costs* be funded as recognized. In addition, *past and prior service costs* of pension plans must be funded over 30 or over 40 years, depending on the circumstances.

funding.   Replacing *short-term* liabilities with *long-term* debt.

funds.   Generally *working capital;* current assets less current liabilities. Sometimes used to refer to *cash* or to cash and *marketable securities.*

funds provided by operations.   An important subtotal in the *statement of changes in financial position.* This amount is the total of revenues producing *funds* less *expenses* requiring funds. Often, the amount is shown as *net income* plus expenses not requiring funds (such as depreciation charges) minus revenues not producing funds (such as revenues recognized under the *equity method* of accounting for a long-term investment). The statement of changes in financial position maintains the same distinctions between *continuing operations, discontinued operations, and income* or *loss* from *extraordinary items* as in the *income statement.*

funds statement.   An informal name often used for the *statement of changes in financial position.*

funny money.   Said of securities such as *convertible preferred stock, convertible bonds, options,* and *warrants* that have aspects of *common stock* equity but that did not reduce reported *earnings per share* prior to the issuance of *APB Opinions* No. 9 in 1967 and No. 15 in 1969.

FUTA. Federal Unemployment Tax Act, which provides for taxes to be collected at the federal level to help subsidize the individual states' administration of their unemployment compensation programs.

GAAP. *Generally accepted accounting principles.* A plural noun.

gain. Excess of *revenues* over *expenses* from a specific transaction. Frequently used in the context of describing a transaction not part of a firm's typical, day-to-day operations.

general debt. Debt of a governmental unit legally payable from general revenues and backed by the full faith and credit of the governmental unit.

general expenses. *Operating expenses* other than those specifically assigned to cost of goods sold, selling, and administration.

general fixed asset (group of accounts). Accounts showing those long-term assets of a governmental unit not accounted for in *enterprise, trust,* or intragovernmental service funds.

general fund. Assets and liabilities of a nonprofit entity not specifically earmarked for other purposes; the primary operating fund of a governmental unit.

general journal. The formal record where transactions, or summaries of similar transactions, are recorded in *journal entry* form as they occur. Use of the adjective "general" usually implies only two columns for cash amounts or that there are also various *special journals,* such as a *check register* or *sales journal,* in use.

general ledger. The name for the formal *ledger* containing all of the financial statement accounts. It has equal debits and credits as evidenced by the *trial balance.* Some of the accounts in the general ledger may be *controlling accounts,* supported by details contained in *subsidiary ledgers.*

general partner. Member of *partnership* personally liable for all debts of the partnership; contrast with *limited partner.*

general price index. A measure of the aggregate prices of a wide range of goods and services in the economy at one time relative to the prices during a base period. See *consumer price index* and *GNP Implicit Price Deflator.* Contrast with *specific price index.*

general price level adjusted statements. See *price level adjusted statements.*

general price level changes. Changes in the aggregate prices of a wide range of goods and services in the economy. These price changes are measured using a *general price index.* Contrast with *specific price changes.*

general purchasing power accounting. See *price level adjusted statements.*

general purchasing power of the dollar. The command of the dollar over a wide range of goods and services in the economy. The general purchasing power of the dollar is inversely related to changes in a general price index. See *general price index.*

generally accepted accounting principles (GAAP). As previously defined by the *APB* and now by the *FASB,* the conventions, rules, and procedures necessary to define accepted accounting practice at a particular time; includes both broad guidelines and relatively detailed practices and procedures.

generally accepted auditing standards. The standards, as opposed to particular procedures, promulgated by the *AICPA (*in *Statements on Auditing Standards)* that concern "the auditor's professional qualities" and "the judgment exercised by him in the performance of his examination and in his report." Currently, there are 10 such standards, three general ones (concerned with proficiency, independence, and degree of care to be exercised), three standards of field work, and four standards of reporting. The first standard of reporting requires that the *auditor's report* state whether or not the *financial statements* are prepared in accordance with *generally accepted accounting principles.* Thus the typical auditor's report says that the examination was conducted in accordance with generally accepted auditing standards and that the statements are prepared in accordance with generally accepted accounting principles. See *auditor's report.*

GNP Implicit Price Deflator (Index). A *price index* issued quarterly by the Office of Business Economics of the U.S. Department of Commerce. This index attempts to trace the price level of all *goods and services* comprising the *gross national product.* Contrast with *consumer price index.*

going public. Said of a business when its *shares* become widely traded, rather than being closely held by relatively few *stockholders.* Issuing shares to the general investing public.

going-concern assumption. For accounting purposes a business is assumed to remain in operation long enough for all its current plans to be carried out. This assumption is part of the justification for the *acquisition cost* basis, rather than a *liquidation* or *exit value* basis, of accounting.

goods. Items of merchandise, supplies, raw materials, or finished goods. Sometimes the meaning of "goods" is extended to include all *tangible* items, as in the phrase "goods and services."

goods available for sale. The sum of *beginning inventory* plus all acquisitions, or purchases, of merchandise or finished goods during an *accounting period.*

goods in process. *Work in process.*

goodwill. The excess of cost of an acquired firm or operating unit over the current or *fair-market value* of *net assets* of the acquired unit. Informally used to indicate the value of good customer relations, high employee morale, a well-respected business name, and so on, that are expected to result in greater than normal earning power.

goodwill method. A method of accounting for the *admission* of a new partner to a *partnership* when the new partner is to be credited with a portion of capital different from the value of the *tangible* assets contributed as a fraction of tangible assets of the partnership. See *bonus method* for a description and contrast.

GPL. General price level; usually used as an adjective modifying the word "accounting" to mean the accounting that produces *price level adjusted statements.*

GPLA. General price level adjusted accounting; the accounting that produces *price level adjusted statements.*

GPP. General purchasing power; usually used as an adjective modifying the word "accounting" to mean the accounting that produces *price level adjusted statements.*

graded vesting. Said of a *pension plan* where not all employee benefits are currently *vested.* By law, the benefits must become vested according to one of several formulas as time passes.

gross. Not adjusted or reduced by deductions or subtractions. Contrast with *net.*

gross margin. *Net sales* minus *cost of goods sold.*

gross margin percentage. $100 \times (1 - cost of goods sold/net sales) = 100 \times (gross margin/net sales).$

gross national product (GNP). The market value within a nation for a year of all goods and services produced as measured by final sales of goods and services to individuals, corporations, and governments plus the excess of exports over imports.

gross price method (of recording purchase or sales discounts). The *purchase* (or *sale*) is recorded at its *invoice price,* not deducting the amounts of *discounts* available. Discounts taken are recorded in a *contra* account to purchases (or sales). Information on discounts lapsed is not made available, and for this reason, most firms prefer the *net-price method* of recording purchase discounts.

gross profit. *Gross margin.*

gross profit method. A method of estimating *ending inventory* amounts. *Cost of goods sold* is measured as some fraction of sales; the *inventory equation* is then used to value *ending inventory.*

gross profit ratio. *Gross margin* divided by *net sales.*

gross sales. All *sales* at *invoice* prices, not reduced by *discounts, allowances, returns,* or other adjustments.

group depreciation. A method of calculating *depreciation* charges where similar assets are combined, rather than depreciated separately. No gain or loss is recognized on retirement of items from the group until the last item in the group is sold or retired. See *composite life method.*

guarantee. A promise to answer for payment of debt or performance of some obligation if the person liable for the debt or obligation fails to perform. Often, the words "guarantee" and "warranty" are used to mean the same thing. In precise usage, however, "guarantee" means a promise to fulfill the promise of some person to perform a contractual obligation, such as to pay a sum of money, whereas "warranty" is most often used to refer to promises about pieces of machinery or other products. See *warranty.*

hidden reserve. The term refers to an amount by which *owners' equity* has been understated, perhaps deliberately. The understatement arises from an undervaluation of *assets* or overvaluation of *liabilities.* By undervaluing assets on this period's *balance sheet, net income* in some future period can be made to look artificially high by disposing of the asset: actual *revenues* less artificially low cost of assets sold yields artificially high net income. There is no *account* that has this title.

historical cost. *Acquisition cost; original cost;* a sunk cost.

historical summary. A part of the *annual report* to stockholders that shows important items, such as *net income, revenues, expenses, asset* and *equity* totals, *earnings per share,* and the like, for five or ten periods including the current one. Usually not as much detail is shown in the historical summary as in *comparative statements,* which typically report as much detail for the year immediately preceding as for the current year. Annual reports may contain both comparative statements and a historical summary.

holding company. A company that confines its activities to owning *stock* in, and supervising management of, other companies. A holding company usually owns a controlling interest in, that is more than 50 percent of the voting stock of, the companies whose stock it holds. Contrast with *mutual fund.* See *conglomerate.*

holding gain or loss. Difference between end-of-period price and beginning-of-period price of an asset held during the period. Ordinarily, realized holding gains and losses are not separately reported in financial statements. Unrealized gains are not usually reflected in income at all. Some unrealized losses, such as on inventory or marketable securities, are reflected in income or *owners' equity* as the losses occur. See *inventory profit* for further refinement, including *gains* on *assets* sold during the period.

horizontal analysis. *Time-series analysis.*

human resource accounting. A term used to describe a variety of proposals that seek to report and emphasize the importance of human resources—knowledgeable, trained, and loyal employees—in a company's earning process and total assets.

hypothecation. The *pledging* of property, without transfer of title or possession, to secure a loan.

ideal standard costs. *Standard costs* set equal to those that would be incurred under the best possible conditions.

IIA. *Institute of Internal Auditors.*

IMA. Institute of Management Accounting. See *CMA* and *National Association of Accountants.*

imprest fund. *Petty cash fund.*

improvement. An *expenditure* to extend the useful life of an *asset* or to improve its performance (rate of output, cost) over that of the original asset. Such expenditures are *capitalized* as part of the asset's cost. Contrast with *maintenance* and *repair.*

imputed cost. A cost that does not appear in accounting records, such as the *interest* that could be earned on cash spent to acquire inventories rather than, say, government bonds. Or, consider a firm that owns the buildings it occupies. This firm has an imputed cost for rent in an amount equal to what it would have to pay to use similar buildings owned by another.

imputed interest. See *interest imputed.*

income. *Excess of revenues* and *gains* over *expenses* and *losses* for a period; *net income.* Sometimes used with an appropriate modifier to refer to the various intermediate amounts shown in a *multiple-step income statement.* Sometimes used to refer to revenues, as in "rental income."

income accounts. *Revenue* and *expense accounts.*

income distribution account. *Temporary account* sometimes debited when *dividends* are declared; closed to *retained earnings.*

income from continuing operations. As defined by *APB Opinion* No. 30, all *revenues* less all *expenses* except for the following: results of operations, including income tax effects, that have been or will be discontinued; *gains* or *losses,* including income tax effects, on disposal of segments of the business; gains or losses, including income tax effects, from *extraordinary items;* and the cumulative effect of *accounting changes.*

income from discontinued operations. *Income,* net of tax effects, from parts of the business that have been discontinued during the period or are to be discontinued in the near future. Such items are reported on a separate line of the *income statement* after *income from continuing operations* but before *extraordinary items.*

income (revenue) bond. See *special revenue debt.*

income statement. The statement of *revenues, expenses, gains,* and *losses* for the period ending with *net income* for the period. The *earnings per share* amount is usually shown on the income statement; the *reconciliation* of beginning and ending balances of *retained earnings* may also be shown in a combined statement of income and retained earnings. See *income from continuing operations, income from discontinued operations, extraordinary items, multiple-step, single-step.*

income summary. An *account* used in problem solving that serves as a surrogate for the *income statement.* All *revenues* are closed to the Income Summary as *credits* and all *expenses,* as *debits.* The *balance* in the account, after all other *closing entries* are made, is then closed to the retained earnings or other *owners' equity* account and represents *net income* for the period.

income tax. An annual tax levied by the federal and other governments on the income of an entity. An *expense;* if not yet paid, a *liability.*

income tax allocation. See *deferred tax liability* and *tax allocation: intrastatement.*

incremental. An adjective used to describe the change in *cost, expense, investment, cash flow, revenue, profit,* and the like if one or more units are produced or sold or if an activity is undertaken.

indenture. See *bond indenture.*

independence. The mental attitude required of the *CPA* in performing the *attest* function. It implies impartiality and that the members of the auditing CPA firm own no stock in the corporation being audited.

independent accountant. The *CPA* who performs the *attest* function for a firm.

indeterminate-term liability. A *liability* lacking the criterion of being due at a definite time. This term is our own coinage to encompass the *deferred income tax liability* and *minority interest.*

indexation. An attempt by lawmakers or parties to a contract to cope with the effects of *inflation.* Amounts fixed in law or contracts are "indexed" when these amounts change as a given measure of price changes. For example, a so-called escalator clause in a labor contract might provide that hourly wages will be increased as the *consumer price index* increases. Many economists have suggested the indexation of numbers fixed in the *income tax* laws. If, for example, the personal *exemption* is $750 at the start of the period, prices rise by 10 percent during the period, and the personal exemption is indexed, then the personal exemption would automatically rise to $825 (= $750 + .10 × $750) at the end of the period.

indirect costs. Costs of production not easily associated with the production of specific goods and services; *overhead costs.* May be *allocated* on some arbitrary basis to specific products or departments.

indirect labor (material) cost. An *indirect cost* for labor (material) such as for supervisors (supplies).

individual proprietorship. *Sole proprietorship.*

Industry Audit Guide. A series of publications by the AICPA providing specific *accounting* and *auditing principles* for specialized situations. Audit guides have been issued covering government contractors, state and local government units, investment companies, finance companies, colleges and universities, stock life insurance companies, brokers and dealers in securities, and many others.

inflation. A time of generally rising prices.

information system. A system, sometimes formal and sometimes informal, for collecting, processing, and communicating data that are useful for the managerial functions of decision making, planning, and control, and for financial reporting under the *attest* requirement.

insolvent. Unable to pay debts when due. Said of a company even though *assets* exceed *liabilities.*

installment. Partial payment of a debt or collection of a receivable, usually according to a contract.

installment contracts receivable. The name used for *accounts receivable* when the *installment method* of recognizing revenue is used. Its *contra, unrealized gross margin,* is shown on the balance sheet as a subtraction from the amount receivable.

installment sales. Sales on account where the buyer promises to pay in several separate payments, called *installments.* Sometimes are, but need not be, accounted for on the *installment method.* If installment sales are accounted for with the sales *basis of revenue recognition* for financial reporting but with the installment method for income tax returns, then a *deferred income tax liability* arises.

installment (sales) method. Recognizing *revenue* and *expense* (or *gross margin*) from a sales transaction in proportion to the fraction of the selling price collected during a period. Allowed by the *IRS* for income tax reporting, but acceptable in *GAAP (APB Opinion* No. 10*)* only when cash collections are reasonably uncertain. See *unrealized* (and *realized*) *gross margin.*

Institute of Internal Auditors. The national association of accountants who are engaged in internal auditing and are employed by business firms. See *IIA.*

Institute of Management Accounting. See *CMA*.

insurance. A contract for reimbursement of specific losses; purchased with insurance premiums. Self-insurance is not insurance but merely the willingness to assume risk of incurring losses while saving the premium.

intangible asset. A nonphysical, *noncurrent* asset such as a *copyright, patent, trademark, goodwill, organization costs, capitalized* advertising cost, computer programs, licenses for any of the preceding, government licenses (e.g., broadcasting or the right to sell liquor), *leases, franchises,* mailing lists, exploration permits, import and export permits, construction permits, marketing quotas, and other rights that give a firm an exclusive or preferred position in the marketplace.

intercompany elimination. See *eliminations*.

intercompany profit. If one *affiliated company* sells to another, and the goods remain in the second company's *inventory* at the end of the period, then the first company's *profit* has not been realized by a sale to an outsider. That profit is called "intercompany profit" and is eliminated from net *income* in *consolidated income statements* or when the *equity method* is used.

interest. The charge or cost for using money; expressed as a rate per period, usually one year, called the interest rate. See *effective interest rate* and *nominal interest rate*.

interest, imputed. If a borrower merely promises to pay a single amount, sometime later than the present, then the present value (computed at a *fair-market* interest rate, called the "imputed interest rate") of the promise is less than the *face amount* to be paid at *maturity*. The difference between the face amount and the present value of a promise is called imputed interest. See also *imputed cost*.

interest factor. One plus the *interest* rate.

interest method. See *effective-interest method*.

interest rate. See *interest*.

interfund accounts. In governmental accounting, the accounts that show transactions between funds, especially interfund receivables and payables.

interim statements. Statements issued for periods less than the regular, annual *accounting period*. Most corporations are required to issue interim statements on a quarterly basis. The basic issue in preparing interim reports is whether their purpose is to report on the interim period (1) as a self-contained accounting period, or (2) as an integral part of the year of which they are a part so that forecasts of annual performance can be made. *APB Opinion* No. 28 and the *SEC* require that interim reports be constructed largely to satisfy the second purpose.

internal audit. An *audit* conducted by employees to ascertain whether or not *internal control* procedures are working, as opposed to an external audit conducted by a *CPA*.

internal control. See *control system*.

internal rate of return. The discount rate that equates the net *present value* of a stream of cash outflows and inflows to zero.

Internal Revenue Service (IRS). Agency of the U.S. Treasury Department responsible for administering the Internal Revenue Code and collecting income, and certain other, taxes.

internal reporting. Reporting for management's use in planning and control; contrast with *external reporting* for financial statement users.

International Accounting Standards Committee. An organization that promotes the establishment of international accounting standards.

interperiod tax allocation. See *deferred income tax liability*.

interpolation. The estimation of an unknown number intermediate between two (or more) known numbers.

Interpretations of Statements of Financial Accounting Standards. See *FASB Interpretations*.

in the black (red). Operating at a profit (loss).

intrastatement tax allocation. See *tax allocation: intrastatement*.

inventoriable costs. *Costs* that "attach" to products. *Product costs (assets)* as opposed to *period expenses*.

inventory. As a noun, the *balance* in an asset *account* such as raw materials, supplies, work in process, and finished goods. As a verb, to calculate the *cost* of goods on hand at a given time or to physically count items on hand.

inventory equation. *Beginning inventory + net additions − withdrawals = ending inventory.* Ordinarily, additions are net purchases and withdrawals are *cost of goods sold*. Notice that ending inventory, to be shown on the balance sheet, and cost of goods sold, to be shown on the income statement, are not independent of each other. The larger is one, the smaller must be the other. In valuing inventories, beginning inventory and net purchases are usually known. In some inventory methods (for example, some applications of the *retail inventory method*), cost of goods sold is measured and the equation is used to find the cost of ending inventory. In most methods, cost of ending inventory is measured and the equation is used to find the cost of goods sold (withdrawals). In *replacement-cost (*in contrast to *historical cost)* accounting, *additions* (in the equation) include holding gains, whether realized or not. Thus the replacement-cost inventory equation is Beginning Inventory (at Replacement Cost) + Purchases (where Replacement Cost is Historical Cost) + Holding Gains (whether Realized or not) − Ending Inventory (at Replacement Cost) = Cost of Goods Sold (Replacement Cost).

inventory holding gains. See *inventory profit*.

inventory layer. See *LIFO inventory layer*.

inventory profit. This term has several possible meanings. Consider the data in the accompanying illustration. The *historical-cost* data are derived in the conventional manner; the firm uses a *FIFO cost-flow assumption*. The *replacement-cost* data are assumed, but are of the kind that the *SEC* requires in *ASR* No. 190.

We use the term *distributable income* to refer to revenues less expenses based on replacement, rather than historical, costs. To that subtotal add realized holding gains to arrive at realized (conventional) income. To that, add unrealized holding gains to arrive at *economic income*.

The SEC, in its *Accounting Series Releases,* uses the term "inventory profit" to refer to the realized holding gain, $110 in the illustration. The amount of inventory profit will usually be material when FIFO is used and prices are rising.

Inventory Profit Illustration

Assumed Data	(Historical) Acquisition Cost Assuming FIFO	Replacement Cost
Inventory, 1/1/XO	$ 900	$1,100
Inventory, 12/31/X0	1,160	1,550
Cost of Goods Sold for 19X0	4,740	4,850
Sales for 19X0 . . . . $5,200		
INCOME STATEMENT FOR 19X0		
Sales	$5,200	$5,200
Cost of Goods Sold	4,740	4,850
(1) Distributable Income		$ 350
Realized Holding Gains		110[a]
(2) Realized Income = Conventional Net Income (under FIFO)	$ 460	$ 460
Unrealized Holding Gain		190[b]
(3) Economic Income		$ 650

[a] Realized holding gain during a period is replacement cost of goods sold less historical cost of goods sold; for 19X0 the realized holding gain under FIFO is $110 = $4,850 − $4,740. The SEC refers to this as "inventory profit."

[b] The total unrealized holding gain at any time is replacement cost of inventory on hand at that time less historical cost of that inventory. The unrealized holding gain during a period is unrealized holding gain at the end of the period less the unrealized holding gain at the beginning of the period. Unrealized holding gain prior to 19X0 is $200 = $1,100 − $900. Unrealized holding gain during 19X0 = ($1,550 − $1,160) − ($1,100 − $900) = $390 − $200 = $190.

Others, including us, prefer to use the term "inventory profit" to refer to the total *holding gains,* $300 (= $110 + $190, both realized and unrealized), but this appears to be a lost cause.

In periods of rising prices and increasing inventories, the realized holding gains under a FIFO cost-flow assumption will be substantially larger than under LIFO. In the illustration, for example, assume under LIFO that the historical cost of goods sold is $4,800, that historical LIFO cost of beginning inventory is $600, and that historical LIFO cost of ending inventory is $800. Then distributable income, based on replacement costs, remains $350 (= $5,200 − $4,850), realized holding gains are $50 (= $4,850 − $4,800), realized income is $400 (= $350 + $50), the unrealized holding gain for the year is $250 (= ($1,500 − $800) − ($1,100 − $650)), and economic income is $650 (= $350 + $50 + $250). Because the only real effect of the cost-flow assumption is to split the total holding gain into realized and unrealized portions, economic income is the same, independent of the cost-flow assumption. The total of holding gains is $300 in the illustration. The choice of cost-flow assumption governs how much holding gain is conventionally reported as realized (SEC "inventory profit") and how much is not.

inventory turnover. Number of times the average *inventory* has been sold during a period; *cost of goods sold* for a period divided by average inventory for the period. See *ratio.*

invested capital. *Contributed capital.*

investee. A company whose *stock* is owned by another.

investment. An *expenditure* to acquire property or other assets in order to produce *revenue;* the *asset* so acquired;

hence a *current* expenditure made in anticipation of future income. Said of *securities* of other companies held for the long term and shown in a separate section of the *balance sheet;* in this context, contrast with *marketable securities.*

investment tax credit. A reduction in income tax liability granted by the federal government to firms that buy new equipment. This item is a credit, in that it is deducted from the tax bill, not from pretax income. The tax credit has been a given percentage of the purchase price of certain assets purchased. The actual rules and rates have changed over the years. See *flow-through method* and *carryforward.*

invoice. A document showing the details of a sale or purchase transaction.

issue. When a corporation exchanges its stock (or bonds) for cash or other assets, the corporation is said to issue, not sell, that stock (or bonds). Also used in the context of withdrawing supplies or materials from inventory for use in operations and drawing of a *check.*

issued shares. These shares of *authorized capital stock* of a *corporation* that have been distributed to the stockholders. See *issue.* Shares of *treasury stock* are legally issued but are not considered to be *outstanding* for the purpose of voting, *dividend declarations,* and *earnings-per-share* calculations.

job development credit. The name used for the *investment tax credit* in the 1971 tax law on this subject.

job-order costing. Accumulation of *costs* for a particular identifiable batch of product, known as a job, as it moves through production.

joint cost. Cost of simultaneously producing or otherwise acquiring two or more products, called joint products, that must, by the nature of the process, be produced or acquired together, such as the cost of beef and hides of cattle. Other examples include central *corporate expenses, overhead* of a department when several products are manufactured, and *basket purchases.* See *common cost.*

joint product. One of two or more outputs from a process that must be produced or acquired simultaneously. See *by-product* and *joint cost.*

journal. The place where transactions are recorded as they occur. The book of original entry.

journal entry. A recording in a *journal,* of equal *debits* and *credits,* with an explanation of the *transaction,* if necessary.

journalize. To make an entry in a *journal.*

Journal of Accountancy. A monthly publication of the AICPA.

Journal of Accounting Research. Scholarly journal containing articles on theoretical and empirical aspects of accounting. Published three times a year by the Graduate School of Business of The University of Chicago.

journal voucher. A *voucher* documenting (and sometimes authorizing) a transaction, leading to an entry in the *journal.*

kiting. This term means slightly different things in banking and auditing contexts. In both, however, it refers to the wrongful practice of taking advantage of the *float,* the time that elapses between the deposit of a *check* in one bank and its collection at another. In the banking context, an individual deposits in Bank A a check written on Bank B. He (or she) then writes checks against the deposit created in Bank A. Several days later, he deposits in Bank B a check written on Bank A, to cover the original check written in Bank B. Still later, he deposits in Bank A a check written on Bank B. The process of covering the deposit in Bank A with a check written on Bank B and vice versa is continued until an actual deposit of cash can be arranged. In the auditing context, kiting refers to a form of *window dressing* where the amount of the account Cash in Bank is made to appear larger than it actually is by depositing in Bank A a check written on Bank B without recording the check written on Bank B in the *check register* until after the close of the *accounting period.*

know-how. Technical or business information of the type defined under *trade secret,* but that is not maintained as a secret. The rules of accounting for this asset are the same as for other *intangibles.*

land. An *asset shown at acquisition cost* plus the *cost* of any nondepreciable *improvements.* In accounting, implies use as a plant or office site, rather than as a *natural resource* such as timberland or farm land.

lapping (accounts receivable). The theft, by an employee, of cash sent in by a customer to discharge the latter's *payable.* The theft from the first customer is concealed by using cash received from a second customer. The theft from the second customer is concealed by using the cash received from a third customer, and so on. The process is continued until the thief returns the funds or can make the theft permanent by creating a fictitious *expense* or receivable write-off, or until the fraud is discovered.

lapse. To expire; said of, for example, an insurance policy or discounts made available for prompt payment that are not taken.

last-in, first-out. See *LIFO.*

layer. See *LIFO inventory layer.*

lead time. The time that elapses between order placing and receipt of the ordered *goods or services.*

lease. A contract calling for the lessee (user) to pay the lessor (owner) for the use of an asset. A cancelable lease is one the lessee can cancel at any time. A noncancelable lease requires payments from the lessee for the life of the lease and usually has many of the economic characteristics of *debt financing.* A noncancelable lease meets the usual criteria to be classified as a *liability* but some leases entered into before 1977 need not be shown as a liability. *FASB Statement* No. 13 and the *SEC* require disclosure in notes to the financial statements of the commitments for noncancelable leases. See *financing lease* and *operating lease.*

leasehold. The *asset* representing the right of the *lessee* to use leased property. See *lease* and *leasehold improvement.*

leasehold improvement. An *improvement* to leased property. Should be *amortized* over *service life* or the life of the lease, whichever is shorter.

least and latest rule. Pay the least amount of taxes as late as possible within the law to minimize the *present value* of tax payments for a given set of operations.

ledger. A book of accounts. See *general ledger* and *subsidiary ledger;* contrast with *journal.*

legal capital. *Par* or *stated value* of issued *capital stock.* The amount of *contributed capital* that, according to state law, must remain permanently in the firm as protection for creditors.

legal entity. See *entity.*

lender. See *loan.*

lessee. See *lease.*

lessor. See *lease.*

leverage. Operating leverage refers to the tendency of *net income* to rise at a faster rate than sales when there are *fixed costs.* A doubling of sales, for example, usually implies a more than doubling of net income. This phenomenon can be studied at *breakeven chart.* Capital leverage refers to the increased rate of return on owners' equity (see *ratio*) when an investment earns a return larger than the *interest rate* paid for *debt* financing. Because the interest charges on debt are usually fixed, any *incremental* income benefits owners and none benefits debtors. When this term is used without a qualifying adjective, it usually refers to the capital leverage and means the use of *long-term* debt in securing *funds* for the *entity.*

leveraged lease. A special form of lease involving three parties—a *lender,* a *lessor,* and a *lessee.* The lender, such as a bank or insurance company, lends a portion, say 80 percent, of the cash required for acquiring the *asset.* The lessor puts up the remainder, 20 percent, of the cash required. The lessor acquires the asset with the cash, using the asset as security for the loan and leases it to the lessee on a *noncancelable* basis. The lessee makes periodic lease payments to the lessor, who in turn makes payments on the loan to the lender. Typically, the lessor has no obligation for the debt to the lender other than transferring a portion of the receipts from the lessee. If the lessee should default on required lease payments, then the lender can repossess the leased asset. The lessor is usually entitled to deductions for tax purposes for depreciation on the asset, for interest expense on the loan from the lender, and for any investment tax credit. The lease is leveraged in the sense that the lessor, who enjoys most of the risks and rewards of ownership, usually borrows most of the funds needed to acquire the asset. See *leverage.*

liability. Usually, a legal obligation to pay a definite or reasonably certain amount at a definite or reasonably certain time in return for a current benefit. Some of the criteria are not met by items classified as liabilities where there are special circumstances. Examples are *pension* liabilities, estimates of future *warranty* expenditures, and *deferred tax liabilities.* See *indeterminate-term liability.* Other items meet the criteria to be a liability but are not shown as such, for example, noncancelable leases, which are sometimes disclosed only in footnotes; see *lease.*

lien. The right of person A to satisfy a claim against person B by holding B's property as security or by seizing B's property.

life annuity. A *contingent annuity* in which payments cease at death of a specified person(s), usually the *annuitant(s).*

LIFO. An *inventory-flow* assumption where the *cost of goods sold* is the cost of the most recently acquired units and the *ending inventory cost* is determined from costs of the oldest units: contrast with *FIFO.* In periods of rising prices and increasing inventories, LIFO leads to higher reported expenses and therefore lower reported income and lower balance sheet inventories than does FIFO. See *FISH* and *inventory profit.*

LIFO, dollar-value method. See *dollar-value LIFO method.*

LIFO inventory layer. The *ending inventory* for a period is likely to be larger than the *beginning inventory.* Under a *LIFO cost-flow assumption,* this increase in physical quantities is given a value determined by the prices of the earliest purchases during the year. The LIFO inventory then consists of layers, sometimes called "slices," which typically consist of relatively small amounts of physical quantities from each of the past several years. Each layer carries the prices from near the beginning of the period when it was acquired. The earliest layers will typically (in periods of rising prices) have prices very much less than current prices. If inventory quantities should decline in a subsequent period, the latest layers enter cost of goods sold first.

limited liability. Stockholders of corporations are not personally liable for debts of the company.

limited partner. Member of a *partnership* not personally liable for debts of the partnership; every partnership must have at least one *general partner* who is fully liable.

line-of-business reporting. See *segment reporting.*

line of credit. An agreement with a bank or set of banks for short-term borrowings on demand.

liquid. Said of a business with a substantial amount (the amount is unspecified) of *working capital,* especially *quick assets.*

liquid assets. *Cash, current marketable securities,* and, sometimes, *current receivables.*

liquidating dividend. *Dividend* declared in the winding up of a business to distribute the assets of the company to the stockholders. Usually treated by recipient as a return of *investment,* not as *revenue.*

liquidation. Payment of a debt. Sale of assets in closing down a business or a segment thereof.

liquidation value per share. The amount each *share* of stock will receive if the corporation is dissolved. For *preferred stock* with a *liquidation preference,* a stated amount per share.

liquidity. Refers to the availability of *cash,* or near-cash resources, for meeting a firm's obligations.

LISH. An acronym, conceived by George H. Sorter, for *last-in, still-here.* LISH is the same cost-flow assumption as *FIFO.* Many readers of accounting statements find it easier to think about inventory questions in terms of items still on hand. Think of FIFO in connection with *cost of goods sold* but of LISH in connection with *ending inventory.* See *FISH.*

list price. The published or nominally quoted price for goods.

list price method. See *trade-in transaction.*

loan. An arrangement where the owner of property, called the lender, allows someone else, called the borrower, the use of the property for a period of time that is usually specified in the agreement setting up the loan. The borrower promises to return the property to the lender and, often, to make a payment for use of the property. Generally used when the property is *cash* and the payment for its use is *interest.*

long-lived (term) asset. An asset whose benefits are expected to be received over several years. A *noncurrent* asset; usually includes *investments, plant assets,* and *intangibles.*

long-term (construction) contract accounting. The *percentage-of-completion* or *completed contract methods of revenue* recognition.

loss. Excess of *cost* over net proceeds for a single transaction; negative *income* for a period. A cost expiration that produced no *revenue.*

lower of cost or market. A basis for *inventory* valuation where the inventory value is set at the lower of *acquisition cost* or *current replacement cost* (market), subject to the following constraints: First, the market value of an item used in the computation cannot exceed its *net realizable value*—an amount equal to selling price less reasonable costs to complete production and to sell the item. Second, the market value of an item used in the computation cannot be less than the net realizable value minus the normal *profit* ordinarily realized on disposition of completed items of this type. The lower-of-cost-or-market valuation is chosen as the lower of acquisition cost or replacement cost (market) subject to the upper and lower bounds on replacement cost established in the first two steps. The method for valuing by lower of cost or market is easier to remember and use when the method is translated into symbols as follows: Let AC represent acquisition cost, RC represent replacement cost. NRV represent net realizable value, and $PROF$ represent the normal profit. Then the lower-of-cost-or-market valuation is

minimum $[AC, NRV,$ maximum $(RC, NRV - PROF)]$.

In words, find the maximum of replacement cost and net realizable value minus normal profit. Call that quantity MAX. Then choose the smallest of acquisition cost, net realizable value, and MAX. (The minimum of NRV and MAX is the "market" figure used in the computation.) The following example illustrates the application of the rule for lower of cost or market when the normal profit margin is nine cents ($.09) per unit.

	Item			
	1	**2**	**3**	**4**
(a) Acquisition Cost	$.90	$.97	$.96	$.90
(b) Net Realizable Value ...	.95	.95	.95	.95
(c) Net Realizable Value Less Normal Profit Margin	.86	.86	.86	.86
(d) Replacement Cost	.92	.96	.92	.85
(e) Maximum [(d), (c)] = MAX	.92	.96	.92	.86
(f) Lower of Cost or Market = Minimum [(a), (b), (e)]	.90	.95	.92	.86

Notice in this illustration that each of the four possible valuations is used once to determine lower of cost or market. Item 1 uses acquisition cost; Item 2 uses net realizable value; Item 3 uses replacement cost; and Item 4 uses net realizable value less normal profit.

Lower of cost or market cannot be used for tax returns in combination with a *LIFO* flow assumption.

lump-sum acquisition.   *Basket purchase.*

maintenance.   *Expenditures* undertaken to preserve an *asset's* service potential for its originally intended life; these expenditures are treated as *period expenses* or *product costs;* contrast with *improvement.* See *repair.*

make-or-buy decision.   A managerial decision about whether the firm should produce a product internally or purchase it from others. Proper make-or-buy decisions in the short run result only when *opportunity costs* are the only costs considered in decision making.

maker (of note) (of check).   One who signs a *note* to borrow. One who signs a *check;* in this context, synonymous with drawer; see *draft.*

management.   Executive authority that operates a business.

Management Accounting.   Monthly publication of the *NAA.*

management (managerial) accounting.   Reporting designed to enhance the ability of management to do its job of decision making, planning, and control; contrast with *financial accounting.*

management audit.   An audit conducted to determine whether the objectives, policies, and procedures for a firm or one of its operating units are properly carried out. Generally applies only to activities for which qualitative standards can be specified. See *audit* and *internal audit.*

management by exception.   A principle of management where attention is focused only on performance that is significantly different from that expected.

managerial accounting.   See *management accounting.*

manufacturing cost.   Costs of producing goods, usually in a factory.

manufacturing expense.   Another, less useful, title for *manufacturing overhead.*

manufacturing overhead.   General manufacturing *costs* incurred in providing a capacity to carry on productive activities but that are not directly associated with identifiable units of product. *Fixed* manufacturing overhead costs are treated as a *product cost* under *absorption costing* but as an *expense* of the period under *direct costing.*

margin.   *Revenue* less specified expenses. See *contribution margin, gross margin,* and *current margin.*

marginal cost.   The *incremental cost* or *differential cost* of the last unit added to production or the first unit subtracted from production.

marginal costing.   *Direct costing.*

marginal revenue.   The increment in *revenue* from sale of one additional unit of product.

marginal tax rate.   The tax imposed on the next dollar of taxable income generated; contrast with *statutory tax rate* and *average tax rate.*

markdown.   The reduction below an originally established retail price.

market price.   See *fair market price.*

market rate.   The rate of *interest* a company must pay to borrow *funds* currently. See *effective rate.*

marketable securities.   *Stocks* and *bonds* of other companies held that can be readily sold on stock exchanges or over-the-counter markets and that the company plans to sell as cash is needed. Classified as *current* assets and as part of *working capital.* The same securities held for *long-term* purposes would be classified as *noncurrent assets. FASB Statement* No. 12 requires the *lower-of-cost-or-market* valuation basis for all marketable equity securities but different accounting treatments (with differing effects on income) depending on whether the security is a *current* or a *noncurrent asset.*

markon.   An amount originally added to *cost* to obtain *list price.* Usually expressed as a percentage of cost. Further increases in list price are called *markups;* decreases are called *markdowns.*

markup.   An amount originally added to cost. Usually expressed as a percentage of selling price. Also refers to an increase above an originally established retail price. See *markon.*

markup percentage.   *Markup* divided by (acquisition cost plus *markup*).

master budget. A *budget* projecting all *financial statements* and their components.

matching convention. The concept of recognizing cost expirations (*expenses*) in the same accounting period when the related *revenues* are recognized.

material. As an adjective, it means relatively important. See *materiality*. Currently, no operational definition exists. As a noun, *raw material*.

materiality. The concept that accounting should disclose separately only those events that are relatively important (no operable definition yet exists) for the business or for understanding its statements.

maturity. The date at which an obligation, such as the *principal* of a *bond* or a *note*, becomes due.

maturity value. The amount expected to be collected when a loan reaches *maturity*. Depending on the context, the amount may be *principal* or principal and *interest*.

merchandise. *Finished goods* bought by a retailer or wholesaler for resale; contrast with finished goods of a manufacturing business.

merchandise turnover. *Inventory turnover* for merchandise; see *ratio*.

merchandising business. As opposed to a manufacturing or service business, one that purchases (rather than manufactures) *finished goods* for resale.

merger. The joining of two or more businesses into a single *economic entity*. See *holding company*.

minority interest. A *balance sheet account* on *consolidated statements* showing the *equity* in a *subsidiary* company allocable to those who are not part of the controlling (majority) interest. May be classified either as stockholders' equity or as a liability of *indeterminate term* on the consolidated balance sheet. On the *income statement,* the minority's interest in current income must be subtracted to arrive at consolidated *net income* for the period.

minority investment. A holding of less than 50 percent of the *voting stock* in another corporation. Accounted for with the *cost method* when less than 20 percent is held, and with the *equity method* otherwise. See *mutual fund*.

minutes book. A record of all actions authorized at corporate *board of directors'* or stockholders' meetings.

mixed cost. A *semifixed* or a *semivariable* cost.

modified cash basis. The *cash basis of accounting* with long-term assets accounted for with the *accrual basis of accounting*.

monetary assets, liabilities. See *monetary items*.

monetary gain or loss. The *gain* or *loss* in general purchasing power as a result of holding *monetary assets* or liabilities during a period when the *general purchasing power of the dollar* changes. During periods of *inflation*, holders of net monetary assets lose, and holders of net monetary liabilities gain, general purchasing power. During periods of *deflation*, holders of net monetary assets gain, and holders of net monetary liabilities lose, general purchasing power.

monetary items. Amounts fixed in terms of dollars by statute or contract. *Cash, accounts receivable, accounts payable*, and *debt*. The distinction between monetary and nonmonetary items is important for general *price level adjusted statements* and for *foreign exchange gain or loss* computations. In the foreign exchange context, account amounts denominated in dollars are not monetary items, whereas amounts denominated in any other currency are monetary.

money. A word seldom used with precision in accounting, at least in part because economists have not yet agreed on its definition. Economists use the term to refer to both a medium of exchange and a unit of value. See *cash* and *monetary items*.

money-purchase plan. A *pension plan* where the employer contributes a specified amount of cash each year to each employee's pension fund. Benefits ultimately received by the employee are not specifically defined but depend on the rate of return on the cash invested. Sometimes called a "defined-contribution" pension plan; contrast with *defined-benefit plan*. As of the mid-1970s most corporate pension plans were defined-benefit plans because both the law and *generally accepted accounting principles* for pensions made defined-benefit plans more attractive than money-purchase plans. The federal pension law of 1974 makes money-purchase plans relatively more attractive than they had been. We expect the number of money-purchase plans to increase. See *ERISA*.

mortality table. Data on life expectancies or probabilities of death for persons of specified ages and sex.

mortgage. A claim given by the borrower (mortgagor) to the lender (mortgagee) against the borrower's property in return for a loan.

moving average. An *average* computed on observations over time. As a new observation becomes available, the oldest one is dropped so that the average is always computed for the same number of observations and only the most recent ones. Sometimes, however, this term is used synonymously with *weighted average*.

moving average method. *Weighted-average method*.

multiple-step. Said of an *income* statement where various classes of *expenses* and *losses* are subtracted from *revenues* to show intermediate items such as *operating income*, income of the enterprise (operating income plus *interest* income), income to investors (income of the enterprise less *income taxes*), net income to shareholders (income to investors less interest charges), and income retained (income to stockholders less dividends). See *entity theory*.

municipal bond. A *bond* issued by a village, town, city, county, state, or other public body. *Interest* on such bonds is generally exempt from federal *income taxes* and from some state income taxes. Sometimes referred to as "tax exempts."

mutual fund. An investment company that issues its own stock to the public and uses the proceeds to invest in securities of other companies. A mutual fund usually owns less than 5 or 10 percent of the stock of any one company and accounts for its investments using current *market values;* contrast with *holding company*.

mutually exclusive projects. Competing investment projects, where accepting one project eliminates the possibility of undertaking the remaining projects.

National Association of Accountants (NAA). A national society generally open to all engaged in activities closely associated with *managerial accounting.* Oversees the administration of the *CMA* Examinations through the Institute of Management Accounting.

natural business year. A 12-month period chosen as the reporting period so that the end of the period coincides with a low point in activity or inventories. See *ratio* for a discussion of analyses of financial statements of companies using a natural business year.

natural classification. *Income statement* reporting form in which *expenses* are classified by nature of items as acquired, that is, materials, wages, salaries, insurance, and taxes, as well as depreciation; contrast with *functional classification.*

natural resources. Timberland, oil and gas wells, ore deposits, and other products of nature that have economic value. The cost of natural resources is subject to *depletion.* Often called "wasting assets." See also *discovery-value accounting* and *percentage depletion.*

negative confirmation. See *confirmation.*

negative goodwill. Refer to *goodwill.* When the purchase price of the company acquired is less than the sum of the *fair market value* of the *net assets* acquired, *APB Opinion* No. 16 requires that the valuation of noncurrent assets (except *investments* in *marketable securities*) acquired be reduced until the purchase price equals the adjusted valuation of the fair market value of net assets acquired. If after the adjusted valuation of noncurrent assets is reduced to zero and the purchase price is still less than the net assets acquired, then the difference is shown as a credit balance in the balance sheet as negative goodwill and is amortized to income over a period not to exceed 40 years. For negative goodwill to exist, someone must be willing to sell a company for less than the fair market value of net current assets and marketable securities. Since such a bargain purchase is rare, negative goodwill is rarely found in the financial statements.

negotiable. Legally capable of being transferred by endorsement. Usually said of *checks* and *notes* and sometimes of *stocks* and *bearer bonds.*

net. Reduced by all relevant deductions.

net assets. *Owners' equity;* total *assets* minus total *liabilities.*

net current asset value (per share). *Working capital* divided by the number of common shares outstanding. Many security analysts think that when a common share trades in the market for an amount less than net current asset value, then the shares are undervalued and should be purchased.

net current assets. *Working capital = current assets − current liabilities.*

net income. The excess of all *revenues* and *gains* for a period over all *expenses* and *losses* of the period.

net loss. The excess of all *expenses* and *losses* for a period over all *revenues* and *gains* of the period. Negative *net income.*

net markup. In the context of *retail inventory methods, markups* less markup cancellations; a figure that usually ignores *markdowns* and markdown cancellations.

net-of-tax method. A nonsanctioned method for dealing with the problem of income tax allocation; described in *APB Opinion* No. 11. Deferred tax credit items are subtracted from specific asset amounts rather than being shown as a deferred credit or liability.

net-of-tax reporting. Reporting, such as for *income from discontinued operations, extraordinary items,* and *prior-period adjustments,* where the amounts presented in *financial statements* have been adjusted for all income tax effects. For example, if an extraordinary loss amounted to $10,000 and the marginal tax rate were 40 percent, then the extraordinary item would be reported "net of taxes" as a $6,000 loss. Hence, all income taxes may not be reported on one line of the income statement. The taxes will be allocated to *income from continuing operations,* income from discontinued operations, extraordinary items, cumulative effects of an *accounting change,* and prior-period adjustments.

net present value. Discounted or *present value* of all cash inflows and outflows of a project or from an *investment* at a given *discount rate.*

net price method (of recording purchase or sales discounts). The *purchase (or sale)* is recorded at its *invoice* price less all *discounts* made available under the assumption that nearly all discounts will be taken. Discounts lapsed through failure to pay promptly are recorded in an *adjunct account* to purchases (or sales) or in the purchasing context, to an *expense* account. In the context of purchases, management usually prefers to know about the amount of discounts lost because of inefficient operations, not the amounts taken, so that most managers prefer the net price method to the *gross price method.*

net realizable value. Selling price of an item less reasonable further costs to make the item ready for sale and to sell it. See *lower of cost or market.*

net sales. Sales (at gross invoice amount) less *returns, allowances,* freight paid for customers, and *discounts* taken.

net working capital. *Working capital;* the "net" is redundant in accounting. Financial analysts sometimes mean *current* assets when they speak of working capital, so for them the "net" is not redundant.

net worth. A misleading term, to be avoided, that means the same as *owners' equity.*

New York Stock Exchange (NYSE). A public market where various corporate *securities* are traded.

next-in, first-out. See *NIFO.*

NIFO. *Next-in, first-out.* In making decisions, many managers consider *replacement costs* (rather than *historical costs*) and refer to them as NIFO costs.

no par. Said of *stock* without a *par value.*

nominal accounts. *Temporary accounts* as opposed to *balance sheet accounts.* All nominal accounts are *closed* at the end of each *accounting period.*

nominal interest rate. A rate specified on a *debt* instrument, which usually differs from the market or *effective* rate. Also, a rate of *interest* quoted for a year. If the interest is compounded more often than annually, then the *effective interest rate* is higher than the nominal rate.

noncancelable. See *lease.*

noncontributory. Said of a *pension plan* where only the employer makes payments to a pension *fund;* contrast with *contributory.*

noncurrent. Due more than 1 year (or more than one *operating cycle*) hence.

non-interest-bearing note. A *note* that bears no explicit interest. The *present value* of such a note at any time before *maturity* is less than the *face value* so long as *interest rates* are positive. *APB Opinion* No. 21 requires that the present value, not face value, of long-term non-interest-bearing notes be reported as the *asset* or *liability* amount in financial statements.

nonmonetary items. All items that are not monetary; see *monetary items.*

nonoperating. In the *income statement* context, said of revenues and expenses arising from transactions incidental to the company's main line(s) of business. In the *statement of changes in financial position* context, said of all sources or uses of *working capital* other than working capital provided by operations.

nonprofit corporation. An incorporated *entity,* such as a hospital, with no owners who share in the earnings. It usually emphasizes providing services rather than maximizing income.

nonrecurring. Said of an event that is not expected to happen often for a given firm. Under *APB Opinion* No. 30, the effects of such events should be disclosed separately, but as part of *ordinary* items unless the event is also unusual. See *extraordinary* item.

normal cost. *Pension plan expenses* incurred during an *accounting period* for employment services performed during that period; contrast with *past* and *prior service cost* and see *funded.*

normal spoilage. Costs incurred because of ordinary amounts of spoilage; such costs should be prorated to units produced as *product costs;* contrast with *abnormal spoilage.*

normal standard cost. The *cost* expected to be incurred under reasonably efficient operating conditions with adequate provision for an average amount of rework, spoilage, and the like.

note. An unconditional written promise by the maker (borrower) to pay a certain amount on demand or at a certain future time. See *footnotes* for another context.

note receivable discounted. A *note* assigned by the holder to another. If the note is assigned with recourse, it is the *contingent liability* of the assignor until the debt is paid. See *factoring.*

number of days sales in inventory (or receivables). Days of average inventory on hand (or average collection period for receivables). See *ratio.*

NYSE. *New York Stock Exchange.*

OASD(H)I. *Old Age, Survivors, Disability, and (Hospital) Insurance.*

objective. See *reporting objective* and *objectivity.*

objectivity. The reporting policy implying that formal recognition will not be given to an event in financial statements until the magnitude of the events can be measured with reasonable accuracy and is subject to independent verification.

obsolescence. A decline in *market value* of an *asset* caused by improved alternatives becoming available that will be more *cost-effective;* the decline in market value is unrelated to physical changes in the asset itself. See *partial obsolescence.*

Occupational Safety and Health Act. *OSHA.*

off balance sheet financing. A description often used for a *long-term, noncancelable lease* accounted for as an *operating lease.*

Old Age, Survivors, Disability, and (Hospital) Insurance. The technical name for Social Security under the Federal Insurance Contribution Act (FICA).

on consignment. Said of goods delivered by the owner (the consignor) to another (the consignee) to be sold by the consignee; the owner is entitled to the return of the property or payment of an .amount agreed upon in advance. The goods are assets of the consignor.

on (open) account. Said of a *purchase* or *sale* when payment is expected sometime after delivery and no *note* evidencing the *debt* is given or received. When a sale (purchase) is made on open account, *accounts receivable (payable)* is debited (credited).

open account. Any *account* with a nonzero debit or credit *balance.* See *on (open) account.*

operating. An adjective used to refer to *revenue* and *expense* items relating to the company's main line(s) of business.

operating accounts. *Revenue, expense,* and *production cost accounts;* contrast with *balance sheet accounts.*

operating cycle. *Earnings cycle.*

operating expenses. *Expenses* incurred in the course of *ordinary* activities of an *entity.* Frequently, a narrower classification including only *selling, general,* and *administrative expenses,* thereby excluding *cost of goods sold, interest,* and *income tax* expenses.

operating lease. A *lease* accounted for by the *lessee* without showing an *asset* for the lease rights (*leasehold*) or a *liability* for the lease payment obligations. Rental payments of the lessee are merely shown as *expenses* of the period. The lessor keeps the asset on his or her *books* and shows the rental payments as *revenues;* contrast with *financing lease.*

operating margin (based on replacement costs). *Revenues* from *sales* minus current *replacement cost* of goods sold. A measure of operating efficiency that is independent of the *cost-flow assumption* for *inventory.* Sometimes called "current (gross) margin." See *inventory profit* for example computations.

operating ratio. See *ratio.*

operational control. See *control system.*

opinion. The *auditor's report* containing an attestation or lack thereof. Also, *APB Opinion.*

opportunity cost. The *present value* of the *income* (or *costs*) that could be earned (or saved) from using an *asset* in its best alternative use to the one being considered.

option. The legal right to buy something during a specified period at a specified price, called the *exercise* price. Employee stock options should not be confused with put and call options traded in various public markets.

ordinary annuity. An *annuity in arrears.*

ordinary income. For income tax purposes, reportable *income* not qualifying as *capital gains.*

organization costs. The *costs* incurred in planning and establishing an *entity;* example of an *intangible* asset. Often, since the amounts are not *material,* the costs are treated as *expenses* in the period incurred even though the *expenditures* clearly provide future benefits and should be treated as *assets.*

original cost. *Acquisition cost.* In public utility accounting, the acquisition cost to the *entity* first devoting the asset to public use.

original entry. Entry in a *journal.*

OSHA. Occupational Safety and Health Act. The federal law that governs working conditions in commerce and industry.

outlay. The amount of an *expenditure.*

out-of-pocket. Said of an *expenditure* usually paid for with cash. An *incremental* cost.

out-of-stock cost. The estimated decrease in future *profit* as a result of losing customers because insufficient quantities of *inventory* are currently on hand to meet customers' demands.

output. Physical quantity or monetary measurement of *goods* and *services* produced.

outside director. A member of a corporate board of directors who is not a company officer and does not participate in the corporation's day-to-day management.

outstanding. Unpaid or uncollected. When said of *stock,* the shares issued less *treasury stock.* When said of checks, it means a check issued that did not clear the *drawer's* bank prior to the *bank statement* date.

over-and-short. Title for an *expense account* used to account for small differences between book balances of cash and actual cash and vouchers or receipts in *petty cash* or *change funds.*

overapplied (overabsorbed) overhead. An excess of costs applied, or *charged,* to product for a period over actual *overhead* costs during the period. A *credit balance* in an overhead account after overhead is assigned to product.

overdraft. A check written on a checking account that contains less funds than the amount of the check.

overhead costs. Any *cost* not specifically or directly associated with the production or sale of identifiable goods and services. Sometimes called "burden" or "indirect costs" and, in Britain, "oncosts." Frequently limited to manufacturing overhead. See *central corporate expenses* and *manufacturing overhead.*

overhead rate. Standard, or other predetermined, rate at which *overhead costs* are applied to products or to services.

over-the-counter. Said of a *security* traded in a negotiated transaction, rather than in an auctioned one on an organized stock exchange, such as the *New York Stock Exchange.*

owners' equity. *Proprietorship; assets* minus *liabilities; paid-in capital* plus *retained earnings* of a corporation; partners' capital accounts in a *partnership;* owner's capital account in a *sole proprietorship.*

paid-in capital. Sum of balances in *capital stock* and *capital contributed in excess of par (or stated) value* accounts. Same as *contributed capital* (minus *donated capital*).

paper profit. A *gain* not yet realized through a *transaction.* An *unrealized holding gain.*

par. See *at par* and *face amount.*

par value. *Face amount* of a *security.*

par value method. The method of accounting for *treasury stock* that *debits* a common stock account with the *par value* of the shares reacquired and allocates the remaining debits between the *additional paid-in capital* and *retained earnings* accounts; contrast with *cost method.*

parent company. Company owning more than 50 percent of the voting shares of another company, called the *subsidiary.*

partial obsolescence. As technology improves, the economic value of existing *assets* declines. In many cases, however, it will not pay a firm to replace the existing asset with a new one even though the new type, rather than the old, would be acquired if the acquisition were to be made currently. In these cases, the accountant should theoretically recognize a loss from partial obsolescence from the firm's owning an old, out-of-date asset, but *GAAP* does not permit recognition of partial obsolescence. The old asset will be carried at *cost* less *accumulated depreciation* until it is retired from service. See *obsolescence.*

partially funded. Said of a *pension plan* where not all earned benefits have been funded. See *funded* for funding requirements.

partially vested. Said of a *pension plan* where not all employee benefits are *vested.* See *graded vesting.*

participating dividend. *Dividend* paid to preferred stockholders in addition to the minimum preferred dividends when the *preferred stock* contract allows such sharing in earnings. Usually applies after dividends on *common stock* have reached a certain level.

participating preferred stock. *Preferred stock* with rights to *participating dividends.*

partner's drawing. A payment to a partner to be charged against his or her share of income or capital. The name of a *temporary account* to record such payments.

partnership. Contractual arrangement between individuals to share resources and operations in a jointly run business. See *general* and *limited partner* and Uniform Partnership Act.

past service cost. *Present value* at a given time of a *pension plan's* unrecognized, and usually unfunded, benefits assigned to employees for their service before the inception of the plan. A part of *prior service cost.* See *prior service cost* for disclosure rules. See *funded;* contrast with *normal cost.*

patent. A right granted for up to 17 years by the federal government to exclude others from manufacturing, using or selling a claimed design, product, or plant (e.g., a new breed of rose) or from using a claimed process or method of manufacture. An asset if acquired by purchase. If developed internally, the development costs are *expensed* when incurred under current *GAAP*.

pay as you go. Said of an *income tax* scheme where periodic payments of income taxes are made during the period when the income to be taxed is being earned; in contrast to a scheme where no payments are due until the end of, or after, the period whose income is being taxed. (Called PAYE—pay as you earn—in Britain.) Sometimes this phrase is used to describe an *unfunded pension plan,* where payments to pension plan beneficiaries are made from general corporate funds, not from cash previously contributed to a pension fund. Not acceptable as a method of accounting for pension plans.

payable. Unpaid but not necessarily due or past due.

payback period. Amount of time that must elapse before the cash inflows from a project equal the cash outflows.

payback reciprocal. One divided by the *payback period.* This number approximates the *internal rate of return* on a project when the project life is more than twice the payback period and the cash inflows are identical in every period after the initial investment.

PAYE. See *pay as you go.*

payee. The person or entity to whom a cash payment is made or who will receive the stated amount of money on a check. See *draft.*

payout ratio. *Common stock dividends* declared for a year divided by net *income* to common stock for the year. A term used by financial analysts; contrast with *dividend yield.*

payroll taxes. Taxes levied because salaries or wages are paid; for example, *FICA* and unemployment compensation insurance taxes. Typically, the employer pays a portion and withholds part of the employee's wages for the other portion.

P/E ratio. *Price-earnings ratio.*

pension fund. *Fund,* the assets of which are to be paid to retired ex-employees, usually as a *life annuity.* Usually held by an independent trustee and thus is not an *asset* of the firm.

pension plan. Details or provisions of employer's contract with employees for paying retirement *annuities* or other benefits. See *funded, vested, normal cost, past service cost, prior service cost, money-purchase plan,* and *defined-benefit plan.*

per books. An expression used to refer to the *book value* of an item at a specific time.

percent. Any number, expressed as a decimal, multiplied by 100.

percentage depletion (allowance). Deductible *expense* allowed in some cases by the federal *income tax* regulations; computed as a percentage of gross income from a *natural resource* independent of the unamortized cost of the asset. Because the amount of the total deductions for tax purposes is usually greater than the cost of the asset being *depleted,* many people think the deduction is an unfair tax advantage or "loophole."

percentage-of-completion method. Recognizing *revenues* and *expenses* on a job, order, or contract (a) in proportion to

the *costs* incurred for the period divided by total costs expected to be incurred for the job or order, or (b) in proportion to engineers' estimates of the incremental degree of completion of the job, order, or contract during the period. Contrast with *completed-contract method.*

percentage statement. A statement containing, in addition to dollar amounts, ratios of dollar amounts to some base. In a percentage *income statement,* the base is usually either *net sales* or total *revenues* and in a percentage *balance sheet,* the base is usually total *assets.*

period. *Accounting period.*

period cost. An inferior term for *period expense.*

period expense (charge). *Expenditure,* usually based on the passage of time, charged to operations of the accounting period rather than *capitalized* as an asset; contrast with *product cost.*

periodic inventory. A method of recording *inventory* that uses data on beginning inventory, additions to inventories, and ending inventory in order to find the cost of withdrawals from inventory.

periodic procedures. The process of making *adjusting entries, closing entries,* and preparing the *financial statements,* usually by use of *trial balances* and *work sheets.*

permanent account. An account that appears on the *balance sheet;* contrast with *temporary account.*

permanent difference. Difference between reported income and taxable income that will never be reversed and, hence, requires no entry in the *deferred income tax (liability)* account. An example is the difference between taxable and reportable income from interest earned on state and municipal bonds; contrast with *timing difference* and see *deferred income tax liability.*

perpetual annuity. *Perpetuity.*

perpetual inventory. Records on quantities and amounts of *inventory* that are changed or made current with each physical addition to or withdrawal from the stock of goods; an inventory so recorded. The records will show the physical quantities and, frequently, the dollar valuations that should be on hand at any time. A perpetual inventory facilitates *control;* contrast with *periodic inventory.*

perpetuity. An *annuity* whose payments continue forever. The *present value* of a perpetuity in *arrears* is p/r, where p is the periodic payment and r is the *interest rate* per period.

personal account. *Drawing account.*

petty cash fund. Currency maintained for expenditures that are conveniently made with cash on hand.

physical verification. *Verification,* by an *auditor,* performed by actually inspecting items in *inventory, plant assets,* and the like; may be based on statistical sampling procedures; contrasted with mere checking of written records.

plant. *plant assets.*

plant assets. Buildings, machinery, equipment, land, and natural resources. The phrase "property, plant, and equipment" is, therefore, a redundancy. In this context, "plant" means buildings.

pledging. The borrower assigns *assets* as security or *collateral* for repayment of a loan.

pledging of receivables. The process of using expected collections on amounts receivable as *collateral* for a loan. The borrower remains responsible for collecting the receivable but promises to use the proceeds for repaying the debt.

plow back. To retain earnings for continued investment in the business.

plug. For any *account*, beginning balance + additions − deductions = ending balance; if any three of the four items are known, the fourth can be found by plugging. In making a *journal entry*, often all *debits* are known, as are all but one of the *credits* (or vice versa). Because *double-entry* bookkeeping requires equal debits and credits, the unknown quantity can be determined by subtracting the sum of the known credits from the sum of all the debits (or vice versa). This process is also known as plugging. The unknown found is called the plug. For example, if a *discount* on *bonds payable* is being *amortized* with the *straight-line method,* then *interest expense* is a plug: interest expense = interest payable + discount amortization. See *trade-in transaction* for an example.

pooling-of-interests method. Accounting for a *business combination* by merely adding together the *book value* of the assets and *equities* of the combined firms. Contrast with *purchase method.* Generally leads to a higher reported *net income* for the combined firms than would be reported had the business combination been accounted for as a purchase. See *APB Opinion* No. 16 for the conditions that must be met before the pooling of interests treatment is acceptable.

positive confirmation. See *confirmation.*

post. To record entries in an *account* in a *ledger;* usually the entries are transferred from a *journal.*

post-closing trial balance. *Trial balance* taken after all *temporary accounts* have been closed.

post-statement events. Events with *material* impact that occur between the end of the *accounting period* and the formal publication of the *financial statements.* Such events must be disclosed in notes for the auditor to give a *clean opinion,* even though the events are subsequent to the period being reported on.

potentially dilutive. A *security* that may be converted into, or exchanged for, common stock and thereby reduce reported *earnings per share: options, warrants, convertible bonds,* and *convertible preferred stock.*

preclosing trial balance. *Trial balance* taken at the end of the period before *closing entries.* In this sense, an *adjusted trial balance.* Sometimes taken before *adjusting entries* and then is synonymous with *unadjusted trial balance.*

preemptive right. The privilege of a stockholder to maintain a proportionate share of ownership by purchasing a proportionate share of any new stock issues.

preference as to assets. The rights of *preferred stockholders* to receive certain payments in case of dissolution before common stockholders receive payments.

preferred stock. *Capital stock* with a claim to income or assets after bondholders but before *common stock. Dividends* on preferred stock are income distributions, not expenses. See *cumulative preferred stock.*

premium. The excess of issue (or market) price over *par value.* For a different context, see *insurance.*

premium on capital stock. Alternative but inferior title for *capital contributed in excess of par (or stated) value.*

prepaid expense. An *expenditure* that leads to a *deferred charge* or *prepayment;* strictly speaking, a contradiction in terms for an *expense* is a gone asset and this title refers to past *expenditures,* such as for rent or insurance premiums, that still have future benefits and thus are *assets.*

prepaid income. An inferior alternative title for *advances from customers.* An item should not be called *revenue* or *income* until earned, when goods are delivered or services are rendered.

prepayments. *Deferred charges. Assets* representing *expenditures* for future benefits. Rent and insurance premiums paid in advance are usually classified as *current* prepayments.

present value. Value today of an amount or amounts to be paid or received later, discounted at some *interest* or *discount rate.*

price. The quantity of one *good* or *service,* usually *cash,* asked in return for a unit of another good or service. See *fair market price.*

price-earnings ratio. At a given time, the market value of a company's *common stock,* per share, divided by the *earnings per* common *share* for the past year. See *ratio.*

price index. A series of numbers, one for each period, that purports to represent some *average* of prices for a series of periods, relative to a base period.

price level. The number from a *price index* series for a given period or date.

price level adjusted statements. *Financial statements* expressed in terms of dollars of uniform purchasing power. *Nonmonetary* items are restated to reflect changes in general *price levels* since the time specific *assets* were acquired and *liabilities* were incurred. A *gain* or *loss* is recognized on *monetary items* as they are held over time periods when the general *price level* changes. Conventional financial statements show *historical costs* and ignore differences in purchasing power in different periods.

primary earnings per share. *Net income* to *common stockholders* plus *interest* (net of tax effects) and *dividends* paid on *common stock equivalents* divided by (weighted average of common shares outstanding plus the net increase in the number of common shares that would become *outstanding* if all common stock equivalents were exchanged for common shares with cash proceeds, if any, used to retire common shares).

prime cost. Sum of *direct materials* plus *direct labor* costs assigned to product.

prime rate. The rate for loans charged by commercial banks to their most preferred risks. For the *earnings-per-share* purpose of deciding whether a security is or is not a *common stock equivalent,* the corporation should use the rate in effect at the bank at which it does business or an average of such rates if the corporation does business with more than one bank. The *Federal Reserve Bulletin* is considered the authoritative source of information about historical prime rates.

principal. An amount on which *interest* is charged or earned.

principle. See *generally accepted accounting principles.*

prior-period adjustment. A *debit* or *credit* made directly to *retained earnings* (that does not affect *income* for the period) to adjust retained earnings. Such adjustments are now extremely rare.

Theory would suggest that corrections of errors in accounting estimates (such as the *depreciable life* or *salvage value* of an asset) should be treated as adjustments to retained earnings. But *GAAP* require that corrections of such estimates flow through current, and perhaps future, *income statements.* See *accounting changes* and *accounting errors.*

prior service cost. *Present value* at a given time of a *pension plan's* unrecognized benefits assigned to employees for their service before that given time. Includes *past service cost.* Such obligations are not recognized as liabilities in the accounting records, but must be disclosed in the notes to the financial statements; contrast with *normal cost.* See *funded.*

pro forma statements. Hypothetical statements. Financial statements as they would appear if some event, such as a *merger* or increased production and sales, had occurred or were to occur. Pro forma is often spelled as one word.

proceeds. The *funds* received from disposition of assets or from the issue of securities.

product. *Goods* or *services* produced.

product cost. Any *manufacturing cost* that can be inventoried. See *flow of costs* for example and contrast with *period expenses.*

production cost. *Manufacturing cost.*

production cost account. A *temporary account* for collecting *manufacturing costs* during a period.

production department. A department producing salable *goods* or *services;* contrast with *service department.*

production method (depreciation). The depreciable asset is given a *depreciable life* measured, not in elapsed time, but in units of output or perhaps in units of time of actual use. Then the *depreciation* charge for a period is a portion of depreciable cost equal to a fraction determined by dividing the actual output produced during the period by the expected total output to be produced over the life of the asset. Sometimes called the "units-of-production (or output) method."

production method (revenue recognition). *Percentage-of-completion method* for recognizing *revenue.*

productive capacity. In computing *replacement costs* of *long-term assets,* we are interested in the cost of reproducing the productive capacity (for example, the ability to manufacture 1 million units a year), not the cost of reproducing the actual physical assets currently used (see *reproduction cost*). Replacement cost of productive capacity will be the same as reproduction cost of assets only in the unusual case when there has been no technological improvement in production processes and the relative prices of goods and services used in production have remained approximately the same as when the currently used ones were acquired.

profit. Excess of *revenues* over *expenses* for a *transaction;* sometimes used synonymously with *net income* for the period.

profit-and-loss sharing ratio. The fraction of *net income* or loss allocable to a partner in a *partnership.* Need not be the same fraction as the partner's share of capital.

profit-and-loss statement. *Income statement.*

profit center. A unit of activity for which both *revenue* and *expenses* are accumulated; contrast with *cost center.*

profit margin. Sales minus all expenses as a single amount. Frequently used to mean the ratio of sales minus all *operating* expenses divided by sales.

profit maximization. The doctrine that a given set of operations should be accounted for so as to make reported *net income* as large as possible; contrast with *conservatism.* This concept in accounting is slightly different from the profit maximizing concept in economics where the doctrine states that businesses should be run to maximize the present value of the firm's wealth, generally by equating *marginal costs* and *marginal revenues.*

profit-volume graph. See *breakeven chart.*

profit-volume ratio. *Net income* divided by net sales in dollars.

profitability accounting. Responsibility accounting.

programmed costs. A *fixed cost* not essential for carrying out operations. Research and development and advertising designed to generate new business are controllable, but once a commitment is made to incur them, they become fixed costs. Sometimes called *managed costs* or *discretionary costs;* contrast with *capacity costs.*

progressive tax. Tax for which the rate increases as the taxed base, such as income, increases; contrast with *regressive tax.*

projected financial statement. *Pro forma* financial statement.

promissory note. An unconditional written promise to pay a specified sum of money on demand or at a specified date.

proof of journal. The process of checking arithmetic accuracy of *journal entries* by testing for the equality of all *debits* with all *credits* since the last previous proof.

property dividend. A *dividend in kind.*

proprietorship. *Assets* minus *liabilities* of an *entity;* equals *contributed capital* plus *retained earnings.*

proprietorship theory. The view of the corporation that emphasizes the form of the *accounting equation* that says *assets − liabilities = owners' equity;* contrast with *entity theory.* The major implication of a choice between these theories deals with the treatment of *subsidiaries.* For example, the view that *minority interest* is an *indeterminate-term liability* is based on the proprietorship theory. The proprietorship theory implies using a *single-step income statement.*

prorate. To *allocate* in proportion to some base; for example, to allocate *service department* costs in proportion to hours of service used by the benefited departments.

prospectus. Formal written document describing *securities* to be issued. See *proxy.*

protest fee. Fee charged by banks or other financial agencies when items (such as checks) presented for collection cannot be collected.

provision. Often the exact amount of an *expense* is uncertain, but must be recognized currently anyway. The entry for the estimated expense, such as for *income taxes* or expected costs under *warranty,* is

Expense (Estimated)   X
    Liability (Estimated)   X

    In American usage, the term "provision" is often used in the expense account title of the above entry. Thus, Provision for Income Taxes is used to mean the estimate of income tax expense. (In British usage, the term "provision" is used in the title for the estimated liability of the above entry, so that Provision for Income Taxes is a balance sheet account.)

proxy. Written authorization given by one person to another so that the second person can act for the first, such as to vote shares of stock. Of particular significance to accountants because the *SEC* presumes that financial information is distributed by management along with its proxy solicitations.

public accountant. Generally, this term is synonymous with *certified public accountant.* In some jurisdictions individuals have been licensed as public accountants without being CPAs.

public accounting. That portion of accounting primarily involving the *attest* function, culminating in the *auditor's report.*

PuPU. An acronym for *purchasing power unit,* conceived by John C. Burton, former Chief Accountant of the *SEC.* Those who think *general price level adjusted* accounting is not particularly useful, poke fun at it by calling it "PuPU accounting."

purchase allowance. A reduction in sales *invoice price* usually granted because the *goods* received by the purchaser were not exactly as ordered. The goods are not returned to the seller, but are purchased at a price lower than originally agreed upon.

purchase discount. A reduction in purchase *invoice price* granted for prompt payment. See *sales discount* and *terms of sale.*

purchase method. Accounting for a *business combination* by adding the acquired company's assets at the price paid for them to the acquiring company's assets. Contrast with *pooling-of-interests method.* Because the acquired assets are put on the books at current, rather than original costs, the *amortization expenses* are usually larger (and reported income, smaller) than for the same business combination accounted for as a pooling of interests. The purchase method is required unless all criteria to be a pooling are met.

purchase order. Document authorizing a seller to deliver goods with payment to be made later.

qualified report (opinion). *Auditor's report* containing a statement that the auditor was unable to complete a satisfactory examination of all things considered relevant or that the auditor has doubts about the financial impact of some material item reported in the financial statements. See *except for* and *subject to.*

qualified (stock) option (plan). Said of a compensation scheme in which *options* to purchase *stock* are granted to employees and in which the implicit compensation is neither tax deductible as an *expense* by the employer nor taxable *income* to the employee.

quantity discount. A reduction in purchase price as quantity purchased increases; amount of the discount is constrained by law (Robinson-Patman Act). Not to be confused with *purchase discount.*

quantity variance. In *standard cost* systems, the standard price per unit times (actual quantity used minus standard quantity that should be used).

quasi-reorganization. A *reorganization* where no new company is formed or no court has intervened, as would happen in *bankruptcy.* The primary purpose is to absorb a *deficit* and get a "fresh start."

quick assets. *Assets* readily convertible into *cash;* includes cash, *current marketable securities* and *current receivables.*

quick ratio. *Acid test* ratio. See *ratio.*

R&D. See *research and development.*

rate of return on common stock equity. See *ratio.*

rate of return on stockholders' equity. See *ratio.*

rate of return (on total capital). See *ratio* and *all-capital earnings rate.*

rate variance. *Price variance,* usually for *direct labor costs.*

ratio. The number resulting when one number is divided by another. Ratios are generally used to assess aspects of profitability, solvency, and liquidity. The commonly used financial ratios are of essentially two kinds: (1) those that summarize some aspect of operations for a period, usually a year, and (2) those that summarize some aspect of *financial position* at a given moment—the moment for which a balance sheet has been prepared.

    The table in Exhibit 6.10 on page 210 lists the most common financial ratios and shows separately both the numerator and denominator used to calculate the ratio.

    For all ratios that require an average balance during the period, the average is most often derived as one-half the sum of the beginning and ending balances. Sophisticated analysts recognize, however, that when companies use a fiscal year different from the calendar year, this averaging of beginning and ending balances may be misleading. Consider, for example, the *all-capital earnings rate* of Sears, Roebuck & Company, whose fiscal year ends on January 31. Sears chooses a January 31 closing date at least in part because inventories are at a low level and are therefore easy to count—the Christmas merchandise has been sold and the Easter merchandise has not yet all been received. Furthermore, by January 31, most Christmas sales have been collected or returned, so receivable amounts are not unusually large. Thus at January 31, the amount of total assets is lower than at many other times during the year. Consequently, the denominator of the all-capital earnings rate, total assets, for Sears is more likely to represent a smaller amount of total assets on hand during the year than the average amount. The all-capital earnings rate for Sears and other companies who choose a fiscal year-end to coincide with low points in the inventory cycle is likely to be larger than if a more accurate estimate of the average amounts of total assets were used.

raw material. Goods purchased for use in manufacturing a product.

reacquired stock. *Treasury stock.*

real accounts. *Balance sheet accounts;* as opposed to *nominal accounts.* See *permanent accounts.*

real estate. *Land* and its *improvements,* such as landscaping and roads but not buildings.

realizable value. *Market value* or, sometimes, *net realizable value.*

realization convention. The accounting practice of delaying the recognition of *gains* and *losses* from changes in the market price of *assets* until the assets are sold. However, unrealized losses on *inventory* and *marketable securities* classified as *current assets* are recognized prior to sale when the *lower-of-cost-or-market* valuation basis is used.

realize. To convert into *funds.* When applied to a *gain* or *loss,* implies that an *arms'-length transaction* has taken place. Contrast with *recognize;* a loss (as for example on *marketable equity securities*) may be recognized in the financial statements even though it has not yet been realized in a transaction.

realized gain (or loss) on marketable equity securities. An income statement account title for the difference between the proceeds of disposition and the *original cost* of *marketable equity securities.*

realized holding gain. See *inventory profit* for definition and an example.

rearrangement costs. *Costs* of re-installing assets, perhaps in a different location. May be *capitalized* as part of the assets' cost, just as is original installation cost.

recapitalization. *Reorganization.*

receipt. Acquisition of *cash.*

receivable. Any *collectible* whether or not it is currently due.

receivables turnover. See *ratio.*

reciprocal holdings. Company A owns stock of Company B and Company B owns stock of Company A.

recognize. To enter a transaction in the books. Some writers use "recognize" to indicate that an event has been *journalized* and use "realize" only for those events that affect the *income statement.*

reconciliation. A calculation that shows how one balance or figure is derived systematically from another, such as a *reconciliation of retained earnings* or a *bank reconciliation schedule.* See *articulate.*

record date. *Dividends* are paid on payment date to those who own the stock on the record date.

recourse. See *note receivable discounted.*

recovery of unrealized loss on marketable securities. An *income statement account title* for the *gain* during the current period on the current asset portfolio for *marketable equity securities.* This gain will be *recognized* only to the extent that net losses have been recognized in preceding periods in amounts no smaller than the current gain. (The Allowance for Declines in Marketable Equity Securities account can never have a *debit balance.*)

redemption. Retirement by the issuer, usually by a purchase or *call,* of *stocks* or *bonds.*

redemption premium. Call *premium.*

redemption value. The price to be paid by a corporation to retire *bonds* or *preferred stock* if called before *maturity.*

refunding bond issue. Said of a *bond* issue whose proceeds are used to retire bonds already *outstanding.*

register. Collection of consecutive entries, or other information, in chronological order, such as a check register or an insurance register, which lists all insurance policies owned. If entries are recorded, it may serve as a *journal.*

registered bond. *Principal* of such a *bond* and *interest,* if registered as to interest, is paid to the owner listed on the books of the issuer. As opposed to a bearer bond, where the possessor of the bond is entitled to interest and principal.

registrar. An *agent,* usually a bank or trust company, appointed by a corporation to keep track of the names of stockholders and distributions of earnings.

registration statement. Statement required by the Securities Act of 1933 of most companies wishing to *issue securities* to the public or by the Securities Exchange Act of 1934 of a company wishing to have its securities traded in public markets. The statement discloses financial data and other items of interest to potential investors.

regressive tax. Tax for which the rate decreases as the taxed base, such as income, increases. Contrast with *progressive tax.*

Regulation S-X. The *SEC* regulation specifying the form and content of financial reports to the *SEC.*

reinvestment rate. In a *capital budgeting* context, the rate at which cash inflows from a project occurring before the project's completion are invested. Once such a rate is assumed, there will never be multiple *internal rates of return.* See *Descartes' rule of signs.*

relative sales value method. A method for *allocating joint costs* in proportion to *net realizable values* of the joint products. For example, joint products A and B together cost $100 and A sells for $60 whereas B sells for $90. Then A would be allocated ($60/$150) × $100 = .40 × $100 = $40 of cost, whereas B would be allocated ($90/$150) × $100 = $60 of cost.

relevant cost. *Incremental cost. Opportunity cost.*

relevant range. Activity levels over which costs are linear or for which *flexible budget* estimates and *breakeven charts* will remain valid.

remittance advice. Information on a *check* stub, or on a document attached to a check by the *drawer,* which tells the *payee* why a payment is being made.

rent. A charge for the use of land, buildings, or other assets.

reorganization. A major change in the *capital structure* of a corporation that leads to changes in the rights, interests, and implied ownership of the various security owners. Usually results from a *merger* or agreement by senior security holders to take action to forestall *bankruptcy.*

repair. An *expenditure* to restore an *asset's* service potential after damage or after prolonged use. In the second sense, after prolonged use, the difference between repairs and maintenance is one of degree and not of kind. Treated as an *expense* of the period when incurred. Because repairs and maintenance are treated similarly in this regard, the distinction is not important. A repair helps to maintain capacity intact at levels planned when the *asset* was acquired; contrast with *improvement.*

replacement cost.   For an asset, the current fair market price to purchase another, similar asset (with the same future benefit or service potential). *Current cost.* SEC ASR No. 190 requires certain large firms to disclose replacement cost data. See *reproduction cost* and *productive capacity.* See also *distributable income* and *inventory profit.*

replacement-cost method of depreciation.   The original-cost *depreciation* charge is augmented by an amount based on a portion of the difference between the *current replacement cost* of the asset and its *original cost.*

replacement system of depreciation.   See *retirement method of depreciation* for definition and contrast.

report.   *Financial statement; auditor's report.*

report form.   This form of *balance sheet* typically shows *assets* minus *liabilities* as one total. Then, below that it shows the components of *owners' equity* summing to the same total. Often, the top section shows *current* assets less current liabilities before *noncurrent* assets less noncurrent liabilities. Contrast with *account form.*

reporting objectives (policies).   The general doctrines underlying accounting. These include *full disclosure, objectivity, consistency, conservatism,* the assumption of *continuity of operations,* and *materiality.*

reproduction cost.   The *cost* necessary to acquire an *asset* similar in all physical respects to another asset for which a *current value* is wanted. See *replacement cost* and *productive capacity* for further contrast.

requisition.   A formal written order or request, such as for withdrawal of supplies from the storeroom.

resale value.   *Exit value. Net realizable value.*

research and development.   Research is activity aimed at discovering new knowledge in hopes that such activity will be useful in creating a new product, process, or service or improving a present product, process, or service. Development is the translation of research findings or other knowledge into a new or improved product, process, or service. The *FASB* requires that costs of such activities be *expensed* as incurred on the grounds that the future benefits are too uncertain to warrant *capitalization* as an *asset.* This treatment seems questionable to us because we wonder why firms would continue to undertake R&D if there were no expectation of future benefit; if future benefits exist, then the *costs* should be assets.

reserve.   When properly used in accounting, the term refers to an account that appropriates *retained earnings* and restricts dividend declarations. Appropriating retained earnings is itself a poor and slowly vanishing practice, so the word should seldom be used in accounting. In addition, used in the past to indicate an asset *contra* (for example, "reserve for depreciation") or an *estimated liability* (for example, "reserve for warranty costs"). In any case, reserve accounts have credit balances and are not pools of *funds* as the unwary reader might infer. If a company has set aside a pool of *cash*

(or marketable securities), then that cash will be called a *fund.*

No other word in accounting is so misunderstood and misused by laymen and "experts" who should know better. A leading unabridged dictionary defines *reserve* as "Cash, or assets readily convertible into cash, held aside, as by a corporation, bank, state or national government, etc., to meet expected or unexpected demands." This definition is absolutely wrong in accounting. Reserves are not funds. For example, a contingency fund of $10,000 is created by depositing cash in a fund and this entry is made:

Dr. Contingency Fund   10,000
  Cr. Cash   10,000

The following entry may accompany this entry, if retained earnings are to be appropriated:

Dr. Retained Earnings   10,000
  Cr. Reserve for Contingencies . . .   10,000

The transaction leading to the first entry is an event of economic significance. The second entry has little economic impact for most firms. The problem with the word "reserves" arises because the second entry can be made without the first—a company can create a reserve, that is appropriate retained earnings, without creating a fund. The problem is at least in part caused by the fact that in common usage, "reserve" means a pool of assets, as in the phrase "oil reserves." The *Internal Revenue Service* does not help in dispelling confusion about the term *reserves.* The federal *income tax* return for corporations uses the title "Reserve for Bad Debts" to mean the "Allowance for Uncollectible Accounts" and speaks of the "Reserve Method" in referring to the *allowance method* for estimating *revenue* or *income* reductions from estimated *uncollectibles.*

residual income.   In an external reporting context, this term refers to net income to common stock (= net income less *preferred stock dividends*). In *managerial accounting,* this term refers to the excess of income for a division or *segment* of a company over the product of the *cost of capital* for the company multiplied by the average amount of capital invested in the division during the period over which the income was earned.

residual security.   A *potentially dilutive security.* Options, *warrants, convertible bonds,* and *convertible preferred stock.*

residual value.   At any time, the estimated or actual, *net realizable value* (that is, proceeds less removal costs) of an *asset,* usually a depreciable *plant asset.* In the context of depreciation accounting, this term is equivalent to *salvage value* and is preferable to *scrap value,* because the asset need not be scrapped. Sometimes used to mean net *book value.* In the context of a *noncancelable* lease, the estimated value of the leased asset at the end of the lease period. See *lease.*

responsibility accounting.   Accounting for a business by considering various units as separate entities, or *profit centers,* giving management of each unit responsibility for the unit's *revenues* and *expenses.* Sometimes called "activity accounting." See *transfer price.*

restricted assets.   Governmental resources restricted by legal or contractual requirements for specific purposes.

restricted retained earnings. That part of *retained earnings* not legally available for *dividends*. See *retained earnings, appropriated*. *Bond indentures* and other loan contracts can curtail the legal ability of the corporation to declare dividends without formally requiring a retained earnings appropriation, but disclosure is required.

retail inventory method. Ascertaining *inventory* amounts for financial statements by using ratios of cost to selling price. That is, *cost of sales* = (1 − *markup percentage*) × *sales;* and *ending inventory* = (1 − *markup percentage*) × *ending inventory* at retail prices.

retained earnings. Net *income* over the life of a corporation less all income distributions (including capitalization through stock dividends); *owners' equity* less *contributed capital*.

retained earnings, appropriated. An *account* set up by crediting it and debiting *retained earnings*. Used to indicate that a portion of retained earnings is not available for dividends. The practice of appropriating retained earnings is misleading unless all capital is earmarked with its use, which is not practical. Use of formal retained earnings appropriations is declining.

retained earnings statement. *Generally accepted accounting principles* require that whenever *comparative balance sheets* and an *income statement* are presented, there must also be presented a *reconciliation* of the beginning and ending balances in the *retained earnings account*. This reconciliation can appear in a separate statement, in a combined statement of income and retained earnings or in the balance sheet.

retirement method of depreciation. No entry is recorded for *depreciation expense* until an *asset* is retired from service. Then, an entry is made *debiting* depreciation expense and *crediting* the asset account for the cost of the asset retired. If the retired asset has a *salvage value,* the amount of the debit to depreciation expense is reduced by the amount of salvage value with a corresponding debit to cash, receivables, or salvaged materials. The "replacement system of depreciation" is similar, except that the debit to depreciation expense equals the cost of the new asset less the salvage value, if any, of the old asset. These methods were used by some public utilities. For example, if 10 telephone poles are acquired in year 1 for $60 each and are replaced in year 10 for $100 each when the salvage value of the old poles is $5 each, then the accounting would be as follows:

Retirement Method

Plant Assets	600	
Cash		600
To acquire assets in year 1.		
Depreciation Expense	550	
Salvage Receivable	50	
Plant Assets		600
To record retirement and depreciation in year 10.		
Plant Assets	1,000	
Cash		1,000
To record acquisition of new assets in year 10.		

Replacement Method

Plant Assets	600	
Cash		600
To acquire assets in year 1.		
Depreciation Expense	950	
Salvage Receivable	50	
Cash		1,000
To record depreciation on old asset in amount quantified by net cost of replacement asset in year 10.		

The retirement method is like *FIFO,* in that the cost of the first assets is recorded as depreciation and the cost of the second assets is put on the balance sheet. The replacement method is like *LIFO* in that the cost of the second assets determines the depreciation expense and the cost of the first assets remains on the balance sheet.

retirement plan. *Pension plan.*

return. A schedule of information required by governmental bodies, such as the tax return required by the *Internal Revenue Service*. Also the physical return of merchandise. See also *return on investment*.

return of capital investment (capital). A payment to owners *debited* to an *owners' equity account* other than *retained earnings*.

return on investment (capital). *Income* (before distributions to suppliers of capital) for a period. As a rate, this amount divided by average total assets. *Interest,* net of tax effects, should be added back to *net income* for the numerator. See *ratio*.

revenue. The monetary measure of a service rendered. *Sales* of products, merchandise, and services, and earnings from *interest, dividends, rents,* and the like. A revenue *transaction* results in an increase in *net assets*. Do not confuse with *receipt* of *funds,* which may occur before, when, or after revenue is recognized; contrast with *gain* and *income*. See also *holding gain*. Some writers use the term *gross income* synonymously with revenue; such usage is to be avoided.

revenue center. A *responsibility center* within a firm that has control only over revenues generated; contrast with *cost center*. See *profit center*.

revenue-cost graph. See *breakeven chart*.

revenue expenditure. A phrase sometimes used to mean an *expense* in contrast to a capital *expenditure* to acquire an *asset* or to discharge a *liability*. Avoid using this phrase; use *period expense* instead.

revenue received in advance. An inferior term for *advances from customers*.

reversal (reversing) entry. An *entry* in which all *debits* and *credits* are the credits and debits, respectively, of another entry, and in the same amounts. It is usually made on the first day of an *accounting period* to reverse a previous *adjusting entry,* usually an *accrual*. The purpose of such entries is to make the bookkeeper's tasks easier. Suppose that salaries are paid every other Friday, with paychecks compensating employees for the 2 weeks just ended. Total salaries accrue at the rate of $5,000 per 5-day work week. The bookkeeper is accustomed to making the following entry every other Friday:

```
(1) Salary Expense . . . . . . . . . . . . .    10,000
       Cash . . . . . . . . . . . . . . . . . . . . .         10,000
    To record salary expense and
    salary payments.
```

If paychecks are delivered to employees on Friday, December 26, 1980, then the *adjusting entry* made on December 31 (or, perhaps, later) to record accrued salaries for December 29, 30, and 31 would be

```
(2) Salary Expense . . . . . . . . . . . . .    3,000
       Salaries Payable . . . . . . . . . .          3,000
    To charge 1980 operations with
    all salaries earned in 1980.
```

The Salary Expense account would be closed as part of the December 31 *closing entries.* On the next pay day, January 9, the salary entry would have to be

```
(3) Salary Expense . . . . . . . . . . . . .    7,000
       Salaries Payable . . . . . . . . . . . .    3,000
       Cash . . . . . . . . . . . . . . . . . . . . .        10,000
    To record salary payments split
    between expense for 1981 (7
    days) and liability carried over
    from 1980 (3 days).
```

To make entry (3), the bookkeeper must look back into the records to see how much of the debit is to Salaries Payable accrued from the previous year so that total debits are properly split between 1981 expense and the liability carried over from 1980. Notice that this entry forces the bookkeeper both (a) to refer to balances in old accounts and (b) to make an entry different from the one customarily made, entry (1).

The reversing entry, made just after the books have been closed for 1980, makes the salary entry for January 9, 1981, the same as that made on all other Friday pay days. The reversing entry merely *reverses* the adjusting entry (2):

```
(4) Salaries Payable . . . . . . . . . . . . .    3,000
       Salary Expense . . . . . . . . . . . .          3,000
    To reverse the adjusting entry.
```

This entry results in a zero balance in the Salaries Payable account and a *credit* balance in the Salary Expense account. If entry (4) is made just after the books are closed for 1980, then the entry on January 9 will be the customary entry (1). Entries (4) and (1) together have exactly the same effect as entry (3).

The procedure for using reversal entries is as follows: The required adjustment to record an accrual (*payable* or *receivable*) is made at the end of an *accounting period;* the closing entry is made as usual; as of the first day of the following period, an entry is made reversing the adjusting entry; when a payment is made (or received), the entry is recorded as though no adjusting entry had been recorded. Whether or not reversal entries are used affects the record-keeping procedures, but not the financial statements.

Also used to describe the entry reversing an incorrect entry before recording the correct entry.

reverse stock split. A stock split in which the number of shares *outstanding* is decreased. See *stock split.*

revolving fund. A *fund* whose amounts are continually expended and then replenished; for example, a *petty cash fund.*

revolving loan. A *loan* that is expected to be renewed at *maturity.*

right. The privilege to subscribe to new *stock* issues or to purchase stock. Usually, rights are contained in securities called *warrants* and the warrants may be sold to others. See also *preemptive right.*

risk. A measure of the variability of the *return on investment.* For a given expected amount of return, most people prefer less risk to more risk. Therefore, in rational markets, investments with more risk usually promise, or are expected to yield, a higher rate of return than investments with lower risk. Most people use "risk" and "uncertainty" as synonyms. In technical language, however, these terms have different meanings. "Risk" is used when the probabilities attached to the various outcomes are known, such as the probabilities of heads or tails in the flip of a fair coin. "Uncertainty" refers to an event where the probabilities of the outcomes, such as winning or losing a lawsuit, can only be estimated.

risk-adjusted discount rate. In a *capital budgeting* context, a decision maker compares projects by comparing their *net present values* for a given *interest* rate, usually the *cost of capital.* If a given project's outcome is considered to be much more or much less risky than the normal undertakings of the company, then the interest rate will be increased (if the project is more risky) or decreased (if less risky) and the rate used is said to be risk-adjusted.

risk premium. Extra compensation paid to an employee or extra interest paid to a lender, over amounts usually considered normal, in return for their undertaking to engage in activities more risky than normal.

ROI. *Return on investment,* but usually used to refer to a single project and expressed as a ratio: *income* divided by average *cost* of *assets* devoted to the project.

royalty. Compensation for the use of property, usually a patent, copyrighted material, or natural resources. The amount is often expressed as a percentage of receipts from using the property or as an amount per unit produced.

rule of 69. An amount of money invested at r percent per period will double in $69/r + .35$ periods. This approximation is accurate to one-tenth of a period for interest rates between $1/4$ and 100 percent per period. For example, at 10 percent per period, the rule says that a given sum will double in $69/10 + .35 = 7.25$ periods. At 10 percent per period, a given sum doubles in $7.27 +$ periods.

rule of 72. An amount of money invested at r percent per period will double in $72/r$ periods. A reasonable approximation but not nearly as accurate as the *rule of 69.* For example, at 10 percent per period, the rule says a given sum will double in $72/10 = 7.2$ periods.

rule of 78. The rule followed by many finance companies for allocating earnings on *loans* among the months of a year on the sum-of-the-months'-digits-basis when equal monthly payments from the borrower are to be received. The sum of the digits from 1 through 12 is 78, so 12/78 of the year's earnings are allocated to the first month, 11/78 to the second month, and so on. See *sum-of-the-years'-digits depreciation.*

ruling (and balancing) an account. The process of summarizing a series of entries in an *account* by computing a new *balance* and drawing double lines to indicate the information above the double lines has been summarized in the new balance. The process is illustrated below. The steps are as follows. (1) Compute the sum of all *debit* entries including opening debit balance, if any—$1,464.16. (2) Compute the sum of all credit entries including opening credit balance, if any—$413.57. (3) If the amount in (1) is larger than the amount in (2), then write the excess as a credit with a check mark—$1,464.16 − $413.57 = $1,050.59. (4) Add both debit and credit columns, which should both now sum to the same amount, and show that identical total at the foot of both columns. (5) Draw double lines under those numbers and write the excess of debits over credits as the new debit balance with a check mark. (6) If the amount in (2) is larger than the amount in (1), then write the excess as a debit with a check mark. (7) Do steps (4) and (5) except that the excess becomes the new credit balance. (8) If the amount in (1) is equal to the amount in (2), then the balance is zero and only the totals with the double lines beneath them need be shown.

This process is illustrated below.

SAB. *Staff Accounting Bulletin* of the *SEC.*

salary. Compensation earned by managers, administrators, professionals, not based on an hourly rate. Contrast with *wage.*

sale. A *revenue* transaction where *goods* or *services* are delivered to a customer in return for cash or a contractual obligation to pay.

sale and leaseback. Phrase used to describe a *financing* transaction where improved property is sold but is taken back for use on a long-term *lease*. Such transactions often have advantageous income tax effects, but usually have no effect on *financial statement income.*

sales allowance. A reduction in sales *invoice* price usually given because the goods received by the buyer are not exactly what was ordered. The amounts of such adjustments are often accumulated by the seller in a temporary *revenue contra account* having this, or a similar, title. See *sales discount.*

sales basis of revenue recognition. *Revenue* is recognized, not as goods are produced nor as orders are received, but only when the sale (delivery) has been consummated and cash or a legal receivable obtained. Most revenue is recognized on this basis. Compare with the *percentage-of-completion method* and the *installment method.* Identical with the *completed-contract method* but this latter term is ordinarily used only for *long-term* construction projects.

sales discount. Reduction in sales *invoice* price usually offered for prompt payment. See *terms of sale* and *2/10, n/30.*

sales return. The physical return of merchandise; the amounts of such returns are often accumulated by the seller in a temporary *revenue contra account.*

sales, uncollectible accounts adjustment. The preferred title for the *contra-revenue account* to recognize estimated reductions in income caused by accounts receivable that will not be collected. Called *bad debt expense* and treated as an expense, rather than an adjustment to revenue, when the write-off method is used. See *allowance for uncollectibles* and *allowance method.*

sales value method. *Relative sales value method.*

salvage value. Actual or estimated selling price, net of removal or disposal costs, of a used *plant asset* to be sold or otherwise retired. See *residual value.*

SAS. *Statement on Auditing Standards* of the *AICPA.*

schedule. Supporting set of calculations that show how figures in a statement or tax return are derived.

scientific method. *Effective-interest method* of *amortizing bond discount* or *premium.*

AN OPEN ACCOUNT, RULED AND BALANCED
(Steps indicated in parentheses correspond to steps described in "ruling an account.")

	Date 1979	Explanation	Ref.	Debit (1)		Date 1979	Explanation	Ref.	Credit (2)		
	Jan. 1	Balance	✓	100	00						
	Jan. 13		VR	121	37	Sept. 15		J		42	
	Mar. 20		VR	56	42	Nov. 12		J	413	15	
	June 5		J	1,138	09	Dec. 31	Balance	✓	1,050	59	(3)
	Aug. 18		J	1	21						
	Nov. 20		VR	38	43						
	Dec. 7		VR	8	64						
(4)				1,464	16				1,464	16	(4)
	1980					**1980**					
(5)	Jan. 1	Balance	✓	1,050	59						

scrap value. *Salvage value* assuming item is to be junked. A *net realizable value. Residual value.*

SEC. Securities and Exchange Commission, an agency authorized by the U.S. Congress to regulate, among other things, the financial reporting practices of most public corporations. The SEC has indicated that it will usually allow the *FASB* to set accounting principles but it reserves the right to require more disclosure than required by the FASB. The SEC's accounting requirements are stated in its *Accounting Series Releases (ASR)* and *Regulation S-X.* See also *registration statement* and *10-K.*

secret reserve. *Hidden reserve.*

Securities and Exchange Commission. *SEC.*

security. Document that indicates ownership or indebtedness or potential ownership, such as an *option* or *warrant.*

segment (of a business). As defined by *APB Opinion* No. 30, "a component of an *entity* whose activities represent a separate major line of business or class of customer . . . [It may be] a *subsidiary,* a division, or a department, . . . provided that its *assets,* results of *operations,* and activities can be clearly distinguished, physically and operationally for financial reporting purposes, from the other assets, results of operations, and activities of the entity." In *FASB Statement* No. 14 a segment is defined as "A component of an enterprise engaged in promoting a product or service or a group of related products and services primarily to unaffiliated customers . . . for a profit."

segment reporting. Reporting of *income* and *assets* by *segments of a business,* usually classified by nature of products sold but sometimes by geographical area where goods are produced or sold. Sometimes called "line of business reporting." *Central corporate expenses* are sometimes allocated to the segments although these reports may be more useful when such expenses are separately disclosed.

self-balancing. A set of records with equal *debits* and *credits* such as the *ledger* (but not individual accounts), the *balance sheet,* and a *fund* in nonprofit accounting.

self-insurance. See *insurance.*

selling and administrative expenses. *Expenses* not specifically identifiable with, nor assigned to, production.

semifixed costs. *Costs* that increase with activity as a step function.

semivariable costs. *Costs* that increase strictly linearly with activity but that are positive at zero activity level. Royalty fees of 2 percent of sales are variable; royalty fees of $1,000 per year plus 2 percent of sales are semivariable.

senior securities. *Bonds* as opposed to *preferred stock; preferred stock* as opposed to *common stock.* The senior security has a claim against *earnings* or *assets* that must be met before the claim of less senior securities.

serial bonds. An *issue* of *bonds* that mature in part at one date, another part on another date, and so on; the various maturity dates usually are equally spaced; contrast with *term bonds.*

service basis of depreciation. *Production method.*

service department. A department, such as the personnel or computer department, that provides services to other departments, rather than direct work on a salable product; contrast with *production department.*

service life. Period of expected usefulness of an asset; may not coincide with *depreciable life* for income tax purposes.

service potential. The future benefits embodied in an item that cause the item to be classified as an *asset.* Without service potential, there are no future benefits and the item should not be classified as an asset.

services. Useful work done by a person, a machine, or an organization. See *goods and services.*

setup. The time or costs required to prepare production equipment for doing a job.

share. A unit of *stock* representing ownership in a corporation.

shareholders' equity. See *stockholders' equity.*

short-term. Current; ordinarily, due within one year.

shrinkage. An excess of *inventory* shown on the *books* over actual physical quantities on hand. Can result from theft or shoplifting as well as from evaporation or general wear and tear.

sight draft. A demand for payment drawn by a person to whom money is owed. The *draft* is presented to the borrower's (the debtor's) bank in expectation that the borrower will authorize its bank to disburse the funds. Such drafts are often used when a seller sells goods to a new customer in a different city. The seller is not sure whether the buyer will pay the bill. The seller sends the *bill* of lading, or other evidence of ownership of the goods, along with a sight draft to the buyer's bank. The buyer is therefore notified that if the goods are to be released to the buyer, the bank must be instructed to honor the sight draft. Once the sight draft is honored, the bill of lading or other document evidencing ownership is handed over to the buyer and the goods become the property of the buyer.

simple interest. *Interest* calculated on *principal* where interest earned during periods before maturity of the loan is neither added to the principal nor paid to the lender. *Interest = principal × interest rate × time.* Seldom used in economic calculations except for periods less than 1 year; contrast with *compound interest.*

single-entry accounting. Accounting that is neither *self-balancing* nor *articulated;* that is, it does not rely on equal *debits* and *credits. No journal entries* are made. *Plugging* is required to derive *owners' equity* for the *balance sheet.*

single proprietorship. *Sole proprietorship.*

single step. Said of an *income statement* where all *ordinary revenue* and *gain* items are shown first and totaled. Then all ordinary *expenses* and *losses* are totaled. Their difference, plus the effect of *income from discontinued operations* and *extraordinary items,* is shown as *net income;* contrast with *multiple-step* and see *proprietorship theory.*

sinking fund. *Assets* and their earnings earmarked for the retirement of bonds or other long-term obligations. Earnings of sinking-fund investments are taxable income of the company.

sinking-fund method of depreciation. The periodic charge is an amount so that when the charges are considered to be an *annuity,* the value of the annuity at the end of depreciable life is equal to the *acquisition cost* of the asset. In theory, the charge for a period ought also to include interest on the accumulated depreciation at the start of the period as well. A *fund* of cash is not necessarily, or even usually, accumulated. This method is rarely used.

skeleton account. *T-account.*

slide. The name of the error made by a bookkeeper in recording the digits of a number correctly with the decimal point misplaced; for example, recording $123.40 as $1,234.00 or as $12.34.

soak-up method. The *equity method.*

Social Security taxes. Taxes levied by the federal government on both employers and employees to provide *funds* to pay retired persons (or their survivors) who are entitled to receive such payments, either because they paid Social Security taxes themselves or because the Congress has declared them eligible. See *Old Age, Survivors, Disability, and (Hospital) Insurance.*

sole proprietorship. All *owners' equity* belongs to one person.

solvent. Able to meet debts when due.

sound value. A phrase used mainly in appraisals of *fixed assets* to mean *fair market value* or *replacement cost* in present condition.

source of funds. Any *transaction* that increases *working capital*

sources and uses statement. *Statement of changes in financial position.*

SOYD. *Sum-of-the-years'-digits depreciation.*

special journal. A *journal,* such as a sales journal or cash disbursements journal, to record *transactions* of a similar nature that occur frequently.

specific identification method. Method for valuing *ending inventory* and *cost of goods sold* by identifying actual units sold and in inventory and summing the actual costs of those individual units. Usually used for items with large unit value, such as jewelry, automobiles, and fur coats.

specific price changes. Changes in the market prices of specific *goods and services;* contrast with *general price level changes.*

specific price index. A measure of the price of a specific good or service, or a small group of similar goods or services, at one time relative to the price during a base period; contrast with *general price index.* See *dollar-value LIFO method.*

split. *Stock split.* Sometimes called "splitup."

splitoff point. The point where all costs are no longer *joint costs* but can be identified with individual products or perhaps with a smaller number of *joint products.*

spoilage. See *abnormal spoilage* and *normal spoilage.*

spread sheet. A *work sheet* organized like a *matrix* that provides a two-way classification of accounting data. The rows and columns are both labeled with *account* titles. An entry in a row represents a *debit,* whereas an entry in a column represents a *credit.* Thus, the number "100" in the "cash" row and the "accounts receivable" column records an entry debiting cash and crediting accounts receivable for

$100. A given row total indicates all debit entries to the account represented by that row and a given column total indicates the sum of all credit entries to the account represented by that column.

squeeze. A term sometimes used for *plug.*

stabilized accounting. General *price level adjusted accounting.*

stable monetary unit assumption. In spite of *inflation* that appears to be a way of life, the assumption that underlies *historical-cost* accounting—namely, that current dollars and dollars of previous years can be meaningfully added together. No specific recognition is given to changing values of the dollar in the usual *financial statements.* See *price level adjusted statements.*

Staff Accounting Bulletin. An interpretation issued by the Staff of the Chief Accountant of the *SEC* "suggesting" how the various *Accounting Series Releases* should be applied in practice. A substantial fraction of the first 20 or so SABs are concerned with the implementation of *replacement-cost accounting,* as required by *ASR* No. 190.

standard cost. Anticipated *cost* of producing a unit of output; a predetermined cost to be assigned to products produced.

standard cost system. *Product costing* using *standard costs* rather than actual costs. May be based on either *absorption* or *direct costing* principles.

standard price (rate). Unit price established for materials or labor used in *standard cost systems.*

standby costs. A type of *capacity cost,* such as property taxes, incurred even if operations are shut down completely. Contrast with *enabling costs.*

stated capital. Amount of capital contributed by stockholders. Sometimes used to mean *legal capital.*

stated value. A term sometimes used for the *face amount* of *capital stock,* when no *par value* is indicated. Where there is a stated value per share, it may be set by the directors (in which case, capital *contributed in excess of stated value* may come into being).

statement of affairs. A *balance sheet* showing immediate *liquidation* amounts, rather than *historical costs,* usually prepared when *insolvency* or *bankruptcy* is imminent. The *going concern assumption* is not used.

statement of changes in financial position. As defined by *APB Opinion* No. 19, a statement that explains the changes in *working capital* (or cash) balances during a period and shows the changes in the working capital (or cash) accounts themselves. Sometimes called the "funds statement." See *dual-transactions assumption* and *all financial resources.*

Statement of Financial Accounting Standards. See *FASB.*

statement of financial position. *Balance sheet.*

statement of retained earnings (income). A statement that reconciles the beginning-of-period and end-of-period balances in the *retained earnings* account. It shows the effects of *earnings, dividend declarations,* and *prior-period adjustments.*

Statement on Auditing Standards. No. 1 of this series (1973) codifies all statements on auditing standards previously promulgated by the *AICPA*. Later numbers deal with specific auditing standards and procedures. *SAS.*

static budget.   *Fixed budget.*

statutory tax rate.   The tax rate specified in the *income tax* law for each type of income (for example, *ordinary income, capital gain or loss*).

step cost.   *Semifixed cost.*

step-down method.   The method for *allocating service department* costs that starts by allocating one service department's costs to *production departments* and to all other service departments. Then a second service department's costs, including costs allocated from the first, are allocated to production departments and to all other service departments except the first one. In this fashion, the costs of all service departments, including previous allocations, are allocated to production departments and to those service departments whose costs have not yet been allocated.

stock.   *Inventory. Capital stock.* A measure of the amount of something on hand at a specific time; in this sense, contrast with *flow.*

stock appreciation rights.   The employer promises to pay to the employee an amount of *cash* on a certain future date. The amount of cash is the difference between the *market value* of a certain number of *shares* of *stock* in the employer's company on a given future date and the market value on the date the rights are granted. This is a form of compensation used because both changes in tax laws in recent years and stock market performance have made *stock options* relatively less attractive. *GAAP* do not allow any entry to be made when such rights are granted. Only when (and if) the cash is eventually paid is there an entry made recognizing *expense.*

stock dividend.   A so-called *dividend* where additional *shares* of *capital stock* are distributed, without cash payments, to existing shareholders. It results in a *debit* to *retained earnings* in the amount of the market value of the shares issued and a *credit* to *capital stock* accounts. It is ordinarily used to indicate that earnings retained have been permanently reinvested in the business; contrast with a *stock split,* which requires no entry in the capital stock accounts other than a notation that the *par* or *stated value* per share has been changed.

stock option.   The right to purchase a specified number of shares of *stock* for a specified price at specified times, usually granted to employees; contrast with *warrant.*

stock right.   See *right.*

stock split.   Increase in the number of common shares outstanding resulting from the issuance of additional shares to existing stockholders without additional capital contributions by them. Does not increase the total *par* (or *stated*) *value* of *common stock* outstanding because par (or stated) value per share is reduced in inverse proportion. A three-for-one stock split reduces par (or stated) value per share to one-third of its former amount. Stock splits are usually limited to distributions that increase the number of shares outstanding by 20 percent or more; compare with *stock dividend.*

stock subscriptions.   See *subscription* and *subscribed stock.*

stock warrant.   See *warrant.*

stockholders' equity.   *Proprietorship* or *owners' equity* of a corporation. Because *stock* means inventory in Australian,

British, and Canadian usage, the term *shareholders' equity* is usually used by Australian, British, and Canadian writers.

stores.   *Raw materials,* parts, and supplies.

straight debt value.   An estimate of what the *market value* of a *convertible bond* would be if the bond did not contain a conversion privilege.

straight-line depreciation.   If the *depreciable life* is *n* periods, then the periodic *depreciation* charge is $1/n$ of the *depreciable cost.* Results in equal periodic charges and is sometimes called "straight-time depreciation."

Subchapter S corporation.   A firm legally organized as a *corporation* but taxed as if it were a *partnership.*

subject to.   Qualifications in an *auditor's report* usually caused by a *material* uncertainty in the valuation of an item, such as future promised payments from a foreign government or outcome of pending litigation.

subordinated.   Said of *debt* whose claim on income or assets is junior to, or comes after, claims of other debt.

subscribed stock.   A *stockholders' equity* account showing the capital that will be contributed as soon as the subscription price is collected. A subscription is a legal contract so that an entry is made debiting a receivable and crediting subscribed stock as soon as the stock is subscribed.

subscription.   Agreement to buy a *security,* or to purchase periodicals such as magazines.

subsequent events.   *Post-statement events.*

subsidiary.   Said of a company more than 50 percent of whose voting stock is owned by another.

subsidiary (ledger) accounts.   The *accounts* in a *subsidiary ledger.*

subsidiary ledger.   The *ledger* that contains the detailed accounts whose total is shown in a *controlling account* of the *general ledger.*

successful-efforts accounting.   In petroleum accounting, the *capitalization* of the drilling costs of only those wells that contain oil. See *discovery-value accounting* for an example.

summary of significant accounting principles.   *APB Opinion* No. 22 requires that every *annual report* summarize the significant *accounting principles* used in compiling the annual report. This summary may be a separate exhibit or the first *note* to the financial statements.

sum-of-the-years'-digits depreciation. SYD. SOYD.   An *accelerated depreciation* method for an asset with *depreciable life* of *n* years where the charge in period i $(i = 1, \ldots, n)$ is the fraction $(n + 1 - i)/[n(n + 1)/2]$ of the *depreciable cost.* If an asset has a depreciable cost of \$15,000 and a 5-year depreciable life, for example, the depreciation charges would be \$5,000 ($= 5/15 \times$ \$15,000) in the first year, \$4,000 in the second, \$3,000 in the third, \$2,000 in the fourth, and \$1,000 in the fifth.

sunk cost.   *Costs* incurred in the past that are not affected by, and hence irrelevant for, current decisions, aside from *income tax* effects; contrast with *incremental costs* and *imputed costs.* For example, the *acquisition cost* of machinery is irrelevant to a decision of whether or not to scrap the machinery. The current *exit value* of the machine is the imputed cost of continuing to own it and the cost of, say, electricity to run the machine is an incremental cost of its operation.

supplementary statements (schedules).   Statements (schedules) in addition to the four basic *financial statements* (including the retained earnings reconciliation as a basic statement).

surplus.   A word once used but now considered poor terminology; prefaced by "earned" to mean *retained earnings* and prefaced by "capital" to mean *capital contributed in excess of par* (or *stated*) *value.*

surplus reserves.   Of all the words in accounting, *reserve* is the most objectionable and *surplus* is the second most objectionable. This phrase, then, has nothing to recommend it. It means, simply, *appropriated retained earnings.*

suspense account.   A *temporary account* used to record part of a transaction prior to final analysis of that transaction. For example, if a business regularly classifies all sales into a dozen or more different categories but wants to deposit the proceeds of cash sales every day, it may credit a sales suspense account pending detailed classification of all sales into sales, type 1; sales, type 2; and so on.

sustainable income.   The part of *distributable income* (computed from *replacement cost* data) that the firm can be expected to earn in the next accounting period if operations are continued at the same levels as during the current period. *Income from discontinued operations,* for example, may be distributable but not sustainable.

S-X.   See *Regulation S-X.*

SYD.   *Sum-of-the-years'-digits depreciation. SOYD.*

T-account.   Account form shaped like the letter T with the title above the horizontal line. *Debits* are shown to the left of the vertical line, *credits* to the right.

take-home pay.   The amount of a paycheck; earned wages or *salary* reduced by deductions for *income taxes, Social Security taxes,* contributions to fringe benefit plans, union dues, and so on. Take-home pay might be as little as 60 percent of earned compensation.

taking a bath.   To incur a large loss. See *big bath.*

tangible.   Having physical form. Accounting has never satisfactorily defined the distinction between tangible and *intangible assets.* Typically, intangibles are defined by giving an exhaustive list and everything not on the list is defined as tangible.

target cost.   *Standard cost.*

tax.   A nonpenal, but compulsory, charge levied by a government on income, consumption, wealth, or other bases for the benefit of all those governed. The term does not include fines or specific charges for benefits accruing only to those paying the charges, such as licenses, permits, special assessments, admissions fees, and tolls.

tax allocation: interperiod.   See *deferred income tax liability.*

tax allocation: intrastatement.   The showing of income tax effects on *extraordinary items, income from discontinued operations,* and *prior-period adjustments* along with these items, separately from income taxes on other income. See *net-of-tax reporting.*

tax avoidance.   See *tax shelter.*

tax credit.   A subtraction from taxes otherwise payable; contrast with *tax deduction.*

tax deduction.   A subtraction from *revenues* and *gains* to arrive at taxable income. Tax deductions are technically different from tax *exemptions,* but the effect of both is to reduce gross income in computing taxable income. Both are different from *tax credits,* which are subtracted from the computed tax itself in determining taxes payable. If the tax rate is t percent of pretax income, then a *tax credit* of \$1 is worth $\$1/t$ of *tax deductions.*

tax evasion.   The fraudulent understatement of taxable income or overstatement of deductions and expenses or both; contrast with tax shelter.

tax exempts.   See *municipal bonds.*

tax shelter.   The legal avoidance of, or reduction in, *income taxes* resulting from a careful reading of the complex income tax regulations and the subsequent rearrangement of financial affairs to take advantage of the regulations. Often the term is used pejoratively, but the courts have long held that an individual or corporation has no obligation to pay taxes any larger than the legal minimum. If the public concludes that a given tax shelter is "unfair," then the laws and regulations can be changed. Sometimes used to refer to the investment that permits tax avoidance.

tax shield.   The amount of an *expense* that reduces taxable income but does not require *working capital,* such as *depreciation.* Sometimes this term is expanded to include expenses that reduce taxable income and use working capital. A depreciation deduction (or *R&D* expense in the expanded sense) of \$10,000 provides a tax shield of \$4,800 when the marginal tax rate is 48 percent.

technology.   The sum of a firm's technical *trade secrets* and *know-how,* as distinct from its *patents.*

temporary account.   *Account* that does not appear on the *balance sheet. Revenue* and *expense* accounts, their *adjuncts* and *contras, production cost accounts, income distribution accounts,* and purchases-related accounts (which are closed to the various inventories). Sometimes called a "nominal account."

temporary difference.   See *timing difference.*

temporary investments.   Investments in *marketable securities* that the owner intends to sell within a short time, usually 1 year, and hence classified as *current assets.*

10-K.   The name of the annual report required by the *SEC* of nearly all publicly held corporations. This report contains more information than the *annual report* to stockholders. Corporations must send a copy of the 10-K to those stockholders who request it.

term bonds.   A *bond issue* whose component bonds all mature at the same time; contrast with *serial bonds.*

term loan.   A loan with a *maturity* date, as opposed to a demand loan which is due whenever the lender requests payment. In practice bankers and auditors use this phrase only for loans for a year or more.

terms of sale.   The conditions governing payment for a sale. For example, the terms *2/10, n(et)/30* mean that if payment is made within 10 days of the invoice date, a *discount* of 2 percent from *invoice* price can be taken; the invoice amount must be paid, in any event, within 30 days or it becomes overdue.

tickler file. A collection of vouchers or other memorandums arranged chronologically to remind the person in charge of certain duties to make payments (or to do other tasks) as scheduled.

time-adjusted rate of return. *Internal rate of return.*

time cost. *Period cost.*

time deposit. Cash in a bank earning interest; contrast with *demand deposit.*

time-series analysis. See *cross-section analysis* for definition and contrast.

times-interest earned. Ratio of pretax *income* plus *interest* charges to interest charges. See *ratio.*

timing difference. A difference between taxable income and pretax income reported to stockholders that will be reversed in a subsequent period. It requires an entry in the *deferred income tax* account. For example, the use of *accelerated depreciation* for tax returns and *straight-line depreciation* for financial reporting.

total assets turnover. *Sales* divided by average total *assets.*

trade acceptance. A *draft* drawn by a seller which is presented for signature (acceptance) to the buyer at the time goods are purchased and which then becomes the equivalent of a *note receivable* of the seller and the *note payable* of the buyer.

trade credit. One business allows another to buy from it in return for a promise to pay later. As contrasted with consumer credit, where a business extends the privilege of paying later to a retail customer.

trade discount. A *discount* from *list price* offered to all customers of a given type; contrast with a *discount* offered for prompt payment and *quantity discount.*

trade payables (receivables). *Payables (receivables)* arising in the ordinary course of business transactions. Most accounts payable (receivable) are of this kind.

trade secret. Technical or business information such as formulas, recipes, computer programs, and marketing data not generally known by competitors and maintained by the firm as a secret. A famous example is the secret formula for *Coca Cola* (a registered *trademark* of the company). Compare with *know-how.* Theoretically capable of having an infinite life, this intangible asset is capitalized only if purchased and then amortized over a period not to exceed 40 years. If it is developed internally, then no asset will be shown.

trade-in. Acquiring a new *asset* in exchange for a used one and perhaps additional cash. See *boot* and *trade-in transaction.*

trade-in transaction. The accounting for a trade-in depends on whether or not the asset received is "similar" to the asset traded in and whether the accounting is for *financial statements* or for *income tax* returns. Assume that an old asset cost $5,000, has $3,000 of *accumulated depreciation* (after recording depreciation to the date of the trade-in), and hence has a *book value* of $2,000. The old asset appears to have a market value of $1,500, according to price quotations in used-asset markets. The old asset is traded-in on a new asset

with a list price of $10,000. The old asset and $5,500 cash (*boot*) are given for the new asset. The generic entry for the trade-in transaction is

New Asset	A	
Accumulated Depreciation		
(Old Asset)	3,000	
Adjustment on Exchange of Asset ...	B or	B
Old Asset		5,000
Cash		5,500

(1) The *list price* method of accounting for trade-ins rests on the assumption that the list price of the new asset closely approximates its market value. The new asset is recorded at its list price (A = $10,000 in the example); B is a *plug* (= $2,500 credit in the example). If B requires a *debit* plug, the Adjustment on Exchange of Asset is a *loss;* if a *credit* plug is required (as in the example), the adjustment is a *gain.*

(2) Another theoretically sound method of accounting for trade-ins rests on the assumption that the price quotation from used-asset markets gives a more reliable measure of the market value of the old asset than is the list price a reliable measure of the market value of the new asset. This method uses the *fair market value* of the old asset. $1,500 in the example, to determine B (= $2,000 book value − $1,500 assumed proceeds on disposition = $500 debit or loss). The exchange results in a loss if the book value of the old asset exceeds its market value and in a gain if the market value exceeds the book value. The new asset is recorded on the books by plugging for A (= $7,000 in the example).

(3) For income tax reporting, no gain or loss may be recognized on the trade-in. Thus the new asset is recorded on the books by assuming B is zero and plugging for A (= $7,500 in the example). In practice, firms that wish to recognize the loss currently will sell the old asset directly, rather than trading it in, and acquire the new asset entirely for cash.

(4) *Generally accepted accounting principles (APB Opinion No. 29)* require a variant of these methods. The basic method is (1) or (2), depending upon whether the list price of the new asset (1) or the quotation of the old asset's market value (2) is the more reliable indication of market value. If, when applying the basic method, a debit entry, or loss, is required for the Adjustment on Exchange of Asset, then the trade-in is recorded as described in (1) or (2) and the full amount of the loss is recognized currently. If, however, a credit entry, or gain, is required for the Adjustment on Exchange of Asset, then the amount of gain recognized currently depends on whether or not the old asset and the new asset are "similar." If the assets are not similar, then the entire gain is recognized currently. If the assets are similar and cash is not received by the party trading in, then no gain is recognized and the treatment is like that in (3); that is, B = O, plug for A. If the assets are similar and cash is received by the party trading in— a rare case—then a portion of the gain is recognized currently. The portion of the gain recognized currently is the fraction *cash received/fair market value of total consideration received.* (When the list price method, (1), is used, the market value of the old asset is assumed to be the list price of the new asset plus the amount of cash received by the party trading in.)

The results of applying GAAP to the example can be summarized as follows:

More Reliable Information As To Fair Market Value	Old Asset Compared with New Asset	
	Similar	Not Similar
New Asset List Price	A = $7,500	A = $10,000
	B = 0	B = 2,500 gain
Old Asset Market Price	A = $7,000	A = $ 7,000
	B = 500 loss	B = 500 loss

trademark. A distinctive word or symbol affixed to a product, its package or dispenser, which uniquely identifies the firm's products and services. See *trademark right.*

trademark right. The right to exclude competitors in sales or advertising from using words or symbols that may be confusingly similar to the firm's *trademarks.* Trademark rights last as long as the firm continues to use the trademarks in question. In the United States, trademark rights arise from use and not from government registration. They therefore have a legal life independent of the life of a registration. Registrations last 20 years and are renewable as long as the trademark is being used. Thus, as an asset, purchased trademark rights might, like land, not be subject to amortization if management believes that the life of the trademark is indefinite. In practice, accountants usually amortize a trademark right over some estimate of its life, not to exceed 40 years. Under *FASB Statement* No. 2, internally developed trademark rights must be *expensed.*

trading on the equity. Said of a firm engaging in *debt financing;* frequently said of a firm doing so to a degree considered abnormal for a firm of its kind. *Leverage.*

transaction. An exchange between the accounting *entity* and another party, or parties, that leads to an accounting entry. Sometimes used to describe any event that requires a *journal entry.*

transfer agent. Usually a bank or trust company designated by a corporation to make legal transfers of *stock (bonds)* and, perhaps, to pay *dividends (coupons).*

transfer price. A substitute for a *market,* or *arms'-length, price* used in *profit center,* or *responsibility, accounting* when one segment of the business "sells" to another segment. Incentives of profit center managers will not coincide with the best interests of the entire business unless transfer prices are properly set.

translation gain (or loss). *Foreign exchange gain (or loss).*

transportation-in. *Freight-in.*

transposition error. An error in record keeping resulting from reversing the order of digits in a number, such as recording "32" for "23." If an error of this sort has been made in a number added in a total, then the incorrect total will differ from the correct total by a number divisible by nine. Thus if *trial balance* sums differ by a number divisible by nine, one might search for a transposition error.

treasury bond. A bond issued by a corporation and then reacquired; such bonds are treated as retired when reacquired and an *extraordinary gain* or *loss* on reacquisition is recognized. Also, a *bond* issued by the U.S. Treasury Department.

treasury stock. *Capital stock* issued and then reacquired by the corporation. Such reacquisitions result in a reduction of *stockholders' equity,* and are usually shown on the balance sheet as *contra* to stockholders' equity. Neither *gain* nor *loss* is recognized on transactions involving treasury stock. Any difference between the amounts paid and received for treasury stock transactions is debited (if positive) or credited (if negative) to *additional paid-in capital.* See *cost method* and *par value method.*

trial balance. A listing of *account balances;* all accounts with *debit* balances are totaled separately from accounts with *credit* balances. The two totals should be equal. Trial balances are taken as a partial check of the arithmetic accuracy of the entries previously made. See *adjusted, preclosing, postclosing, unadjusted trial balance.*

turnover. The number of times that *assets,* such as *inventory* or *accounts receivable,* are replaced on average during the period. Accounts receivable turnover, for example, is total sales on account for a period divided by average accounts receivable balance for the period. See *ratio.*

turnover of plant and equipment. See *ratio.*

two-T-account method. A method for computing either (1) *foreign exchange gains and losses* or (2) *monetary gains or losses* for *general price level adjusted statements.* The left-hand *T-account* shows actual net balances of *monetary items* and the right-hand T-account shows implied *(common) dollar* amounts.

2/10, n(et)/30. See *terms of sale.*

unadjusted trial balance. *Trial balance* before *adjusting* and *closing entries* are made at the end of the period.

unappropriated retained earnings. *Retained earnings* not appropriated and therefore against which *dividends* can be charged in the absence of retained earnings restrictions. See *restricted retained earnings.*

uncertainty. See *risk* for definition and contrast.

uncollectible account. An *account receivable* that will not be paid by the *debtor.* If the preferable *allowance method* is used, the entry on judging a specific account to be uncollectible is to *debit* the Allowance for Uncollectibles account and to *credit* the specific account receivable. See *sales, uncollectible accounts adjustment.*

unconsolidated subsidiary. A *subsidiary* not consolidated and, hence, accounted for on the *equity method.*

uncontrollable cost. The opposite of *controllable cost.*

underlying document. The record, memorandum, *voucher,* or other signal that is the authority for making an *entry* into a *journal.*

underwriter. One who agrees to purchase an entire *security issue* for a specified price, usually for resale to others.

unearned income (revenue). *Advances from customers;* strictly speaking, a contradiction in terms.

unemployment tax. See *FUTA.*

unexpired cost. An *asset.*

unfavorable variance. In *standard cost* accounting, an excess of actual cost over standard cost assigned to product.

unfunded. Not *funded.* An obligation or *liability,* usually for *pension costs,* exists but no *funds* have been set aside to discharge the obligation or liability.

Uniform Partnership Act. A model law, enacted by many states, to govern the relations between partners where the *partnership* agreement fails to specify the agreed-upon treatment.

unissued capital stock. *Stock* authorized but not yet issued.

units of production method. The *production method of depreciation.*

unlimited liability. The liability of *general partners* or a sole proprietor for all debts of the *partnership* or *sole proprietorship.*

unqualified opinion. See *auditor's report.*

unrealized appreciation. An *unrealized holding gain;* frequently used in the context of *marketable securities.*

unrealized gross margin (profit). A *contra* account to *installment accounts receivable* used with the *installment method* of revenue recognition. Shows the amount of profit that will eventually be realized when the receivable is collected. Some accountants show this account as a *liability.*

unrealized holding gain. See *inventory profit* for definition and an example.

unrealized loss on marketable securities. An *income statement account* title for the amount of *loss* during the current period on the portfolio of *marketable securities* below beginning-of-period *book value* of that portfolio. *FASB Statement* No. 8 requires that losses caused by declines in price below market be *recognized* in the income statement, even though they have not been *realized.*

unrecovered cost. *Book value* of an *asset.*

use of funds. Any transaction that reduces funds (however funds is defined).

useful life. Service life.

valuation account. A *contra account.* When *inventories* or *marketable securities* are shown at *cost* and the *lower-of-cost-or-market* valuation basis is to be used, often any declines in market value below cost will be credited to a valuation account. In this way, the acquisition cost and the amounts of price declines below cost can both be shown.

value. Monetary worth; the term is usually so subjective that it ought not to be used without a modifying adjective unless most people would agree on the amount; not to be confused with *cost.* See *fair market value.*

value added. *Cost* of a product or *work in process,* minus the cost of the materials purchased for the product or work in process.

variable annuity. An *annuity* whose periodic payments depend on some uncertain outcome, such as stock market prices.

variable budget. *Flexible budget.*

variable costing. *Direct costing.*

variable costs. *Costs* that change as activity levels change. Strictly speaking, variable costs are zero when the activity level is zero. See *semivariable costs.* In accounting, this term most often means the sum of *direct costs* and *variable overhead.*

variance. Difference between actual and *standard costs* or between *budgeted* and actual *expenditures* or, sometimes, *expenses.* In accounting, the word has a completely different meaning from its meaning in statistics, where it is a measure of dispersion of a distribution.

variance analysis. The investigation of the causes of *variances* in a *standard cost system.* This term has a different meaning in statistics.

variation analysis. Analysis of the causes of changes in items of interest in financial statements such as net *income* or *gross margin.*

vendor. A seller. Sometimes spelled "vender."

verifiable. A qualitative *objective* of financial reporting specifying that items in *financial statements* can be checked by tracing back to supporting *invoices,* canceled *checks,* and other physical pieces of evidence.

verification. The auditor's act of reviewing or checking items in *financial statements* by tracing back to supporting *invoices,* canceled *checks,* and other business documents, or sending out *confirmations* to be returned. Compare with *physical verification.*

vertical analysis. Analysis of *percentage statements* of a single firm as of a given date, as opposed to *horizontal* or *time series analysis* where items are compared over time or across firms.

vested. Said of *pension plan* benefits that are not contingent on the employee continuing to work for the employer.

volume variance. *Capacity variance.*

voucher. A document that serves to recognize a *liability* and authorize the disbursement of cash. Sometimes used to refer to the written evidence documenting an *accounting entry,* as in the term *journal voucher.*

voucher system. A method for controlling *cash* that requires each *check* to be authorized with an approved *voucher.* No cash *disbursements* are made except from *petty cash funds.*

wage. Compensation of employees based on time worked or output of product for manual labor. But see *take-home pay.*

warrant. A certificate entitling the owner to buy a specified amount of stock at a specified time(s) for a specified price. Differs from a *stock option* only in that options are granted to employees and warrants are issued to the public. See *right.*

warranty. A promise by a seller to correct deficiencies in products sold. When warranties are given, good accounting practice recognizes an estimate of warranty *expense* and an *estimated liability* at the time of sale.

wash sale.   The sale and purchase of the same or similar *asset* within a short time period. For *income tax* purposes, *losses* on a sale of stock may not be recognized if equivalent stock is purchased within 30 days before or 30 days after the date of sale.

wasting asset.   A *natural resource* having a limited *useful life* and, hence, subject to *amortization* called *depletion.* Examples are timberland, oil and gas wells, and ore deposits.

watered stock.   *Stock* issued for *assets* with *fair market value* less than *par* or *stated value.* The assets are put onto the books at the overstated values. In the law, for stock to be considered watered the *board of directors* must have acted in bad faith or fraudulently in issuing the stock under these circumstances. The term originated from a former practice of cattlemen who fed cattle large quantities of salt to make them thirsty. The cattle then drank a lot of water before being taken to market. This was done to make the cattle appear heavier and more valuable than they would have been otherwise.

weighted average.   An average computed by counting each occurrence of each value, not merely a single occurrence of each value. For example, if one unit is purchased for $1 and two units are purchased for $2 each, then the simple average of the purchase prices is $1.50 but the weighted average price per unit is $5/3 = $1.67. Contrast with *moving average.*

weighted-average inventory method.   Valuing either *withdrawals* or *ending inventory* at the *weighted average* purchase price of all units on hand at the time of withdrawal or of computing ending inventory. The *inventory equation* is used to calculate the other quantity. If the *perpetual inventory* method is in use, often called the "moving-average method."

where-got, where-gone statement.   A term used by W. M. Cole for a statement much like the *statement of changes in financial position.*

window dressing.   The attempt to make financial statements show *operating* results, or *financial position,* more favorable than would be otherwise shown.

with recourse.   See *note receivable discounted.*

withdrawals.   *Assets* distributed to an owner. *Partner's drawings.* See *inventory equation* for another context.

withholding.   Deductions from *salaries* or *wages,* usually for *income taxes,* to be remitted by the employer, in the employee's name, to the taxing authority.

without recourse.   See *note receivable discounted.*

work in process.   Partially completed product; an *asset* that is classified as *inventory.*

work sheet.   A tabular schedule for convenient summary of *adjusting* and *closing entries.* The work sheet usually begins with an *unadjusted trial balance.* Adjusting entries are shown in the next two columns, one for *debits* and one for *credits.* The horizontal sum of each line is then carried to the right into either the *income statement* or *balance sheet* columns, as appropriate. The *plug* to equate the income statement column totals is the income, if a debit plug is required, or loss, if a credit plug is required, for the period. That income will be closed to retained earnings on the balance sheet. The

income statement credit columns are the revenues for the period and the debit columns are the expenses (and revenue *contras*) to be shown on the income statement.

An example work sheet is shown here for Caralex Stores, Inc., for the quarter ending September 30, 1979. The company last closed its books on June 30, 1979. The Expense Control Account is used to record various expenses not shown in separate accounts (see *control account*). The numbers in parentheses on the work sheet correspond to the adjusting entries explained below.

(1)   A deposit of $1,250 was made up, journalized and posted on September 30, but actually was not deposited in the bank until October 1.

Undeposited Cash   1,250
  Cash in Bank   1,250
To reverse entry prematurely recorded.

(2)   The net debit balances of accounts receivable from customers is $94,000. A review of individual customers' accounts reveals that several individual accounts have credit balances totaling $650. Thus, the gross amount of accounts receivable is $94,650.

Accounts Receivable   650
  Advances by Customers   650
To set up advances by customers who have made payments on accounts or returned goods for credit.

(3)   The merchandise inventory on hand at September 30 is $13,000.

Cost of Goods Sold   246,000
  Merchandise Inventory   246,000
To record reduction in inventory as cost of goods sold. $376,000 − $130,000 = $246,000.

(4)   The insurance policies all expire on January 1, 1981. No payments on insurance policies were made this quarter.

Expense Control Account   260
  Prepaid Insurance   260
The insurance policies provide 18 months' coverage as of June 30, 1979. To record insurance expired for three months; $3/18 \times \$1,560 = \$260$.

(5)   The rent is $1,200 per month and has been paid through November 30, 1979. When the rent was paid, it was debited to Rent Expense, a component of the Expense Control Account.

Prepaid Rent   1,200
  Expense Control Account   1,200
To set up 2 months' prepaid rent as of September 30. Prepaid rent was $1,200. As a result of this entry, it is $2,400.

Caralex Stores, Inc.
Work Sheet—Quarter Ending
September 30, 1979

	Unadjusted Trial Balance		Adjustments				Income Statement		Balance Sheet	
	Dr.	Cr.	Dr.		Cr.		Dr.	Cr.	Dr.	Cr.
Undeposited Cash	500		(1) 1,250						1,750	
Cash in Bank	8,270				(1) 1,250				7,020	
Accounts Receivable	94,000		(2) 650						94,650	
Allowance for Uncollectible Accounts		1,400			(6) 3,200					4,600
Interest Receivable	80		(10) 240						320	
Merchandise Inventory	376,000				(3) 246,000				130,000	
Supplies Inventory	1,200		(8) 1,400						2,600	
Prepaid Rent	1,200		(5) 1,200						2,400	
Prepaid Insurance	1,560				(4) 260				1,300	
Notes Receivable	9,600								9,600	
Furniture and Fixtures	25,000								25,000	
Accumulated Depreciation		17,000			(7) 500					17,500
Accounts Payable		32,400								32,400
Advances by Customers					(2) 650					650
Interest Payable		400			(11) 100					500
Bonus Payable					(12) 752					752
Sales Tax Payable		9,600								9,600
Withheld Income Tax		1,970								1,970
Payroll Taxes Payable		360			(9) 1,680					2,040
Income Taxes Payable					(13) 2,160					2,160
Notes Payable		24,000								24,000
Capital Stock		160,000								160,000
Retained Earnings		13,860								13,860
Sales		326,000						326,000		
Sales Returns and Allowances	6,000						6,000			
Sales, Uncollectible Accounts Adjustment			(6) 3,200				3,200			
Interest Revenue					(10) 240			240		
Cost of Goods Sold			(3) 246,000				246,000			
Expense Control Account	62,960		(4) 260		(5) 1,200		62,800			
			(7) 500		(8) 1,400					
			(9) 1,680							
Interest Expense	620		(11) 100				720			
Bonus Expense			(12) 752				752			
Income Tax Expense			(13) 2,160				2,160			
Column Totals	586,990	586,990	259,392		259,392		321,632	326,240	274,640	270,032
Net Income for Quarter							4,608			4,608
							326,240	326,240	274,640	274,640

(6) The estimated uncollectibles to arise from sales of the quarter are 1 percent of sales, net of returns and allowances.

Sales, Uncollectible Accounts
Adjustment 3,200
   Allowance for Uncollectible
   Accounts 3,200
.01 × ($326,000 − $6,000) = $3,200.

(7) Depreciation on furniture and fixtures is 8 percent of cost per year.

Expense Control Account 500
   Accumulated Depreciation 500
3/12 × .08 × $25,000 = $500.

(8) The cost of all supplies purchased is debited to Supplies Expense, a component of the Expense Control Account. The Supplies Inventory at September 30 is $2,600.

Supplies Inventory 1,400
   Expense Control Account   1,400
To set up supplies inventory at $2,600.

(9) The employer's share of payroll taxes has been paid through September 1. The employer's share for September is calculated to be $1,680.

Expense Control Account 1,680
   Payroll Taxes Payable   1,680
To record Payroll Tax Expense for September as a component of the Expense Control Account.

(10) The Notes Receivable account contains a 10-percent note for $9,600 dated June 1, 1979, and due December 1, 1979.

Interest Receivable 240
   Interest Revenue   240
$3/12 \times .10 \times \$9,600 = \$240.$

(11) The Notes Payable account contains a single 10-percent note for $24,000 dated July 15, 1979, and due January 16, 1980. Interest has been accrued on the 15th of each month.

Interest Expense 100
   Interest Payable   100
Interest expense per month is $200 $(= 1/12 \times .10 \times \$24,000)$. The balance of Interest Payable on the note should be $500 $(= 2\frac{1}{2} \times \$200)$. To adjust interest expense for the quarter and interest payable as of September 30.

(12) The manager is to be paid a bonus of 10 percent of the pretax income of the enterprise exclusive of the bonus.

Bonus Expense 752
   Bonus Payable   752
From Income Statement columns: .10 × ($326,000 + $240 − $6,000 − $3,200 − $246,000 − $62,800 − $720) = $752.

(13) The income tax for the quarter is estimated to be $2,160.

Income Tax Expense 2,160
   Income Taxes Payable   2,160
To record income tax expense for quarter.

    Work sheet is also used to refer to *schedules* for determining other items appearing on the *financial statements* that require adjustment or compilation.

working capital. *Current assets* minus *current liabilities.* The *statement of changes in financial position* usually explains the changes in working capital for a period.

working capital equation. The *balance sheet* states that *Assets = Equities.* The information in comparative balance sheets from the start and end of a period can be restated as:

$$\text{Change in Assets} = \text{Change in Equities}.$$

This equation can be further broken down to say that

Change in Current Assets Plus Change in Noncurrent Assets	=	Change in Current Liabilities Plus Change in Noncurrent Equities

which is equivalent to

Change in Current Assets Less Change in Current Liabilities	=	Change in Noncurrent Equities Less Change in Noncurrent Assets

The left-hand side of this equation is the change in *working capital* for the period. The items on the right-hand side cause the change in working capital during the period. The *statement of changes in financial position* typically shows the causes of the changes (right-hand side of the equation) at the top of the statement and the way working capital has changed (left-hand side of the equation) at the bottom of the statement.

working papers. The schedules and analyses prepared by the *auditor* in carrying out investigations prior to issuing an *opinion* on *financial statements.*

worth. *Value.* See *net worth.*

worth-debt ratio. Reciprocal of the *debt-equity ratio.* See *ratio.*

write down. *Write off,* except that not all the asset's cost is charged to expense or *loss.* Generally used for nonrecurring items.

write off. Charge an *asset* to *expense* or *loss;* that is, *debit* expense (or loss) and *credit* asset.

write-off method. A method for treating *uncollectible accounts* that charges *bad debt expense* and credits accounts receivable of specific customers as uncollectible amounts are identified. May not be used when uncollectible amounts are significant and can be estimated. See *sales, uncollectible accounts adjustment* and the *allowance method* for contrast.

write up. To increase the recorded *cost* of an *asset* with no corresponding *disbursement* of *funds;* that is, *debit* asset and *credit revenue* or, perhaps, *owners' equity.* Seldom done because currently accepted accounting principles are based on actual transactions.

yield. *Internal rate of return* on a stream of cash flows. Cash yield is cash flow divided by book value. See also *dividend yield.*

yield to maturity. At a given time, the *internal rate of return* of a series of cash flows, usually said of a *bond.* Sometimes called the "effective rate."

zero-base(d) budgeting (ZBB). In preparing an ordinary *budget* for the next period, a manager starts with the budget for the current period and makes adjustments as seem necessary, because of changed conditions, for the next period. Since most managers like to increase the scope of the activities managed and since most prices increase most of the time, amounts in budgets prepared in the ordinary, incremental way seem to increase period after period. The authority approving the budget assumes operations will be carried out in the same way as in the past and that next period's expenditures will have to be at least as large as the current period's. Thus, this authority tends to study only the increments to the current period's budget. In ZBB, the authority questions the process for carrying out a program and the entire budget for the next period. Every dollar in the budget is studied, not just the dollars incremental to the previous period's amounts. The advocates of ZBB claim that in this way: (1) programs or divisions of marginal benefit to the business or governmental unit will more likely be deleted from the program, rather than being continued with costs at least as large as the present ones, and (2) alternative, more cost-effective, ways of carrying out programs are more likely to be discovered and implemented. ZBB implies questioning the existence of programs, and the fundamental nature of the way they are carried out, not merely the amounts used to fund them. Experts appear to be evenly divided as to whether the middle word should be "base" or "based."

zero salvage value. If the *salvage value* of a *depreciable asset* is estimated to be less than 10 percent of its *cost,* then the tax regulations permit an assumption of zero salvage value in computing *depreciation* for federal *income tax* purposes. This convention is often used in financial reporting as well.

INDEX